1 John

1 John

On Docetism and Resurrection
Revised and Extended

L. Daniel Cantey Jr.

WIPF & STOCK · Eugene, Oregon

1 JOHN, REVISED AND EXTENDED
On Docetism and Resurrection

Copyright © 2021 L. Daniel Cantey Jr. All rights reserved. Except for brief quotations in critical publications or reviews, no part of this book may be reproduced in any manner without prior written permission from the publisher. Write: Permissions, Wipf and Stock Publishers, 199 W. 8th Ave., Suite 3, Eugene, OR 97401.

Wipf & Stock
An Imprint of Wipf and Stock Publishers
199 W. 8th Ave., Suite 3
Eugene, OR 97401

www.wipfandstock.com

PAPERBACK ISBN: 978-1-6667-0808-0
HARDCOVER ISBN: 978-1-6667-0809-7
EBOOK ISBN: 978-1-6667-0810-3

Manufactured in the U.S.A.   MAY 24, 2021

Contents

Book I

Lay Introduction: To the Devout Christians in the West | 3

1 John 1:1–2 | 15

1 John 5:18–21 | 29

1 John 1:3–4 | 68

1 John 5:16–17 | 85

1 John 1:5–10 | 115

1 John 5:6–15 | 134

1 John 2:1–2 | 152

1 John 5:4b–5 | 169

1 John 2:3–6 | 183

1 John 5:1–4a and 2:7–11 | 208

1 John 4:16b–21 | 233

Book II

Preface | 269

1 John 2:12–14 | 272

1 John 4:13–16a | 289

1 John 2:15–17 | 312

1 John 4:7–12 | 348

Epilogue | 371
Appendix to the Academics | 373
Select Consulted Works | 381

Book I

Lay Introduction

To the Devout Christians in the West

To Western Christians who have sought the Lord to the best of their ability, who have yearned to know and to be known by God, who have labored to live in a manner pleasing to him, who have sought him in suffering, prayed to him and beseeched him in trials, and who have trusted him in adversity and temptation: greetings in the name of the Lord Jesus Christ. My heart goes out to you devoted ones, who include friends whom I respect as well as the family that I cherish. To those who are not my acquaintances I offer my hope and concern that God will look upon you with compassion here and at the judgment.

Do not be fooled, for many deceivers have gone out into the world. Men now proclaim that there is no God and no judgment, they accuse and impugn God as unjust and a tyrant, they declare that they are without sin and they announce that God has left the world. They decry the notion that nature has a meaning other than what men deign to give it while they burst the bonds that hold men together, so that all that makes a claim to truth they brand as propaganda, agendas, and falsehood. Men today wander in a sea of lies and do not know which way to turn, with believers often overlooking their participation in the deception. For there is another falsehood, one not as obvious, one to which Christians turn a blind eye as they sing their songs, as they—we, you and I—pray our prayers and perform our worship. This falsehood ensnares and spoils us, driving us away from Christ while speaking in his name.

The ancient church faced a heresy called Docetism. As a premise, the Docetists believed that the spirit is good and that matter is evil, and that the two cannot mix. They then affirmed that God sent his Son, Jesus Christ, but with the attendant claim that Christ had no physical body. Shall God, who is all goodness, light, and truth, combine with depraved matter? According to Docetism, certainly not! Christ therefore comes as the Son of God but without a body, and all that he did, the walking on water, the teachings and healings, the feedings of thousands, the Last Supper, he did without a body. He appeared as if he had a body to those around him, but in fact he did not have one. He even climbed the cross not in the flesh but as a seeming. This Christ without a body did not die in the body nor did he raise the body from the dead.

Thus in Docetism there is no resurrection, no life, and no salvation, and those who believe in Christ in the docetic way are deceived.

In like manner we also are deceived, for Western Christians also believe that Christ has no body. I speak not of the body of the man Jesus, but of the body of Christ, the church. "But," you say, "I go to church every week and have for years! How could I not believe in the body of Christ?" Listen: when a man's body dies it does not vanish into air, but over time it decomposes, disintegrating and scattering into dust. This has happened to Christ's body in the West. Over many centuries it has decomposed, breaking through schism upon schism until today it is all but lifeless. To say "I accept these multiplied and multiplying Western denominations," to regard their collective existence as a matter of indifference or personal choice, to consider each sect as justified according to its own rationale, and to participate in one or another of them—or worse, to say "It does not matter how or whether one worships, it only matters what one believes in the heart"—to say any one of these things is effectively to accept the disintegration and scattering of the body of Christ. To accept the scattering of the body of Christ, however, is to accept its death, and to worship a Christ with a dead body is to worship a Christ without a body. That one says "I believe in Jesus Christ" makes little difference here, as even demons acknowledge that Jesus is the Christ. What matters is that one worships the Christ correctly, according to the way he has given,[1] as a Lord not only of spirit but also of the flesh, who came to redeem both the body and the soul. How can Christ redeem the bodies of men when his own body, the church, is torn into pieces? Western Christians, inasmuch as we worship a Christ without a body, are Docetists, all; we have been deceived, despite our devotion, to the last one of us.

"Every kingdom divided against itself becomes a desert, and house falls on house . . . whoever is not with me is against me, and whoever does not gather with me scatters" (Luke 11:17, 23). These are the words of our Lord and they are true. He is the great gatherer, who aims to bring all things together in his body the church. But Western Christendom is the great scattering, the intensifying division of the body of Christ. Juxtapose Christ's assertion that "he who does not gather with me scatters" beside his admonition that "you will know them by their fruits" (Matt 7:15–20), so that the fruit that witnesses to the Holy Spirit is gathering and its opposite is scattering.[2] Then examine the history of Western Christendom, which amounts to scattering

---

1. When the Israelites made the Golden Calf, God said to Moses that "they have been quick to turn aside from the *way* that I commanded them" (Exod 32:8, emphasis added), and this despite the fact that the Israelites believed that they still worshipped God (32:4). One must therefore have more than the name of God or Christ on his lips. He must also live and worship according to the way that God requires. To deny the way denies the God who commands it.

2. Many Christians read "you will know them by their fruits" as a reference to moral purity, and not without reason. But can one be morally pure and also divide the Church? Is the love of God justifiable as the breaking of Christ's body and the hatred of brethren? Schism witnesses against the moral purity of its proponents.

after scattering. You will see that throughout Western history the Bible, and the Christ whose name we hope to exalt, indicts that history's witness.

Can one find a page in the Scripture where God does not affirm the unity of the church? "I am the good shepherd," says the Christ. "The good shepherd lays down his life for the sheep. The hired hand, who is not the shepherd and does not own the sheep, sees the wolf coming and leaves the sheep and flees—and the wolf snatches them and scatters them" (John 10:11–12). The false leader cannot stand against forces that threaten and divide Christ's body, while Christ, seeing the wolf coming, lays down his life for the sheep. "I have other sheep," he continues, "that do not belong to this fold [referring to the Gentiles who are added, in the church, to the flock of the Jews]. I must bring them also, and they will hear my voice." Of these two peoples Christ makes "one flock" under one shepherd, joined in the witness to resurrection and life in Jesus (10:15–16).

Hear also the prayer of Christ before his passion, when in the Garden awaiting his betrayer (John 17). Concerning his disciples he asks, "Holy Father, protect them in your name that you have given me, so that they may become one, as we are one . . . I ask not only on behalf of these, but also on behalf of those who believe in me through their word, that they may all be one. As you, Father, are in me and I am in you, may they also be in us, so that the world may believe that you have sent me. The glory that you have given me I have given them, so that they may be one, as we are one, I in them and you in me, that they may be completely one." These are the words of Christ to his Father, his last testament and the prelude to his death, and in them he petitions for the unity of the faithful. Above all they must be one, united in Spirit and in truth, lest they do not accomplish the earthly purpose for which he calls them. The Christ seeks their unity so that "the world may know that you have sent me and have loved them even as you have loved me." The unity of the body of Christ witnesses to its truth, and to the truth of God who enlivens and maintains it through his Spirit. When the body divides unto incoherence, what is left of its witness except that Christianity, rather than engendering peace, is a seed of faction and conflict?

The unity of men in the church stands at the center of God's cosmic plan. "With all wisdom and insight God has made known to us the mystery of his will," writes St. Paul, "according to his good pleasure that he set forth in Christ, as a plan for the fullness of time" (Eph 1:9–10). Westerners might be astonished that this plan is not for individuals *per se*, not for the lonely man before God. The divine plan gathers up "all things in Christ, things in heaven and on earth." Recall that Christ is the great gatherer, and see here that the eternal purpose of God gathers all things in him! God has "raised Christ from the dead and seated him at his right hand in the heavenly places, far above all rule and authority and power and dominion, and above every name that is named, not only in this age but also in the age to come. And he has put all things under his feet and has made him the head over all things"—for what reason? What manifests and embodies the rulership of Christ, exemplifying his lordship over all? Where is this headship located and for what is it established?—"*for the church,* which is his body, the fullness of him who fills all in all" (1:20–23, emphasis added). We must affirm that Christ is the head of his body, the church; that Christ is put over all things for this body as his fullness; and that in it he gathers all things in heaven and earth under himself. For "through the church the wisdom of God in its rich variety . . . [is] made known to the rulers and authorities in the heavenly places. This was in accordance with the eternal purpose that he has carried out in Christ Jesus our Lord" (3:10–11). Should we deny the centrality of the church for God's purposes, we deny also the words of Christ and his foremost apostle.

I urge you to pray for those who divide the body of Christ, who attempt to reconcile God's plan of gathering all things in Christ with the scattering of his body! I further urge you to pray for those who say that they can believe in Christ without submitting to the church. Beware those who say "I am loved by God and will be gathered to him in eternity" but who spurn Christ's body now. Those who reject the body of Christ in this world may well be shut out from it in the next, for God is not mocked.

God saves men by grace through faith, "and this is not your own doing; it is the gift of God—not the result of works, so that no one may boast" (Eph 2:8–9). Paul directed this statement to Jews who used their inheritance, including the law, the prophets, and the covenant of the Old Testament, to raise themselves up above Gentiles. Paul declares that the Jews do not find justification in this inheritance but in the faith of Jesus Christ, a message that applies equally well to believers today. The upshot of this justification in the first century was that Christ "is our peace; in his flesh he has made both groups [Jews and Gentiles] into one and has broken down the dividing wall, that is, the hostility between us. He has abolished the law with its commandments and ordinances,[3] that he might create in himself one new humanity in place of the two, thus making peace, and might reconcile both groups to God in one body through the cross, thus putting to death that hostility through it" (2:14–16). Justification in Christ does not occur without man's assimilation into his body, which reconciles him to those against whom he formerly raised himself up. Christ means to create one humanity out of believers at peace with one another and devoid of hostility, men who manifest the divine wisdom in which Christ gathers all to himself.

Faction in the church contradicts both the cosmic plan of God in Christ and the reconciliation brought about for those justified in him. For this reason Paul berates the Corinthians who would segregate themselves from one another. "Each of you says, 'I belong to Paul,' or 'I belong to Apollos,' or 'I belong to Cephas,' or 'I belong to Christ.' Has Christ been divided? Was Paul crucified for you? Or were you baptized in the name of Paul?" (1 Cor 1:12–13) Those who divide according to their apostolic teachers misunderstand what it means to follow Christ. They raise up leaders against one another when they should bear in mind that Christ, the Lord of all, led by humbling himself. When Paul came to the Corinthians, he knew "nothing among [them]

---

3. Christ abolishes the law in this passage as it might raise the Jews over the Gentiles, dividing the peoples. In other aspects he fulfills the law, not one iota of which will fall away (Matt 5:17–20).

except Jesus Christ, and him crucified" (1 Cor 2:2). He knew nothing of leaders puffed up in pride, nothing of men in competition for human honor or recognition, but he knew the Lord who lowered himself to become a servant of sinners. Faction according to leaders undermines this example because it sets men up as antagonists, tending toward the division of Christ's body as though the servants and stewards of God's mysteries surpassed their master.

"Do you not know that you are God's temple and that God's Spirit dwells in you?" Paul asks in the midst of this discussion. "If anyone destroys God's temple, God will destroy that person. For God's temple is holy, and you are that temple" (1 Cor 3:16). These words should send chills down the modern spine. Faction is the destruction of the church, according to Paul, and men who destroy the church through faction shall be destroyed by God. But what are Christians of the West if not totally at home in and approving of faction? Do we not see that the body of Christ has fallen, that it has become a desert and been destroyed, overwhelmed by schism, secularity, and disregard for the church? If we turn our back toward the dissolution of Christ, will he not also turn his back upon us?

As Paul exhorts, let us "lead a life worthy of the calling to which we have been called, with all humility and gentleness, with patience, bearing with one another in love, making every effort to maintain the unity of the Spirit in the bond of peace. There is one body and one Spirit, just as you were called to the one hope of your calling, one Lord, one faith, one baptism, one God and Father of all, who is above all and through all and in all" (Eph 4:1–5). Where there is "one body" there is "one Spirit," as the Holy Spirit holds all things together for the glory of Christ, but where there are many bodies, separated by indifference if not by disdain and violence, there are many spirits that goad men to conflict with one another. The Christian cannot affirm one Spirit, one faith, one baptism, and one God and Father of all, and at once affirm a multitude of bodies born out of antagonism and mutual condemnation.[4]

One discovers the New Testament's emphasis on the unity of God's people in the Old Testament also. When God promises Abraham that he will make him a great nation, bestowing upon him land and blessing, and giving him a great name (Gen 12:1–3), one does not need to add that this nation will be unified. When God announces of Israel through the prophets that "I will be their God, and they shall be my people," it goes without saying that this people is one, strengthened in their singularity by their worship of God and their obedience to his law. We learn more of the necessity of Israel's unity not through direct assertions of national solidarity, which the Old Testament often presumes, but through the forms of punishment leveled on the people: division and exile, both of which are kinds of scattering.[5]

---

4. Other examples of the New Testament's focus on unity include 1 Cor 12–14 and the letters of 1–3 John, although one could multiply instances of the warnings against dissension and conflict and admonitions toward unity.

5. The idea of scattering has a notable place in the Old Testament. One finds it in the Tower of

When Solomon sinned by idolatry, following the gods of his foreign wives, God announced that "Since this has been your mind and you have not kept my covenant and my statutes that I have commanded you, I will surely tear the kingdom from you and give it to your servant... I will not, however, tear away the entire kingdom; I will give one tribe to your son, for the sake of my servant David and for the sake of Jerusalem" (1 Kgs 11:11–13, 29–36). God fulfilled this sentence by dividing the kingdom from Solomon's son, Rehoboam, who enforced harsh labor on the people and so drove them to rebellion under Jeroboam. The line of David lost 10 tribes but retained the kingdom of Judah and Jerusalem.

Later and more prominently God punished the people through exile, uprooting them from the land. This happened in two events, each a turning point in the history of Israel, and each the result of the people's turning from God. In each case, the prophets brought accusations against Israel for the two sins of idolatry and disobedience. The conjoining of these two infractions signaled the impending judgment of God. In the first manifestation of that judgment, the Assyrian Empire defeated the Northern Kingdom around 721 BC, deporting the people. By this action the Northern Kingdom died, being wiped out completely. As the prophet Amos proclaimed, "The end has come upon my people Israel," for "Israel must go into exile away from his land" (8:2, 7:11). The second instance, with the Exodus perhaps the most important pair of events in the Old Testament, is the Babylonian exile (ca. 586–538 BC). Here God removed the remainder of his people, the Judeans who had survived the Assyrian threat roughly a century earlier, and subjected them to life in a foreign kingdom under foreign gods. One cannot overstate the impact of this event on the Jewish consciousness. The prophets predicted it and God carried it out, and the Israelites mourned until restored to their homeland. The scatterings of the Jews in the Old Testament are twofold: the division of the kingdom, a national schism that separates man from man; and the division of the people from the land, which forcibly removes men from their ancestral home.

Consider closely the biblical witness, how the words of Jesus and Paul exhort believers toward the unity of the faith, how the Old Testament presumes the unity of the people of Israel, and how God punishes and all but destroys his people for their sins through division. The Bible nowhere justifies schism; it nowhere says that the body of Christ ought to be rent for one or another reason; it nowhere says that the people of Israel ought to seek division rather than regard one another in friendship and brotherhood. It says that followers of God must love one another and give to one another, humbling themselves before God and serving the neighbor. The Bible's teaching on these points is unqualified.

Consider now the history of the church in the West. As we move briefly through this history, we shall see that at juncture after juncture the body of Christ has divided,

---

Babel (Gen 11:1–9), in the punishments promised for Israel in Deuteronomy (28:64 and implicitly in 28:7, 25), in the Deuteronomic promise of restoration, or gathering after scattering (30:1–5, cf. Nehemiah 1:8–9), and in the prophetic corpus (e.g., Ezek 34:1–6, 11–13, 20–24).

Lay Introduction

that men who claim the name "Christian" have turned against one another, sometimes killing one another because of their faith. Can this scattering and eventual demise of the body of Christ be directly harmonized with the gathering that is his purpose?

For approximately a millennium the church was one, spanning roughly from Spain to the Middle East, fighting heresies and enduring contrary religions with an ostensibly unified front. About 1054, with the excommunication of the Patriarch of Constantinople, this attitude changed in the Catholic West. The papal circle saw the Eastern leader as schismatic, a view that eventually took hold throughout Western Christendom. The Crusades, carried out over the course of the twelfth century, greatly widened the division that was growing between East and West, until after the sack of Constantinople (1204) the Eastern Christians could not affirm communion with their Western counterparts.

Who was at fault for the Great Schism? Modern Christians do not like to ask such questions. Surely there was blame to go around, surely the fault was not entirely on one side. Therefore, all were equally guilty and consequently all are equally innocent, and therefore no one can judge the guilty from the innocent, and there is no judgment to be had. One can nonetheless raise another question: who was punished for the Great Schism? God's punishes his people's sin through division, as shown above.[6] Their pride precedes the destruction that is scattering. In the wake of the Great Schism, who suffered the scattering? Who bore the wrath of God in the likeness of the Israelites who turned from him? The Roman Catholic Church alone can claim this distinction.

In the centuries following the finalization of the Great Schism, the Catholic West suffered amazing peril to its unity and authority. In successive order, it endured exile from its land in Italy and the internal debacle of the Great Western Schism. For roughly 70 years in the fourteenth century, the Church relocated from the Italian peninsula to Avignon, on the French border. At this point the papacy, which had garnered international respect and power particularly through Innocent III (1198–1216), became a pet of the French monarchy. The popes who reigned from Avignon often lived in luxury, enjoying a court whose splendor surpassed that of kings and emperors. They did not tend to mourn the loss of their homeland, but the testimony of history stands against them. Has any other church been exiled from its home for such a duration?

Upon the return to Rome things went from bad to worse. Pope Gregory XI had brought the papacy back home, but he died soon after this in 1378. The election of the new pope faced the challenge of a divided group of cardinals and the potentially negative reaction of the Roman people, who desired that a Roman should become pope. The candidate originally chosen was Barolomeo Prignano, Archbishop of Bari. The cardinals chose him because they outranked him, and seeing him as their inferior, they believed that they could govern him. Prignano was elected and enthroned as Urban VI, and his power went instantly to his head. The cardinals had badly miscalculated when they considered him governable and he became such a nuisance to them

---

6. In the case of the Great Schism, the punishment of division for the guilty party intensifies the prior infraction. Those guilty of division become further divided.

that they claimed that the original election was invalid and moved, as a group, outside of Rome. There they formally repudiated Urban VI and elected a new pope, Robert of Geneva (also known as the "Butcher of Cesena" and the "Man of Blood") as Clement VII. But Urban would not step down as the cardinals had hoped. Two popes claimed authority at the time, with each elected by the same college of cardinals.

Rather than resigning, Urban created a new college of cardinals and went to war against his enemies. At this point the schism was an acknowledged fact throughout Europe. With one pope and college of cardinals relocated to Avignon (Clement VII) and another pope and college of cardinals in Rome (Urban VI), the nations were forced to take sides for one or the other. This state of affairs divided national rulers and their clerics in some places, while it in others it separated the clerics from the people. The monarchs on the side of Urban included England, Flanders, the Holy Roman Empire, Hungary, Poland, and Scandinavia. Those on the side of Clement included France, Scotland, and eventually Spain and Portugal.

The effect of the schism on the general public was horrendous. Each pope had excommunicated the other and those who followed him. Every Christian, then, found himself excommunicated by one or the other pope, with little way of being sure that he followed the correct one. Imagine baptizing one's child in the hope that God will have mercy on his soul, but being told that God will not have such mercy because the pope one recognizes is invalid. Therefore one's child will endure perdition if he dies in such a state, and this despite being baptized. In some areas, there were two bishops who proclaimed the ceremonies performed by each other as sacrilege. The soul of Catholic Europe could hardly have been more divided.

The Great Western Schism continued for roughly 40 years, well beyond the adversarial claims of the original pair. The councils called in the early fifteenth century sought to invalidate both lines of popes by introducing a new ruler, but the introduction of a third pope only caused more confusion, so that for a time there were 3 claimants to the papal throne. The Schism eventually died by attrition, with one line of popes outlasting the others. Coupled with the exiling of the papacy to Avignon, the Schism testifies against the Catholic Church as scattered, divided from both its land and its people.[7]

---

7. History testifies against the East to a lesser degree. Constantinople fell to the Turks in 1453, and one can reasonably ask if this was not a punishment for wrongdoing. I respond that the Orthodox Churches are not without fault in the Great Schism, but history does not testify against them as it does for the Catholics. Being conquered by a foreign people is at best an equivocal judgment upon the followers of God. The Church grew under the reign of the Roman Empire and men do not see this as a punishment. Nor does the Old Testament treat every experience of the Jews under foreign rule as negative, as seen with the Persians. The New Testament further reminds Christians that they must suffer on earth (1 Peter), a suffering that often takes place under pagan authorities. The witness of a restricted and burdened life under other peoples is not nearly as strong as that of geographical displacement and schism, both of which troubled the Catholics and neither of which have plagued the Orthodox. The evidence stands against the West, not the East.

Lay Introduction

Perhaps more than any other event, the Schism provoked the various movements of reform that welled up in the fifteenth century. These sought a new foundation for authority, occasionally looking to the Scripture alone rather than the popes, and often raising cries of heresy from defenders of the Catholic status quo. These movements eventuated in the Reformation, the most important occurrence in Western Christianity in the second millennium. Many Protestants look on the Reformation as the saving of the church from Catholic crimes and doctrinal errors. They see it as the birth of all that is true and good in Christianity, as the transformation and revitalization of the church away from what had ailed it. To these I respond by looking again to the words of our Lord, "You shall know them by their fruits." What is the fruit of the Reformation? How should we assess its effects?

The most forthright defender of the Reformation, who lists the perversions of medieval Catholicism with confidence, must also admit that the Reformation was schismatic. Before the Reformation one church stood in the West, and in it the one gave way to the many. This schism did not divide the church in two or three but into multiples of two or three. Rather than competing Catholics, one finds denominations divided by leadership, belief, and practice, Lutherans, Calvinists, and Zwinglians, various strands of Anabaptists, and eventually Anglicans in addition to smaller groups forgotten by history. The Western church became the Western churches, a collection of houses of worship without communion or collegiality, divided by assertions of truth. All that bound the Protestant sects was their rejection of Catholicism and often the doctrine of justification by faith alone, but beyond this they splintered as a ship crashed upon rocks. If one affirms that the Reformation saved the church, he must simultaneously affirm that this salvation fractured the body of Christ, intensifying the tragedy of the Great Western Schism.

In the Reformation the body of Christ suffered from a deeper schism, that between the body and the soul as between works and faith. Justification by faith alone, the doctrinal anchor of the Protestant revolution, announced that what is outward has nothing to do with what is inward, that the works of the body have no relevance for the state of the soul. Faith alone belongs to salvation, and the works of the body, while notable, are qualitatively lesser in importance. But just as one separates the soul of man from his body and the latter dies, with the flesh breaking down into uncountable pieces, so if one separates the faith of Christians from the physical reality of Christ's body in the Church and its' good works, then that body also dies, fracturing into bits.

The result of the Reformation consists in no small part in the Wars of Religion, in which Protestants fought Catholics to the death, with each side persecuting the other when it was able. One can recall Mary Tudor, Queen of England, who imposed a series of repressive measures against Protestants in returning England to subservience to the pope. During her reign, open persecution of Protestants became the official policy of the English kingdom, for which she earned the name "Bloody Mary." France saw various periods of killing, from the St. Bartholomew's Day Massacre, which murdered thousands of Protestants in 1572, to further oppression of Protestants under Cardinal Richelieu in the 1620's (despite the Edict of Nantes (1598), which allowed for Protestant religion), with Protestantism officially outlawed in 1685 under the Edict of Fontainebleau. Religious war in Germany occurred on multiple occasions, from the War of Schmalkald, fought during the life of Luther, to the 30 Years' War (1618–1648). The latter, known in Germany as "The War of Total Destruction," was the bloodiest period in German history prior to the twentieth century. It also involved powers outside of Germany who came to the aid of one side or the other.

How is it that Christians can kill one another, with each side denouncing the other as heretics and spilling blood in the confidence of its righteousness? How do Christian motives (the desire for purity of worship and the glory of God) intertwine with political intrigue and yearnings for freedom, so that the claim of divine authority validates lethal force? The Bible allows no justification for schism and exhorts Christians to love one another! Yet schism broke out with the Reformation, in whose wake those who called themselves Christian hated others who took that name, and in which the confusion and competing claims of righteousness raised such a clamor that men doubted that God deserved recognition in human affairs. It is no wonder that, after the Puritan Revolution in England (1640–49), the political philosopher Thomas Hobbes envisioned a world with God distanced from politics and human nature, and in which men lusted for combat with each other. The house divided becomes a desert indeed.

During the early modern era religious men began to reject the organized church, with notable persons leading the charge. George Fox imagined a church without a liturgical structure, eventually founding the Quaker religion. This version of Christianity does away with all form in worship, believing that the Spirit must flow freely through the individual conscience to contribute to communal life. Here there is no pastor and of course no priest, and freedom reigns supreme. Anne Hutchinson also found herself outside of the organized church of Puritan New England, although not because she rejected that church but because she supposed herself to stand above it. She began to preach beyond her rights according to local authorities, drawing people by her knowledge and asserting that God had spoken to her directly. The Massachusetts colony exiled her but she had made her mark on the American consciousness. Not far from her was Roger Williams, a Baptist whose pursuit of a pure worship of God drove him out the church and toward the Indians before convincing him to take leave of religious society altogether. Such persons serve as the template for the modern disavowal of the church, the body of Christ torn this way and that by those who believe that they can adhere to it according to their own judgment.

Reliance on individual conscience flowered further in the United States following the American Revolution. From the 1790's to the 1820's, the period referred to as the Second Great Awakening, a multitude of Christian movements and new denominations exploded onto the American scene, expanding as the population moved West. The Baptists and Methodists were skilled at making converts along the frontier, adding daily to their numbers, gathering the people at camp meetings characterized by emotional preaching and occasionally raucous behavior. The Black church gained a foothold in the United States during this era, breaking away from white society in the North in order to found communities in which race did not entail second-class citizenship.

The age suffered from anxiety regarding religious authority. In this time and land the pope was forgotten and truth was supposed to come from the Bible alone. As each man read the Bible for himself the interpretations proliferated, and with numerous interpretations came conflicts, denomination against denomination and sect against sect, man against man, until the heads of devout believers spun on their shoulders. In such circumstances men went to their private rooms in order to discern truth for themselves, reading the Bible in solitude and without thought for the authority of pastor, priest, or church council. The times provided ample room for men like Alexander Campbell, Barton Stone, and their peers to found new movements. Those originally known as the Christians rose dramatically before eventually settling as the Church of Christ, while Joseph Smith proclaimed revelations from an angel and additions to Scripture as the authority supporting his teaching. Everywhere one looked, one saw that "All Christendom has been decomposed, broken in pieces, and resolved into new combinations and affinities," while "every theological vagabond and peddler may drive here his bungling trade, without passport or license, and sell his false ware at pleasure." This assessment comes from Philip Schaff, a nineteenth century historian, who adds that "what is to come of such confusion is not now to be seen."

But what has come of it is now, in the twenty-first century, very much accomplished: the Christian house has divided and continues to divide, and it has become a desert. The American nation has left God behind in fulfillment of the words of Christ, as the house divided falls upon itself. Although churches still have members, liberal Protestantism has all but died and Evangelicalism senses that it is next, struggling to retain its children. Scholars speak of a post-Christian society, a world in which religious moorings are antiquities, in which men grow distant from one another as they forget God.

I urge you, you devout and God-fearing churchgoers, you men and women who take your faith to heart, to think soberly on the testimony of Scripture against the Western church. Consider the words of Christ and of Paul, consider the design of God to unify men in the Son, and then consider the breakdown of the church in the West, the theological disputes and competition of the Awakenings, the blood and desolation of the Wars of Religion, the exile of the papacy from its home and the sorrow of the Great Western Schism. Think about the modern age in which men have become atomized and self-determining, in which they believe that they can worship Christ and forsake their fellow men. The worship of a bodiless Christ was known as Docetism and castigated as a heresy in the first century; we in the twenty-first century have our own Docetism, the worship of Christ apart from his body the church. Or has the church not died through division? And are we not accomplices in that death so long as we embrace the corpse?[8]

I exhort you, brethren, to look to the Eastern Church. Although not without its own challenges and practical flaws, Orthodoxy has not endured the division that plagues the West. It has also struggled to maintain the spirit of the ancient councils, of the tradition of meekness and gentleness in mind and heart, of self-control and love of neighbor. It teaches how to practice the presence of God and to strive for union with Christ. I gently encourage you to look to the East, foreign as it is for many Western believers, and to pray upon it as a home for those dismayed by the fate of Western Christendom.

---

8. Some may object that those in their churches are good people. The challenge is, then, to set the history of violence, schism, and uproar in the Western church against the concrete experience of worship with people who are friendly, agreeable, and devout. It would seem that such people cannot be deceived, and that the Holy Spirit is among them.

But there are friendly, agreeable, and devout people in every religion. If this becomes our standard of judgment, what of the Hindus, Sikhs, Muslims, and Buddhists are who are agreeable, friendly, and devout in their faith? Are they also followers of Christ according to their own way? There must be some standard other than the friendliness of people in order to determine the Holy Spirit's presence: the biblical standard of unity.

We have such a standard in the assertion that the Holy Spirit gathers the body of Christ. It is present in unity and absent from schism. The question is not whether people are amicable but whether they have forgotten their deeper division, and by forgetting condoned a spirit of schism that hides beneath an otherwise sincere desire for God. Cannot Satan, who makes himself into an angel of light (2 Cor 11:14), secretly turn man's yearning for the divine to his own purposes? He would be a poor deceiver who could not hide his plans from the casual observer or whose ruses were obvious. One must consequently hold fast to the criterion of Christ, who looks at the church as well as the individual heart, and ask whether one accepts the church as dissolved or affirms it as unified. As for what we moderns know as unity, is it anything more than the ruin left by repeated wars of attrition?

1 John 1:1–2

That which was from the beginning, which we have heard, which we have seen with our eyes, which we have looked at and our hands have touched—this we proclaim concerning the word of life. The life appeared; we have seen it and testify to it, and we proclaim to you the eternal life which was with the Father and has appeared to us.

THE SENTRY, DECKED OUT in full colors and bearing the seal of his king, gazed at the old man from across the doorway. The latter squinted at the visitor. He stood leaning over his cane, his face wrinkled, his hands hardened by labor.

"I do not mean to impose on you, sir, but the hour is late, I come from another land, and I seem to have lost my way. Will you show me hospitality by allowing me to stay for the night?"

"Of course. Please come in," said the old man, who was overjoyed to entertain a guest affiliated with wealth and station.

After dinner the two fell into conversation. The old man asked about the royal way of life, its comforts, its delicacies, and its esteem. He also asked about the customs of the distant land, trying to discover how they differed from his own. For much of the night the man prodded the sentry to divulge all he could about his affairs, and the guest obliged.

The sentry then inquired about the old man's way of life. "I have lived humbly," replied the man, describing the difficulties and joys of the peasantry. "Now I am old, burdened by fatigue and wounded flesh, stooped with an injury that follows me like a shadow of death. But I am most troubled by the loss of my sight, which has faded in recent years and makes my getting around more dangerous. I wish that I could see with the clarity of my youth. I could at least then enjoy the world around me and make my way more safely."

The sentry smiled. "I believe that I can help you with this desire of yours," he said. "My king employs many sorcerers, and they have lately developed a weapon meant to counter death and suffering and empowered to give life. I carry this weapon with me as a part of my errand. Would you like to see it?"

The old man responded skeptically that he would like to behold this weapon, if its powers were true. The sentry then removed a cloth from his blouse, unwrapping it to reveal a double-edged dagger. Its blade gleamed in the firelight, and its handle was gilded and studded with gems. The old man held it up to his face, noticing an inscription that he could not make out. It reads, "To conquer death, and to achieve life immortal," said the sentry in answer to the old man's curiosity. "Would you like to use it, regaining the powers of sight that you once had, and escaping the danger of your condition?"

"Yes," said the old man. "What must I do?"

"It is simple," replied the sentry. "Take the dagger and apply it to that part of your flesh that is ailing, making a deep wound so that the blood flows, and the power of the dagger will so transform the wound that it will shortly heal with a greater strength than the body had before the defect. In your case, as you wish to repair your sight, you must strike your eyes. You will lose your sight for a few moments, but soon afterwards it will be restored and you will see with the eyes of youth."

The old man hesitated, doubting the promise of the sentry. Would he really gouge out his eyes in order to see? "I sense that you do not believe," said the visitor. "Have you not heard of the resurrection of the one called Christ, who overcame death by dying and rising from the grave? He suffered greatly in order to bring life to mankind, and it is his power that animates this dagger. If you wish for it to heal your infirmity, you must die to what you see by purging your eyes. Only after you have wiped away the vision of death will you receive life."

The old man had heard of the resurrection, though his faith in it had waned. Trusting that power anew, he took the dagger in his hands. "I will do it," he said. "Good," responded the sentry. "You must puncture each eye with a powerful stroke, leaving nothing to sight. The purgation must extend to all that you see."

Closing his eyes and bracing, the man tightened his grip on the dagger and drove it into his eye. He shrieked and fell forward onto the table. "Again!" cried the visitor. "You must strike the other eye! Resolve to do it and you will see again!" Straightening, the old man gathered his courage and plunged the dagger into the other eye, cutting off his sight entirely. All was dark, and blood poured over his face. "I see nothing!" he burst out to the sentry. "Strike again, and harder!" exclaimed the guest, "The blade must penetrate all the way through!" And so the old man, bewildered and enfeebled, thrust the dagger into his eyes again and again, yearning for new sight in spite of his pain. After many strokes he dropped the dagger and fell to his knees.

"I am lost!" he cried. "The devil has deceived me and I have succumbed, and my blood witnesses against my pride! What do I have left but to grow old in darkness and die without sight?"

"Indeed," said the other, now standing over the old man, his eyes glowing and his teeth blackened and gnarled. "But are you not at least saved from the sight of your ailing flesh?" And he vanished with the dagger, leaving the old man to himself.

In the first beginning "was the Word, and the Word was with God, and the Word was God. He was with God in the beginning." The Word, the Son and Second Person, dwelled with the Father in eternity. This dwelling-with alone fails to sum up the interpenetration of Father and Son, for the Word was God, one in substance but different in person from the Father. The Father is an eternal and immutable person, a mystery subsisting in the fulfillment of its requirement, being as he ought to be and without possibility of improvement. In his fulfillment the Father transcends his form in the begetting and procession of persons, reaching out from a life perfect in its singularity to a mutual dwelling-in in which law ascends into love. The Trinity means the internal outpouring of a perfection in being so magnificent that it abides in a shared and personal celebration of that perfection. The love between Father, Son, and Spirit consists in the origin of the latter two in and from the Father and the unbroken harmony between the three. An untarnished obedience within the singularity of the substance and an irrepressible joy in that obedience within and among the persons, the transfiguration of the rhythm of conformity into a differentiated union, is the oneness of the God who is both three and one. God exists in the plenitude that seals Father, Son, and Holy Spirit with bonds so impregnable that by the divine will they extend into the creation of being from nothing.

"Through him all things were made; without him nothing was made that has been made." Father, Son, and Holy Spirit created all that is as one God, the Father giving being, the Son bestowing law and life upon being in its form, and the Spirit sealing creation in communion. Yet one cannot parse the roles in the creation as if the persons stepped forward in distinction from one another and acted individually. God acted as one, so that the giving of being means the giving of form and communion: He creates no being that does not imply the destination of and growth toward form, limit, and unity, or in a word, toward nature.

What, then, of the formless matter that had yet to take shape, the waters over which the Spirit breathed when the earth was formless and void? As created by God, formless matter possessed an intrinsic vector toward form, with Christ present in it as He is present in all things. As created from nothing, and like all created natures after they receive their shape, this matter also possessed mutability, the possibility and freedom by which matter could advance toward form or shrink from it, in this case remaining in a state of formlessness. When the Spirit breathed over that which was formless and void, the inclination toward form had yet to distinguish its drive toward nature from the mutability. The inclination existed at such an embryonic state that it equaled and did not yet surpass the pure possibility of change. Thus matter's freedom from form, not a freedom bereft of a drive toward form or of form annulled, not an empty and directionless matter, but a matter pregnant toward form as if having a will and desire for it, but not yet possessed of the power to assert that form over the mutability.

1 John: On Docetism and Resurrection

"Let there be," says the Father, and the Word creates, elevating and limiting the matter destined for but lacking definition into the defined and the natural. In the Son who is the life of all things being created from nothing rose from indifferentiation into law, receiving grace. Formless matter gathered into particular beings, each receiving its nature as it received its law, molded by the beneficence of God into its particular beauty. Now being inseparable from law as way of being, now life inseparable from way of life. The tree receives a way of being with bark, leaves, and seeds, and in some instances fruit, and this is its law; likewise the fish receives its fins, scales, eyes, and the motion of swimming as its law; the leopard receives its paws, fur, tail, and skill to strike without warning by the same principle. These ways of being, bequeathed and instilled by the creator into the natural world in the words "let there be," entail that creation was as it ought to have been, that God shaped each nature by a particular design and that each nature conformed to the design. This is the righteousness of the natural world and individual natures, their adherence to the way of being specified for each part and for the whole, nature's living in the law that God decreed for it in the Son.

God fashioned man with a law unique and unparalleled in the physical order, a single law manifest in two, one being and one way of being in body and soul. The soul has its own law and way of being, its particular inscription toward life and fulfillment, and likewise for the body. The two laws are one for one man, a law that on one hand mandates the shape of the flesh, its ears, eyes, hands, and feet, and all the characteristics that identify the body as man's body. The manifestation of these characteristics is the activity of man *qua* body, his visible and intrinsic obedience to the law by which he is what he is as a body. The same single law dictates a way of being for the soul, a law fit for it as the higher element in man's nature. God molded the soul to contemplate him, intending its focus on his love so that the soul should orient both its own nature and that of the body toward harmony with the creator. The more the soul turns toward God, persisting in the contemplation of and obedience to him, the more it abides according to the law that defines and fortifies it as a soul, while man equally abides according to the single law that is his life as a man.

At its creation, the law of man's nature established both the limits of body and soul and the mutual limitation between body and soul. The body discovered its limit in the boundary of the flesh, the acknowledgment of the space it does not occupy gained through physical feeling and encountered as an imposition. Then another, more profound limit confronted the body: though created good and without sin, God did not create it incorruptible. The body faced its finitude in the possibility of death, a potentiality necessitated by the freedom in which man might turn back toward nothingness, disobeying God. The soul likewise discovered its limit: as to origin, created by God; as to power, licensed to rule creation only under the rule prescribed by God; as to knowledge, allowed to know only what God saw fit for it to know. The soul knew that it is not the body and that its connection with the body does not entail confusion between the one and the other. The two abided as one in their respective limits, their definition the logical prerequisite for nature's unity. This is the law of man, that his elements in their mutual limitation and solidity should interpenetrate, grounding his singularity. The soul thus understood the body as its link to the physical world and the lower limit to which it bestows life; it simultaneously encountered the law of God, the origin, rule, and knowledge prescribed for the soul by him, as the upper boundary. Beyond this, the soul faced the possible limit of death not in a physical perishing but in the life turned away from God.

Body and soul originally existed without confusion, division, or separation, with man enjoying the image of God in which law abides in and ascends toward love. In the rhythmic conformity of the powers of nature to the will of God and nature's design man both dwells in God and finds his being at rest in God and his neighbor. The soul's being gathered into God parallels its union with the body, its submission to the higher limit elevating it in the same overlapping harmony by which the soul grasps the body as its instrument and dedicates that instrument to life. Completely attuned to his intended way of being, man abides in the obedience that is joy and the joy that is love, a worship that humbly and gratefully desires God's lordship at the same time that man discovers in that lordship the mercy that is law poured out and giving birth. This grace invigorates man's appreciation of nature and his interpenetration as a nature, fortifying the elements in their solidity and giving them weight. Man seeks God above all and as Master, Creator, and King, yet he cannot enjoy God's grace without giving thanks for his nature, he cannot know God without knowing body and soul as God's creation, he cannot love God without loving body and soul as God's handiwork and possession, practicing peace with his fellow men. So the divine nature bestows its likeness upon a unified man, filling man's nature in its fulfillment, and men live in the finite divinization that is beatitude.

But man could fall, he could relinquish the divine image and descend toward formlessness. Though bolstered by the grace of God he was not totally secure, and the possibility of descent attended to him as a creature corruptible and free. He could disobey the law of his nature and the divine law that would lift that nature to incorruption, abdicating his purpose as the prize of God's creation. A necessity intrinsic to both his finitude and his capability for communion with God, man's freedom is the limit upon the law of his nature in which he, as a spiritual being, encounters the formlessness of possibility. There lies his mutability and, as that mutability annuls its contingency in acquiescence to law, the affirmation of God as a merciful lord and man as a blessed slave. Man's freedom is embedded in the law of his nature and is meant to validate it in his active reception of the divine love, but in freedom also lies the threat, the chance that man could abdicate the image and fulfillment in which soul and body are married in God. There were therefore in the first man's nature these three aspects: the physical body as the lower element, created without sin but capable of death by physical disintegration; the soul as a higher element beyond disintegration other than its alienation from God; and the mutability attendant to both, the possibility of a life in incorruptible form or its opposite, the life tending toward corruption and death.

The devil seized upon man's mutability, tempting and deceiving him with the knowledge of good and evil. In the tree of the knowledge of good and evil man encountered his soul's upper limit, acknowledging the lordship of God and the right order of creation as well as the penalty for breaching that order. Should he eat of the tree or even touch it man would die, rending the fullness of the image of God from his nature at the same time that nature grows despoiled. "But the serpent said to the woman, 'You will not die; for God knows that when you eat of it your eyes will be opened, and you will be like God, knowing good and evil.' So when the woman saw . . . that the tree was to be desired to make one wise, she took of its fruit and ate; and she also gave some to her husband, who was with her, and he ate."

In eating the fruit the soul acquired a wisdom beyond its limit just as it turned from God, abandoning the orientation that is its life. Deceived by the serpent, the soul misunderstands the defect that upends the peace of nature by grasping emptiness as though it were fullness, as though the life apart from God possessed significance because the soul had ascended toward the place of God. The soul does not see, it is fooled in the belief that it can rise beyond its limit without simultaneously falling, as though the illegitimate ascent did not entail descent. The serpent says, "Rise without falling!" So it conceals the essentially dialectical character of the demonic, of the disobedience with which it entices the soul. The fruit of the knowledge of good and evil is a delight to the eyes and desirable for wisdom, but that wisdom belongs only to God and to those spiritual beings to whom he deems fit to grant it. For man to embark upon the rise, to arrogate a wisdom beyond the form of his nature in the hope that it will elevate his capacities and augment his fullness, is the deception. It begins the alienation of man from both God and his neighbor, and from his life as a man.

The soul abdicates its law when it eats of the tree, forfeiting the solidity and rule of its being as shaped according to God's will. Simultaneously rising above and falling below the measure of its integrity, the soul grows more like God with respect to the content of the mind but farther from him in the loss of the ontological knowledge of God's presence. In the fall man trades the knowledge of God for God's knowledge, appropriating a modicum of infinity as though he could contain an illicit likeness to God within his finitude. The soul expands but it also contracts, transgressing its created form from both directions, surging beyond its limit in the knowledge that would judge good and evil at the same time that man feels this knowledge as a loss of being and as distance from the divine love. In the divorce from its nature the soul relinquishes what abides for the dialectical transition between greater and lesser, jettisoning the stability of being that is according to its law for being which is both itself and its opposite, an ascent that approximates divinity necessarily accompanied by the descent which recognizes the upward reach as a crime. The soul's new existence is finally punishment, tending toward nothing inasmuch as the finite's theft of the infinite results in its dissolution *qua* finite, the death of distance from God. Sin therefore means the diminution of being in which man no longer looks to God, no longer trusts, obeys, loves, and worships God, replacing God with a nature divided and estranged, an object at once of love and of hatred, a life he cherishes and despises and which he wants to imbue with meaning despite its despair. Man would think that he has become like the God who is immutable Form, but he has sacrificed what form he possessed. He thinks that he has risen in the likeness of He who Is, but this very rising portends his descent toward what is not.

The descent corrupts the whole creation, turning birth into a cry of pain and the search for sustenance into combat against thistles and thorns, demanding that the body return to the dust from which God shaped it. But the curse thundered upon the body means more than physical demise; it means the body's release for a life of rebellion as well. Once the good and God-pleasing instrument for the soul's acquisition of life, the body remains that good and God-pleasing instrument, but at the fall the reins change hands and it is redirected under a law unto death. In its sin the soul oriented the whole man away from God, carrying the bodily nature with it into the rise that falls, entangling the body in the dialectic in which the appearance of divinity achieved and form grasped whispers the penalty of humanity lost and form dissolved. The body draws its life from the soul and imitates its habit, embarking after the fall upon the dialectical greater-lesser by scoffing at the soul's governance and rising in annulment of bodily limits. The lower element pursues the pleasures of this world as though possessed of its own mind, hoping for meaning in worldly delights, but every grasping inasmuch as it implies the surpassing of the body's limit cannot but evaporate in the hand that seizes it. Food rots in the mouth that chews, comforts leave man stale and vapid, and should he come to the remarkable place where he knows no bodily inconvenience, gratifying every desire with ease, man there finds his body reduced to invisibility and no longer relaying the meaning stamped upon his being. The rise of the body foreshadows its fall, the ascent dialectically mediates erosion, the unhindered bodily appropriation of this world facilitates the liberation of man from both body and world.

The soul enraptured by the semblance of divinity and the body enslaved to lust, both married to the dialectic of finitude disintegrated through infinity seized, means that each loses the solidity of its measure. Rightly formed, body and soul interpenetrate as grounded in the integrity of definition, each element fortified within its limit and bearing out that fortification in the mutually supporting harmony of grace. The infinitizing dialectic dissolves the limit of both body and soul, undermining the internal stability of the elements and poisoning their intermarriage. That which reaches out toward the infinity of an impervious form suffers toward the infinity of form annulled, the endless possibility of form without its achievement. What was solid, distinct, and particular devolves into what is liquid, amorphous, and obscure. The union that was without confusion yields to the indistinguishable permeability of fluid with fluid. Man melts down so that he can no longer endure, no longer withstand the forces that would drag him to the pit, no longer counter the temptations that exploit the malleability of his being.

Man experiences the confusion of body and soul as an alienation in which each part illicitly communicates its properties to the other. The body desires rule over man and would live as though immortal, seeking pleasure without end, undermining the soul as if the latter were the element destined to die. The soul unwittingly authorizes this venture, for in grasping the infinite it turns away from both God who is its life and the body that lives through it, willing a world apart from finitude, without physical feeling, a world in which the body forgets death. This confusion of properties entails separation between body and soul as two elements so distorted by infinity that they lack the cohesion necessary for fellowship. Body and soul know nothing each of its own limit and thereby of its complement, and though they flow freely into one another their nearness only exacerbates the distance between them. That nearness, that joining in division, is the war of soul against body or spirit against flesh. In this combat the infinity sought by the soul alienates it from the finitude of the body and puts the body to death, while the infinity sought by the body means its revolt against the soul and the relegation of the latter to despair. The mortality of its turn from God characterizes the soul as it increasingly strives after infinity absorbed in the finite, the same infinity that promises the body a life without inconvenience, want, and death. The soul thereby becomes the instrument of the body, the element apparently destined to die while the body appears immortal, with both parts drowning in the deception that this is life abundant. Each hastens toward death as man descends into a constant and irregular aggression, his attempts to regain definition marred by the homogeneity in which both soul and body are negated. At the consummation man trades his nature and the divine image for privation's power, dissolving in an unfeeling hopelessness in which he has only enough of the soul to apprehend the loss of the body.

This is the vector of man's mutability in the wake of the fall and as corrupted by sin, a scattering dedicated to the dialectic of disobedience and seeking the confusion and alienation of soul and body. The scattering is that dialectic embedded in man's nature, the power of privation seeking the disfiguration of form. Whereas in his body and his soul man retains definition, particularity, and differentiation after the fall, existing to some extent according to the pattern of nature and thereby possessed of some righteousness, the scattering would, at its summit, pervert the way of being by which man is a specific creature into the dialectical contradiction in which he is at once a thing and its opposite. Rather than a finite creature located within the specificity of God's order, the scattering would unmake man into the universal-particular, a being tied to a place without boundary or locale; rather than a creature blessed with an appropriate knowledge of his world and his God, the scattering would reduce man into an omniscient ignoramus, combining a seemingly endless knowledge of his world with blindness toward the God to whom that world testifies; rather than a creature ascending in the love of his natural form and the God who fashioned it, the scattering would so curse man that his love of nature conceals his hatred of it, that because he loves nature as though it were infinite he infects its finitude with his own thirst for death. At the extreme, at a point not dreamed of at the fall, man appears to cherish and even divinize the natural world while he despises and destroys it, constructing another in its place. The greater power the scattering gains within the nature of man, the more he relinquishes that nature and slides into contradiction and indefinition, left with the name of man but not the substance, a man only in appearance, a seeming.

From his throne God saw man's tendency toward formlessness and how it would doom his beloved, he perceived the groaning of man and his world under disorder and demise. If the fall had not occurred, God would have sent the Son as the most perfect grace and communion between God and man and an exemplar of the love meant to join them. After the fall he sent the Son for this reason but also for another, condescending in Christ to make right what sin had stained and direct toward life what sin would carry into perdition. Man's being was beset by the infraction of his rise and his inclination to repeat it, an urge toward disobedience plaguing his nature and subjecting it to death. Christ came so that the fall following the rise, the death that had become man's negative knowledge of the law of his being, might become his path to life. It is the love of God that through the Son he should transform the curse of bodily demise into the means for new life, that God the Son should address the dialectic of rise and fall by beginning with the downward vector, emptying himself and becoming man, even suffering a heinous death, and taking up that fall so that it becomes the preliminary for a rise to eternal life. That is the beauty and mercy of God, that the sinless lamb should grant life to sinners, calling them to bear the cross toward life on the other side.

The incarnation is the great mystery, the pivot on which the universe turns. Whereas the dialectic of perdition pretends a finite man who seizes a lasting and impervious infinity, thinking that he could grasp the divine and absorb it into his limit, and whereas this grasping produces the opposite effect by erasing man's finitude in an abyss of possibility, the dialectic mediating destruction through the promise of a higher, divinized life—against all this and as its inverse Jesus Christ empties the divine nature and takes on flesh so that the infinite descends and conceals its nature in the finite. Through this descent Jesus rises glorified and honored to the throne above all thrones, while he restores man to life through faith in him. The dialectic in which the finite arrogates the infinite is contradiction and impossibility, but that in which the infinite empties itself and is incarnate in man is the mystery.[1] When the infinite mediates its glory through the finite, this is the love of God and the salvation of man; when the finite seeks its glory as mediated through the infinite, this is the death of man and the destruction of faith. In the latter man rejects obedience to the descent in which

---

1. The ancient councils and biblical wisdom stand behind what I say about the Christ, and I have no desire to contradict or transgress these sources. If the reader should have any confusion regarding my words on this subject here and throughout this book, I ask that he keep this intent in mind.

he, following his Lord, would be lowered in order to rise, choosing instead the ascent destined for perdition, the rise that is inevitably a fall.

The dialectic of salvation stands behind John's second beginning, that "which we have seen with our eyes, which we have looked at and our hands have touched," the message that Jesus Christ came as fully God and fully man. In order for the Physician to accomplish salvation for man he must become man in all aspects except submission to sin, joining both soul and body with his divinity. A Christ who does not take on the soul cannot redeem that part of human nature nor nature in its entirety, nor can a Christ who does not take on the body redeem that part of human nature nor the whole. Jesus came that man might come to know the grace by which God cures soul and body of sin, reversing man's depravity by wiping away the punishment for past crimes and directing him toward *theosis*. Arriving in body and soul, the Second Person dies in the most inexplicable manner, magnifying the miracle of incarnation with the end of resurrection and restoring his humanity through the divine life. Thus the Christ opens the door so that every man who places faith in him might imitate the descent, casting off pretensions to infinity in favor of the love in which man is known by God and in which death succumbs to life. Body and soul return to and edify one another, man comes to know his nature as blessed, and the image of God convalesces unto eternal health.

Having come as the unity of God and man, Christ also came with the power of resurrection. This way through death to new life is love, the perfected unity of law and grace, the command that is eternal life and whose end is sacrifice and compassion. For in harmonizing law and grace Christ requires what appears as the greatest severity just as he replenishes what is taken away. The command is to die, but its implication is to live again. This resurrection, this love, is the taking of life resolved in a greater life being given. The cross is the first and lesser aspect of this dynamic in the Son, the mystery in which the infinite and immutable God, in its union with man, somehow perishes. In this death God integrates the denial of life into life beyond measure, overwhelming the horror of death and reconstituting it as a law unto renewal. The cross has no meaning apart from that renewal. Otherwise Christ's death is only death, only God dying pitifully. But love accomplishes the retrieval in which God conquers sin and invites man into heavenly communion, the life which draws man through absence and into fullness. On the other side of death comes exaltation, the glorification of the Son as Risen and as having completed the purpose of the Father, the promise to man of blessing beyond the curse.

The Christian's path of salvation imitates the fall and rise of his Lord, engaging in death in the hope of the life beyond. "Love others as I have loved you," Christ commands, pushing the disciple into and through inconveniences and sufferings, requiring him to be submerged in them. The disciple's facing death in the likeness of his Lord means the assimilation of non-being into his being, standing against its force as imposed upon him in the sensible recognition of mortality. Man gains in being by enduring what transience throws at him, enduring his own transience and striving to live on the other side of it. Getting to the other side is not a hit-and-run affair, not a strike against one's mortality followed by flight from it in the name of grace, but a tarrying with mortality in order to be engulfed in it. This is the call and command of Christ: in his name endure your mortality. For his love and his glory, die to sin and abide beyond death.

Through this way of being Christ bestows the fullness of soul, the weight of *gravitas* and the joy of *misericordia*. Man finds, as he abandons the world and pursues the soul, that the Spirit of God descends from on high as a welling up within. The soft emptiness of sin recedes, and in its place he matures as a man of sharpened stone on the one hand and as a well of compassion on the other. *Gravitas* chastens him against the lassitude in which being slips imperceptibly away, while *misericordia* calls him to comfort the suffering of others. Are you a man of grit, able to bear harsh treatment, public scorn, the blows of nature and ill fortune? Good! But know that men do not rest in God apart from their rest in one another, and know also that the giving of rest is intrinsic to your nature. Without a properly guided pathos, without a sense for suffering and a willingness to be humbled before one's brother as one feeds him and visits him when sick, one's grit amounts to Stoicism, not salvation. Are you a man of sensitivity, feeling the suffering of others and empathizing with them, shedding tears for the neighbor's tribulation? Good! But know that without the heaviness of *gravitas*, without restraining one's passions, man does not follow the way of God but turns being toward non-being, indulging a proud sentimentality. Salvation requires and grace provides both the steel and the pliability, both the resistance and the empathy. By grace man delves into law, even into death in the name of Christ, and dwelling there he rises by grace into what abides. Love rushes over him and he finds that rather than being consumed as an object for its nourishment, he is nourished.

Salvation through the Christ faced enemies within the first generations after his resurrection, including the Docetism that threatened John's congregation and provoked his first letter. Docetism claimed that Christ did not come as a man of flesh, asserting that he came to save man but not with a real body and therefore not as a real man. Those who saw him might have believed him to be a man and to inhabit a body, but Docetism rejected this appearance as a seeming. All that one could ascribe to Christ's bodily life the docetists dismissed: the body to be torn down and rebuilt in three days was a chimera, Christ the bread from heaven came as spiritual bread only, the one who walked on water did not do so with human flesh, the one who bore the nails and hung on the cross neither endured this pain nor later rose as a body. In this way Docetism denied the emptying of the divine nature and the taking on of full humanity at the heart of Christ's redemption, insisting that the infinite could not perform the mystery in which it descends into the finite and cleanses man's faults.

This denial presumed the division of the world into two realms, positing a strict duality between the material and the spiritual. Docetists considered the material realm as flawed and abased, outside of redemption and a divine mistake, whereas they regarded the spiritual as pristine and exalted, the locus of knowledge and salvation. In man's spirit resided the divine spark that called him to a higher existence, a spark in which the body had no part but contradicted in its materiality. The docetists applied this duality to Jesus Christ with the consequence that they could not understand him as truly God and truly man, for a divinity of spirit could not stand contact with the flesh. The heterogeneity of the realms would not allow that God could assume the profanity of the material and remain God. In this way the dualism of spirit and body intervened and perverted Christ's incarnation in the docetic mind, separating Christ from flesh and confining him to spirit. The docetists discarded the Christ of flesh and bone, full humanity as well as full divinity, and in his place affirmed an ethereal being. In this manner they lost what was preached from the beginning, that Christ came as fully man in order to redeem men and bring them to eternal life.

The church overcame the old Docetism, vanquishing it with other ancient heresies that threatened fellowship within Christ's body. Yet with the passing of centuries another Docetism has emerged, a New Docetism of profound and subtle strength, a recapitulation of the infinitizing dialectic cloaked under the promise of exaltation here of the church and there of man, an enemy whose power has unfolded over millennia and whose bloodlust goes unchecked. The original Docetism denied the dialectic of salvation that is the Son incarnate, refuting the notion that the divine could be joined in a single person with the finite, at once remaining infinite and saving sinners. The New Docetism, the inverse of the old, affirms the dialectic in which a finite man ascends toward the infinite as though he could both contain divinity and remain in the particularity of finitude, as though this ascent does not eventuate in formlessness. By the New Docetism man leaves off the law of form and definition in order to dedicate his energies to his disintegration, and this in the belief that he is rising as man, that he is fighting the good fight of justice, peace, and progress.

The New Docetism has swallowed the history of the West, undergirding the long story of conflict between church and kingdom on the one hand and man, state, and society on the other as a single dialectical progress in which form rises and falls with the boundlessness of law. For the New Docetism is above all the dialectical abolition of the law by which God shaped man according to nature and would elevate that nature to incorruption, a devertebration of church and kingdom in parallel with the internal decay of men. Docetism annuls the law as natural and divine, giving rise to the scattering as the principle of man and his environment until it has pummeled both into existence as a set of contradictions, a flurry of changes set against everything opposed to their continual transitions. Like its predecessor, the New Docetism thrives upon the implication that its object is not substantial or tangible, and therefore no longer real. It would devolve man and his world into a vapor without body or soul.

In a breathtaking and unperceived stroke, Docetism long ago twisted the meaning and glory of Christ to its purposes. The spirit that would flatten man's fortitude does so under the banner of gospel and grace, righteousness and justice and mercy, while disemboweling his world in the name of the kingdom of God. Docetism has not only found room for Jesus Christ within the infinitizing dialectic, but at the turning point in its maturation Docetism proclaims the Christ-Idol as the pulse of its movement. All that precedes the cataclysm known as the Reformation is Docetism's determination to corrupt the name of Christ by confounding the gospel of life with the scattering. The grace of Christ there merged with the structureless infinity of being divested of law and thereby of form, decapitating the divine aspect of the law and initiating in earnest Docetism's attempt to infinitize the natural realm. Rather than he who takes up death and transfigures it into life for those who perdure in his name, Jesus Christ became the license by which man annuls the law until death becomes his way of life.

For the Protestant adherent of the New Docetism, the gospel speaks of Christ overcoming sin and death at the cross. There the docetic believer assumes that his iniquity will be conquered because Christ has conquered it, there the docetist claims to see blessing secured because evil has fallen. But Docetists, whether Catholic, Protestant, or secular, do not understand their own logic, they do not perceive that the liberation that they have preached and sung for centuries means not freedom from sin, death, and the law as their crier, but freedom from the law and thereby from the acknowledgment of sin and its penalty. The law and its giving of form Docetism secretly identifies as sin, redefining as enemies the institutions and nature expressive of that law and responsible for man's limits. With shocking mendacity Docetism defines the graces given to keep sin at arm's length as death-dealing and strives to liberate itself from them. Docetic man therefore works to remove the mediations that guard him from violence, laboring until they are destroyed and envisioning the destruction as a final liberation. Docetic man deceives himself by believing that in destroying the mediations he will confront a reality in which sin and death have no part. This reality without the mediations *is* death, for upon dismissing his protections the combat comes hand-to-hand. The life beyond death of which docetic man might dream comes not into and through death but to death. At the end of his striving against the mediations he perceives evil lodged within himself and prepared for carnage. Rather than being swallowed by love, docetic man is enveloped by hatred.

The deprivation of man's form has arrived at the most recent and thus the most urgent of the crisis points embedded in Docetism's history. He flutters as the confusion of higher and lower, repudiating nature and limit in favor of the infinite. Man has seen eternal life, hearing it and touching it with his hands, but rather than this life descending from eternity in Christ it has ascended in earth lifted to heaven. Docetic man has abandoned contact with the ground, rejecting natural existence and its submission to and envelopment in death-unto-life, each generation having pulled the ground further from beneath its children. Man at his most prominent now abides in the clouds, high above in his cities, looking out over the millions. He flies from place to place, forgetting time and location, plucking his life out from locale, season, and rhythm. The typical docetic man partakes in a lower but no less devastating habit of flight, floating a few feet above the ground thanks to engines that distort his consciousness and erode his soul. He neglects dawn and dusk, sun and moon, living by the artificial command that there be light or its absence. He forgets heat and cold as if these did not compose the natural world, constructing a world without discomfort, without feeling, and finally without conscience. Replete with marvels, delights, and magic, this world covers him in darkness and fuels his pride.

Docetic man feels the descent intrinsic to this ascent in his internal ruin, his yearning for the meaning that he hoped to acquire by unwittingly obliterating all meaning. Though he does not know how to conceptualize it, docetic man senses that his way of being is not and that he exists as war. He senses that he is both an accomplice to and a cry of revolt against the evisceration of his nature. Docetism has reduced him to this cry, whose intensity reflects the ease with which his world invades and passes through his being—as well as his surrender to this invasion and his taking up its cause. Everywhere docetic man believes that he will receive fulfillment through release, that transgression and the eradication of boundaries will rescue him from emptiness, but he does not understand that expenditure is the undoing of the form by which he preserves his significance. He strives upward and outward in his pride as if he could absorb the whole earth, believing that then he would no longer wander, no longer be violated. This externalization tightens his shackles, divorcing his divinity from the interiority proper to it. Surveying the modern city, man bows before the altars he has erected in the name of alienation. Concrete and steel stand surrogate for the soul, capturing the natural longing for God and reversing its potency, parading the allure of man undifferentiated and deprived of law.

What shall save docetic man from the morass into which he has fallen, or from the consummation that looms ahead? What shall heal him of the pride that charms him to descend deeper into his blindness? Man will never find resurrection in what terminates in death, he will not escape his fluidity in what intensifies the stream. Let him, then, comprehend his darkness and its rule over him, that though it purports to save him from death Docetism has stolen the vision that gathers him into life. Let him therefore, and more importantly, see again that which was from the beginning, the Word of life that was with the Father and has appeared in Jesus Christ. Like the incarnation, what is here seen can be heard and touched. It is a life that, in addition to being formed in the truth, is also a way. With this new sight man apprehends the way as love, from God who created all things in and for love, given to man whom he loves.

1 John 5:18–21

We know that anyone born of God does not continue to sin; the one who was born of God keeps him safe, and the evil one cannot harm him. We know that we are children of God, and that the whole world is under the control of the evil one. We know also that the Son of God has come and has given us understanding, so that we may know him who is true. And we are in him who is true—even in his Son Jesus Christ. He is the true God and eternal life. Dear children, keep yourselves from idols.

THE MOUNTAIN DOMINATED THE countryside, puncturing the sky like a needle, peaking in the heart of the heavens. It loomed over a village, separating the people from points east with such height that they endured its shadow until late morning. The people complained that the darkness delayed production, that it stunted the growth of crops, and that it hindered their fullness of life. They longed to be out from under the mountain.

At length a man of unusual ability arose among the people, surpassing his companions and their ancestors in discernment, knowledge, and strength. His fellows envied him, the elders respected him, and the women sought him. The villagers made him their leader and he promised them an age of prosperity and justice. He made plans to improve the common way of life, but found time and again that the darkness hindered his pursuits. "If only I could bring my people into the full light of day," he thought. "We shall never advance while this mountain hangs over us."

He expressed his frustration to one of the women who courted him, and she responded with a way that he could draw the town out of darkness. "You, who are like a god among us, must become a sun for yourself and bring your light down for the rest. Listen to what you must do: ascend the mountain, arriving at the summit before dawn and hiding yourself there. When the sun rises just above the mountain's topmost point, seize it with your hands. Wrestle with the sun by laying hold of it, and though you melt from its heat, do not let go until it gives you its blessing. At that moment you will become the light of the sun, and when you return to the town as walking light, you will bless us all by your glow until we, too, have become our own suns. Then there will be no more darkness, and our people will make progress."

The man decided upon this idea at once, setting out for the peak. For days he scaled cliffs and endured the wild, descending into his depths and testing himself there. He reached the apex in darkness and hid himself. Dawn came and evolved into late morning, and the sun slowly awakened to the western lands. At the moment of total exposure, just as its light neared the village below, the man leaped out and grasped the sun with both hands. He immediately caught flame, his fingers and forearms turning black, his whole body shaking. Fire darted all around, the peak trembled, the sky rolled. The horizon twisted and coiled, and the man felt his feet dissolve into the earth. But he would not let go. "I will have your blessing!" he shouted, and with all his energy he held tightly and impeded the sun's course across the heavens. At last the sun was exhausted and gave in. A dazzling and concentrated beam flowed into the man and swelled in his flesh, an eternal light received. He let go and fell to his knees, where he noticed that all the colors, all difference and vivacity, fluttered within him and illumined his body. Smiling at his blessing, he looked at the sun to find that it was no longer bright in the same way, but had become another moon. "It is no matter," he thought as he stood up. "I do not need the sun. I am now my own sun!"

But then his light withered in a gasp and retreated beneath his skin, abandoning him to the dark. His skin began to ripple and crawl, his fingernails grew into claws, and hair sprouted on his face, hands, and feet. He looked again at the moon and howled with lust. The man that he had been departed; the people never saw him again. In his place they knew perpetual night, and fear of the monster that roamed the mountain.

∽

"We know that anyone born of God does not continue to sin; the one who was born of God keeps him safe, and the evil one cannot harm him. We know that we are children of God, and that the whole world is under the control of the evil one."

"Amen, the word of God is truth. The whole world lies under the evil one, and all men are born not of God but of the deceiver. Where now are those kept safe by the one born of God, who have not sinned with the world but who worship Jesus Christ?"

"We know that the Son of God has come and has given us understanding, so that we may know him who is true. And we are in him who is true, even in his Son Jesus Christ. He is the true God and eternal life."

"Amen, the word of God is love. But where today are men of understanding, who are coming to know Jesus Christ the Son, who abide in him and obey his commandments? Where are those who recognize Jesus as the true God and seek him as eternal life? The light of men has nearly left the world, and the hour is dark."

"Dear children, keep yourselves from idols."

∽

1 JOHN 5:18–21

I

The nature of man so exemplifies his social world that a rough congruence holds between the elements of his being and those of his society. As the higher and spiritual element most oriented to the worship and contemplation of God, the soul corresponds to the church. As the lower element more oriented to the temporal world and its necessities, the body corresponds to the kingdom, which includes various forms of social organization not immediately referred to the *ecclesia*, especially the political. The soul rules over the body not as another body but spiritually, delivering the moral guidance needed to humble the body toward immortality; so also the church's guidance of the kingdom. Attendant to both church and kingdom and representative of the mutability by which soul and body might rise or fall in their fellowship with one another and with God, not an element but an aspect of the two elements, are the individual man and groups of men as abstracted from their institutional homes. The individual-group so abstracted and universalized into a mutability that stands above all law, then tacitly declared as the ruling element in man's nature and his interactions, is the social meaning of the scattering. That man might justify this universality by reference to the name of Jesus is the essence of the Christ-Idol, the savior who invites man into the scattering both within his nature and as the principle of his social order. The Christ-Idol deceives by coaxing man into formlessness as though it were the beatitude of God.

The historical rise of the Christ-Idol conforms in a general way to the anthropological pattern exemplified at the fall. Through various personalities, political intrigues, machinations, and misunderstandings between well-meaning men, in short, in and through the details of history and men freely willing their place in history, Docetism accomplished its purposes as a guiding dialectical spirit, goading man to rise before compelling his fall. This transformation occurred over the medieval era, intensifying and proceeding from hints, unforeseen implications, occasional brazen announcements, and critical periods of corruption, schism, and war, until the infinitizing dialectic had opened the chasm necessary for the Christ-Idol. Just as the soul in deciding to eat the fruit exceeds its measure and rends its nature away from its proper form, so the papacy in its excessive assumption of primacy divorced the Western church from the East. Just as the soul achieves this rending in the grasp toward infinity, so the medieval papacy raced after the infinite in a plurality of ways. From the desire to reform the world to the papal excommunication of Eastern patriarchs; from claims of universal jurisdiction and theories of world-monarchy to the Crusades; and, most importantly, in the transformation of ecclesiastical law away from liturgy and theology and into a distinct system of statutes, with the church established as a legal institution; through all these the church seized the infinite and abandoned the law of its being. Just as the soul dies in its distance from God at the fall, suffering the loss of its being at the same time that it struggles under the flesh, so the papacy lost touch with its spiritual purposes as a prelude to falling to the French kings and eventually enduring the Western Schism. All the while the scattering, the universal man, germinated in consciousness and power until the docetic dialectic culminated at the Reformation, the breakthrough in which the infinite law was exhausted, divine law annulled, and the Christ-Idol raised on high.

The first cycle of rise and fall began with the crowning of Charlemagne by Leo III, a stratagem by which the pope secured a protector for Rome against the Lombards. Leo never intended to have a hand in docetic processes, not foreseeing the claims of papal power that later arose on the authority of his action. Nor did he desire a break from the Eastern church, taking care on other fronts not to offend the Eastern sees by including the *filioque* in the Western creed. Yet in establishing a new emperor Leo brought to life the docetic dialectic in both the Roman Church's break from its ecclesiastical nature (i.e., its union with the other sees) and its dismissal of a stable form for the transition of the greater-lesser. Though one should not overstate the impact of his action at the Constantinopolitan court and among the Eastern patriarchs, none of whom considered it schismatic, they were dumbfounded that their Roman brother should concoct a new emperor in an unheard-of assertion of papal prerogatives. The application of that prerogative symbolized the docetic dialectic at this embryonic stage, for after crowning the emperor as one authorized to institute his empire, Leo paid homage by humbling himself. Some say that Leo knelt before Charlemagne and others that he kissed the ground, but in either case the spiritual authority that had risen above the temporal proceeded to fall below it. In a most surreptitious and obscure way, the crowning of Charlemagne set in motion the series of events by which the church would fall and the scattering would rise.

Only occasionally does the docetic dialectic concentrate in a single event or individual man, more often tracing its arc from rise to fall over generations and centuries. Here the rise of the church and of Western lands continued from Charlemagne through the Carolingian Renaissance, with the papacy asserting its power under Nicholas I (858–867). Bolstered by confidence in his office as God's representative on earth, Nicholas initiated that separation and confusion between the church and the kingdom that approximates the corruption of soul and body at the fall. On one hand he decreed that no secular authority could appoint men to ecclesiastical office, fighting in particular cases to overturn a practice common at least since Charlemagne. In this way Nicholas announced the separation of the church as independent from the kingdom. Nicholas simultaneously exercised his power to force the hand of kings and discipline them when they did not pay him respect, invading their affairs in order to safeguard the dignity and interest of the church. "By me kings reign, and princes decree justice; by me princes rule, and nobles, and even all the judges of the earth," Nicholas wrote to Charles the Bald, manifesting the papacy's rise above its limits.[1]

---

1. Nicholas adopts these words, spoken in Proverbs by the wisdom that is humble before God, and transforms them into an expression of hubris. The word of God may be on one's lips while the heart is far from him.

The rhetoric of separation that justified Nicholas's reasoning regarding ecclesiastical appointments, and which would defend the distinct position of the church, combined with a supposed right of supervision over temporal affairs whose rationale allowed the pope to interfere in the lower order, to include judging temporal laws and mandating the resistance of clerics against kings when he deemed it necessary. Whereas it would define itself as a higher spiritual authority, the church confused its jurisdiction with the temporal, lording over the business of the body as well as the soul.

Events during the reign of Nicholas also temporarily rent the Western church from its Eastern brethren, introducing issues of lasting importance for the Great Schism. The sudden appointment of the lay scholar Photius to the patriarchate of Constantinople dismayed Nicholas, who considered the controversy that developed between the two sees as an opportunity to assert the primacy of Rome. Though he at first refused to recognize Photius as the legitimate patriarch, Nicholas later offered to accept his title on the condition that the lands of Sicily and Illyricum be handed over to the supervision of Rome. Neither Photius nor the Eastern emperor would yield to these terms, which so incensed Nicholas that he excommunicated Photius without consulting the other patriarchs. At the Lateran Council of 863 Nicholas ordered that Photius step down, declaring the supremacy of Rome over the whole church in spite of the protesting emperor. These actions put Rome and Constantinople in a temporary state of schism.

The rivalry that soon developed between Rome and the Byzantines over the lands of Moravia and Bulgaria intensified the breach. Both parties believed that they possessed the right to proselytize these lands, with the Byzantine missionaries first arriving and establishing their churches. When the Roman missionaries followed, they were reported to have attacked Eastern clerical customs regarding marriage and to have insisted on inserting the *filioque* into the Nicene Creed. Photius and the other patriarchs would not tolerate this doctrinal addition, considering it mistaken and unauthorized by the councils. In light of these developments Photius convened a synod in 867 that deposed and excommunicated Nicholas, who passed away before news of the decision arrived at Rome.

Though the schism did not last long, it highlighted questions of papal authority and the legitimacy of the *filioque* that would eventually lead to permanent division. Indeed, the course of the papacy under Nicholas represents the dual movement at the heart of the docetic dialectic. The separation of the Western church from its natural union with the East as exemplified in the schism, a break resulting on the Western side from unwarranted claims of papal power, is the break of the soul from its nature as it grasps for a knowledge beyond its limit. At the same time, in Nicholas the papacy manifested the upward movement of the docetic dialectic in which the soul leaps away from the temporal body—the political kingdom—before becoming confused with it, the latter a sign of the fall below that body that is to come. For in Nicholas the papacy ascended to a height from which it would soon descend.

The initial fall of the Western church occurred not long after Nicholas, when from the second half of the ninth century into the eleventh the papacy suffered devastating corruption. With the decline of the Carolingian Empire the popes found themselves without an external protector, with the result that they became the victims of local power brokers. Prominent Roman families and their factions engineered sedition against pope after pope, occasionally submitting the pontiff to brutal treatment. The popes themselves collaborated in plots to preserve their position while indulging in various immoralities. There were many low points during the nearly two centuries of the fall, with perhaps the lowest coming during the reign of Stephen VI (896–897). The pope ordered that the corpse of his predecessor Formosus be exhumed and placed on trial for numerous crimes, finding lifeless flesh guilty and punishing it for infractions supposedly committed during Formosus' pontificate.

Though still respected by the church throughout Europe as the throne of Saint Peter, during this era the papacy became practically irrelevant to wider religious and secular affairs. Europe faced external enemies from multiple directions and lacked rulers with the strength to maintain peace on the local level. The people lived under a more or less constant threat of conflict, while congregations continued under local military aristocracies that reigned through a combination of military and spiritual authority. In this context the appointment of local clerics by temporal rulers took a turn toward the overt subordination of the church to the kingdom. The buying and selling of bishoprics by local rulers introduced morally unworthy characters into the service of God, sullying the sanctity of the spiritual office under political affairs. The priestly ranks swelled with simoniacs who cared predominantly for their livelihood with little thought for delivering grace to parishioners. Just as Leo had placed the crown on Charlemagne's head before bowing in homage, the church descended from papal superiority over temporal rulers in Nicholas to the decay of the papacy and the servitude of the church before local magnates.

In addition to the subordination of the spiritual beneath the temporal, the fall during this time was characterized by externality in the religious life of the individual. As late as the eleventh century practices of penance, which followed confession and preceded absolution, had no noticeable emphasis on inward sorrow. This is not to say that the individual's motives were irrelevant, but that the idea of reconciliation with God consisted principally in bodily activity without a complimentary recognition of the turning of desire to God's will. Confession occurred rarely and possessed a character more communal than individual, concentrating on obvious and heinous infractions against God's law and the well-being of the group. The idea of searching one's heart to its depths, discovering the multitude of one's sins and laying them before God for pardon, had yet to flower in the Christian mind. In the 900s, officers in the church would have considered such an exercise unnecessary if not impossible. The practical understanding of the religious life and its devotion, in its diminished attention to the inner man, resonated with a social reality in which the kingdom trampled over the church and local clerics had scant regard for the qualities required by the religious office.

By the first half of the eleventh century the initial rumblings of a second iteration of rise and fall, the medieval Grand Dialectic, had begun to appear. The monastic tradition of the tenth century typified by the monks at Cluny had advocated a life of withdrawal into the cloister, discipline according to the *Rule of Benedict*, and prayer for a disordered world. The monastery during that century provided a singular alternative to the chaos of secular existence, and during the eleventh century much of that singularity remained. But an alternative also grew to prominence during the early 1000's that embodied the docetic dialectic in both its arc as the greater-lesser and its tendency to strife. Energized by the disease of simony and driven toward the reform of society, independent monks and occasionally entire monasteries appeared that modified the tradition of Benedictine and Cluniac monasticism in favor of a more active engagement with the society beyond the cloister.

The monks advancing the new perspective saw themselves as paradigms of Benedictine obedience, practicing a severe eremitical life or hailing from monasteries that maintained an unusually strict observance of the *Rule*. They were not dropouts or apostates from the Benedictine way but its perfecters, super-monks whose rigor outperformed the common monastic habit. The attitude of moral superiority inherent in such self-recognition ironically justified contact with the laity, a practice forbidden by traditional interpretations of the *Rule*. The confidence of being the greater coincided with the practice of the lesser as those supposedly above the *Rule* granted themselves the liberty to break it. Citing *caritas* as their motivation, the new monks poured over the boundaries of the monastery, leaving the neighbor-love enclosed within it in order to purge the secular church of simoniac clergy. Their harangues against tainted representatives of Christ threw the church into turmoil in various places, threatening it with local schism as the price of purification.

The attitude and activities of the reforming monks illustrate the contradictions inherent in the docetic ethos. On one hand they viewed themselves as justified in preaching to society because of their moral holiness, but on the other their arguments in support of their activities referred to the duties of Christians considered in general. The monks therefore appeared as a higher and distinct order vis-à-vis other monks and the laity at the same time that they defended their activities by reference to "universal" Christian principles. The ideological paradox that joins the especially separate and holy to the universal and common went hand-in-hand with the monks' habit of contact with the laity in breach of the *Rule*. The monks are among the earliest examples of the higher lawbreakers that reappear as Docetism's vanguard of social conflict and division, a group so possessed of its superiority that it can fuse with average men without sacrificing its sense of privilege. This pattern of confusion and separation emerged on a larger and more destructive scale as the Grand Dialectic matured into the war of the church against the kingdom, a conflict in which the church affirmed its distinction from the temporal order only to use that distinction as a rationale for lording over temporal affairs.

The interests of reforming monks and the papal leadership intersected only occasionally, but found a mutual champion in Leo IX (1049–1054). Two months after assuming the pontificate he convened a synod in Rome that denounced simony and violations of clerical marriage, the first papal proclamation regarding these issues in the eleventh century. Yet the most important events ascribed to Leo's reign do not concern the denunciations, which he did not vigorously enforce, but the divisive affair in Constantinople involving legates acting in his name.

The controversy included intransigent and volatile figures on both sides, with Cardinal Humbert sent as a Roman legate to negotiate with Michael Cerularius, the patriarch in Constantinople. Cerularius had heard that Roman leaders in Norman Italy were prohibiting Greek forms of worship in their territories, and used this as an excuse to return the favor by prohibiting Roman-style worship in the Byzantine capital. The papacy dispatched its legates in response, hoping to settle the differences between the two sees. Their efforts resulted in a series of miscommunications and inflammatory exchanges that worsened the conflict, which culminated in July of 1054. Fed up with Greek insouciance and led by Cardinal Humbert, the legates strode into the Church of Saint Sophia and presented a Bull excommunicating Michael Cerularius and his high officials. The Bull refused the title of patriarch to Cerularius and accused him of multiple crimes, condemning him for failing to insert the *filioque* into the Greek version of the Nicene Creed. When news of the Bull spread through the city, the people exploded into riots. The emperor then demanded that the Bull be publicly burnt and the legates anathematized in order to restore calm. By this time the legates had embarked for Rome, declining to return to negotiate a new concord when summoned by the emperor.

The Eastern emperor and Cerularius did not envision a permanent break with the papacy in the wake of these events, pinning the blame on the legates rather than the papal office *per se*. A later pope could have acted to reverse the growing ill will between the two sees without losing face as the patriarch of Rome, still regarded as *primus inter pares* by the remaining sees. The officials at Rome interpreted the matter differently, lending to it the centrality that it has maintained in the Roman tradition as the beginning of the Great Schism. The legates had friends of high rank in Rome, including the future Pope Gregory VII, and from this circle the view took hold in the West that the pope's representatives had acted with righteousness and that the excommunication of Cerularius was legitimate. The legates, it was thought, had acted upon the authority of the pope as ruler among the patriarchs, justly expressing the papacy's qualitatively higher position. Though the papal team had not included the church in Constantinople in the excommunication of its leader, the West would come to see its Eastern counterpart as continuing to elect and approve of schismatic bishops. The

West had a stronger consciousness of its break with both the leaders and the laymen of the East, a consciousness that bore tremendous significance for the vigor of Docetism.

The Grand Dialectic presumed the break of the church from its nature not only in the growing chasm between West and East, but in the West's confirmation of that distance as righteous on the grounds of its ecclesiastical superiority. At the fall, the soul breaks from its limit in an unwarranted and disobedient grasping for knowledge, an illegitimate attempt to rise above its station. In like manner, the papacy broke from the East in an assertion of authority unwarranted in light of the tradition of the councils. Thus the papacy initiated the first aspect of the double movement in which the church, like the disobedient soul, becomes divided from its nature at the same time that it rises as a prelude to its fall. With the debacle in 1054 Rome unwittingly turned its attention toward the infinite, a trajectory raised to violence during the reign of Gregory VII.

The dialectical rise and fall began in earnest during the reign of Gregory, who initiated the church's laborious and painful division from the kingdom. Taking up the problem of simony with a determination well beyond his predecessors, Gregory rejected the lay right of investiture as the solution to the church's ailment. In February of 1075 he issued a decree making lay investiture illegal, and in the next month the papal register records the *Dictatus Papae*, a series of proclamations that asserted unheard-of powers for the pope in the spiritual and the temporal realms. The *Dictatus* proclaimed that "the pope alone can depose or reinstate bishops," that "the Roman Pontiff alone is rightly called universal," that "the Pope is the only one whose feet are to be kissed by all princes," and that "he himself may be judged by no one." These affirmations signaled the elevation of the papacy to a power in excess of its limit and representative of the infinitizing dialectic, summoning the spirit of Nicholas I while declaring the supremacy of the pope before spiritual and temporal authorities. Nor did the *Dictatus* stop with these pronouncements, going on to declare that the pope "may depose emperors" and that he "may absolve subjects of unjust men from their fealty." Gregory's affirmation of these rights insulted Europe's royalty and threw society into an uproar, consequences he tolerated in light of the authority he believed that God had bestowed upon his office.

Lay investiture remained the principle point of contention, bringing the pope and the kings into direct conflict. Temporal rulers were used to installing men they trusted as bishops—often relatives and cronies—and did not look favorably on having local bishoprics, with their land and wealth, transferred to papal control. In this context, Gregory's proclamations split local officials of the temporal and spiritual orders according to their loyalty: would they side with the local temporal ruler or, in the case of Germany, with the emperor? Or would they join the reform instigated by the pope? The emperor Henry IV refused the pope's demand to invest German bishops, and Gregory answered by deposing and excommunicating him. Henry's enemies in Germany then took the side of the pope, using papal policies as grounds to incite a revolt against the emperor. The friends of the deposed ruler subsequently viewed the lord of Rome as having facilitated civil war across German lands, castigating him as a disingenuous and belligerent pontiff whose severance of the church from the kingdom had provoked the flow of blood.

Gregory defended his program of reform by assembling a team of legal advisers and tasking them with the development of arguments that would substantiate his agenda. From roughly 1080 forward the pamphlets distributed in support of papal claims display a preoccupation with grounding the pope's positions in reputable authorities. Both the papists and the imperialists soon showed a concern to bolster their rationale by appeal to biblical verses and canonical traditions. The papists produced the "Collection in Seventy-Four Titles," a compilation of ecclesiastical rules culled from the Church Fathers and presented as a guide for settling disputes in Germany. In the archives of the Lateran the pope's advisors also found the *tomi*, accounts of early papal correspondence that made their way into Cardinal Deusdedit's *Collectio canonum*. Similar collections took shape in the hands of papal advocates like Anselm of Lucca, whose work gathered the rules of the Fathers and the early councils into a single book of laws. In this manner the pope's legal specialists sowed the seeds for the most insidious and devastating form of infinity that struck the church. The development of the *ecclesia* as a legal institution with codices distinct from theology and liturgy, a tendency that ran amok in the twelfth century and beyond, defined the church's alienation from its nature and its path toward indefinition. It laid the groundwork both for man as the scattering and for the Christ-Idol who validates him.

Shades of the scattering were outlined in the work of Manegold of Lautenbach, a supporter of Gregory's excommunication of Henry and of the papal right to release subjects from unjust kings. In Manegold one finds the scattering intimated from the perspective of both the individual and the universal, though in each case in an understated and embryonic way. In the first instance, whereas a generation earlier Peter Damian had employed the notion of *officium* to justify the power of the office over potential moral lapses in the individual holding it, claiming that the grace of the priesthood overcame the deficiencies of those who gained their position by simony, Manegold reversed the logic with respect to temporal rule such that morally insufficient individuals negated the power of good order inherent in royal station. He shifted the crucial consideration to the moral worthiness of the office-wielder rather than the good of the office, subtly denying the efficacy of the office to correct the wayward holder. Such an attack suggests the new consciousness of man *qua* individual that flowered in later centuries in both religious affairs and in society on the whole, witnessing to the gestation of the scattering in the Gregorian era.

Manegold introduced another important shift by altering the theoretical relation of the people to their temporal rulers. The notion of contract, which based royal authority upon the will of the people (that is, the nobles) rather than divine ordination, had already appeared in the writing of Bernhard of Hildesheim, a member of Manegold's circle. This development was momentous on its own, but Bernhard restricted it by arguing that in the wake of choosing the king the people had no right to remove him. Manegold denied a permanent rule based in the contract in favor of the people's judgment on whether and when the king might have broken the agreement through injustice, at which point they could legitimately overthrow him. By this theory Manegold justified revolution in temporal affairs given appropriate circumstances, a rationale that he exploited in support of Gregory's conflict with Henry. In addition to suggesting an advanced awareness of the individual as office bearer in lieu of consideration of the office borne, Manegold fought for a new consciousness of the popular will as sitting in judgment on temporal rulers. He abstracts both the individual person and the collective from the outward office or law that would prescribe the boundaries for action, empowering the abstraction as an element potent enough to overturn its limits. Man rises above the law that would contain him in a logic that foreshadows the fuller emergence of the scattering.

Gregory died ignominiously in 1085, but the docetic spirit that had stormed through him continued after his passing. To the forms of infinity birthed during his reign, including claims of universal papal jurisdiction and the seeds of a distinct legal consciousness in the church, the papacy presently added a third. Under Pope Urban II, the Western church embarked on the first of its Crusades, the military and economic ventures that projected Western might over international boundaries in search of conquest. Of the forms of infinity that Docetism introduces into religious and temporal affairs, international expansion is perhaps the most obvious. The docetic spirit can hardly survive apart from such expansion, which has accompanied its development from these early centuries until the present day.

The First Crusade manifests Docetism's recurring treachery, here personified in the high expectations of Urban. He believed that the Crusades would help mend the breach between Eastern and Western Christians, pleasing the Eastern churches and the Byzantine emperor while uniting Christendom against a pagan enemy. Urban did not understand the docetic logic and its deception. He did not comprehend the infinitizing content of international military action nor its destabilizing tendencies, but unintentionally used that which divides in the hope that it would bind Christians together. So the Crusades, developed with the best papal intentions, exacerbated the divergence between West and East. Besides engaging in a holy war whose concept was suspicious to the Greeks and conducting themselves in an unruly and disrespectful manner while traversing Byzantine lands, the Crusaders aroused the ire of the Eastern sees by forcing the sitting patriarch out of occupied Antioch and replacing him with a Latin bishop. Their supposed Latin benefactors consequently appeared to ecclesiastical leaders in the East as foreigners rather than fellow-Christians, an impression worsened by the expedition against Constantinople in 1107. The march on the city had the blessing of then-pope Paschal II, whose approval was viewed in the East as a declaration of Holy War on the empire. The venture was short and an unqualified failure, but it cast a long psychological shadow. In conjunction especially with the ousting of the Antiochian patriarch, the military threat against Constantinople heightened the antipathy of the East toward the West in the opening decades of the twelfth century. The advances begun with high papal hopes terminated in unforeseen and utterly contrary results, irritating the rift that Urban had hoped to close.

The twelfth century saw the maturation of the three modes of infinity initiated in the eleventh: the popes launched new Crusades from the middle of the century to its conclusion, intensifying the breach between West and East; they embraced exalted estimates of papal supremacy vis-à-vis temporal rulers and fought to impose their might in worldly affairs; and the Roman church progressively transformed into an institution with a distinct legal identity. The last of these stands above the others, for the expansion of ecclesiastical law beyond its roots in theology and liturgy constitutes the side of the infinitizing movement that most directly brings man to his consummation in universality. The detachment and growth of the law intertwines with the consciousness of the individual *qua* individual, who knows himself in abstraction from his public and institutional life to the extent that those institutions embrace an expansive legal platform. As the institution devolves through an alien and limitless law, so the individual regards his new self-consciousness with both delight and confusion. It comes as no surprise that the twelfth century embodied both sides of this phenomenon in a single age, boasting a burgeoning ecclesiastical edifice met step-for-step with a graduated emphasis on the individual.

In that time the Western church spawned a new kind of cleric concerned less with the administration of the sacraments than the business of administration. A managerial class swelled the ranks of Catholic officials, men trained in law and prepared for political careers as much or more than the holier duties of their order. They directed the Western ethos toward legal philosophy, system, and logic, dedicating their energies to the justification of the church's political prerogatives as an institution at once set apart by its spiritual functions and licensed to weigh in on if not decide temporal disputes. As the church widened its distance from the kingdom, protecting the separation of the two spheres, it also broke with its own theological consciousness, infusing a new and evolving body of law into the institution through experts trained at universities. These new schools responded to the demand for men capable of constructing arguments that would validate the changing ecclesiastical order and its claims regarding the temporal realm. Soon the universities began supplying lawyers on both the papal and royal sides of political disputes, serving as centers of learning for an age confident in its ability to reform society despite persistent legal conflict.

The revolutionary upheavals that pitted the church versus the kingdom provoked a new method for solving the problems of law that they implied. The dialectical reasoning of the twelfth century, which seems innocent enough on the surface, stands as the first instance of a philosophical pattern that reflects the docetic dialectic as a systematic intellectual phenomenon. Mirroring the practical quandary of the law of the pope set against the law of the king, the dialectical method begins not with a single, indisputable authority but with questions raised by gaps or contradictions between authoritative legal texts or within the same text. The dialectic places the contradictions side by side in the effort to establish a new harmony, resolving the contrasting elements until rules that appeared broken or antithetical are reconciled within a broader synthesis. In this way the method hoped to find unity where there was discord.

The dialectical method presumed a view of the law largely unknown in the West. Whereas the Roman legal texts that medieval lawyers used as a starting point did not necessarily imply general maxims or a comprehensive understanding of law, handling particular cases in their particularity and without extending them into universal rules, dialectical legal philosophy sought a system defined by its universal scope and which integrated separate matters of legal doctrine into a coherent whole. This method found itself in a state of contradiction illustrative of the docetic logic. Beginning in the uncertainty of questions and contradictions, the method rises upward in the reconciliation of opposing cases into a new maxim. The new maxim, however, forms the first of two new competing principles that require adjudication, a recognition that submerges what had risen into discernible legal guidance under a new antagonism. While seeking a comprehensive, unified system of legal truth, the dialectic ends up with an asymptotic approximation of that truth that never achieves final answers. The psychological consequence of such an undertaking is not pride at the approximation but despair at a truth that appears more distant as it comes closer, for the comprehensive and systematic grasp of truth for which the system strives is increasingly understood as an impossible goal. In the process the law—and in medieval times this included both natural and ecclesiastical law—becomes seen as programmatic, growing, and reformable, but by that same standard also pliable and, in an implication with which the optimistic legal technicians of the day would not have agreed, unstable. The dissemination of laws in works such as Gratian's *Decretum* (1140) testify to an age that hastened legal development while lacking a consciousness of its negative implications. These surfaced only later and in a more personal setting, leading to the dialectical innovations of the docetic genius Martin Luther.

The ballooning class of clerical administrators and lawyers did not ascend without opposition. Humanists of letters and learning, men of literature, poetry, and the arts whose activities define the twelfth century as a time of renaissance, looked on the managerial class with a mixture of concern and disdain. While religious humanists lambasted the new officialdom in satires, others indulged a novel awareness of the individual as seen in the development of self-portraits, deepened explorations of affect in troubadour love songs, and meditations on friendship between pairs thought to mirror one another's soul. Through these practices the humanists cultivated new, inward attitudes and mores, offering a meaningful alternative to the careerism of ecclesiastical affairs.

The trend toward the individualized consciousness influenced religious no less than secular life. The concern for the judgment of the individual implicit in Anselm's satisfaction theory, the increased devotional emphasis on participation in Christ's sufferings, and the inward turn that permeated such writings as Hugh of Fouilloy's *On the Cloister of the Soul* prove the presence of a religious personality conceived in relative detachment from the outward affairs of church and society. In the spirit of the worldly monks who preceded Gregory VII, Hugh argued that a holy man attentive to the thoughts and commitments of the inner cloister can engage in worldly activity without detriment to his soul. Like the institutional breach separating the kingdom from the church, the break between the body and the soul had progressed enough that the pious could posit a soul protected by its distance from bodily habits.

The new focus on man's inner life as opposed to outward action also influenced the Western practice of confession. The popes in the eleventh century had altered the traditional pattern of confession, penance, and reconciliation so that reconciliation followed the admission of sin. This change preceded the twelfth century's turn to inner sorrow as the crucial element in the sinner's restoration before God, a stress that went hand in hand with a wider and more consistent adoption of confession among Christians. Though the church did not impose annual confession upon every member until the Lateran Council in 1215, the spirit that recognized its necessity had matured over the course of the 1100's, advancing with an accent on the remorse of the penitent rather than the absolution given by the priest. In this age men became more concerned with the inner state of the confessing sinner, and in lieu of the focus on externals indicative of earlier penal codes one finds a penchant for self-examination among the devout. Men as prominent as Bernard of Clairvaux developed their conceptions of the spiritual life around the notion of intention, while Peter Abelard defined sin according to the individual's inner aims in *Ethics: or, Know Yourself*. The confession booth became an important locus for the assurance of salvation at the same time that the purity of one's conscience measured the soul's standing before God.

The age had much to confess in the eyes of the satirists, who saw the ascendance of the managerial class as the betrayal of the church's ideals. Viewing the technocratic order from the outside and despising the church's machinery as an arena for opportunists, the satirists felt that things had gone mournfully awry in both the spiritual and temporal orders. They perceived the distortion of reality that lurches behind a society flushed with its sense of progress, whose optimism confuses the accumulation of worldly power with the advance of God's will. Writing in the latter decades of the twelfth century, Walter of Châtillon contrasted the lawful order of the natural world with the disjuncture that man faced within his society and his nature:

> God, who by a fourfold rule
> Chaos regulated
> Things unequal equalized
> And by laws related
> All interrelationships

> Duly calculated—
> Why do you leave only man's
> Nature dislocated?

The discontent inspired by social conditions and the felt fragmentation of man led Walter and his ilk to espouse eschatological views. It seemed to them that the disorder among men presaged the antichrist and the return of Jesus, for how could a state of affairs in which greed and ambition had run rampant go unpunished? How could the Lord not return to set right what had gone wrong?

More than others in this era the satirists apprehended the docetic spirit in their midst, recognizing the fraying of the form that holds man together. The law by which man knows his nature as embedded in institutions, those mediations meant to train him away from sin, was dissolving. By the twelfth century those institutions had lost sight of their purpose just as man felt his abstraction from them, an alienation manifest in his pronounced awareness of the inner life. Thus appeared that simultaneous experience of expectation and uneasiness that accompanies man as his form slides from solidity into possibility, the internal dialectic of raising and lowering that reflects the rise and fall of institutions that throw off their boundaries. The proliferation of ecclesiastical canons and their scholastic study, though they tempted him with the hope of a just society grounded in the rule of the church, signaled man's ontological distance from the divine law and the undoing of the church's institutional form as the body of Christ. Through these canons and their twin in the individualized consciousness one discovers man slouching toward universality, approaching the formlessness in which he celebrates his indifference to God's command. Man imperceptibly melts into the scattering as the principle of his existence, though this movement had yet to achieve the religious validation that would enhance its assault.

That assault raised the war between church and kingdom to ecclesiastical crisis during the reign of emperor Frederick Barbarossa, whose decisions eventuated in dual popes for nearly two decades. From the 1150s into the 1170s one pope claimed authority under the emperor while another proclaimed himself the leader of an independent Rome. During these same decades papal jurists developed arguments that sought to augment papal rights over the temporal sphere. The claim that the church as the soul had priority over the kingdom as the body had been advanced since the time of Cardinal Humbert, with papists often grossly distorting the doctrine in support of Roman aims. They now argued that the "power of the keys" conferred to Saint Peter included the pope's right to crown emperors, though historically this affirmation derived from Leo's crowning of Charlemagne. By the end of the century some among the papacy's advocates leaned toward a theory of papal world-monarchy in which the pope possessed complete sovereignty over temporal and spiritual government.

This theory found its nearest embodiment in the pontificate of Innocent III (1198–1216), whose rule presents the apex of the Grand Dialectic. In Innocent multiple forms of the infinitizing movement came to a head: his willful exercise of supreme authority in temporal as well as spiritual government, his push for the Crusade that finalized the Eastern schism, and his codification of a mountain of Roman laws dovetail in a singularly potent expression of the finite's transgression of its limits. Innocent sums up the advance in which the church breaks from its nature by striving to bottle the infinite within the finite. He is the docetically-empowered giant whose height foreshadows the depths to which the papacy would fall.

Innocent never bluntly argued that the pope possesses supreme temporal authority when justifying his interventions in international affairs, but his theological rationale and his actions imply this conviction. In addition to informing the emperor at Constantinople that the priesthood surpassed the kingship as the soul over the body, Innocent construed the position of the pope by reference to the description of Jesus as a priest of the order of Melchizedek, a man who had been both priest and king. By this argument and others like it Innocent reserved the supreme right of judgment in worldly affairs for the papacy, a right put to work in his resolution of the dispute between two aspirants to the throne of the Western emperor and in his arbitration of controversies between the kings of France and England. Innocent also deposed a king in Norway and had another established in Bulgaria, while laboring to enlarge the Papal States in Italy. Innocent wielded papal power with an authority relatively undisputed by the temporal dignitaries involved, as if all recognized that the augmentation of spiritual powers into temporal rule reflected the order desired by God. This is the unique achievement of his papacy, the height to which no pope before or after would ascend.

The expansion of Innocent's power reached no less to the East, although the bad consequences of the Fourth Crusade resulted more from indecision than arrogance. Animosity had grown between average Byzantines and the Westerners who had settled in their lands, flaring in the massacre of Latins in Constantinople in 1182. The Crusade of 1204 returned the insult with an intensity not sought by Innocent but not stridently condemned by him. While Innocent had roused Europe to a Crusade meant to reassert the Christian presence in the Holy Land, the nobles who executed the assault turned their eyes upon the Byzantine capital. Prince Alexius, the son of the dispossessed Byzantine emperor Isaac Angelus, had approached the Crusaders with promises of money if they should install him as ruler of the empire. The nobility did not consult the pope in taking up the prince's cause, which failed with the riots that immediately followed his establishment by Latin hands.

Seeing that the coffers in Constantinople were empty, and that they consequently would not receive the expected payment, the Crusaders conspired to seize Constantinople and make it the capital of a new Latin empire. This plan was concocted again without notifying the pope. The three-day sack of the city ensued, in which the Crusaders perpetrated one of the most heinous and unruly crimes in the history of the West. They set the Byzantine libraries on fire, destroying ancient manuscripts and decimating collections of antique art, while committing outrages against Byzantine men, women, and children as well as monks, nuns, and priests. It is reported that a French prostitute strolled through the Church of Saint Sophia and sat on the patriarchal throne while Latin soldiers paid her homage. The Crusaders helped themselves to whatever they pleased, compiling a trove of booty so enormous that it included the city's priceless treasures as a fraction of the take. The desecration of the city and its shrines grieved the Easterners deeply, especially as a crime committed by supposed brothers in Christ. The memory of Constantinople's ruin and the sacrilege involved catapulted the dissonance of earlier disputes into overt schism, permanently severing the East from the West.

Innocent's reaction to the seizure of the city exacerbated Eastern discontent. In fairness, the first report he received did not mention the horrors that the Crusaders had poured out upon the people. Innocent was frustrated to learn that the Crusade had diverted its focus from the Holy Land to Constantinople, but he exulted at the prospect of an eastern Latin Empire that seemed, for the moment at least, to bind the whole of Christendom under Roman rule. His congratulations of the new Latin emperor stung the Byzantine population, while his later dismay upon hearing the details of the sack did nothing to mitigate the resentment inspired by his initial reaction. Far from resolutely denouncing the Western assault upon the city and its churchmen, Innocent supported the imposition of a Latin patriarch in Greek lands, a sign that he accepted the overthrow of Constantinople despite the obscenities carried out during the conquest. The leaders of the Eastern sees and their parishioners could not help but conclude that the Romans were no longer Christian brothers, for how could the pope tolerate such abuses and indulge the illusion of a unified Christendom?

Neither Innocent nor his followers had a satisfying answer to such questions, soon turning from Rome's relationship with the East to business more pertinent to the Western churches. About a decade after the Crusade Innocent headed the Fourth Lateran Council. Preceded in 1179 by the Third Lateran, together the two councils issued hundreds of new statutes that solidified the church's grounding in a concept of law independent from theology and lacking an apparent limit to its expansion. With the councils the twelfth century culture of lawyers took a significant step forward, as from the 1190s into the first decades of the thirteenth century the church composed no less than five major systematic collections of decretals. Innocent thus stands at the center of the congealing of the legal consciousness so pivotal for the earlier century into a detailed codex of rules with the formal stamp of the papacy. In 1234 Pope Gregory IX completed the process by amassing a comprehensive collection of decretals including roughly two thousand sections. Joined with the *Decretum* of Gratian, Gregory's collection served as the foundation for further political theory as well as the canon law that remains in force in the current era.

The hundred years after Innocent saw the decline of papal supremacy over the temporal sphere, a development ironically forwarded by the grand pope. When

Innocent introduced prince Frederick II as the successor of Otto IV, the emperor whom he deposed in 1215, he unwittingly raised up an adversary who harassed the papacy until mid-century. As emperor, Frederick ruled a Sicilian government that operated with brilliant efficiency while setting his sights on subduing all Italy under his authority. Innocent, who died in 1216, would not have dreamed of allowing Frederick such power, and the popes who followed him shared the same aversion to the emperor. For the duration of Frederick's reign they found themselves on the defensive side of political squabbles and military threats.

Aside from convening a council to condemn and depose Frederick in 1245, Pope Innocent IV used every means at his disposal to gain supporters from across Europe for his duel with the emperor. Spiritual claims and privileges were deployed to effect temporal ends, debasing the papacy in the minds of those it hoped to influence. The papacy was fighting for its political life and, in order to protect its position, had vigorously adopted the habits and attitudes of a temporal political establishment. The popes continued to argue for Rome's supremacy, claiming that the papacy was imbued with both the sacerdotal and the royal powers of Christ, but their rhetoric was marred by the reality of an emperor determined to ignore papal assertions and annul Roman power.

The philosophy of Thomas Aquinas lent intellectual credibility to the distillation of the kingdom from the church that developed in the first half of the century. Drawing on Aristotle, Aquinas affirmed that political life derived from man's nature as a social animal. Reflection on the nature of man provided a framework for a political life fit for that nature and that facilitates the kinds of activity inherent in its design. By this reasoning Thomas crafted a theory of politics without overt reference to the supernatural or divine law. This theory had a noticeable impact, for just as one could conceptualize the kingdom with lenses that were not self-evidently theological, so kings could justify their powers in distinction from popes. If the pontiffs pointed to the royal rule handed down to them by Christ, after Aquinas the kings could answer that the temporal order possessed legitimacy independent of such rationales.

The dispute over national sovereignty and the right of popes over the nation's churchmen brought the papacy to its knees, pitting the French king Philip IV against Pope Boniface VIII (1295–1303). The first of their battles concerned the right of kings to tax the clergy. When Boniface announced that kings had no power over the persons and goods in their realms that belonged to the church, Philip answered by halting all exports of currency and precious metals to Rome. This decree deprived the papacy of its principle source of revenue, with the result that Boniface succumbed to Philip's right of taxation. The second dispute arose over Philip's arrest, trial, and imprisonment of a French bishop, a matter carried out in spite of canon laws stating that only a pope could put a bishop on trial. After a multitude of papal bulls against Philip that met with the king's own propaganda campaign, Boniface proclaimed his unqualified supremacy as pope in *Unam Sanctam*. Promulgated in 1302, the bull affirmed that all the church's sheep belong to one shepherd, lest they not constitute one flock. It also argued that "the spiritual power has to institute the earthly power and to judge it if it has not been good," a perspective that elevated Boniface over Philip as a lord over his subject. The bull so emphasized the pope's authority that it pronounced it "altogether necessary to salvation for every creature to be subject to the Roman pontiff." One could hardly imagine a more explicit and forceful combination of the papacy's spiritual foundations with its supposed temporal authority.

Philip responded to *Unam Sanctam* by commissioning a military attack on the person of Boniface, who had recently taken up residence in his hometown of Anagni. In 1303 the king's leading minister and an army of mercenaries assaulted the town in an effort to find the pope, discovering him after an afternoon of fighting. The minister and an associate entered the papal chambers and saw Boniface, an old man, dressed in pontifical attire and clutching a crucifix. The invaders insulted and mistreated him but could not finally decide what to do regarding their captive. A delay of three days permitted the people of Anagni to expel the mercenaries, with the pope escaping and returning to Rome. Yet the humiliation of the affair had done its work, with a shocked Boniface dying a few weeks later. His successors capitulated to Philip, even lauding the king for the piety he had displayed in his conduct with the earlier pope.

The opening of the fourteenth century intensified the fall initiated in the thirteenth. During this period, the Grand Dialectic hastened its descent as the papacy plummeted beneath the temporal power both in concrete circumstances and on the level of theory. Not long after Boniface the papal throne relocated to Avignon, where it stayed for roughly 70 years. The popes during this period amounted to little more than lackeys of the French kings, having been deprived of their independence and in complete contrast to the superiority of Innocent III. The hierarchy also fell prey to the ills that had troubled it prior to Gregory, permitting the practice of simony that had provided an immediate cause for the eruption of the Grand Dialectic. The fall of the papacy was nearly exhausted in the "Babylonian Captivity" in which the spiritual authority devolved into a partisan of a particular ruler while suffering internal corruption. Its sorry condition was obvious to monarchs both within and outside of France.

Changes in political theory in the early fourteenth century were delicate and profound, indicating Docetism's maturation into a new phase in its progress toward the Christ-Idol. Some canonists continued to advocate papal world-supremacy in the time of Boniface, with Giles of Rome contending that the authority granted by the papacy's spiritual functions implied that the pope owned all the world's material goods. The ocean between the language of spiritual purity and the reality of worldly ambition that characterized papist arguments had rendered them unconvincing to European leaders for decades, and this was no less the case with Giles. At this point royal thinkers continued to take cues from the papists, as a theory appeared in France that mirrored Roman claims inasmuch as it dreamed of the consolidation of vast territories under French rule. The philosopher Pierre Dubois advanced a scenario in which France would gain control over Germany, Constantinople, and Rome in addition to

England and smaller European provinces. The fantasy of papal world-domination met its twin in the illusion of a universal temporal empire standing over the West as well as much of the East.

At the fall the soul aspires toward infinity and so descends toward the formlessness of possibility, with the body as the lower imitating the higher in the same dynamic. In like manner the kingdom duplicated the theoretical errors of a church in steep decline, justifying royal rule in the direction of the limitlessness that had progressively characterized papal aims since Gregory. The royal theorists who posited an infinite kingdom found their precedent in the theoretical application of that infinity to the church. This conceptual confrontation of infinite versus infinite equalizes the spiritual and the temporal and so undermines the higher by negating its superiority. Just as in fallen nature the flesh wars against the spirit in order to subdue it, the late-medieval kingdom pressed the church under its heel both through the physical relocation of the papacy to Avignon and in its claims to royal universality.

Nor is this all. John of Paris, arguably the most sophisticated thinker in his time, also maintained that the church and the kingdom each possessed a distinct and universal dominion, the church in spiritual affairs and the kingdom in temporal government. John then proceeded to redefine the pope's authority in terms of his administration of ecclesiastical goods that belonged in fact to the people. Like temporal rulers, the pope exercised power for the benefit of the community and gained legitimacy from the righteousness of that exercise. This view had been popular regarding kings at least since Manegold, and John's innovation was to apply it to ecclesiastical rule. The point was not that popes and kings did not retain legitimacy from God, as they did for John and would for some time, but that in John's thought pope as well as king owed a substantive debt of responsibility to the populace, who could depose the pope through temporal rulers if he failed in his duties. In John one therefore finds both the dualism of universalized and distinct spheres of temporal and spiritual government and the grounding of each in a constitutional responsibility to the people.

John's theories carry disturbing implications in light of the docetic logic, which they exemplify in a nascent but striking degree. For the universalization and distinction of the church and the kingdom, institutions designed to train man in his finitude, implies their foundation in the negative infinity of appeals to the people. Their growth toward the infinite in principle matures as they realize their legitimacy in the moment when law has not yet become concrete, in the will of a people unconditioned by an understanding of their lives as embedded in that law. John did not explicitly conceive of the people as so unconditioned, but in the constitutional principles that he helped set in motion the law in its divine and natural expressions eventually became detached from and subordinated to the community rather than the community being embedded in it. By this inversion the law relinquishes its validity inasmuch as it falls beneath a principle of change. Isolated and extracted in a way that would develop out of John's constitutionalism, the people are that uninterrupted motion that is the abolishment of law and the fulfillment of its universalization. To base both temporal and spiritual institutions in the people is thus to base natural and divine law in the scattering. Such a direction prepares the way for Docetism's annulment of law as the prerogative of man and his social world.

That world appeared, in the fourteenth century, to have relinquished the last vestiges of beneficent order. When the popes returned to Rome from Avignon, the Western Schism erupted as a new punishment. In the schism the papacy descended into jaw-dropping legal and practical confusion, with a multiplicity of popes advocating for the throne. That each made his case with cogent arguments presented a unique threat to papal legitimacy, undermining the viability of the office until the schism's resolution in the fifteenth century. The same age saw Europe's entrenchment in the Hundred Years' War (1337–1475), a conflict in which the papacy lacked the moral authority to criticize participating nations. Defined in the fourteenth century by papal alienation from Rome and the onset of war, not to mention the horrors of the Black Death (1348–1350), Western Christendom had fallen into such disrepair that rebirth might not have seemed possible.

During this age theological transformations emerged that mysteriously resonated with the foregoing legal changes in the Church. When the institution developed a new and ever-expanding law in canons distinct from theology and liturgy, it unintentionally introduced a new ontology and a new nature into the Church in contrast to the old. In earlier periods the mystery of the sacraments limited the reach of the law, but the legal apparatus knew no such limits, affirming in their place a systematic striving for perfection. The rest of the Church's nature in the habit of grace thus came under threat from the infinite, and how long would it take before a new understanding of God took hold that mirrored the ontological shifts in Christ's institutional body? If the Church could adopt a nature based on an infinitized law, could men not conceptualize God in the same manner? Could they not imagine him as an infinite law unbound by rest and reason, by the habit and pattern of nature? The nominalist God envisioned in the fourteenth and fifteenth centuries does just this. The essence of this God as absolute power extends without boundary over all things, asserting itself beyond reason as well as good and evil. If something is good, it is so because God decrees it and not because of the thing's intrinsic rationality. A thing is evil likewise because God decrees it, not because of the corruption of a nature that is good as rational. The meaning of the thing moreover lies not in its nature but in the use to which God puts it, so that the form of the nature becomes immaterial to its content as an object of use. God himself arguably has no limiting nature or reason, but is an infinite will.

If men conceived of God as an infinite law, they could equally well portray themselves in his image. The Renaissance thus introduced the third rise in Docetism's ongoing dialectic, a period of apparent resurrection unto life, of pride in man's capacities after the preceding time of suffering. A few men of genius towered at the Renaissance's cultural peak, determining the tastes and sensibilities of countless others across

Europe. The universal man, the man of the Renaissance, mastering as many activities as he could, dedicating himself to various and unbounded pursuits, manifested the heights latent within the human spirit. Painter, engineer, and anatomist Leonardo da Vinci exemplified the ideal. He enjoyed the life of unlimited possibilities praised by Pico della Mirandola, who stressed the choice of man in reaching his potential while lauding him as a chameleon who could change for the better. So does the scattering deceive, so does it lead its captives into the hope of betterment through paths that conceal decline. What appears as his freedom and his exaltation unto universality belies the ontology of formlessness. The man of possibility is man scattered, a man celebrated in the Renaissance by those who lacked a consciousness of his deeper meaning. That new depth's bottom, however, would not be touched until the Reformation, where man's religious orientation suffered perhaps its profoundest blow. It was not the Renaissance but the Reformation that catapulted man into formlessness, that launched the scattering into domination of man and his world. There, and there alone, came the revelation of the Christ-Idol.

II

Docetism's Grand Dialectic undermined the papacy as a channel of divine law in a number of ways. The collapse under Boniface VIII diminished the popes into puppets of French kings in the same era that John of Paris defined papal legitimacy in terms of the pope's administrative responsibility to Catholic believers, suggesting a novel theory of ecclesiastical constitutionalism. While the church relinquished spiritual authority under the supervision of a particular nation and as its partisan, on the level of theory the grounding of the pope's legal authority in substantive appeals to the people based his right in the collective as an entity subtly distinguished from the law and granted the power to judge it. These two challenges to a Catholic law grounded in the supreme rule of God joined hands in the early fourteenth century with the silent and more stunning transformation in which the practice of confession grew to require the enumeration of absolutely all of one's sins in order for one to receive assurance of pardon. If in the prior two developments Docetism lay coiled and ready to strike, in the latter it delivered the venom. For the infinite law imposed upon the conscience in confession, the inward parallel to the multiplication of the church's legal canons, served only to undermine that law's viability. From the Christian's imprisonment in this confessional cocoon would be born the Christ-Idol as the god of man liberated and universalized, indifferent toward and without the law. Thus Docetism unveiled the dagger supposed to bear the name and power of Christ, a weapon that executed its first strike in the Reformation.

In the fourteenth and fifteenth centuries Western man grew increasingly anxious over the state of his soul, fomenting that anxiety through a progressively burdensome requirement in confession. Theologians and church officials deemed it necessary that man count what lies beyond counting, that he present each and every sin to God so that the Savior might wipe it away, cleansing the conscience and relieving guilt. The Christian pursuing salvation embarked upon the most stringent inner examination, holding up the smallest sin as much as the greatest in order to expose and eliminate it in the grace of God. This trajectory flowered as the infinitizing of the law in the conscience and the consequent demolition of natural righteousness, and at its apex it dominated the minds of two men. Towering above the preceding age as its paradigmatic product is Martin Luther, the melancholy monk who obliterated the bonds of man's spiritual being. Luther brought the docetic dialectic to a new pitch, redefining the spiritual freedom of man as the necessary maturation of inner tyranny under the law. At his side stands John Calvin, the mastermind who applied the dialectic of the liberated conscience to man as such, energizing powers that have alienated him from his neighbor, his society, his natural environment, and from the law of his being *qua* man.

As a young monk, Luther took up the law with unusual vigor, trusting in it as a way of righteousness. His years of confidence in devotion, fasts, ceremonies, and worship as if these could save defined his early efforts toward salvation, in which he sought justification via the law. When this way of justification brought on anxiety, Luther felt the temptation to continue to trust in the law, promising God that he would fulfill all of the law's commands while doubling his determination along that course. Looking back on this way of life in the *Commentary on Galatians* (1531), Luther observes that "those who perform the works of the Law with the intention of being justified through them not only do not become righteous but become twice as unrighteous . . . I have experienced this both in myself and in many others." He then explains in some depth the dynamic of the conscience that seeks justification via obedience. This passage, a reflection of Luther's personal development, hints at the docetic innovation in which the oppression of the conscience under the law precedes its liberation in the grace of the Christ-Idol:

> "Therefore anyone who seeks righteousness through the Law does nothing by his repeated actions but acquire the habit of this first action, which is that God in His wrath and awe is to be appeased by works. On the basis of this opinion he begins to do works. Yet he can never find enough works to make his conscience peaceful; but he keeps looking for more, and even in the ones he does perform he finds sin. Therefore his conscience can never become sure, but he must continually doubt and think this way: 'You have not sacrificed correctly; you have not prayed correctly; you have omitted something; you have committed this or that sin.' Then the heart trembles and continually finds itself loaded down with wagonloads of sins that increase infinitely, so that it deviates further and further from righteousness, until it finally acquires the habit of despair. Many who have been driven to such despair cried out miserably in the agony of death: 'Miserable man that I am! I have not observed the rules of my monastic order. Where shall I flee from the countenance of Christ, the

> wrathful Judge? If only I had been a swineherd or the most ordinary of men!' Thus at the end of his life a monk is weaker, more beggarly, more unbelieving, and more fearful than he was at the beginning, when he joined the order . . . The Law or human traditions or the rule of his monastic order were supposed to heal and enrich him in his illness and poverty, but he became weaker and more beggarly than the tax collectors and harlots . . . Therefore neither past nor present works are enough for him, regardless of their quantity or quality; but he continually looks at and looks for ever-different ones, by which he attempts to appease the wrath of God and to justify himself, until in the end he is forced to despair . . . Therefore it is impossible for men who want to provide for their salvation through the Law, as all men are inclined to do by nature, ever to be set at peace. In fact, they only pile laws upon laws, by which they torture themselves and others and make their consciences so miserable that many of them die before their time because of excessive anguish of heart. For one law always produces ten more, until they grow to infinity. This is shown by the innumerable *Summae* that collect and expound such laws . . . "

Though in it Luther describes the way of perdition by sustained trust in the law rather than justification as the transition from law to grace, this passage informally outlines the law's transformation from presenting a temptation to seek one's righteousness through it, which Luther elsewhere refers to as its abuse by the believer, to what he calls the law's proper theological use, that of bringing the Christian to a robust knowledge of sin, reducing nature's powers to nothing and denying their contribution to justification while nourishing despair of the law as the way of righteousness. Applied to Luther's own experience and given a voice in the passage, the mediating term between man's approach to the law as that meant to "heal and enrich" and its eventual terminus in despair is the recognition of the law's infinite demands. Everywhere the Christian looks, good deeds required but undone swallow obedience performed. As the commands multiply, pressing down upon man by their uncontrolled expansion, he perceives that the law has become limitless, even infinite. The law mutates from a promised way of justification into a tomb and a prison because it lays an unlimited demand upon a finite creature. Yet in this movement the law also begins to perform its right theological use in convincing the believer of the utter insufficiency of works for justification, driving him to despair at nature's "wagonloads of sins that increase infinitely." So long as man continues to trust in the law despite this despair, a sinful agony consumes him. This is the docetic tyranny of the law over the Christian, the inward manifestation of an ecclesiastical power that transgresses its limits without restraint.

The passage implies an interaction between law and nature that moves in contrary directions. The law initially appears as the way to justification and man clings to it as such. This hope in the law remains present despite the contrary pressure exerted by the expansion of the commands to infinity, whereby the Christian finds that the law undermines its own lure toward justification and destroys confidence in nature's power to procure that justification via obedience. The law holds out assurance of salvation and peace of conscience only to pull them back, submitting Luther and his believer to a deadly teasing from which there appears to be no escape.

The law's growth to infinity undergirds its role in the "conflict of conscience" or spiritual trial, in which the contradictory vectors of the law attain their highest intensity. "It is the devil's habit" in this conflict, Luther says, "to frighten us with the Law and to set against us the consciousness of sin, our wicked past, the wrath and judgment of God, hell and eternal death, so that thus he may drive us into despair." As the product of its increasing boundlessness, the law's tendency to annul its apparent offer of justification loomed over Luther's consciousness in moments of angst, so that when he considered the law he immediately perceived its terror. At these times it seems "that the devil is roaring at us terribly, that heaven is bellowing, that the earth is quaking, that everything is about to collapse . . . that hell is opening up in order to swallow us," in other words, that perdition is sure because nature has no available means to secure grace against its sin. Nature endures its "reduction to nothing" under a merciless law, experiencing its wrath as a "true taste of death." This anxiety under the law presupposes the promise of justification via obedience toward whose annulment the law itself tends; the law's ability to terrify depends upon its apparent validity as the way to salvation, a way that the believer endures as the limitless revelation of anguish.

The law's limitlessness in application to a finite creature means likewise its limitlessness in the realm of being, an infinity achieved by the eradication of its limit in nature's freedom of will. The law's commands everywhere convincing man that he is under the curse, allowing no respite from their assaults and convicting him of multiple sins for each single act of righteousness, condemn nature before it acts. This ubiquitous and inescapable condemnation renders human freedom meaningless; it is the law as a tyrannical infinite victimizing the finite will that would hold its boundary. It is also the experiential source of Luther's dictum that the will is powerless with respect to justification, which is to say that the will suffers the curse no matter what it has done or will do. The insufficient righteousness that the will might claim for itself dwindles into no righteousness at all, just as the individual in the midst of spiritual trial endures the law's infinity as the roaring of hell and the devil. As the law progressively expands, squeezing its limit into insignificance, it simultaneously abdicates its form, casting off its definition in the believer's experience as the loss of mercy. The law as a direction toward righteousness given for nature's benefit transforms into something cold and cruel, a terror to the conscience.

Grace as "the righteousness of God" shatters this process by announcing a way of righteousness completely apart from works and by faith alone, with Luther turning to the righteousness of Christ given freely and received in total passivity. This new way of justification rescued Luther from the torment of the infinite law because it successfully negated that law's presupposition, that he should take it up as the way of redemption. In the wake of justification grasped by faith alone, the law has lost all power to frighten because it has lost all power to tempt, with its validity as a path to heaven decisively denied. Faith accomplishes what the law's expansion to infinity could not, overcoming the apparent acquisition of righteousness via the law by the realization of the total lack of righteousness, and thus the utter insufficiency for justification, of nature as well as the law. But in another sense justification by faith alone fulfills the law's movement of self-annulment, completing the nullification of the law as a way to justification with a power greater than its own unbounded expansion. The total annulment of the law, and therefore the quieting of its terrors, is the passive righteousness that struck Luther as though he had entered "through open gates into paradise itself." He construed this experience as the sigh of faith in the midst of spiritual trial: "In every temptation and weakness, therefore, just cling to Christ and sigh! He gives you the Holy Spirit, who cries 'Abba! Father!' Then the Father says: 'I do not hear anything in the whole world,' neither the terrors of the devil nor the threats of hell, 'except this single sigh'" that is the Christian's acknowledgment that justification belongs to Christ alone, and that nature and the law play no part.

The final deforming of the law, in which it loses all authority for justification at the same time that it relinquishes all limits, occurs at the hands of grace as a new and different power. Only through this new path of assurance, this justification grounded solely in the work of Christ, does the sabotage of the law's authority begun in its infinite expansion find its explosive consummation. The law gives up all authority as a way of justification in the believer's acknowledgment of Christ's grace "for you and me," the sigh of "Abba! Father!" that expressed Luther's turn exclusively to Christ in abdication of the righteousness of the law and nature. In that moment, the law's movement to infinity gains an equal footing with its temptation as a supposed means to heal and enrich, annulling the temptation and negating the law's claim to compel. The growth into a tyrannical infinity that is the law's annulment as merciful concludes in the annulment of the law *per se*.

In this latter annulment the limit that gave the law definition as law succeeds in its withdrawal at the same time that the law's authority is abolished. Nature's turn to Christ by faith alone entails the proclamation that the will is utterly powerless and thereby utterly bound, reducing its freedom as well as its supposed righteousness to nothingness. The free will squeezed by the law's advance to infinity becomes the limit abolished by the individual's own abdication of it. This abdication destroys the law's object in the will, and the destruction of the will means the destruction of the law. The latter no longer has a limit because it has no will to limit it, just as it has no authority because it meets no will to receive its commands. The law no longer makes sense as law, both as uncontained and lawless in its boundlessness and as inchoate in its lack of strength to command. In this vein Luther writes of Christ's grace as "the death of death": "Thus in my flesh I find a death that afflicts and kills me"—the law and its punishment for sin—"but I also have a contrary death, which is the death of my death and which crucifies and devours my death," that is, the death of Christ, appropriated by Luther through faith, that vanquishes the law's terrors. "Thus the law that once bound me and held me captive is now bound and held captive by grace or liberty, which is now my law."

The undoing of the law means the liberation of nature, which finding the accusing law accused and the condemning law condemned, grasps its existence under "the law of liberty." And yet, because the law put to death by grace is also the natural law that gives nature its form, nature suffers a parallel devolution. Because the death of the law negates the principle by which nature possesses definition, one cannot distinguish nature's liberty from law from its life apart from definition. The liberty realized through faith alone, the righteousness of God through Christ experienced as the gates of paradise thrown open, drives home the fiat in which the law melts into mist so that nature might follow it there. The same grace that proclaims "the death of death" for the law as the giver of nature's definition announces "the law of liberty" for nature as deprived of form.

This is the work of the Christ-Idol, that man should scale the summit of a draconian demand and at its peak lay hold of a power thought to liberate him from darkness, breaking the bonds of his taskmaster and bursting his limit as if the sun's light had permeated his flesh. But in his freedom from the law, in his indifference to its commands and his rejection of it as a way of righteousness, standing over it by the blessing of the Christ-Idol, man proclaims for himself a freedom in which he relinquishes his definition. Whereas man cannot absorb the infinite-unto-dissolution by his own power, crying out under the burden it impresses upon his conscience, the Christ-Idol delivers that power and dissolves the law at the same time that nature crumbles into the scattering. Justified by a righteousness acquired through faith alone, man arrogates universality as a curse concealed as blessing, a death concealed as new birth, a de-formation paraded as Reformation. Docetism unmakes his nature into the contradiction that believes in its conscience that it resides above the law when it cannot help but break the law, and indeed has nullified the law.

The Christ-Idol erupted from the dialectical innovation implicit both in Luther's experience and in the doctrine of justification that he built upon it. The medieval age had developed dialectical reasoning as a juxtaposition of contrary legal cases meant to close the gaps between the principles they espoused, but it did not suggest the realization of one of those principles as accomplished in the movement through its opposite. Dialectics at that early stage acknowledged no intrinsic connection between the alternatives beyond their shared grounding in a more fundamental concept of law. Luther's experience of the law in the matter of the justified conscience—the same law collected and ordered in the *Summae* of the preceding centuries—accelerated the interrelationship of the opposites at the same time that it redefined them according to universal categories. Rather than a single legal case or maxim set against another for adjudication, Luther set the oppression of the conscience under an infinite and dominating law against the freedom of the conscience as the total liberation from its oppression. The dialectic now called a comprehensive, inescapable, and merciless demand into battle against an indifference to law that renders its legal character obsolete. The genius of the dialectic consists in Luther's assertion that man cannot know the liberty of Christ, cannot receive righteousness by faith alone nor assurance of pardon, until he has passed through the hell of the law's limitless requirement. The law must crush man's nature, including all his powers of reason and will, until he knows no natural freedom and no hope apart from Christ. The liberty of grace presumes man's oppression under the law, germinating in the progressive tyranny in which man bows to the infinite demand. The dialectic concludes in the achievement of joy-through-terror, the explosion that Luther errantly understood as forgiveness and a new communion with his creator.

This explosion reveals the Christ-Idol in man's experience as the validation of his universality. The whole process of docetic grace means man's liberation from law natural and divine, a process crystallized in Luther's conscience and brought to dialectical fruition in the electrifying discovery of Christ "for you and me." For the dialectical expansion of the law divides man against his nature, rending him into two parts. One side of his nature stands with the infinite law, imposing the boundless demand upon the finite creature as if man were the infinite, as if his nature could absorb infinity. Cowering beneath this terror, oppressed and horrified like Luther before the Judge and Tormentor, is that same nature as hopelessly unable to fulfill the law's demands. Man at once becomes executioner and victim, destroyer and destroyed. The interweaving of nature and law, two realities bound under the grace of form, splinters in a dual and antagonistic movement toward the infinite. The law and nature as its ally accept expansion to infinity as legitimate at the same time that each shrinks into nothingness, though the law better expresses the expansion and nature the diminution. Docetic man does not understand (and Luther never understood!) that the dialectical culmination of brutality in the grace of the Christ-Idol means man's absorption into the infinite and the disintegration of his being. In the Christ-Idol man stands above the law because he renounces all law; he feels the exuberance of chains broken because he has torn his nature into pieces. Man confuses this advance toward the scattering with beatitude and assurance, with Luther trumpeting the deformity of the conscience as justification by faith alone.

If Luther introduced the dialectical intensification that provokes inner terror for the sake of man's liberation from it, he did so primarily in the spiritual order. His breakthrough cast down the ramparts of an infinitized ecclesiastical and divine law, destroying the monastery and holding out a new way of life that called itself Christian though it rejected the habit of finitude. Luther nonetheless fancied himself no revolutionary, no disturber of the peace nor political gadfly, but saw himself rescuing sinners from a God depicted as hot with anger by the church. At least in his own mind Luther would keep the natural order and its political systems intact, and this despite his consideration of divine law as a restatement of the natural and as fundamentally synonymous with it. Luther did not rigorously press man into the annulment of the natural order either in its ecological or its political manifestations. It fell to John Calvin, the lawyer of Geneva, to wear the crown as ruler of the new age. Whereas Luther stood as the apex of the docetic movement to decapitate the divine law, summing up the trajectory of his medieval predecessors, Calvin transferred the docetic spirit into the natural order with a logical vivacity no less enthusiastic than the pride of Gregory VII and no less subtle than the philosophy of Manegold of Lautenbach. In the single move of the Reformation Docetism thus captured the queen and placed the king in check, turning its canons upon the natural order before the corpse of the spiritual had grown cold. For it was Calvin's lot to take up the infinite law in the conscience in a way not far from Luther, but more importantly to unleash the mayhem of infinity into the ethical life of man.

Luther gives an account of man and the law: nature initially trusts in the law for justification; the law then grows into an infinite and merciless tyrant; finally the righteousness of God, given through faith alone, liberates the believer from the law's horrors. Calvin provides an account of man before God's judgment: the believer first takes confidence in nature's abilities; one then comes under an infinite law in the form of God's unyielding holiness, "descending into the self" until one recognizes nature's "nothingness"; then the grace of Christ, again the resolution of the dynamic, announces the believer as justified by faith alone, propelling nature into a life of ceaseless obedience. Unlike Luther, however, Calvin applies the infinite character of the law to both the inner and the outer aspects of man's nature and sees the law's infinity as illustrative of its embedding in grace.

For Calvin, Christ grounds the law or Old Testament as its foundation; Christ is likewise at work, in a muted way, within the law through its ceremonies and the promises that point to him; and he is the law's goal as the terminus in which it finds fulfillment. Man approaches the law in its proper context as enfolded within the gracious covenant established in Christ, whose delivery of justifying grace entails engagement in the non-justifying but necessary law allied with it. If, at this point, Luther should accuse Calvin of blurring the antagonism between law and gospel, Calvin would respond that while the law certainly does not justify, God is always one and unified. So also is his revelation through Christ's grace and the law embedded within it one and unified, a revelation consistent throughout salvation history. Applied to the life of man, this revelation entails not only saving grace, but the uninterrupted obedience that accompanies it.

Calvin's version of religious experience begins with nature's temptation to ascribe righteousness to itself in light of its gifts, which include natural virtues and the goodness that men can achieve by human standards. Concentration on these gifts results in pride in one's merit and a consequent sluggishness toward the obedience demanded by the law. Nature always wants to flatter itself, but this flattery is anathema to justification in Christ. For this reason Calvin directs the believer to the law, not that it should justify, but that by it men might "shake off their sluggishness" and be "pinch[ed] awake to their imperfection." This "pinching" amounts to a terrifying confrontation with God's holiness that decimates man's former confidence. Calvin describes this "descent into the self" from two angles, one focused upon the holiness of God and the other upon the depravity of nature. This movement stands at the center of Docetism's logic for the inner man, described by Calvin at various points in his writings alternately from the perspective of God and from that of the sinner:

> Our discourse is concerned with the justice not of a human court but of a heavenly tribunal, lest we measure by our own small measure the integrity of works needed to satisfy the divine judgment . . . Yet surely it is held of precious little value if it is not recognized as God's justice and so perfect that nothing can be admitted except what is in every part whole and complete and undefiled by any corruption. Such was never found in man and never will be . . . for [before God's justice] we deal with a serious matter, and do not engage in frivolous word battles. To this question, I insist, we must apply our mind if we would profitably inquire concerning true righteousness: How shall we reply to the Heavenly Judge when he calls us to account? Let us envisage for ourselves that Judge, not as our minds naturally imagine him, but as he is depicted for us in Scripture: by whose brightness the stars are darkened; by whose strength the mountains are melted; by whose wrath the earth is shaken; beside whose purity all things are defiled; whose righteousness not even the angels can bear; who makes not the guilty man innocent; whose vengeance when once kindled penetrates to the depths of hell. Let us behold him, I say, sitting in judgment to examine the deeds of men: Who will stand confident before his throne? "Who . . . can dwell with the everlasting fire?" asks the prophet. "Who. . .can dwell with everlasting burnings?" . . . "If thou, O Lord, shouldst mark iniquities, Lord, who shall stand?"

Calvin's vision from the vantage point of the Judge is calculated to inspire trembling and consternation. He elsewhere describes this vision from the perspective of the nature so judged:

> [Under the teaching of the law] we must then . . . descend into ourselves. From this we may at length infer two things. First, by comparing the righteousness of the law with our life, we learn how far we are from conforming to God's will. And for this reason we are unworthy to hold our place among his creatures—still less to be accounted his children. Secondly, in considering our powers, we learn that they are not only too weak to fulfill the law, but utterly nonexistent. From this necessarily follows mistrust of our own virtue, then anxiety and trepidation of mind. For the conscience cannot bear the weight of iniquity without soon coming before God's judgment. Truly, God's judgment cannot be felt without evoking the dread of death. So also, constrained by the proofs of its impotence, the conscience cannot but fall straightway into deep despair of its own powers. Both of these emotions engender humility and

self-abasement. Thus it finally comes to pass that man, thoroughly frightened by the awareness of eternal death, which he sees as justly threatening him because of his own unrighteousness, betakes himself to God's mercy alone, as the only haven of safety. Thus, realizing that he does not possess the ability to pay to the law what he owes, and despairing in himself, he is moved to seek and await help from another quarter.

These two passages capture the spirit of the observation with which Calvin opens the *Institutes*, that true wisdom consists in two parts, "the knowledge of God and of ourselves." This knowledge elevates God to the highest while it strips nature of any claim to righteousness. The sinner comes before the God by whose power the earth was formed, and before whose wrath it quakes with anguish, with the result that he feels the full severity of the law and the unqualified powerlessness of nature to appease its Maker. To know the immeasurable greatness of God is to know the antithetically immeasurable smallness of man, and beyond this, the perdition awaiting sinners apart from grace. The knowledge of God for Calvin presupposes this dual realization of the justice and majesty of God and the worthlessness of his disobedient creatures, a realization constitutive of the descent into the self.

At the heart of this descent is man's acknowledgment that nature's powers are "utterly nonexistent," the perception that immediately precedes the experience of grace. His consideration of that grace "will be foolish and weak unless every man admit his guilt before the Heavenly Judge, and concerned about his own acquittal, willingly cast himself down and confess his nothingness." To be cleansed of its "thousand sins," what can a nature that is nothing do? Thus the denigration of nature unto nothingness that Calvin repeats throughout the *Institutes*, illustrating the progress of the descent into the self until one "betakes himself to God's mercy alone, as the only haven of safety."

Looking to Christ out of nature's depravity, man observes "a wonderful consolation: that we perceive judgment to be in the hands of him who has already destined us to share with him the honor of judging! Far indeed is he from mounting his judgment seat to condemn us!" The man stricken unto nothingness discovers a great solace, a righteousness imputed by the Son's grace "that he may care for the consciences of his people." This turn of events elicits the "feeling of delight" in which the heart throws off the threat of perdition just as it is remade in its eagerness to obey, now a heart of flesh rather than stone. The destined graced firmly stamped upon the will, the Christian sets about the life of ceaseless obedience with the zeal of an assured conscience.

The docetic logic pervades this account of inner religious experience. As for Luther, for Calvin the law and nature combine in an initial leaning toward form countered by their eventual reduction to shapelessness. Also like Luther, for Calvin the law loses its form via its expansion to infinity while nature suffers as the object of that expansion, with grace consummating the dissolution of both. The terminology of the story changes from Luther to Calvin, but its ontological meaning does not.

Nature's initial estimation of itself as capable of some righteousness, relying on its powers of obedience as at least partially sufficient for justification, implies an ontological hope in the acquisition of form through obedience. Nature seeks to rise in form as it seeks justification via obedience to the law. Yet Calvin wants to destroy the impression that nature could add to its justification by completely denying natural righteousness. He insists that man abandon the "human tribunal," coming before the unmitigated requirement of the law in the person of the divine Judge. Calvin's descent into the self mirrors the growth of the law to infinity experienced by Luther, though couched in the language of the majesty and wrath of God rather than the multiplication of commands. In each reformer, the power and judgment of the law expand beyond all expectation that obedience could fulfill it. This produces, for Calvin as well as Luther, dual and antagonistic qualities within the law itself. The law promises to give life as the way of justification while its expansion to infinity would annul that promise, and by extension the law's capacity as life-giver.

The increasing chasm between the righteousness of the Judge and the weakness of the believer presses in upon nature's earlier confidence in its capacities. Where the will seemed capable of choosing the good, one finds that capability progressively neutered. Where one might have thought reason sufficient to discern saving truths, its conclusions evaporate as smoke and foolishness. For Calvin, the righteousness that nature would hold up as its achievement shrinks before the "thousand sins" that the Judge brings in accusation, just as, for Luther, each single act of obedience is dwarfed by nature's "wagonloads of sins that increase infinitely." Surveying the nature that tempts man to pride, Calvin finds it all but helpless before the immensity of God's judgment. Like Luther's exhortation that the law reduce the believer to nothing, imposing a "true taste of death," Calvin insists that nature come to recognize its "nothingness" under a law that bears "the most immediate death."

By this process both the law and nature reverse their assumed tendency toward form. The law loses definition in its growth to infinity at the same time that God appears unforgiving, severe, and bent upon punishment. Whereas Calvin elsewhere identifies divine law as a restatement of natural law, the identification of the same divine law with the character of God suggests an intriguing distortion, as if the nature of the creature should replicate the ineffability of the Creator. So the law's infinity crushes the individual by a mercilessness in step with the looming holiness of the Judge. Terrified under this judgment, nature endures the opposite diminishment of form, shedding its definition in the lessening confidence that it possesses intrinsic righteousness. The law expands without boundary while nature contracts into the infinitesimal, with both progressively abdicating the form with which they were designed. The ontological pattern of growth to infinity and reduction to nothing by which Luther's believer experiences the deformation of the law and nature resurfaces in Calvin.

When man at last releases the claim to natural righteousness *in toto*, acknowledging nature's utter emptiness and submitting to the inevitable curse of disobedience, when the descent into the self hits bottom in a psychological hell, then one meets the grace that comforts the conscience, liberating the believer unto joy. Ontologically speaking, when the law has so expanded as to completely annul its support of nature's inclination to form, its movement to infinity equaling and thereby conquering its appearance as a way of righteousness, nature sincerely perceives its own nothingness, that is, it is freed from form as freed from the law. Just as for Luther, Calvin's law perishes in the equality in which the movement to infinity annuls the law's claim to justify, an annulment that renders nature free from the law's curse. Again like Luther, Calvin implicitly links this culminating ontological event to the appropriation of grace in the heart, the felt knowledge that the Christ, secretly redefined as Christ-Idol, justifies the sinner in nature's total abdication of form.

This shared ontological story joins Luther and Calvin despite their differences, notably the latter's embedding of the law within grace. In Calvin's thought, the underlying ontology and the embedding combine in the ceaseless obedience that he requires of Christians. His calls to "unceasing progress" in and "unwavering attention" toward the law, with a heart "zealously inclined" to obedience by grace and on guard against all kinds of sloth, invest the infinity of the law into ethical life. In the descent into the self, the law expands to infinity as one approaches God's judgment seat, while in the ceaseless obedience exhorted by Calvin man submits outwardly to the law so expanded. The law whose commands provide no rest, and that goads man on to an apparently limitless expectation of conformity, is the practical meaning of a law whose tendency to infinity is its participation in grace. This life of obedience, according to Calvin, is grounded in, oriented to, and in a muted way expressive of the grace by which God calls his children. It is the sanctification inseparable from the justification to which God destines his elect.

Herein lies the most significant difference between Luther and Calvin: Luther views the law's infinity, experienced in the conscience, as the antithetical enemy that grace conquers by consummating the law's regression from form, whereas Calvin, applying the law's infinity to both the inner and the outer life, embeds a ceaseless obedience within the grace that consummates it. It is implicit in Calvin that the law in its tendency toward form, but especially in the infinitizing movement that annuls that tendency, springs forth from the promise of annulment in grace; that the law's increasing unboundedness, by advancing toward annulment, expresses the destined abdication of form in an incomplete and muted way; and that grace, at its advent, fulfills the destiny of the law as the obliteration of the form that remains. The law's fulfilled dissolution differs from its infinitizing progress toward that end, one might say, as a difference in "clarity of manifestation," Calvin's distinction between the law and the gospel. The law also meets that end as predestined in a way resonant with the procession of the elect to heaven according to God's eternal decree. Both Luther and Calvin teach the believer to advance toward grace through an infinite law, a road by which both nature and the law begin to lose their form. Only Calvin makes the law's inward and outward infinity a participant in grace, destining the law's path in parallel with the chosen embarked upon it.

That path injects the infinite law into man's dealings with the natural order, expanding the docetic advance beyond the conscience and the church to the political world as well as the natural environment. Under Calvin's aegis, man strives to achieve freedom from political and natural law through the annulment in which the infinity that undermines the law equals and negates its authority. Along the way his social existence operates according to a frantic and chaotic intensity, with man sensing that he must perform all his works to their limit and beyond. His economic and scientific ethos push him to undreamed ingenuity in the accumulation of wealth and bodily comforts, while his political ethos celebrates the destruction of a well-ordered society in the name of democratic liberation. In both the divine and the natural orders the docetic spirit rules over man by enslaving him to an ethic that erodes his being, whipping him to reach further above his limit so that his form might descend further below it. Through so cherished and misunderstood an event as the Reformation, Docetism forwarded its reign under the name of Christianity, cloaking its deception under the Christ-Idol. Now disclosed, its principle is a grace that destroys the law, its promise a liberation in universality. Docetism is man's well-meaning entanglement in the undoing of his world.

III

The spiritual element in man so determines the physical that he always strives to model his physical existence after the image of the god he worships. Man cannot exist apart from such an authority, he cannot live and move without unspoken and often unthought adherence to a divine ontology that both explains his nature and directs him toward conduct in conformity with the explanation. This unconscious adherence appears with full force in men who misunderstand the ontological foundations of their god, losing no potency even if man disavows all gods and declares himself an atheist. The ontology remains though the theological language has dried up, guiding man according to forces that, in the advanced stages of Docetism, he considers mythology and superstition if he recognizes them at all. If the divine ontology instills law and rest, mercy and peace, then man shall move in no small part according to these realities; if the ontology entails lawlessness, cruelty, and war, then man shall suffer their excesses. The ontology of Docetism, whose anti-god reigns over the contemporary world, is the formlessness of law dialectically annulled. Its image is an indefinite universality, its imprint upon man his unraveling as a nature.

Docetism does not work the truth as the conformity of being with its law but falsehood as the dialectical bifurcation of being and combat between its elements. Its god is at once the positing of the law and its negation, at once the construction of form and order and its being torn down. At one pole stands the docetic god as law, a form reminiscent of the eternal changelessness of the true God, of he who is mercy to man and all creation. Whereas the true God infuses grace into men so that they might come to the knowledge of the divine and better obey the law implicit in their natures, however, Docetism vilifies its law-god and announces him as the enemy. Justification by faith alone, the Christ-Idol's doctrinal fortress, knows the law finally as wrath and cruelty and will not tolerate it. At the other pole the Christ-Idol trumpets a grace alienated from law and thereby from form, redefined as the adversary of both. Thus law and grace, form and formlessness, distilled and opposed within the docetic opposition-god, the divine war-in-act. All law, immutability, wrath, holiness, and authority, which man ought to know among the attributes of the true God's being, represent one half of this bifurcated god. All grace, compassion, mercy, forgiveness, and gospel, what man should also know as attributes of the true God, comprise the other half as the scepter of the Christ-Idol. Law stands against grace as sin against righteousness, two armies arranged for the battle in which the Son negates the negation that is the Father.

That the docetic God proclaims itself fundamentally as grace, love, and compassion, affirming that man can know it through the Christ-Idol alone, means that it exists fundamentally as formlessness. Utter emptiness and indifference ground the docetic divinity as the putative void behind all that is, possessed of neither form nor content, subsisting in its purity as a cloud or a mist. This primordiality cannot continue its existence on its own, for it has no principle of continuity intrinsic to its indefinition. It is deceptive to think of it as an independent principle, as if non-being could claim actuality apart from being or evil were not dependent on the good. Docetism's primordial abyss must therefore posit its negation, it must affirm the form that is its opposite, but it can do this only because from the start it relies upon the goodness of actual being, including its finite measure. The initial work of Docetism, which it accomplishes through deception, is to invite itself into this being, to become attached to it like a parasite and feed off of it, infinitizing the good measure of being unto mercilessness and fragmentation. Thus the docetic development through the medieval era presupposed the divine law as measured, gentle, and oriented toward salvation, invading that law and perverting it as a preparation for the Christ-Idol. Docetism then furthers the deception by redefining the law in terms of the perversion. Insofar as it is authoritative, docetic law has become this infinity, this terror, this assault upon man, and it cannot but be so. Docetism supposes this infinite law to have arisen from the infinity of the abyss, and in a sense it has. In the docetic logic, law and form burst forth from formlessness in an inexplicable and ultimately false vision of creation, for what Docetism construes as the birth of form from formlessness conceals its reliance on the givenness of nature. Hiding this foundation, Docetism's god proclaims the evolution of form out of formlessness by an unnamed power, even the power of nothingness. Life, it would seem, evolves willy-nilly out of death, and light proceeds from darkness.

The dialectical advance of the docetic god projects a form, a "Father," that at first appears congenial, even merciful, maintaining the harmony of being with its law, rising like the bell curve. The mist wavers as though its potentiality would bear fruit, producing a certainty that steadies its uncertainty and a knowledge that qualifies its unknowing. It seems that the unnatural and unlimited shall acquire nature and limit, achieving a higher reality. This is another deception, for the law that seems to bring limitation will later reveal its lack of limit. The infinity of possibility has only withdrawn for the moment to allow the growth of form, but it will reapply its hand. As the nascent form progresses it reveals that the law intrinsic to it knows no end, multiplying and reproducing its demands with each moment, disclosing the law's intent to impose an infinite possibility upon a divine being supposed to have a definite and singular nature. The more harsh the application of the law, the more unflagging its persistence, the more the form sinks toward indefinition, the unnatural, and the ambiguous. The law increasingly appears cold, remorseless, magnificent, and cruel, pressing down upon form with the unattainable standard until both the form and the law descend toward the primordiality from which they emerged.

The Christ-Idol then appears as the void, unsheathing his sword and issuing the death-blow in which form finally collapses into the deep. This onslaught finalizes the liberation of being from definition in a devastating moment. Formlessness had evolved into form as its negation just as the promise of docetic grace presumes the encounter with the law, and now formlessness negates the negation just as the grace of Christ negates the terror of its legal antithesis. The form of the Son as an unmeasured release slays the content of the Father, bringing the latter's loss of limit to its conclusion. Though the Father and the Son meet, they have neither communion nor rest and there is no Holy Spirit. In the place of mutual humility and love the combat rages until the Christ-Idol conquers. He receives glory for his victory as the bringer of freedom, the liberator of being from a law that lays an infinite burden upon its definition. He simultaneously receives praise as an equalizer who matches form's previous rise toward discernibility with its full descent into shapelessness. Yet the Christ-Idol does not oppose the law's terror but consummates it, he does not limit the infinite requirement and the slide of form into formlessness but brings being into full conformity with limitlessness, releasing it from the horror of the infinite burden only to subject it to universality. In the wake of its liberation this being has no definition, and so oscillates in suspension between being and nothingness, unstable and unsure, an unnatural internal turmoil.

The dialectic of the docetic god evolves into its dissolution: the infinite law comes forth out of grace because grace cannot exist but through this law; the law then ascends and descends in its progress along the infinite; lastly the Christ-Idol arrives to negate the negation, driving what was left of form into formlessness. Docetic man experiences his god and follows his commandments according to this general pattern, replicating its movements within his own nature as a dialectical creature.

The image of the docetic god that man appropriates as his nature and the foundation of his being is freedom. This is man's unwitting secret, the haughty proclamation whose meaning he does not know, its message obscured like Hebrew read from left to right. Docetic man declares that he is free and stakes his pride upon this declaration, so embracing freedom that he would have it sprout into the largest and most prosperous of trees, defining his dreams, his activity, and his philosophy until it controls his whole way of being as man, until he wakes, moves, and returns to sleep with the unconscious recognition that what he is as man is freedom, and that to pilfer his freedom defaces his dignity. He does not understand, he is frighteningly deceived, because he has failed to uncover the reality underlying his freedom. He does not see that he rightly allies his nature with possibility only when the latter is subordinate and bounded, whereas to exalt possibility as the ground and assumption of his life implies a foundation of quicksand. His freedom is formlessness and indefinition not as a principle oriented to the acquisition of form but isolated as its own end, elevated to the annulment of form and the lawlessness of universality. To this freedom he sings his hymns and odes without realizing that it cannot fashion his being because it strives to liberate him from all fashioning principles. His foundational freedom is a boundless boundlessness, the unrestrained newly untethered to demolish all restraint, the unending positing of a nullity. The freedom that man identifies as his essence casts his origin into the wind. It is the popular word for his existence as the scattering.

Like his divine exemplar man-as-freedom subsists through positing freedom's opposite, a process to whose inner mechanisms man is ever blind. He begins time and again with trust in the law born out of freedom, a law that has taken on various religious, cultural, and political manifestations across the era since the Christ-Idol. He believes here that through the law he will become what he is meant to be as a man, or there that by the law he can craft an existence shining with significance, or again that he can affirm his life in the face of absurdity through the grace of autonomy. In short, man believes that by positing the law he will find salvation and experience the totality of his nature as free. He believes with unshakable conviction that the law offers a way respectful of his freedom and destined to its fulfillment. He throws his energy into the law with the alacrity and meticulousness of the early Luther, or with the discipline and austerity taught by Calvin. Ignorant of the final antithesis between freedom and form, it appears to him that the law of freedom is an unequivocal form rising, that he is advancing, that life according to this law promises a higher vision of his being.

Yet just as freedom authorized the law's growth to form, freedom also demands form's decline. The law that appeared fertile continues along its path unhindered, increasing in intensity and demand at the same time that its benefits fade. Man experiences the dissolution of his form as terror under the law he trusted, whether that law imitates Luther's anxiety under the internal whip or, in a later expression of the docetic logic, consists in the cruelty of a state constructed to liberate man from want. Man places his hope in a law that must become oppressive inasmuch as he grounds that law in freedom, for freedom achieves itself through the loss of form progressively accomplished as the law loses its limit. Thus the brightest hope of an earlier generation, or even the same generation in its younger years, morphs into a curse for those subject to its later stages. Though he might identify it with outward phenomena, this way of being fundamentally exists within man. It is always his law, his nature, his form that simultaneously expands and suffers under the expansion, that comes to revile what he celebrated a short time ago. To his mind something has gone wrong, and he wonders how plans joyfully laid should result in such ironic and devastating consequences. He fails to perceive that the law grounded in freedom must extend to infinity, undermining its authority through oppression. The law born out of freedom necessarily arrives at man's fear of his own nature, a fear that, though it seems to contradict the expectation of liberty, proceeds logically from that expectation.

By this point man has assumed the image of the docetic god by bifurcating into two antithetical elements. He is fundamentally the promise of freedom, the child of god destined for a grace that is formlessness, but he is also nature experienced as an infinite and oppressive law, a self-annulling authority that enslaves him. Man endures his nature-as-law as sin and terror against the grace that he seeks, that is his liberation. The law's self-annulment intensifies, it has not achieved its purpose, and it cannot do so on its own. The law cannot effect an annulment equivalent to and therefore superior over its positing as authoritative, but waits on a unique and special power in order to reach its conclusion as annulled. Man cries out for aid and the Christ-Idol appears with this power, imparting the docetic essence that passes through man as a participant. Man experiences this participation, the gates of heaven thrown open and the embrace of the grace of Christ, as the transfer of righteousness.

The Christ-Idol permeates man in his bifurcation by fusing with the divided elements, nature or man-as-law versus grace or man-as-freedom, and the meaning of the Idol's arrival turns on the character of the permeation. The Christ-Idol, himself a putative form at war against a putative content, allies his form (the "righteousness" that is his power of total annulment) with man-as-freedom, so that the power of Christ and the possibility of man become a single element. The Christ-Idol simultaneously identifies his content (his name falsely presented as Christ) with man-as-nature or as possessed of form, a shape writhing under the infinite law as immediately identified with it. This bifurcation means that the name of Christ takes on man's sin while man defines himself by Christ's power or righteousness. Both man and Christ are present in the anguish of sinful nature under the law and the potential freedom of the law's annulment, with man assuming the pole of righteousness as annuller while Christ stands at the pole of sin and form to be annulled. Man then channels the Christ-Idol's power of annulment into an attack upon his content, sacrificing the name of Christ at the hands of Christ's own righteousness. This channeling completes the dialectic of a divinity divided against itself, the dialectic of form or righteousness divorced from content or name that achieves its demise through man as its mediation. The same channeling turns man-as-freedom against his nature, his form, and the law, with all three subtly understood as his sin, and slaughters the latter in a qualitatively distinct expression of violence. Man executes his own dialectic, moving through the total annulment of his positing as form and nature in order to realize his freedom in formlessness. This double dialectic, presuming the bifurcation of both man and Christ-Idol, constitutes the transfer: man appropriates the Christ-Idol's power against nature as the defeat of sin, and therefore as both the victory of Christ and the liberation of nature, but man achieves this annulment at the expense of Christ's name and unto the exaltation of man as annulled or liberated. Both man and the Christ-Idol come to annulment, with name of Christ destroyed and man elevated to grace.

In the transfer the Christ-Idol and man swing from pole to pole, suspended in the equality of form and formlessness, of positing and annulment. There is no longer discernible being, no longer true form, no longer peace, because the instant those things are suggested the annulment equals and obliterates them. The Christ-Idol locks man in the from-to in which his nature knows no solidity and the law has rescinded into mist, so that man is all fluidity and motion. The severance of his being would confuse and overwhelm man if the Christ-Idol had not deceived him into believing that this freedom is blessing, that he has received eternal life and a profounder humanity. Man has become both the executor and the victim of a power of privation breathtaking in its universality, a force so grand that docetic man announces that God is known through Christ alone. Only the Christ-Idol offers grace as the annulment of form, only he redefines man as the freedom and equality whose purity is disintegration.

This is the basic ontological pattern by which man conforms to the image of the docetic god, but it is one multiple, diverse, and often discreet in its manifestations and development. For every distinct law, order, hierarchy, and form that man might assume as a permutation of the definition intrinsic to his nature, Docetism implements a distinct version of its dialectic to undermine and eradicate that definition. Nor does Docetism's progress move with such strength that it can annul all law at once, but its advance reiterates the cycle of confidence in the law, horror at the law's enormity, and destruction of the law's rule. Since the advent of the Christ-Idol, Docetism has proceeded from the destruction of weaker and more peripheral forms of law in the natural order to more central ones, growing to the power of devastation needed to equal the law it wishes to conquer. In this way the docetic spirit has spread over peoples and lands who have never or no longer recognize the name of Christ, until it sets all men against the life given to them.

1 John 1:3–4

> We proclaim to you what we have seen and heard, so that you also may have fellowship with us. And our fellowship is with the Father and with his Son, Jesus Christ. We write this to make our joy complete.

IN MERCY GOD APPROACHES man, desiring to draw him up out of the nothingness toward which he has turned, waiting for him to learn the fruitlessness of the world so that he should submit with goodwill. Longsuffering and gentle, the Lord remains faithful and calls off destruction, so unwillingly does he bear the loss of his children. Just as he forgave Israel's iniquity and did not utterly destroy them for their sin, so at length he restores mercy to the sinner. The Word that pierces man's heart and lifts up his hands, branding him as the prize and possession of God, is love. God writes it upon his lips, serving it to him as a scroll bitter to the taste but filling to the stomach, flowering as praise. God cultivates his love into the course of man's life, casting him into the pit and subjecting him to slavery so that, in the fulfillment of time, he should establish him in security and save him from famine. The revelation under which man currently labors, the penultimate statement of the Word, declares the love with which the Father loves the Son and the glory that the Father gave to the Son because he loved him before the foundation of the world. God entered the darkness and cast it out in the incarnation, in the display before peoples and nations of the love in which Father and Son dwell, in which they are completely one, and which the Father reveals through the Son so that God might abide within man. The impartation of this love, the very presence of God, is man's fellowship and his joy fulfilled.

Man comes to know Jesus Christ first through the natural world formed through him. There the creature encounters the Father through the Son, one God creating being from nothing and instantaneously giving it form, instilling within it a law of finitude and mercy. Beyond this original and natural law, man meets the Son through the Mosaic law meant to heal his sin, the combination of command and sacrifice, of law and grace, that God bestowed as a direction for his people toward their savior. The natural and the Mosaic laws are the precursors, lacking the potency of eternal life and the fulfillment of the love of God while pointing toward their dispensation. The full revelation, the perfect fusion of law and grace, the great taking resolved in giving, is Jesus Christ. In him law and command do not merely combine with sacrifice and mercy but become unified with them in a single entity, so that Christ's following the law means his handing over the highest sacrifice. Like the caterpillar emerging as the butterfly, Christ's obedience matures into compassion and the giving of being. The savior accomplishes this metamorphosis in a person whose incarnation, crucifixion, and resurrection mark the divine work of atonement. In nature, in the Old Testament law, and in his incarnation Jesus Christ is one in mission, everywhere healing, everywhere love.

Man's knowledge of God through Christ begins with the givenness of the natural world and the characteristics it displays to him. Within this world he discovers the attributes of the divine in a diminished form, and by concentrating on those attributes man attends, at length if not immediately, to nature as a bridge over which he can begin his journey into love. In nature man witnesses the preliminary revelation of law and thereby of mercy because God created this world and called it good. Opening his eyes to that world and dwelling in it, removed from the docetic spider web of images and words, man appropriates his being in its orientation to law and in the righteousness of form. He lodges his way of being within the natural order and finds that, despite its subjection to sin, the order is very good. Man discovers that God created him as good and righteous, that his existence on earth is the divine mercy poured out and that human life is the blessing of God bequeathed to him. He perceives that God fashioned him to tend toward peace and joy, that he is fashioned for harmony within his nature, with his neighbors, and with God. Man's recognition of his law is God's helpful and necessary initiation of the creature into fellowship, though that initiation is not fully salvific, not yet unto eternal life.

Observing nature man discerns a multiplicity of laws that manifest a single law, a unified principle of finitude and form. God imbued nature with form as he shaped it in beauty, and the natural series of species, landscapes, and seasons converge to overwhelm man with the love and mercy of the designer. Each creature abides in its integrity, enjoying the definition that assigns the creature's proper activity and harmonizes the activity of each within the whole. Feathers, wings, thin legs, and clawed feet, uniquely combined for flight, denote the bird created in its way of being. Scales and fins for swimming and gills for drawing oxygen out of water denote the fish whose proper way of living is in the sea. Man can make similar judgments of the reptiles and the mammals that populate the earth, in addition to his appreciation for the multitude of plants that envelop his natural existence. For each type of plant and animal God has provided a law of definition that implies activity in accordance with it, a finite shape given to every creature so that each might abide in the way that the creator saw fit. The law of finitude limits the comings and goings of all life as a presupposition and an expression of the joy that their creator takes in them, the one who looks at them and calls them good.

These finite beings come together in an arrangement that subjects the lower to the higher. The plants reside below the animals and provide sustenance for them.

Likewise herbivores provide nourishment for carnivores who hunt and devour their prey. Among the meat-eaters there is still higher and lower until one arrives at man as head and lord over the animal kingdom. In virtually all cases the lower serve the needs of the higher, submitting their strength, their good health, and their lives to the well-being of the stronger species. The law that the higher lords over and devours the lower might appear uncivilized if not barbaric to the docetic mind, but let the observer look more closely. The division of the eater from the eaten does not deny all freedom to the lower species, for all animals and plants have room for growth, all contribute to the order by maturing and reproducing. So also the higher, though they kill the lower for food, do not consume their bodies with an infinite lust or a limitless domination. The cheetah does not run down one gazelle, then a second, and then a third, until he has left nothing of the herd. The killer whale does not seek out whole populations of seals in order to devastate their numbers. Nor do the higher animals terrorize the lower by ever and always hounding them, pressing in upon them with the constant fear of death. The hunt occurs regularly and out of necessity, but the victims are free from dread in the intervening times and are almost always caught in isolation. The higher and devouring animals instinctively know their limits, they are not creatures of bloodlust and rapacity, animals that would lay a strange and unnatural psychological burden on their victims. The ruling species kill what they need for the day and no more, building up no storehouses and laying waste to no class of subordinates. They rule but do not oppress, they kill as they must and manifest no tyranny or injustice in satisfying their hunger. Thus the law of nature integrates all creatures into a hierarchy of superiors and subordinates while maintaining a certain peace in their interactions, assuring that no creature excels the measure appropriate for the maintenance of its kind or imposes horror and extinction upon others.

Together with the law among living things, man recognizes a deeper and more profound abiding in the surrounding landscape. The earth that he treads does not wobble beneath his feet, the forests do not hide at a whim, the rocks do not dissolve perceptibly into dust, the rivers do not change their course unpredictably. The ocean's horizon does not lose its grandeur, its breathtaking silence and enchantment, for the whole span of man's days on earth. He encounters the natural environment, the finitude that encompasses physical life, as a monolith and a surety. He admires the hills and mountains as immovable and transcendent expressions of power, reminders of the ages that have passed before him and that will pass after he has gone. In the seasons he learns a rhythm that becomes stitched into his way of being, a concourse with the gradual circles between warm and cold that teaches him patience with nature's bounty and joy at its arrival. As man surveys the natural world he drinks in the abiding of that which abides, and finds comfort in the law of abiding as joy.

Joy is the content that springs from the form of nature, it is man's appropriation of a nature in conformity with its law. When man perceives that each thing abides in accordance with its design, that the way of being for each animal remains consistent between what it ought to be and what it is, he senses the joy of being within its measure. God fashioned wings to fly, and so they do; he fashioned fins to swim, and so they do; he fashioned noses to smell, and so they do, and in their activity each part dwells in the harmony in which it acts as it should, as God intended. Only man distracted and defiled experiences nature without a sense for this joy, having lost his memory of natural existence. Joy nonetheless remains as the first and basic apprehension within man of the natural world and his own nature. It is the overflow of law and abiding in law apprehended as mercy in the heart.

Joy circumscribes man's being and impinges upon him as a tutor by which he learns his limit. Through joy he learns that he is meant to be, that he possesses righteousness and purpose, that the law of his being is good and directs him toward goodness. He learns that like the rest of the order he has a place, that he is positioned between higher and lower, that the righteousness of the creation extends through him and through his society. He learns durability, integrity, and definition, patience and discipline as a man satisfied with his lot, not seeking what lies above his limit and not descending beneath it, obedient to the way of being instilled within the temporal world and so within his body. He finds pleasure in what is small and simple: the cultivation of the earth, the love of his wife, the youth of his children. He adds to the fraternity of men bound by their mutual limitation, their agreement that nature is a law to which they must submit and that inclines toward their benefit.

In his inculcation within nature does man not also come to know its freedom and transience, to say nothing of its ills and pains? The philosophers have rightly said that man does not step into the same river twice. Are the waves that crash upon and caress the beaches not a constant change and do the sands not erode under their force? Do the birds not play in their mating and chase one another in the struggle for life, and do they not sing as they will? Does man not engage the natural world out of his freedom, putting its bounty to use for his good and that of his loved ones? Does he not rise to every day as new, and to every year as a passage from the strength of youth to the helplessness of old age? Do the seasons not here bless man with sunshine and there pelt him with thunderstorms? Does he not suffer the severity of winter and the drought of summer? Does he not quiver in fear of tornadoes, hurricanes, earthquakes, tsunamis, volcanic eruptions, and any number of natural disasters that can crush him without warning or apparent reason? To all of these questions, yes. To nature's freedom and its transience, and to its capacity to destroy and inspire fear, yes. These also contribute to man's enmeshment in nature and his learning of its law, and insofar as nature's freedom and transience do not embody the curse, they also are joy.

It might seem that the freedom of nature and its penchant for disaster annul the abiding and the pleasure bestowed by it, and that in consequence man can know no law of nature and no joy. But this man learns from nature, a lesson of the utmost importance: freedom depends upon the law and presumes it, and the freedom of transience and change and the joy that these afford, and even the unfortunate freedom of destruction, cannot exist apart from the abiding within law that allows for their possibility. The river would not flow twice if it did not follow its laws of motion, the waves would not crash and caress the beaches if they did not adhere to the laws that determine their course, the birds would not chase and cajole one another if they did not conform to the laws of flight. Nature could not terrorize man with disasters if it did not execute these according to laws, suffering the corruption of life-giving rhythms toward annihilation and ruin. And man, that most free and remarkable of creatures, could not exercise his freedom if he were not first a lawful combination of soul and body created for communion with God just as he is grounded in the material world. Without law freedom fades into a vapor and a nullity, an emptiness lacking the foundation necessary for its movement. In the creation man discovers not merely law and freedom, but law as the foundation of freedom and freedom ensconced within law.

Either the law provides the presupposition and ground for freedom, a case in which natural form possesses mutability, or freedom provides the presupposition for law, an instance in which form is embedded in and arises from formlessness. One can embed mutability comfortably within form so long as the change, if negative, does not imply the total diminution or loss of form. The possibility of change can also offer the opportunity in which nature rises to incorruption, as man could have achieved in the Garden had he not fallen. Form does not ground mutability and share room with it as an antithesis but as a complement, a space from which a free nature can consent to its law as limited by that freedom. The law permits an opening for freedom so that it should integrate its liberty back into the law, fulfilling the law and not breaking it. If freedom should ground the law another kind of integration takes place, one not of harmony but of war. Absolute freedom is absolute possibility and the denial of all form, it is universality as the primal shapelessness prior to coming-to-be. This coming-to-be in its emergence toward form does not complement formlessness but directly opposes it. Form contradicts and negates formlessness as soon as it becomes discernible. Although the form might at first appear pleasant, the expectation of maturity in this case is a deception, for as born out of the infinity of formlessness the rise of form proceeds according to an infinite law, a law destined by that infinity to return to indefinition. Formlessness gives birth to its antithesis in order to re-integrate it according to a law of boundlessness and expansion; the form that appears to assert its limit will at length reveal its limitlessness.

Man's life under the limitless law follows the rise and fall of form, experiencing an initial joy at form's rise that succumbs to horror at its expansion. Man believes at first that blessing has arrived and will continue to arrive, that this supposed nature is not only good but improving and that according to this law he will achieve his potential as a man. Then comes the disappointment, the discovery that what seemed so promising is tyrannical and indifferent, a deceiver and a brute. Man is shattered and forgotten under such a law and its self-depleting growth. He eventually sees the law as a curse and a whip, inescapable and all-devouring in its boundlessness, a pain and a scourge.

1 JOHN 1:3–4

Has this ever been or is it now man's experience of nature's law? Has he ever trusted in nature only to find its joy transformed into unrelenting punishment? Do the trees bend down and lash him with their branches, torturing him with their buds and leaves? Do the birds gather into numberless flocks in order to assault him in a bloody frenzy, destroying his peace and deafening him with their screeches? Does the natural air burn his eyes and poison his lungs as a carrier of disease, as though it meant him ill? Does man, in short, encounter nature as an internal war set against him as a participant in the conflict? Does he know nature as a reality that contradicts its essence, a reality shaped according to a self-destroying law? Does man meet nature as a form that yearns for liberation from definition, wanting to throw off the laws that bind it? Is the beauty and splendor of the natural world only a magnificent and ubiquitous lie, a halcyon harbinger of death rather than a cradle of life? Ever and always no! In nature man discovers no law leading into infinity, neither in the past nor in space nor in any fashion, insofar as he does not experience that infinity as an immeasurable weight laid upon him, his loved ones, and mankind throughout its history. Let docetic theorists gather their evidence and say what they will. They shall claim that time reaches back billions of years, that the universe is expanding *ad infinitum*, that man's scientific possibilities know no boundaries, and that the observed universe is therefore fundamentally infinite. But let them also understand that their science tacitly presumes man understood as an infinity, confirming his infinitude within a world construed to mirror it. Docetic science reconceptualizes physical reality after a foregoing spiritual universality, the ontological conception of man that gained its foothold in the Reformation. Docetism's deeply religious scientists have little to say that does not arise from the temple where they serve as high priests. Their oracles are hypotheses and interpretations of nature's law that contradict that law as man experiences it by dwelling in the natural world.[1]

---

1. This is not to say that the findings of docetic science are false. The universe may be expanding beyond human measurement, time may extend backwards millions of years. The point is not to deny the infinite but to embed it within the finite, so that it does not become an errant foundation for man's understanding of God or his own nature. God's work of creation exists between his definition as God, including his personhood and his coherence as the giver of law, and the manifestation of finite laws in created natures. If life comes to be through the infinite as a middle point, one could expect such finitudes to emerge through some form of the infinite, even apparent infinitudes in space and time.

One might also ask: could the universe actually be infinite, born from the abyss and destined to it, without disclosing the felt contradiction of finite natures with the universe's more fundamental and formless infinitude? Could a powerful deception last for millennia, even the known history of men, so that they did not perceive the truth while the revelation of darkness waits until the very end? It is logically possible, but I see no evidence for this view. Were it the case, men would surely observe smaller but regular manifestations of the infinite in the day-to-day life of nature, perceiving hints of nature's undisclosed warfare if they looked closely. Moreover, the docetic age has produced the unmistakable sense of the deception that the finite contradicts a supposed underlying infinite, for that society lives on the perception of finitude as the prelude to revolt against it. If docetic society cannot avoid the experience of the contradiction, a docetic universe could not either.

Man must not mistake the magnificence of nature and the awe that it inspires in him, a grandeur shown in his inability to comprehend the vastness of space or the sands of the beaches, as though these witnessed to a universal law of nature and his being as a participant in that universality. Nature is not an order of finitudes testifying to an intrinsic and more fundamental infinity, as if the creation in its variety bespoke an orientation to possibility more basic than its grounding in the form it has received. Nor does nature breathe through man as a creature born of and made essentially for possibility, as though he were raised above natural processes into self-determination. Man should not dive into his inner recesses as if a divine All is manifest in him and his emotions, as if his soul contains a universal, everlasting, and evolving assertion of truth indivisible from an unlimited natural world. These heightened emotions and false intuitions deceive man into believing that he can appropriate the infinite as though he were a god. They are the scent of man's alienation from his true and finite nature and invitations to the dissolution thereof.

Docetism scorns the humility of the natural man because the latter recognizes his nature not in freedom but in obedience. Docetic man grounds his consciousness in liberty and it offends his pride when one suggests that he has arrogated his freedom and annulled his limit. By Docetism's logic, the natural man approaches as a slave and a usurper, one conditioned by form and willing to impose that conditioning on others. Docetic man cannot fathom how one could find contentment in a law of limit, for his infinity immediately castigates such a law as oppressive. Yet the natural man seeks this law, a command robust and limited, just as he seeks mercy. His pursuit is not wild and erratic, not given to frustration, anxiety, and excess, but it is planted in a rhythm of patience, an abiding in contemplation and the hope of purity. The maturation of the natural man requires law and his positioning as its instrument, a law that stands over and directs him in ways that his passions might not desire but that his apprehension recognizes as necessary.

The design of higher over lower reigns within the natural man as the rule of the will over the body. As he considers nature man might not yet have considered its source in the eternal, he might not yet perceive the infinite beyond the finite or an undying soul as the counterpart to the body. He will nonetheless perceive the incorporeal portions of his nature as the higher, for just as the higher animals put the energies of the lower to use for their own well-being, so the will puts the body to use for its benefit. There is no devouring within man, however. The will does not consume the body but uses it as an instrument by which both achieve a better harmony within the law of his nature. The will must command as rational and conscious, it must guide the body by virtue of its comprehension and its judgment. Otherwise the body will overrule the will not as an adversary with its own consciousness but by the ubiquity of its urge to avoid inconvenience. The revolt of the body against the will and the undoing of both essentially consists in the inclinations by which man flees the hardships and vulnerabilities of his natural existence. As soon as man perceives the possibility of ease and averted displeasure his pulse quickens. His thoughts hurry in with rationalizations that convince the will to permit these pleasures until they become habitual. Man can always respond to the passions in his conscience, he can sense the temptation and refute it so long as he recognizes the limit that he would cross and can identify the complicity of his thoughts with his passions. He affirms his nature against perversion when he gains this sensitivity and determines that he shall resist the temptation, when he understands that the mind's rationalizations do not outweigh the benefit of discipline, which is the formation of the soul. Then man grows into a manifestation of law, a nature heavy and moving toward completion, blessed with the development of *gravitas*.

As the weight congealing in his breast, his fortitude as a man planted and watered in the created order and bearing its law, in *gravitas* man apprehends his natural existence. *Gravitas* is a plenitude not felt but apprehended, an ontological substance acquired through years of inconvenience and endurance, through discipline and rank. Man apprehends a hardening like a shotput in his diaphragm, a heaviness coalescing silently and unquantifiably as the conformity of his being with its law. This is his truth, his knowledge, and his memory not as an individual but as a man, as a nature formed to dwell within an order of longsuffering and mercy. In *gravitas* man apprehends the natural and public design that yearns to breathe through him, ossifying through his obedience both within the creation and among men. In it, though man remains a sinner, and though he knows nothing yet of the salvation given through Christ, it remains for him to enjoy some measure of the righteousness and purpose of his being and to draw upon its depths.

Late docetic man has never experienced *gravitas* and is virtually ignorant of it. He might even call it a lie or a myth. How sorrowed and distraught is he, who flitters about the world in instability? Docetic man lies awake at night with no companion but his emptiness, and with this he suffers a powerful psychological deceit, a lie that has fooled him for hundreds of years. He apprehends his emptiness, his purposelessness, and his wasting away, but he does not realize this apprehension as his inverted knowledge of *gravitas*, a knowledge gained by its absence rather than its presence. Instead of identifying the true source of his loss, that he lives in defiance of the law of his nature, docetic man interprets his emptiness as though it reflected his distance from others—an interpretation that is not altogether untrue. Apprehending the hole in his nature he says in his heart, "I miss these others, even my loved ones, my wife, my children, my larger family and my friends." Docetic man then seeks to conquer his alienation by removing the legal and social boundaries that separate man from man just as he idealizes intimacy and unhindered relationships. He strives in ignorance of the fact that his outward annulment of the law further loosens the inner bonds of his nature, excavating his fullness like oil drawn from the earth. By tearing down the walls that he believes to block his contentment, docetic man finds his nature emptier than before and he falls deeper into despair. He thinks that by his removal of boundaries he will liberate men for brotherhood, but he has freed his nature from both its integrity and its fellowship with other men.

When man enters the technological world, leaving his nature and the natural world behind, he loses the understanding of the latter as doors from the finite into the positive infinitude that is the knowledge of God. As long as man abides in the natural world and meditates on it he discerns the finitude of its law, a finitude proving that nature is not utterly boundless. Although man cannot count the stars in the sky he feels their presence as mercy and thereby as finitude, and this finitude must have a cause. If the physical universe were infinite, if it were without beginning and without end, it would subsist according to an infinite law, a law without mercy, a law in which the forms that man experiences have risen out of the abyss and are destined to return to it. The limit of particular beings within nature would contradict the limitlessness of their origin and he would experience their particularity as contradiction and, with the passage of time, as horror. The establishment of the natural world and its particular forms must consequently rely on a power sufficient not simply to shape a matter already present and understood as eternal but strong enough to create matter out of nothing. This power instills matter with the vector toward form by which it takes definition, drawing it up from nothingness into certitude. Man recognizes this cause as the eternal, the ground and goal of existence, as that which has no beginning and no end. Otherwise he is left with a cause for the natural world that requires its own cause, with this latter cause requiring another behind it, and so on to absurdity.

The eternal cause behind natural finitude is God, the one instance of an infinite law that is merciful. Man cannot comprehend how this is, he cannot fathom how an infinite being should not live according to a law of terror, or how that being should embody the infinite in an ordered fashion. He believes in the mercy of such a being and its law because he has experienced the natural world as merciful. That world cannot be its own origin because as infinite it would be tyrannical (which it is not), and so it requires a cause; the world experienced as finite is also experienced as merciful and ordered; the infinite cause of the world must therefore be without a prior cause in order to avoid absurdity but it must also be merciful in order to produce a merciful world. In this way man arrives at God who is infinite, without cause, and merciful in his creation of the universe.

But is the natural world not fundamentally merciful? Does it not also possess aspects that are beyond man's comprehension, such as the stars that he cannot count? Is the natural world itself not both infinite and merciful? If these presuppositions are granted, why can the natural world not be its own cause, an eternity unto itself? It cannot because it is corruptible and already corrupted. A world that is by nature infinite and merciful implies the fusion of the attributes, so that this world would be infinitely merciful and merciful in its infinitude. There is no place where this world would not show its mercy, no time where mercy succumbs to despair. The world would neither grow nor decrease in mercy because the mercy is infinite, lying beyond corruption.

Now consider the natural world, where environmental disasters, war, injustice, and other defects show the fallenness of man and nature. Is this world, although grounded in mercy, everywhere and infinitely merciful? Does it not suffer iniquity? Does it not labor under the curse? Its mercy is not infinite because it is subject to corruption. *Ergo* this world is not its own cause and its mercy points to a higher reality, the God who grounds its finitude in a blessed infinity.

God has stamped the world with mercy as his seal, signing it in beauty. Just as man surveys the creation and finds joy in life abiding in law, life conforming to its design and continuing the species, so he discerns that the creator takes a similar joy in all that he has made. How could man, the lone rational creature in the physical order, take such delight in the physical world if the creator did not feel the same joy to a greater degree? And how could that divine joy not pervade all life? Man is illumined by grasping that the joy of the creator is everywhere present and fills all things, including the realms beyond his purview and the time before and after his time. God has smiled upon his handiwork and called it good. Through this recognition man embraces his part in the abiding of what abides, the physical in its orientation to life and resplendence, and moves from the form of the finite and its content in joy to the necessity of the present and benevolent infinite, advancing from that which abides to that which Is not only as being but as mercy and goodness.

This joy of what Is recasts the meaning of the world inasmuch as man comprehends that the physical does not exist without reference to the spiritual and that the goodness of the natural world abides in and witnesses to the spiritual power. The spiritual does not collapse into the physical but stands as a higher nature while the physical is a lower world imbued with the delight of God. Yet the physical world is the spiritual world not because physical realities determine spiritual ones or because nature is God but because there is one nature in which both the spiritual and the physical, the higher and lower natures, intertwine. In this unity the spiritual power breathes through the physical and is inescapably present within it. Like the physical traits of man transferred from father to son, or like the psychological and emotional habits bequeathed from parent to child, the physical world bears an intrinsic and internalized impression of its spiritual origin. Inasmuch as the form of creatures and the magnificence of the earth bear testimony to their creator, therefore, they manifest a law that is not only natural but an image of the divine.

Man perceives the divinity of the natural order most directly by contemplating his own nature. In experiencing joy as the content of the finite he discerns that God desires to take joy in him as he abides in his form. The law by which man abides thereby ascends from what is natural into what is natural and divine, with the overlap between the two laws not confusing the finite creation with the infinite creator but acknowledging the former as a law originating from the latter. In light of this recognition, when man acquiesces to the requirements of his nature he simultaneously obeys the will of God. Man's obedience brings him closer to his Maker and bestows the joy of knowing that God desires communion with him. Likewise when man abdicates his integrity by submitting to the rise and fall of formlessness he knows the infraction against his nature as a sin against God. Man feels this breach of law as guilt and disruption, a betrayal of his natural fullness and a descent toward emptiness. The diminution of his being, a loss of *gravitas* apprehended as yearning and sorrow, chases him until he cries out to God for salvation.

As an answer to this cry God handed down the law of Moses, commands intended to orient the men of Israel to the God who sought them. The law came to the Israelites as moral instruction, as ordinances by which they might close the gap in their natures and gain communion with the Lord. From Moses forward God sent prophets to set his laws before the people, counseling them in the way that they should go and warning them of wrath should they grow negligent. From the law and the prophets the Hebrews learned first of the interrelation between God and the land, that their obedience to the one secured their prosperity upon the other. They also gained a foreshadowing of judgment and the soul, hearing that man endures beyond this world and receives his due in the afterlife, that his existence as spirit outlives the death of this body. They also saw that the God of mercy is holy, turning away when his people repeatedly break his commands. How often they failed, seeking other gods and refusing the voice of the Lord, not correcting their iniquities or reflecting on the Lord's fidelity! How he laid waste to Jerusalem and its sanctuary, handing his children over to foreign powers for their misdeeds!

The Israelites incurred such penalties despite God's offer of atonement. In the Pentateuch God addressed his people with a way for returning to him, that in addition to the people's obedience the priests could appeal to the divine mercy through the blood of animals. Through sacrifice the Hebrews understood their God as holy, requiring redress for transgressions and desiring that his people come to him contritely, while also finding him compassionate to forgive the repentant. The individual and the nation bowed before God by acquiescing to his demand for payment, worshipping him in a sacrificial habit of confession. The sacrifice entails the acknowledgement of sin before God in the hope of pardon, presuming confidence that in the shedding of blood God will look upon man and cool his wrath, extending a healing hand. Sacrifice is the critical means for God's convalescence of his children. It brings strength to what had fallen and purges the soul of corruption, so that man might better attain the obedience intended for him. Sacrifice exists in partnership with the moral law, each of profound importance to the life of God's creature and never to exist apart from one another, together the path by which man regains his being and returns to fellowship with his Maker.

In Jesus Christ command and sacrifice merge in an indivisible unity, a singularity expressed in the history of the Son of Man as he consummates the law. The Christ is law as incarnation, grace as crucifixion, and both of these to the reaffirmation of law in the resurrection, but all along he embodies the harmony of a law that is grace and a grace that upholds the law. In this way he descends as the love that rescues life from death, and that for the sake of sinful men.

The incarnation confounds and disturbs the man who looks into it because he cannot comprehend its truth. Logically, it seems that God cannot become man because of the contradiction between the two laws. The law of God that defines his being as the eternal, impervious, immutable, and infinite, cannot reside within the finite law of man without either crushing it under the infinite weight or swelling it to explosion. From the opposite angle, Docetism's deformation of man depends on the delusion that a finite man can directly seize the infinite and retain his definition as man, which is plainly false. Shall God, then, become one with the finite creature without obliterating that finitude beneath the infinite? How does the infinity of the divine being fuse with the finitude of man without the deity becoming a tyrant and oppressor over the humanity? How does the man Jesus of Nazareth not dissolve in body and soul under the pressure of the Second Person? The mystery consists in the coinherence of the two laws whereby the one does not negate the other. More than this, each law retains its fullness inasmuch as Jesus Christ subsists in perfect obedience to both standards. In descending to become man the Second Person does not cease to be God or exist in a manner that is less than divine. He remains the principle and lawgiver through which all nature has form, though in an inexplicable and miraculous way he has emptied himself in order to join the unborn and unending with what has beginning and end. In this joining the humanity not only continues in its finitude but is imbued with perfection, so that, far from being strangled by the deity, the human body and soul abide without sin, enjoying a spotless integration and the full image of God. Jesus Christ embodies the two laws as an obedience without blemish, perfectly expressing the law of God in its infinity and the law of man in its finite integrity. Through this obedience he reconciles man with God, with his neighbors, and with his nature as man, offering these unto eternal life.

Holding every thought, every action, and every word captive to the law inseparable from grace, the soul of Christ looked without sin to the Father. So his body, drawing its life from the soul, knew no sickness. In body and soul Christ manifested the unstained obedience to law that is the incarnation just as faith led him forward as the Messiah of God. The law drove Jesus into the desert for temptation and guided him to the mountain where he delivered the beatitudes, it led him to transform water into wine and to cleanse the temple of the money-changers. By the law Jesus visited the house of Zaccheus and filled the fishermen's net to the brim, by the law he fed thousands on the meal of a single man and healed the lame. By the law Jesus gave sight to the man blind from birth, cured the woman who had bled for many years, and raised the little girl to life. By the law he stood at the tomb of Lazarus and called the dead man forth, by the law he rode on a colt into Jerusalem as the people paid homage. The law led Jesus to wash his disciples' feet and to lay down his life for them, even lifting him up on the cross. In all this Jesus humbled himself to obedience in faith, testifying to the command that is life.

If man could capture the sun and enclose it in a jar, its light would not rival Jesus Christ, the spiritual light of the world. At the cross that light goes out, darkness covers the skies, and all appears lost. The ruler of creation, its Lord and Redeemer, endures the defect of the fall and takes on its penalty. The Incarnate receives the sin of the world, he who was unspotted righteousness bears the creation's tendency to nothingness. The forces of evil have their say, condemning the Savior to death among criminals and mocking him as king when his following had scattered. As he hung upon the cross, a sacrifice for men who have no hope apart from him and who turn to their own desires, he cried out: "My God, my God, why have you forsaken me?" In these words Christ exclaimed the despair of one who knows the turning of God from the soul, who knows the emptiness of existence apart from the divine love. He confessed the death of the soul as its distance from its source, the haplessness of man left to sin and its punishment.

Yet one also reads: "It is finished." Following this statement Jesus bowed his head and gave up his breath. Having lamented his forsakenness, Jesus completes the punishment for sin in the passing of the body. The finite and infinite natures that had fused in the incarnation separate as the body dies. The crucifixion is Jesus' liberation and his freedom, in which he has taken on sin so profoundly that he has no contact with the body for which he is the principle of form, having relinquished the lower law of human nature. The lawgiver and lifegiver no longer bestows law or life, while the freedom of the body from Christ means its death, a liberty of physical perishing in which the body becomes equal with the soul as totally divorced from it. In this sacrifice Jesus unifies the highest obedience and the divine mercy, for he submits to the divine will by drinking the cup that the Father had assigned to him, a cup ordained for pardon.

Through death Christ accomplished not the full salvation of man, not the bestowal of light and redemption that belong to the whole dynamic of incarnation, crucifixion, and resurrection, but the minor key within that dynamic. The crucifixion as the severance of the finite and the infinite presupposes their joining in the incarnation and looks forward to their renewed singularity in the resurrection. When Christ rose he rejoined the laws that had split apart, sealing them in a unity beyond death. The miracle of the resurrection consists in the divine's absorption of death but moreso in the reinvigoration of the lifeless man, resuscitating him into reconciliation with his source. Form returns to man's nature in good health and toward the destiny of eternal life, and whereas the cross affirms the necessity of death, of sacrifice, and of freedom, the resurrection subsumes their necessity under the reconsolidation of the lawgiver and lifegiver with his beloved. In Christ's new life the Christian discovers the ultimate grace, the divine power given so that man might have fellowship with his law and rest in God and neighbor. This is the love of the Father through the Son and his joy made complete, the delight of the creator in his creation and his desire to see it furthered, the extension of imperturbable being to heal the corrupted.

The life of the disciple conforms to the pattern of God's love as a practice in the fusion of law and grace. Whereas Christ joins the law of the infinite with that of the finite as the mystery of the incarnation, man receives the power of that fusion as the grace that invigorates his attempt to obey the law. Man does not seek the power of the infinite or desire to cast off his finitude in following Christ but wants to appropriate the power needed to conform to his measure. He already exemplifies that measure to the extent of his bodily form and the rational mystery of the soul, the soundness and definition of his arms, toes, and eyes on the one hand and his reason and capacity for music on the other. His adherence to his law is nonetheless flawed. The body bears imperfection and disfigurement and is subject to death while the soul languishes in pride and deception, failing to pursue the creator in humility. When man embarks upon the law, therefore, he knows from the start that he adds to his salvation by virtue of the form of body and soul. More importantly he knows that he will never accomplish salvation on his own. Although he can assume his contribution on the grounds of his form, looking to his righteousness as one shaped by God, who would brag in such a contribution as though it was not received totally as a gift? Who looks at his physical form and the capacities of the soul and says "I have made this and it is mine"? Only the deceived boast or take pride in this given righteousness, while the humble recognize that man's contribution does not begin to approach the sufficiency that raises him to eternal life or that puts off judgment. Man has no grounds for arrogance but must seek grace as a remedy, as the power received through faith in Jesus Christ.

Man's pursuit of Christ, a venture impossible apart from his adherence to nature, means first the combat against sin in the flesh, against the sickness and disease illustrative of fallenness. Sickness is no less moral because it is bodily, for in sickness man encounters the fact of his revolt against his nature. Man has inflicted pain upon his flesh that he cannot truly understand apart from acknowledging its moral quality as guilt. The religious man experiences this truth as God imposes it upon him, recognizing illness and death as an affirmation that he does not live as God intended, that he has foregone his finitude and bears the penalty for seeking the infinite. God has handed man over to the boundlessness brought on by the fall and man in desiring to turn from that boundlessness must seek health as a moral good. This pursuit admits the necessity of sickness and the inevitability of pain as right in their place. Seeking to obey his law, man does not strive for an existence utterly exempt from pain and inconvenience because, as fallen, this would imply an existence without the law he means to obey. He does not work toward a life utterly removed from vulnerability and suffering nor does he lust after a life liberated from death. Man seeks a finite health received through God's healing, a health that reaffirms his law as finite. In this manner he conforms to his law and humbly draws near to Christ the physician.

As man continues in obedience he faces the spiritual aspect of his law, which poses the challenge of spiritual sickness. Man grows up in the soil of habits, many of which orient him to the world rather than God and which tempt him toward the infinite. All around him forces beguile and deceive and he feels their pull as the lure to so many transgressions, habits of mind, heart, and body that trade the law of what is noble, good, and right, the law of heavenly things, for the satisfaction of the flesh. Evil habits make man's soul a slave to his body, his will the assistant to desires that he lacks the strength to withstand. The world assails him with uninterrupted distractions and pleasures, freedoms of gratification and pride, of sophistication and indulgence, and it would convince him that giving in to his lusts will fulfill his nature. In this way man entertains the delusion that having what he wants, when he wants it, and without worry that others might take it, will not leave him barren and inept.

In his combat against habits and temptations man performs his penance, a spiritual sibling of the natural progress toward *gravitas*. The habits of *gravitas* and penance so overlap that one could in many respects call them the same. Where *gravitas* disciplines man under the guidance of the natural order, penance gathers that discipline under the mercy of the spiritual, channeling it through man's recognition of the spiritual order and his place within it. Penance transfigures the habit of *gravitas* inasmuch as man comprehends his sins against nature as sins against God and lives in light of the judgment of the soul. It elevates the heaviness of man's natural way of being by directing that way of being toward incorruption. Penance looks to the cross of Christ as the unique model of divine judgment, where Christ provided the exemplar for man not only in the sacrifice of the body but in the possibility of disobedience relinquished as a petition to God. The disciple replicates Christ in the penitential habit of soul, the life of prayer, fasting, and almsgiving that trains the body in mortality while it seeks the pardon of grace.

Whereas the perfect obedience of Christ issued in the Sermon on the Mount, the rebuke of the Pharisees, the healing of the sick, and the forgiveness of sinners, and led him finally to its paradigmatic expression at the cross, man's imperfect obedience and his inevitably insufficient penance lead him to confession. The act of confession in the life of man approximates the cross in the life of Jesus Christ. Where Jesus brought his body as a sacrifice sufficient for the sins of the world and as a gift unto eternal life, man brings the sacrifice of his soul's orientation away from God in the hope of receiving that eternity, a sacrifice necessary but insufficient for his own salvation. On the cross Jesus announced his forsakenness and suffered his freedom, with the human and the divine splitting into an equality that is death. So man comes to confession and offers up his forsakenness and his freedom, the division of his body from his soul, that is, his acknowledgment of sin. In confession he imitates the severance of Christ from the body by annulling his righteousness, he replicates the freedom and equality of Christ's death by admitting his disobedience, his qualified freedom from and equality with God. Man then asks that Christ receive the defect, that he cast it into the tomb and roll the stone over the entrance. Thus does he receive pardon and hope for a life released from judgment.

The crucifixion is not an end in itself, not the *terminus a quo* and the *terminus ad quem* of salvation, but a middle point incomprehensible as divorced from the resurrection. Neither does man's repetition of the dynamic of the cross in confession stand alone. It points to man's acceptance of the mystery as the renewal of his life. God opened confession as a gateway to the eucharist, where the grace of Christ gathers man's insufficient sacrifice into the sufficiency of the cross. There the blood of Christ wipes sins away and gives man strength for a better obedience. In the cup man imbibes the capacity for form restored, in the bread he chews on the one who rejoined soul and flesh in the resurrection. Man accepts the vitality of Christ for the sake of a similar reconciliation in his own nature, so that through a joyful, patient, and longsuffering obedience the interpenetration of body and soul might congeal within his union with his Lord. Progressing along that habit man enjoys the reconsolidation of his nature as a spiritual and a natural being. The love that made the Son incarnate and raised him from the dead envelops its beloved, and man discovers fellowship with his God.

The troubles and inconsistencies, the pains and fracturing of life fall into blessed being as so many pebbles cast into the ocean. Love is the splash on the surface; it is the drift downward through the deep; it is the rest upon the ocean floor. At all times love surrounds man's infirmities like waters over the stone, at all times God stands before and behind, below and above and beside, even within, and the indwelling of love comes to man as delighted desire. Like one enjoying the first course of a banquet, his mind turning to following courses as he clears his plate, so the one in whom God dwells delights in his presence as he desires it, longing after the God who rules in his heart. God dwells and in faithfulness promises always to dwell in the heart and the fortified soul, so long as man does not expel him. Man can delight in God as the present source and object of hope, trustworthy because his integrity is law and obedience to law, a perfect faithfulness rivaled by his mercy. The divine promise gives surety that man has the joy of immediate presence and that of the gift to come, the life with God beyond mortality. Man's soul looks to this life as his hope and reconciliation with his Lord, and as the consummation of his present obedience in eternity.

God commands the believer not only to endure his suffering but to engage the suffering of the neighbor, the one close to him, as an exercise of love against the transient. In this manner God, through church and fellow-worshipper, consoles the afflicted as the water encompassing the stone. Love enters the sufferer's life in the Christian's sacrifice, his being handed over to his brother's dark places, not pretending that they have been eradicated or neglecting his neighbor's enslavement to them, but knowing and believing God's abiding through them. When a man knows the long suffering, the intractable boring of the worm into the flesh, he is brought to the doorstep of the knowledge of God. When he endures with faith, trusting that the one inside shall answer, he knocks upon the door. When, out of the discipline of *gravitas*, he dedicates his time, his money, his thoughts and prayers, as well as his freedom to come and go as he desires, to associate with whom he will, to think and strive as he likes, to shape his life according to his own judgment and prerogatives, when he abandons these things to the long suffering and its prisoners, serving the orphan and the widow, feeding the hungry and the thirsty among Christ's brethren, befriending and housing the estranged, visiting the sick within the fellowship and helping the imprisoned, when those sufferings persuade and compel him that they are his own and he takes them up as such, when his whole life is compassion and service to the neighbor, when his heart is full, then he loves, entering through the door thrown open to him. Then he finds the presence of God in *misericordia*, and the delight that expected the gift has grown into gratitude for, even union with, the giver.

In this love man draws near to God in this world, while the body and the soul approach their intended reunion. Man embodies the knowledge that law ascended into love binds man to man, and that love does nothing greater than lay down its life for one's friends. Man will still sin, but not unto death. He will still face the perishing of the body, but not of the soul. Humbled by the inevitability of his failings and overjoyed by the grace that conquers, he carries on in thanksgiving and mercy, gathered toward the father through his son Jesus Christ.

1 John 5:16–17

> If anyone sees his brother committing a sin that does not lead to death, he should pray and God will give him life. I refer to those whose sin does not lead to death. There is a sin that leads to death. I am not saying that he should pray about that. All wrongdoing is sin, and there is sin that does not lead to death.

A VILLAGE STOOD AT the edge of a forest. As a part of their habit, the men of the village would take to the forest in order to learn from it. They dwelled in its silence and meditated on its sounds. They admired the height and breadth of its trees. They enjoyed its creeks and ponds. They observed the nesting birds, the fish, and the animals of the ground. They saw as well the bramble, the fallen logs, the half-eaten leaves, and the brush. In all these things they learned of life and death, and while nature did not give the height of this knowledge, it gave the basic lesson. Living in this way the men endured heat and cold, they tasted wind and rain, they knew dawn and twilight. They were grounded, heavy, and full, brothers in fellowship and travail.

Among the residents of the town lived a man of nobility, one wise and patient, stout and kind. In earlier times, he would teach the people the full lesson of life and death, perfecting nature's teaching. Then in his later years he grew sick, and his knowledge was twisted away from the truth. When he had come to the edge of death, his three sons came to him. They prayed that his spirit would revive, longing that he would return to health, but at length the sickness consumed him and he died. The young men, brothers of devotion and sincerity, mourned his passing.

While in mourning the brothers took a walk through the forest. The oldest of them saw a large tree strangled by vines, its branches withered. "Brothers," he said, "do you see this tree? Years ago we walked through the forest and marveled at the vine's flowers. But the vine is a parasite that has killed the tree." He paused, and the three of them surveyed the branches. "Is this not our nature?" the brother exclaimed. "Our mortal lives are beautiful but they end in death, and how shall we be saved? Would that I could be saved apart from the flesh, that my salvation did not stumble over what is cursed. This body is damnation, a contradiction of life. I shall never move beyond it, and I can only be pure apart from it." He and his brothers were shocked at his words.

The trial of this brother moved the second in his heart. "Listen," said the second brother. "Death and the flesh have been conquered, if only you believe it. And it is for us to live in this belief and bring it to life. This is our father's spirit, which we shall carry on though he is dead." The first brother replied: "This work is more yours than mine, but I shall be with you." The two brothers resolved to bring death to an end, to find a way of being in which it no longer reigned. The third brother, who was younger than the other two, watched in silence.

The elder brothers introduced the task of ending death to the village as freedom, and the people agreed to it. They refashioned their lives and surroundings so that death played a diminishing role. They became busy and anxious, occupied with escaping their demise. They put the natural world to use toward this task, so that their bodies grew comfortable and physical pain faded. At the same time the villagers lost their habit. Men no longer heard the forest's sounds or dwelled in its silence. They forgot the brush and the trees, the twilight and the dawn, the cold and the heat. The villagers changed, growing strange each to himself and one to another. Man's heaviness dissipated, his substance hollowed, and his fellowship thinned. He grew ignorant and blind, and forgot compassion.

These developments enraged the younger brother. Seizing control of the village, he expelled the elder brothers and the memory of the father. He promised the return of what was lost, that man would return to his being, that he would live in fellowship and peace. With great hope the brother then continued the project of his predecessors, for he too yearned to be free from death and the flesh.

After a time the younger brother sensed that his project had failed, and he became exasperated. Man's heaviness had not returned, his fellowship had not revived. The brother himself moved as though lifted off the ground, ethereal and porous, without direction or root. He took a walk through the forest to calm himself, but the forest was not the same. Once there had been bramble and fallen trees, broken limbs and dead leaves, and smaller plants entwined in one another. The villagers, under the brothers' guidance, had rejected this. Now the trees grew exceedingly large, planted in rows and columns to ensure maximum freedom. The brother looked but he saw no birds. He listened but could not dwell in silence. He rather heard a terrible grating sound. Just then a villager who tended the trees approached him. "These trees are so beautiful," said the brother. "Before our work began they would never have grown to such heights."

"They will not stand much longer because their wood is of use," the villager answered. "The saw is sharpened, and the trees, which have grown so large, were planted in order to be cut down." At these words the younger brother was filled with dismay.

∽

1 John 5:16–17

I

God gave man science as a path into beauty, where creation and creator intersect. By inquiring, scientific man discovers the harmony of what is, finding the laws that govern nature and discerning the principles that govern him as a part of it. Science guides him through temporal integrity toward its eternal source, introducing him to the rules that order and unify the physical world as bound to the spiritual one. Though death, sickness, and disaster taint this world as fallen, man can come to know it and, God willing, be known by God through his knowing. Man is meant to study the land that supports him with its mountains, plains, forests, and jungles; he can admire the rivers and lakes, the oceans vast and foreboding, brilliant and deep; he can trace the clouds and the sun by day and the stars at night. He can observe land animals, fish, and birds, as well as his own nature, just as he develops agriculture, weaving, and other natural means to enjoy the earth and to prosper in life. In this way man engages the earth as one obedient to the law of God, inhabiting it as a fellow-creature by virtue of that law, subordinate in his knowledge to the conviction that God ordered him here. With this disposition man orients his science to the life of the soul in God, and to healing, peace, and mercy.

Docetism invades the science of nature and poisons it with a new prerogative, submitting phenomena once investigated under the presumption of unity to a new spirit. Rather than lifting its discoveries to the heavens, docetic science pulls man down to the pit, while the knowledge meant to confirm nature's harmony turns on itself, dividing what it should join. This science surveys the world and, beginning from the assumption of indefinition, it severs unity in pursuit of fracture. The finite and general law of nature morphs into an absolute and universal law before shattering into infinite and innumerable laws. The unforgiving and exceptionless dissolves into numberless exceptions, bifurcating into two, four, sixteen, two hundred, two thousand. Clarity mutates into complexity as the particular example of a general phenomenon becomes a phenomenon unto itself. In the last state all the particulars differ but they are also universalized, made the same under the broadest and most objective of categories. Docetism sets about its ultimate task: discover the smallest, most miniscule particular, the universal particle whose division seems impossible, the very element and building block of life, and divide *this*. From this rending erupts the catastrophe beyond man's understanding, the atrocity that annihilates all.

The proper object of science is righteousness and life, the joining of man to God and nature according to the law given him. Science has a both spiritual foundation and spiritual orientation as a way of knowledge attuned to man as God's creature. It is a method of discovery that furthers the mutual edification of body and soul just as it harmonizes man with the created order, limiting him within a world of right limit. Science studies the righteousness of man's nature so that, as one instructed and nourished by grace, he might discover his form in the embrace of the eternal. It presumes that God created man for unity with him, imbuing man with a natural law that directs him to what he ought to be. Science also recognizes the divine law that overlaps with and supersedes the natural and admits that man can obey neither law fully. Man asks, as a scientist, "Where is my righteousness?," and finds it in the form of his nature and of the natural world. The presence of righteousness is the starting point for all scientific investigation, for the furtherance of life within limit is the joy of scientific man. This joy immediately encounters its problem in sin, the defect of form that cries out for a remedy. The practice of science, as much as it is pleasure in the beauty of nature, is no less the search for the knowledge that reconciles man to God and his limit, a healing of spiritual disease and of bodily misfortune.

In the spiritual order man practices his science in the proper alignment of penance and confession. In the medieval era Docetism defiled this alignment, substituting confession and absolution before penance for the order in which penance precedes confession and absolution. It further landed the weight of salvation upon the acknowledgment of sin, as if man should count each and every one of his sins and find rest in the conscience purified by the counting. These were the steps in Docetism's transformation of confession into an anti-science, a mode of knowledge that tears man away from God and divides the soul from the body.

In confession man exercises the freedom intrinsic to his nature, mirroring in his cry for mercy the freedom in which he could accept or reject God's will. Just as matter called into form out of nothing must pass through indefinition, the formless state that is a something-nothing or an is-that-is-not, so the man who would know his nature as spiritual must recognize his freedom. This liberty does not disdain the law or annul it, but is nestled within the law as the law's boundary. The law must encounter freedom, a possibility intrinsic to man's form and significant in power, as a bridle upon its demands. In the decision to obey the law stops at this bridle, respecting freedom as its threshold in order to receive freedom's blessing and pass through. The encounter between freedom and law implies the limit of both, with the two supporting one another in their mutual limitation. Law upholds freedom and freedom upholds law as man exercises freedom for the purpose of living according to his nature. Without the freedom to conform or disobey and its penitential mirror in confession, man would lose the limit and thereby the form of the law that defines him. The law would become boundless and lawless, a universality applied to a finite creature. To deny freedom as the limit meant to confirm the law is to abolish both man and the law, reducing them to objects without definition.

When man disobeys the law, he announces both his freedom from it and his equality with it. In a word, he annuls the law. In disobedience man proclaims his freedom from the law by declaring that it has no authority over him, that the law does not stand above him as the presupposition and goal of his freedom. Man simultaneously proclaims his equality with the law, that his freedom is its own law equal in power to the command and in revolt against it. This combination of freedom and equality bears the secret of annulment, that for man to abolish the law as command and authority, and by extension its definition as law, he needs only to exert a power of annulment equal to that authority. When a power that annuls authority equals the power that posits it, the annulment matches and immediately overcomes the positing. To say "equality of positing and annulment" is simply to say "annulment," because there remains no power of positing or establishment of the law distinct from what is annulled. In the act of disobedience man stands in a new freedom from the law just as he asserts that freedom as a force equal to the law, ignoring God's command and exalting himself.

The moment of annulment does not obliterate the whole law, as if man abdicated his entire form as the result of a single sin. Adam and Eve did not fall straightaway into dust when they fell, but persisted as God's creatures despite being cast out of Eden. Though one infraction renders man guilty of breaking the whole law, this means that he is no longer sinless, no longer perfect in form and abiding. In the sense that he is no longer whole, man has broken the whole law. The single sin does not so counteract the law that it annuls all of man's form, although it does distance the soul from God and subject the body to eventual death. The crime annuls the law in the particularity of the confrontation in which man rejects a particular command. This requirement is annulled, but much of the form of man and the law, and much of man's natural righteousness, continues intact. It would take over a millenium for man to arrive at the point where his sins nearly wiped out the law of his nature while blinding him to the divine law meant to guide him to incorruption.

In the wake of sin man feels the horror and the sickness, the remorse in which he apprehends his loss of being. Out of the depths he comes to penance and confession as the way of healing, and to confession especially as his plea for forgiveness. In the act of confessing man recapitulates and sacralizes the original infraction in its freedom and equality. When the words pass from his lips they relate a specific sin, with man recollecting his theft, lust, greed, gossip, pride, or any of a host of crimes against God and man's limit. Though man comes a suppliant for grace and contrite in heart, he must walk through his rebellion again, verbally re-enacting his disobedience, briefly re-affirming his liberation from his righteousness and the command that he seek God's will. In the admission of sin the words implicitly say: "I am free of the law; I am equal with the law; I annul the law." The words that pass from his lips re-present his sin, and in this manner he annuls in a qualified way the righteousness in which God created him. Awaiting absolution he remains annulled, having recognized the diminution of form equivalent to his sin. His acknowledged need for grace sustains him, and once given that grace succors him. Without this grace he remains suspended in annulment, in freedom.

Confession presumes the law as its origin and seeks the law as its end; it is the freedom of sin harnessed within a recapitulation dedicated to reversing the infraction. Confession looks back to the goodness of the law as the way of righteousness and of man's destined form, but with the memory of the failure before his finitude, that is, his attempt to supersede his boundary. Man then engages in freedom's representation so that he might offer up his sin on the altar, dividing his righteousness from his sin and externalizing the latter through speech. In this way man sacrifices his loss of being in the humility that beseeches God for mercy. If he has properly lowered his pride in outer penance and inner contrition, providing the condition necessary but not sufficient for his healing, man turns rightly to God's grace in Christ as the only effective balm. Grace arrives in absolution and more fully in the mystery, in God's taking on man's sin and delivering him from death, strengthening man's spirit to withstand future temptations and to proceed toward union with Christ. The law surrounds confession in the same way that it surrounds man's freedom, and confession is that freedom humbled by its hubris and subordinated anew in its orientation to law, hoping for mercy from God.

It was the purpose of Docetism throughout the Middle Ages to emaciate the law's power and ultimately revoke its priority as the context in which confession is embedded. The distillation of the Western church's legal essence away from liturgy and theology and into a corpus of canons marks the opening stage of that emaciation, withering the church's sacramental-legal strength. That the church should become a distinctly legal institution with a class of technicians devoted to the development of canon law divides the upbuilding and healing power of the mystery and lodges the divided portion in an unnatural home, instilling it within an endless dialectical process that forgets the forming power handed down through Christ. To add to the church's dialectical-legal machinery drains the mystery and shifts the acquisition of salvation away from penance and confession as fulfilled in absolution and liturgy, replacing the proper means of reconciliation with a confession defined by its confrontation with the canonical infinity. One can hardly conceive how subtle the series of modifications, how silent and apparently innocent the powers that turn man one degree at a time until his orientation has changed without his recognizing it. So docetic forces readied man for their next move, in which confession intensified toward the annulment of the law.

Docetism's progress had isolated confession in the encounter with the infinite law by the early fourteenth century. At the turning point in Docetism's Grand Dialectic, when the popes fell to the French kings and saw their political legitimacy grounded in a new way in responsibility to the people, the law lost the independent validity necessary for it to surround confession as embedded within it. The outward law instantiated in the papacy could no longer command with the authority of God, it could no longer meaningfully proclaim its authority as the guardian of a divinely wrought way of salvation, at the same time that its legitimacy appealed to the mutability of the populace. The inward law likewise lost its vitality, so that the law no longer stood behind confession as its origin or before confession as its goal, having no authority to justify its demands beyond its role in confession itself. Confession was already the definitive practical means of salvation, it was already the locus at which man could approach God and petition for assurance. Now this petition faced the challenge that the law that confession presumed no longer possessed its own justification, nor could it carry confession forward to the mystery. But Docetism had trapped man in the confessional method of salvation, with the church's legal apparatus and its claims to worldly power blocking the thought of a return to the mystery as grace and rest from the law. In essence, all that was left to the law was its role in the act of confession, which is its annulment. The abrogation of the law in the conscience subtly became the means of salvation for Catholicism's spiritual avantgarde, its most pious and devoted monks. This means frustrated and terrified those who dedicated themselves to it in earnest, for aside from facing the systematized infinitude of Western canons, man is always and everywhere law insofar as he is formed as a nature, and the annulment of the law as his means of salvation implies the annulment of form as his path to eternal life.

In this way Docetism sowed into man's mind a new understanding of his being and a new goal for his existence, though the flower would not bloom until Martin Luther. If the annulment of the law—and at this point the annulment concerned principally the divine or spiritual law in the conscience—is the means of salvation, the completion of that annulment is the restoration of man to grace. The end of man's spiritual life and his restoration *qua* man becomes a movement into a freedom realized inasmuch as without law, a freedom of formlessness. Further and more shocking, this achievement supposedly signals his return to the blessedness he enjoyed before the fall, a formlessness hidden under dreams of beatitude. The assumption and goal of man, inasmuch as his way of salvation consists in the annulment of the law that gives him form, is the formlessness of total annulment. Between these ends man knows he is a sinner, but his sin denotes not the diminution of his being but its rising into form. This is his crime against the freedom from form that Docetism means for him to be. Man's salvation within this docetic understanding necessitates the annulment of form and its depletion toward formlessness, so that he as a spiritually distinct and lovingly fashioned being descends toward infinity. The law no longer surrounds freedom as embedded within it, but freedom becomes the presupposition and goal of a law destined for dissolution.

To the extent that the annulment of the law stands as man's means of grace and he acts according to that means, man implicitly accepts the docetic account of the ontological foundations of his nature with respect to the spiritual order. This is his first and partial accommodation to the reconstruction of the creaturely image after the docetic god.

Under Docetism man engages in confession as a science directed not to the edification of righteousness but to its undoing. In the original science man asked, "where is my righteousness?," meaning ontologically "where is my form?," and discovered the sin that is his deprivation of righteousness and diminution of form. Penance and confession were then his way of healing and reconciliation with his creator and his nature, restoring lost righteousness through the grace of Christ. In a secret and powerful way Docetism distorted this process by changing the terms, so that righteousness means not form but formlessness and sin means not the diminution of form but form's congealing into nature. Under these assumptions confession ceases to imply a limited division of righteousness (as form) from sin (as diminution) that sacrifices the sin for the sake of a greater life in God. Confession becomes instead a method that posits law, form, and nature as sin and executes an infinite division of that sin in order to return nature to its righteousness (as formless). The method is infinite because sin as the deprivation of form cannot act without positing the form that it must deprive. Sin then divides that form ever and anew, all the while leading man to believe that the infinite division will fulfill his nature, cure his anxiety, and guide him into the embrace of Christ. Whereas the mystery once covered unnamed sins under grace and allowed respite from the law, under Docetism confession must bring every sin to the surface. Man must raise everything to light, dividing and externalizing all, interrogating every action, every word, every thought and feeling, everywhere severing his natural form and vocalizing its diminution. The law expands infinitely as a power that annuls its presumption in man's unity, breaking down the form that defines man as man.

This occurs while the individual thinks that he is confessing in the traditional way; he remains unaware that the ontological meanings of sin and righteousness have switched. One now sins not by breaking the law but by positing the law outside of its orientation to annulment, as if it did not bow to this orientation. Cursing and gossip, lust and theft, curiosity and greed constitute sins not because they have disobeyed the command but to the extent that they presume a law not subordinated to its sacralized annulment in confession. These docetic "infractions" need not entail an unsubordinated law because they can be part of a positing of the law in which the believer tacitly acknowledges the law's consummation in disintegration. In this case they amount to an obedience set against an unknowingly confessed "sin," the implied understanding of the law as forming or righteous, a law whose corruption in fact consists in its submission to annulment.

When confession takes charge of salvation in its extension to infinity, freedom's rule over righteousness and law becomes the actual mode of sin. The freedom of confession once embedded within the healing of form gathers the law that forms within itself and so cancels the law. The confessed specific sin, one's gossip, lust, or theft, is not necessarily sin, because the docetic method secretly redefines the fault as the law affirmed in its righteousness (as forming). The confessional representation, the infinite admission of specific sins, thereby constitutes sin in fact, the actual sin. The representation here confuses the breach and the command broken, so that the breach is a sin because of its implicit confirmation of the command and not because of the command's rejection in disobedience. One cannot distinguish in practice the "false sin" (the specific sin that is not, according to the infinite law, directly and unequivocally sin) from the actual sin that is the annulment of law elevated into the means for attaining grace.

The infinite law so connects the false and the actual sin that the actual sin hides beneath the false at the same time that the false appears as the actual. Man believes that he pursues righteousness because he confesses a specific sin, acknowledging that it contradicts the law. This specific sin is the false sin, it is not the sin that Docetism would have man confess. The believer fails to discern that the mode of his confession, that it offers a way of salvation through the infinitized negation of the law, undermines his stance with respect to the law and renders the specific sin that he confesses a matter of indifference. He confesses, "I have indulged in lust," but he secretly confesses, in a manner that he does not recognize, his submission to the law as independently valid, as legitimately possessing righteousness and as a temptation away from its own annulment. That the law should receive respect in its power to compel and retain its definition as law, competing with if not overcoming the annulment, is the sin that Docetism compels man to face down. The believer must overcome this temptation and render the law into formlessness through confession, but this rendering is man's sin in fact.

Just as the false sin conceals the docetic sin of presuming a valid law (a law both authoritative and limited by freedom), so man's despair at his inability to measure up to the kind of being that the docetic god has commanded him to be conceals the betrayal in which he unknowingly accepts the law as the substance of his sin and formlessness as his proper way of being. Docetism's destruction of the law involves an illicitly baptized and astoundingly deceptive habit of misrepresentation. In the confession oriented to the mystery, misrepresentation is allowed in a diminutive rather than an ultimate form inasmuch as the believer seeks grace as the *telos* that rectifies the sin confessed, whereas in docetic confession the misrepresentation is ultimate because unconditioned. In the misrepresentation oriented to the mystery man says "I am a sinner," but the representation of nature *qua* sinner bears the subtle and overriding acknowledgment that God created man in righteousness (that is, with form) and that the sin he confesses does not strip all of this righteousness away. When the Christian confesses his sin, he says that sin has suppressed but not wiped out nor equaled his righteousness, but also that he cannot surmount this sin without grace. This misrepresentation is not unqualified and whole because the antagonism between the admission of sin and the righteousness of nature does not achieve the equality in which the spiritual law of man's nature is completely annulled. In docetic confession, on the other hand, the antagonists achieve this equality because the declaration hopes not for the restoration of natural righteousness lost but the denial of the righteousness that remains. The collapse of the law into confessional freedom exalts a diminutive misrepresentation into a genuine antithesis, an equality that transforms the sin, so that man sees his nature as his fault. In docetic confession he juxtaposes equal and heterogeneous elements that pit "I am not" against "I am," as though man could both be and not be at the same time. His words give the account in which he says "I am a sinner," while his nature cries out that a merciful law has sculpted him in righteousness. The misrepresentation elevated to actual sin consists in man's unequivocal verbal annulment of the law that he is, a movement of freedom from and equality with the law in confession that enhances the annulment because the announcement of the sin in its unqualified suppression of righteousness has become the apex of salvation. This is the meaning of justification by faith alone, the doctrinal expression of triumphant docetic science, that just as the law becomes an infinite inquisitor over the conscience and an oppressor that destroys man's free will, so the infinite confession totally annuls man's righteousness by compelling him to abdicate it. Man believes that salvation comes to him by the means and in the moment that salvation recedes; he believes that the soul experiences grace in the event that obliterates the soul in its orientation to God.

Docetic confession is the boldest genius under which man has ever toiled, the most brilliantly conceived perversion that the deceiver could dream. Evil has seized confession and, in the wake of grace's collapse, turned what God gave as a passage point toward salvation into a passage point toward perdition, all the while maintaining the impression that confession is a supplication for grace. The devil's art is not to openly define his science as the annulment of righteousness and law, celebrating an ethic that man knows to be turned toward the pit, but to bury that annulment under its holy reflection, the confession in which man regards the annulment as a prelude to healing. Docetic man has dismembered both the spiritual law unto form and the grace of form conferred, tearing law and grace apart through his science until they are no longer felt realities or imaginable as such, the whole time believing that he works toward salvation, that a good future awaits him and his children as agents of God's will. Docetists are indeed confessors of sin, but their confessional essence is the unknown and all-controlling sin. They supplicate not for the grace of eternal life but the grace of life eternally denied.

The application of the science of confession to the natural order began before the Reformation, sprouting in circles not immediately connected to Luther's monasticism or Calvin's Geneva. If the Reformers did not cultivate new ideas of natural science into the West, however, they did much to water the plant. When Calvin transferred Luther's infinite law into man's ethical life, jump-starting the ceaseless activity of Reformed Protestantism, he imbued the infant natural science with a powerful spirit of advance. Under Calvin's hand, Docetism's inward science strode forward as the *modus operandi* of man's dealings with the natural world, with Calvin's ethic unwittingly enlivening the new science as a means of knowledge that located the order of nature and its political expression in the crosshairs. Freedom in the natural order would come to ground the law and demand that the law return into it, while man's "righteousness" entailed seeking the annulment of his physical form as well as the spiritual. Man embarked on a path of freedom and equality that he accepted as his destiny, believing that he would receive salvation through obedience to its law. He hoped for a fuller and more blessed existence, even a proper communion with God, although he made his way on the road that annuls the body in the shadow of the annulled soul. This is man's natural science under Docetism, the sin that leads to death by endlessly dividing the natural order and man as its resident, a pestilence mortal to both his social world and his earthly home.

II

The infinite man: fired out of the Reformation like artillery, hurled at the structures by which he and his world retain definition and bent upon annulment as his salvation. He has known many names in the docetic development following the Christ-Idol: here reformer, revolutionary, capitalist, imperialist, scientist, inventor, there missionary, democrat, activist, liberator, communist. In all cases, whether attached explicitly to docetic Christianity or floating in a secularized docetic stream, he has drunk to a greater or lesser extent the draughts of Docetism, twisting his efforts under the grand goal of ignorance of his being, misrepresenting his nature. This man is not what he is, his comings and goings a formlessness in which the priority and thus the connection between soul and body lies in disrepair. In the wake of this emasculation he calls himself a man only by lying to himself, by disguising his nature within the self so successfully that he has no concept of natural existence. Docetic man, breed and slave of the infinite law, stands upon the rubble of the natural world and says "I am natural"—but he denies any given meaning to nature, exploits his environment, and only knows the natural world through his alienation from it. He stands upon the ruin of his society and says "I am a social animal, my world is mutuality and network"—but his social existence is loneliness and his relationships a collective unknown. He says "I am a liberator, the breaker of bonds and rescuer of the oppressed"—and yet the peace that he establishes is a prelude to war, a bondage that appears sweet as long as he delays its consummation. He surveys his science and says "I am the possessor of infinite knowledge, having unlocked the secrets of my world"—but he has abdicated the knowledge of the infinite and has no inkling of the powers that he claims to control.

For centuries docetic man has languished under the infinite science, making double the bricks without straw or, in the modern metaphor, locked in the cage where his being gnaws at him like a worm. Concentrating his efforts in economics, politics, technology, philosophy, history, or religion, he works tirelessly, giving over all time, energy, and pride to a scientific task that judges him expendable, a cruelty that tabulates men as interchangeable parts and quantifies life in currency, and in his moments of reserve his abyss wells up as an echo: why this task, this rush, this fury, this necessity, this anxiety, when it exacerbates the dizziness of a freedom he is taught to love but which has no substance to offer him and wears away what substance he has? Shall docetic man continue to justify the choice to annihilate his nature and the natural law on the ground that he chooses it, and that his thirst is slaked? Or shall he perceive that the goal of his toil, the freedom that he worships as his house god, feeds upon the annulment of nature and demands that he live without meaning as the smell of sacrifice in its nostrils?

The science of confession that preceded the Christ-Idol and the natural science that followed it are one science of freedom, one release of nature from the form by which it retains coherence as nature. Just as Luther believed consciously that he possessed form as a man, so Docetism's natural scientists have believed that man, his society, and the natural world are each fundamentally formed and fundamentally a unity. In the early centuries following the Christ-Idol men assumed this unity with the further belief in progress, reform, and the possibility of bettering the human condition. Like Luther they set upon a course that they thought would take them to salvation, a redemption now understood as freedom, equality, and the achievement of man's fullness. This science replicates docetic confession in the natural order; it too is a science of infinite division. Where the earlier practice of confession divided sin from righteousness in order to annul the righteousness by externalizing the sin, extending this practice to the infinity of the total annulment of the spiritual man, the new science divides the docetic sins of physical pain and social limit from the docetic righteousness of physical satisfaction and freedom in order to externalize and wipe out the former. By this means Docetism's natural science divides not only sin from righteousness but men from men and man from man, alienating man from the natural world and numbing his bodily existence. This result intensifies until the last externalization, the natural infinity that mirrors its spiritual predecessor.

Many docetic men have believed that man's form accomplishes its fullness through the division of sin from righteousness, which provides the opportunity for him to work off the sin and so better his condition. In this view, the severance constitutes the mediating step between man as he is and the achievement of his best capacities, principally the realization of his freedom. After the division and the conquering of the sin, he thought, his nature would return to itself aggrandized and heightened, ennobled by the challenge of difference and coming once more to its own. The dialectical method in which man juxtaposes freedom against its supposed opposite, the infinite task, in order to pass through the latter and return to freedom from the mediation with greater strength—a freedom mistakenly thought to be synonymous with form and definition—underlies docetic man's explicit conceptions of his natural science and his politics, as if the eradication of suffering should lead to his plenitude as a nature, or as if the unraveling of a hierarchical social order should give birth to brotherhood. Docetism has misrepresented the infinite division of nature as a means toward paradise, blinding its adherents to its actual effects.

The presuppositions of docetic man's dialectical science have reversed without his knowledge. They reside not in the explicit claims of Docetism's most brilliant philosophers but in the understanding of man secretly brought to life in the Reformation doctrine of justification. There the docetic science of confession achieved the redefinition of man as free and equal, indefinite and formless, and tasked him with the burden of executing that formlessness. Docetism's dialectical science begins not with unity, form, and solidarity but with shapelessness and conflict. This assumption grounds Docetism's science of nature and kicks it into action, so that its mediation consists not in the division of what is formed according to its defect but in the positing of form from what was formless. Docetic science asserts form, unity, and order, a law for man, his society, and the natural world, as a middle term. They become the sin, the infinite law through which he must pass. Politically, his sin in this dialectic remains a society of limit and thus of finite form, although docetists both experienced and theorized this finitude as infinite and an oppressor. More fundamentally, the sin is now not so much the pain involved in bodily life as the body itself. For pain and inconvenience are but the negative experience of his bodily law, and he cannot abolish them without abolishing bodily feeling. The nature that man is in fact, the expression of his nature as formed, shifts from the presupposition of his existence to the inescapable and sinful mediation of his being as unformed. The practical focus of his science, the drive behind his technological breakthroughs and political revolutions as the conquering of his sin, likewise shifts so that it tends not toward unity and improvement but returns man's form to its supposed origin in formlessness. Docetic man will find no unity on the other side of division because he labors at a method whose end is dissolution and limitless alienation. His science affirms what it loves and cherishes only to undermine the affirmation, his infinite technological and political divisions advance toward the annulment of nature and society. He posits the state in order finally to negate it, while his science of the natural environment claims to love the nature that he despoils.

Docetism's great political philosophers, its new lawgivers and social theorists, sensed the docetic assumption of formlessness as it were unconsciously, applying the deformation of man's spiritual nature to the political world in a new conception of its origins and development. Prior to the Christ-Idol man's political freedom and equality had existed within constraints inasmuch as man situated the democratic assembly within a society of structure and rank, circumscribing the political moment of annulment within the hard walls of form. After the Christ Idol this moment broke its bonds and became the unconditioned. The moment of freedom and equality wherein man stands apart from the law in order to consent to it or reject it was extracted from the order in which it found its proper place and made the defining principle for man and his society, so that he understood his nature by its distance from the law. As entirely freedom from the law and entirely equal with it man envisioned a new state descriptive of his original existence, a new nature bestowed in theory upon all men, a state of lawlessness with no command other than "do not die" or, in its more naïve versions, "do no injury," a state that inverts the order of nature by establishing man in his freedom over the law rather than having the law stand over and limit him. This state of nature, the Docetic Eden, the initial explication of a world born out of formlessness for a man without form, the blueprint for a society oriented to annulment and filled with false hope, followed the Reformation and its wars of religion as the political anchor for docetic man.

Taking up formless man, the philosophers placed him in a group without structure or mold, in which he lived upon his freedom and recognized the law as a constraint upon his natural right. To each that right was infinite. Whatever he desired and his strength could attain for him was his, with little to stop him beyond the fear of retribution from others. This world without industry, arts, letters, commerce, and security; this life, solitary, poor, nasty, brutish, and short; this man without boundary, fellow-feeling, discipline, and peace, much less joy, patience, kindness, gentleness, and control over his lusts, a man barely distinguishable from beasts and bereft of the love for which God has shaped man in fact. This man assumed his place as natural and proper, a scapegoat if not a model for the vices that docetic man houses in his soul. Thrown together as so many criminals and upstarts into a primal gaggle, Docetism's natural men knew little other than the violence that defined their inner existences, applying the inward and ontological annulment of the law within their natures to the outer world in their attacks upon one another. With this formless society as a presupposition docetic science initiates its political dialectic.

Can it surprise the astute thinker that honest formulators of the state of nature knew it immediately or almost immediately as a state of war? Hobbes could not distinguish the two states, Locke knew the state of nature as a preliminary to the state of war, and only Rousseau, the most sanguine of the early expositors of Docetism's political logic, could accept the lie that the natural state was not immediately one of conflict, claiming that it is too slippery for definition. The state of nature inevitably pits man against man, as if beings divinely-wrought and pleasing to their Lord in fact should be born for the aggression of absolute freedom and equality. When man comprehends his nature in this state and looks upon others, he sees the enemies that would subdue and impose form upon him, the other to whom his inner and outer violence estranges him and whose capacity for violence he must overcome. In his mind, his neighbor plays the attacker and he the defense, just as his adversary reverses these roles, so that each is an adversary to all others and righteous in his own estimate, each justified in his assault upon the others and dignified in the outworking of his inner combat. This state of mutual annulment of law cannot long abide because its end is death. Its inexplicable product and the annulment of the continuous war between man and man is a new law, one strange and nefarious, a puzzle and a fright.

Docetic man named that law the social contract, a hypothetical mutual agreement among men who wished to escape the danger of the state of nature. According to the philosophers, in the state of nature the mutual annulment of law between man and man (that is, his violence) terrified but did not annihilate him, so that he sought an escape from his fear through the power of the contract or the state. Docetic man believes that he can trust the state, which is responsible for his defense and the protection of his well-being, bestowing upon it the power to quell the insatiability of his natural existence. In the contract each man gives up his power to the sovereign, whether an individual or an assembly, for the better preservation of all. This decision does not eradicate the horror of man's natural existence but hides it under a false confidence, for when individual men transfer their capacity for violence onto a collective entity they only relocate that violence under a cloak that they believe acts for their good. They believe that the state will guard their safety and support their endeavors, when they have created a product which is the sum of the antagonism that reigned between them. The state might appear at first as a blessing and a relief, but it has not yet revealed its true nature. Those who favored such a state did not realize that they created a monster of limitless power, a dragon whose boundlessness implies that it will turn malignantly upon its subjects.

The contract is the mediating element in Docetism's political logic of formlessness. The Leviathan, the government designed to punish and inspire fear, is the infinite law rising from the state of nature, it is the form dialectically opposed to the formlessness from which it springs. In it the anarchic power that ruled in the direct conflict of man against man temporarily withdraws, allowing nature's factual tendency to form to assert its definition. Docetism's secret involves the infiltration and perversion of that form so that what appears to rise into being will finally fall into infinity. As it initially takes shape this form appears beneficent, not yet disclosing its lack of boundary in practice, and man trusts in the contract as an emergent principle of freedom, peace, and prosperity. With time and development the self-annulling vector of the form becomes apparent, with the contract's validity declining through the unlimited expansion of political power and law. As the state imposes its strength without restriction it transforms into a tyrant, and man encounters it as an enemy to his freedom.

Docetism's political science turns on the question of state power and popular rebellion, and in the rationale for revolution Docetism's man carries out his political confession. As early as Locke man sought to limit the power of the government by subordinating it to the people. The state, Locke assumed, possessed validity and thereby form, but it could err by exceeding its boundaries. By these terms he distinguished the righteousness of the state, its necessity and legitimacy as a protector of the persons and possessions of its citizens, from the sin of the state, its tendency to exceed its limits through arbitrary assertions of right. The spiritual science of confession that eventuated in the Christ-Idol and remained active in Protestantism for centuries after the Reformation finds its political match in this science of power, which forces the state under its microscope in order to divide its sin from its righteousness. Docetic man says at one point that the state exercises its power within its bounds and so justly, and thus is righteous, while at another point—at the crux, the test of conscience and the path to salvation—man discovers the state surpassing its boundaries and acting as a brute. In the latter case man externalizes the sin of state power by announcing it to the public, doing this as a prelude to the resistance intended to eradicate what he has externalized. With Locke man has the right to push back against the government when the people surmise that it has breached the contract and forfeited their trust. This is docetic man's grace, the reform unto revolution that conquers the sin of the state, annuls its power, and negates its law in the direction of a more expansive liberty for all.

The spiritual law relinquishes its form as its commands multiply into infinity, a loss of form made concrete in the endless requirement of confession. This slide into indefinition climaxes in the explosive and total annulment of the law in the docetic experience of grace. The two experiences that seem opposed, the terror of the conscience under the law and the joyous liberation of grace, are ontologically unified as one dialectical descent into formlessness, one movement of mediation through the infinite and horrifying spiritual law that returns to its origin in the indefinite. Political confession works according to the same logic: it posits the contract as the law, the mediation arising from the state of nature, but does so in order to apply its science of division and externalization until the mediating form returns to its roots in shapelessness. Man's experience under an increasingly burdensome political power denotes the slide of the government toward illegitimacy and its ontological loss of form, a loss that climaxes in the unhindered release of revolution. In the political case as well as the spiritual the pair that seem to exist as opposites, man's terror under tyranny and the exultation of his rebellion, combine as a single and unified process of the dissolution of form.

In Locke's day this science of politics had not achieved the infinite either in theory or in practice. In the face of their rulers, he and his contemporaries agreed that the government maintained a legitimate power of coercion. They did not dream of an infinite confession of political sin, of man's finding injustice and oppression beneath every assertion of state power, nor of the comprehensive liberty affirmed in later centuries. Men in Locke's day nonetheless contributed to the annulment of political law, subtly articulating the science of division by which man negates the monster that he has created. This monster develops not all at once, and not exactly in a linear fashion, but in dialectical cycles not fundamentally dissimilar from those observed in the buildup to the Christ-Idol. In his political science, the docetic spirit moves man to consider a legal power as unjust or in transgression of its boundaries, and in this sense a partisan of the infinite. He revolts against this law and overturns it, placing a new legal standard in its stead. Man trusts in the new law as a better justice and a greater freedom, unaware that his revolt has diminished the form of political law *per se*, and that the new law is more subject to the cruelty of the infinite than its predecessor.

In the first political cycle Docetism set to work against the system of rank intrinsic to the natural political order. Docetic man discovered through his science that kings too often wield an arbitrary, unwarranted, and unlimited power in contradiction to the freedom of the common man and in supposed opposition to the contract. Assessing that monarchies lead almost by necessity to tyranny and oppression, docetic man enervated or annulled their power in the same centuries that the merchant classes threatened the nobility. These developments peaked in the revolutionary eruptions in the American colonies and France, a period consummated in the Napoleonic Wars. Napoleon, the first docetic liberator and executioner, the logical conclusion of the French Revolution, who burned away what remained of the old political hierarchy! Through his bloodletting Docetism wiped away the old form of political order and placed a novel one in its stead, a law more beholden to freedom and equality than any before it.

In the wake of the Napoleonic wars Europe replaced the hierarchy of birth with the hierarchy of wealth. The vocational drive to formlessness known as the Protestant ethic, an ethos which denotes the application of Docetism's infinite law to the individual's economic life, had already done much to undermine the feudal hierarchy. By the mid-nineteenth century this ethos had helped funnel the diversity of monarchical rank into two classes, antagonists that exemplify economic freedom and equality. The bourgeoisie lived at the height of material power and leisure, possessed of a multiplication of superfluous pleasures and increasingly detached from the inconveniences of life. This class obeyed the infinite law in their ceaseless activity and, as managers, forced that law upon others as a tyrant. The class burdened by that law, crushed like human nature under the demand that terrified Luther and Calvin, is the proletariat. A horde subjected to squalor, deprived of necessities in a way not fitting for men enshrined with God's image, the proletariat endured the oppression of the bourgeoisie as its alter ego. The infinite law raised its champions at the expense of its slaves, squeezing the latter into oblivion in order to exalt the former into luxury. Docetic man surveyed the chasm between the classes and could not tolerate it, sensing the injustice of the infinite law and its need for redress, even revolution.

This assessment provoked Karl Marx's philosophy of communism, which promised a better and more egalitarian world. A life without the alienation of man from his nature and from other men, an existence without oppression and tyranny, called to men from the other side of the class war and the leveling of economic castes. The conviction of this promise as a historical inevitability, as the meaning of history at whose edge the West stood, took its cues from the docetic belief that man and his world need reform unto a better way of being. Docetic progress, a worldly form of salvation encapsulated in the drive toward economic, technological-scientific, and political improvement and supposed to break down divisions between men, found expression in communism as the certainty that such an improvement is man's destiny. This certainty seized Europe's brightest minds and political will and turned them to its purposes. Who could resist a future so resplendent, in which the pride of man beamed through each and every individual in his own way? Who would dismiss a future in which each thrived in the consciousness of his own true humanity, shared real brotherhood with others, and in which the dehumanization of the masses had no part? The promise of salvation in this world, the conclusion of political history in a collective defined by unbounded freedom and equality, with the laws that had hung over them annulled—who would forsake this vision or call it a lie? Only the most selfish and stupid, the most backwards, the unjust usurpers of the collective power and their religious dupes, would hesitate to work toward the realization of progress and the fullness it entailed.

In Marx's mind, the revolution necessitated the dismantling not only of bourgeoisie law but of all law. State and religion as coverings for bourgeoisie power had to fall, unveiled as injustices that point toward the revolt that cancels them. With the economic drive to classlessness undergirding history all appeals to a society in which some rule while others are ruled become suspect. The working classes had to throw off the chains of religious illusion so that, setting their eyes upon the sensuality in which they believed their lives to consist, they could battle the bourgeoisie through the state as the functional origin of law. With Marx, the earlier docetic attack upon the particular religion of priest craft, popery, and sacramental magic expanded into an attack upon religion in general just as the attack upon a particular form of the state that restricts rule to monarchs, nobles, or a specific class expanded into an attack upon the state as the arm of any particular group or class excepting the proletariat, the universal class. The communist revolution would destroy all lawgivers and with them all law, with the goal of unlocking the handcuffs of economic distinction by terminating private property. Recast as ineradicably unjust insofar as not supportive of an unlimited freedom and equality, the law that gives society form, differentiation, and structure came under thoroughgoing assault. Its enemies wished to tear it down for the sake of the liberated man, the one who revolves about himself as his own sun.

Man achieves this self-referentiality as he grasps himself in his social universality, at once as the citizen or representative of the human species in its collective aspect and as a being unrestricted in individual freedom and equality with others. In order to live within this universality, man-as-citizen must deny the private differentiations that spring from private property and that set him against others, relinquishing claims to privilege and status. On the collective level, this denial means the abolition of civil society and its elements, a violent and permanent conflict of the state against man's life as detached from it. Political life in Marx's philosophy constantly wages war against the differentiation inseparable from economic and cultural existence. Whenever a class or social faction would rise to power in civil society and in politics, as classes consistently want to do, the universal man must combat it both in civil society as a would-be economic and cultural power and as that power already expresses itself in the political-legal edifice. Forces of universal freedom and equality see the upward progress of a single group as destined to oppress, and for the sake of universality they must annul it. Only through this permanent revolution does society preserve the freedom and equality at its heart, preventing the return of the class struggle and the upending of history.

In this way Docetism elevates its political science toward an infinite freedom and equality, stultifying the possibility that political life might take a definite shape. Every push of society toward order and coherence, and toward the distinction between higher and lower that this order implies, means ontologically its attempt to acquire form. Marx's docetic science keeps a vigilant eye on this form in order to attack it as soon as it appears, executing the division fundamental to Docetism's political confession. Seeing the emergence of form through the law Marxism divides the righteousness of valid law from the sin of distinction and hierarchy, employing an absolute freedom and equality as its standard. Beneath this absolute judgment all law becomes sin because law inevitably privileges some above others, protecting one group and placing another at risk. The unrelenting and infinite division that scrutinizes political assertions as expressions of economic injustice undermines the legitimacy of the law as a phenomenon independent of its overturning in revolution. Political law in Marx's thought does not circumscribe freedom and equality as a presupposition and goal. The law rather collapses under the rapacity of an unlimited political liberty and an equal right for all, so that the annulment surrounds, consummates, and gives meaning to the law's positing. The docetic pattern of confession surfaces in Docetism's political philosophy as a threat to the political manifestation of the natural order, applying the science of Luther's inward annulment of righteousness to the form of the political world.

That Marx aligns permanent revolution with brotherhood rather than war proves his folly. In that ideal situation man possesses full rights and capacities to express his desires, taking turns among possibilities so that he becomes fisherman, hunter, and critic without any of these activities imposing a definite way of being upon him. Inasmuch as everyone enjoys this liberty of expression, it is supposed that all will be happy, each taking pleasure in the products of his labor and no longer alienated from others by the division of tasks. But each also exists in the ubiquitous struggle to suppress those factions and individuals who would force their wills upon society through the state. Permanent revolution and the indifferentiation that it espouses, having achieved the goal of equality by abolishing the upper classes, only widens the war against the powerful and the monied so that all become potential rulers and oppressors. Every man perceives his neighbor as an enemy ready to usurp what is mine as though it were his and subjugate me to his prerogative. In the midst of man's celebration of his individuality he must suspect the individuality of others, suppressing it inasmuch as power might reside in it or insofar as others might use their individuality to establish power over him. This is no euphemistic revolution, but war; not the end of alienation, but its perfection; not the fulfillment of man, but his emptying as deprived of righteousness and given over to suspicion; not a joyful return to nature, but the reign of an unnatural fear.

The communist theory of Marx and Engels is the paradigmatic political expression of the docetic logic. It presumes an original freedom and equality among persons, an order in which the division of labor had yet to differentiate and structure men and women according to their economic functions. Like their Enlightenment predecessors the communist theorists placed their hypothetical ancestors in a state of formlessness without legal or natural stability. Out of this condition emerged an economic law unjust and reprehensible in Marx's mind, a division of labor that alienated the consciousness of individuals one from another and initiated man's history of class struggle. The division of labor and its various forms of dehumanization, as well as the attempt at their justification through state and religion, negated the ideal and natural mode of men's relations by arbitrarily raising one group to economic power while alienating all from genuine existence as human beings. Communism seeks to negate this negation of true humanity, to destroy the oppressive law and end the class struggle while returning man's society to its original equality. The theory of communism conforms in this manner to the dialectical pattern at the heart of Docetism: it posit the origin of man and his society as without law and thereby formless; it envisions a law emerging out of this formlessness that diametrically opposes its source and which man must annul; and it resolves the opposition by executing the annulment and re-introducing man to a version of the initial order.

In its history Marxism moved through a different and unforeseen dialectic, producing some of the cruelest governments that man has known. The communists formulated their doctrine after the fall of feudalism and so faced a lesser barrier between their aspirations for an unlimited freedom and equality and the construction of the political apparatus intrinsic to their dreams. Marx celebrated man as defined by political existence, the universal man or man as a species being, but he did not understand that the creation of a society of universal men entails handing absolute power to an absolute state. Men only become universally and completely political, being defined by their standing before the state, inasmuch as the state pulverizes and incarcerates them under its power and compels them into total combat with it as their enemy. To borrow a term from Marx's forerunner Rousseau, the "total alienation" of the individual as handed over to the state means the bestowal of unlimited power to its administration at the price of the unchecked terror of the citizen. Man must then run to the assembly as fast as his legs will carry him not because of his love of democracy or pride in his equality with his fellows, but to invent ways of defeating the demon that he has conjured. Only when he has accomplished this task and relieved his anguish does man feel his concepts enlarged and his soul ennobled. Only when man has propped up the political power as an unaccountable and reckless despot that he must then vanquish can he suppose to gain the protection of the collective power while each rules himself, remaining as free as he was outside the contract.

Man's yearning for freedom tricks him into the dialectic underlying communist theory. Communism proclaims a government that will bless individuals with freedom and equality, protecting their well-being and raising the commonwealth to brotherhood. Man believes this rhetoric and hands his powers to the government expecting the dawn of a new age, so that the state seems not to require the compulsion that forces man to be free. Man must learn the lesson that he cannot become free apart from being so forced, even being crushed and oppressed, and so his efforts at improving his political life, born from the best intentions, create not a communist haven but a fantastic and unheard-of platform for tyranny. Rather than the advent of a new era that has outgrown alienation, man languishes under a breathtaking and lawless beast, the totalitarian state.

The most important features of Luther's experience of the spiritual law resurface in the prerogatives of totalitarian government. In the former case Docetism mounted a devastating and climactic assault on the spiritual order, and in the latter case it mounts a similar attack upon the political aspect of the natural world. Luther trembled before a law limitless in its ubiquity, hounding every thought, action, and feeling, a law that punished each sin with the immediate threat of eternal damnation. Under that law he felt his spiritual freedom shrink until it was destroyed, reducing his moral choices to insignificance and stripping him of confidence in human nature and the law as means to justification. Luther understood the essence of that law as terror, a startling fear intrinsic to the Christian's earnest supplication for grace. Totalitarian law duplicates these characteristics in the political order. It oppresses everyone within its purview as a law limitless and ever present, bent outwardly upon world domination just as it presses upon its captives without interruption, everywhere confronting its subjects with the power of the totalitarian leader. This law abolishes the political freedom of its citizens, condemning them to permanent guilt. Like the law in Luther's conscience, this law is sheer terror, a vehicle whose motion thrives on strangling men into submission.

Totalitarian government is the logical outgrowth of the fantasy that man should discover his consummation in the state, a deception alive in the twentieth century in both communism and fascism. Such governments desire a political order totally divided from abuses of power and consequently from political sin, but in order to purge the state of its potential for sin they eradicate the form of political order itself. The righteousness of the political world consists in differentiations of rank and power rightly fashioned according to their limit. By unequivocally rejecting these differentiations, totalitarianism melts down the limits of position and power and leaves nothing to the political order but its corruption. The undoing of the political law of righteousness, the order of a measured and finite governmental form, might appear as the joyous revolution of the commonwealth whereas it is fundamentally the unleashing of an infinite capacity for oppression. The limitlessness of the Party leaders, expressed in their brutality and inescapable surveillance, is the morbid but truthful reflection of their belief in an unlimited humanity. On the other hand, the state pulses through its subjects as its agents while it simultaneously condemns each man as separated from his political responsibility. The citizen embodies both the infinite law of the political authority (as its secret spy) and his total guilt under that law *qua* individual (as spied on by others). In this world all men are alienated and fearful while the state is unlimited and whimsical.

Totalitarianism's lack of limitation compelled its leaders to annihilate the divine within the political order. The Holocaust and the persecution of the Russian church, the religious insanity of unbridled Docetism, spared no means in pursuit of this end. They sought to cut off man's faith in a beneficent and divine presence moving through the political order, destroying the possibility of a politically relevant and merciful providence by destroying the Christian and the Jew. Having rejected God in these crises, docetic man descends into near total darkness. God leaves him to feast on his own vomit, to wonder how he could commit such evil when just a short time earlier he considered history destined for utopia. In docetic persecution man sees the world without mercy, the ugly infinity that he has unwittingly pursued, in the trauma that wipes out the legitimacy of political order because it has wiped out the divine purpose of political life. Surveying his atrocity man realizes that politics divorced from a merciful providence, without a God who watches over it as a means not toward the maximization of freedom but toward the limit designed for his creatures, is an order that liberates men by reducing them to rubble.

During the conflict provoked by totalitarianism docetic man invented weapons of such grand demolition that the obliteration of nature became possible. In nuclear weaponry Docetism's annulment of political life intertwines with its capacity to annul the natural world. Such weapons are the current height of Docetism's technological science as a process of division, a progressively narrowed and precise breaking down of natural elements until the last severance. This break releases an inestimable and catastrophic power, an energy meant not to defeat armies but to level cities and incinerate civilians. Such weapons helped complete Docetism's political dialectic while they anticipate the final annihilation of nature, a battle that makes the world wars appear like the removal of a splinter next to the amputation of a limb.

The World Wars inflicted a mortal wound upon the Western state; in them, the state lost its efficacy as a binding institution, opening the door to the latest cycle in Docetism's advance against the natural order. On the one hand, the reinvigoration of boundless law after the World Wars reaches above and beyond nations, undermining them in favor of the global nexus. On the other hand, the revolutions following the Second World War enacted the political scattering, the obsolescence of political solidarity and prior forms of constraint, just as they heightened man's infinitude. Though man announced his freedom from hierarchies of race, though woman proclaimed her liberty from the rule of man, and though today new forms of sexual liberation assert themselves, these witness to the preceding and essential liberation that is man's rejection of political power. They are the grace of indifference to political rest, the realization of a freedom and equality that spurns the commanding authority of the legislators. Through these movements man carries out the docetic logic against more fundamental forms of social life such as the family, or against hierarchies, like that of race, that are not natural but are products of Docetism's earlier trajectories. In this way man continues his alienation from his nature and the natural world, unaware that his efforts work against their stated aims, and that rather than creating a world of brotherhood he sets the conditions for conflict.

With the Christ-Idol the Reformation secretly established a new dialectic in man's relation to his entire nature, extending from the soul to the body and likewise to the physical environment. This dialectic energized the nascent modern science with a religious spirit foreign to earlier forms of scientific inquiry, embedding its explicit processes within a religious context that its practitioners did not discern. Docetic man learned the scientific method as best articulated by Newton: as an experimenter, man asks a question, forms a hypothesis, carries out his experiment and gathers data, and later issues a conclusion in response to the question. This method gave science the appearance of moral neutrality, as if because it was merely a method science had no implications or assumptions regarding good and evil or right and wrong. In the maturing scientific view, those questions belonged to categories of religion and philosophy that did not enjoy the value-free prerogative of scientific investigation. Modern natural science, docetic science, has progressed for centuries under this charm and without a clue to its own deeper meaning, ignorant of the moral and religious foundations that provide it with an unspoken and powerful warrant. Underlying the science that understands itself only as a method is the docetic science that divides and severs, the science that means to annul the law of man's nature and the natural world.

The application of the docetic dialectic to the body begins, as in the political realm, with the unspoken assumption of man's nature as bereft of form. Rather than man affirming his freedom and equality in the chaotic hypothetical origin of the commonwealth, Docetism here implies a natural state of anthropological universality, or man's life in perfect freedom from the law of his nature and in unrestricted equality with it. Man's liberation from the natural law means his liberation from both the order of the soul over the body and his nature as the interpenetration of these two, defacing the integrity of both elements. He no longer knows his soul, which has turned wholly from God and toward what is other than God. Nor does he know his body, which has so lost its capacity for feeling that it lives as though it were dead. Each dwelling in a form that is the negation of its content, man's body and soul exist in contradiction against their own natures and in near complete freedom from one another. This freedom is their equality, a perversion in which the properties of the soul become confused with the body while those of the body become confused with the soul. The mortal but unfeeling flesh lives as though it will not die, though this not dying is itself a kind of death, while the undying soul relinquishes its will to live. Man floats as a ceaseless motion without order or rhythm, lacking the measure required for his existence. Though its best philosophers have not perceived or thematized this theoretical starting point, it serves as the foundation for Docetism's recasting of man's bodily life and the ontological presupposition of its scientific endeavors.

As the antithesis to this unspoken assumption regarding his natural existence and as the mediating element within the docetic dialectic, man encounters his nature as imbued with form, even beauty and blessing. He surveys the strength of his body and the reason of his intellect, he acknowledges his capacities for securing his existence and for joy in the natural world. These testify to his natural definition and man recognizes them, on the surface, as the goodness of his nature. He nonetheless faces a considerable evil. It is not that docetic man has consciously experienced the natural law with revulsion and horror, nor that the law of his body weighs upon him with an infinite and unmitigated requirement. Such experiences are not the conscious origin of his distaste for his nature. In a way often subtle if not unconscious, man recognizes his enemy as the limitation inherent in the body. The restriction in a particular place, the hard wall of time experienced in waiting, as well as the natural encounter with the elements, contradict the presupposition of his limitlessness. Thus the existence for which he strives, the assumption and goal of his technological paradise, arrives at a world in which there is no space, in which man has overcome time, and in which he tolerates no bodily discomfort. This pursuit of boundarylessness underlies what man consciously recognizes as the great wickedness: the suffering of pain and his inevitable mortality. These decisively prove his constraint under limit, and the infinite man cannot stand them. From these positive and negative experiences of bodily existence man tacitly develops his conceptions of the righteousness of nature and its sin. Nature's righteousness consists in man's natural shape, power, and intelligence as fashioned by God, whereas its sin is located in his limit, especially bodily pain and death.

Man looks everywhere and, discovering his pain, he exclaims: "Here I suffer, here I am vulnerable, here I am inconvenienced, and at the end I must die!" On a deeper level these exclamations boil down to one announcement: "Here is my sin." This is the confessional origin of docetic man's natural science, his limitless division of sin from righteousness in the ubiquitous identification of pain, want, and vulnerability, and these terminating in demise. This division is moral inasmuch as it prescribes a way of being in which man must eradicate the enemies that threaten and limit his existence. It is religious because it discreetly names his subjection to these enemies as his sin and wishes to save him from it. Docetic man has failed to perceive this truth, as well as one more fundamental and ironic. He does not see that the same law undergirds both his joy in the body as God's creation and the punishment that it suffers. One side takes pleasure in the partially fulfilled form of man while the other recoils at the penalty for his abdication of total fulfillment at the fall, but both sides imply an encounter with the one law. The negative side further presumes the positive because man can only revile the corruption of form where form is already present. His science, in which he seeks to eradicate the negative by dividing it from the positive and destroying its law, thus entails his inadvertent eradication of the law of the positive. The elimination of pain and vulnerability unto death necessitates the elimination of feeling and thus of the body *per se*. The deepest sin of docetic man emerges not as the physical suffering of the body but as its form and life. Docetic man strives to blot out suffering in the body by unknowingly pursuing the death of a life without the body.

He carries out this pursuit in a two-pronged fashion, a division of the body from the soul that moves in parallel with the body's division from its own nature. The body draws its life from the soul, so that the destruction of bodily form implies its distance from the soul as a logical preliminary for the division of its own nature. Man finds his suffering and hastens to negate it, fashioning a world without hunger and thirst, without heat and cold, without diseases and disabilities, and in which men might live apart from the fear of death. His work to this end produces a bodily way of being severed from the soul, nourishing a consciousness that lacks a sense for the eternal and for spiritual forces, and that silences suggestions that man will live beyond the physical world. The consequent orientation of the soul to the natural world sentences it to a devastating loss of meaning, a despair in which his pursuits devolve continually into means rather than ends. He attempts to imbue the finite with the infinite, subscribing to a method that enslaves him beneath discoveries, improvements, and values that have no significance beyond his unending quest for an orientation that gives rest. His pursuit of a life without bodily suffering incarcerates the soul as divorced from both the body and God.

Through the same ethic docetic man constructs a world in which war, sickness, misfortune, and old age, all the bringers of death against which he can erect defenses, should fail to impinge upon the ramparts. He lives a danger-free life to an extent unlike any before him, separating himself from the perils of bodily existence as though he were immortal, chasing an indefinite future. This love of the body, this invulnerability, means at once man's hatred of the body. He has so thoroughly sequestered himself from death that he has removed his capacity for feeling. Docetic man fought bodily feeling for centuries, controlling it first by discipline and then by the technological comforts that discipline produced. He can now escape bodily feeling almost at will, avoiding pains and inconveniences with little effort. Docetic man increasingly finds his sensations, his fear, his compassion and joy, his love, and his longing, not through flesh and blood, not through mutual interaction with his fellows, but through make-believe. He possesses no emotional profundity, no patience and will to longsuffering, having lost a taste for the beauty beyond hardship. There is for his wife no labor cry, for him no toil with the land, and for both none of the fullness of the natural world as the world of attachment. God designed the body to feel but docetic man repudiated that design and rendered the body numb, alienating it from its natural livelihood. This is his hatred of the body, the flip side of invulnerability, the disgust that poses as love.

The principle of man's nature as soul and body reflects his world, which includes both the spiritual and the temporal orders. No difference pertains between the lower nature and the higher inasmuch as these compose one cosmos, just as the body and the soul compose a unified man. The docetic science that aims at man's formlessness and especially that of his body therefore aims by necessity at a physical world that tends toward formlessness. Just as man unconsciously presumes a formless human nature as the starting point for his anthropologico-scientific dialectic, so he unconsciously presumes a formless physical world as its counterpart. Man then encounters the antithesis of his presumption, seeing the natural world in its magnificence as formed by God. Just as he surveys his body and appreciates its beauty, so he regards the natural world with delight, identifying the sublimity of nature as its righteousness. He locates the sin of the natural world in its capacity to cause him hurt and inflict distress, to subject him to physical pain, disaster, and death. Docetic man then implements his infinite confession, everywhere finding and removing the sin that threatens him until he has constructed a world in which physical suffering and death have no place. He imposes confession upon the natural world, but just as his elimination of bodily pain disintegrates the law of his body, so his imposition upon nature entails the despoiling of the natural world. Man executes a double division upon that world that mirrors the division of the soul from the body and the body from its own nature. He erects a physical world that has expelled its spiritual companion, a world simultaneously emancipated from natural rhythms and ways of being and in equality with their laws.

The division of the physical world inverts Docetism's attack against the spiritual order as seen in the buildup to the Christ-Idol. In the medieval era Docetism divided the spiritual order of Christendom in two, at once alienating the divided element, the Roman Catholic Church, from the temporal kingdom of the West. In the wake of the Christ-Idol Docetism divides the physical world in two, drawing technological life out from the natural world just as it alienates the divided element from the spiritual kingdom of faith.

This new world, docetic man's technological Babel, expands over space and time to imprison docetic man in his severance from the spiritual. It ostracizes heaven and hell, angels and demons, Satan and the love of God, by so distancing them from man's consciousness that they evoke no earnest apprehension. Ostensibly religious men have come to view them without fear, joy, or gratitude, while mockers laugh at them as unprovable if not mythical or as crutches for the weak. The technological division of nature has closed man off to the spiritual order within an existence that it convinces him is natural, the new mundanity in which the world no longer parlays its mystery and in which its witness to its creator fades.

The docetic split of the physical from the spiritual world dovetails with the internal bifurcation of the lower order: their single root is docetic technology, which mediates the division of the body from its nature by dividing the physical power of the natural world. Ensconced in the technological world, the modern temperature-controlled self trades the natural imposition of darkness for the control of the light switch, giving up the sweat of manual labor for the ease of the office and abolishing the finitude of travel on foot for the miracle of automobiles and airplanes. Man has raised physical existence to a level unimagined for most of history, engineering a society in which fleshly gratification races to meet him at the inception of desire, in which his eyes everywhere see light and external glory, in which his divinity towers in the sky, and through which his pride courses like electricity. Production and manufacturing have refashioned the natural elements into a world apart from and dismissive of man's environment, coaxing him into its clutches as a circus of ease.

Inured to this world and unable to conceive life apart from it, docetic man knows it as his beloved, as though taken from his rib and woven together while he slept. Now in the dream: is this world real? Its glory vanishes, its pride lacks substance, it delights the tongue but impoverishes the heart. He knows its light does not come from sun, moon, or fire, and is unnatural. He knows that its glory dimly reflects the beauty of mountain and brook, coast and vale, while undermining them. Docetic man senses that with every advance in the splendor of this world that he thinks a companion to the natural one, that other world draws further into the shadows. Natural existence becomes a folk tale, its inner conviction the bliss of idiots. He thinks himself natural, but his natural existence amounts to non-existence, a blur, the scraping of mud from one's shoe. He dwells in an otherworld in which the neighbor has become the other and nature is Other. Docetic man hates this unnatural existence that he preserves despite its deprivation of soul, he hates the emptiness of the technological world's successes and its inability to pacify him, he hates how the dissonance between technological society and the natural environment subtly expresses the dissonance within his being. He loathes the society that compels him to believe that he is by nature a man without a nature, the same society that tickles his pride and overwhelms his eyes, the world that loves the flesh, and by loving annihilates it.

An empty and haphazard laughter, disjointed contradictions, frames that hang together loosely if at all, linked by disagreement, a universal difference, the tempo and cacophony of his being, his movement evil as neutral, inchoate, divided, borne by titillation and spite, docetic man passes and transitions through until an end without end, a perpetuity crammed and oblique, dull and scrolling, a murmur in which voices rise but do not enunciate, in which despair crests and joy falls, an evanescence in which what passes, passes through man, so that passing through is absorbed into passing away. Without rhythm or rest, without testing, sharpening, or winnowing, without knowing or being known, without past or future, ignorant of *gravitas* and too languid for *misericordia*, wanting the will to offer the being he lacks, crippled and drowned, a fog envelops him. This infinite man is born along in an infinite world, his way of being universal as defined by possibility and bereft of form. Docetism presents this world and his existence in it as naturally unbounded, as though time reaches backwards into an indefinite darkness while space extends into a limitless abyss. It would impose the infinite upon man's consciousness as if his potentiality and unceasing progress reflected the way of the natural world, as though this way were real and genuine. That way is falsehood and deceit, its promise a mirage, its end perdition.

Now man asks how anyone could lodge such a comprehensive critique of the docetic world. What of its breakthroughs that have bettered his existence, particularly the advance of medicine? How can one condemn a science that has developed vaccines, mended broken limbs, replaced hearts and other vital organs, and cured deadly diseases? Does medicine not save lives, and does it not improve man's physical, moral, and spiritual welfare? Was Jesus Christ not a healer, and does docetic medicine not follow his example through healing? Why castigate it as a part of the docetic edifice? Does this edifice have no redeeming qualities? Why sentence man to an existence in which maladies riddle his bones and eat at his flesh, and in which the blight of age purloins his joy? Is this not taking pleasure in pain, and a denial of the benefits that God has wrought through docetic science?

I answer that Docetism accomplishes its purposes by stretching a good and divinely ordained law to an unnatural infinity, and that this is no less the case with the science of medicine than with other sciences. The end of the medical art is health. The law of medicine is to guard and preserve the health of the body, and I add that this health, as meant for a finite being, must remain within its limits. The pursuit of health does not entail the search for a life devoid of all pain, nor a life in which death is all but absent, nor a life technologically lengthened as if man will not die. In the latter cases the law of medicine reaches beyond its boundaries and toward the infinite. This is the vector of docetic medicine, which has in the last century progressed to an infinite application by virtue of its technological advances and its political importance. Docetic medicine facilitates man's attitude toward the body as that which he must negate, which he must escape at all costs. Docetic man seeks not a finite affirmation of health for an intrinsically finite being, but unlimited access to balms that eradicate his disease and enable him to live as though not destined to perish. His is not a finite medical science humbled by his finitude, but an infinite science leading him into the infinite.

The alternatives of a finite and an infinite medical science overlap to a significant extent, adding to the docetic deception. One could reasonably argue that all docetic treatment does not immediately entail an infinite application of the law of healing. This is so much to the good, but there are men who stop at this good as though it justified all techniques and their aims. One must look deeper. Saying of a particular creature "there is good here," on the ontological level, means no more than asserting "there is being here," because all being is good and so long as it subsists it will remain good *qua* being. The question turns not on the mere presence of the good but on the form of the good. Ontologically, it matters whether the creature lives according to the law of form that God employed in fashioning it, or whether it suffers a perversion of that law unto the dissolution form. In the case of a science, it matters not whether it accomplishes any good at all because all sciences assume some principle of good in order to function as sciences. It matters whether the trajectory of the science conforms to the finitude of its law or presumes the law's expansion to infinity. Does the particular example of the science tend toward an infinite application of the law, is it embedded within and does it presume such an application, or does it recognize man's finitude and not transgress it in the pursuit of health? To which trajectory does the application of the science belong?

Much of docetic technology confirms man's life in a world divorced from his natural vulnerabilities and capacities for spiritual healing, a world that disguises the hangman's noose as the champion's garland. Through his reliance on docetic advances man loses his limit, grasping an unnatural life, a life emptied of both his consciousness of materiality and the substance of conscience. He affirms his body as his highest good and the soul as an afterthought (if at all), abandoning the knowledge of both. Heal the sick by natural means, then, but do not let them be a party to docetic technology and its lies. Do not teach them that all diseases are meant to be cured and that pain has no moral purpose, do not let them go with the silent conviction that suffering and death must be ubiquitously feared and avoided or otherwise subject to man's will. Do not let the sick believe that the health of the body summarizes man's well-being as a child of God.

Men now live their victory over death and want, reveling in a splendid carnage, taking pride in a pleasant if precarious freedom. They are deceived: man's science has not removed physical suffering from his life but, withdrawing diffuse experiences of inconvenience and pain from the course of his days, it gathers and concentrates those experiences into periods of incalculable harm. These cataclysms arise from and accelerate the unraveling of the political and natural orders, witnessing to the success of docetic science against man and his world. Often with little warning or foreshadowing, natural and political disasters seize man's property and good fortune and transform them into squalor and war. Ventures that docetic man undertakes with high expectations turn out to his ruin and he wonders how the world could descend so quickly into madness.

The World Wars were the most recent and most devastating docetic catastrophes up to this point, but this violence was neither Docetism's greatest nor its last. Already the docetic spirit approaches the end of its third cycle in the natural order, coaxing new peoples toward freedom, and to what lengths will its drive to infinity push them? What universal bloodshed, what unbounded political order and environmental chaos remain for it to achieve? Its purposes are already in motion, its weapons lie ready at hand. Docetic man has sown the wind; he shall soon reap the whirlwind.

III

Docetism is religion unto death, its spirit the animus of modern Christianity and the secular world. Facilitation of Docetism's science is the sin unto physical death, but God alone knows that science's power for the spiritual death of perdition. How then shall Christians pray?

For those well-meaning churchgoers, the generous and the patient, who have shown kindness, gentleness, self-control, and compassion to their fellow men, and who have sought God as best they knew how, yet who unwittingly worship now or have lived and died in the grip of Docetism: pray regularly for these. Due to their ignorance of the forces that shaped their lives and practice, their sin is not necessarily unto spiritual death. God will have mercy on them as he will, and if he judges negatively, he will not fail to take their ignorance into account.

Concerning those Christians who have heard the error and destiny of Docetism and do not repent, who cling to it as the truth though informed that it is a lie, who embrace it as the divine will and devote their energies to the further elimination of being, hastening man into formlessness: pray for these. Although they cast their lot with Pharaoh as objects devoted to destruction, pray for them. God will have mercy on them as he sees fit.

For secular men who have participated in Docetism's science and live through its effects, from the most arrogant unbeliever to the religiously inclined, all of whom Docetism has set up to endure the consequences of its confession: pray for mercy, that they and their children will acknowledge God and find rest in him. Continue in prayer for all of these even if they despise and persecute you. Do not fail to bring them before God for clemency.

But that judgment might be averted, that the avenging angel will sheath his sword and God turn a blind eye to wickedness, that the men whose sins have piled up to heaven will not plummet to an equivalent depth, that the guilty will not reap the corruption they have sown: do not pray for this. The sin of Docetism must lead to death, the laws of the cosmos must run their course, and each man must receive his due. Those upon the narrow path will be saved, the humble, the remnant.

1 John 1:5–10

This is the message we have heard from him and declare to you: God is light; in him there is no darkness at all. If we claim to have fellowship with him yet walk in the darkness, we lie and do not do live by the truth. But if we walk in the light, as he is in the light, we have fellowship with one another, and the blood of Jesus, his Son, purifies us from all sin. If we claim to be without sin, we deceive ourselves and the truth is not in us. If we confess our sins, he is faithful and just and will forgive us our sins and purify us from all unrighteousness. If we claim we have not sinned, we make him out to be a liar and his word has no place in our lives.

I

From all its history and regions since the Christ-Idol, spanning centuries and continents, including denominations and sects, races, tribes, and tongues, worshippers, theologians, pastors, and leaders, the docetic church came together as one. The disputers, teachers, and preachers quieted, the missionaries and revivalists gathered, the prophets grew still. The contests and movements that divide docetic Christendom receded. As a congregation they joined in song, myriad voices in one spirit, one people under one lord. When the hymn ended, they turned to the charges laid against them. No docetist believes himself to be such, no docetic preacher considers himself a blind leader of the blind, no born-again believes he has received a deceiving spirit, no advocate for peace believes himself a soldier of war. The docetic church has come together to repudiate the accusation that it has destroyed salvation by dividing man against his nature, making him a contradiction. Let us hear what it has to say.

A dignified and solemn man comes forward, erect, well-mannered, and self-assured. He tells how Docetism fashions man in good works poured out from faith:

"We cannot sufficiently thank God for leading us by the blessed work of the Reformation out of the Babylonian captivity of Rome and setting us down in blessed freedom. For the very doctrine itself whereby they claim to be the church, is a deadly butchery of souls, a firebrand, a ruin, and a destruction of the church. They cannot bear that the whole praise and glory of all goodness, virtue, righteousness, and wisdom should rest with God, but, as far as I can see, they are characterized by a completely depraved, hopeless, and notorious godlessness. The Romans all would wish to be Christ's vicars, and I fear that most of them have been this too literally. A man is a vicar only when his superior is absent. If the pope rules, while Christ is absent and does not dwell in his heart, what else is he but a vicar of Christ? Indeed, what is such a vicar but an antichrist and an idol? In Rome faith has died, and the word of faith is dumb. Works have taken its place, and the tradition of works. That is what has happened to Christianity in Rome: it has been transformed, by the teaching of godless men, into a good work.

I have another law which strikes the law of works dumb. This law is liberty, and what liberty is that? The liberty of Christ, for by Christ I am utterly freed from the law. Works do not make a man a believer, nor do they make him righteous. A Christian has no need of any work or law in order to be saved since through faith he is free from every law and does everything out of pure liberty and freely. Christ gives this most pure spiritual touch through faith alone, and without works justifies the soul by the Word of God. A Christian therefore has all that he needs in faith and needs no works to justify him; and if he has no need of works, he has no need of the law; and if he has no need of the law, surely he is free from the law.

A man cannot and should not trust in works for salvation. The pastors of churches would not be doing ill if, when they see ruin hanging over the necks of their people, they were to cry out to them to hasten to fasting and weeping; provided—and this is the principal point—they always urge with greater and more intent care and effort that they should rend their hearts and not their garments. If a man has all those benefits that God vouchsafes to people in the face and bosom of his Church, its preaching and sacraments, its community and discipline, these would not do him any good at all without the circumcision of the heart. Take now one who lacks the power of godliness in his depths. He keeps his fingers from filching and stealing, he abstains from gross acts of sin and from open profaneness, but what strength of grace is there in his soul? What mortification shall you find of his secret lusts? What subduing of sin? Ask him what rules in him, at whose command he is, at whose call he comes, and he shall reveal himself truly. For all outward privileges, and outward acts of obedience, are not able to make a man a true saint of God.

These works, being inanimate things, cannot glorify God, although they can, if faith is present, be done to the glory of God. The faith that dwells in the heart is the source and substance of all righteousness, and while it is a blind and dangerous doctrine which teaches that the commandments must be fulfilled by works, it is true that faith follows from the Word of God; then love succeeds faith, and gives rise to every good work. In faith, the Spirit gives us the happiness and freedom at which the law aims, so that the law no longer increases our guilt but is done with a willing heart, and not in fear, or under compulsion. In faith we meet the law's requirements gladly and lovingly, living virtuous and upright lives without the constraint of the law, and as if its penalties did not exist. By grace through faith, we learn more thoroughly the nature of the Lord's will to which we aspire and are confirmed in the understanding of it. We become like servants, already prepared with earnestness of heart to commend ourselves to our master, who must search out and observe the master's ways more carefully in order to conform and accommodate ourselves to them. Works of spontaneous love in obedience to God flow from our faith, and from the righteousness God has imputed to us.

Man must experience this imputation of righteousness fully, grasping it with his whole soul as a New Birth. He must submit to the Word of God, whose words teach him first of sin and the law. This Word, the one thing needful, penetrates into our hearts, and looks at the root and the very source of all sin, i.e., unbelief in the depth of our heart. It uncovers our exaltation of our flesh and our desire to do works that are plainly wrong. Descending into ourselves, we see that we are estranged from God through sin, are heirs of wrath, subject to the curse of eternal death, excluded from all hope of salvation, beyond every blessing of God, slaves of Satan, destined finally for a dreadful destruction and already involved in it. The holy glory of God so shakes and strikes us dumb that we are almost annihilated, laid low by the dread of death. In this way are we humbled, faced with the rottenness that we cannot cure.

Turning in this darkness to Christ, we see a great light. Far indeed is he, who has mounted his judgment seat, from condemning us! How could our most merciful ruler destroy his people? How could the Head scatter his own members? In the depths we feel Christ transfusing us with his power, taking from us our heart of stone and giving us a heart of flesh. In grace we receive our conversion, the creation of a new spirit and a new heart. A feeling of delight is imparted from God, and man finds his soul united with Christ as a bride is united with the bridegroom. With faith between man and Christ, sins, death, and damnation will be Christ's, while grace, life, and salvation will be the soul's. The believing soul by means of the pledge of its faith is free in Christ, its bridegroom, free from all sins, secure against death and hell, and is endowed with the eternal righteousness of Christ.

The riches of this inner kingdom are then poured out as man descends beneath himself to his neighbor. The man of faith no longer seeks to be righteous in and for himself, but has Christ as his righteousness and therefore seeks only the welfare of others. His faith is living, busy, active, and mighty, and it is impossible for it not to do good works incessantly. It does not ask whether there are good works to do, but before the question rises it has already done them and is always at the doing of them. The faithful one thus lives in the midst of wealth, business, honors, pleasures, feasts, and religious ceremonies, as so many dangers, engaging in them not for themselves but in love for his neighbor. This love is his earthly end, the unity of his soul with Christ in faith expended in sacrifice for his brothers. In faith's outflow into love man's unity is presumed and assured. The lasting fulfillment of faith in love, to which man ever looks forward, is in the blessing of heaven and life eternal with God."

The man stepped down and another replaced him. The latter, a man brimming with optimism, spoke of unity, care, and peace:

"The purpose of Christianity is to illustrate, at all hazards, this doctrine or theory that man, properly trained in sanest, highest freedom, may and must become a law, and a series of laws, unto himself, surrounding and providing for, not only his own personal control, but all his relations to other individuals, and for a society of justice. Man has found in the fantastic reality of heaven, where he sought a supernatural being, only his own reflection. We have called man to abandon his illusions about his conditions, to liberate himself from the other-world of truth and to establish the truth of this world. We celebrate the central divine idea of All, suffusing universe, of trains of purpose, in the development, by however slow degrees, of the physical, moral, and spiritual cosmos. Time and space, in the will of God, furnish successive chains, completions of material births and beginnings, solve all discrepancies, fears and doubts, and eventually fulfill happiness.

We believe, therefore, not in one reality among the many but One beyond all the many. Inclusive and creative, it is the source of all being for the significance of the self and all that exists. It is the assurance that because I am, I am valued, and because you are, you are beloved, and because whatever is has being, therefore it is worthy of love. We hope not in some "soul" that has its immortality independently of God and finds liberation in the death of the body, but trust in the powerful and creative Word of God that calls a cosmos out of chaos and gives light to the darkness and light to the dust. This Word, the One suffusing All, is in our flesh. Whole selves—embodied selves, mortal and dependent, creatively and powerfully gifted—are flesh, and God moves in them as flesh.

Peering into the universe and himself, man learns that his being is without bound; that to the good, to the perfect, he is born, low as he now lies in evil and weakness. He is alone: only in the perfect uncontamination and solitariness of individuality may the spirituality of religion positively come forth at all. Alone, and identity, and the mood—and the soul emerges, the interior consciousness beams out its wondrous lines to the sense. It is exclusively for the noiseless operation of one's isolated Self, to enter the pure ether of veneration, to reach the divine levels, and commune with the unutterable. Man sees that, insofar as a man is at heart just, then so far is he God; the safety of God, the immortality of God, the majesty of God do enter into him with justice. Such a one is to others a divine man, is to them thought and virtue.

His divine power is an ecstatic openness to participation in the world, the achievement of an immediate relation to other existents, and a going beyond himself to meet the future. The divine power liberates man through this sense of social responsibility, of dissent and criticism. His purpose, like Jesus and the prophets before him, is the Kingdom of God. This is not a matter of getting individuals to heaven, but of transforming life on earth into the harmony of heaven. It is the society to be established, a fellowship of justice, equality, and love. The Kingdom of God regenerates all human relations and reconstitutes them in the will of God. An end based on human needs and capacities, and universal in scope, its Messianic salvation is a reversal on the grand scale. It leaves the regular guests out in the cold, while the halt and blind are gathered to enjoy the fat things.

This justice for which law and order exist, this freedom, is never voluntarily given by the oppressor. It must be demanded by the oppressed. The creation of tension is therefore necessarily part of the work of the Christian. He creates the kind of tension in society that will help men to rise from the dark depths of injustice and nobodiness to the majestic heights of understanding and brotherhood. He creates a situation so crisis-packed that it will inevitably open the door to negotiation between oppressor and oppressed, offering his very body in nonviolent resistance as a means of laying his case before the conscience of the community.

This task might involve the breaking of unjust laws, and one who breaks such a law must do it openly and lovingly. We submit that any person who breaks a law that conscience tells him is unjust, and willingly accepts the penalty in order to arouse the conscience of the community over its injustice, is in reality expressing the very highest respect for law. Such a one does not tolerate the negative peace in which the oppressed passively suffer, but seeks a positive peace where all men respect the dignity and worth of human personality, a common life so radically different from the present that it involves a displacement of existing inequalities.

The demands of the oppressed embody the eternal will of God, who wills that in some not too distant future the radiant stars of love and brotherhood will shine over all people with all of their scintillating beauty. Then all will say together: Free at last, free at last; thank God almighty, we are free at last."

As he finished speaking, a train of priests, bishops, and cardinals entered. Attention turned to them and they announced as one:

"We declare that the human person has a right to freedom. In religious matters everyone should be immune from coercion by individuals, social groups and every human power so that, within due limits, no men or women are forced to act against their convictions nor are any persons to be restrained from acting in accordance with their convictions. The right to this freedom is based on the very dignity of the human person as known through the revealed word of God and by reason itself. The practice of religion of its very nature consists primarily of those voluntary and free internal acts by which human beings direct themselves to God. Acts of this kind cannot be commanded or forbidden by any merely human authority. We urge everyone to form their own judgments in the light of truth, to direct their activities with a sense of responsibility, and strive for what is true and just in willing cooperation with others. By this peaceful relations and harmony in the human race are established."

1 John: On Docetism and Resurrection

II

The proponents of Docetism have repeatedly adorned their doctrine in promises that it offers the way of unity, peace, and salvation. Flushed with the conviction of truth and seeking a closer approach to their Lord and his Kingdom, they have announced the path to God as grace in the heart, brotherhood in the church, and justice in the social order. The docetic spirit has filled men with the best intentions, enlivening them with hopes of moral edification and collective improvement, pressing them forward with expectations of blessing. It has whispered redemption in their ears, but taking them gently by the hand, it has blinded them to their course and destination. Leaders have spoken the words that Docetism would have of them, painting images of personal and social beatitude while they and their listeners stumble in darkness. Docetism has led its man through the breakdown of church and social order, sealing the alienation of man from man despite visions of fellowship. His eyes have yet to open to the contradiction between his words and the reality that they foster, he has yet to perform the confession that would rescue him from disunion and hand him over to God.

The course through schism and liberation has involved various and particular persons, men and women of docetic charisma and daring, as well as unique historical events. The docetic dialectic connects their disparate times and places within repetitions of its revolutionary pulse. In this dialectic man begins with the unconscious conviction that his nature is universal and formless, and by extension he unknowingly assumes that the institutions that shape and preserve nature in its form possess no intrinsic structure. The church as his religious institution and the institutions of his social world possess no form according to Docetism's theoretical starting point, from which man imagines them as parties to his grasp toward the infinite. He then encounters the institution in fact as limited, as law, coherence, and integrity, possessed of the power to coerce him into a particular way of being and an obstacle to his freedom. The institution stands as the antithesis and mediating element, the middle term through which the dialectic progresses and the legal burden that cries out for liberation. Man moves through the mediation by disintegrating its structure, propelling the institution toward the infinite, toward terror and self-exhaustion, so that he can trounce it as sinful and announce his liberty from it. The inner movement of the soul toward the Christ-Idol, which subjects man to the infinite law before liberating him into indefinition, finds an outward parallel in the dissolution in which institutions, even the church, embody a law without limit that expires in negation.

At points in the history of Protestantism the desire for grace in the heart (that is, the grace of the Christ-Idol), although considered an evidence for salvation and the spring of a holy life, has dragged the church into schism. The same leaders who sought the church's good have been bewildered to see it torn in two, rent along divisions between revivalists and their detractors. Such was the case in the Great Awakening, in which the Presbyterians in America's middle colonies endured a separation lasting

1 JOHN 1:5-10

17 years (1741–1758). The strife began because the revivalists sought a special experience of grace in their followers, advocating a potent and dramatic upheaval supposed to signal the renewal of individuals toward God. The New Side party, led by pastor Gilbert Tennent and centered in the presbytery of New Brunswick, NJ, worked to spread this experience within its own territory and into neighboring districts. Their efforts threw congregations into tumult and confusion, irritating pastors installed in the presbyteries visited by New Side itinerants. The New Side's tactics disgruntled those in the Philadelphia synod, the higher governing body for Presbyterians in the region. The synod was led by the Old Side, a party suspicious of the revival and hoping to restrain it, and the higher body took measures to quell the disruptions caused by revivalist preaching. In this way the pursuit of grace in the heart provoked a confrontation between a superior lawgiving body and those under its law. Beneath both this institutional battle and the experience of grace at its core lies the docetic dialectic, a movement unto formlessness that deceived the historical actors and put them to its purposes.

The presumption of this dialectic that man is fundamentally free, universal, and bereft of form, cloaked itself behind the revivalists' pursuit of inner grace among the laity. With this starting point they set out to do good by a method that leads to evil. Imitating the dialectic's earlier formation in Luther and especially Calvin, the revivalists followed the dialectic from its basic assumption to its mediation through a boundless law and finally to the grace of formlessness.

Tennent and his cohort employed a method known as "preaching terrors," in which they sought to shake their hearers out of the confidence of righteousness based on deeds. Those who would cover inward injustice with an outward pretense of piety needed terror to shake them from their deception. This pretense, in Tennent's view, posed the main threat to the salvation of the soul, introducing the sickness for which terror is the cure. Echoing Calvin's assertion that the law must force believers to "shake off their sluggishness" and be "pinch[ed] awake to their imperfection," Tennent employed the law to terrify and awaken. When in "The Justice of God" he depicts God as a consuming fire, filled with "hatred, revenge, and judgment" against sin, and when he expands upon the divine wrath as impartial, universal, inexorable, incomprehensible, and intolerable, Tennent channels Calvin's exhortation that the sinner come before the heavenly Judge as he "by whose wrath the earth is shaken; by whose purity all things are defiled; whose righteousness not even the angels can bear; who makes the guilty man not innocent; whose vengeance when once kindled penetrates to the depths of hell." When Tennent further instructs his hearers to survey the "prodigious multitude" of their sins, which "rival the stars" in number and "for aggravation, are as red as crimson," a subject that "speaks to terror," he repeats Calvin's conviction of the believer's "thousand sins" under the law, introducing the fear of eternal death constitutive of Calvin's descent into the self. Tennent's preaching of terrors so mirrors Calvin's descent that they are virtually indistinguishable. In both cases man feels the infinite requirement as the infinite burden, despairing of salvation as he abandons his pretense. For Tennent as for Calvin, the wrathful God grows infinitely large while the guilty believer shrinks into the infinitesimal. The judgment of God looms over the believer as the mediating element in the dialectic, imposing the horrifying middle passage on the way to freedom.

Tennent's preaching of terror culminates in the believer's hastening to Christ, wherein the individual receives him "by faith, as the gospel offers him, so that we may be justified by faith." In this unilateral turning, made in abdication of works and in the hope of a justification that is "wholly gracious," Tennent's Christian experiences the New Birth. The grace of Christ wipes out the curse of the law, liberating the conscience and transforming the heart. Tennent's believer enjoys the "feeling of delight" taught by Calvin, if not the exultation of Luther when he felt the gates of heaven thrown open. In "The Grace of God," Tennent describes this inward conversion by echoing Calvin's use of Ezekiel, noting how God takes away the sinner's heart of stone and replaces it with one of flesh. The dialectic concludes in the annulment of the law and man's grasping of liberty, or in Luther's terms, "the death of death" combined with man's newfound "law of liberty." What the revivalists interpreted as the onset of grace expressed man's relative achievement of formlessness.

This grace produced results in opposition to those expected by Tennent and his comrades. They thought that man's inner liberty would give rise to moral piety, with Tennent encouraging parishioners to attend to duty and charity as the ethic of the transformed heart. Like Calvin, Tennent preached that the realization of grace, far from providing an excuse for laxity, drives the believer to a stricter obedience. To feel the grace of God inwardly, for both men as well as for Luther, is to carry out the habit of grace outwardly. Rather than observing moral improvement and the renewal of church and society, however, Tennent's methods provoked strife in congregations and landed him in controversies with his denominational superiors. In the conflict between factions standing for and against the revival, the docetic dialectic applied to the inward life of the believer extended to the institutional life of the church, severing the fabric of the people of God just as it severs the nature of the individual man.

The dialectical accomplishment of the inward experience of grace marks the beginning of a parallel institutional dialectic inasmuch as it legitimizes practices that tend toward the division of the church. This outward dialectic begins not with the promise of grace in the inner life but with the promise of an institutional order in which that grace proliferates without hindrance. Such conditions constitute revival, which advocates see as indispensable to the well-being of the church. The revivalists of the Great Awakening, in addition to seeking to transform the inner lives of men, set out also to open the institutional order to those transformations, transgressing the limits of the ecclesial establishment as necessary to attain their goals. By so doing they set in motion events that snowballed into the synod's imposition of an infinite law, a law resolved in the freedom of schism.

The obedience inspired by the New Birth destabilized the church order in diverse ways. The New Side habit of itinerancy in particular drew the ire of the Old Side as a threat to the status quo. Itinerants flaunted established ministerial boundaries in light of the "necessity" of spreading the New Birth, upsetting their fellow clergy and stoking an uproar among ministers and the laity. The Old Side also grew suspicious of William Tennent's Log College because of its role as a training ground for revivalists. In their view, the Log College questioned the legitimacy of traditional forms of pastoral education, as if outlying institutions were the genuine centers of God's work. In both cases the New Birth as an inward annulment of the law moved in harmony with an outward challenge to institutional norms, fostering habits that contributed to the schism of 1741.

The New Side's practices stirred the synod to implement regulations meant to suppress its activities. The synod's 1738 acts against itinerancy and requiring synodical examination of ministerial candidates would have suffocated the New Side if their pastors had obeyed them. Instead the New Brunswick presbytery issued its "Apology," in which its pastors stated their case in rebuttal of the synod's decrees. The New Side first objected to the itinerancy act because it allowed one minister to suspend the itinerating practice of another "not for any real fault committed, or so much as alleged; but upon suspicion that some bad consequences will follow upon his preaching." They added that this rule "would condemn men . . . before they be heard in their own defense" and "without the least pretense of fault committed." The New Side also argued that if the synod can arrogate a presbytery's powers of licensure to itself, there is no limit to what other powers it might strip away. "For, if the synod can take away, at its pleasure, one privilege and proper business of presbyteries, what hinders but by the same power they may take away another, and another, 'til they take away the whole, by the same rule that this act is made?" This progress would result in "the end of presbyteries altogether," removing the substance and leaving only the name.

In these two arguments the New Brunswick presbytery refuted the synodical acts by envisioning them as part of an infinitely expanding application of law, implying the further conclusion of that law's annulment in freedom. That men should be condemned prior to committing a crime implies a law without bound, for it erases the freedom in which men can either follow or transgress the command. The claim that synodical power could bring about "the end of presbyteries altogether" is equally troublesome because it hints at a higher governmental body's reduction of a lower authority "to nothing" in the same way that the law would reduce Luther's individual into a nullity. The "Apology" went on to argue that the synod had no power to make laws that supersede the right of conscientious objection. The New Brunswick party asserted that the synod or any judicatory's crafting and imposing new laws as if these were terms of communion provides a ground for schism between authorities and dissenters by undermining Christian liberty and placing believers under "an intolerable Bondage." In lieu of this imposition of law, the New Side would radically reduce the coercive force of authoritative bodies for the sake of individual liberty, relegating them to advising rather than commanding their constituents. The "Apology" finally contends for the annulment of synodical authority on the ground of liberty of conscience, posing the freedom of the individual as a counter to a law that would assume the characteristics of the infinite.

"The Danger of an Unconverted Ministry," a sermon preached by Tennent in 1740, intensified the New Side's provocation of the synod by castigating those without and opposed to the New Birth as unregenerate tyrants. Tennent's attack on the Pharisee-teachers who "violently oppress" vital religion, and which the Old Side correctly saw as Tennent's judgment on themselves, struck at the heart of their claim to pastoral legitimacy. To lack the experience of grace, Tennent insisted, left the pastor in the natural and unsaved state. The Old Side received this condemnation gravely if not indignantly, but Tennent went further. Chaining parishioners to such unregenerate pastors, he claimed, amounted to "a cruel oppression of tender consciences, a compelling of men to sin," and a slavery not unlike that of the Hebrews under the Egyptians. In Tennent's sermon the Old Side perceived a challenge to both their right to the pastoral office and their worthiness as guides over their congregations.

In this sermon the New Side's proposed annulment of synodical law extended beyond published arguments between pastors, encouraging parishioners to ignore the authority of Old Side clergy who would restrict them from the New Birth. Tennent's admonition that parishioners quit their unregenerate pastors in a respectful manner aside, the thrust of his argument comes in his granting the laity the liberty to go where they must in order to receive spiritual nourishment. This, he proclaims, is their duty, despite the disruptions in congregations that might result. Tennent enjoins his listeners to go where they can to procure the New Birth, not requiring that the laity find a pastor from a synod-approved college or that they avoid itinerants but just the opposite. He calls for "faithful laborers" from "private schools," hinting toward itinerants from his father's Log College, as needed to bring saving grace to the same people whom he authorizes as free to seek it beyond local boundaries. Such public exhortation virtually begged the Old Side to assert its power more forcefully in the synod in the attempt to suppress the revival's threat to its legitimacy.

That assertion arrived in the protestation of 1741, presented at the synodical meeting that transformed the threat of schism into a reality. The five points of protest announced by the Old Side stand out as a coercion of the New to either relinquish its revivalist habits or abandon the synod. The Old Side's affirmation that (1) the synod must maintain the Westminster Confession, catechisms, directory, and acts implemented by its own authority in their entirety; that (2) no person who breaks any point of doctrine or conduct in the aforesaid can sit and vote in the synod; that (3) the New Side had no right to sit and vote due to various infractions, including the denial of synodical authority versus dissenters, the breaking of the examining act, and the disruption of others' congregations; and that (4) whatever ordinances the New Side might establish have no binding force upon their opponents—these led to the final point of protest, that (5) if the revivalists sustained their divisive practices they would be guilty of schism, whereas the Old Side would constitute "the true Presbyterian church in this province." With this protestation the Old Side attempted to slam the door upon the Awakening through the unimpeded application of synodical power. Effectively proclaiming themselves to be the synod, they would impose a law upon the New Side that would reduce the latter's cause to nothing, crushing it under the weight of the Confessions, catechisms, directory, and synodical legislation.

The protestation shows the increase of synodical power as a law extending to infinity, an authority so expanded that it squashes all adversaries and denies substantive freedom to its constituents. The New Side would fade into nothing beneath its demands, through which the synod grew into the mediating element between the New Birth's promise of institutional freedom and that freedom's achievement. As the middle term in the dialectic, the synod enforces a law so full with its own power, and so unremitting in that power's application, that it undermines its legitimacy as law. The revivalists who sought grace in the heart through "preaching terrors," bringing their listeners to despair under the weight of sin and the divine holiness, met the parallel of that terror in a church authority that demanded unqualified obedience, a self-righteous and holy synod bent upon exterminating its opposition.

While it is hard to retrace the public tumult that followed the reading of the protestation, there is no doubt that the gathering concluded with the rending of the New Brunswick party from the synod. Given the force of the protestation it is also difficult to say whether the New Side ministers left of their own will or were forced out by their brethren. When the Old Side presented its protest, the animosity between the two factions reached an impossible intensity. With its announcement the Old Side declared itself to be the Presbyterian church, but in the ensuing chaos the New Side effectively declared itself to be the same, with both parties seeing their cause in the right and refusing to back down. The Old Side demanded a conformity so relentless that the revivalists arguably had to secede, but was their secession not the culmination of developments that the New Side had provoked? Goaded on by both parties, the infinite law of the synod gave out in the "grace" of schism, the outward severance of men from men that replicates the inner severance of man from his nature. Whether in the inner man or among the society of men, the docetic dialectic peaks in the freedom of disintegration.

Tennent related his version of events and justified the New Side point of view in his *Remarks Upon a Protestation*. Here Tennent rebutted the protestation by arguing that if every rule in the directory, including those passed by the synod, constituted a term of communion and possessed such authority that to object to it barred members from sitting and voting, these regulations "may be multiplied yearly into an immense volume. And if one did adopt the directory, in the strictest sense, it is no sufficient security against exclusion, unless he can swallow all the after canons, which shall be contrived by the majority." The requirement to obey every rule in the directory permitted "no mercy for scrupulous consciences, and renders synodical communion as precarious as the variable humours and fancies of men." Tennent then returned to the theme of liberty of conscience first expressed in the 1739 "Apology," asserting that the dictates of conscience supersede the enforcement of oppressive laws upon the minority by the majority. "We know of no authority on earth," Tennent writes, "that can bind us to the Word of God, and it is our own and not another's judgment of that Word, which we are to follow." When the conscience faces a choice between obeying an unjust authority and the will of God, it must follow the will of God.

With these arguments the New Side, represented by Tennent, again interpret the Old Side's actions in the synod in terms of an infinitely expanding law. When Tennent refers to the protestation's implicit mulitiplication of terms of communion into an "immense volume" that would require members of the synod to "swallow all the after canons" that the majority might contrive, he imagines the synod's authority expressed in a gargantuan and unbounded, even infinite, number of commands. The perceived innumerability of synodical requirements, each a sufficient cause for ejecting dissenters, is so unrealistic a standard in Tennent's view that the Old Side pastors themselves fail to adhere to it at numerous points. When Tennent goes on to criticize this expression of authority as permitting "no mercy for scrupulous consciences," he echoes the ruthlessness and inexorability of the infinite law as expressed in Luther and Calvin. Taking the New Brunswick "Apology" and Tennent's *Remarks* together, one finds a consistent reference to an unjust and oppressive authority unbounded in its requirement, and liberty from that authority proposed as the solution to its claims. The dialectical coercion leading to the believer's inward experience of grace manifests itself in the reasoning of the minority party in its reflections on the causes of difference leading to schism.

The New Side pastors returned to obey the law after the schism, submitting themselves out of the grace of freedom. This return did not imply a new submission to the Philadelphia synod or the end of the schism in 1758, but the establishment of an ecclesiastical organization representative of New Side perspectives on authority. In 1745, a new "law" was formed in the synod of New York, a law that denied its own legislative powers and affirmed the Scriptures as the only valid rule over the church. In addition, the synod's founders agreed that when conscientious objection posed an insurmountable disagreement on essential matters between synodical authorities and a dissenter, the individual could peaceably withdraw. In this way an organization formed upon the Scriptures as supreme negated its authority to compel before the right of individual conscience. That authority existed in annulment with respect to the matters that it considered most important, for the minority could conscientiously object to the majority with unquestioned liberty, and with the default of the community leaning against its own prerogatives and toward the objecting individual or group. The institutional order of freedom that the revivalists desired had arrived, but not according to their expectations. Where they had hoped for a church transformed by grace and freed for holiness, they worked toward and received a church broken by the grace they had administered, and given to a freedom birthed in division.

Docetism evolved and changed shape as orthodox Protestantism morphed into its liberal heir, applying the dialectic more vigorously to society as well as the church. Through this late religion and into the secular world Docetism carried its assumption of freedom into new forays against law, aggrandizing man's liberation. Liberal Protestantism has identified barriers to liberty on all sides, calling multiple forms of hierarchy unjust, oppressive, and obstacles to the fulfillment of man, identifying multiple mediating elements through which the dialectic has progressed on its way to universality. In perhaps the greatest of its cultural identifications, Docetism funneled its energies through liberal religion in order to destroy the hierarchy of race, annulling an infinite law erected through Docetism's own drive toward economic prosperity. In what follows concerning slavery and racial inequality the reader must not think for an instant that the elevation of one race over another conforms to natural or divine law. It categorically contradicts the law of God that one race should claim superiority over others and there is no place for such superiority in a society seeking the love of Jesus Christ. I say directly that there is no justification for racial hierarchy. I say again: there is no justification for racial hierarchy. Yet both the rise and the fall of this hierarchy in recent centuries exemplifies the docetic dialectic. Although men currently excoriate the rise and its cruelties while celebrating the fall as the denouement of freedom, the two parts constitute one movement. They are both culpable, both driven by the docetic spirit, both subject to the deception that unbinds man from God, his nature, and other men.

Every man requires some limited amount of freedom in accordance with the limit of his nature. Some men will rule, others will be ruled; some will have greater freedom, others will have less. But no man may exercise such power over another that he may separate what God has joined, tearing him from his wife in a manner contrary to the Scriptures or as an arbitrary assertion of power. Nor may a man remove children from their mother and father in defiance of the bonds that God has established. The mourning lady shall weep no more, her child shall slumber on her shoulders, and the father shall love and protect his family. No just law wantonly severs men from their loved ones, no righteous power undermines the joys of nature and eradicates rest. For its destruction of the ties of fidelity and progeny if for no other reason, the docetic institution of slavery embodied the assault of the infinite law upon nature's mercy.[1] Grinding its subjects into dust and tears, its tyranny cried out for revolt and thereby for fulfillment.

Liberal Protestantism carried out that fulfillment as an active agent in the dialectical process, decrying the injustice of the slave system in the abolitionist movement, the civil war, and beyond. From the nineteenth century into the twentieth it has held

---

1. One could fill many pages cataloguing the crimes committed by this odious institution. That I touch upon it briefly here does not intend disrespect or forgetfulness of those who suffered under it.

high the standard of freedom, its soldiers marching in determined and irrepressible phalanxes, their weapons keen to finish off the racial application of the infinite law. A century after the civil war, when the American South had held on to an attenuated version of the preceding racial order, there arose a man and a movement to bring the dialectic to completion, ushering in an unprecedented racial equality. The latest of freedom's great prophets, the hero of liberal Protestantism, its secular friends, and eventually the whole of the United States, Martin Luther King, Jr., led a civil rights movement that found its glory in the annulment of law and in whose logic the docetic spirit crystallized with remarkable subtlety.

King's ideas and actions embody the docetic dialectic: he assumes the promise of freedom and equality for all men as the core and presupposition of his gospel; he encounters an infinite law in the segregation that permeated the South, reducing the negro to constant fear, disenfranchisement, and a debilitating sense of nobodiness; and he fights to put that death-dealing system to death and grant its prisoners a new liberty, hoping to join all men in solidarity. Like Martin Luther's gospel of a justification that liberates man from the law, a gospel that moves through the law's terror before realizing freedom by faith alone, Martin Luther King proclaims the freedom of man as his assumption and goal, teaching that men must traverse the mountain of despair before realizing their freedom in racial equality. At the heart of the civil disobedience by which King pursues this new reality stands a claim in defense of his activities and the good that he expected them to bring about. He submits "that an individual who breaks a law that conscience tells him is unjust, and who willingly accepts the penalty of imprisonment in order to arouse the conscience of the community over its injustice, is in reality expressing the highest respect for law." By this statement King declares himself a benefactor of the law and the forerunner of a society in which unjust laws no longer divide men along racial lines. On the other side of the imprisonment of the witnesses, when the community conscience admits the need for a just racial law, the era of love and brotherhood, of peace and freedom, is supposed to arrive.

The marchers, freedom riders, boycotters, and other protesters of the civil rights movement said to the Southern state: "We do not respect your law because you do not respect us as men. We reject your law because you have rejected us as men. We are indifferent to your law because you are indifferent to our dignity as men." Imprisonment manifests this indifference in the most paradoxical way because there the dissenters validate their superiority over and dismissal of the law by submitting themselves to its penalties. Men, women, and children might suffer verbal and physical abuse in jail, but with every exertion of the law to discipline them into obedience the protesters strike back with the confidence that the law does not limit them, that it will not define their natures, that they remain spiritually independent of this law regardless of its brutality. They have chosen this imprisonment in order to accomplish a higher purpose, provoking the infinite law to its extreme in order to publicly endure its wrath and expose the tyranny of its burden. They seize the law as a means to their own ends, so influencing the conscience of the community that those who do not suffer under the law perceive its terror and the whole populace can agree to dissolve the statute that puts the protester behind bars. The protester damns the law that damns, binds the law that binds, and accuses the accusing law, until all damning, binding, and accusation cease.

The march prepares the way for the docetic transfer that is the meaning of the protester's imprisonment. Man under the infinite law has split in two: man-under-law and bound, the slave of the infinite imposition, is contrasted against man-as-freedom, the promise of man as liberated from bondage. King's protester as man-under-law is the negro reduced to nobodiness by segregation, whereas the same individual is man-as-freedom according to his conviction of equal dignity with all men. The transfer requires that man-as-freedom realize his power so that freedom defines his nature in victory over the law, with the protester no longer suffering his nobodiness. In pursuit of this realization the protester begins his march, consciously asserting his freedom over-against the law and unconsciously desiring to bring that law to its consummation. The driving force behind this pursuit for King and his followers is the Christ-Idol. The promise of Christ the revolutionary, Christ the bringer of justice, and Christ the liberator from law invigorates the protesters as bearers of the will to annulment. They march valiantly and defiantly, in the hope of redress and with the discipline of nonviolence, seeking the resolution of their bifurcated natures and the overturning of the law.

In the most imperceptible way, a way unnoticed by the protesters and their champions, the docetic spirit takes advantage of man's revolt against the law in the name of the Christ-Idol. Cloaking itself in the sermons, songs, and prayers of Christianity, the docetic spirit bifurcates to cover man's dual elements. Only in this way can it accomplish the exaltation of man and the destruction of the law. In a way reminiscent of Luther's transfer, the name of Christ takes sides with the law, assuming the "sin" of man-under-law. In its deepest sense, man-under-law is man formed by his life under the state, but Docetism has distorted this law toward the infinite so that man cannot but consummate it through rebellion. In the fight for civil rights, Christ's name thereby aligns with the boundless law that enslaves the negro to nobodiness.[2] As divided from his name, the power of Christ morphs into another infinite as man's pride over the political law, aligning with man-as-freedom in his pursuit of realization, the protester as he marches. The table is set, the contest begins: in the confrontation with the police, in the line of water hoses and dogs and in physical aggression, the augmentation of the political law approaches its apex. The coercion that had maintained a constant pressure upon the negro achieves its highest intensity, inflicting pain and deprivation. As arrested and detained beneath the infinite law the prisoner grasps his bars, suffering physical dislocation and humiliation, but his soul wells up. He is filled with the power

---

2. That Christ's name aligns with the boundless law is also necessitated by the victory, presently to be described, of man-as-freedom over man-under-law. For man-as-freedom is man as the infinite and without rest, but Christ, properly understood, is man's rest. Therefore the victory of man-as-freedom is the annulment of the name of Christ.

of the Christ-Idol. In prison the protester seizes his identity as man-as-freedom and channels the Idol's power upon the political law, his nature under the law, and the name of Christ subtly identified with the law. In prison man obeys and upholds the law only to prove his equality with it and thereby to negate it. He says, "I preserve you as the law—but it is I who preserve you!" and so he abolishes the authority by which law is law. He seeks a law that he could obey by disobeying the current law, he seeks a law worthy of recognition by refusing to recognize the law. He desires a law of equality, a law of order and harmony, but in order to gain his goal he has raised himself above the law and undermined order. The law is, but it also is not; man exists under the law, but more fundamentally he exists in freedom from the law. Both man and the law are what they are and what they are not as simultaneously above and below one another, each subsisting as a thing and its opposite, both in confusion, both without limit.

Man rises empowered from the confusion, having realized his existence as man-as-freedom. The law of the state served as his mediation, the middle term between his potential as free and the actuality of his liberty. He has cast the power of the Christ-Idol against the law and defeated it, so that the name of Christ and the law of the state have received all sin, punishment, and ignominy, enduring the penalty for injustice, while man appropriates the encounter as dignity and as victory over his oppressors. Man receives the glory and the grace, all blessing and freedom, basking in the advent of a more just society. He reigns, newly exalted and newly crowned, a king over the small and slippery terrain that is left of his nature, a citizen in an earthly Kingdom of Heaven and a Christless Kingdom of God. As he leaves the prison with buoyancy and satisfaction, he embraces this new standing as the fulfillment of his humanity, the pure expression of his universality.

I say without equivocation: racial inequality is an unjust hierarchy, and the burden imposed on subjected peoples has therefore been unjust. It was good that King desired to remedy this injustice and seek a society of brotherhood, just as it was good that Tennent and his companions desired a society shaped by God's grace in the heart. Yet both Tennent and King, despite their good intentions, chose means contrary to the end of social unity. King speaks of an "individual who breaks a law that conscience tells him is unjust," a law that raises some above others, limiting the personalities of some while not limiting others in the same way. In truth, if a law limits some, at least in theory it limits all through their mutual difference. Also in truth, King's assault against the law touches not only inequalities attendant to race but between individuals *per se* inasmuch as the standard for the justness of law is the expression of individual personality. The law that does not establish higher and lower, that does not limit some and thus all, instead limiting none, secures the lack of limitation for all. It is an infinite law, a law meant to draw man into the ocean of possibility while sabotaging its coercive power, the strength needed to safeguard the public good. While it might forward equality, such a law does not finally contribute to peace, brotherhood, and stability, but seduces men into the pride of entitlement and antagonism. It is this law for which King unwittingly shows "the highest respect," while not realizing that such a law presumes oppression and its overcoming in protest, even in incarceration. I now say again: this point does *not* argue for racial hierarchy, but highlights the dubious ontological assumptions implicit in the method of Docetism's most cherished freedom fighters. The claim that they pose no threat to peace and order, or that they are not harbingers of social discombobulation, rings hollow. The society of fracture and grievance in which docetic men now live attests to this.

The civil rights movement's annulment of the racial law enhanced the more basic annulment of the American state, a negation largely accomplished through the World Wars. The protesters facilitated the primary social liberation of contemporary life, a freedom not from the various "isms" that men castigate as enemies but from the state that limits him with the rank of citizen. Man has traded in this rank and its responsibility for a formlessness manifest in his unwillingness to identify with and submit his nature to authorities that place a concrete boundary upon his freedom. Such authorities, as bestowers of form, inspire horror in him as a creature of formlessness and his meaning consists in their refutation. As one beyond the political authority man wanders as one beyond judgment and critique, beyond commitment and discipline, beyond friendship and trust. In spite of the mantra of autonomy he sighs, pressed like putty by images and words that promise him community within his nature and with others. He has no such community because he has no state or natural order, and he floats instead among the variety of cultures and groups whose clamorous confusion testifies to Docetism's conquest. He has little option beyond docetic community, and what is that? The collision of formless individuals with one another through their emotions, fluid spilling into fluid, blood into blood. It is the illusion that man dwelling in the repudiation of law, divorced from his nature and from the distance that binds him to other men, can find meaning in the society that he has all but destroyed. The rhetoric of community (if not also of intimacy, of authenticity, of flourishing, of brotherhood and peace) conceals the alienation that man experiences as disappointment and ethereality, in which Docetism has reduced him to a seeming, and in which the world yawns at his tragedy.

The more solidly it has allied its efforts with the struggle for civil rights and the other movements of annulment that followed, the more the liberal Protestant church has withered. With the name of Christ vanquished, why should such men worship? With the power of Christ transferred to man, what need has he of salvation? Hegel rightly asserted that the goal of Christianity (in its liberal Protestant-docetic form, at least) is the state, but he did not discern that the church worked toward this goal by furthering the logic of annulment within the political order. With that annulment accomplished in the main, what is left for liberal Protestants to do *qua* Christians? The church of liberation has thus spawned children who fulfill its mission by racing out of its doors, leaving the elderly to caress empty pews. Receiving the prize won by their predecessors, the youth have grasped the infinity unleashed by the freedom fighters and embarked upon secular life. They have sunk into the multitude, witnessing to the failure of religious belief to convict and shape man's nature, testifying to the victory of depletion. The disintegration of the liberal church in the United States has consummated the docetic ethos that was its heartbeat and life, and that church, having satisfied its destiny in annulment, has laid down to die.

The evangelical Protestant churches have fared little better. Although they have retained a number of worshippers, the churches keep them through a remarkably decadent worship. In the evangelical churches men converge out of the distance of liberation, recognizing no law that binds. They come together to seek a foothold within the arbitrariness of their choices, a context exemplified by their ability to move from church to church and stay as long as they are pleased. The preacher who in former eras gave at least some form to his congregation through law and the recognition of sin—though this form, as docetic, was a prelude to formlessness—has disappeared, and in his place one finds men enraptured by the infinite. Together with their liberal Protestant and Catholic brethren, they are motivational speakers, comedians, provocateurs, and entertainers, men promising wealth to the poor and fulfillment to those complacent in their riches, ghosts deflated by Docetism's successes, men without authority whose gospel validates the ennui of their hearers. They are autumn trees without fruit, twice dead, uprooted; wild waves of the sea, casting up the foam of their own shame; wandering stars at home in darkness; waterless clouds carried along by the winds. A formless mist has invaded this house of God, whose people do not perceive the nature of their worship just as they do not perceive the nature of their liberation from one another. The evangelicals and the Catholics, following their liberal brothers, are already relinquishing their children.

Beloved church of Christ, what has become of you? Where has the spirit of salvation gone, and why do demons dance on your ruins? You fathers and mothers, you young men and women, you pastors, elders, deacons, and bishops, you who seek God sincerely, you who would hand over your bodies for the good of your souls, why do you toil in disunion? Why do you claim to live in the truth, when you walk in darkness? Why do you not confess and turn so that you may be forgiven, purified, and gathered into the fellowship of God?

III

In the first Docetism Satan denied that the infinite God could join with the finite and material man, and in this way he rejected the Incarnation. In the New Docetism Satan has tricked man into believing that he can grasp infinity without destroying his finitude, or that he can become the incarnation apart from the Resurrection of Christ. Docetism deceives man through the appearance that this grasping is life, that it leads to a better world, that it will justify him and bring grace to his society. Through the semblance of blessing, Docetism leads to death; through the Christ-Idol it guides not to the fortification of man but to his dissolution. His undoing comes upon him suddenly and unaware, for he is hopeful according to the docetic ruse, always seeking greater things. Deceived, docetic man follows a way of life-unto-death, coaxed by the promise of enrichment to a termination in divorce. Docetism is history's confirmation of biblical wisdom, its proof that a misled pride comes before destruction.

The promise of the true Christ, of true gospel and freedom, is the boldness to endure through the tomb because Christ has conquered it. In him, truth and love converge in unceasing union, with each edifying the other in the mutual giving of life. Man's goal is to be an object in this overlapping and rhythmic edification, to be caught up and suspended in it. To be so caught up and suspended, he must bear his cross and die. Thus his practical and ontological fusion of *gravitas* and *misericordia*, of discipline and mercy. Thus his humbling under the finitude of his nature and his acceptance of the commandment, and his handing over of this humility to his neighbor. Swallowed immediately by death, and mediately by truth and love, man finds that his embrace of his finitude presages his earthly approach to the eternal. Present suffering opens into the beyond, is revealed as a stepping stone to the everlasting. Horror and ugliness recede, and man beholds beauty.

God orchestrates all creation to this single point, directing temporality to this end. He stands behind all motion, diversity, agency, and decision, a unitary and singular fullness that calls to man in his trials. Expectation, discipline, and joy rest in God's love, as do disappointment and sorrow. The harmony of all things, even suffering and death, is their envelopment in that love's comprehensiveness. Love is all being, all history; it is the secret of time. The man of understanding longs for this secret. Patience, peace, and gentleness have been imposed upon him, and his wisdom is to desire a deeper imposition.

Docetism's pull away from love does not amount to an absolute break, but identifies it as the great rebellion that love absorbs. Although Docetism turns from union with Christ, from the necessity of death and the promise of life on its far side, from obedience as faith and fusion with the divine, it never leaves love's orbit, it never escapes love's extension. This is the faithfulness of God: love will take up Docetism in its own image, locating it in history as the lawlessness that, despite its material glory, its knowledge, and its air of triumph, shall fall before the revelation of mercy.

That revelation approaches with the final movement in man's descent into universality. In a day of terror and judgment man will suffer his total alienation from his nature, from his society, and from the natural world. He will endure a scarcity and violence of his own making, a catastrophe beyond anything he can currently conceive. His darkness will be full. Those who continue to live by Docetism and pledge their adherence to it ask to perish in the purging. Those who turn from Docetism and seek righteousness, humbling themselves before God's law and beseeching him for compassion, should know that the days will be hard, but that God will give them rest.

1 John 5:6–15

This is the one who came by water and blood—Jesus Christ. He did not come by water only, but by water and blood. And it is the Spirit who testifies, because the Spirit is the truth. For there are three that testify: the Spirit, the water, and the blood; and the three are in agreement. We accept man's testimony, but God's testimony is greater because it is the testimony of God, which he has given about his Son. Anyone who believes in the Son of God has this testimony in his heart. Anyone who does not believe God has made him out to be a liar, because he has not believed the testimony God has given about his Son. And this is the testimony: God has given us eternal life, and this life is in his Son. He who has the Son has life; he who does not have the Son of God does not have life.

I write these things to you who believe in the name of the Son of God so that you may know that you have eternal life. This is the confidence we have in approaching God: that if we ask anything according to his will, he hears us. And if we know that he hears us—whatever we ask—we know that we have what we asked of him.

We ask that God will save us, that he will refashion us according to the ancient beauty of his likeness and re-create us after his image. We ask that he will hear us, that he will have mercy and compassion on us, forgiving us for the ways in which we have walked. We ask that God will enlighten the eyes of our understanding so that we may not sleep to death in sins, that he will remove all darkness from our hearts and seal us in the testimony of his Spirit. May we who receive out of his kindness have eternal life in Jesus Christ. May God guide our steps in the way of peace. By God's grace, may we abide in the testimony of redemption, of water, blood, and Spirit, conforming our lives to the Savior and life-giver.

All creation occurs after the image of the Trinity. In the divine faithfulness, present throughout the Trinitarian illumination as well as in the Father, Son, and Spirit in their distinction, and in the moments of possibility, in the internal life-givings of God unto joy complete, man contemplates the original mystery. In this contemplation God allows men to know enough to adore and worship him, so that he might draw them into union with him. Concentration upon the divine being invites man to acknowledge the limits of his understanding and to remain silent before what surpasses him. Mystery surrounds what follows regarding the Trinity, which seeks no more than what the Fathers have asserted. With them, we bow before both questions that man cannot answer and the God whose love intoxicates as it gathers, whose mystery elevates those who lower their minds before it.

God the Father, source and unoriginate, abides in eternity as the faithfulness of being with nature and nature with will, so that the unity of the Father baffles man when he meditates upon its simplicity. In many ways this being abides beyond measure: in righteousness, in holiness, in justice, in peace, in mercy. The Father's faithfulness is a structure and law without imperfection and limit in its magnificence and magnanimity, and yet, speaking of the logical beginning of the Trinity (there is no temporal beginning, no time when the Son and the Spirit were not), the Father is one and alone. Though unbounded and beyond understanding in measure, and beyond Pure Being as beyond comprehension, the Father remains singular and defined as source and unoriginate. In his person he is one, and by this number definite and limited.

How does the finitude of the one become more than one? How does the Father share his being and mystery without diminishing his existence? The Father begets the Son so that men recognize the Son as the Only-Begotten, whereas the Spirit proceeds from the Father. Begottenness belongs to the Son and procession to the Spirit, these two types of generation not being the same. Christians do not know the substance of the difference but we submit to it. The Father begets the Son, the Spirit proceeds from him, and men worship and obey in faith.

Both begetting and procession involve the stretching of the finite toward the infinite. The Father, singular and defined in his personhood, gathered in solidarity and solitude, sacrifices the finitude of his person in the Son and the Spirit. One imagines the Father's definition expanding until the Son is begotten, opening and extending as the Spirit proceeds. How else shall the mind of man understand it? Let us dispense with images, let us dispense for the moment with the attempt to describe begetting and procession. We know only that the One becomes Three, that what is logically source and unoriginate produces in a mysterious fashion the Son and Spirit, and by implication we know that the finitude of singularity passes through possibility. No temporality taints this passing through. To contemplate the "moment of begetting" or a time "before procession" misunderstands the relation between logic and time in God. In the logical emergence of the persons, between their appearance as formed and faithful to their distinct personhood and the preceding finitude of the Father, there exists the freedom, the infinitude, the possibility. What is one cannot become two and three without passing through this freedom.

Forgive me if I speculate upon the transition from One into Three, and forgive me if I speak beyond my bounds. I speak here, if I err, at least out of joy. The faithfulness of God, the harmony of being, law, and will in the Father, grounds all that is. All that men know and experience, all that is possible for them to know and experience, abides to a greater or lesser extent in this faithfulness. This ground, Christians, is the most immense, most gracious, most tender, and most persevering joy! As being in uninterrupted faithfulness to being, as "I am who I am" and "I will be who I will be," God the Father abides as the matchless harmony of a being that is as it should be. This is the great and stupendous joy that fills the created order as formed in God's image, that surrounds man and pervades him if he has eyes to see. This joy of the Father in his own being prompts and goads the infinite. I am tempted to say that this joy is the infinite, an unstoppable ray of light emanating from the divine sun. For the Father, flushed with the joy of his being and willing in step with his nature, desires that this joy should be made complete. In this manner one begins with the faithfulness of the Father, with the impregnable law of his being and the mystery of I am, and seeing the abundant joy that flows from this being one brushes up against possibility. The joy of being opens toward generation and procession, the diversification in which a single essence multiplies toward a greater fulfillment.

The expansion of the Father's joy through possibility into being, a joy made complete in the unity of the divine persons, at once expresses the Father's humility. In sharing there is lowering: as source and unoriginate, the Father gives wholly of his being in the begetting and the proceeding. He holds back nothing as though he were too high, as though he wished to raise his nature above the persons who originate in and from him. The title "unoriginate" does not give the Father an excuse for pride but identifies him as the great Giver of being. He bestows this being not to the Son as his opposite (there is no opposition in the Trinity, only complementarity), nor to the Spirit as superfluity (there is no superfluity in the Trinity, but a merciful rationality). The Father humbles his nature in begetting the Son, who is a complement and a part of his joy, but the union between the two is not complete. He humbles himself again in the Spirit, whose holiness is to make the Trinity whole, to perfect the harmony of the three by dismissing any hint of opposition, antagonism, or selfishness, and to bring the divine joy to fruition.

Son and Spirit emerge differently, but both take logical form as perfect sharers in the divine nature. From the perspective of the divine unity they are one with the Father, embodying the entire divine faithfulness, but each also possesses a distinction as to its person. The Son is begotten and formed as Son, not as Father or Spirit, while the Spirit proceeds and is formed as Spirit, not Father or Son, and so for the Father who maintains form as Father in distinction from Son and Spirit. The personhood of each does not suffer, but the point is this: the infinite through which the Son and Spirit emerge is not an end in itself. It exists as gathered into the new and distinct expressions of the divine faithfulness. The possibility, even the indefinite within the divine being appears as an outgrowth of the Father's joy but its meaning consists in the transition from faithfulness to faithfulness, law to law, form to form, Father to Son and Spirit. The freedom of the Father to beget the Son and have the Spirit proceed is not an isolated and independent freedom nor freedom for its own sake, but exists as a medium unto life.

The fulfillment of joy occurs through a subsequent pair of infinites, two moments that turn first on the freedom of the Son and secondly on that of the Father. In the Trinitarian illumination the Son wills to give his life to the Father and the Father reciprocates by freely giving all to the Son, each laying down his life within the indwelling Spirit. As three expressions of faithfulness and the one faithfulness, as three unique persons and one God, the Father, Son, and Spirit do not abide at a distance from one another or merely coexist. The coinherence of the three in the one means that each abides within the others, offering the unhindered life-gift in which the independence of the particular person comes under threat. Whereas the Father alone humbles his nature in the begetting and the procession, here all three humble their natures, challenging the definition of the person as the life of each actively persists within the other two. In this mutual sharing the solidity of faithfulness is humbled into completion, an accomplishment that hinges on the infinite moments. Through freedom the Father and the Son lower their natures into each other, each sacrificing his singularity and putting his distinction to death.

Or so it appears. In the mutual life-gift among the persons, each simultaneously giving all for the others and erasing its own distinct existence, that distinction stands reaffirmed. When each is sacrificed into the others, the result is not the death of any but the fulfillment of all. Father, Son, and Spirit abide in the uniqueness of personhood at the same time that personhood appears lost, each nature persevering on the other side of the sacrifice, dwelling distinctly in unhindered sharing. The lowering of each into the others rises to a final unity and the exaltation of joy fulfilled. Such is the illumination within the Trinity, a restful rhythm not fundamentally structureless and free but gathering within it possibility and freedom, not lawless but the supreme expression of faithfulness and law, the mystery of a perfect union that maintains and upholds distinction. As John tells us, God is love.

All creation occurs after the logic of the Trinity: in a way that both recalls the distance between the Creator and the creation and recognizes the stamp of the Designer upon the designed, the process of creation imitates the pattern of the triune God. God's act of creation entails his faithfulness toward what he has created, his dedication that he shall form his creation according to law. This faithfulness underlies God's work and secures its accomplishment. The creative process requires two moments of infinity, two points that punctuate the trajectory toward the law's fulfillment in finitude and form and that replicate the pair of infinites within the Trinitarian illumination. These points appear in various ways expressive of the infinite's challenge to finitude. Prior to the fall one meets them as formless matter and the dwelling of God in man, whereas after the fall, in the creation of Israel, one confronts them as the infinite pressure, a force that means to disintegrate its object.

The creation of the cosmos begins with God's will, for without the divine determination the creation does not emerge. The divine faithfulness stands under and behind all that is, sustaining and preserving creatures and their surroundings. In his faithfulness God wills to bring the world into being and give it form, in his Wisdom he shapes the universe that he calls good. God's humility and his faithfulness intertwine as rather than resting in the eternal and divine abundance he looks down, as it were, into what is not, calling life out of nothingness. He then carries out his will to create by forming the world, giving it distinction and structure.

The creation immediately involves the infinite: "In the beginning when God created the heavens and the earth, the earth was a formless void and darkness covered the face of the deep." Without contour or substance, without structure or differentiation, without law or definition, formless matter is the first infinity in the creation, the infinitude of the physical order. Men cannot imagine this matter except perhaps as a kind of mist, although even this description gives an ephemeral space and shape to what is utterly shapeless. Its structurelessness entails pure freedom, pure possibility, unrestricted openness, an infinite capacity to come-to-be in an infinite number of shapes or ways. Only after the formless void and the deep does Genesis mention the water over which God's spirit hovers. After the infinity of formlessness comes the near-infinity of water, the great life-giver and destroyer, whose shape is determined by what contains it.

Like the logical moment of begetting and procession, the moment of formlessness does not end in itself. Its infinity serves as a transition between God's will to give law and the law's taking concrete shape. Freedom exists embedded within law, as a way-station between the promise of form and its actualization. Creation rises as the division of day and night, sky and sea, and the gathering of the seas to uncover the land. There follows the population of day and night with sun, moon, and stars; the population of sky and sea with birds and marine creatures; and the population of the land with beasts and men. It would seem that creation occurs in two distinct steps, with the first three days establishing the realms of the natural order and the second three populating those realms. This distinction holds except for the appearance of vegetation on the third day, whose growth constitutes an overlap between the two phases. Out of the infinity of formlessness emerges a law of form accomplished through separation followed by gathering in the first days, and through generation in the last, two steps by which God fashions life where there was none.

At the apex of God's creative activity, when he has formed heaven and earth and filled the latter with all kinds of creatures, he creates men. "Let us make mankind in our image, according to our likeness" and so God creates them male and female. Leaving aside a host of questions that men could raise regarding the mystery and meaning of the image, let us focus on the communion meant to join men and God. Creating a man as the image-bearer, God has made a finite creature, even a creature of the flesh, and endowed him with free will. A form of the infinite God has thereby made intrinsic to man, so that man's communion with God must traverse it. This infinity of free will, a freedom in the likeness of the divine persons, leads to a second and more definitive infinitude, the unity of man with his creator. To say "Man bears God's image" means no less than that God wills to dwell within man, making a home in his soul and abiding in union with it. The second infinity in the creation thus occurs as God abides with and in man in the spotlessness of the image. For this indwelling of God in men, though not at its highest in Adam and Eve, tends in the direction of the incarnation as it implies the residence of the infinite within the finite.

How does man endure the indwelling of the infinite, which should gobble up his finitude and pulverize it, destroying soul and body? How does he survive his union with God intact? Like the fire on the bush, the Spirit of God should consume man's finitude—but he remains unconsumed, for this infinitude radiates mercy and gentleness. Beyond this, God fulfills man's nature, raising his form into the divine peace. Not unlike the re-affirmation of the divine persons on the other side of the perichoretic life-gift, the mortal nature bearing the divine image enjoys re-affirmation on the other side of a union that should wipe that nature away. How this occurs surpasses the mind of man, who gives his life to God to discover it fortified and gathered in him. Man hereby ends in the rest that is union, a unity first and fundamentally of the soul with God but also of the body with the soul and between man and his neighbors. The more earnestly man surveys his bearing of the divine image prior to the fall, as well as the union with the eternal implied in that image, the more humbled he becomes before the mystery and love of God, the more spellbound by God's desire to share life with his creature.

In the creation of the cosmos as in the Trinity, two infinities adorn an underlying faithfulness. In the Trinity that faithfulness refers to the God's integrity in harmonious abiding, while in the creation it refers to his will to form the cosmos. In the Trinity the first infinity occurs logically as the Son freely gives his life to the Father, while in the creation of the cosmos it occurs in the appearance of formless matter. The second infinity takes place in the Trinity as the Father freely reciprocates in his life-gift to the Son, while in the creation the second infinite appears at God's taking up residence within man. In its resemblance to the Trinity, the creation gathers within it moments of apparent indefinition, even the threat of dissolution, orienting these toward life.

All creation follows the pattern of the Trinity: in the creation of Israel no less than the cosmos, the bestowal of structure and definition to what God calls out of nothing entails encounters with the infinite. In the wake of the fall, these moments of freedom involve subjection to an infinite pressure, a near-dissolution that squeezes the maturation toward form through the brink of formlessness. The brushes with the infinite here imply anguish, uncertainty, and ruthless oppression, if not the near-certainty of death. In these moments freedom means death, for sin so perverts the created order that life must now come to be through death, and the pressure that men feel bears the weight of God's holiness against our fallenness. In Israel's creation story men observe two pairs of infinites, often horrifying events that nonetheless lead to rest. The first pair takes place in a cycle involving the patriarchs, the second follows the people from Egypt to Canaan.

God wills to create Israel and remains ever-faithful to that will. "I am who I am" does not change because his object has shifted from the cosmos to his chosen people. When God declares the covenant to Abraham, he supports it with the fullness of the divine commitment. He repeats the promise multiple times, moving between the halved carcasses, ensuring that his people will take shape and receive structure. God's integrity does not permit the denial of form to Abraham's descendants. He has promised them a law of form, a law that portends definition and substance, a law that will establish the Israelites as his possession. God puts his own divinity at stake as surety that his promises will come to fruition, that this people will grow and thrive. When God pledges land, offspring, and blessing to the father of his beloved nation, without doubt this thing shall come to pass, God will certainly establish this people.

How baffling, how tragic and inconceivable, that the same God who issues the promise with all confidence should in the next breath command the unthinkable. "Take your son, your only son Isaac, whom you love," God says to Abraham, "and go to the land of Moriah, and offer him there as a burnt offering on one of the mountains that I shall show you." The God who issues the covenant and foretells the birth of Isaac as heir, so that the hope of the promise rests on this son of Abraham, now apparently destines both the son and the promise to destruction. "Is this God love? Is this God compassion? I will never worship such a God!" says the atheist. "How can God do such a thing? Why the command? Why the sacrifice?" says the Christian, no less stupefied than the non-believer.

God tests Abraham and Abraham takes the long journey to Moriah because creation requires the encounter with the infinite. Here the infinite confronts men as disintegration and dissolution, the threat of formlessness embedded within the maturation toward form. At the earliest moment, a negative reflection of the formless void which initiates the creation, God subjects the people borne in Isaac to the unqualified pressure, the freedom of death. Abraham must lead Isaac up the mountain, he must build the altar and lay his beloved son upon it, he must raise the knife, he must peer over death's rim as an expression of the infinite pressure placed upon the Israelite nation. How incomprehensible the Trinitarian grounds of creation and how disruptive the power of sin, that after the fall men must perdure into death, if not beyond it in mind and heart, in order to proceed toward life? How baffling and absurd, how insulting to the mind that requires perfect clarity and efficiency to concede that creation cannot come to be without a certain dumbfoundedness that man accepts by faith and then acts upon in that faith! Not the direct and progressively clarified but the mysterious and occasionally frightening faithfulness of God leads men into life. Without the brush with the infinite, this movement through death, creation does not occur, law and life do not emerge.

When God issues the covenant to Isaac well after his near sacrifice by Abraham, and when God delivers his promise to Jacob the son of Isaac, he twice re-affirms the promise of a law for Israel: this people shall receive form as God's people. This people will take shape, they will come to be and abide in God. The Father gives the promise to Abraham entirely as promise, that is, as focused entirely on his descendants. Inasmuch as Isaac is the first of those descendants, and Jacob the furtherance of Abraham's line especially in fathering the twelve sons, God repeats the law as promise to those who represent the earliest stages of its fulfillment. Isaac and Jacob embody the maturation of the law-as-promise in the growth of Israel out of the nothing from which God called it toward its definition as his people. The infinity of Abraham and Isaac on Moriah stands between God's will to form as expressed to Abraham and the double repetition of that will to Isaac and Jacob. The infinity does not stand on its own, it does not exist as plucked out of the story of form, but is nestled within a preceding expression of law as promise and a following double expression of law on the way to fulfillment.

The people of Israel soon encounter a second brush with death, a threat powerful enough to wipe out Jacob, his sons, and their families. The famine that loomed over the world knew no mercy, threatening all people with demise. It is the second infinity confronted by Israel in the patriarchal cycle, the second encounter with freedom as death, but it is more. The dreams of Pharaoh reveal the famine as the end of a trajectory in which seven years of destitution follow seven years of plenty. In Egypt, the famine reached such severity that the anguish of the seven years of want made men forget the seven years of abundance. The pattern of rise and fall, understood as a historical force that determines the fates of men, belongs to the ancient world no less than the docetic, and with no less devastating consequences. The success and prosperity of civilizations, as they expand without limit, pass through the turning point in which the joy of growth empties into the horror of want. The suffering comes at the end of the trajectory that seemed promising, which appeared at first as wealth and affluence but which gives way to the infinity of annihilation. The pattern of destruction does not change from the biblical era to the millenia following it. Nor, fortunately, does the pattern of life for those who seek to avoid the harshest aspects of the punishment.

Joseph rescues Israel from the famine and brings the people into security. His story reverses the dynamic of rise and fall, illustrating that humility comes before honor. His brothers cast him into a pit as into a tomb, later selling him into slavery, and they convince his father that an animal has taken his life. Joseph then lives as a slave in Egypt, eventually wallowing in an Egyptian prison as one wrongly accused. From this humble position God raises him up as the benefactor of Egypt and the savior of Israel. After interpreting Pharaoh's dream, Joseph becomes prominent in Egypt, leading the efforts to prepare for the famine. Because of his plans, Egypt has more during the years of want than any surrounding people. His brothers must come to him for grain, and when he sees them he struggles to restrain his emotions. Joseph carries no bitterness or anger against them, but in disclosing himself he reveals the wisdom and discernment of one lowered for the sake of others. "God sent me before you," he states, "to preserve for you a remnant on earth, and to keep alive for you many survivors. So it was not you who sent me here, but God; he has made me a father to Pharaoh, and lord of all his house and ruler over all the land of Egypt." This lord of Egypt delivers his family from the terror of famine, introducing them to safety and rest. With prosperity in Egypt the first iteration in the account of Israel's creation closes.

The faithfulness of God, expressed in the promise to Abraham, Isaac, and Jacob, underlies the formation of Israel. That formation encompasses two points of virtual destruction in the patriarchal cyle, two encounters with the infinite that threaten the promise and coming-to-be of God's people. The first occurs in God's command to Abraham to sacrifice Isaac, the second occurs in the famine during the time of Joseph. God saves the people from both of these moments through sacrifice, the almost and apparent release of blood to stave off annihilation. This blood of creation looks forward to Christ, in whom man knows it conjoined with water and Spirit.

When Abraham lifts the blade to thrust it into Isaac, when the angel halts him at the last possible moment, when the sacrifice is interrupted and Isaac feels life return to his bones, the action does not end with his descent from the altar. God still requires a sacrifice, he demands the flow of blood as the conclusion of the infinite pressure. Abraham sees the ram caught in the thicket and sacrifices it in lieu of Isaac, who receives life as one reborn from the dead. In the case of Joseph, the sacrifice precedes the pressure. The apparent sacrifice: his brothers throw Joseph into the well, they tear his coat and smear it with blood, they persuade his father that Joseph has perished while God saves him from death, shepherding him through his troubles. In this way God sets Joseph apart as one plucked from family and home, one given to death, in order to resurrect him as a preparation and a guard against the infinite burden. The sacrifice of Isaac is expected until the end, while the sacrifice of Joseph is apparent because the evidence hides his life. In neither case does salvation come without blood, the same blood by which Jesus came and that testifies to him, for the people of Israel do not mature without sacrifice. They attain neither rest nor rescue from the infinite without one handed over to all but death for their sake.

The first cycle in the creation of Israel ends with the people in Egypt; the second cycle begins with the transformation of their prosperity into slavery and oppression. The promise of God to the patriarchs and his continuing faithfulness to it underlie both cycles. These cycles, in their presumption of God's faithfulness and their embeddings of the infinite within the maturation of the finite, imitate the Trinity.

The second iteration plunges immediately into its first encounter with the infinite. The Egyptians desired that the Hebrews should not "increase and . . . escape from us." For this reason they set taskmasters over the Israelites "to oppress them with forced labor," so that the Egyptians "became ruthless in imposing tasks on the Israelites, and made their lives bitter with hard service in mortar and brick and in every kind of field labor. They were ruthless in all the tasks" to which they subjected the Hebrews. This was not only slavery, which is compatible with the gentleness of the master and the rest of the slave. The Egyptians imposed upon God's people an infinite law, a burden of cruelty and oppression, a work bitter and unremitting, a labor meant to paralyze the people and grind them into dust. Under the weight of this infinity the Israelites cried out to God and he heard their groans, remembering the covenant he made with their ancestors.

God appears to Moses so that he should become God's instrument for the salvation of the people, commanding him to go to Pharaoh and demand the release of the Israelites for "a three days' journey into the wilderness, so that [they] may sacrifice to the Lord" their God. Pharaoh receives this request with derision. "Get to your labors!" he exclaims. The Israelites are now "more numerous than the people of the land and yet you want them to stop working!" Pharaoh then directs his taskmasters to deny straw to the slaves, though still requiring the same quantity of bricks. "So the people scattered throughout the land," falling to their lowest point. Torn apart by the injustice of their superiors, the Hebrews were fragmented, divided, and overcome.

God had foreseen Pharaoh's refusal of Moses and announced judgment upon Egypt: "Israel is my firstborn son. I said to you, 'Let my son go that he may worship me.' But you refused to let him go; now I will kill your firstborn son." Egypt had proudly imposed the infinite law unto scattering upon the Hebrews, but God punishes the oppressors by turning the tables, placing a similar law upon the Egyptians in the plagues. Water turned to blood, frogs, gnats, flies, diseased livestock, boils, thunder and hail, locusts, and darkness together amount to the infinite pressure. How long shall the Pharaoh exalt himself against God by not letting his people go? How much calamity can the Pharaoh absorb before his pride collapses? How much can his people withstand? "How long," God asks him, "will you refuse to humble yourself before me?"

The final plague presents the conclusion of the infinite law and the saving power of sacrifice. The Egyptians give the firstborn of their children and their livestock as an unwilling sacrifice, as those taken by God as his vindication. God scatters Egypt in tearing the souls of firstborn children from their bodies, cutting the higher nature from the lower; in the tearing of father and mother from their sons; and in the tearing of the future from the present. As the reward for the pride of Pharaoh, the life of the people becomes death, unity descends into division. Having received the warning from God and performing the sacrifice of the lamb, the Israelites avoid this fate. Seeing the lamb's blood on the doorposts, the angel passed over the houses that made the sacrifice and spared the children within. Both the Egyptians and the Israelites make a sacrifice just as both suffered under a form of the infinite law but these sacrifices do not have the same meaning. The Israelites had already suffered under the infinite oppression, they were already scattered, and their sacrifice portends not their dissolution but their coming liberation from the infinite and their later maturation according to God's law. The Egyptians also endured a form of the infinite, but their scattering comes as its conclusion. In the wake of Pharaoh's pride, God humbles the Egyptians beneath the full force of the infinite and their sacrifice marks the terminus of its development. The Israelites humble themselves before the God who will exalt them and the sacrifice is part of their humility. The Pharaoh rose up against God in his pride, and the sacrifice of the Egyptian firstborn results.

The Hebrews plundered the Egyptians as they left the country, gathering the gold of their oppressors on the way to the sea. There they performed the unthinkable. The waters parted when Moses held out his hand, allowing the Israelites to pass through the sea on dry ground. Not unlike the cosmos in Genesis 1, God draws the people out of water so that they come to life on the other side. The Egyptian army, bearing down upon the Hebrews and intent on returning them to slavery, is not so lucky. As the pursuers passed through the sea the waters returned to their normal depths, covering the chariots and chariot drivers so that "not one of them remained." The same water that served as the way of life for the Israelites destroyed the Egyptians, wiping them out utterly.

God did not free the Israelites for the sake of freedom, he did not release them from the bonds of their oppressors so that they might live without bonds. God liberated the people from the infinite law, a law that strangled and crushed them, in order to form them according to a law of mercy. "I shall be your God, and you shall be my people," says the compassionate God of the Jews. He does not say, "Be liberated, and indulge in your freedom!" Nor does he say, "You are free to rule yourselves!" God stakes his claim upon the Israelites as expressed at Sinai and again at Moab. Twice does God issue the law through Moses, twice he shapes the people as his people. The Exodus, though a glorious liberation and a testimony to God's faithfulness, does not fulfill the covenant nor secure the closeness between God and his people. That security comes as God weaves the people into his way of being through the law, opening to them the path by which they might humble themselves before him.

The law consists of ordinances concerning worship and commandments that require obedience. Command and sacrifice, humility in one's moral habits and in the ceremonial honoring of God, ground the Israelite religion and appear in both issuances of the law. At Sinai Moses receives the 10 commandments and the Book of the Covenant but he also receives instructions regarding the size and equipment for the tabernacle, the duties of the sacrificial cult, and the ordination of priests. Worship so intertwines with law that Leviticus, a book concerned principally with priests and sacrifices, also includes an extensive list of regulations meant to preserve Israel's holiness. This combination of command and sacrifice appears no less prominently in Deuteronomy, which contains a repetition of the 10 commandments together with a host of laws while it stresses the relocation of worship to "the place that the Lord your God shall choose." The way bestowed upon the Israelites for worshipping God, a way of humility later offered to all men in Jesus Christ, unequivocally affirms both law and worship, command and sacrifice.

Through this law God forms the Israelites as his people. They worship God in the particular way specified for them, a way not of their own creation but given to them from above. The Jews complete the reception of the law at Moab with a covenant that admits that they, as the people obedient to God, shall receive the benefits of life that he promises in case they are obedient, whereas they will endure the horror of punishment should they go astray. When the people agree that God's wrath should come upon them if they disavow him, they testify against themselves that they are his people. Like the bride who pledges matrimony to the groom, the Hebrews acknowledge God as their husband and their God, their protector and their watchman, and they commit themselves to remember all that he has done for them.

Memory plays a central part in the last infinity through which the Israelites assume form. In this case, they do not immediately suffer the pressure, they do not directly endure the brush with death. No new threat emerges to match the command to sacrifice Isaac, the famine, and the oppression under the Egyptians. The final infinity occurs in memorializing the liberation from Egypt in the Passover. Before the Israelites enter the Promised Land under Joshua, they mnemonically re-enact their suffering as slaves. They place themselves again under the infinite law of oppression, they are scattered under their taskmasters, they look to God for salvation. In the mind and the heart they return to the point of near death, so that the liberating power of God and his wrath upon the Egyptians comes alive for them again. They recall the plagues witnessed by the previous generation, they look back to the death of the Egyptian sons and livestock, and they sacrifice the Passover lamb. They carry out the sacrifice in practice as well as in memory, performing the ritual as they did while in bondage, awaiting the deliverance of God.

The entrance of the Israelites into Canaan mirrors the Exodus from Egypt in many ways, so that the former replicates the latter. At both times, the Israelites ensure that all males are circumcised in conjunction with the Passover; in both cases, the enemy is destroyed so that "not one remains." In both circumstances, though first in physical experience and later in the soul, the Israelites suffer the infinite weight. In both the people also gain life through water, taking shape as a people who have passed through the waves. As the Israelites travel through the Red Sea at the Exodus and later the Jordan, the water withdraws so that the people walk on dry ground. God fashions his people as those who burst the bonds of slavery by passing through water, just as they pass through water in order to assume the land that he has given them.

In the second cycle of Israel's creation God shapes his people not only through blood, but also through water. To the emphasis on sacrifice in the stories of Isaac and Joseph, an emphasis repeated in the Passover and the ritual prelude to entering Canaan, God adds the rite of passage through the Red Sea and the Jordan. The elements of the creation are now two rather than one. Israel comes to be not only by blood, but through water and blood. By these same elements Christ comes, and together these testify to him.

The water and blood in the account of Israel's formation signify the mutual support of law and sacrifice as the means through which the people take shape. God speaks to his people through the law, calling them to worship him just as he sets them apart for his commands. In this manner God plants his people as a tree nourished by water and producing its fruit in season, in this way he calls his people to the day when the law shall flow from the temple as a stream, deepening with distance from its source. This law molds the Israelites under the compassion and mercy of God, who forms them not according to the infinite but as finite, imposing upon finite creatures the mercy of a finite law. As the complement and guardian of the law's finitude, the blood indicates the salvation of the people from the infinite requirement. Just as God created the earth by drawing form out of formlessness, so he creates the people of Israel by drawing them through the threat of infinitude. That God sometimes initiates that threat is the great mystery but his purpose is always life, the salvation of man on the other side of the test and the proliferation of joy. In sacrifice God provides the means of escape, the giving of one so that the infinite should not destroy the many. In sacrifice God says that life comes through the infinite, through the freedom of death as a necessary moment or passage point, but he does not allow that moment to undermine his beloved.

The law and the blood exist together, limiting one another as a safeguard against death. Law underlies the process of creation, for God's promise that he shall give to Abraham's descendants land, offspring, blessing, means that he shall give them a law. Within this context of law God embeds encounters with the infinite, the confrontations with death in which sacrifice saves. The necessity of sacrifice limits the law that forms the Israelites, so that the law does not become the infinite, while the embedding of sacrifice within the law assures that sacrifice shall not itself become a law without boundary. The two foundations, water and blood, preserve the life formed through them by limiting one another.

That life is rest, a peace given to the Israelites after they conquer and apportion the land of Canaan. As settled, they acknowledge that the Lord gave to them "all the land that he swore to their ancestors that he would give them," giving them rest all around as sworn to their forebears, so that "not one of all the good promises that the Lord had made to the house of Israel had failed; all came to pass." From the call to Abraham to the occupation of the Promised Land God remains faithful to his people, not turning from the covenant nor forgetting them in their distress, not abandoning them to folly but forming them through his wisdom.

God's work comes to completion as the Israelites distribute the land, with each tribe settled within its boundaries. The people as a whole and as individual tribes achieve their form in their attachment to the land given by God and their acceptance of its boundaries as his determination. They can now say "God has planted us here" at the same time that they acknowledge God as God. The Hebrews apprehend their definition as the fixity of their feet upon the ground, within their limits, and as the turning of their hearts toward their Lord. One limits them from above, the other from below, but in each case they humble themselves in view of their limit and enjoy rest in their space. Is this rest not eschatological? Does it not foresee the reign of God in peace and prosperity, with land and people nourished by the law? Will the waters not flow from the temple, giving life and verdure to everything near them? Will Jerusalem and its land not receive the blessing of fruit that does not fail and leaves that bring healing? When God has completed the last restoration, so will his people again receive their boundaries, both as a whole and as tribes, dwelling within their limits, one above and one below, satisfied in the rest that gathers them under God and unto one another.

The creation of Israel progresses through two cycles, each grounded in the faithfulness of God and punctuated by two encounters with the infinite. The first cycle meets the infinite in the command to sacrifice Isaac and the famine in Egypt, escaping both through the near and apparent sacrifice. The cycle's two "laws" appear in Isaac and Jacob not as lawgivers, but as representative of the early growth of Israel into a nation formed under God and defined by his promise. The second cycle confronts the infinite as ruthless slavery in Egypt and in its ritualized remembrance prior to entering Canaan, with the people performing the sacrifice in both instances as pleas for rescue from the pressure. The two laws occur in this cycle at Sinai and Moab, with commandments and ordinances that fashion the people as God's possession through worship and obedience. The first iteration is one of blood, or of sacrifice as salvation from the infinite. The second iteration is of water and blood, adding the mercy of a law limited by sacrifice. At the end of these cycles, God blesses the Israelites with rest in his presence and fulfillment within their limits.

The creation of Israel presumes the divine faithfulness, it progresses through a pair of infinite moments, and it concludes in rest and joy complete: thus does the creation of Israel imitate the Trinity. Though the sounds differ as spoken through what is created rather than in the creator, and though those sounds suffer the distortion of sin among the fallen, the meaning remains discernible. God so stamps his creation with his image that men can identify the creation as this God's and no other's.

All creation imitates the Trinity: yet now "the Lord your God is in your midst, a warrior who gives victory; he will rejoice over you with gladness, he will renew you in his love; he will exult over you as on a day of festival," for he who bears the new covenant, who writes his law on the hearts of men, so that they shall be his people and he their God, man knowing him through the outpouring of his presence, has arrived! God forgives man's iniquity and remembers his sin no more! See that the former things have passed away and God declares new things, a light for those who walked in darkness, a child born to us, one on whose shoulders authority rests, whose might grows unto endless peace for the kingdom of David. The Righteous Branch has sprung up and executes justice in the land, so that David never lacks a man to sit on the throne of Israel and the levitical priests never lack a man in God's presence to offer burnt offerings. The age turns in him through whom God brings Jacob back, who binds up the injured and strengthens the weak, rescuing men from the places to which they have been scattered, gathering them from the nations and bringing them to the land.

It is he who, though in the form of God, did not regard equality with God as something to be exploited, but emptied himself, taking the form of a slave, being born in human likeness. And being found in human likeness, he humbled himself and became obedient to death, even death on a cross—he who is the image of the invisible God, the first born of all creation, in whom all things in heaven and on earth were created, things visible and invisible, whether thrones or dominions or rulers or powers, he whom God designated for our redemption as a plan for the fullness of time, to gather up all things in him, things in heaven and things on earth, reconciling all men to God through his death, setting the minds of men upon the things of the Spirit, on things honorable, just, pure, pleasing, commendable, and worthy of praise, he who buries men by baptism into his death so that they might walk in newness of life, not letting sin exercise dominion in their mortal bodies, Jesus Christ the power and wisdom of God, a wisdom that destroys the wisdom of the wise and the discernment of the discerning, so that he might come to have first place in everything—therefore God highly exalted him and gave him the name above every name, so that at the name of Jesus every knee should bend, in heaven and on earth and under the earth, and every tongue should confess that Jesus Christ is Lord, to the glory of God the Father.

Being therefore exalted at the right hand of God, and having received from the Father the promise of the Holy Spirit, Jesus Christ has poured the Spirit out upon all men, so that the sons and daughters prophesy, the young men see visions, and the old men dream dreams. This is the Spirit of truth, whom men know because he abides with them and is in them. This Spirit guides men into all truth, so that they abide in the Christ as the Christ abides in them. The Spirit sanctifies them in the truth, so that the followers of Christ bear fruit and become disciples, loving one another and abiding in the love of Jesus, who abides in the love of the Father. Through the Spirit men lay down their lives for their friends, just as they love the Lord by obeying his commandments. Those who abide in the Spirit abide in truth and in love, to the glory of the Son.

The Advocate convicts the world of sin and judgment not by arrogance and presumption, but by its unifying power. Through the Spirit, Christ bestows the glory given to him upon his followers, so that they might be one as the Son and the Father are one. Through the Spirit, God protects them so that they might be one, as the Trinity is one. As the church abides in the Spirit, the world sees its communion and recognizes that God has sent his Son, perceiving that the Father loves men even as he loves their Savior. Through the Spirit, those who see come to believe, so that they with the others become completely one. Those divided by language hear the gospel proclaimed each in his own tongue, as men scattered according to region, culture, and era come to bear a single witness to Jesus Christ, gathered by the Spirit into the divine power. The Spirit of truth perfects the unity of men as they kneel before the Son.

All creation imitates the Trinity: division, scattering, and breaking is death; reconciliation, gathering, and bonding is life. The mystery of Jesus Christ gathers what was scattered, binds what was broken, and reconciles what was divided, but more than this, the mystery locates a certain scattering within the gathering, it assimilates a certain division into reconciliation, it provides for a certain breaking within bonding. Through this mystery of Christ men have access in one Spirit to the Father. Through water, blood, and Spirit, they find nature and communion restored.

In the mystery of the Savior abides the covenant of God with men, not with Jews only but the whole world. God promised Noah that he will never again destroy all flesh by water, a promise for all men. In the same manner, God's salvation extends to all mankind in Jesus Christ, the herald of the divine faithfulness. For God, seeing his creation turned toward darkness, mired in corruption, and dreadfully deceived—how gullible are men, how dense and ignoble their most celebrated and skilled philosophers, how lost the leaders of their ignorance—willed mercy upon men out of the abundance of his love. He offers them union with and in the divine faithfulness, approaching them graciously, patiently, and with longsuffering, proving his honor in the death and resurrection of the Son. God has said to the world "I will be your God," just as God has always willed that not one perish, that men return his faithfulness with their own, that they become his as he becomes theirs.

Heavenly mystery, heavenly love, a stumbling block to Jews and foolishness to Greeks, God the Son has become man. After the fall the infinite denotes the brush with death, and this is no less the case with the Redeemer than in the formation of Israel. Is it any less stupefying that the Father should say to the Son, "Become man in all his finitude, frailty, and weakness," than that God should say to Abraham, "Sacrifice your son as a burnt offering on Moriah"? Is it any less necessary that God should descend into commonality with the humble in order to save them, than that he should submit his people to ruthless slavery in order to form them in his embrace? An infant born through pregnancy, through labor, through water breaking and blood poured out, the infinite and incomprehensible God suffers the infinite, he undergoes the infinite pressure by becoming one with the finite. When God becomes man, that which stood at the infinite's immeasurable remove from the finite crosses the sea, becoming one person with two natures, fusing the human with the divine. Is it not humiliation and a sacrifice, an infinite pressure and freedom unto death, that the Son "empties" his nature and so becomes man? How does the divine nature become so emptied and remain divine? How does it sustain full divinity within the body of man? How also does that body receive the divinity and not die at once? How does it retain its definition without either exploding due to the divine power or collapsing under the divine weight? How do both sides not sacrifice their structure, how do both subsist as what they are, how do they not form an unnatural coexistence at war with its components and suffering mutual contradiction? Surely the world has turned upside down, surely God and man are rent asunder, surely this incarnation both ought not and cannot be.

But Jesus Christ lives, and his word, whispered to all who consider the incarnation with wonder and humility, is peace. He has brought peace into man's heart, directing his mind as a horseman holding the reins until bitter envy and selfish ambition cease, until man abides in the wisdom that is first pure, then peaceable, gentle, kind, willing to yield, disciplined against all silly and profane talk, without the slightest hint of partiality or hypocrisy. When Jesus lowers himself into incarnation in wisdom, his life as man abides in wisdom as well. In Jesus Christ human nature lives within its natural limit. Far from dying, the mortal nature receives such succor from the immortal that it is humbled toward eternity. In this way Jesus Christ fulfills the natural law, disclosing to man the meaning of a nature whose fullness consists in the contentment of a limited life. Grand visions, extraordinary measures and achievements, worldly wonders and trivialities, not to mention the schism, division, faction, and isolation that typically result from these, gaze upon this perfection of law within limit as distant and unwelcome strangers. They know nothing of peace because they know nothing of obedience, they know nothing of obedience because they know nothing of humility, they know nothing of humility because they know nothing of limit, and they know nothing of limit because they are deceived regarding the law, which they abolish. On the other hand, Jesus Christ fulfills man's nature as all of these things: law, limit, humility, obedience, peace, and beyond this, love.

"Greater love has no man than this," Jesus says, "to lay down one's life for one's friends." Love is the very life of God. In love the Father begets the Son and the Spirit proceeds; in love the three lay down their lives for and in one another; in love the three abide as mysteriously affirmed beyond their mutual effacement. What could the Son of God do other than love? Will the faithfulness of the Father that loves the Son and the Spirit, and which they share without hindrance, not issue in a love beyond human understanding? Will the Christ, having accomplished the miracle of the infinite in the incarnation, not complete a second and more dazzling miracle, multiplying the infinite by the infinite, so that the indestructible and eternal life of being descends not only to the miniscule proportions of man, but traversing this in peace, passes on into death? What tongue does not cease, what mouth does not close, what mind does not reel at the maturation of Christ's perfection of the natural law in his life as a man into the perfection of the divine law in his death on the cross? Throughout his life Christ obeyed the law divine and natural without sin, dwelling in both aspects of the one law, justifying each in their unity. At the cross, however, Christ temporarily suspends the natural law that orders man to subsist in his bodily limit in order to hand the flesh over to death. Hence he turns wholly and completely to God, hence he suffers the agony of the severance and becomes the sacrifice.

"But when they came to Jesus and saw that he was already dead, they did not break his legs. Instead, one of the soldiers pierced his side with a spear, and at once blood and water came out." The death of Jesus picks up the elements of Israel's formation and recasts them in a new light. The water refers fundamentally to law, just as the Christ perfectly obeyed the will of the Father and the law in its stipulations and commands, just has he passed the command on to his disciples: "As I have loved you, love one another." The blood represents sacrifice, which Christ performs as both High Priest and offering, handing himself over according to the divine love. "As I have loved you, love one another": love in sacrifice fulfills the love manifest in obedience, with the two fused in the supreme giving. The Son takes in death and judges evil so that men might participate in the divine nature. This scattering of the divine from the human, this division of Christ's flesh from his spirit wrapped into gathering and reconciliation, this infinity embedded within the way to finitude, is the cross.

The Christ then welds together what death had severed, reaffirming the life of eternity in its superiority over death. Like the bush engulfed by fire but not burning, suffering the certainty of death only to persevere through it, Jesus Christ lives beyond death. He has passed through the darkness, the dissipation of the human nature where all is cold and alone, and his renewed life announces the victory of God over the grave just as God absorbs the grave into his very life, trampling down death by death. Like the mutual life-giving of the persons within the Trinity, the Christ effaces the human nature, lowering the body into death. Like the renewed affirmation of the persons, each grounded in everlasting faithfulness, Christ returns to the world perfected and without blemish, the expression of the Father's faithfulness to men and the cosmos. This is the testimony of God offered through his Son, that the life of Christ is the truth of unification and the love of one who extends life's power to others.

The resurrection is also rest: Jesus has accomplished his work, he has fulfilled his task of glorifying the Father and testifying to the truth. The work of reiterating the divine pattern in the world completed, Christ rejoins the Father in a new glory. He also promises the Spirit of truth to his disciples, who comes to them as reconciliation. Through this Spirit God reconciles with man, allowing the soul to reconcile with the body and men to reconcile with one another. The Spirit of mutual contrition blesses men with internal and external order, a law of humility and limit, but also with the heart and mind of service in which peace achieves perfection. With faithfulness as its presupposition, the Spirit nourishes men to extend outwardly in sacrifice, to be immersed in suffering as a temporary suspension, a suffering even to death because they know that though the bush burns, it lives, and though Christ cries in agony on the cross, he rises. Men can die because Christ has testified to life eternal, he has proven that the faith and love of God ground all that is.

Beloved, we do not ask for life in this world, not for the desire of the eyes and the things of the flesh, not for freedom and possibilities wrongly understood, not for grace perverted into license. We ask for that to which God has testified, the eternal life that gathers death up in order to judge it, that proclaims the truth in love and lives a love grounded in the truth. We ask for eternal reconciliation and rest, for the perfection of form within limit, for the Spirit to abide in our minds and hearts. This calls for wisdom, for patient endurance, and for the faith that conquers all.

1 John 2:1–2

> My dear children, I write this to you so that you will not sin. But if anybody does sin, we have one who speaks to the Father in our defense—Jesus Christ the Righteous One. He is the atoning sacrifice for our sins, and not only for ours but also for the sins of the whole world.

I HAVE LONGED TO write to the brethren of the immeasurable blessings pledged to us in Jesus Christ, who unifies us in his love. May you learn humility before God, who searches minds and hearts, so that you can approach the throne of Christ with confidence that his sacrifice confirms your salvation. Beyond this, I urge you to keep yourself from idols.

The days drown in darkness, men race from deception to deception, indulging in violence, licentiousness, and immorality, and having on their hearts only evil continually they consume themselves in self-exaltation. Soon this wickedness will plunge into fullest darkness. On that day they will be happy who have bowed low before Christ, who have become foolish before the world so that they might walk in God's wisdom, who have repented in meekness, circumcising the foreskins of their hearts and rending their inward garments. These are the living stones built into a spiritual house, the holy priesthood that offers spiritual sacrifices acceptable to God through Jesus Christ. Members of the chosen race, the royal priesthood, the holy nation, they are God's people though they reside in the present age. Christ has made them a kingdom, priests serving his God and Father, or again, "priests serving our God," or again, "priests of God and of Christ," who will reign with him for a thousand years.

What does it mean to serve Christ but to offer one's life as a sacrifice? Or to seek union with Christ through the mystery of the sacrifice? Or to pursue the healing of soul and body through the same mystery? Are Christians not, then, and above all, priests? But Docetism has destroyed the priesthood, wiping away the mystical reality of God in the world by dividing the spiritual from the material. Over centuries it has desecrated and ridiculed the priestly office until men regard priesthood and sacrifice as relics of a lesser world. Whether they give no thought for the name Christian, having abandoned God long ago, or whether they accept that name enthusiastically, men wander in unknowing, ignorant of the meaning of sacrifice for the nature of worship and their nature as God's creatures.

Docetism's ostensibly devout, conscientious, and religiously astute, including those trained in theology and tempted to pride in their erudition, leaders of congregations and churches, teachers and trendsetters, all claiming allegiance to Jesus Christ, do indeed make sacrifices—but to the wrong god! These worship the Christ-Idol, immersed in the powerful delusion that their lawlessness, their grace unwittingly perverted into licentiousness, brings the world into harmony with God's will. Such men might call themselves priests though many of them have hardly laid eyes on priest or sacrifice. They might affirm a priesthood of all believers though they have no practice of sacrifice as a part of their worship (an unthinkable anti-worship). They might cry out, "Lord, Lord," but he will say to them, "Get away from me, I never knew you." The docetic deception has hidden from these men the meaning of sin and of salvation in Christ.

Paul teaches that "if it had not been for the law, I would not have known sin." Faced with the command not to covet, he writes that "sin, seizing an opportunity in the commandment, produced in me all kinds of covetousness . . . I was once alive apart from the law, but when the commandment came, sin revived and I died, and the very commandment that promised life proved to be death to me. For sin, seizing an opportunity in the commandment, deceived me and through it killed me." The law, Paul concludes, "is holy, and the commandment is holy and just and good," but sin "worked death" in him through the good law, "in order that sin might be shown to be sin, and through the commandment might become sinful beyond measure."

Sin lies in wait in man's nature, and when it encounters the command it springs to life in defiance. The order not to covet thus produces covetousness, the command not to lust produces all kinds of sinful thoughts, the command to be humble tempts men to pride. This occurs, as Paul argues, not because sin resides in the law but because it taints man's inner life, wanting to turn him away from God and toward death. Sin spurns the measure and restraint required by the law, preventing self-control and obedience. Under sin's direction, men ignore blocks upon their desire and move as the passions impel them. In this way sin reveals its life as sin, using man's meeting with the law that limits and forms in order to push him over the limit. According to sin, man meets the law only to break it, and every such meeting amounts to a chance to prove that the particular command has no authority over him. Restrained by no law and dominated by sin, men living this habit show how sin, working "through the commandment" as its antithesis, "becomes sinful beyond measure."

In this scenario sin maintains a dialectical relationship with the law. The limitlessness of sinful desire requires the law as a mediating term whose strictures it must overturn. The encounter with the prohibition serves as a necessary middle step for sin's actualization as sin, which comes to be in the opposition against and conquering of the commandment. Throughout the scenario so described sin and the law remain opposites. Sin refuses all limits and checks upon desire while the law embodies and enforces those limits. There is little room for conceptual confusion or overlap between the two. But must sin always confront the law objectively and more or less obviously as an antagonist? Is sin no cleverer than this? Can it not achieve a synthesis with the law, in which sin becomes law and law becomes sin?

Consider the law of man's being, stated religiously: humble your nature before the Lord your God. Now consider that same law stated philosophically: abide within the limit of nature. Though much separates the two laws, they overlap substantially. Man cannot perfectly abide within the limit of nature without humbling that nature before God, nor can he regain the form lost in sin without that same humility. The Greeks perceived that man has a nature that limits him, grasping the philosophical law, but they did not know the wisdom of God that leads to salvation. On the other hand, it is not only the docetic age that has dreamed of infinite men.

An infinite man subsists according to an infinite law, a law that opens up a life in which nothing is impossible because all limits have eroded. As the men of Shinar said: "Come, let us build ourselves a city, and a tower with its top in the heavens, and let us make a name for ourselves; otherwise we shall be scattered abroad upon the face of the whole earth." Then the Lord came down and saw the city and the tower, and said: "Look, they are one people, and they all have one language; and this is only the beginning of what they will do; nothing that they propose to do will now be impossible for them." God saw his creatures not simply constructing a tower to the heavens but refashioning their own natures, making themselves men not of form and limit, not men of the earth and its restrictions upon existence, but men without form and boundary, men arrogating the life of immortals both in the height of their tower and in the pursuit of an infinitized life. For this reason he brought their aims to their logical conclusion, "scattering them abroad over the face of all the earth" and confusing their language.

At the Tower of Babel men did not confront a particular and promulgated law such as "Thou shalt not covet." They did not, insofar as the story tells us, dismiss prohibitions upon individual actions but faced the single commandment implied in human nature. The command to live within nature, to dwell in humility under God and in subjection to creaturely limits, is fundamental to man's life, and while men rarely find it directly stated they can grasp it rationally. At Babel men rebelled against the law of their creation and so against their Creator, and in the denial of natural limit sin became sinful beyond measure. This "beyond measure" does not mean that sin broke the law by addressing it objectively and as an antagonist. When sin here breaks the law of nature it becomes one with that law and distorts it. One can hardly perceive this synthesis when examining particular prohibitions, but when one faces the limits of creaturely existence in the abstract and repudiates them, the repudiation entails the transformation of man as one who embodies both the commanding function of natural law and nature's immediate if partial conformity to it. Sin here exists as synthesized with the law, interposed as a foreign but controlling element within the law, turning the dictate of nature away from its God-given function in providing limit to the opposite. The sin-dominated law becomes a limitless law that drives man to limitlessness. His work, his obedience, his hope, his devotion, his energies, all cooperate with the imperatives of limitlessness and their restless pace. Rather than man humbled before God, he grows proud, self-exaltant, dismissive of checks on his prerogatives, and consumed by the importance of his task. He believes that he shall make a name for himself and that he shall make the nations one, unifying heaven and earth while he lives in the former in place of the latter.

Just as a balloon has limits entailed by the size of the rubber, so with man's nature. For men to pursue a limitless activity, a limitless achievement, and thereby to live according to an infinite law, amounts to filling a finite balloon with an unlimited quantity of air. The pressure of the air against the balloon inevitably equals and immediately surpasses the amount that the rubber can bear so that the balloon explodes into fragments. The infinite law works upon man's nature in a similar fashion, so that his pursuit of boundlessness leads to an explosion, a fracturing and scattering, even death. When the Lord scattered the men of Shinar "abroad from there over the face of the earth," confusing their language, he hastened the logical conclusion of their own actions. He did not introduce a new principle or impose an otherwise unrelated punishment upon men for their pride. Sin had invaded the law and turned it to limitlessness, to infinite possibility. Scattering as boundarylessness fulfilled represents the inevitable end of that turn.

Men do not foresee the scattering, they do not anticipate that their course of action will produce results opposed to their desires. The men of Shinar wanted to make a name for themselves, they wished to be unified and not scattered and so they built a tower. They show their pride already in the desire for fame but they show it more glaringly in the decision to build the tower, which acts as a means for their goals. How shall they attain unity and a good name? By putting themselves in the place of the gods, ceasing to be men of earth and residing with the heavenly beings, by becoming infinite men. They proceed according to the infinite law, rushing toward the scattering without knowledge of their direction. When the balloon bursts, when they find that man cannot abide according to an infinite aspiration and demand, they meet the contrary of their desires. They sought a name that men would remember as the people who unified the world, a name of glory and wisdom. They received a name of ignominy as those punished by God and their memory remains as a warning against sin. They sought to be one, to gather all the world in unity, but they provoked the dispersal that they meant to avoid and the confusion of their language. The men ended up with either an ironic distortion of their original desire or with results antithetical to their stated aims. This occurred because they followed a law transformed by sin, a law that deceives at the same time that it promises men the infinite.

The infinite law does not always burden men through the deception in which they take it up believing that it will lead them to glory. Sometimes the law comes upon them directly and against their wills, imposed on them as ruthless oppression. When the Egyptians made the lives of the Israelites "bitter with hard service in mortar and brick and every kind of field labor," they subjected their slaves to an infinite weight. Moses then came to Pharaoh from the Lord and on behalf of the people to request a three days' journey into the wilderness so that the people could sacrifice to God. Pharaoh responds by commanding the slaves to make bricks without providing them straw and accusing them of laziness. "You are lazy, lazy," he declares. "That is why you say, 'Let us go and sacrifice to the Lord.'" The request of Moses and Pharaoh's reply juxtapose the relentless work of the Israelites, the unceasing tasks that embody the infinite burden, against the request to sacrifice. This contrast captures the relation between sacrifice and the infinite at the heart of man's right orientation to God: sacrifice restricts and provides a respite from the infinite law. It ensures that the law does not assume infinite size, demanding the infinite requirement. Sacrifice thus corresponds to and honors the freedom implicit in man's form. As a break upon the infinite law, it is peace and rest.

The finitude of man's nature intertwines law and freedom. Law denotes the command to form and life written into man's way of being, a way that subsists both in the limits of his body as situated in the natural environment and in the limitations implicit in the soul's quest for knowledge. Freedom, or free will, limits the law, ensuring that it does not contradict the mercy of form by expanding to the infinite. As free will limits the law or form of nature, so the law limits freedom, so that natural law implies these two in their mutual limitation. Extract and isolate one from the other and both lose their integrity. What subsisted harmoniously within limit aggrandizes, expanding unto rapacity and malice, dismissing its former measure. The two that shared in limit as in friendship transform into antagonists as each pursues boundlessness. The law becomes tyrannical, dominating, and merciless while freedom makes arrogant proclamations of right, necessity, and prestige. The two still exist in mutuality but their intersection involves not harmony but discord, not friendship but hatred. An infinite freedom matures through the infinite law and not without it, while the law's infinity at once assumes and grows toward the liberation of man from form. Yet neither of the pair trusts the other and each wants to assert its supremacy over the other.

God understands that the peace of his creature turns on the mutual dependence of law and freedom. Shall he, then, place an infinite burden on his finite creation, on man whom he loves as a son? Will God not recognize the dual nature of man and, in issuing the way of salvation, fashion that way to reflect the necessities of human nature? Is the divine law, like the natural law that it surpasses and perfects, not a law of mercy, a law of command and freedom? In the divine mandate handed down from Sinai and in the words of Christ, the law embodies the command whereas freedom, expressed in terms of the divine requirement, consists in sacrifice. In the latter God places a bridle upon the law, saving man from the prospect of the divine command becoming the infinite. Sacrifice and command must exist together as components of the divine way, molding man's approach to God, or all is lost. As long as the two mutually limit one another, man can obey the law of God as a law of mercy, a law that does not extort an unceasing and relentless burden. In the sacrifice man finds rest; in the cult and its ceremonies, God honors the freedom of man at the same time that he proclaims his compassion, recognizing the finitude of his creature.

Isolate and extract the law of God from sacrifice and what God bestowed in mutual limitation, and thereby as adapted to man's nature as a means for its transfiguration, becomes a means of despoliation. Like the mutual antagonism of free will and the law of form when one rends them unto limitlessness, the severance of command and sacrifice in the divine law subjects both to a boundlessness that perverts the creature away from salvation. Rather than drawing man up to God, the infinite command oppresses him no less ruthlessly than the Egyptian taskmasters over the Israelites. Rather than confirming man's peace in God's mercy, the infinite sacrifice deceives him into believing that he will receive eternal life while it abdicates the power of rest. Sacrifice here means not a break upon the infinite or peace and union, not the liberation of the Passover lamb, but the logical conclusion of the infinite, the tearing of life from life, the loss of the Egyptian children and livestock as a consequence of pride. When men divorce command and sacrifice they give up the knowledge of God as longsuffering, patient, and kind, replacing him with a despot and an iron hand. They rob God of his mercy while they envision him as the infinite coercion and the author of restlessness.

Man must come to God humbled in law and freedom, lowered before the necessity of command and sacrifice. He must confess his sin in repentance, turning away from violence and the heart's war against the neighbor, conquering his passions, abandoning the delight of the eyes and the insolence of the tongue. He must change his habit of mind so that murder, lust, and covetousness fade, while meekness, generosity, and patience take their stand. In these ways, among other concrete obediences, man humbles his nature before the command. He must also humble his freedom, performing the sacrifice in faith. In sacrifice man says, "I have tried to obey the law and often failed. But had I obeyed perfectly, as fallen I must still bow before God, who fashioned me in my limit, in light of my natural freedom and the freedom of the divine way. I seek him not only in works but in faith, in sacrifice." Man thereby acknowledges that his effort shall never gain him heaven because God's law cannot exist apart from its boundary, the offering in freedom. Man lifts up his hands to a merciful God in that offering: "Here I have come, and no farther! Without your gracious action, your free acceptance of the humbled heart, I am lost!" Far from a manipulation or an *opus operatum*, the sacrifice is a work of freedom and is therefore self-annulling: through it man abdicates hope in his deeds including the effort expended in the sacrifice. Man gives the whole of his nature, handing over his life and his struggle against sin as an offering so that God, whose mercy resides principally in the divine freedom, may bless him with grace and beatitude. Man begins with humility but only God completes it by bringing it to honor. Only God sees the humility of the creature and, out of his kindness, grants the life of union with him. Only God, observing the creature's self-despising, brings soul and body back to the mean of friendship, so that man's union with God entails his internal union as man.

Sacrifice thus accomplishes much more than breaking the power of the infinite law; it reverses man's bent toward the infinite, turning man's proclivity to division and internal combat back to harmony. This transformation does not happen without man's effort of humility but it belongs wholly to God's compassion and grace.

Sin locates man within the dynamic of the infinite, the rise and fall in which he exalts himself in his achievements as a prelude to destruction. This trajectory came alive in the social world in the time of Joseph, who saw seven years of plenty before the seven of famine. God gave it to Joseph to foresee the infinite expansion and to warn the Pharaoh of its coming. In the story, the sacrificed son of Israel rescues the people by saving grain from the years of abundance for the time of destitution. Joseph reduces the extravagance of the plenty, applying the excess during the years of want so that men could live through necessity. He lowers the years of rise so that the fall should not utterly destroy. Instead of two periods that abandon the mean in which each has what he needs, one period reaching far above that limit and the other frighteningly below it, Joseph helps to approximate the mean through both periods, diminishing the fullness of the former in order to mitigate the emptiness of the latter. His sacrifice saves by contradicting the pattern of sin, directing society toward its right measure.

Men seek a similar elimination of extremes when they seek salvation from God. In their pride, which hounds them like a shadow, they reject their limits for the sake of something supposedly higher. They desire pleasure, knowledge, power, prestige, and comfort, as any number of worldly goods and honors convey these things, while they consistently look upon their neighbor as an inferior and unworthy of service. By acting upon this pride or by indulging it in their hearts they call upon themselves the destruction that follows, sometimes enduring this destruction both inwardly and outwardly in the present world, sometimes inwardly in this life and fully in the next. When man pursues salvation he wants to avoid the destruction inherent in his pride, and beyond this he yearns for union with God. This unity precedes the reconciliation of man with his nature both logically and in practice. How could men become unified in their natures while remaining impudent toward nature's author? How could the inward elements at war lay down their arms apart from practical submission to the king of peace? Man thus seeks God's mercy so that he should avoid the destruction that his sins deserve, but more fundamentally that God should welcome him into eternal harmony.

Man humbles his nature through his obediences and this lowers his pride a certain distance, but only a certain distance. He humbles his nature again through sacrifice, turning to God in the freedom inherent in the law, and this lowers his pride once more. Neither of these humiliations return man to the mean of his nature. He cannot save himself, he cannot manipulate God's union with him, he always remains raised above the limit in which God fashioned him and consequently worthy of condemnation. In the sacrifice, however, man not only acts in light of the freedom that limits the law but recognizes a more fundamental liberty: the freedom in God's nature, intertwined in the divine being with God's faithfulness and out of which God responds to his creature in compassion and love. Out of his grace God turns to the creature who seeks him and answers with kindness. In the sacrifice, the freedom of man calls to the freedom of God that the author of salvation should make the divine work effective, joining man to God and gathering the nature that sin had scattered. Not because of man's humility but not without it, God restores the union of creature and Creator, healing the image borne in man's soul and body and replenishing it by the Holy Spirit. This application of God's power occurs through the paradigmatic sacrifice, the offering of the savior Jesus Christ.

Our Redeemer, "who for a little while was made lower than the angels, sharing in flesh and blood, becoming like his brothers in every respect, tested as we are yet without sin, became through his abasement a merciful and faithful high priest in the service of God, making a sacrifice of atonement for the sins of the people, through death destroying the one who has the power of death, becoming the source of salvation for all who obey him. This Christ came as a high priest of the good things that have come, entering once and for all into the heavenly Holy Place, not with the blood of goats and calves, but with his own blood, thus obtaining eternal redemption. For if, under the old covenant, the blood of goats and bulls, with the sprinkling of the ashes of a heifer, sanctifies those who have been defiled so that their flesh is purified, how much more will the blood of Christ, who through the eternal Spirit offered himself without blemish to God, purify our conscience from dead works to worship the living God!"

"For Christ did not enter a sanctuary made by human hands, a mere copy of the true one, but he entered into heaven itself, now to appear in the presence of God on our behalf. Nor was it to offer himself again and again, as the high priest enters the Holy Place year after year with blood that is not his own; for then he would have had to suffer again and again since the foundation of the world. But as it is, he has appeared once for all at the end of the age to remove sin by the sacrifice of himself. And when he had offered for all time a single sacrifice for sins, he sat down at the right hand of God, and since then has been waiting until his enemies would be made a footstool for his feet. For by a single offering he has perfected for all time those who are sanctified. And the Holy Spirit also testifies to us, for after saying, 'This is the covenant that I will make with them after those days, says the Lord: I will put my laws in their hearts, and I will write them on their minds,' he also adds, 'I will remember their sins and their lawless deeds no more.' Where there is forgiveness of these, there is no longer any offering for sin."

Through his sacrifice, Jesus Christ reverses the dynamic of sin not only for the church and the individual believers within it, but for the cosmos. When Adam fell the created order rose up in rebellion. The hierarchy of men over beasts and beasts over plants capsized as the ground revolted against the planter, requiring men to draw produce through toil while serving them thistles. Pride appeared everywhere and humility faltered, until God destroyed the race of men by the flood, preserving Noah and his family. Unlike the antediluvian era, in our age God sent his son, the perfect and complete overturning of the fall who absorbs the destruction inherent in pride at the same time that he embodies humility. Jesus Christ thereby reveals the love of God for mankind and all creation as well as the tremendous power of sacrifice, for in Christ men and the creation discover the rest that averts destruction, with the creation longing to be set free from its bondage to decay through him, obtaining the freedom of the glory of the children of God. Christ's sacrifice declares that man shall not descend into the infinite, shall not retrogress into chaos and the unformed, but shall, by the Savior's victory over death, be re-established in harmony with God and nature. Christ's sacrifice also proclaims that, insofar as man lives in submission to him, the earth inhabited by humble men shall not be submerged beneath the waters but shall persevere though the wicked suffer annihilation. Jesus Christ is the rhythm of the divine wisdom, a rhythm accomplished through sacrifice; out of that accomplishment, he bestows life.

Men make sacrifices as a way of conforming to that life, the being of God alive in and sustaining the world, healing what sin had made sick. Because man desires above all to know and be known by God, he turns after the model of Christ to the Lord, "continually offering a sacrifice of praise to God, that is, the fruit of lips that confess his name." What is man's prayer if not incense, and the lifting up of his hands if not the evening sacrifice? What first should man offer God if not his whole mind in prayer and his whole heart in yearning? Following upon these, man does not "neglect to do good and to share what he has, for such sacrifices are pleasing to God." Man gives his life over inwardly and outwardly, in thought and feeling as well as in material goods, until that life replicates the sacrifice of Jesus Christ as a disciple to his teacher and Lord.

These sacrifices reflect the faith that Jesus Christ has restored all things, that God will place all things under his feet and that he will reign, gathering all things under him as head, having sealed his victory in the resurrection. Man has faith that the Holy Spirit has and will continue to collect him into this gathering, that as man makes his way along the path of life, recovering his form as he proceeds, drawing closer to the divine union in which he finds his terminus, he participates in that broader, cosmic restoration. Man sacrifices, therefore, in faith that Christ has conquered death and dissipation and that, as the bearer of God's mercy, Christ will apply that victory to him as he pleads for forgiveness. For this reason man's sacrificial prayer asks that the Lord Jesus Christ will have mercy on him, a sinner, while his alms ask that Christ should gather him into the peace of a world in which none surpasses his limit, and in which each loves his neighbor.

The eucharist embodies the believer's desire for the life of God in a unique and powerful way. "Very truly, I tell you," states the Christ, "unless you eat the flesh of the

Son of Man and drink his blood, you have no life in you. Those who eat my flesh and drink my blood have eternal life, and I will raise them up at the last day; for my flesh is true food and my blood is true drink. Those who eat my flesh and drink my blood abide in me, and I in them." When men partake of the bread and the cup, they pledge themselves to God in full, as sacrifices whole and entire. To eat the flesh of the Son of Man and to drink his blood means no less than that the communicant wills to die as the Son has died, to engage in the way of life that compels men to perdure through death. Here man acknowledges that salvation does not belong to him as though it were his work. He humbles his nature by giving over his being to the unifying power of the Spirit, through which Christ gathers all that is his. In the mystery man lays down in his freedom in order that the Spirit, the executor of the free mercy of God, should pick him up. All of man's sacrifices amount to this humiliation, this laying down before God, but only the eucharist bears the promise that those who make this sacrifice shall abide in Christ and he in them. This abiding weds man to the eternal, securing him in the divine wisdom after the fashion of the Son, blessing him with power for obedience and life. It guides and protects him along the path of the everlasting, of *theosis*.

In addition to the mystery and as its preliminary, the sacrifice of confession owns a special place in the life of the believer. This sacrifice also plays a pivotal role in the historical development of Docetism, even in the perfecting of its ontological pattern through the spiritual law. Confession consists first in the division of man's sin from his righteousness, distilling the former so that man can bring it before God through a sacralized repetition, externalizing his unrighteousness in the hope that God will wipe his sin away and restore his nature. The sacrifice remains in its proper boundary so long as the announcement of sin or unrighteousness does not equal and at once annul the assumption of natural righteousness, that is, so long as the practice of confession does not grow to infinity. The perversion of this sacrifice through its expansion to the infinite, an expansion dependent on the foregoing expansion of the law, has produced the remarkable deception in which men believe that they worship Jesus Christ when they worship the Christ-Idol. In the wake of the transformation of the meaning of sacrifice, men make their offerings to a malevolent god falsely called the Christ. They claim to believe in Jesus Christ when they worship a god whose ontological *telos* is death.

I speak specifically of those docetists called Protestants, whose believers through centuries would respond to my charges with incredulity: "We have staked all on the grace of Christ, on his sacrifice on the cross, on his giving his life for our sin. We talk only of Christ and his giving, and we have done so earnestly. How can you say that we have worshipped an idol?" Many of them will turn immediately from this claim with contempt, unwilling to listen. Yet to those whose hearts yearn for God and bewail the disintegration of the world, who stare confusedly into lands marked by religious fracture and difference (the forerunner of institutionalized religious indifference), and who apprehend the emptiness of modern life just as they cannot extricate their own religious heritage from that emptiness, I say: Western Christianity moves and breathes through idolatry, subsisting according to a pattern of dissolution rather than life. Docetism thrives under virtually all talk of Jesus Christ in Western Christendom and especially under talk of faith in his sacrifice.

According to the science of justification by faith alone, men must come under the law not as limited and merciful but as unlimited and tyrannical. When one records a single act of obedience, a dozen infractions and doubts storm the stronghold and raze it to the ground. According to Luther, in this science "one law always produces ten more, until they grow to infinity." As the law grows, so grows one's consciousness of sin, as each command, applied always and everywhere, suffocates the conscience until it wilts, convicting the mind and the heart of an ever more comprehensive guilt. "The heart trembles," Luther writes, "and continually finds itself loaded down with wagonloads of sins that increase infinitely, so that it deviates further and further from righteousness, until it finally acquires the habit of despair." The believer took this habit with him into confession in Luther's day with the requirement that he recount each and every one of his faults. Salvation rested upon the cleansed conscience and purification necessitated that the believer lay out all his sins, not forgetting any but providing an exact and exceptionless account of his miscues in order to receive assurance of pardon. In this circumstance the sacrifice grew toward the infinite. Driven forward by the infinite law and burdened by an infinite sin, what remedy could man seek if not the culmination of his endless confession, an infinite sacrifice accomplished by his savior on the cross?

Not only Luther and Calvin but a whole lineage of docetic believers have discovered the infinite sacrifice in Jesus Christ, by whose blood alone they believe they have acquired salvation. At the end of his inner tortures Luther found the righteousness of faith alone, given freely by Christ and received in total passivity by the believer. He felt himself rescued from the law, whose power to frighten was destroyed. He entered "through open gates into paradise itself," and later taught this experience by saying that one must accept Christ in the heart, that the Lord must become Christ "for you and me," interpreting his personal experience as the believer's victory over the law and handing it down to others as such. But Luther handed down the wrong faith, a faith in the docetic wolf dressed up as the lamb. He did not teach faith in Christ, and particularly faith in Christ's sacrifice on the cross, as a limited respite from a limited law. He knew nothing of the harmony in which law and freedom, or law and sacrifice, intertwine and mutually limit one another in the practical rhythm of Christian struggle. Instead, he assumed the infinite reach of the law as necessary for and intrinsic to the experience of grace, and his stress upon that infinity, upon the terror of the law that makes one flee to Christ, proves that Christ's grace upon the cross and delivered to the believer does not secure the merciful limit of the law but consummates the horror of its limitlessness. If the law's infinite expansion encounters no limit, no rest, no stop upon its advance (for which God in fact provided sacrifice), then it proceeds to the point at which the boundlessness of the requirement overwhelms the finitude of the creature and scatters his nature. At this moment the law collapses, having attained its end. Luther experienced this conclusion as paradise, unwittingly misunderstanding his liberation from the law's pressure as grace. He went on to condone an ontology of dissipation and fracture inasmuch as he retains the infinite law and allows no place for sacrifice as rest.

But do docetists not lay all upon the sacrifice of Christ? Do they not look solely to Christ's work on the cross for justification? Of course they do, and in this lies the deception. Docetic language conceals the belief not in law and sacrifice intertwined and limited but severed as the consequence of limitlessness. Appropriating this limitlessness, docetists distill law and sacrifice as two discrete infinities, drawing them away from one another unto alienation and antagonism. At the same time, both law and sacrifice dissolve in their lack of boundary while implying the infinite burden. To say "we believe in the sacrifice of Christ, we look solely to his cross" helps none at all, for the docetist, particularly in Protestantism, proclaims both the infinite law and the infinite sacrifice, the infinite imposition of the command and the infinite freedom from the command. When the Protestant insists that the whole accent of salvation lands upon the cross, he means that the infinite law leads to the infinite liberation from law, unknowingly advocating a liberation that is not reconciliation but scattering and which portends destruction. For the announcement of the infinite sacrifice in faith, made in conjunction with faith alone's severance of the soul from the body, abolishes sacrifice in practice. The infinite sacrifice is in this way no sacrifice at all. It is not a break upon the infinite but a cloak that conceals it.

One can perceive the ontology of division within Protestantism, this advanced and pristine religious trapping of Docetism, in its theology of the cross. Inasmuch as Protestant theology elevates the crucifixion above the incarnation and the resurrection, locating salvation on Good Friday rather than the following Sunday, it isolates and extracts the death of Christ from its home within the divine affirmation of life. In this manner Docetism replicates, in its conception of Christ, its theoretical isolation of freedom from law and the infinitizing of both. Protestant justification all but destroys the theology of the incarnation as a practical ethic and so emphasizes the cross that the resurrection falls into the shadows. This isolation of the cross means not the right worship of Christ and the freedom from sin he provides but a worship of freedom that means no less than the secret worship of death. Docetism so perverts the divine encounter with the infinite at death, and the divine's conquering of death in fact, that death has clandestinely become the victor, hiding its sting within the assertion that Christ has defeated the tomb.

The worship of death has proceeded under the name of Christ but with equal stealth under the ideals of freedom and equality. The Reformers advanced the Christian's freedom from the law and the equality of all men before God, the latter seen for example in Luther's doctrine of the universal priesthood. Religious and secular docetic men have not perceived that freedom and equality before the law conclude in death, that by destroying the law these two destroy life and are themselves death. Docetic men forget that God structured man as a soul ruling a body, a higher law with priority over the lower. Separation of the lower from the higher frees the body to do as it desires, throwing off the law of the soul and issuing its own orders. This severance ends in demise; the total liberation of the body from the rule of the soul, and the total equality of both elements, is the death of the body. In rejecting the law that rules it the body rejects its own life and in completing that rejection it seals its death. Docetism exalts this moment of perishing in the life of Jesus Christ as it occurs between the divine and human natures, at a point where the ontological deception is especially crucial. Looking at the cross, Docetism proclaims the salvation of men in the death of Christ. But because docetists have dislodged that death from the teleology of life, they worship not death-unto-life and resurrection but death as such. Where docetists say "we worship Christ the conqueror of sin and death," thinking that they worship a Christ who gathers freedom into mercy, they worship a Christ conquered by death and exemplifying death, who consummates the infinite burden of death in the freedom of the death-moment. They replace Jesus Christ with the Christ-Idol.

Must we multiply examples of the scattering effected by Docetism's doctrine of faith alone? Has the Western body of Christ not splintered into fragments? Has the social world not burst into autonomous spheres, each demanding unbending allegiance and content within its own logic? Has man not disavowed nature as a reality and a philosophical concept, dismissing it in favor of limitlessness? Have docetic men not torn the body from the soul with regard to salvation, turning the latter against the former? Have they not divided works from faith, as if the form of one's life had no substantive implications for salvation? Have they not absolved Christianity from public life, divorcing it in particular from government, sequestering the divine law from its politico-natural form? Have men not plummeted into the theological isolation in which salvation becomes an individual and private affair, with others not to be trusted? Does one need greater evidence that Docetism, under the veil of the Christ-Idol, has seduced men into worshipping and practicing not sacrifice wrapped within the pattern of life but sacrifice distilled from life and tending toward death? Here fissiparity, there strife, everywhere suspicion, everywhere loneliness; such is the world formed through the Christ-Idol, the lord of division and infinite freedom dressed as the God of fellowship.

In both Judaism and the Christianity that fulfills it sacrifice limits the law, prohibiting its expansion to infinity and preserving the mercy of God toward his creatures. This recognition of man's freedom occurs in the eucharist, where men sacrifice themselves *qua* free and submit to the inadequacy of their efforts at obedience. If the eucharist is no longer a sacrifice, it no longer provides this stop upon the law, no longer representing man as finite and free in his finitude, no longer curbing the infinite requirement. But what do Luther and the Protestant Docetism formed in his wake have to say? "There is another misconception to be done away with which is more serious and specious . . . the common belief that the mass is a sacrifice offered to God." Christ's words of institution, he adds, "contain nothing about a good work or a sacrifice," while "it is a self-contradiction to call a mass a sacrifice; for a mass is something we receive but a sacrifice is something we offer. But one and the same thing cannot be received and offered at the same time . . . it would be safer to deny everything rather than to grant that the mass is either a good work or a sacrifice." Finally, "The gospel offers no warrant for calling the mass a sacrifice." I leave aside Luther's charge that the Catholic Church misunderstood the eucharist as a repetition of the sacrifice of Christ on the cross. The correction of this misunderstanding should assert the believer's sacrifice of himself at the mystery, not the abdication of sacrifice as such. When Luther carried out this abdication he did the unthinkable, effectively removing sacrifices from the docetic-Christian temple. Under the leadership of Luther as well as Calvin, whose disgust toward sacrifice is evident, the Protestant prince has reared his head until this hour.

Docetic man believes in the infinite sacrifice just as he abolishes all sacrifices. Christ's work on the cross distilled and infinitized in faith conceals the appropriation of the infinite ethic in both the soul and the body. Now man's conscience must suffer under the infinite torture as required by Luther, now man's ethic must proceed ceaselessly and without interruption, restless and without contentment as implied by Calvin. Man can look for solace but he will not find it inasmuch as the Christ-Idol allows no place for freedom-as-rest. Man himself becomes an exceptionless and universal law, transforming and transformed by the secret transfer of his worship to a god that allows no respite. Prayer, alms, and all of Christian practice but especially the eucharist, having lost their sacrificial character, become handmaidens of the infinite. On his lips man calls sacrifice the highest, even the object of faith and the locus of salvation, but in his heart he has forgotten it.

Yet he has not forgotten sacrifice entirely, having become himself a sacrifice to the Christ-Idol. Whereas sacrifice naturally exists as lodged within the divine law, providing a periodic and regular break upon it, Docetism extracts the sacrifice in order to relocate it. Removing sacrifice from its mutually supporting tempo with the law permits the latter to devolve into stress and cacophony, while the sacrifice shifts to the end. In Christianity, sacrifice embedded in the law prevents the infinite; in Docetism, sacrifice concludes the infinite and consummates it. In Christianity, sacrifice prevents scattering at the hands of the infinite; in Docetism, sacrifice is scattering as the infinite's finality. Man therefore sacrifices under Docetism but sacrifices himself to death as his end and his object of worship. He hands over not the Passover lamb but his firstborn child and ultimately himself. Lord, have mercy upon us: all the while the docetist has meant to believe in Christ, all the while he has suffered the deception. So often men know not what they do.

Having divested the eucharist of its sacrificial meaning, Luther redefines it as a memorial to the promise of Christ. For Luther and for the heirs who follow him,

Christ promises the believer "with these words, and apart from any deserts or undertakings of thine, to forgive all thy sins, and give thee eternal life. In order that thou mayest be most assured that this my promise is irrevocable, I will give my body and shed my blood to confirm it by my very death, and make both body and blood a sign and memorial of this promise. As often as thou partakest of them, remember me." Luther and his Protestant descendants have conceived of the eucharist as a place for memory and the confidence of faith alone, as "nothing else than faith is needed for a worthy observance of the mass." Standing on the side of the promise, the Protestant mass opposes all works and commandments, reinforcing the conviction that salvation comes to the Christian apart from human effort.

"Little children, I write this to you so that you will not sin." If the sacrifice on the cross is only a testament and sign, only a memorial for faith, where is its deeper significance for the promise? *Qua* memorial or sign, could not Christ have assumed any one of a number of forms of death in order to validate his pledge of forgiveness and life eternal? Does the freedom of God, so emphasized in the century prior to Luther and implicit in his ontology, not demand liberty at this point? If the giving of the body and blood confirms a promise whose dependence upon the form of the memorial is at least uncertain, if form and content, in other words, bear no clear and intrinsic relation to one another, are the cross and its sacrifice not somehow arbitrary? "Christ must die and be resurrected," says the docetist. "Christ must face the greatest humiliation possible," he adds. True enough. But is the form of death a matter of happenstance? Is the greatest humiliation located on the cross in a way that it is not upon other ways of dying?

We tread dangerous ground here inasmuch one might wish to establish the logical necessity of the cross. Pursuing logical necessity as the absence of freedom in both the agent and the act, as the unmitigated requirement that things had to occur in this way, that they had to unfold according precisely to this plan, at this hour, with these details, and with a complete comprehension of the meaning of the specifics, implies man's confidence that he can attain a total and exact knowledge of the divine event on which history has turned. No such knowledge is possible for man, who knows nothing exactly and comprehensively, nor does such knowledge exist, for the freedom that exists within the divine life touches God's actions such that they do not assume a merciless legality. When men search for the deeper meaning of divine actions, even the paradigmatic love for men on the cross, they seek the harmony of the action with the divine life rather than an exceptionless necessity.

Jesus Christ dies not only as a sign and memorial for the promise of forgiveness, eternal life, and union with God, but as a continuation of his repetition of the Trinitarian life in his existence on earth. The Trinity subsists in perichoresis, in which each person dwells within the others through mutual life-giving, with each "dying" as a life handed over in fellowship, facing the infinity of apparent death no less than the bush consumed by fire. Like the bush unconsumed before Moses, the persons perdure through immolation unscathed, reaffirmed beyond the infinite unto eternal blessedness. Jesus takes up the infinite as the incarnate God-man and, by accepting the severance of the divine and human natures, makes the severance the prelude to life. Only by death does he conquer death, only by death does he absorb the conclusion of Docetism's infinitizing dialectic and embed it as a moment within the divine life. At the same time Christ replicates the perichoretic infinity within the Trinity, accomplishing his life-giving work as incarnate as a prelude to his glorification by the Father. The Christ thereby saves man just as he abides in God. He remains fully man as one whose body dies as mortal bodies die but he retains Godhood according to the Trinitarian pattern, gathering death into life. It is Christ's unsurpassed humiliation and his wisdom to participate in both mortal death and immortal life.

Christ dies under particular authorities and at the hands of particular men, judged as the supreme lawbreaker by the created order. As judges and rulers according to the divine law, the Pharisees cry out that he is a blasphemer and require his death. The High Priest tears his clothes, his companions shudder at Jesus' acknowledgement of himself as Christ, and from that moment the authorities bear down upon him. The Pharisees hand him over to Pilate, the Roman executor of the political law, who has him beaten and taken before the people. Pilate offers Jesus and Barabbas before the crowd, pledging to free whomever the people choose. When they choose to kill the Savior, Pilate washes his hands before ordering the crucifixion. This action annuls the authority of the political institution in the death of Christ, transforming it into a channel between the religious authority and the people as distinct from their political form. The authorities of the divine law convict the Savior and insist on his death, handing him to the political authority to carry out the sentence, while the people confirm it as necessary. The collective soul, body, and mutability all have a hand in the indictment of the Lord; his condemnation by the social body is total. When the soldiers drive the crown of thorns into Christ's head, so that the thorns and thistles that revolted against the old Adam now revolt against the new, the natural environment adds its condemnation to the others. The divine law, the politico-natural law, and the physical order combine to proclaim their lordship over the Savior and announce his guilt, asserting that this man has undermined their prerogatives and that he deserves death at their hands. Why is this death a perfected humiliation? Why does Jesus die in this way? Because he bears the infinite burden under each manifestation of the single law, convicted by the order created through him.

Christ nonetheless dies as one lifted up, raised above the ground in his humiliation. After he hears the voice in John, Jesus tells the crowd that "Now is the judgment of this world; now the ruler of this world will be driven out. And I, when I am lifted up from the earth, will draw all men unto me." Jesus understands that the lowest moment of his humiliation foreshadows, even begins, the honor that follows upon humiliation. The "lifting up" of Christ on the cross expresses the wisdom in which humility and honor embrace one another, the latter following the former. Those who hear his words do not see the kinship between the two, just as we do not see without the Spirit training us unto sight. Jesus' lifting up is his humiliation, his humiliation is his lifting up; his humility begins his glory, it is essential to his glory. Here Christ conquers death, here he judges the world by gathering in death in order to subordinate it to life. The cross is not merely a sign or memorial but the wisdom of God manifest among men that they should be gathered to Christ no less than his body and soul are gathered in the Resurrection.

Brothers, in all humility I exhort you to deal circumspectly with those who deny the sacrifice of Jesus Christ! Beware their ceremonies, their festivals, their doctrines, and their music, for these carry the spirit of deception to a greater or lesser degree, sanctioning the infinite as a way of life whether the church and its believers are conscious of this or not. The history of Docetism, in which the infinite matures as an ontological ethos moving through the Western Church into the unbelieving world, progresses no less through the undermining of sacrifice in the medieval West to the bitter rejection of all things sacerdotal in the present age. Contemporary men, whether they proclaim the name of Jesus Christ or reject him outright, are the product and apex of this devolutionary progress. They have together disdained the sacrifice of Christ and embraced the infinite as their mantra. Pray for them and show them mercy and kindness, but as a protection of your salvation and a guard over your union with Christ do not join with them. Doing so risks losing the freedom of rest in Christ in favor of the freedom of death and scattering; it risks misunderstanding the meaning of Christian faith until man relinquishes his faith in Christ.

1 John 5:4b–5

> This is the victory that has overcome the world, even our faith. Who is it that overcomes the world? Only he who believes that Jesus is the Son of God.

THE DAYS CRY OUT for the faith that men have abandoned, that they no longer remember, that the form of their lives repudiates and which they have consigned to irrelevance. Some openly malign this faith and pour out their energies to discredit it, some view it as an obscure and vestigial curiosity, many assume they have received it without travail or obligation and therefore indulge a certain ignorance toward it, while few know this faith and live according to it. It asks too much of men who desire all at no cost, so that the whole has written it off through misremembrance until it has died. What shall we say of this faith? Can that which received the death-blow conquer the world? Can the convictions and confidence that men have mocked come again to life? I speak not of the faith that puffs up, not of the temptation of those who crown themselves as benefactors of men, who clamor for "a better world" and a "redeemed" social order. I speak of faith in Jesus Christ and his Resurrection, the faith that suffers because of the glory that follows, the faith that is humbled as a premise before honor. This faith looks out into the time ahead and trembles, but it stands firm and perseveres to the end, believing that God is merciful, that he turns with clemency to those who seek him. Though the righteous endure the scattering, though they face want, hardship, shame, hatred, imprisonment, torture, and even death, they abide in the belief that after the scattering, once the dark forces have completed their work, God will draw them into the final and irrevocable gathering, the coming together in harmony of God with his children.

We believe in God the Father Almighty, Maker of heaven and earth, and of all things visible and invisible; and in one Lord Jesus Christ, Begotten of the Father before all worlds, Light of Light, Very God of Very God, by whom all things were made; and we believe in the Holy Spirit, the Lord, and Giver of Life, who proceeds from the Father, who with the Father and the Son is worshipped and glorified. We affirm the mystery of the Trinity and worship the God who is three in one and one in three, whose being surpasses man's mind. That we can say that the Son is only-begotten and the Spirit proceeds does not diminish this mystery. Nor does God's abiding in faithfulness and man's description of the Trinitarian illumination encompass the divine being or make it quantifiable. Man experiences this being not in what is calculable but not thereby in what is irrational, and what is more, while man encounters God as incomprehensible and resplendent man encounters him no less as personal, near, and loving. For God created man in his image, and man cannot approach God, the knowledge of whom guides him into silence, without being silenced in faith.

We believe in Jesus Christ, who for us men and for our salvation came down from heaven and was incarnate of the Holy Spirit and the Virgin Mary, and was made man; and was crucified also for us under Pontius Pilate, and suffered and was buried; and the third day he rose again, according to the Scriptures; and ascended into heaven, and sits at the right hand of the Father. The center of our faith is Jesus Christ and his Resurrection. We proclaim the good news of a person, a member of the Trinity who calls us to abide in him. The end of our faith is life, a mystical union in which the whole man shares in the life of God according to the creaturely nature, in which the personhood of God and that of man embrace, in which the Creator takes up his creature as a father his child. God calls men to share in his infinitude and thereby to the truth that is also a way.

Personhood does not exist without law or form, much less does it exist against or in opposition to law or form. The personal transcends the law but does not contradict it, affirming the law as a necessary precondition and foundation for ascension into the mystery. So the Trinity has a foundation in the faithfulness of *I am*, so one does not come to know Christ the person apart from his work. Man begins in faith by conforming to its pattern, discerning the way that is true, holding fast to it and enduring unto life in God. Jesus Christ, the object of faith, lowered himself from equality with God into the form of a slave, and having assumed this form he descended to death, even death on a cross. In the initial lowering he is emptied, in the further lowering he dies: in the latter he bears the scattering in which life submits to death, in which the mortal body perishes. What had unity and coherence fractures and is divorced, what was one separates. On the far side of the cross, as the culmination of his earthly existence, Christ gathers together what was scattered. The reconciliation of the body with the soul and the revivification of the man Jesus Christ, the power and wisdom of God summed up as Resurrection, means no less than that gathering follows scattering, that what experienced division comes to life in its solidarity. The experience of Christ and his mystery means more than this inasmuch as it involves union with his person, but that gathering follows scattering is the principle of faith in our Lord. It encourages and guides the Christian's humility as it motivates him toward mystical union with the Savior. It is also the form of faith's victory over the world, the path by which those who believe that Jesus is the Son of God conquer the forces set against them.

Throughout the Old Testament faith concerns gathering and scattering. God punishes by scattering and rewards by gathering, and at a deeper level, when men peer into the pattern of creation and life exemplified in the Scriptures, they find scattering as a prelude to gathering.

When God tells Abraham to take Isaac to the mountain and sacrifice him there, commanding his servant to kill the heir of the promise, the Lord says, in effect, that Abraham must perdure through the scattering, that the scattering must take place by his very hand and at the cost of Isaac's life. This is the test: Abraham, the father of faith, must believe in God's promise and in the covenant, he must believe that God will make good on his repeated intent to gather his descendants as a people, to give them land, offspring, and blessing, and in light of the command Abraham must believe that God will accomplish this gathering not in spite of but through the scattering. Isaac is the heir; Isaac must live. The people must come about through him, though Abraham appears to have lost all at the behest of the God who promised all. But Abraham "considered the fact that God is able even to raise someone from the dead," that is, that the scattering that appears final can yield to gathering, "and figuratively speaking, he did receive [Isaac] back. After he has passed the test and proven his faith, when the angel has held back the knife at the last moment, God proclaims to Abraham: "Because you have done this, and have not withheld your son, your only son, I will indeed bless you." Why this "because"? Has Abraham forced the hand of God? No, but Abraham has responded to God's promise of gathering with the faith that he will gather, though Abraham arguably does not understand that gathering proceeds through scattering. When God says "Because you have done this," he says to Abraham, "By faith, you have passed through the preliminary," the premise through which the people's coalescence unto form must move and that the faithful must bear. The progress toward form will continue until God makes Abraham's offspring "as numerous as the stars of heaven and as the sand that is on the seashore."

God further promised Abraham that "your offspring shall be aliens in a land that is not theirs, and shall be slaves there, and they shall be oppressed for four hundred years; but I will bring judgment on the nation that they serve, and afterward they shall come out with possessions." Just as he commanded Abraham to kill his son, a test that Abraham passed by faith, God foretells the subjection of the Israelites to Egypt, hinting at their scattering there and raising the question of faith for those enduring ruthless oppression. Who shall believe there that gathering follows scattering? Who shall remember God's commitment to gather Israel unto form, fearing not men but God and believing that the divine power excels the powers of men?

God appears to Moses as a bush enveloped in flames but not consumed. Moses says "I must turn aside and look at this great sight" because before his eyes stands what ought to be scattered into ashes, what ought to blacken and die, here persevering through scattering as life and health. God initiates the fire and thus the scattering and God overcomes it in the life of the bush. In this way God provides an image for his nature as well as the principle of faith in him; God says "*I am He who Is*" and "believe in me, despite apparent death, as *I am*." Moses removes his shoes from his feet before the theophany as directed, for the place on which he stood was holy ground.

Already Moses had separated from the Egyptians and sought unity with his fellow Israelites, denying the privileges of Egypt to protect his kin. Already he had humbled himself to the level of the slave, forgetting the pride of the master. Having fled Egypt and at the mountain of God he received the directive through the bush. "I have observed the misery of my people who are in Egypt . . . I know their sufferings, and I have come down to deliver them from the Egyptians, and to bring them up out of that land to a good and broad land, a land flowing with milk and honey . . . So come, I will send you to Pharaoh to bring my people, the Israelites, out of Egypt." Moses believed this promise despite being a poor speaker, taking it to the people so that they should take heart, believing that God had heard their cries and purposed to release them from cruel bondage.

When Pharaoh hears the request that the people leave their work to go three days into the wilderness, he scoffs and increases their burden. Forced to make the same number of bricks without a given supply of straw, "the people scattered throughout the land of Egypt to gather stubble for straw." Here the people scatter not as a premise to their maturation as a people but as the preliminary to the formation of the object in which their oppression congeals, the brick for which they labored but whose glory belonged to Egypt. Holding the small brick or gazing on the larger one meant for the pyramids, the slaves confront an alien object held over them, a product whose value superseded their value as workers and made concrete the injustices imposed upon them. They scatter so that the might of their oppressors should gather, their masters' psychological power reinforced and intensified with the creation of each brick. Thus faith seems lost, thus the pattern in which the people's scattering precedes their gathering is cut off, sabotaged by the insertion of a foreign and diabolical object. The people easily lose heart, castigating Moses and Aaron. "The Lord look upon you and judge! You have brought us into bad odor with Pharaoh and his officials, and have put a sword in their hand to kill us."

The people cannot bring themselves to believe that their scattering leads to anything other than the increased power of their lords. They see the bricks with their eyes but at the moment they do not see the power of God. They will see this power soon in plagues that devastate Egypt, and through the liberation, the law, and the conquest of Canaan to follow they will find that the scattering in Egypt indeed presages their formation as a people. They must traverse the scattering in the form of cruel slavery, in the ruthless oppression of their masters and the coercion of uninterrupted labor, a burden severe enough to cast the Israelites across the land like seed over a field. Through this terror they initiate their development toward the maturity in which God takes them as his people and he is their God. That God will accomplish this is the faith of Moses, who believes that God will make good on his pledge to bring the people to prosperity in the promised land.

The same faith led Moses to believe that God would spare the people from the angel of death. When God promised to send the destroyer, he added that the blood of the Passover lamb "shall be a sign for you on the houses where you live: when I see the blood, I will pass over you, and no plague shall destroy you when I strike the land of Egypt." At the end of God's application of the infinite to the Egyptians, an application meant to terminate in their scattering and in the liberation unto form for the Israelites, God pledges to Moses that the blood of the sacrifice stands in the place of the blood of the Israelite children and livestock. The Israelites practice humility by performing the sacrifice according to God's instructions and by believing in the replacement, submitting in their hearts to the proclamation that God preserves and has mercy on those humbled in this way. Like Moses, the people have faith that the sacrifice is effective to stave off God's wrath, that in ordering the sacrifice he has confirmed his compassion toward them, and that though the rulers and privileged of the land cry out under the destruction everywhere imminent, God will spare his people.

Gathering and scattering appear not only in the formation of the people through Moses but in the promises to Israel as formed. God says that Israel's obedience will lead to the exaltation of the people over others, as "the Lord your God will set you high above all the nations of the earth . . . you shall be only at the top, and not at the bottom" if the Israelites humble themselves beneath his commands. In that case they would "abound in prosperity, in the fruit of your womb, in the fruit of your livestock, and in the fruit of your ground in the land that the Lord swore to your ancestors to give you," that is, in the land where God pledged to gather and nurture his people. Because of their obedience, "the Lord will cause your enemies who rise against you to be defeated before you; they shall come out against you one way, and flee before you seven ways." Or again, "You shall give chase to your enemies, and they shall fall before you by the sword. Five of you shall give chase to a hundred, and a hundred of you shall give chase to ten thousand." Whereas the Lord will bless the Israelites at the same time that he sets them on the path of life, showering them with fertility and produce, he will scatter those that threaten their peace. These point to the underlying gathering of the people by God to himself, for the people that humbles itself before God finds communion with the divine. "I will place my dwelling in your midst, and I shall not abhor you. I will be your God, and you shall be my people." This is the promise of gathering into God's presence.

The opposite will occur in the case of disobedience: "Cursed shall you be in the city, and cursed shall you be in the field. Cursed shall be your basket and your kneading bowl. Cursed shall be the fruit of your womb, the fruit of your ground, the increase of your cattle and the issue of your flock . . . aliens residing among you shall ascend above you higher and higher, while you shall descend lower and lower. They shall lend to you but you shall not lend to them; they shall be the head and you shall be the tail." Having spurned and forgotten God, the source of life, the Lord shall cut the people off from life's blessing. Embracing the infinite, they orient themselves to death in God's absence and they shall bear profoundly the scattering destined for the unrighteous. "The Lord will cause you to be defeated before your enemies; you shall go out against them one way and flee before them seven ways," relinquishing solidarity to the weakness and terror of division. And when the Israelites have achieved the height of pride, when they disdain worship and mock God with idols, when they have made injustice their way of life, the air they breathe, and the food they eat, "The Lord will bring a nation from far away, from the end of the earth, to swoop down on you like an eagle . . . it shall consume the fruit of your livestock and the fruit of your ground until you are destroyed . . . Although once you were as numerous as the stars in heaven, you shall be left few in number." They shall suffering the scattering as death and dissolution, the end of gaiety and joy, because throughout Israel's years of disobedience and stubbornness "you did not obey the Lord your God." Therefore, "just as the Lord took delight in making you prosperous and numerous, so the Lord will take delight in bringing you to ruin and destruction: you shall be plucked off the land" that God gave according to his promise, and "the Lord will scatter you among all peoples, from one end of the earth to the other." Among those foreign peoples, worshipping their gods, the Hebrews enslaved by the infinite will find "no ease, no resting place" for the soles of their feet.

Through Moses God makes the further promise, the commitment reflecting his faithfulness and the order of his being, that he does not forget his covenant but remains at the side of his people. When they have endured the scattering, and in the midst of their isolation they remember God and turn to him, obeying him with all their mind, heart, soul, and strength, "then the Lord your God will restore your fortunes and have compassion on you, gathering you again from all the peoples among whom the Lord your God has scattered you. Even if you are exiled to the ends of the world, from there the Lord your God will gather you, and from there he will bring you back," returning Israel again to the land, to offspring, and to prosperity. In this instance redemption presumes the scattering as punishment for sin, but this scattering also precedes gathering.

The prophets echo the divine promise of gathering, looking forward through the scattering to life on the far shore. Long before Babylon's coming, Isaiah sees that the God who created and formed Israel will also redeem her, reminding the people that God has "called you by name, you are mine." Though Israel passes through waters that destroy, through rivers that carry off life and cast it to death, though they walk through fire, enduring imminent dissolution, clashing with the infinite and apparently succumbing before it, scattered from land and hope, though it appears that God has turned away from them, "Do not fear," says the Lord, "for I am with you." God sees the undoing of Israel under foreign rulers, his people terrorized and displaced, alienated and forgotten, and remembering his covenant he announces that "I will bring your offspring from the east, and from the west I will gather you; I will say to the north, Give them up, and to the south, Do not withhold; bring my sons from far away . . . everyone who is called by name, whom I created for my glory, whom I formed and made." Jeremiah affirms that "David shall never lack a man to sit on the throne of the house of Israel, and the levitical priests shall never lack a man to offer burnt offerings, to make grain offerings, and to make sacrifices for all time." Staring Babylon in the eyes, watching the clouds gain strength and the storm brew before erupting, the prophet still proclaims that God's covenant with David rivals his faithfulness to the day and the night, a promise announced in the ancient world to Noah. Only if the day and night did not follow their appointed time would God not honor his servant David, for the same Wisdom, Jesus Christ the Lord in creation, lies behind both promises. The implications of the Davidic covenant for Israel's exile in Babylon are clear: the Lord will re-establish his people and their suffering must end. "Hear the word of the Lord, O nations, and declare it in the coastlands far away; say, 'He who scattered Israel will gather him, and will keep him as a shepherd a flock' . . . their life shall become like a watered garden, and they shall never languish again." Where God watched over his people to break down and pluck up, he will watch over them also to build and to plant.

God's character and life, even the divine nature, rests on his faithfulness and the surety of his commitment. As the laws of pride run their course into destruction, so the Israelites bore their punishment in Babylon, suffering both in the deprivation of the body and in the soul's separation from God. But God did not finally dismiss his people, and his fatherly hand struck them neither in malice nor in absolute rejection. "For a brief moment I abandoned you," says the Father through Isaiah of his withdrawal, "but with great compassion I will gather you. In overflowing wrath for a moment I hid my face from you, but with everlasting love I will have compassion on you . . . for the mountains may depart and the hills be removed, but my steadfast love shall not depart from you, and my covenant of peace shall not be removed, says the Lord, who has compassion on you."

Rejoice, you children of Jerusalem! Take heart, you who are brought low by trial! For the Lord saw the destitution of his children in Babylon before the time arrived, looking further ahead to the new dawn of Israel, a day when Jerusalem would again enjoy its inhabitants, when the cities of Judah would be rebuilt and their ruins raised up. Then the heavens and the earth will exult, "for the Lord has comforted his people, and will have compassion on his suffering ones," so that they do not hunger or thirst, and neither wind nor scorching sun strikes them down and springs of water guide them home. Truly the Lord observes his people, this valley filled with dry bones, and commands that what had died shall again know life, that what had neither breath nor heartbeat, neither thought nor emotion, neither will nor action, should revive with full flesh, with a new heart, with a renewed mind and spirit, breathing life when all that once was, no more than bones, lacked only fire to reduce it to ashes. This life drawn up from death, this form subjected to darkness and restored, this temple rebuilt and this way confirmed! This faithfulness, this promise, this loving-kindness of the creator and Father!

1 John: On Docetism and Resurrection

The Christian gospel proclaims not only release from Babylon and the gathering of the Jews, but that God works for the salvation of all men in Jesus Christ. Our gospel says "gathering through scattering" in a single word, "resurrection," for in this signal event, this turning of the age, God opened to men the divine nature that scatters on the way to a final and joyous gathering. In the theophany at the bush what ought to have died did not, and the mystery is its survival unconsumed. So Jesus Christ who died ought to have remained dead but did not, reviving unto life as man redeemed, a dying body resurrected unto eternity. With Paul, our gospel is resurrection. "For David, after he had served the purpose of God in his own generation, died, was laid beside his ancestors, and experienced corruption"; the Israelites in the wilderness likewise ate the manna from heaven and they died; the exiles returned from Babylon, though they laid the foundations of the temple and raised up the walls of Jerusalem, also submitted to death; "but he whom God raised up experienced no corruption," conquering death by death, defeating Hades and validating his reign over the tomb no less than all else. He proved the faithfulness and liberality of God by scattering unto death, absorbing the scattering into gathering and new life. That is his principle and his work. Yet our faith is not in a law, not in a principle or in a work *per se*, but in a person inseparable from this work and mystically completing it, a being whose love is not a pattern but not without a pattern, not without rhythm and meter though not reducible to a formula, life and truth as parable. With this in mind we acclaim Jesus Christ as Lord who heads up all things just as he invites us into union with him.

This union occurs in part in the present world, finding fulfillment in the next. Christ has come as an exemplar and a paradigm, but more than this, as the first fruits of the resurrection of the faithful. Man sees in the resurrection the divine person for whose love and compassion he yearns, to whom he cries out in mercy, and he sees also the promise that just as Christ died unto rising, celebrating life remade, so man conformed to Christ also dies unto rising. As with Israel, the scattering is temporary but the covenant is eternal, and in the case of believers the covenant points to and rests in the next world, in eternity in Christ. "What you sow," Paul writes to the Corinthians, "does not come to life unless it dies . . . so it is with the resurrection of the dead. What is sown is perishable, what is raised is imperishable. It is sown in dishonor, it is raised in glory. It is sown in weakness, it is raised in power. It is sown a physical body, it is raised a spiritual body." This is our hope of salvation, that we should know and be known by God in the life everlasting. On the other hand, if we claim to believe in Christ for this world only we have given the last word to death and the scattering. Do not be deceived: Docetism proclaims that Christ remains true while it rejects the resurrection of the body, by elemental philosophies injecting the spiritual and eternal power into the world of transience. To accede to such philosophies and distortions of the gospel loses the principle without which we cannot know the person, secretly trading the scattering that precedes gathering for the gathering that precedes scattering. In accepting such teachings one therefore accepts a gospel other than that known to the church, submitting the good news of Christ to the desire to eat and drink. In such a case "Christians are of all people most to be pitied."

Jesus consistently predicts his scattering (that is, his death) as a prelude to his gathering in the resurrection. That the gospels rarely use the terms "scattering" and "gathering" in this connection should not distract believers from the harmony between the Old Testament language and the New Testament gospel. Or does the story of Esther not illustrate the wisdom teachings of "pride before destruction" and "humility before honor" without explicitly mentioning these teachings? In like manner, the seven years of plenty followed by seven years of famine in the story of Joseph exemplify unbounded expansion, and thus the pride that precedes destruction, without direct mention of sin or an avowed focus on wisdom. One does not need the words to perceive the ontological implications. So one does not need Jesus to say directly "I shall be scattered on the cross before being gathered in the resurrection." One needs only the wisdom to discern the principle and the humility to follow the example of the Christ who lives it.

Three times Jesus predicts his death and resurrection and three times the disciples misunderstand it, and how arrogant is the man who would look down on the disciples as if he knows what they did not know, as if all would have been plain to him then as it is supposedly plain to him now! Peter first acknowledges Jesus as the Messiah only to prove that he does not perceive the significance of messiahship. When Christ announces the suffering and rejection that he must undergo, describing his dying and rising, Peter rebukes him. But such must occur for the Messiah, he must be scattered before being gathered. For this reason Jesus scolds Peter, commanding Satan to get behind him. "For you are setting your mind on human things," on the direct acquisition of glory by the Son of God, as though he came not to suffer but to sit directly on David's throne. Jesus then teaches that those who follow him must be scattered from the world by taking up their crosses and following him. "For those who want to save their life" by raising it immediately to glory, and one might add "those who want to save the world" by lifting it with themselves up to heaven, will lose their life as well as the world they hoped to save. On the contrary, "those who lose their life for my sake, and for the sake of the gospel, will save it." A second time Jesus tells the disciples that "The Son of Man is to be betrayed into human hands, and they will kill him, and three days after being killed, he will rise" to life, gathering together the divine and human natures that had scattered. The disciples do not understand what Jesus says nor its implications for their lives. Not long after his revelation Jesus sees that they have been arguing, and when he asks about the matter they admit that they have quarreled over who among them is the greatest. He responds by proclaiming that "Whoever wants to be first must be last of all and servant of all," welcoming little children in his name. The disciple must live in humility as a servant not only among men but among children. He must abide in such lowliness that he looks up even to the young, addressing them with a heart of service appropriate to his position as an elder. The third time Jesus informs his disciples that they are heading to Jerusalem, where the chief priests and the scribes will condemn the Son of Man to death before handing him over to the Gentiles, who will kill him. Three days after these events he will rise. The Son of Man will endure scattering before gathering, he will be humbled under death before being honored over it. A third time the disciples fail to grasp this teaching and its consequences for their hearts, with James and John asking for places of honor at Jesus' side in his glory. Even in the presence of Christ who is humility, meekness, and service, men desire direct exaltation. Jesus answers James, John, and the others by instructing them in servitude. Whereas the Gentiles have rulers who lord it over them, those who are great among Christ's followers are the servants, and "whoever wishes to be first among you must be slave of all. For the Son of Man came not to be served but to serve, and to give his life as a ransom for many."

The principle and work of Christ consists in enduring the scattering of death as a premise to gathering in renewed life. This is the ontological meaning of the resurrection, the victory of life over death, expressed in the language of the Old Testament and manifested at its height in the New. This same principle and work Jesus taught to his disciples as humility, obedience, and slavery to others. To be gathered to him they must be scattered from pride if not, at the extreme, from bodily life.

The gathering effected concerns the body of Christ understood both as the flesh of the man Jesus and the institutional collective that bears his mystery, the church. Through the one death both forms of the body come together as attested in the Scripture, a fact foreseen even by those who rejected Jesus as Lord. Caiaphas the high priest, no friend to the lowly man from Nazareth, insisted that Jesus die so that the Jewish nation might endure. Yet as one inspired by God he also prophesied that "Jesus was about to die for the nation, and not for the nation only, but to gather into one the dispersed children of God." Jesus died, then, to rejoin the body and the soul in eternal life and to be the first fruits of the resurrection, but he did not die only for this. He rose again to initiate the reconciliation of all men and all things by bringing together the faithful who were scattered. As Christ says when he looks to the cross, "Now is the judgment of this world; now the ruler of this world will be driven out"—the one who finally scatters and the world that indulges in scattering now flee—"and I, when I am lifted up from the earth, will draw all men unto me." Jesus' lifting up at the cross signals not the victory of scattering over gathering but the subsumption of scattering within gathering. In this manner life prevails and death dies, while men oblivious to God, their natures, and one another are called to all of these. "I am the way, the truth, and the life," Christ proclaims. "No one comes to the Father except through me." The way prescribes scattering unto gathering, the truth exults in the harmony of the divine being opened to man through this way, and the life celebrates the victory of God over the grave.

Jesus acts so that the harmony of the divine being should extend into and define the harmony between men, enacting this harmony by his suffering unto death. "I am the good shepherd," he affirms. "The good shepherd lays down his life for the sheep."

This contrasts with the hired hand who "sees the wolf coming and leaves the sheep and runs away—and the wolf snatches them and scatters them." The hired hands saves himself over and against the sheep and the wolf scatters them, but the shepherd works "so that there shall be one flock, one shepherd." The prayer of Jesus shortly before his arrest likewise turns at multiple points to his concern for the unity of his flock. "Holy Father, protect them in your name that you have given me, so that they may be one as we are one . . . [I ask] on behalf of those who will believe in me through their word, that they may all be one. As you, Father, are in me and I am in you, may they also be in us, so that the world may believe that you have sent me. The glory that you have given me I have given them, so that they may be one, as we are one, I in them and you in me, that they may be completely one, so that the world may know that you have sent me and have loved them even as you have loved me." Jesus desires that men discover and abide in the mystical unity that joins them to God and one another, a unity lost upon those who overlook the destruction of the church through schism. Did Christ rise from the dead missing an arm or a leg? Was his resurrection not physical? How then can the church be called alive and exemplify the resurrection when the eye does not recognize the foot nor the hand touch the ear, but when severed limbs acknowledge one another at a distance, looking at each other as if to say "I used to know you"? The body of Christ perishes as it ignores the prayer of its Lord, while its believers accept the scattering as their spirit when they boast of their allegiance to one or another alienated organ. Yet through this death as well God will bring forth life.

We believe in the Holy Spirit, the Lord and giver of Life, who proceeds from the Father, who with the Father and the Son together is worshipped and glorified, who spoke by the prophets. We believe in one holy catholic and apostolic church. We acknowledge one baptism for the remission of sins.

The history of the Holy Spirit's activity in the church pivots on the gathering that presumes and follows upon scattering. When the divided tongues of fire appeared among the disciples in Jerusalem, with a tongue resting on each of them and the Holy Spirit blessing them with foreign speech, Jews staying in Jerusalem from many nations came together to see. Then each one heard in his native language the good news of God's power. Here the Holy Spirit overturned the Tower of Babel and the infinite movement there implied, calling all who were dispersed into a new body through the announcement of Jesus Christ. Peter then proclaims to the Israelites the gospel of our Lord, who was handed over to the Jews "according to the definite plan and foreknowledge of God," whom they "crucified and killed by the hands of those outside the law. But God raised him up, having freed him from death, because it was impossible for him to be held in its power . . . Being therefore exalted at the right hand of God, and having received from the Father the promise of the Holy Spirit, he has poured out this that you both see and hear." The Holy Spirit drew the Jews of Jerusalem to its activity in the miraculous tongues, but neither the tongues nor the preliminary gathering of the crowd is the end of its activity. The Spirit comes to those who stand outside of the gospel as a witness so that they might believe and be baptized. Through baptism the Spirit accomplishes its purpose of gathering the scattered, unifying them through the proclamation of the Savior who was scattered prior to his gathering. The Spirit does nothing unconnected with the upbuilding and unification of the church, nothing that does not bind new believers to others and fortify the harmony of the body. The Spirit is, as it were, the soul of the body that is the church, and where the Spirit has left the body dies and begins to decompose, to break apart and scatter. The tongues of fire serve as a means to the goal of baptism and the life of peace: those who accepted the message of Christ "were baptized, and that day about three thousand persons were added." These converts shared the true life with their brethren, giving themselves "to the apostles' teaching and fellowship, to the breaking of bread and the prayers," and having all things in common, "they would sell their possessions and goods and distribute the proceeds to all, as any had need."

The speech of the Pharisee Gamaliel gives no small testimony to the ways of God vis-à-vis the ways of man. When the council was considering the proper punishment for the apostles, who disobeyed the authorities by speaking the gospel publicly, he had them put outside before making the following speech: "Fellow Israelites, consider carefully what you propose to do to these men. For some time ago Theudas rose up, claiming to be somebody, and a number of men, about four hundred, joined him; but he was killed, and all who followed him were dispersed and disappeared. After him Judas the Galilean rose up at the time of the census and got people to follow him; he also perished, and all who followed him were scattered. So in the present case, I tell you, keep away from these men and let them alone; because if this plan or this undertaking is of human origin, it will fail; but if it is of God, you will not be able to overcome them—in that case you may even be found fighting against God!"

Gamaliel recalls two examples of men who "rose up," but the consequences of their rising up are nil. The followers of Theudas "were dispersed and disappeared" in the wake of his death, while the adherents of Judas "scattered" after he had perished. Gameliel is a good wisdom teacher; he knows that those who rise up against God come to destruction. Men do not need to exert themselves to bring this destruction about, as God will see that the wicked receive their due. For this reason Gamaliel advises his colleagues not to trouble Peter and the apostles. If these are like Theudas and Judas, God will reduce them to nothing. On the other hand, if they speak from God, then those who oppose the apostles oppose the Lord as well.

Gamaliel argues that those who raise themselves up will be scattered, but this pattern only vaguely implies its opposite, that God works through the humiliation of scattering as a prelude to gathering. But how does the church spread in Acts? Stephen insults the Jewish leaders as "stiff-necked people," enemies of the Holy Spirit, persecutors of the prophets, murderers and betrayers of the Righteous One, and lawbreakers, inciting them to drag him out of Jerusalem and stone him. As a result, "That day a severe persecution began against the church in Jerusalem, and all except the apostles were scattered throughout the countryside of Judea and Samaria."

The church grows through this turn of events, as "those who were scattered went from place to place, proclaiming the word." In contrast to those who raise themselves up and come to nothing, the church grows through scattering as a medium oriented to gathering. According to this plan Philip goes to Samaria, where he meets the Ethiopian eunuch. In the latter's case the Spirit acts to effect his baptism, directing Philip to the eunuch's chariot so that he should explain the good news about Jesus to the eunuch as he searched Isaiah. As they traveled, the two came upon water and the man exclaimed that he wished to be baptized then and there. When they came up out of the water the Spirit "snatched Philip away," its work in baptism being accomplished. The one scattered from Jerusalem guides in the one who is gathered; the scattering of the first precedes the gathering of the second. This pattern was the norm across the region near Jerusalem, where "those who were scattered because of the persecution that took place over Stephen traveled as far as Phoenicia, Cyprus, and Antioch," speaking at first only to the Jews but later also to Gentiles.

The scattering and gathering of Christians does not end with the apostolic age. Inasmuch as the plan of God comes to fruition "in the fullness of time," and inasmuch as that plan purposes to gather or head up all things in Christ, things in heaven and on earth, today Christians should acknowledge that God has destined them to this mystery. God chose believers "before the foundation of the world" and destined them "for adoption as his children through Jesus Christ," making known to them "with all wisdom and insight" the mystery of his will. Wisdom refers to the humility of Christ as he passed through the incarnation and the crucifixion, traversing from equality with God to abasement as a man, while the mystery is that the passage through the infinite, even death, leads to resurrection and life. This mystery is an immeasurable power, one "far above all rule and authority and power and dominion," a power that subjects all things under its feet. Death, the final enemy, has fallen before the God who wills to bring all things together under his rule, securing Christ as head over all things "for the church," creating a single humanity by making peace between men, reconciling them through his blood on the cross. Those in the church "are citizens with the saints and also members of the household of God" with Jesus Christ as the cornerstone, in whom "the whole structure is joined together and grows into a holy temple in the Lord." That the church should embody a unity hardly less mystifying than the resurrected body of our Lord, that its members should so lower themselves that each views the interests of others as higher than his own, that men should suffer in myriad ways in the present age because of the hope given them in Christ, is the "wisdom of God in its rich variety" made known to the heavenly powers through the church. There men give to others according to their gifts, but all sacrifice in the image of their Lord, faithful to the mystery of salvation.

Let us not, therefore, be surprised that a time of scattering greets us, for all who wish to be gathered to Christ will endure some form of scattering. We believe "in the Resurrection of the dead, and in the Life of the world to come," that is, in the final gathering of our souls and spiritual bodies, so no less should we blink when danger, wants, hardship, and threats enter our lives. Do not fear, for Christ has already "appeared once for all at the end of the age to remove sin by the sacrifice of himself," ensuring the forgiveness of those who follow him in faith, while he also "saves those who are eagerly waiting for him," who are made perfect as they approach his sacrifice as imitators. I say again, "Do not be surprised at the fiery ordeal that is taking place among you to test you, as though something strange were happening to you. But rejoice insofar as you are sharing Christ's sufferings, so that you also may be glad when his glory is revealed . . . let those suffering in accordance with God's will entrust themselves to a faithful creator, while continuing to do good."

Dear Christians, humble yourselves beneath the trials imposed upon you, not resisting or revolting when adversaries accost and despoil you. Though you defend the teachings of Christ and manifest his love for men in prayer, alms, and hospitality, regard with caution arguments based upon rights and equality, and do not be deceived by freedom, but recall always the example of the Lord, who "when he was abused, did not return abuse; when he suffered, did not threaten; but he entrusted himself to the one who judges justly." Just as his wounds have healed us, returning we who had gone astray to the shepherd and guardian of our souls, our suffering shines to the world as a witness to the gathering of all things in Christ. Men may suffer and even die for the name of Christ, and in their suffering his body perdures. The bush burns unconsumed and the virgin gives birth to God and is refreshed, for the mystery of our religion is great.

This suffering is our patient endurance and our victory, inasmuch as our victory in this world consists in the integrity of our testimony to the truth. Do not shrink back or rebel in unbelief, but considering this victory look beyond the present struggle to the reward in which God gathers in Christ those scattered because of his name, introducing them to eternal rest. "A Sabbath rest," the Scripture teaches us, "still remains for the people of God," a rest not of the present age, not the rest of Israel in its land but a heavenly and everlasting respite in which men enjoy full fellowship with God. "Let us therefore make every effort to enter that rest" through faith, setting our minds and hearts on the love of God for his children.

1 John 2:3–6

> We know that we have come to know him if we obey his commandments. The man who says, "I know him," but does not do what he commands is a liar, and the truth is not in him. But if anyone obeys his word, God's love is truly made complete in him. This is how we know we are in him: whoever says, "I abide in him" must walk as Jesus did.

FAITH TRULY OVERCOMES THE world! In it the Christian braces against threats, hardships, pain, ignominy, and all kinds of danger in order to endure them, bearing all in the hope of a victory not his own but Christ's, a resuscitation and revivification impossible apart from the work of Christ and the Holy Spirit. When men ask how God saves, the Christian responds "by faith" because faith is the *sine qua non*, the heart of the covenant by which God grants mercy to man. This covenant and salvation belong to God because they rest upon his gift in Jesus Christ, looking to the compassion of the Son who saves the unworthy. So men have faith as a foundation, a cornerstone upon which the whole stands and falls and the opening of communion between creatures and the creator. But brethren, though we could say so much about faith, though we could deliver homilies and hymns of praise, songs of wonder and thanks to God for faith, recall now that faith is not an end, not a goal, not the highest, not a terminus but a passage point. Man should not exert all the energy of his mind, heart, and strength upon faith as though it were the destination that God meant for him, as though all stopped with faith, as though man could and should isolate faith as a monarch over the spirit. God desires to know men and that men should know him, and men come to this only through faith, only by faith, only with faith and in submission to Jesus Christ, and through, by, and with nothing other than faith and in submission to none other than the Christ. As John writes in the beginning, "But to all who received him, who believed in his name, he gave power to become children of God, who were born, not of blood or of the will of the flesh or of the will of man, but of God." Men receive a new birth in faith so that they should mature in new life, growing as that faith gives them the power to become children of God. Faith presides at the beginning of this transformation and moves with man through it, but faith is not the transformation's end! John writes at the end of his Gospel that he has recorded the words and deeds of Christ "so that you may come to believe that Jesus is the Messiah, the Son of God, and that through believing you may have life in his name." To believe is the first and utmost necessity and one comes to life through belief, but yes, *through* belief! Belief must gird the Christian in confidence, trust, perseverance, fortitude, and hope, and faith accomplishes this girding to lead men through the trials to come, the struggles in which faith escorts men into the knowledge of God.

Why does Jesus assert that "Those who believe in me, even though they die, will live, and everyone who lives and believes in me will never die," laying the whole accent on belief as if it alone saves, asking his disciples, "Do you believe this?", when he also affirms that "the Father who sent me has himself given me a commandment about what to say and what to speak. And I know that his commandment is eternal life"? Does faith give one life though one dies, or does the commandment from God enliven the believer because it is eternal life? Do belief and the commandment stand opposed? To put the question in the language of the verses at hand, how is faith our victory and our salvation, the anchor and compass by which men overcome the world, when the one who says "I have come to know him" but disobeys the commandments is a liar, and "if anyone obeys his word, God's love is truly made complete in him"? One apparently comes to know God and loves in perfection by the commandments as much as if not more than by faith.

Man is saved as he is humbled into union with God through Jesus Christ. At the same time and as a consequence salvation restores and heals man's nature and strengthens the bond among and between men. Salvation re-creates man, insofar as pride has de-created him, so that through God's wisdom and power in Jesus Christ man should again take form as the creature with whom God enjoyed the original communion, upon whom God smiled in the unbroken pleasure of a Father with his children. This communion is a matter of both faith and obedience, without which man can neither come to know God nor love him perfectly.

The nature of man encompasses both the definition in which he dwells, the form of the body and the soul designed and unified by the creator, and the soul's freedom to choose toward or away from God. Freedom limits man's definition in the distance of choice, a distance in which freedom consummates itself by choosing humility. In this way freedom annuls its distance and reinforces man's law, so that freedom and law exist in mutual friendship and support one another. As the means of re-creating man in the Old Testament, command and sacrifice mirror his constitution as law and freedom. Just as freedom limits man's nature, sacrifice limits the reach of God's law; just as man's nature finds rest in freedom, the law finds rest in sacrifice. At least inasmuch as the means harmonize with man's nature, they appear well suited for covenanting him with God. Man bears the image of his creator: does this image not somehow involve the intertwining of law and freedom? God gave man the law and the sacrificial cult through Moses: does this set of ordinances expressing the divine will and good pleasure not guide man toward him? If the image of God and the form of the Old Testament law are not enough, the incarnation says much more. The Savior embodies both elements in their union, serving as both the highest and final sacrifice and the giver of the law, illustrating the peace between the two. He is additionally God in the form of man, God unified with the definition of man as soul and body and God with the freedom of man's will. When men look into the faithfulness of God, when they peer cautiously into the divine life, they should therefore not balk at finding the elements constitutive of man, law and freedom, within the Trinitarian existence—although one must use such language cautiously, recognizing the inadequacy of all attempts to speak of God and the necessity of respecting the divine ineffability.

God reveals himself in this way at the burning bush, whose mode of appearance indicates the middle role of freedom. When Moses sees the bush unconsumed, approaching in curiosity and wonder, he surveys the miracle of form persevering through death. Phenomenologically, he does not see the fire, which bears death and freedom from form, and then the bush, and lastly the fire again. Such a progression would imply the bush's perishing by the fire, its form a middle term lodged between two affirmations of death. No, Moses sees the bush, then the fire that engulfs it, and then the mystery of form affirmed despite and through the flames. The miracle requires that the form of the bush come at the beginning and the end with the death-moment in the middle, not unlike the crucifixion's placement between incarnation and resurrection. Thus God shows himself as he who exists through death, whose abiding transfigures death and freedom toward the renewed expression of life.

The faithfulness of God can refer to the full being of the Trinity, including the Father, Son, and Holy Spirit as they share in joy complete. It can point toward the passage through begetting and procession as well as the mutual life-giving, affirming in the *I am* that God will always remain He who moves through death into life, who is scattered in subordinate ways and an ultimate way before being gathered in subordinate ways and an ultimate way (the subordinate ways dealing with the scattering of law unto freedom and back to law within the persons, the ultimate way having to do with the scattering of the Father in the Son and Spirit unto their teleological union). God will always be this God because he always will exist and has existed in this fashion. For the being of God in the illumination from joy to joy complete hinges on the mystery of life-through-death and gathering-through-scattering. The faithfulness of God cannot not be what it is without and apart from this mystery.

This faithfulness has a preliminary and simple referent in the Father. Considered alone and as the origin of the Son and the Spirit (whereas there is no temporal "beforehand," no time when the Spirit or the Son were not) the Father abides. In this abiding he is faithful as he dwells in an integrity that consists of the unbroken harmony of being and law. The Father has a "law," a definition implicit within his being, to the extent at a minimum that men can call him "Father," that one can recognize this divine being as coherent, ordered, and at peace. To deny such a law to the Father, whatever philosophical questions and conundrums the acknowledgement of such a law might entail, would make him structureless and without form, one scattered rather than gathered in his being. May men never envision God the Father in this way! He has a law that says "Father," that makes his personhood recognizable and definitively present. The law implies the prescription that God ought to be in this way—personal, righteous, immutable, impervious—and finds its match and complement in the Father's actual existence in this way. The harmony between the two imbues the divine life with a peace and simplicity for which men lack words. Where law and abiding cohere, where they hold hands like dear friends, there is fullness and contentment, a rhythm that senses no lack and knows no harshness, no anxiety, no worry. There is "no darkness at all in God," as John writes with good reason, because the fundamental harmony within the divine life, the incomprehensible peace, is at once an immeasurable joy. What peace can abide apart from the harmony of things living as they ought to live? What peace does not spur upwards a great joy at the goodness of that which abides in this way? What joy is not simultaneously gentleness and compassion? God the Father is perfect harmony and thereby perfect peace, perfect peace and thereby perfect joy, perfect joy and thus perfect gentleness.

The Father's coherence as the Father, his abiding according to the law definitive of his singularity as origin, implies the limit of freedom. This limit is, at the very least, a space of non-abiding, a step away from the abiding and its temporary cessation. Yet as the limit that upholds and maintains the law, it is intrinsic to the law. Descriptions of the Father's nature or essence, if one wishes to use these terms, must include both elements, not conceiving the Father as an abstract freedom nor mere subsisting being. Each of these implies the other, and neither precedes the other. Together they express the divine personhood, together they say "Father." For the freedom is inevitably personal, revealed as *I am*.

The harmony within the Father does not abide in isolation from the Father's will but turns on it, for God cannot abide without willing to do so. In his freedom, the Father eternally affirms and governs his abiding in harmony with his law. In and through this freedom God announces his name as *I am*, as that which abides in eternity and immutably. One might ask in light of this announcement if it is possible for God not to be God, if the Father in his freedom could abdicate the harmony of his being and become something other than God. Certainly not! God the Father is always God and always will be. But if God will and must always be God, how is God the Father truly free? His choosing *I am* apparently cannot be a real choice because it does not issue from a substantive freedom (or so one might argue). How can men, then, affirm freedom for the Father? Because God the Father is not scattered but gathered. If God the Father had no freedom to limit his law, nor to gather his abiding according to the divine measure, then his being would lack coherence of person and be structureless, indefinite, a negative infinity, and without any power to beget the Son and have the Spirit proceed. Yet the Father does have such power and he does abide in order and peace, and therefore he must have freedom. This is the case regardless of how puzzling the Father's freedom seems to men.

From the harmony of the Father's abiding wells up the pressure, the joyful force that the Father feels as the inclination to life. "Let the Son be begotten! Let the Spirit proceed!" So says the joy of harmonious being implicit in the Father's abiding. Though he apprehends this pressure its weight remains ever gentle, ever tender. Never does this pressure become the infinite as fallen men experience it, never is it harsh, impersonal, draconian, tyrannical, savage, and cruel. It leans upon the will of the Father like the disciple who reclined upon the Lord, like one at rest in the presence of his master. This pressure is, as it were, the abiding's transition into freedom, its fade into stillness. Turning toward and delving into freedom, the abiding acknowledges its limit and supplicates it. The abiding meets with the Father's freedom such that the freedom at first retains the upper hand and rules in the affair, as though the servant had met his superior. The joy of the Father's being implies within it the request for more, the desire for new life, but it submits to the fact that even perfect abiding cannot eventuate in new life if it abstracts away from will and freedom. Only the divine will can bring about the mystery of life-through-death; its faith in the power of the abiding is the locus of this mystery. The affair thus involves a mutual respect and sharing of place between the abiding and the free will. For all its exuberance, the joy that exerts pressure on the Father stops short as tied to the abiding while the will takes up the request with magnanimity.

I say again: when the law passes the request for life to the Father's freedom for blessing and furtherance, holding back its hand and awaiting the response, the abiding and the joyful inclination along with the law come to rest. Steady in quiet and anticipation, stilled in the hope of a life to be given through freedom, they turn the bestowal of life over to the Father's liberty as their necessary co-worker. The law scatters from its nature as work, somehow dividing itself from its nature and temporarily becoming what it is not as a work at rest. Now the task begun in the law belongs to freedom, now the movement toward life transitions through scattering and death. Freedom is the undefined, the mystery that some would call darkness, the incomprehensible and unknown. In God this indefinition points to definition, it facilitates the work of life by dying to itself, it provides a rest sufficient for the abiding to bloom.

Having received the request for life from the abiding of his being, the freedom of the Father obliges by humbling itself into the abiding. The distance of freedom that provided rest for the law's growth toward life draws closer and closer into the abiding, until the freedom is submerged in the original harmony. Thus freedom is fulfilled in the Yes to life, a Yes in which it annuls its distance and thereby its own existence. This fulfillment reverses the relationship found at first, in which the law looked to freedom as a servant to its master, granting freedom the upper hand due to it. In possession of the request, the freedom of the Father acts upon its faith by cutting itself off, recognizing that only the abiding has the power to absorb death. That which was higher becomes lower, with freedom submitting to the law in the pursuit of life. The mystery of gathering-through-scattering requires the contribution of both elements, of the law first humbled before and limited by freedom and the freedom that gives up its place for the furtherance of law and life. The law possessed the power of life all along but only as it temporarily gives up this power to freedom; the latter, not puffed up with pride, responds toward life by similarly handing over its priority and bowing back into the law. This dual humility and mutual support surround the mystery in which the unalterable alters and yet remains unalterable, in which origination within and from the origin's being does not change the origin, in which the transcendence of God's being becomes partially manifest before the puny minds of men. God the Father has borne the means of death in the movement from the deity's initial joy, a somehow lower joy, toward the finality of joy complete.

It is not that the Father wills to actually die (as if such a thing were possible), but that in blessing the inclination toward life in which he abides the Father accepts the cessation of his singularity and his independence, and his way of being inasmuch as defined by these, to the extent that he accepts the begetting of the Son and the procession of the Spirit. The Father descends, we know not how, dividing from his way of being in a manner that transcends men's understanding but leaves us in awe of his humility. He lowers the divine nature before the promise of life and for the sake of life in a great act of faith. In his freedom, the Father believes that the harmonious abiding at the core of his being can withstand the infinite, that the abiding possesses the mysterious power of life that overcomes all scattering, all cessation, all division. The Father believes that he can descend in this way and persevere as an immutable and unchanging person. For this reason he performs the double annulment, humbling both his freedom into the abiding and his nature into the scattering unto new persons in the confidence that his life will continue unabated, even prospering beyond the passage point.

Out of this comes the annulment of the Father's nature in its singularity, the scattering and diversification of the Father toward a new gathering, the miracle of the divine form congealed and celebrated in the Son and the Spirit. On the one hand the begetting of the Son, a mystery surpassing man's understanding and propelled by joy. On the other, the procession of the Spirit, another mystery distinct from the begetting and aimed toward perfecting the Trinitarian form. These two abide just as the Father, who continues to abide in perfect harmony with the law of his being. Yet now the Father abides in the unanimity of being with the Son and the Spirit. Each of these three exists as a perfect life while sharing one life, one essence; indivisible, inseparable, and yet unmistakable in their distinction, the three share in a harmony that repeats and augments the preliminary harmony of the Father with its peace and joy. For now not one but three exist, each in perfect harmony with its nature, each willing that nature, and each at peace in its nature and thereby with the others, each basking in the joy that permeates its nature as well as that of the others, each gentle and warm toward the others. All along these three were not three but one while also one-in-three, a multiple unity born out of the Father.

Like the bush that endured the means of death without succumbing to them, the flames leaping over leaves and branches unconsumed, so that the sight struck Moses with wonder and compelled him to turn and investigate; and as the Father announced his name from this would-be dissolution, this mystery of perdurance, as *I am*; so in the Trinitarian illumination the Father endures the infinite unscathed and absorbs into his abiding what should amount to death. The Jerusalem Church in Acts provides a creaturely image: suffering persecution as a catalyst for its spread to Judea and Samaria, bearing the infinite pressure meant to squelch the gospel and that cast it into neighboring regions, from this scattering new churches emerge, communities who receive the good news of Jesus and exhibit a similar willingness to suffer. The Jerusalem church withstood the scattering but did not die and its scattering planted the seeds of new churches and new life. Although the Father does not experience the infinite as persecution or a paradoxical "tyranny of joy," nor does he become less in begetting the Son and as the Spirit proceeds, he accepts the joy of his being willingly, bestows life willingly, and so submits willingly to a kind of scattering. The abdication of his way of being, an act incomprehensible to men, eventuates in the other persons of the Trinity, begetting the Son and proceeding in the Spirit. The church that abides in the Spirit and life of God on earth replicates, according to its nature and in its own fashion, the mystery of the divine life as the Father assents to the life of the other persons.

The plan of the Father for men replicates the unity within the Trinity as a model, gathering them with one another and all things in Jesus Christ. Speaking of Christians, Saint Paul writes that God the Father "chose us in Christ before the foundation of the world to be holy and blameless before him in love. He destined us for adoption as his children through Jesus Christ, according to the good pleasure of his will... with all wisdom and insight he has made known to us the mystery of his will, according to his good pleasure that he set forth in Christ, as a plan for the fullness of time to gather up all things in him, things in heaven and things on earth." For this end Christians have "been destined according to the purpose of him who accomplishes all things according to his counsel and will, so that we, who were the first to set our hope on Christ, might live for the praise of his glory."

Saint Paul expounds on God's plan to gather all things in Christ and the Christian's part in that plan, with believers conformed to the providential good pleasure of God as his will guides things to their predetermined end, with such certainty that one can ask if faith and effort matter in the quest for salvation. Does not all rest on God's action? Does he not choose believers before the foundation of the world? Does he not destine them for adoption through Christ Jesus? Does the Father not position them according to his purpose, aligning them with his plan for the fullness of time? If so, what is left to man with respect to effort, to freedom, to conscience and the struggle for virtue? What of his path toward *theosis*, his working out his salvation with fear and trembling? Even what faith is left to him if God controls all universally, ineluctably, and insuperably?

God does order all things according to his will, he does align all things according to his purpose, and his providence directs the course of history in ways that men neither see nor comprehend. His guidance does culminate in gathering all things in Christ, a gathering that begins with men as formed into one people, the church. In this sense men do fall into the plan of God, fitting together as so many puzzle pieces within the divine plan, submitting to the Father's will as an overriding mandate for human affairs. Yet this submission does not destroy man's effort, freedom of will, the struggle of conscience, the striving for virtue and control of the passions, nor does it deny that men must work out their salvation. God does not snatch the fate of each man out of his hands and hide it in the heavens, as if the destinies of peoples and individual men belonged to a clandestine and shadow-dwelling deity. God controls history because it is his just as the creation is his, but he does not rule with a ubiquitous, irresistible, and unqualified providence, nor does the certainty of his plan obliterate the freedom of man but requires it.

How can God control and direct history to his preferred end, the gathering of all things in Christ, and also allow that men have freedom? Such freedom, it seems, is illusory at best and a bald deception at worst. In response, look again to the Father who says *I am*, affirming that he will always be as he is, while also retaining an eternally substantive freedom. God can affirm both the apparent predetermining of *I am* and the freedom because if he were not free, then the uninterrupted and universal character of his law, coupled with his abiding according to it, would undermine and eventually shatter its own integrity by prohibiting rest within the divine being. The Father would be scattered and no longer be Father in the way Christians understand, nor would he be able to beget the Son and have the Spirit proceed. Freedom limits the Father's law so that *I am* implies coherence rather than chaos. The same reasoning applies to the plan of God with respect to men. If the Father imposed the mystery of his will upon men unremittingly, encompassing all eras and regions as an exceptionless inevitability so that men acted as automatons or machines moving lifelessly from one item to the next, synchronizing perfectly in their coordinated activities, this infinite law would not gather but divide. In the single-mindedness of their manner men would relinquish all soul, all humility, all fellow-feeling, and all desire for the neighbor's company. They would endure life as a bane managed by a merciless and all-seeing despot, themselves deprived of the love and compassion that binds man to man. Such men would consist in the task and only the task, and in this way each would forego knowledge of his brothers.

What would become of the church in such a situation? Could anyone call "gathered" men brought together under the pressure of duties comparable to the slaves in Egypt? Men might be unified in a strange and secondary way by their suffering, as indeed they all suffer, but consider the attitude engendered by the infinite as it fills man's heart. The will of God conquers and crushes him, permeating him everywhere and without intermission, and while he can experience this presence as fear, dread, and the nearness of judgment, at other times he perceives that God has seized and possessed him for a particular purpose and task. He sets about this restless task with the knowledge that he belongs fully to God and that God has marked him for this work, a knowledge that naturally lends him to contempt toward his fellows. "Has God so marked them? Has he raised them up from among others to accomplish his desires as he has done for me?" Thus could such a man speak, proud in the confidence that the Holy Spirit moves in and through him. Convinced that God has elected him for grace, such a man easily rises above nature's limit and presumes to judge others, placing himself and his ilk on the side of the saved while his adversaries, the sluggish, backwards, and falsely content, he places on the side of the lost until his thought rolls to its conclusion and schism burns down the whole. Men divided in heart and mind divide also in body and society, abdicating mutual space and fraternity. Does Docetism not illustrate this trajectory especially in Protestantism, which has collapsed under the hidden infinitude of justification by faith alone? The shattering of the church testifies to false doctrine! If men abandon their freedom to preserve the power, providence, and freedom of God, they simultaneously invite the slow dissolution of the same church that God meant as a first and principle witness to his intent to gather all things in his love.

Men must have a substantive freedom lest God's plan to gather them in Christ contradict itself and devolve into nonsense. If they possess this freedom, a merciful God gathers them in. Men cannot say how God's providence and man's liberty work together for salvation and over the ages, and they can only affirm that God plays the decisive role and man's effort the lesser one. We affirm this mystery with bold confidence in the goodness of God who shapes us, content that much lies beyond man's knowing. On the other hand, if men possess no meaningful freedom in matters of salvation and of history, then God coerces them through a universal and tyrannical law, crushing their finitude beneath the infinite weight until they are severed within their natures and from one another. In this case men must sadly acknowledge that God wills not to gather but to scatter, leaving them suspicious, lonely, and spiritually barren.

If men do not come to God as machines or robots, if the law that would draw them as though they were such amounts to scattering and de-naturing, if they consequently have freedom with respect to God and the natural law, then when men ask how they come to know and be known by God they can speak of faith and works, of worship and obedience, and of sacrifice and commandment as the latter appeal in greater or lesser ways to the freedom and law constitutive of man's nature. These two categories do not sharply and strictly divide and still less do they oppose one another. The two elements, man's natural law (as definition) and his freedom underlie commandment and sacrifice and the divergence between the latter pair arises as one or the other of these elements receives the stress. The relationship between law and faith in this instance resembles Greek words whose accent shifts when the case changes. *'O ánthropos* becomes *tou anthrópou* in the change from the nominative to the genitive but the word remains the same, "man." So faith and works, sacrifice and obedience share the same root in God and his desire for communion with men. The accent shifts, sometimes subtly, in the life of the believer but the overlap between sacrifice and law does not fully disappear. At this point man should nonetheless remember that the analogy is not perfect, that the priority always belongs to faith inasmuch as faith or its lack determines the character of the work as good or evil.

The two elements constitutive of faith and works are man's exertion and the cry to God for mercy. Both worship and obedience consist in these two in some proportion, while it is useless to try to exactly distinguish the composition of either faith or works when considering these two elements. One can say in general that faith, sacrifice, and worship accent the cry to God for mercy over man's exertion whereas works, law, and obedience, leave a greater place for man's efforts. Consider for now the act of faith as sacrifice. When men bring their sacrifices to God, humbling their natures before God's altar, they do the bringing and the humbling. Man's effort gives his possessions, whether his livestock as in the Old Testament or his alms as in the Christian era, yet the act of bringing and giving shrinks before their meaning. When man offers the sacrifice his work means that he places no confidence in his works, that he grasps their insufficiency. The work annuls itself inasmuch as it means directly that the believer gives up confidence in his own doing, despite that doing's necessity, and calls upon his maker for compassion. Salvation, says the sacrifice, belongs in the hand of the Lord.

The ten commandments require much: do not have other gods before the Lord; make no graven image; take not the Lord's name in vain; observe the Sabbath rest; honor thy father and mother; do not murder; do not commit adultery; do not steal; do not bear false witness; do not covet. Not one of these mandates in a direct and unqualified way that men call upon God. Not one says "abandon trust in your contribution and call upon me as the keeper of salvation." The commands do not have this quality because they accent the "do" or "do not," directing the believer to his action. Sacrifice, by contrast, points the believer away from his contribution as its overriding concern. The believer gives his sacrifice, his exertion, as a means to the cry for mercy. The cry, if he gives the sacrifice properly, swallows up this exertion's significance *qua* exertion while retaining its necessity.

If man exerts his nature as a means to the cry for mercy in sacrifice, it might appear that the inverse holds for law and obedience. Man comes to God and says, like the rich young man, "What must I do to receive mercy and be saved?" Man then receives the command to exert his nature, to live within his boundaries and cleanse his mind and heart, to battle his passions. He cries out for mercy as a means to receiving the commandments so that he can then work out his salvation in fear and trembling. But this is not the whole story. In performing the act of obedience man still cries out to God for mercy: his exertion is humility before the God he serves; he calls upon this

God to aid him in obedience, blessing him with the strength he lacks due to sin; and most importantly, man's obedience occurs with the knowledge that salvation belongs principally and essentially to God's mercy and therefore within the ambit of faith. This recognition reduces man's exertion to a figurative nothingness in his own eyes, adding to the humiliating character of his obedience. The suggestion that man's effort does not imply the cry for mercy, on the other hand, founds that effort in the pride that man can construct his salvation with his own powers. An effort of this sort is necessarily infinite, without faith or rest, ending in the idolatry of misplaced sacrifice.

Obedience and sacrifice cohere as points along a continuum of increasing values defined simultaneously in terms of works and faith. Faith defines the continuum because all along man trusts in the power and wisdom of God shown forth in the mystery of Christ Jesus and poured into believers in the Holy Spirit. Faith in the Savior delivers from death and promises union with the Lord: God "made us alive together with Christ . . . for by grace you have been saved through faith, and this is not your own doing; it is the gift of God—not the result of works, so that no one may boast. For we are what he has made us, created in Christ Jesus for good works, which God prepared beforehand to be our way of life." Grounded in faith, the continuum is also of works because man must exercise his faith lest it be formless and therefore meaningless. Any man who says "I believe in Jesus Christ and his resurrection"—that is, that he believes in the gathering beyond scattering—but who has not taken on the work of scattering, of divorcing his mind, heart, and strength from the pride of the world, the desire of the eyes, and the rule of sin deludes himself. Faith always necessitates and consists in the work that brings it to life, and as faith without works is dead, so the continuum of faith is one of works.

On this continuum obedience lies at a lesser point where man's exertion stands without direct annulment. God says "Do" and man does, though he does in the hope that God will judge him mercifully. In obedience man is humble, contrite, and submissive before the limits of his God-given nature and the commands of the divine law. Sacrifice occurs at a more developed point where man's exertion undergoes full annulment. God says "Do" but the doing-as-sacrifice effectively cancels the doing so that only the cry for mercy and the humiliated heart remain. Mystery and cloudiness, however, surround the distinction that might appear so tidy. Is obedience to limit not, after all, a kind of sacrifice? Does one not already give oneself over to God? Does sacrifice, on the contrary, not imply obedience and a recognition of one's limits? To ponder such a continuum and say "here is obedience and only obedience, and there is sacrifice and only sacrifice" is foolishness because the two always coexist and imply one another, collaborating to some degree. The subject demands acknowledgement of the vague, undefined, and mysterious, and comfort with what men cannot grasp. Man might call one point "obedience" and another one "sacrifice," but the transition between the two mystifies him and he cannot determine a precise shift from one to the other.

The law has a strangely self-annulling character that lowers it into faith like a casket into the earth. Conceived in the light of faith, the law progresses from humility before man's limit (obedience) to raising the neighbor's interest before one's own and serving him (love) to the handing over of one's life for God and neighbor (after the fall, martyrdom as sacrifice), although one should not draw strict distinctions between any of these stages along the law's progress. The annulment occurs in that the death of the body means the destruction of the limit that the original obedience was supposed to preserve. The man of God ends by destroying the body that was an early guide into the knowledge of God (a destruction of man's lower, bodily nature in the service of his higher nature, the soul, and looking to the promise of a new body). This self-annulling character of the law also appears in commands that contradict each other on the surface: "honor thy father and mother" in the Old Testament matures into "anyone who does not hate father and mother, brother and sister, wife and children is not worthy of me" in the New, and "an eye for an eye, a tooth for a tooth" matures into "turn the other cheek." These passages reflect the maturation of obedience to man's God-given and lawful limits into the all-giving of sacrifice.

Exactly how the law travels the path into annulment I cannot say, although it must travel this path in faith or it never comes to the sacrifice. Or what is the same in the latter case, the law comes to the wrong sacrifice. "Through the law I died to the law" Paul writes because the law shows man his sin but lacks the power to save him from it. The evangelical Protestant version of Docetism sees this passage in light of the law's growth to the infinite and proclaims, "This law is a tyrant! It is boundless and cruel and reduces me to nothing!" The infinite severity of this law casts man onto Christ, compelling him to the freedom in which he gives up the last ounce of hope in works and nature so that he can say that "it is no longer I who live, but it is Christ within me." Confident in his reasoning, this docetist claims not to "nullify the grace of God; for if justification comes through the law, then Christ died for nothing." He fails to perceive that the players in his spiritual drama are an infinite law and an infinite freedom, nor does he see that in infinitizing both he has critically misunderstood their relation and brought both to a bad end. His infinite law lands in infinite freedom and thus the dissolution of law. "Through the law" he dies to the law because he walks in faithlessness instead of faith. Faith does not deform and destroy; it preserves law and freedom in mercy. Setting aside for a moment the reality of committed sins—though this reality is secondary so long as an infinite law sets upon a finite man, for such a law causes him terror and proves him sinful whether he acts against it or not, his very finitude constituting a sin against it—how does one die to the law and come to faith "through the law"? How does the law, more specifically, die to itself in order to make room for freedom and faith? Here Christians should consider not a boundless and oppressive law but a gentle and humble one, a law that progresses quietly into sacrifice inasmuch as, while commanding the believer to lower his nature before others, the law is also lowered, also humbled away from its own commands and into God's mystery.

The law culminates in sacrifice, works reach their end in the testimony of faith, obedience is consummated in worship not because the law transgresses all limits, advancing beyond all that would restrain it, becoming the infinite. The law comes to sacrifice because of its gentleness and mercy, just as the abiding of God joyfully transitions toward his freedom. "If justification comes through the law, then Christ died for nothing"—indeed! "For if a law had been given that could make alive, then righteousness would indeed come through the law"—yes! Apart from the consideration of sin, the Christian affirms these because the law leads of its own nature toward the faith that saves, the faith that upholds the law inasmuch as it affirms the law's limit.

Obedience allows man some integrity with respect to the law and his exertion, whereas faith exists at the point of the law's annulment and thus when the law and man's effort have relinquished this integrity. Faith abides in the freedom of the law's annulment not as a force contrary to the law but as its temporary end. For freedom and faith, though they abide as rest from the law, exist in order to hand over their abiding to the law that came to rest in them. In faith, the infinite in man appeals to the infinite in God and this appeal is freedom's annulment of the annulment of law, its drawing of itself back into the law and effort that had apparently died. Faith accomplishes this because through it God gives man a new life drawn from the divine immortality. Faith thus seeks the power of the abiding that traverses death unto new life. Through faith, the law, man's effort, and the striving in fear and trembling arise as those broken free from the casket, forever transformed by God's life-giving.

The conversion of man to God begins in a law that leads to faith, although fallen man should not consider this apart from the experience of sin. Just as God commanded the people of Israel to rest, ordering them to remember the sources of that rest alternately in the rest of God at the creation and his liberation of the people from slavery in Egypt, the converted mind and heart draws upon two sources as it approaches the rest of faith: the gentle joy of the law natural and divine and the infinite pressure that accompanies the recognition of sin. Through these two experiential sources—and working in them, the miraculous, praiseworthy, and mysterious action of the Holy Spirit—man grows toward the new birth in baptism, toward the wonder of faith.

Conversion to God and the new life always presumes faith in the goodness and mercy of God. Without this faith, miniscule as it may be as man begins his walk, he does not exert the effort needed to know God and love him perfectly, nor does man come to know his own nature. In its least mature moments this faith might misidentify God by worshipping the wrong deity or magnifying nature or "that which is," so deeply rooted is this conviction within human nature and so subject to perversion as man thinks consciously upon it. For good reason St. Paul writes that "ever since the creation of the world" the eternal power and divine nature of God, "invisible though they are, have been understood and seen through the things he has made." Confidence in the goodness of what is, a trust in the bounty of nature and in its rhythms, is a preliminary and tacit, often unrecognized knowledge that a faithful God has fashioned the natural order and man within it. Man must first address nature and say "this is good" in his heart, a conviction that floods over him as he considers the majestic harmony of the world. The joy of this statement, a consequence of the joy of God in which all creation abides, leads him to the faithfulness of the one who designed and apportioned its beauty.

Recognition of natural beauty implies recognition of the natural law, but man must rightly comprehend this law if he should benefit from it. In his innermost heart, the unspoken disposition and attitude that weigh upon his will and shape the moral quality of his life, he must believe that he is a creature of nature, that he is subordinate to its law and, inasmuch as he abides according to nature, that it prescribes the limits of that abiding, determining his habits and sealing him in givenness. Man must understand that, although God seated him higher than all the animals and honored him with dominion, his place belongs within the natural order rather than outside it. Man is therefore a limited creature belonging to a world not of his making and subject to its hardships, its cadences and tempos, as well as benefiting from its mercies. Docetism has labored tirelessly to eradicate this disposition and ridicule its way of thinking as absurd, backwards, and useless. It deceives men into thinking that they have no limits and that natural limit is oppression, that the natural world and his own nature are fundamentally a formless freedom, and that he properly resides as one afloat from nature rather than grounded within it. Docetism has constructed an alternative nature with an alternative norm, a new world in which its assumptions seem indubitably true, in which man's inward disposition transforms without his awareness. Some docetists openly mock natural limits of any kind, others falsely believe that they remain natural and God-fearing while their political and cultural adversaries do not, and by far the majority give no thought to their anthropological bearings, assuming that the docetic life ready-made for them is right and veracious because it is all they have known. It is among docetic man's greatest challenges to see that he is no longer a creature of nature, that in virtually every aspect of his way of being the ground has shifted so subtly and fully that he now simultaneously walks on air and drowns, gasping for it. His mind must retrieve the knowledge once innate and now apprehended as void so that his thinking admits consciously and his heart carries silently his belonging to God and nature. Then, as a man within nature, is he humbled beneath its law as God's.

With such thoughts and their faith as preconditions man experiences the natural aspect of the law. By this experience he understands that the antithesis of technological society/nature, or infinite law/infinite freedom, distorts the harmony of law and freedom regnant within nature itself, presenting nature as though it were escape and total liberation. Nature is limit, harmony, rhythm, and man within nature, subordinate to it and content with his lot, is also limit, harmony, and rhythm as a natural creature, conformed to the seasons, to geography, and to social obligations dictated by birth. Man corralled in an automobile cannot know the natural law, man imprisoned in artificial heat and cool air dwells in pride against that law, man incarcerated in airplanes obliterates his bodily statutes, and man enveloped by screens, the sad and tortuous figure of humanity adrift and angered, has died to natural ways of being. Man cannot abandon the experience of natural law without eventually abandoning the law as a whole. Abdication of the lived form destroys the moral content. Men of nature, on the other hand, everywhere apprehend their finitude and the necessity of accommodating that finitude to the natural world. Knowing that he cannot plant his crops at any time of year, the farmer follows the seasons and the weather in order to gauge the correct time. He knows the earth's habits because he abides by them, taking daily care of the crop until it bears fruit, tending it for 45, 60, or 90 days until the plant is ripe. The knowledge of natural law as man lives it means humility before patterns and regularities that are dependable but not precise, and with this humility comes discipline and patience to engage nature on its terms. Man does not seek to exploit, despoil, or abuse nature but to learn and gather from it, just as he is lowered within it rather than being puffed up above it.

"Thou shalt not murder, thou shalt not commit adultery, thou shalt not steal." Underneath these and other commandments that compose the moral law stands the ontological assertion of limit. Why should men not murder, commit adultery, or steal? Because these actions imply that man has exceeded his God-given limit, that he has cast off the obligations and emoluments of natural existence in the pursuit of higher station or illicit satisfaction, elevating himself above his being. The men who pursued these sins prior to Docetism and without its aid were far more likely to feel the inward sting of the law to the extent that they and their society had not lifted off like a rocket from natural mores. Advanced docetic man hardly feels the sting, so thoroughly has Docetism removed him in thought and experience from the natural *habitus*. His religion of darkness has progressed until he calls murder, adultery, and theft by other names, deceiving himself by varied and ingenious twists of logic. For the law's commands enunciate and specify limits woven into natural existence, and when that existence has fallen into disrepair the commandments cease to carry weight. As incitements to and reminders of form, they crash down upon formless man as so many burdens, as intolerable and ripe for revolt.

Natural institutions embody the ethos of the natural law by limiting men within their boundaries. The kingdom, the family, the farm, and the military (in garrison and in defense) all represent the natural order when properly understood. One can distinguish natural institutions from the unnatural and docetic by posing the question of limit: does this institution, in the form and organization being considered, affirm the finitude of man? Does it discipline and humble him while providing him respect and rest? Does the political institution in particular limit man at the same time that, aberrant personalities aside, it limits its own reach into his life? Or does the institution seduce man toward the infinite, toward excess, lasciviousness, and uncontrolled passions? Does the political institution compel man toward the conviction that he deserves more and to covetousness, and from there to revolution? Does the institution bear down upon him like a magnificent stone, pulverizing his spirit and tormenting him with restlessness? Or does it expand into meaninglessness as subject to man's desires, stripped of definition by men who require everything from it? Does the institution descend into limitlessness by failing to limit its prerogatives? In sum, does the institution lower man before and within nature or does it raise him up in pride? The natural institution bestows a lot upon man and commands him to find contentment in it, just as it is disciplined to remain within its own constraints. The unnatural, infinitized institution foments man's anger until he casts off his lot and puffs up into the universal, just as that institution becomes universal in order to support its man. This becoming, for man and institution, entails the destruction of the boundaries in which each is blessed according to God's order. Universality is therefore finally unhappiness despite its appearances to the contrary, ending in the will to conquer others rather than the will to peace.

Natural marriage takes care to gather man up within its impositions, announcing that he has a duty to genealogy, that he belongs to a line of fathers and mothers and that he must take his place in that line. His vows thus bind him to the woman who joins his life and flesh, binding him to her people and his, to the land that they share, and above all to the name. It is unthinkable that man should strike out on his own or reject the name handed on to him. He carries that name as the tradition of the fathers, furthering the line through the children whom he sires for its sake. Such joy, this obligation of children! Such wonder and delight delivered to men through nature, that they should facilitate life and find warmth in youth! Man fathers a child and knows that life continues after him, that the blessing shall outlive his short time in the world, that his natural home is the fulfillment of this blessing. He has little choice in this matter so long as he stays within the natural realm. He produces children as an obligation that gives contentment and rest, until at the end of life he looks down at the little ones on his knees, joyful in his years, and is at last laid down with his ancestors.

Docetic marriage disembeds man from nature's impositions and subordinates nature's requirements to his lack of boundary. At Docetism's most developed stage, man approaches marriage in total liberation from his body. He has forgotten history and rejects the obligations of genealogy as well as his duty to life. Given his self-conception as free and unrestrained, his desire governs his engagement in the institution, which cowers before his autonomy. The institution and the relationships implied in it exist so that he should better craft his life according to his demands. He chooses whom he shall marry by emotion and taste; he selects vows that determine his bonds to his partner rather than receiving these from the tradition; he allows his partner reign over her life as if she did not belong to him and he to her; he regards children as entirely distinct from marriage, envisioning their arrival at the time and circumstances of his choosing. He views children as if they must fit into his life plan rather than lowering his agenda before the necessities of bodily existence. Everywhere that the man of advanced Docetism looks, he sees others put to his service. He takes a wife so that she will enrich his life, he has children so that they will make him happy. If they cease to do this, if he finds life too grand a struggle and that fortune has pierced him and his family with cruelty, he feels a powerful temptation to leave. The institution is often too attenuated, too feckless to compel obedience to it in light of his difficulties.

All sides within Western society belong more or less to the docetic way and to the institutional arrangements it implies. They agree fundamentally that man is free and unwittingly that man is limitless, and their traditions teach that marriage belongs to man rather than man to marriage. It is no wonder that the institution has eroded under the burdens that men place upon it, surrendering its last boundaries to forces that disdain it.

Docetic institutions generally abhor the idea of sacrifice, for how can a man sacrifice himself when his goals center upon his pre-eminence before and above others? How will he give up his freedom when it is the *sine qua non* of his existence? For this reason Docetism reserves sacrifice for very special cases and not for the mass of men, whom it swallows in indifferentiation and indifference. Not so natural institutions, which build various forms of sacrifice into their ethos and assumptions. After the fall, the limited man might need to make the sacrifice for land, kin, and kingdom, and in this way affirm their worth and attempt to prolong their blessing. With respect to all three the soldier gives the sacrifice of defense so that others might endure, carrying on the name, the history, and the solidarity of his people. His death reminds the populace and their rulers of what is highest, humbling noble minds before the bodily sacrifice that makes the present life possible. In this way that sacrifice guards against despotism and the infinite. When kings, princes, and rulers remember the sacrifice of the soldier, they should recall that the kingdom of governors and governed precedes and will outlast them. They should recognize, as in natural marriage, that they belong to a lineage and a collective whose soul encompasses and supersedes the here and now as well as the current generation. The virtuous among the high and low recall the sacrifice with gratitude for what they have been given, the gifts bestowed prior to their asking. These sacrifices and their memory reckon that each man must face his limit and dwell within it, that the tyranny of the high and the low lies beyond these limits, and that the duty of rulers especially is to retain the limited character of governance by bridling their wills and protecting the commoner. The death of the soldier pleads that land, kin, and kingdom should be worth dying for and that memory should not die, for with the memory of sacrifice comes humility before what has been given.

Ensconced within the *mores* of natural institutions man feels the obligation that presses gently upon him. He also finds that he does not meet the criteria of his natural limits, that he is imperfect. In terms of the divine law man discovers that he sins against his nature. In politics he lusts for power, among his neighbors he covets greater possessions and honor, and in his home he is tempted to mistreat wife and children. He struggles for the mean of virtue and often fails, a shortcoming that leads him to meditate upon the weakness of his will to the good and the ubiquity of his faults. He might then ask where he should turn for aid in his striving or seek a power that offers him salvation from his passions and their empty promises. What can show him the way to beatitude and to victory over his troubles? Such questions could lead him from the natural toward the divine law, the law of Christ. More often than not men do not ask such questions, nor do they experience the natural law as distilled from the divine, as if in the first phase of life they knew only the natural law and later came into contact with God's revelation in Jesus Christ. The latter is the experience of some. Others come under the tutelage of the law as natural and divine early and at once, as children baptized at birth by their parents, who in their submission of the child to God fuse the natural and the divine for the salvation of their little ones. The experience of one law and the other varies with era and circumstances, but both laws in their gentleness are necessary to man's coming to faith.

Although men fight valiantly for virtue and in some cases seem to achieve it, how can they truly achieve life according to nature without obeying the God who fashioned it? Man's coming before God introduces him to a new way of seeing the world and to the spiritual consequences of his actions. Formerly man knew the rational soul as the ruler of the appetites and of the body. The Christian perspective retains these qualities and adds the soul's destiny as union with Christ. Now love, which transcends but does not contradict self-control, is man's object and he looks to eternity as his resting place. With the divine law man acknowledges the soul's judgment by the Lord who wills to gather all under his headship, and man sees the outcome of his choices not only as virtue and happiness or vice and malcontent on earth, but also reckons that his thoughts, words, and deeds will locate him among the blessed in the new age, wherein the soul receives its new body, or curse him with torment. Man understands the history of peoples, kings, and empires, of achievements, glories, and war, of tragedies and horrors as bound up within the will of God, whose providence chose the Jews as his people before opening his hand to all men in the church. Man sees the moral quality of his existence and his eternal end through the lens of the incarnate one, Jesus Christ crucified and resurrected, who died so that men might receive life.

Like the natural law, man must experience the divine law in order to grasp its implications. In its fullest and most direct form, Christian worship is this experience. One must guard here against the docetic assumption that any and all worship that says "Jesus Christ" counts as Christian worship, as if that worship could digest an infinite number of forms without vomiting them out. Just as heresy means the subtle perversion of the doctrine of Jesus Christ to painful and destructive ends, even to schism, all the while claiming his name as exalted and glorified, so false worship proclaims the name of Jesus Christ while it puffs men up in pride. This pride can take many forms: pride in doctrine, pride in tradition, pride in supremacy over other churches, pride in supposed social advances and civility, pride in wealth and institutional pomp, pride among the disadvantaged who exploit worship as hope for material gain, pride in ethnicity and nation, and perhaps the worst sort of pride, that which asserts that these worshippers are saved while others are doomed. These variants of pride slip in and despoil worship, swiveling its focus away from the humility of men before God and toward God's usefulness to man. True worship therefore begins in a submission of mind and heart not unlike man's submission to the natural law, in which he approaches God as a subordinate, recognizing God's goal of union with men as pre-eminent.

Man worships rightly when he has trained his mind into unity with his body and thereby orients his heart fully to God. Though he might not yet have joined the church, receiving baptism and the eucharist as one betrothed to Christ, this man arrives early to the liturgy in order to better learn the message of the Scriptures that Jesus Christ has risen from the dead, that the Savior has come to have mercy on mankind. Man hears this message week after week, over and over, until the reality of the resurrection fills him as the turning point of his existence, provoking a yearning to be part of God's gathering. This man comes to worship to plead for salvation through Jesus Christ and to receive power to resist temptation, power that sets him apart from pride and destruction, a grace that humbles him into love of neighbor. In the repetition of the gospel, of prayers and praises, of preaching and singing, of exposure to the mystery of God who brought man into the world, worshippers are conformed to worship. The liturgy weaves its way into the mind and the body, making a home for itself in the soul in order to teach man its ways and means. In this way the liturgy transforms the willing heart into a lover of God, a desirer of his plan of gathering, and a servant of his son our Savior and Lord.

Loving the God experienced in the liturgy requires obedience to the divine commands, living daily in light of grateful and humble thoughts, singing praises of wonder, and resisting temptations to harmful words and deeds. By the divine law men seek to find their limit, as in the natural order, and more than this, to descend beneath it into poverty of spirit. The natural law commands men to discern their limit and attain virtue by living according to it; the divine law recognizes the same limit and commands men to take on the mind of Christ, who, being equal with God, became a servant and humbled himself to death on a cross. In this manner the Christian according to divine law might see his nature in its equality with others, yet as Christ's slave and imitator he lowers himself, blotting out the memory of equality and eschewing all claims to it, and assumes the heart and air of a servant. In all thoughts he humbles his soul before God in prayer, in all deeds he loves God and the neighbor, in all words he remembers his sins and the condemnation they deserve, the various logs boring into his eyes, and he refuses to judge or condescend toward the one close to him. Shaped by the eternal love of God expressed in the liturgy as resurrection, the Christian struggles to live that resurrection as one battling his passions and fleshly addictions in order to better commune with God and others.

What evils confront him, what quicksand, a morass of habits and pleasures dragging him into darkness, so many demons lined in phalanxes, spears and swords drawn, helmets glimmering and eyes thirsting for war, ready to shed his blood and capture his soul! Everywhere man looks the heart faces its desires, every word is pride and arrogance, every thought disdain and haughtiness, his disposition presuming superiority, his will constantly giving in, unable to withdraw his nature from wickedness. For docetic man arguably more than his ancestors, the social world works in concert with the demonic so that its forces circumscribe his thought life and his bodily existence. He must dislodge his mind from the multitude of images that attack and fill it, from films, commercials, and television, these technologically-mediated thieves who replay in his thoughts as invaders he once and sorrowfully invited in. All kinds of false memories swim in his head: of lust, of perversion, of man's exaltation, of lewdness and distraction. All kinds of information concerns him: news from the planet, headlines that convince him that he is a universal man, that the whole world is his home, that his neighbor resides on continents afar; news here of trouble and aggression, there of disease and corruption, and again of scandal and turpitude; news broadcasting the private lives of others and holding them up for shame or adulation. He meditates on games, seasons, and competitions; on money, prowess, and material acquisition; on politics, ambition, and his hatred for those who disagree with him; on whatever might fill his mind. And what might not fill his mind? His mental world belongs to the possibilities of the material and the present until God and the soul fall among what is unnecessary and useless, until the ubiquity and vociferousness of the world's siren silences the summons of God to prayer and worship.

If violence and pleasure enslave the mind, of necessity they control the body. Contemporary docetic man believes in the eradication of violence in theory, searching with all his heart for a world in which no one suffers. He desires the end of all threat and punishment against the body, a world wherein no one hungers and no one thirsts, where none die for their crimes and children do not endure the rod. He is blind, he does not see: the desire that the body should live apart from all violence infinitizes the body against its nature and so brings it to death. All this pleasure, the docetic denial of contact with the nature created by God, man's avoidance of discomfort and his contempt for dis-ease, his demand that he satisfy his wants immediately and his lusts posthaste, slashes the body asunder with violence, hollowing its capacity for feeling. With the limitlessness that melts men down in the satisfaction of their wants comes as well the horrifying one, the man of limitless violence, the docetic destroyer destined to bring formlessness to its conclusion. Man is blind, he does not see: but were he convinced of the infinite's culmination in death and the need for repentance, would he humble himself before God? The seduction of the docetic world is so overpowering, its delusion so enrapturing and its deception so convincing, its aura of factuality and force of habit so impervious to resistance, that man can easily despair before it. From where shall he gain the strength to obey? How shall he conquer the lust and theft that reigns in his heart? How shall he cast out anger, malice, slander, sarcasm, and vengeance? How shall he come again to know his body, to sweat in the summer and feel the chill of winter, to work manually for his bread? How shall he come again to walk like a man, without machines and engines? How shall he fend off pride and remove the haughtiness that contains him like a straightjacket?

Through his repeated failure in controlling his thoughts and passions man grows toward an experience of the infinite at odds with the experience of the infinite in God. In the Father, the joy of the divine integrity pushes subtly and peacefully toward possibility and new life, toward the humility in which the Father's freedom says yes to begetting and procession and to the sharing of being. In man's descent from obedience into faith, considered as abstracted from sin, obedience to the law guides him gently into the humility of negation, in which works cease to be present apart from their annulment, leaving space for faith. In this space man's freedom turns to God and his neighbor so that he hands his life over to them. The third case differs dramatically from the prior two, for here man has sinned. Whereas the law would lead him gently into faith, his sin condemns man before the law. He thereby experiences the law's gentleness as the severest guilt and anxiety, as powerlessness and perdition. He strains under his burden, paralyzed by his turn away from God and his inability to correct it, quivering under the infinite pressure. "For we know that the law is spiritual," writes St. Paul, "but I am of the flesh, sold into slavery under sin. I do not understand my own actions. For I do not do what I want, but I do the very thing I hate. Now if I do what I do not want, I agree that the law is good. But in fact it is no longer I that do it, but sin that dwells within me. For I know that nothing good dwells within me, that is, in my flesh. I can will what is right, but I cannot do it. For I do not do the good I want, but the evil I do not want is what I do. Now if I do what I do not want, it is no longer I that do it, but the sin that dwells within me. So I find it to be a law that when I want to do what is good, evil lies close at hand. For I delight in the law of God in my inmost self, but I see in my members another law at war with the law of my mind, making me captive to the law of sin that dwells in my members. Wretched man that I am! Who will rescue me from this body of death?"

Man has faith that God gathers but he lacks the strength to make progress along the scattering implied in gathering. He believes but he can hardly bring his nature into concord with his belief. This causes him tremendous consternation and sorrow so that he turns to another power to aid him, a power that comes to him in and through Jesus Christ. For the Savior, who walked in obedience and apart from sin, moved through obedience to the limit of man (and so fulfilled the natural law) and further descended below that law, giving up the body as a sacrifice. He fulfilled the divine law in this manner, passing once and for all from the realm of bodily obedience into freedom, even death. "Yes," says Christ to the abdication of the lower, bodily law, "yes" to death as the passage point that he must traverse. When the law of the body has been annulled, therefore, as humbled before sacrifice and faith, handing its life over to freedom, the emphasis shifts. The freedom of Christ's divine nature receives, as it were, the appeal to renew bodily life, and this freedom appeals in turn to the divine integrity, the unconquerable essential being of God in Christ, and ultimately submits into its faithfulness. Freedom closes the gap as the "yes" in which the divine will and the divine faithfulness coalesce in harmony, with the power of their union flowing into the body that had died. What had scattered under death is reborn, gathered again unto eternal life and glorification with God. Men know of this effusion of power and the following revivification as the third day resurrection and the victory of God over the grave.

An echo of this power flows beyond the renewed body of Jesus Christ into the souls and bodies of those who call upon him in faith. Recognizing both the gentleness of the law and the infinite pressure of sin, those who come to Christ in penitence lower themselves after the model of the Savior. They will to sacrifice themselves in baptism, descending into burial with Christ so that they might rise with him as well. Baptism is a second, different kind of infinite. Whereas man first experiences the infinite pressure of sin, with the burden of inescapable habits, guilt, shame, and eternal perdition lying heavily on his conscience, in baptism he encounters the infinite as the freedom that bounds his works. In that freedom man is called to be faithful as he looks to his Savior. These forms of the infinite are involved whether men experience them for themselves as adults or whether others stand in as for infants. In both cases baptism is mystery and transformation, the bestowal of life to the sinner in Christ's name.

When the Christian ritually hands over his nature in the baptismal sacrifice, to that extent giving over his law, his effort is submerged in freedom. From this space man cries out to God, voicing the same appeal for life that the Son received regarding his human body. The Son again says "yes," closing the distance of the divine freedom from the divine faithfulness, and again their union pours forth power. The faithful man receives this power as strength of will and new birth, a life transformed in and through the Holy Spirit and bestowed through faith in distinction from works. For now, "apart from the law, the righteousness of God has been disclosed, and is attested by the law and the prophets, the righteousness of Jesus Christ for all who believe . . . they are now justified by his grace as a gift, through the redemption that is in Christ Jesus, whom God put forward as a sacrifice of atonement by his blood, effective through faith. He did this to show his righteousness, because in his divine forbearance he had passed over the sins previously committed; it was to prove at the present time that he himself is righteous and that he justifies the one who has faith in Jesus. Then what becomes of boasting?"—that is, boasting in one's obedience to the commands, and pride in one's supposed moral achievement—"It is excluded. By what law? By that of works? No, but by the law of faith. For we hold that a person is justified by faith apart from works prescribed by the law."

Faith gives the life that the law cannot give, handing the power of renewal down to man in the space of freedom. The law had lowered itself into this freedom, humbled by its inability to accomplish salvation and appealing to God's grace in the baptismal and eucharistic sacrifices; taking up the appeal, faith becomes singularly alive in freedom and the sacrifice, crying out to Jesus Christ for mercy; and the Christ, in giving the power of life to man in faith, facilitates the reciprocation in which faith returns to the law, in which man's freedom reproduces the law's humility by humbling itself in turn. Freedom is absorbed into the law as fortification, peace, and life, all manifest in the believer's obedience and gentleness of heart, while faith survives the absorption. For man knows that this new life, this peace and joy, this gratitude and confidence did not originate in him but in Jesus Christ in whom he has believed, whose sacrifice portends resurrection and union with God.

"If justification comes through the law, then Christ died for nothing," writes St. Paul. Justification does not come through the law: this means that justification comes principally in the moment of distinction, faith's mediation between the law that precedes and the law that follows. Just as the turning point in begetting and procession is the Father's freedom, which binds the integrity of the Father to life in the Son and the Spirit, so faith stands between fallen man's attempt to obey under sin and his regenerated obedience. If freedom, the space of faith and the intervening infinite, should collapse or be dismissed, if salvation hangs on the law as unmediated by faith and freedom, or if one neglects the new life received through these two, then Christ indeed died for nothing. "For if a law had been given that could make alive, then righteousness would indeed come through the law. But the Scripture has imprisoned all things under sin, so that what was promised through faith in Jesus Christ might be given to those who believe." For if a law had been given that might make alive: man cannot search for righteousness by the law alone inasmuch as the exclusion of faith and full confidence in works necessarily infinitize the commandment and orient it to death. Law without freedom is law without faith and vice versa, and the law as abstracted from freedom or faith loses its limit and grows to boundlessness. The Scripture has imprisoned all things under the power of sin in the way usually understood, in which all men fail to keep the law's commands. It further implies that the law, when liberated unto boundlessness, becomes sin as a means of perdition rather than life. The promise comes through faith, granted to those who believe in the name of Jesus.

"For through the law I died to the law, so that I might live to God." What sadness and deception have dogged man's thinking about this passage! Working especially through Luther, Docetism has ensared men in the thought that "through the law I died to the law" implies the law's growth to infinity, its metamorphosis into a monster and a tyrant, until this growth terminates in self-exhaustion and liberation-as-destruction. "I died to the law"—because the infinite law dies to itself, scattering at last, just as it disintegrates man's nature! The deceived imagine the consequent release from anxiety and terror, man's severance and undoing, as "living to God" because the burden has disappeared. No life, no peace, no union replaces what was lost, and free men experience their liberation as emptiness and despair. This stands ages apart from the meaning of the verse. Man under sin "dies to the law" because the gentle law shows him his sin but cannot help him overcome it. As abstracted from sin, however, "through the law I died to the law" presumes the law's gentle lowering through limit and humility into sacrifice, where the law is temporarily annulled unto faith. The law "dies," and man's effort with it, in hope, steadfastness, and confidence instead of exasperation and despotism. The Lord responds to the believer's hope with life and blessing, a renewed energy and a new beginning. It is no wonder that Docetism, which concludes its pattern with the scattering, knows of no life beyond escape from the infinite pressure, lacking a practice of restoration and renewal. The docetic faith expends all its resources in defeating itself, and has no power for what comes after the perishing.

Properly embedded between the law before and after, faith gives strength and girds man on the path of beatitude. Its power binds man at once to Christ, his own nature, and Christ's body the church. The grace of Christ bestows a mystical union, an inner comfort and closeness with the Savior that is the bonding of man with his God and his fellows. This bonding heals the sinner in soul and body, renewing the union dashed into pieces at the fall. The bonding further appears in the believer's submission to the ways and rhythms of Christ's body the church and in his humility before other believers. Now the infinite pressure fades and the gentleness of the law emerges unalloyed, now man looks to new life with joy, thanksgiving, and peace.

New life comes to man first and foremost as a change of mind. Before he should transform his actions, before he achieves gentleness and humility of heart, his mind must discover its content in uninterrupted and continual prayer. Without this practice he floats from pride to pride, from distraction to distraction, unlike the man of God who breathes prayer as his heartbeat, as the measure of his thoughts and the rope that draws him up to the Lord. "For those who live according to the flesh set their minds on the things of the flesh, but those who live according to the Spirit set their minds on the things of the Spirit. To set the mind on the flesh is death, but to set the mind on the Spirit is life and peace. For this reason the mind that is set on the flesh is hostile to God; it does not submit to God's law." Or as St. Paul adds, "Do not be conformed to this world, but be transformed by the renewing of your minds, so that you may discern what is the will of God . . . [do not] think of yourself more highly than you ought to think, but . . . think with sober judgment." And again, "Likewise the Spirit helps us in our weakness; for we do not know how to pray as we ought, but that very Spirit intercedes with sighs too deep for words. And God, who searches the heart, knows what is the mind of the Spirit, because the Spirit intercedes for the saints according to the will of God." Those transformed unto God think according to the mind of Christ and by the Holy Spirit, which labors so that they should no longer attend to worldly loves. You men of God who live under grace, who strive to love God with all your heart, soul, mind and strength and to love your neighbor as yourself, seek first a mind resolute and unwavering in prayer. "Lord Jesus Christ, Son of God, have mercy on me, a sinner": this is your inward law and the rudder of your heart.

Apart from prayer man can hardly undertake the ethical way of scattering that precedes God's gathering. Without it he cannot obey Christ's commandments, though man may outwardly say "I have come to know him." The love of God will not reach perfection in men without the continuous habit of prayer, nor will man walk just as

Christ walked though he say "I abide in him." To walk just as Christ walked requires that man knows Christ's heart, which is gentle and lowly, and as a preliminary that man know his mind, which is the humility exemplified in the incarnation and crucifixion. Should the Christian walk with God in his mind and heart, he will also walk with Christ in his body, loving God fully and the world in its place. This prayer, this obedience of the heart, is given by the Spirit as a gift through faith, and in no small part it is the work of faith.

1 John 5:1–4a and 2:7–11

Everyone who believes that Jesus is the Christ is born of God, and everyone who loves the father loves his child as well. This is how we know that we love the children of God: by loving God and carrying out his commands. This is love for God: to obey his commands. And his commands are not burdensome, for everyone born of God overcomes the world.

Dear friends, I am not writing you a new command but an old one, which you have had since the beginning. This old command is the message you have heard. Yet I am writing you a new command; its truth is seen in him and you, because the darkness is passing and the true light is already shining. Anyone who claims to be in the light but hates his brother is still in the darkness. Whoever loves his brother lives in the light, and there is nothing in him to make him stumble. But whoever hates his brother is in the darkness and walks around in the darkness; he does not know where he is going, because the darkness has blinded him.

MEN CANNOT LOVE GOD without resting in him; they cannot love Christ without faith in the rest ascertained through his sacrifice, eternal life; they can love neither God nor Christ without loving their neighbors, easing the burdens of their brothers; and man does none of this without also affirming the rest intrinsic to his nature, an affirmation that at once and more or less subtly affirms God as his creator, Christ as his savior, and the neighbor as his friend. In this rest man discovers his union with the divine intertwined with his union with other men, his life with God overlapping and bound up in his life with his fellows. Like God, who is fulfilled not in the Father alone but in the Trinitarian harmony, not in the singular but in the plural, man does not attain the height of nature in an isolated task but in the melody of shared being. Reaching this height comes not without a certain burden, but it is not burdensome.

Against this, Docetism: the inestimable burden, the flood advancing to the last breath, the unstoppable pressure, the infinite law disguised as freedom, peace, and rest. Docetic man says that he loves his brother, that together he and his brother shall march toward the promised land, that they shall come to know and have joy in one another. Yet the promiser stumbles. He walks in darkness and does not know where he is going, he cries out for his brother and desires friendship when his own being is war and his totalizing fabrication, his ersatz world, conjoins the endless task with endless gratification. He tolerates no gap, no disjunction, no hesitation, no wavering, no stopping, no inefficiency, no repetition, no slackening of the reins, no barriers, no judgment, no waiting or patience, no rest, and no freedom-as-rest. Docetic freedom demands that its worshippers disrupt the peace left intact after the last liberation, that they widen the infinite chasm until all mankind has fallen in. "Come to the festival of violence, for we include everyone!" exclaims the docetist. "Come and enjoy the world! Sate your eyes and your stomach! Put your skin and muscles at ease! Come to frankincense and myrrh, come to your salvation! We offer it to you free of charge, we love you enough to give it without obligation, asking only that you do nothing, a nothing accomplished by doing everything! May you never wait for your salvation to arrive, but only strive for it without ceasing!" In this manner Docetism, exalted by expectation and primed for glory, closes man off simultaneously from rest and from love. It alienates him from God, from Christ, and from his neighbor, including all men in mutual exclusion until those who love the entire world hate their neighbors, until the world is awed at freedom but knows no peace.

Beloved, God is perfect faithfulness and perfect peace, the faithfulness of the full being of the Trinity, including Father, Son, and Holy Spirit, a faithfulness that matures through begetting and procession as well as the mutual humility of life-giving. In his faithfulness God moves through death into life, scattering as the Son and the Spirit in their differentiation before being gathered into the teleological union of the Godhead. God will always be this God because he always will exist and has existed in this fashion, conforming to the rhythm of life affirming life, repeating the miracle of life-outpouring as mediated through freedom, the locus of mystery. For the being of God in the illumination from joy to joy complete hinges on the mystery of life-through-death and gathering-through-scattering, the mystery to which God testifies at the burning bush. The faithfulness of God cannot not be what it is without and apart from this mystery.

As the Only-Begotten of the Father, the faithfulness of God has a simple referent in the Son. Considered alone and in his distinction from the Father and the Spirit, the Son abides. In this abiding he is faithful as he dwells in an integrity that consists of the unbroken harmony of being and law. The Son has a "law," a definition implicit within his being, to the extent at a minimum that men recognize this divine being as coherent, ordered, and at peace. To deny such a law to the Son, whatever philosophical questions and conundrums the acknowledgement of such a law might cause, would make him structureless and without form, one scattered rather than gathered in his being. May men never envision the Son in this way! He has a law that makes his personhood recognizable and definitively present. The law implies the prescription that God ought to be in this way, as personal, righteous, immutable, and impervious, while it finds its match and complement in the Son's actual existence in this way. The harmony between the two imbues the divine life with a peace and simplicity for which men lack words. Where law and abiding cohere, where they hold hands like dear friends, there is fullness and contentment, a rhythm that senses no lack and knows no harshness, no anxiety, no worry. There is "no darkness at all in God," as John writes with good reason, because the fundamental harmony within the divine life, the incomprehensible peace, is at once an immeasurable joy. What peace can abide apart from the harmony of things living as they ought to live? What peace does not spur upwards a great joy at the goodness of that which abides in this way? What joy is not simultaneously gentleness and compassion? God the Son is perfect harmony and thereby perfect peace, perfect peace and thereby perfect joy, perfect joy and thus perfect gentleness.

The great joy of the Son emerges not only from his own abiding, but from the rest that the Son enjoys in the Father. His joy derives in an immediate sense from his own being, but this being is no less the being of the Father, just as the Son is mysteriously one with the Father. The Son therefore can bear all burdens with the impregnable power of being, knowing no fault or defect, abiding with the perfection of the Father while also resting. The Son's resting at least means that he does not bear certain burdens, including the work of self-begetting (in itself a nonsensical idea). The Father does not beget him as an inert and shapeless mass, nor does the Father insist that this supposed formlessness form itself, drawing itself up from darkness into nature. The Father does not command that which cannot muster firmness of will to will itself, as such chaos in any case cannot "will itself into existence." On the one hand nothing comes from nothing whereas being produces being, and on the other hand there is something, formless matter, that is also nothing and can only ultimately remain the infinite darkness. In the sense that the Son is not formlessness choosing itself, that such an idea is a contradiction and an impossibility, in this sense the Son does not choose life nor does he consciously affirm his begetting as a precondition for his own maturation. With respect to the burden of self-generation that he does not bear, the Son looks to the Father with gratitude. He thanks the Father for the work of begetting, for blessing life as its font and origin. This gratitude is also rest, for the thanks of the Son refers to a work accomplished on his behalf and which he does not take up, a work of life that the Father performs for him.

The Son's life repeats the Father's and is not whatever the former might like it to be. In other words, the Son abides not fundamentally as freedom but fundamentally as form, as fundamentally the life that surpasses all life as the creator surpasses all creations. As begotten in eternity, the Son is God and is given in the form of God. The Son thereby rests in the Father in both his freedom from the burden of self-begetting and from the burden of maturation, of attaining destiny. The form of the Father is the destined form of the Son. The Son gives thanks to the Father for this destiny and rests in him because the aforementioned burdens are not his; his work is to be, to abide, but the genesis and parameters of this abiding do not originate by his will. In this manner his abiding affirms work and its burden without becoming burdensome. God bestows upon the Son an abiding gathered according to the divine mercy. His begetting allows the Son to take comfort in the coherence of singularity as the Only-begotten.

Although the form of the Son derives from the Father, the harmony within the Son does not abide in isolation from the Son's will but turns on it, for God cannot abide without willing to do so. The Son has a limited nature insofar as his being is not scattered and man perceives this limit in the admission of the Son's freedom, which eternally affirms and governs the abiding of the Son in harmony with his law. In and through this freedom God announces his name as *I am*, as that which abides in eternity and immutably. One might ask in light of this announcement if it is possible for God not to be God, if the Son in his freedom could abdicate the harmony of his being and become something other than God. This might seem not to be the case inasmuch as freedom is an infinite law. As the infinite it must presume some finitude unto itself, a distinct being under the reign of freedom, and yet as freedom it must press that preliminary finitude according to the infinite pressure, undoing both the finite being and itself *qua* freedom as the consequence. In this sense freedom is determined to undermine itself, annulling its power and submitting to the larger context of limited being. If this determination is true, is it possible that God cannot be God? Does the deity possess a meaningful freedom? Is freedom itself truly free? Is it not somehow determined? On the one hand the infinite law necessarily comes to exhaustion, but on the other hand this infinitude recognizes no confinement or predictability, no boundary or restriction. Freedom is the mystery, this formlessness at once itself and its opposite, an infinitely determined liberty. One affirms freedom as free and as mystery because it resists all explanation, because to pin it down to the infinite law *qua* law limits it in some sense, defining it by the determination without the liberty. This liberty is the law's presupposition and goal, the purpose of its expression as law, which is to say that freedom's character as law is subordinate to its finality as freedom, to its undefinability. Is there, then, a meaningful freedom for the Son? Yes, but in a way that men cannot fully comprehend, a way that depends on and incorporates determinism. So men must affirm freedom while admitting that they cannot explain it.

From the harmony of the Son's abiding wells up the pressure, the joyful force that the Son feels as the inclination to life. Though he feels this pressure its weight remains ever gentle, ever tender. Never does this pressure become the infinite as fallen men experience it, never is it harsh, impersonal, draconian, tyrannical, savage, and cruel. It leans upon the will of the Son like the disciple who reclined upon the Lord, like one at rest in the presence of his master. This pressure is, as it were, the abiding's transition into freedom, its fade into stillness. Turning toward and delving into freedom, the abiding acknowledges its limit and supplicates it. The abiding meets with the Son's freedom such that the freedom at first retains the upper hand and rules in the affair, as though the servant had met his superior. The joy of the Son's being implies within it the request for more, the desire for new life, but it submits to the fact that even perfect abiding cannot eventuate in new life if it abstracts away from will and freedom. Only the divine will can bring about the mystery of life-through-death; its faith is the locus of this mystery. The affair thus involves a mutual respect and sharing of place between the abiding and the free will. For all its exuberance, the joy that exerts pressure on the Son stops short as tied to the abiding while the will takes up the request with magnanimity.

I say again: when the law passes the request for life to the Son's freedom for blessing and furtherance, holding back its hand and awaiting the response, the abiding and the joyful inclination along with the law come to rest. Steady in quiet and anticipation, stilled in the hope of a life to be given through freedom, they turn the bestowal of life over to the Son's liberty as their necessary co-worker. The law scatters from its nature as work, temporarily becoming what it is not as a work at rest. As rest for the law, the Son's freedom takes up the request in the Holy Spirit, whose existence the begetting of the Son implies and who becomes especially active here. The Spirit is present to the Son as a testimony and a guide, as the model of the Trinitarian illumination and the escort to its fullness. By the Spirit, the illumination takes a critical turn as the Son considers the orientation of his inclination toward life. Like the Father, the abiding of the Son requests greater life through his freedom, but unlike the Father the product of life's passage through freedom and its renewed affirmation, the life-outpouring of the Son, returns to the Father at the behest of the Spirit. Just as the Spirit guides believers into all truth and promises them words of testimony, so the Spirit guides the Son into union with the Father through its testimony to the latter's faithfulness. The Holy Spirit guides and testifies in the Trinity no less than on earth.

The testimony of the Holy Spirit in the Trinity confirms the righteousness of the Father. The Spirit approaches the Son, as it were, with the request that he direct his life-outpouring to the Father, giving the Son's being in its overflow back to the source and unoriginate. We can hardly imagine that the Son would keep his life-energy for himself or beget another person in the Godhead, as though the divine life-outpouring should produce new persons without end. Rather than these possibilities (if either of them are at all possible), the Spirit calls the Son to return to the Father. The call includes the promise that the Father will reward the Son's life-outpouring—that is, the outpouring of his very life—by responding in kind. This is the Father's righteousness as expressed in the Holy Spirit, who is the Spirit of mutual humility and thus of union. Turn to me, says the Father to the Son through the Spirit, and I will turn to you. Humble yourself before me, says the Source to the Only-begotten through that same Spirit, and I will honor you.

The Son already looks to the Father with gratitude, recognizing in the Father the source of his life and the giver of the divine form. Now the Son believes the promise of the Father given in the Spirit, and through that same Spirit the Son acts on his belief. It is not only that the freedom of the Son believes that his abiding can pour out life and retain its nature, that it can discharge the fullness of being and remain unchanged, moving through death-as-transformation and not sacrificing immutability, dividing and yet remaining undivided. The Son's freedom also believes that the Father will reward this outpouring when given as a gift, and consequently through the Spirit he orients freedom's traversing of the infinite, his rest-unto-life, to the Father. In addition to resting in the Father as the unoriginate and the begetter, and resting also in the Father as the bestower of the divine abiding, recognizing each of these as fundamentally the Father's work and not his own, the Son now rests in the Father in a new way. By believing the Father's promise the Son rests in the Father for what is to come, looking forward to the unsurpassable joy complete that the Father pledges through the Spirit. In what logically precedes the Son's freedom and what logically follows it, as these derive from the Father's action and his promise of logically subsequent action, the Son rests. He acknowledges in the Father's motion a life-giving work that both begins and finishes the divine union.

In the life of Jesus Christ, the Spirit is present from the first of his ministry to its end, from the baptism to the admission of his divinity before the religious leaders to the cross. That the Spirit arrives in a new way at Christ's baptism requires no explanation, as the Gospels state it plainly enough. That the Spirit accompanies Christ at his questioning the Scripture also implies, as Christ affirms that when believers come before the authorities "Do not worry about how you are to defend yourselves or what you are to say; for the Holy Spirit will teach you at that very hour what you ought to say." Or does the Spirit aid Christians without being present with Christ as he came before the Jewish leaders and Pilate? There he testifies in the most direct terms of his status as Messiah, replying when asked that he is the Blessed One, and that "you will see the Son of Man seated at the right hand of the Power and coming with the clouds of heaven." In the Spirit he gives this testimony, just as the Spirit gives appropriate words to Christ's followers in their hour of witness. The Spirit also directed the Christ to the cross and the darkness of the tomb. On the cross Jesus cried out "My God, My God, why have you forsaken me?" It seems as though the other persons of the Trinity, the Father if not also the Spirit, have abandoned him utterly. Yet the cross implies the Spirit's influence not directly and as one suffering (as the Spirit had no body that could suffer) but at a certain remove, as a guide accompanying the Son's return to the Father. Exactly how the Spirit presides at the cross we cannot say except to affirm that, despite the forsakenness of the Son, his crucifixion looks to his resurrection, his scattering directs us to his gathering on the other side. Inasmuch as this implication remains, the suffering of Christ on the cross presupposes the unifying work of the Spirit.

Just as the incarnate's suffering presumes the Spirit's guidance unto resurrection, in a like manner in the Trinitarian illumination the Spirit guides the Son through the latter's freedom or death-moment, the moment of the apparent scattering of life unto the consequent life-outpouring. The Spirit then acts, in a way that men cannot specify but step back from as mystery, in the offer of the Son's effulgence to the Father as a gift. As the Son rests in the Father through the Spirit, the Spirit leads the Son back to the

Source and is intrinsic to the life-giving from the one to the other. To state it in words whose insufficiency goes without saying, the Spirit somehow turns with the Son so that the latter figuratively faces the Father and then is humbled beneath him, handing over his gift to the original giver.

Within the Son, the moment of freedom-unto-life repeats the dynamic found in the Father in important ways. The Son's freedom receives the gentle pressure for life, the experience of profound joy emanating from his being and conjoined with his gratitude to the Father, a freedom further motivated by his faith in the Father's righteousness. From the distance of freedom and the rest for his law intrinsic to it, the Son wills the infinite. That is, he wills life, but in the will-to-life the Son affirms a subordinate and mediating absorption of death. Not that the Son wills to actually die, but that in blessing the inclination toward life in which he abides the Son accepts the mystery of scattering through which new life emerges, here not a begetting but a life-outpouring. In order to pour out life the Son descends, erasing the distance of freedom in the Yes to life. This passage through freedom enriches and augments his being toward the life-outpouring, in which he gives his life in its fullness to the Father, lowering his nature before the Father's promise of life in a great act of faith. In his freedom, the Son believes that the harmonious abiding at the core of his being can withstand this total giving, that the abiding possesses the mysterious power of life that overcomes all scattering, all cessation, and all division, even the scattering of the Son from his nature in the gift. The Son believes, he knows, that he can descend unreservedly into the Father and persevere as an immutable and unchanging person. For this reason he performs the double annulment, allowing first that freedom shall come to its conclusion, annulling itself by submerging into the finitude of the law thereby refreshed, and secondly by annulling himself in the outpouring given to the Father. The Son perdures through these two moments in faith that his life will continue unabated, prospering beyond the passage point.

When the freedom of the Son humbles itself into the abiding, announcing the Yes to life in which it annuls its existence, this fulfillment reverses the relationship in which the law looked to freedom as a servant to its master, granting freedom the upper hand. In possession of the request, the freedom of the Son acts upon its faith by cutting itself off, recognizing that only the abiding has the power to absorb death as a means. That which was higher becomes lower, with freedom submitting to the law in the pursuit of life. The mystery of gathering-through-scattering, of the burning bush, requires the contribution of both elements, of the law first humbled before and limited by freedom and the freedom that gives up its place for the furtherance of law and life. The law possessed the power of life all along but only as it temporarily gives up this power to freedom; the latter, not puffed up with pride, responds toward life by similarly handing over its priority and bowing back into the law. This dual humility and mutual support surround the mystery in which the unalterable alters and yet remains unalterable, in which the transcendence of God's being becomes manifest before the puny minds of men. God the Son has borne the means of death as a movement from the deity's initial joy, a somehow lower joy, toward the finality of joy complete.

Out of this bearing comes the gathering of life, the miracle of divine abundance showered upon the Father as a gift. On the one hand the life-outpouring of the Son, a mystery surpassing man's understanding and propelled by joy. On the other the guiding hand of the Spirit, another mystery aimed toward perfecting the Trinitarian form. The Spirit and the Father abide just as the Son, who abides after the life-outpouring just as he dwelled before it (that is, logically earlier, not to be confused with a temporal before and after). Each of the persons exists as a perfect life while sharing one life, one essence: indivisible, inseparable, and yet unmistakable in their distinction, the three share in a harmony that repeats and augments the preliminary harmony of the Father with its peace and joy. For not one but three exist, each in perfect harmony with its nature, each willing that nature, and each at peace in its nature and thereby with the others, each basking in the joy that permeates its nature as well as that of the others, each gentle and warm toward the others. All along these three were not three but one while also one-in-three, a multiple unity born out of the Father and forwarded by the rest of the Son in the Father.

The Son rests in the Father as the incarnate Messiah as well as in the Trinitarian life, evincing the faith that looks confidently to God although the scattering looms. Jesus knew that he had to set his eyes toward Jerusalem, he knew that men would betray him there, that they would hand him over to the religious leaders and the political authorities, that these would beat, mock, and kill him. He knew that his body must fall away lifeless and that he must enter the tomb. In the face of this he retained his conviction that the life of God can absorb death and by this absorption vanquish it. He further believed that, in turning to the Father in this novel way, working an act of God for the restoration of man and his world, the Father would reciprocate. If the Son turned to the Father by lowering his nature, emptying himself and taking on the form of a slave, humbling himself even to death on a cross, he had faith that the Father would also turn to him, highly exalting him and giving him the name above every name, so that at this name every knee should bend and every tongue confess that Jesus Christ is Lord. This occurs "to the glory of God the Father" inasmuch as the Father bestows this honor upon the Son, but also because the Son suffers as an affirmation of his rest in the Father. The Son rests in the Father's love and faithfulness in the Trinitarian life, and on earth again he rests in the faith that God will glorify him above the creation under which he was lowered. In light of this rest the Son suffers humbly and patiently, without anger, bitterness, and vengefulness.

Jesus offers this rest to men as eternal life, a life inseparable from their gathering as men into his body. "Therefore," says Hebrews, "while the promise of entering his rest is still open, let us take care that none of you should seem to have failed to reach it . . . For we who have believed enter that rest," and for believers "a Sabbath rest still remains for the people of God; for those who enter God's rest also cease from their labors as God did from his" at the creation. The Christian believes that the death of Christ has procured a salvation for mortals that they could never attain by their works. This allows men first to rest in the understanding that, though they must struggle, the work of salvation belongs to Christ and not to them. Man rests in the knowledge that God works while he does not and that God's work far outweighs his own. Man secondly understands that he can perdure through the scattering in a manner after Christ, imitating the Lord's faith because the believer trusts in him. The faith of Christ as the confidence of glory after suffering saves men first because Christ exercised it and then because they participate in it as the foundation of their willingness to suffer. The sacrifice of men does not accomplish their salvation, it does not usher them into the rest of eternal life. Yet that sacrifice, as grounded in faith and therefore as a form of the believer's rest in Christ, as a work that annuls the power of works just as it looks to God, Christ appropriates and wraps into his redemptive work. Man rests and Christ works, and his work brings man into the ultimate rest.

Man cannot enter that rest apart from Christ's gathering him into the church. The Redeemer does not save the solitary individual who must bear his conscience in faith, but incorporates him into the divine body. Salvation does not occur apart from this incorporation; it is unthinkable that a man could find union with Christ and lack union with his fellow men. One cannot distill concepts of "the believer" and "salvation" from salvation's goal as Christ's reconciliation of all things under his lordship. The individual's faith rather implies a salvation shared by those who struggle together for it. The path of salvation, embarked upon in faith and hope, necessarily reconciles man to Christ as a foundation and, as a matter inextricable from that foundation, reconciles man to his neighbor. A salvation that does not envision this multifaceted unity as both the presupposition for individual faith and its guiding orientation, that does not acknowledge the fundamentally shared and reciprocal nature of the striving, and that fails to comprehend that the sacrifice of man to God simultaneously strengthens and encourages his neighbors, plucks believers out from the overlapping harmony toward which all things tend in Christ and, having isolated them, leaves them to languish in their infinitude.

God chose Abraham not for Abraham's sake, not that the individual man should have communion with God, but so that he could make of Abraham "a great nation," one in whom "all the families of the earth shall be blessed." God chose Jacob over Esau not principally so that the one should have communion with God over the other, but so that the line promised to Abraham should continue toward the fulfillment of Israel in Canaan. In creating, God elects individuals as necessary to his election of entire peoples, the primary object of his election. It is similar with redemption, at least in that the saving action of Christ implies not only the honor of the Father given to the Son. It also implies the people formed and reconciled through Christ (although Christ resides above the people as God and Lord, and is no mere means to them). Among men, the cosmic plan of God does not specify individuals but the church, not monads extracted from one another but a *corpus* joined in love. God elects this people in Christ as a priestly kingdom and a holy nation, a collective grounded in faith in the rest secured by Christ, eternal life, and in this encouraged to give rest to one another on earth. Believers might begin in a practical sense as individuals, but their salvation casts off the appearance of individualism via the shared path of sanctification, of faith, prayer, self-control, struggle, rest-giving, love, and sacrifice, in the approximation of that path's end in this world as well as its attainment in the next. One cannot comprehend the apparent beginning of this path (the individual bearing God's image) without understanding the end as implied in him (the body of Christ). Men cannot gain Christ apart from the mutual giving of rest, nor can they love him without loving their neighbors. For one cannot be born of God without loving the Father, resting in his faithfulness; one cannot love the Father without loving the Son, resting in the faith of his cross and resurrection; and one cannot love the Son without loving his body, providing rest to one's brothers according to their need.

Rest belongs to the nature of man no less than the nature of God. It serves as a critical element in man's ontological constitution, as God has woven it into his very depths. Just as God rests in the mutual life-giving in the Trinity, and just as he rests upon completing the work of creation, so man rests as a creature bearing the divine image.

By telling us that "no plant of the field was yet in the earth and no herb of the field had yet sprung up . . . for there was no one to till the ground," Genesis prepares us for a story about man and his work. Otherwise, why would the text specify plants and herbs "of the field," why would it note that there was not yet rain and no one to till? No plants of the field had grown because neither God nor man had worked to make this occur. In this setting the Scripture informs us that "the Lord God formed man from the dust of the ground" and gave him life. The Lord then planted a garden and "took the man and put him in the garden to till it and keep it." The Lord placed man in the garden, in other words, to work. God's design of man as his creature involves labor, a task tied to the land given by God.

To this point God has judged everything that he has created as good. The light, the vegetation and all kinds of trees and plants, the sun to rule over day and the moon to rule the night, the sea creatures and the birds, the cattle and the wild animals, and finally mankind God saw and judged to be "very good." Not until God sees Adam in the garden does he judge something as "not good." For God said, "It is not good that the man should be alone; I will make him a helper as his partner." This "not good" does not at all mean that God created man as evil, for God creates nothing wicked. It means that God had not completed his work regarding man, that in placing him in the garden something was lacking. And why would God make man a helping partner if not because of his work? Why do any one of us ask for help except that the task is too great? The woman is man's helper at his work, which is to till and keep the ground provided by God. She is simultaneously his rest, his relief from the exigencies of his earthly burden.

Here is a striking thing: Adam resided alone in Eden and without sin, and in such conditions he surely enjoyed unbroken communion with God. His soul was thereby perfectly at rest in its creator. How could it be otherwise when sin does not divide man from God? And yet Adam was not perfectly at rest inasmuch as his bodily tasks weighed upon him and required a helper. God obliges, providing a bodily helper for the tasks of a bodily man. For although man has a dual aspect to his nature, possessing a body and a soul, these so intertwine that a disturbance in one disturbs the other. As God made man as one nature, not two, the perfection of the soul's rest in God does not stand apart from his bodily respite, nor is his bodily respite isolated from the well-being of the soul. God gave a perfect rest to Adam's soul but, according to the divine will, only a secondary rest to the body. When the physical tasks became demanding, so that the loss of physical rest threatened and provoked God to judge that "it is not good that the man should be alone," God fashioned a helper to give rest primarily to the body and secondarily to the soul. Man's rest-givers are two according to the dual aspect of his nature, the soul being higher and the body lower, but the gift received from these two sources is one. Together they bless the singular rest that protects the singular definition of his nature. In this sense one cannot separate the rest that man enjoys in God from the rest he receives from others, while without resting in those others he cannot rest in God. This singular rest preserves and edifies his being as both an ontological and a practical manifestation of his freedom from the infinite burden.

Ontologically, rest is a gap, a pause, an interruption, a barrier, an inefficiency. It bounds the pulse of nature, the abiding by which it lives and breathes, the work of life. In rest this work stops and man practices the limit of his creatureliness in stillness. Nature requires this stillness for its preservation, as without it the abiding might expand unto the infinite pressure and become an oppressor and a perversion to itself. So that this does not happen, so that the evil one should not twist nature toward its own dissolution, man must submit to the necessity of rest and regard his dealings with others as opportunities for rest. Not only the man and the woman but man and man should encounter one another as rest-givers. No human interaction falls beyond the reach of the mutual need for and provision of rest, for at no point should man pretend the infinity of his being and so lord it over another, nor can he deny the necessity of rest with respect to one neighbor without denying its necessity for his own nature, thereby denying it to all neighbors. Man should never look to his neighbor and say, "I have no obligation of rest toward him," ignoring if not actively oppressing his neighbor, as this asserts the one's independence from the other. Man is not self-contained, complete, and whole apart from rest and thus apart from his neighbors. In forgetting this man makes himself the infinite, transforming into a death-dealer to his neighbor and threatening him with the scattering.

Not without reason does Exodus recall Jethro's advice to Moses. He saw the lawgiver sitting "as judge for the people, while the people stood around him from morning until evening" and Jethro assessed this as troublesome. "What is this that you are doing for the people? Why do you sit alone, while all the people stand around you from morning until evening? . . . What you are doing," Jethro surmises in echo of Genesis, "is not good. You will surely wear yourself out, both you and these people with you. For the task is too heavy for you; you cannot do it alone." Jethro then advises Moses to find men who are trustworthy and hate dishonesty, setting them over the people as judges in minor affairs while more important matters come to Moses himself. "So it will be easier for you, and they will bear the burden with you. If you do this, and God so commands you, then you will be able to endure, and all these people will go to their homes in peace." In this manner Moses, having carried out Jethro's advice, continued his work without excessive toil while the people received guidance from their leaders. The aid of the men he appointed removed the oppressive character of the work, providing him freedom from the overwhelming task. This surpasses mere practical advice, providing an insight into the nature of man as the reflection of the God who rests.

Later Moses comes to God as the people are crying out to him for meat. "Why have you treated your servant so badly?" he says. "Why have I not found favor in your sight, that you lay the burden of all this people on me? Did I conceive all this people? . . . I am not able to carry all this people alone, for they are too heavy for me. If this is the way you are going to treat me, put me to death at once—if I have found favor in your sight—and do not let me see my misery." God then answers Moses' anxiety by taking some of the spirit that is on him and distributing it among 70 elders, who are to "bear the burden of the people" along with Moses. When this occurs, two of the men remained in the camp rather than going to the tent of the Lord to receive the spirit. When they received it nonetheless and prophesied in the camp, Joshua brought news of this to Moses with the plea to stop them. "Are you jealous for my sake?" Moses replies. "Would that all of the Lord's people were prophets, and that the Lord would put his spirit on them!"

When Moses utters these words, he wishes that all the people could have a share in the spirit of judgment, of wisdom and leadership. He harbors no jealousy, as though he prized his possession of the spirit as something that exalted him above others. For Moses "was very humble, more so than anyone else on the face of the earth." He desired rather that he could look upon all the Israelites and find rest in them as given by God for this purpose. Do not think, Christian, that Moses desired that all could have a share in prophesy so that each could rule himself in isolation, liberating Moses from the task with respect to his brethren. Moses desires that all men have God's spirit so that he can look to them as sources of rest, as helpers in a task that is collective, the formation and preservation of God's people. Again do not think, Christian, that Moses wished to see these others as objects or instruments for his own use, as though their help toward his burdens amounted to his power over them. It is the opposite, as Moses wished to look up to each of them as possessed of God's power, as channels of the divine used by God, who condescends through them.

For man can find no rest in the help given by others without maintaining a space in his heart from which he wills their rest; he cannot will to give them rest without approaching them in his heart with gratitude, as divinely wrought opportunities for him to both receive and give rest and so fulfill his nature; and he cannot so approach them in the highest sense without first being at rest in God, believing in the faith of Christ. Again there are two aspects of rest, man's rest in other men and his rest in God, one first of the body and one first of the soul, while fundamentally there is one rest for one man.

God gives man rest in physical ways, providing rain and sunlight for his crops as well as animals that assist with his tilling the ground. Man finds rest in God's gifts inasmuch as he understands that these are not his work. Man must till the soil, he must tend the plants and collect the harvest, but he cannot cause the rain to fall or the sun to shine. God alone provides these things, which make by far the more significant contribution. Man can till the ground all he wants, he can plant seeds without end, but what good will his work do without rain? Or if he lives in perpetual night? Man must contribute to the production of life resting in the knowledge that God has the larger part and that he will perform that part faithfully. The same reasoning applies when one looks to spiritual matters, for in the affairs of the soul no less than the body man must do his lesser part while he rests in the faith that God has done the greater. In the work of salvation he must practice self-control, presenting his members as instruments of righteousness rather than sin. He must turn his thoughts away from all wickedness, from idolatry, licentiousness, greed, lust, and jealousy, as well as from anger, malice, strife, contention, and pride, directing his mind to prayer, hymnody, and thanksgiving. He must train his nature toward the sacrifice to which Christ calls him, the cross his Lord commands that he should bear. These make up the lesser work. The greater work God has effected through Jesus Christ, the Lord and life-giver who opens the way for man to return to God. Like tilling the ground in a drought or without sunlight, man's work comes to nothing apart from the work of God. Although man must act toward his salvation, the work belongs essentially to Jesus Christ, who provides what man could never provide for himself. Man rests as he has faith that Christ has accomplished the once-for-all sacrifice and opened eternal life for those who seek him. Man must struggle and work, yet he breathes comfortably in the realization that the work is ultimately God's and that God is faithful. The man who believes in Jesus is born of God, and so he regards his salvation and says "not my work," although he must work. The Savior clarifies this tension when he calls his people. "Come to me, you who labor and are heavy laden," he declares, "and I will give you rest. For my yoke is easy and my burden is light."

The Christ gives this rest on Golgotha and in the resurrection, completing the sacrifice for sin and calling man to *theosis*. In light of this ultimate rest he calls men together as his body, reconciling them according to the divine wisdom. Just as God gives rain and sunlight to aid man in keeping the ground but sawthat he needs a physical helper as protection from an undue burden, so the Christ gives the cross and the resurrection for the soul's healing but man cannot work toward this healing alone. Man receives his secondary spiritual rest from other men just as he receives his primary spiritual rest through Christ. Man therefore looks at God in both his spiritual and his physical work and says, "I rest in you. Though I must work, the work is not mine." In this manner God relieves him of the threat of the infinite. Man also approaches his neighbors in both his spiritual and his physical work and says "I rest in you as gifts from God. He has given us to one another for mutual rest, and though we must struggle together, the work is his and not ours." Men thus overlap in the interiority in which they simultaneously commune with God and one another, sharing in both the outward task and the inward rest as a single body, abiding in the Son as he abides in the Father so that the church is one in the likeness of God. In this manner the collective task given to man by God is not burdensome, and men do not threaten one another because their rest in God has removed the likelihood of their burdening one another with ruthlessness.

The task commands what Christians have heard from the beginning, that we love one another. Christians strive in this task as they see others as God's gifts, and so with humility and gratitude. They strive for minds and hearts unified and disciplined in prayer, fashioned in the goodness and gentleness of God and quiet before his providence, so that out of the rest in their souls they can give rest to others. Christians understand that God has given men to one another as helpers, and that in helping one's neighbor one both relieves his burden and gives him life. By such action, surveying the neighbor's predicament and responding to it in faith and compassion, man fulfills his function not only as a fellow-worker with others but as a fellow rest-giver among them. Humbled by the faithfulness and love of God and stilled in thanks for and expectation of his mercy, individual men know their natures as strengthened through the rest they give to their neighbors and supported by the rest received from them. They manifest this knowledge as each asks his neighbor "How can I give you rest?" Or what is the same, "How can I love you?"

The subtlety of Docetism's transformation of this love into hatred leaves one speechless. How imperceptibly it misleads the traveler along the way of life, nudging his mind with thoughts whose hopefulness veils their vanity, whose supposed humility conceals their pride, until Docetism has turned the life-seeker onto the path of death. The deceived one never comprehends the meaning of his actions, his mind and heart never open to the truth of his doings. Outwardly things seem right at times, and inwardly man's confidence, though sometimes challenged, does not fatally flag. His lips can speak daily, even hourly, of salvation in Jesus Christ and of men's need to find communion with God, his mind can think regularly on the name of God and his work among men, but docetic man's heart remains far from the Lord.

The way of life, from nothingness toward an impervious form, is an abiding punctuated by moments of freedom. In these moments man traverses the infinite as a bridge toward greater life. They possess essential importance, as without them man cannot proceed and will never attain his end. They are themselves not the end but inescapable passage points, axes on which the advance toward beatitude turns and matures. Especially at the Christ-Idol Docetism affects its ontological ruse, plucking out the freedom moment so that it no longer acts as a through-way to life. Taking up freedom in its hands, Docetism casts it as an end-in-itself and proclaims the infinite as man's goal. In so doing Docetism transforms the character of freedom's culmination and the path of man has he seeks his supposed salvation. As embedded within abiding freedom consummates itself in dissolution, but one can hardly distinguish the dissolution from the life-outpouring that occurs through freedom. The movement through freedom in this case leads ultimately to life. Disembedding the freedom-moment divorces its dissolution from the life-outpouring so that the consummation of freedom consists solely in self-annihilation, the conclusion of its character as the infinite law. Freedom embedded within the abiding contributes critically to life, whereas freedom isolated and abstracted from abiding, even prioritized over it, is death.

When he unwittingly follows freedom elevated in this way, man's path of salvation changes in dramatic and horrifying ways. Along the path of life man meets infinite moments as subordinate elements, as necessary and protective devices within the harmony of abiding that succor him because he finds rest in them. Inasmuch as an elevated freedom defines both man and his way according to the infinite, Docetism's plucking out and aggrandizing of freedom prohibits these rest-moments. For freedom's character as the infinite allows no gap, no barrier, no exception, no stoppage or interruption. On this path man sees his peace and solace dwindle and his rest fade away until the only freedom left to him is liberation. Just as Moses' and Aaron's request for sacrifice, and by implication rest, tacitly transforms into a drive toward liberation from ruthless oppression, so docetic man experiences the constant denial of his need for respite until his only option is revolution. This option presents the consummation of freedom, the total annulment of the law, as though it were the salvation offered by the way of life. But it is the ontological destiny of freedom in destruction, whose agent is docetic man-in-revolt. The purest theological expression of this revolt, the onset of the Christ-Idol, appears in Luther's doctrine of faith alone.

Luther could not have been without the men who preceded him, who developed the infinite law in Catholicism and carried it forward, if implicitly, as the way of salvation. The law began in earnest with Gregory VII, whose desire for the church's freedom from temporal rulers provoked an expanse of ecclesiastical-legal argument and investigation. Gregory's announcements abolished the old order and set another one in its place, promulgating that the pope alone is to be called universal, that he may be judged by no one, that his feet alone are to be kissed by all princes, and that he may depose emperors. In his mind Gregory made these announcements for a good end, as he sought to cleanse the church of simony and nicolaism. One can easily agree that the ends were good, as money and lust should not pervert Christ's body. Yet Gregory's means for reaching his goals could not have been worse. In gathering power to his office and to himself, Gregory raised up not God but his person as pontiff, trusting not in the providence of God but exalting his official superiority. The infinite expresses itself in man's character fundamentally as pride, which affirms that it is higher while the neighbor is lower. Behold the docetic contradiction: while Christianity teaches that man must lower his nature before God and neighbor in parallel, Docetism claims that man humbles his nature before God while he raises himself up over his neighbor. In Gregory this contradiction made enemies of his duties to the church and to the temporal order inasmuch as he supposed that he served God by lording over men. In him this tension combines as well with the original growth of canon law toward the infinite. This law provided arguments justifying Gregory's war with the emperor and thus injured the church's rest with its temporal neighbor, while it later ballooned into the monster that eradicates man's rest in Jesus Christ.

That this law evolved toward the infinite, becoming the means of salvation for Catholicism's religious elites, means that these found progressively less satisfying and regular rest as they sought the Lord. It is no surprise that the late medieval age saw the withering of sacrificial and sacramental efficacy, which opens man to rest in God. The infinite law means to undermine such experiences if not to squeeze them out entirely. It is also no shock that, when the law reached its culmination in Luther's doctrine of faith alone, believers found themselves isolated in their spiritual lives, alienated by their shared faith. The Protestant revolution declares that God saves men in distinction from one another, for one cannot share the faith of another, nor does one's faith count for another, but each man faces God alone in his heart. The same law that squeezes out man's rest in God in the sacrifice likewise outlaws man's rest in his neighbors as aids to salvation.

In the age immediately following the Christ-Idol, Docetism used the Protestant prayer of confession as a medium for its infinite pressure. One has only to compare the Eastern practice with the early Protestant one to discern this. In the former, the one who prays strives to constantly remember his sin in the Jesus Prayer. "Lord Jesus Christ, Son of God, have mercy on me a sinner" echoes in his thoughts from morning until evening until he has focused his whole heart on his transgression and the desire for grace. The believer yearns for union with Christ through this prayer, always humbling himself before God, occasionally coming to tears because of his sins and his slavery to the flesh, although also out of thanks for God's compassion. But at no time does the Christian feel his sin as a terror or a total fright, and at no time especially does God loom over him as a suspicious or belligerent lawgiver or a scrutinizing and exacting judge. God does not cry out to him, "Where is your sin, that I may damn you for it?!," but "Where have you practiced mercy and humility, so that I might show you mercy and honor you?" Thus the Eastern man of prayer always remains at peace in his recognition of sin, resting as he acknowledges his iniquity because he knows all along that God desires to exercise his mercy, seeking to draw the repentant to him.

How sharply this diverges from the spirit of early Protestantism, in which Docetism coerces man to cower before the thunderous wrath of the Almighty! That the early Protestant knew his God as "Holy, Holy, Holy" meant that he knew his God from a great and awe-inspiring distance, a chasm of terror and anguish brought to life in confession. Luther demands that men encounter God as the tyrant-lawgiver and oppressor of consciences, while Calvin requires that they tremble before the dread judgment seat of the Lord. This happens not because man has turned from the God who is fundamentally gentleness but because God meets man as the Judge who seeks his total condemnation. Some early Protestants "preached terror" to bring man precisely to this point, at which the believer shudders that he has no direction in which he can turn, no place of respite or help against his sin, no moment of rest in which the law and the holiness of God do not convict. In this docetic case the law accelerates and expands to the exclusion of spiritual rest. All works, all sacraments, the prayers and assistance of others, and the guidance of religious leaders add nothing that mollifies the severity of this total confession, whose intensity leads the devout to tears of anxiety and despair as often as joy. The practice of confession between Protestant West and Orthodox East appears ostensibly the same as each urges that man constantly remember his sin. Yet the form of confession differs in the most remarkable and significant way. The Eastern practice presumes the goal of confession in rest, proceeding toward it, whereas the docetic practice aims to abolish rest *in toto*, replacing it with liberation via the infinite law.

The docetic denial of rest in the conscience implies man's rejection of a singularly important neighbor, the deputized representative of man to God and God to man, the priest. For the inward denial of rest implies the denial of freedom, the repudiation of sacrifice, and the exclusion of the neighbor inasmuch as these offer rest, and in the priest freedom from the law, sacrifice, and the neighbor come together. As the neighbor who officiates the sacrifices and so practices the limit of the law, he personifies man's rest before the divine command, mediating the law in mercy rather than terror. By providing rest as both a man and as the representative of God, the priest embodies all that Docetism excoriates; he sins against its spirit by his very presence, which Docetism anathematizes.

Docetism asserts that "All men, as equals, can meet God without mediation," an appointment in the conscience that the believer appropriates as liberation from sin. But even in Eden man did not rest wholly in God apart from others. As it was "not good" that man had no helper for his physical tasks, and as he could not rest in God without the physical rest provided by this helper, in Eden man finds rest in God as mediated through his neighbor. The latter does not stand over man as a channel for rest (or grace, if one wishes to call it that), but man needs his neighbor in order to rest in God. As equals men find rest in God, mediating through one another the divine rest given to each. There is no "meeting God without mediation" in the sense that mediation is unnecessary or ruled out, but quite the contrary.

The introduction of sin alters the tranquility of Eden especially by requiring the punishment of death. Due to the fall man must leave the Garden because God does not want him to eat from the tree of life, and beyond this man must now pay the penalty for his transgression. That penalty per the divine law and in the practice of worship is sacrifice, but why is it needed?

In sinning, man raises himself above his God-given boundaries, seeking to be like God in ways that the Lord prohibits. Prior to the fall he could experience God without dying, he could have communion with God without traversing the negativity of physical death. His living within his limit, turning to God's command in soul and body, preceded his contact with the infinite in Eden. As long as man retained the finitude of obedience, he could experience the infinite of communion with God. First comes the affirmation of man's law and his boundary, and through this man could access God in their shared freedom. In sin man casts off the finitude presumed in his being, asserting that his existence should extend without bound. He disobeys God in his soul, turning away from the Lord there, and in his body, eating the fruit. Rather than saying, "I retain my finitude and the infinite will descend to affirm me in my limit," the sinner says "I cast my finitude away and seek the infinite as the law of my being." He grasps infinite possibilities at the expense of the possibility of the infinite.

God then turns away from man in punishment, announcing that the man who has chosen the infinite as his law shall reap the consequences of his choice. Man must therefore die; his body will become the infinite, although not in the way that man desired. He sought the infinite as eternal life, but he gains it as dissolution unto dust. Now if man would commune with God he must first address the curse of death. The negative infinitude must be fulfilled or consummated before he can meet peaceably with God. Sin's trajectory of rise and fall must complete its course. Sacrifice acknowledges this requirement and performs the infinite descent, as if the sinner said, "I must die, for it is the end of my pride." Sacrifice further puts forward a substitute for the sinner as the means for reconciliation. It acknowledges that the sinner deserves death while pleading for salvation, asking for rapprochement and the renewed rest of the creature in his creator. In this context God designates the priest as the helper who offers sacrifice for the people, seeking rest from death for them in this most direct, intense, and effective way. By performing the sacrifices the priest both brings the people back into peace with God and opens the path for new life in him. This mediation raises the priest above the people as chosen by God, for unlike the case in Eden, men do not mediate the presence of God to one another equally as not all men perform the sacrifice.

Docetists will agree with much of this understanding of sacrifice and then argue that Jesus Christ is the Great High Priest, that he has performed the once-for-all sacrifice and reigns in the Heavenly Temple. They therefore affirm the spiritual sacrifice while not affirming the physical priest who sacrifices, just as they affirm the communion as a form of remembrance rather than a sacrificial offering. They ignore the irony that in their communion they presume to remember rest given by God while denying rest in and through their neighbors. They both affirm and deny their creaturely need for rest in the same act—although the denial is deeper and the affirmation is deception. For if man affirms in the ritual that he is God's creature fashioned according to the limits God planned, and that he desires eternal rest with God and has received that rest (according to Protestant conviction), how can he simultaneously deny the creaturely rest embodied in the help he receives from others by rejecting the priest? How can man ritually announce his rest in God while ritually refusing rest in his neighbor? Of course Christ has provided an eternal rest through his sacrifice, but has he also changed human nature? Have Golgotha and the resurrection transformed men into creatures who do not need one another, whose rest in God is independent from their rest in others? Has redemption in Jesus Christ reversed the implications of Genesis 2? Does the divine plan to gather all things in Christ alienate those implied in the gathering, closing them off from one another? If not, then without the priest the sacrifice makes no sense! Its object changes from Christ to the Christ-Idol, which blesses man in his lack of rest just as it redefines him as the infinite law.

Make no mistake, Christian! The repudiation of the priest implies the repudiation of rest in the neighbor as one seeks rest from God. This repudiation is a contradiction inasmuch as man seeks to restore his finitude in the sacrifice but does it by affirming his infinitude, his lack of rest in his brother. As man pushes out the priest he pushes out the neighbor until he presumes his nature in its detachment from others. In this ontological exile, this individualism, man conceives himself as a monad, perhaps as an individual "alone before God," a complete and unified whole in distinction from other individuals as complete and unified wholes. Man in this way envisions his life as unto himself, without interruption, stoppage, or gap, without intrusion against either his work or the fulfillment of his desires (and thus as an infinite law), but also as isolated. Whereas the Christian and the natural man presume their rest in others as they abide in the rhythm of toil and company, of individual labor embedded in collective struggle, worship, and blessing, Docetism recasts man as alone in his toil, irritated by company, and disdainful of true and priestly worship. Over centuries Docetism has stripped him of neighbors and neighborliness until man resembles the atomization that is his ontological ideal. Whenever man goes to the sacrifice without the priest he submits to this ideal and worships the god who excludes men from one another rather than joining them together, the god who whips men toward the infinite rather than granting them rest in their finitude. Ritual service to this docetic god, the Christ-Idol, grounds a way of life in which devotion to the task squeezes out the divinely-intended rest until the believer cannot but see all neighbors as oppressors and yearn for further liberation from them.

The sacrifice without the priest combines the two great sins against God, idolatry and violence or oppression. In the docetic sacrifice man approaches the table like the Israelites at Sinai, who exclaimed "Here are your gods who brought you out of Egypt" to the Golden Calf. The Jews desired the presence of God and wanted to worship him but did so wrongly, as if his presence meant festival. So the docetic adherents to *Christus Liberator*, the docetic deity, believe that they worship Christ while celebrating the distillation and shattering of nature. They claim to worship the God of communion and life while they have perverted his meaning, so that they offer their acclamation to division and death! At its profoundest level the docetic hatred amounts to this, that one does not need one's neighbors to commune with God and they do not need you nor each other for the same. Lying to himself, each says "I rest in God" without saying "I rest in you" and "You rest in me." Thus violence against the creator, whose design and intent men reject when they refuse mutual rest! Thus the violence of men against their own natures, as they reject the necessity of rest and the humility it implies, asserting that they need no neighbors to meet their God! Thus the violence of men against others, who can hardly rest in God nor find fulfillment without the mutual provision of rest among creatures! In the docetic age, these subtle hatreds lay the foundation for the grosser forms in which the powerful take from others, gathering all right and wealth unto themselves while their neighbors suffer; these hatreds undergird the taskmasters who lay heavy burdens on workers and subjects without concern for what they endure; these silent abandonments bolster those who push aside the needy in the gate and take no thought for the sick, the forlorn, and the estranged; they bolster those who worship their god but know nothing of the orphan and the widow. Alas, you "who say in your heart, 'I am, and there is no one besides me' . . . your wisdom and your knowledge led you astray, and you said in your heart, 'I am, and there is no one besides me.'" For shame, "you who join house to house, who add field to field, until there is room for no one but you, and you are left to live alone in the midst of the land!"

Docetism has woven violence and oppression into the hearts of men, cloaking its idolatry and its hatred under the most respectable and cosmopolitan of terms, "the individual." For men cannot carry out their lives as individuals in the modern sense, nor understand themselves as such, apart from their independence from the neighbor and the denial of his rest. When docetic men think on the individual, when they assume him as the starting point for the consideration of human nature and the social order, when they envision him as abstracted and isolated, as an atom sequestered for reflection and study, as a type set against other types and especially as raised against the institutions supposed to entrap if not enslave him, when they posit him as contrasted against God in his holiness and majesty or dream of him as the savior and superman, when they exalt him in a total freedom conjured as his complete communion with others, in short, when they indulge the proliferations of the docetic imagination, in each case docetic thinkers assume man as the infinite law and therefore as one who does not rest in others. The modern individual and the philosophy of individualism, as well as its apparent opposite in communism or communitarianism, presume the docetic ontology in which man ought to exist in liberation from his fellows. This ontology grounds his distillation from others on the one hand and his total freedom-as-communion on the other. On the one hand he exists as atom and on the other within the formless mass of the mutually liberated. In each case he has forgotten rest in God, in the natural world, and in those close to him, a forgetfulness first practiced in the docetic sacrifice.

The machinations of Docetism slither deeper still in the religious consciousness, hiding beneath the believer's assurance of salvation. By Luther's day, the elite Christians in the West agonized over the question of assurance. Asking whether one had done enough good works, doing all that is in one, and examining whether one has accomplished these works correctly seemed to decide the question of one's eternal fate. By seeking assurance with regard to the question of salvation Luther and his ilk perpetrated a pernicious and crucial ontological error. For the Christian should walk in the harmony of struggle and good works on one hand and sacrificial supplication on the other. He should recognize the necessity of his contribution while acknowledging that salvation belongs to God. In this frame of mind he struggles against sin while making the sacrifice and resting in God's provision. In the sacrifice and in rest man is humbled before God, whom he cannot manipulate or compel, and in that rest he submits to the justice and grace of the lifegiver. Man also recognizes that, inasmuch as salvation presumes the mystery of the appeal to God, man could at any time withdraw the appeal and desert his Lord. In that event God would continue to call to him while beginning also to withdraw. In the mystery of his freedom God can always react to man according to the integrity and fecundity of the divine being, with the two communicating in the mutual giving and receiving constitutive of relationship. The idea of the assurance of salvation, by which one counts oneself among the saved or in some cases among the predestined, casts off this conception of the Christian God and the life that seeks union with him as salvation. How deceptive the enemy is at this point! The believer, after the docetic Reformation, says that he is saved and that he knows this by faith and solely because of the work of Christ. But in this knowledge he has removed the mystery from his salvation, he has ceased to allow God's freedom of responsiveness, and this especially in the case of predestination. He abdicates the struggle as the contribution of man that leads through sacrifice to rest in God's provision. Nor is there any true sacrifice inasmuch as man denies the priest. In the place of these man encounters God the tyrant, the giver of the death-dealing and infinite law as the prelude to docetic grace, the liberation that annuls the infinite burden. While under the law he asks with accumulating intensity whether he is saved, and after being convinced that he is damned, that the law and the holiness of God could never allow him a moment's rest, he finds an unqualified rest, even the certitude of salvation, through faith alone in Jesus Christ.

In this dialectical process the progressive squeezing out of the possibility that man is saved leads to the undeniable confidence that he is saved. But what the docetic god and his adherent have squeezed out on the most basic level is possibility itself, the freedom of movement along the path of salvation in which God responds to the particular actions of men by drawing nearer to them or pulling away. In the context of assured salvation, especially as refracted through justification by faith alone, the freedom of both man and God become irrelevant. Man proclaims that he is certainly among the blessed because the god who grants him this certitude operates via the ontological destruction of liberty, the exclusion of the spontaneous back and forth of daily interaction between God and man, an exclusion that conceals the obliteration of rest under the lie of liberation. Rather than trusting the grace of the God who overlooks man's faults and reciprocates for man's mercy, rather than making his contribution and beseeching God's goodness through sacrifice, for the docetist salvation becomes a game of confidence. Has one convinced himself that God's mercy applies to him? Has one said to himself enough times that "yes, I am saved"? If so, for what reason? By faith alone? But how does one know that one's faith is real? How does one know that one's doctrine, one's morals, one's church is the right one? Does man claim that he has felt the grace of God in his heart? I have shown elsewhere how that feeling hides the scattering of his nature beneath the conviction that the Holy Spirit has arrived. Furthermore, if in the case of predestination man can appeal to no order in his actions as they add or take away from the possibility of salvation, and if, contrary to the biblical witness, he can cite no rationale in God's character for the divine mercy, in what does he trust? The works of God can seem arbitrary and unfounded even to the committed believer while he forgets the rhythm of salvation as work and rest in God.

Those who claim certitude of salvation take no rest in God but are liberated from him; they confuse their liberation in the docetic god with rest in God. Despite their protests at this point, their lack of rest in others testifies to their lack of rest in the Lord. The history of Protestantism especially witnesses to this, repeating the docetic contradiction seen in Gregory VII that those who claim humility before God raise themselves up against their brothers. The children of the Reformation put the contradiction this way: "We are saved by no work of ours and through faith alone. How humbled before God we are! And *we*, the saved who hold to true and right doctrine, will countenance no heretics or breaches of truth!"

Along these lines Docetism perpetrated a barbaric alienation of man from man, speaking through the mouths of Western Christendom words that shredded the unity of the body of Christ. Far from ushering in an age of mutual trust and rest-giving, the Reformation era saw an explosion of doctrinal battles in which each side rose up against the other with zeal and self-righteousness. Christians disagreed with one another about the priority and meaning of biblical texts, the relationship between the Old and New Testaments, the connection between the Bible and the sacraments, the practice of worship, infant baptism, the exercise of reason in discerning theological truth, and God's work on the individual's heart. As the spectrum and content of truth claims proliferated indefinitely, who can doubt that the competing sides saw themselves less as brothers in a shared search for truth and more as adversaries, with each side suspicious of heresy presented as divine teaching? Zwingli defended his doctrines by affirming that "I know for certain that God teaches me, because I have experienced it," whereas Luther, no less convinced that he had experienced the grace of Christ "for you and me," admonished his followers to "Beware of Zwingli and avoid his books as the hellish poison of Satan, for the man is completely perverted and has completely lost Christ." As historian Brad Gregory summarizes the age: "With controversialists transposing the sometimes contentious discourse between scholastic theologians and humanists from the 1510s, rebuffs tended to trigger rhetorical rants: angry insults often replaced textual evidence or even assertions based on experience when antagonists dared to resist and reject one's own claims, as is known to anyone familiar with the era's doctrinal controversies. Such frustration is readily intelligible, because neither dueling biblical interpretations nor compelling allegations about God's direct influence *could* resolve disputes among determined adversaries. Hence the repeated recourse to vituperation and name-calling. Or, if one was in a position of sufficient power against a vulnerable opponent—say, Zwinglians against Anabaptists in Zurich—there was always recourse to execution, a time-tested medieval practice (of Catholic authorities with unrepentant heretics) that persisted in the sixteenth century. That never failed to shut them up. But it frequently strengthened those whom it sought to cow and silence: fellow believers of the slain victims memorialized them as heroic martyrs, with social and political consequences that would endure for centuries and indeed persist in the present."[1]

Buoyed by the assurance of their salvation, men on all sides of these debates embodied the docetic ontology. Their certitude annulled not only the freedom of God to respond to the actions of men, which actions the Protestants saw as irrelevant, but the freedom of men to debate charitably the doctrines of the faith. The annulment of God's moral freedom with respect to salvation dovetails in this manner with the annulment of man's doctrinal freedom with respect to the same. In each case the assured believer must deny the possibility of error if not ambiguity on his own part, affirming his certitude by rejecting the freedom of the other party. As the guardian of saving doctrine this meant stifling dissent, trampling others by the multitude of one's proof texts, the coherence and systematicity of one's logic, or the veracity of one's experience. Doctrine became the infinite law as wielded by all factions without economy or generosity and as oriented toward the exclusion of the neighbor rather than the offer of rest. For the man who bears a certitude understood as absolute and unchallengeable and who wills to impose that certitude on others without exception and to the death lives and breathes by the docetic spirit. His means incline toward terror, his heart shrinks from mercy, and his actions energize a broader scattering.

---

1. I have taken the historical quotations on the following pages from Gregory's *The Unintended Reformation*. While Gregory does not frame his account in terms of ontology or the infinite law, he provides historical evidence of that law in action.

The battles played out in ecclesiastical circles infiltrated the temporal realm without a hitch. As religious authorities enlisted secular powers on their sides, they encouraged temporal rulers to ensure that their realms adhered to the true version of the faith. The highest duty of both churchly and temporal authorities, in the emerging docetic-confessional age, demanded protecting Christian truth and inhibiting error for the benefit of the people. This goal implied a swift and forceful response to heresy, so that efforts at "Christianization" in various lands led to "the exercise of [a] more consistent, surveillant, coercive power" than previously known in Christendom. Those whose beliefs transgressed right doctrine had to face correction meant to convert them to the desired harmony of church and state while purifying them of spiritually subversive views. Only in this way could those who posed a threat to the local order return to it, whereas those who refused to repent suffered exile or execution. The implementation of these policies facilitated the congealing of confessionally-defined states, some Catholic and others Protestant, and among Protestants, those Lutheran, Reformed, and less often Anabaptist.

The intensification of religious rigor in internal political affairs impacted inter-regional relations as well. The docetic-Reformational era "created opportunities for a new martial motivation in the eyes of devout rulers: the clear defense of God's truth and opposition to his enemies within a divided Christendom. If a ruler was willing to levy taxes, hire troops, and marshal force of arms for his own sake, or that of his family dynasty, how much more ought he to have done so out of love for his creator and obedience to his savior? Which was the nobler motivation: to wage war for oneself or for God?" The latter question, which "seemed to answer itself" during this age, introduces the docetic contradiction at another, more physically destructive level. The ruler says "I am humbled before God, I must do my duty before him," as if believing in right doctrine and being blessed with the right way of salvation had lowered his nature before his creator, but the ruler then says "I go to war against others on God's behalf." In this version of the docetic contradiction, the supposed humility of the political ruler before God provokes his exaltation against other men, even to the shedding of blood. In the name of purity and the defense of God's truth he embarks upon a path diametrically opposed to both truth and purity. In the name of love he carries out hatred.

The contradiction deepens when one sees that both the stepping up of internal efforts toward religious purity and the external willingness of kingdom to rise against kingdom produced effects contrary to the aims of their instigators. In contrast to the practices of containing heresy in the Middle Ages, which did little to seriously undermine the Catholic status quo, "the coercive, prosecutory, and violent actions" of early modern docetic-confessional regimes "proved catastrophically destructive to the ambitions of their proponents and apologists." Those who dreamed of cleansing Europe of its sin ended up dousing it in blood, laying heavy burdens on their comrades to ensure that they conformed to right order while urging men into combat for God's

Word. Europe's various armed conflicts illustrate how, by the late seventeenth century, Catholics and Protestants hated each other without reserve. "The era's polemical severity and ferocious intolerance" further grounded an unforeseen and unspeakable alternative, the decisive break of politics from religion. The wars between Christians died down but an intellectual war between secularists and religionists replaced them. In this manner men who rose up against one another in the name of God gave way to those who rose up against God himself. For who can stand the violence of a God who demands that his followers be humble before him, and so slaughter one another?

"Whoever says 'I am in the light' while hating a brother is still in the darkness . . . whoever hates a brother is in the darkness, walks in the darkness, and does not know the way to go because the darkness has brought on blindness." This warning applies to the religious and political conflicts of the docetic-confessional era without question. It applies no less to the rejection of the priest, and by extension the rejection of the neighbor as such, in the name of the individual. The ontology of the individual decrees that he submit to the infinite law, to singularity, to self-sufficiency and self-governance, and so mandates that he exclude his neighbor as intrinsic to his nature and his salvation. This hatred of the neighbor ranges from bloodshed to indifference, but in all cases man's ontological exile seeks to widen the space between men rather than unify them in love. This remains the case today, when docetic processes have grown so strong, and their roots have penetrated so stubbornly into men, that any alternative to mutual exile fills them with horror and indignation. Thus men go on without knowing the way to go, proclaiming their humility before God, or the task, or history, freedom, equality, or progress. They remain incredulous to the blindness in which they rise up against and hate one another, having forgotten the fulfillment of nature as it rests in God and neighbor.

1 John 4:16b–21

God is love, and those who abide in love abide in God, and God abides in them. Love has been perfected among us in this: that we may have boldness on the day of judgment, because as he is, so are we in this world. There is no fear in love, but perfect love casts out fear; for fear has to do with punishment, and whoever fears has not yet reached perfection in love. We love because he first loved us. Those who say, "I love God," and hate their brothers are liars; for those who do not love a brother whom they have seen cannot love God whom they have not seen. The commandment we have from him is this: those who love God must love their brothers also.

"Thus says the Lord: 'If any of you could break my covenant with the day and my covenant with the night, so that day and night would not come at the appointed time, only then could my covenant with my servant David be broken, so that he would not have a son to reign on his throne, and my covenant with my ministers the Levites . . . only if I had not established my covenant with day and night and the ordinances of heaven and earth, would I reject the offspring of Jacob and of my servant David, and not choose any of his descendants as rulers over the offspring of Abraham, Isaac, and Jacob. For I will restore their fortunes and will have mercy on them.'" God has made a covenant with day and night and has established the ordinances of heaven and earth, and he has made a covenant with David, a covenant of the Messiah and of salvation. He cannot break one covenant without breaking the other because he has bound the two together, because the two mysteriously overlap and intertwine. The lower provides an image of the higher because, in a way that ultimately lies beyond man's comprehension, the lower participates in the higher. The ordinances of heaven and earth, including the covenant of day and night, call men to contemplate the Messiah of God, even that God is love.

Night is like a womb. All is dark, still, and quiet as the hours pass. At last the light whispers onto the horizon, pressing against the softened blue. The colors and beauty of life to come, the expectation of fulfillment, smile upon the world. The star-punctured veil gives way to dawn's rosy fingers, the gold of the heavens yields to a glimmering white, and soon the horizon gives birth to the orb, the unsurpassable light of the world, the heavenly giver of life.

As it ascends the sun shines on all things, spreading life to plants, animals, and men. Man goes forth to his work, to plant and harvest, to build and celebrate. Life carries on with regularity if not with gaiety throughout the day, the sun proceeding through its arc from morning to midday to afternoon, at length nearing the dusk. With the sun approaching its end, the scene of the dawn reappears: the sky turns gold, a rosy purple, and white, while darkness and light exchange places across the heavens. Observing dawn and dusk as distilled from temperature and the body, one could easily not know what one sees. Is it morning or night? Is the great light bursting forth or is the horizon absorbing it, laying the light to rest in the darkness? It is the latter, the spectacle of the immovable horizon gathering in the magnificence of the sun.

Some men think only of dawn and dusk, believing that the day begins in darkness, experiences light, and descends back into darkness. These might believe that the universe and history work according to this pattern, progressing from the long dark through the light of form and beauty before returning to the pit. Such men forget that the day and the night must come at their appointed times according to God's covenant. Just as man's need for rest implies his return to work, so the night implies the following day and the dusk looks forward to the dawn. Man should never stop at the darkness because God's covenant does not stop there, nor should man distill one day from the next because God has established them in their mutual dependence. Day will follow night until the eschaton, and so will the apparent end in darkness yield to new light, new birth, and the re-affirmation of life. The sun will again burst forth from the horizon in brilliant colors, again the light of life will dance across the sky, incandescent in glory. This time the joy of the sun will be greater, however, for through the sun's return from its rest men understand that God not only gives life but is faithful, that he both allows men rest and gives them light again that they might live. The light of life first emerges and is then absorbed, and lastly emerges once more. For God has made all things as an image, however rudimentary or opaque, of his love.

To explore another image of this love: one holds a seed in one's hand and observes only the shell. This outer covering conceals the embryo, a life dormant and asleep. Plant the seed in nutrient-rich ground, protecting it from birds and thorns. Then add water, so that its inner life begins to stir. The embryo awakens, unfolding in captivity, stirring against the hardness of the exterior. As this inner development increases the embryo expands and exerts a certain pressure on the shell. When this pressure achieves the needed strength, the plant breaks through the covering, which falls away. The seedling that has broken free ascends toward the surface, striving for further life. The pressure of the embryo against the shell, the breakthrough, and the appearance of new life resemble the first infinite within the Triune life. Just as the Son feels the gentle and joyous pressure of being within and upon his person, a pressure oriented toward life, so the shell feels the pressure of the embryo within until it matures into life without. For God has shaped all creation in the image of his wonder.

The seedling grows over time, sprouting a stalk and leaves according to its design. At the near apex of this growth, when the plant has sufficiently developed, the buds appear. The bud is like the seed inasmuch as it holds the blossom within. The latter is not ready all at once, but gestates until the right moment. It gains strength and form within the bud in a way reminiscent of the embryo within the seed, waiting until the proper time to break out of hiding and show forth in glory. At that moment, when the gentle pressure of the blossom so advances that the bud must give way, the latter does so unto life, a beauty and splendor radiating toward the sky. The pressure of the blossom as it matures within the bud and the joyfulness of that blossom as unveiled remind us of the second infinite within the Triune life. The Father feels the Son's life-outpouring as a delighted yearning for being and responds to its pressure by giving life in turn. So the bud feels the pressure of life in all its beauty, acquiescing to its expression in the flower. For God has shaped all creation in the image of his joy.

The flower reminds us that life emerges through the two infinities, the two joyful pressures of being as it seeks fulfillment. In this way it calls us to the Triune life as one also achieved through two joyful pressures of being.

The blossom looks upward, singing the song of life and inviting the pollinators. It says to the bee, "Come to me, I am yours! See what I have to give, take and eat! And in accepting what I give, I beseech you, give me life." So the lower humbles itself before the higher, the plant before the animal, in seeking the gift of reproduction. The bee obliges by lowering itself to the blossom, taking what it needs for sustenance and blessing the flower with fertilization, a critical step toward renewed life. When the lower opens itself to the higher and the latter agrees, offering itself likewise to the lower, the plant lowered before the animal and the animal lowered to the plant, their mutual humility again provides an image of the Triune life. In that life the Son gives all his outpouring of being to the Father as one subordinate to both the Father and the way of life intrinsic to Father and Son, while the Father lowers himself to the Son by returning life unto joy complete.

The natural order fashioned by God reflects the way of its creator inasmuch as that way, as sustaining and productive of life, implies the two pressures and mutual humility. For God has shaped all life-giving as an image of the divine communion. This is the case no less with the animals, and in particular with man and woman, as it is with the plants.

When husband and wife come together for the sake of life, the women opens herself to the man like the blossom to the bee. "Come to me, I am yours," she says. "See what sweetness I give to you, and you also shall give life to me." She thereby lowers herself before the man in heart if not literally in her body, handing her flesh to him without reserve. When he has set his heart and mind on life, the man responds to the woman in kind. "I see your humility before life and our union, and I also am humbled," he says, "so I lower myself likewise to you. I am present to you and dwell within you, giving my life to you." In intercourse as ordered within and subordinate to life the man and the woman come together in humility, with each lowered in the proper way. In this manner they make one flesh if not also one soul, providing a likeness of the Triune life. For God has formed all the cosmos in the image of his unity.

Although man and woman encounter one another in procreation as body and soul, the pressure belongs primarily to the body. The desire and commitment of husband and wife surround their coming together, a joining illumined in the buildup of sexual intensity, the mounting of energy toward expulsion, the tightening that yearns for release. This tension overcomes the man and the woman until they experience the breakthrough. For the man this means the giving of life, the issue of seed within his mate, while the woman receives it in the hope of conception. This increase of pressure to the breaking point, the pleasure involved, and the orientation of the act toward life resemble the first infinite within the Triune life. Just as the Son wells up within his own being toward the life-outpouring, so the man wells up toward the giving of the seed. For God has shaped all creation after the promise of life in him.

The pregnant woman carries the child in her womb, bearing within her one beloved of God. Over months the little one grows fingernails, hair, eyelids, and a heart, it learns to grasp, kick, and play, becoming as much man or woman as God had designed from the beginning. After many months in the dark its time draws near and in the last weeks the mother can barely avoid discomfort. Then comes labor, the excruciating agony of birth after the fall. The womb, like the bud of the flower, must give way to life in all its glory in the arrival of the newborn. The pressure of the child within the womb up to and including labor, extending as well to the great joy of the new son or daughter, reminds us of the second infinite within the Triune life. There the Father absorbs the life-outpouring of the Son in its fullness and responds by bestowing life in return. Absent sin and the pain of childbirth, the Father feels the gentle pressure of life received and gives it back. With this second giving there is not only joy but joy complete, something portrayed obliquely in the amazement of parents before their child. For no life-giving in this world fails to bear the image of its Maker.

Docetic man scoffs at these images as simplistic if not childish and inane. He knows more, he thinks, because he has accessed the unseen laws of the universe through his science, explaining the smallest and most basic forces by which the physical world works. He knows the atom, and in his mind anyone who knows the atom cannot really believe in God.

Yet bonding between atoms, the most basic coming together of life, is a natural image of the divine. Atomic bonding calls the mind to God inasmuch as the gathering-forces at the heart of creation portray a likeness of the divine unity.

When a metal atom bonds with a non-metal, the metal gives up electrons and the non-metal receives them. Dislocating the electrons from the grasp of the giver, which holds them by the pull of its nucleus, requires the giving atom's absorption of energy.

This absorption places a progressively intensifying pressure upon the atom until the accumulation of energy threatens its solidarity and structure. When the absorbed energy equals the gravitational pull of the nucleus the electrons are released from their usual orbit, threatening the makeup of the atom and opening it to a new possibility. In this way the pressure of the absorbed energy and the release of electrons that follows it enact a severance embedded within bonding, a dawn oriented to new life. Is this not also like the first pressure in the Trinity, in which the buildup of life-energy in the Son leads to its outpouring toward the Father?

According to the natural law, the electrons discharged from the metal atom traverse their path to the non-metal, arriving at their new home without exceptional effort. As they proceed further from the nucleus of the giver, the latter's pull diminishes so that the electrons easily join with the receiver. Like the sun descending at dusk, the electrons pass into the receiving atom, which absorbs them as its own. The receiver takes them in as life, as a force of transformation and augmentation, of beauty and increase. Thus the receiving atom accepts them as a joyous pressure, a mystery of ingathering that calls upon the recipient to act in kind. The receiving atom does not take without giving in return or run away with its prize, it is not selfish or an oppressor but a benevolent superior. It responds to the life-giving of the metal by welling up to a tremendous outpouring of energy, a burst that defines the accomplishment of unity. Like the celebration of a new dawn after rest, the outpouring proclaims the attainment of a state higher if not the highest. It is a natural image of joy complete, a joy reminiscent of the divine communion.

The two infinities again occur within an image of mutual humility. By giving its electrons away, the metal atom lowers itself before the receiving non-metal. When the non-metal receives these electrons, it gives life to the metal in the form of presence and union, of a shared way of being. In this manner the metal lowers itself before the non-metal, while the non-metal lowers itself to the metal. But the peace established is more profound: all along the electrons given by the metal amounted to a kind of excess, surpassing the proper capacity of the atom's fields. By giving them away, the atom attains a state of maximum stability through optimum balance. The loss of electrons lowers it to the level of the nearest noble gas. When the non-metal gains the electrons, its new members fill the vacancies that existed in its energy fields so that the number of electrons matches the atom's intended capacity. Just as the loss of electrons in the giving atom lowered it to a full limit, the gain of those electrons raises the recipient to plenitude. It achieves maximum stability through optimum balance, ascending to the level of the nearest noble gas. In their engagement the one is lowered while the other is raised, with each coming to the other in the humility of union.

Christ teaches the crowds that "Blessed are the merciful, for they shall receive mercy." If one practices mercy toward others, God will see what one has done in faith and, as a faithful God, he will reward your mercy to others with his own toward you. "Blessed are the pure in heart," Christ also teaches, "for they will see God." Those who dedicate their hearts to what is undefiled, to prayer, thanksgiving, humility, and hymnody, who summon God into their minds with every breath, who beseech God in his compassion to dwell within them, will find the Lord softened, making the soul his home. In this way the man who purely calls to the great purity discovers it abiding in him as the blessing of God in his heart. "Blessed are the peacemakers, for they will be called children of God." Those who avoid the strife, disputes, factions, and divisions of pride, who hold fast penitently to the will of God that peace should reign through Christ, who set their minds on gentleness and the refusal to lay burdens on others and do not make war against others in their hearts, calling God into them through these habits, shall discover God as their Father by the tranquility that he pours within them and the equanimity of their souls. To the merciful God shows himself merciful, to the pure in heart he reveals himself as the great purity, and to the peacemakers he comes as the Father of peace.

The Old Covenant promises "an eye for an eye and a tooth for a tooth." Such is the original measure of justice against those who would go too far or perhaps not far enough in punishment. Or as God says to Pharaoh, "Israel is my first born son. I said to you, 'Let my son go that he may worship me.' But you refused to let him go; now I will kill your firstborn son.'" When the Pharaoh denied the Israelites the opportunity to sacrifice and thereby for rest, scattering them throughout the land to gather straw and denying his child to the Lord, God imposed his will in kind. He unleashed an incomparable scattering upon the Egyptians in the plagues, which climaxed in the sacrifice of the Egyptian firstborn. Or as Joseph's brothers understood about their treatment of him: "Alas, we are paying the penalty for what we did to our brother; we saw his anguish when he pleaded with us, but we would not listen. That is why this anguish has come upon us." What one does to others, especially the weak and vulnerable, becomes one's destiny. Consider the punishment of David for his actions with Bathsheba and Uriah: "Why have you despised the word of the Lord to do what is evil in his sight? You have struck down Uriah the Hittite with the sword, and have taken his wife to be your wife . . . therefore the sword shall never depart from your house . . . and I will take your wives from before your eyes, and give them to your neighbor, and he shall lie with your wives in the sight of this very sun." By bringing the sword down upon Uriah, David brought it down upon himself; by taking the wife of another, he provoked the Lord to take his wives. Absalom the son of David fulfilled both of these promises, sleeping with David's concubines on the rooftop while attempting to usurp David's throne, bringing civil war to David's house. For good or ill, what a man works returns to him. For God is a reciprocator.

The Christ teaches us to pray, "Forgive us our sins, for we ourselves forgive everyone indebted to us." Just as men forgive others, practicing forbearance and patience while overlooking the faults and infractions of their neighbors, forgetting the sins that neighbors have committed against them, in this manner they request that God look on them with the same patience, forbearance, and willingness to remit the evil that they have done. Our kindness to our neighbors petitions God to show kindness to us; our softness of heart toward others pleads with God to exhibit a similar softness toward us; our patience with others calls out to God to show patience to us; and our forgiveness of others asks that God should forgive our faults, which are many. "In everything," says the Lord, "do to others as you would have them do to you; for this is the Law and the Prophets." If you would have men be merciful to you—and God also!—show mercy. If you would have even those who persecute you change and bless you, then bless them—and God will not neglect to bless you as well. If you would have men lend freely to you in your need, when you have come into your time of poverty—may God look graciously upon you in that hour—then give freely to those who beg and give to those who wish to borrow from you. If you would have men suffer with you when you suffer and rejoice with you when you rejoice, then do likewise for them—and God will bestow his grace upon you in both your suffering and your rejoicing. For in both the law and the prophets and in Jesus Christ, God is a reciprocator.

"Whoever sheds the blood of a man, by a man shall that person's blood be shed; for in his own image God made mankind." Men can easily read this passage and observe the dignity with which God regards man. So highly does the creator esteem his creature that whoever takes the life of a man will die, and the Scripture affirms that this is so because God made him in the divine image. This is not all: by stating that any man who sheds the blood of another shall have the same done to him, the Scripture promises that man's action today foreshadows a future that mirrors and inverts the present, a judgment inconceivable apart from the design that plants men among their neighbors in love. For the society of men, insofar as it is governed according to the divine nature, conforms to the image of that nature. Insofar as reciprocation reigns within the Trinitarian life, characterizing the communion of the God who is three and one, it also reigns within the life of men. God's creature may accept this reciprocal humility, this binding love, and abide within it joyfully as a member of Christ's body the church, or he may reject his destiny and become one who takes. In this event he calls down upon himself the cruelty he has rendered to God and others. In either case man cannot escape the reciprocal nature of the cosmos in which God has embedded him and his neighbors, for God has fashioned the company of men and their world after his own image.

The Trinitarian illumination begins with God the Father as source and unoriginate. Out of the joy of the Father and through his Yes to its petition for life, the gentle pressure of the paternal abiding, the Father begets the Son in the Spirit. The Son matures after the divine form, immutable, perfect, wondrous, incomprehensible, peaceful, and abundant in the joy present also in the Father. This joy presses upon the Son that he should give life in the Spirit, a life that does not beget another person but looks to the Father in faith and thanksgiving. In humility and as guided by the Spirit, the

Son moves through the infinitude of freedom and directs his life-outpouring to the Father. Upon receiving this gift the Father reciprocates by honoring the Son, turning through a second infinitude to the Son who has turned to him. This latter turning occurs no less in the Holy Spirit.

The life-outpouring of the Son is a mystery, the very life of the Son augmented through freedom and permeated by joy. We cannot define this life-outpouring more specifically except to say that the Son does not beget a new person, nor does he offer something external to his nature but that nature itself. This giving does not destroy his personhood, as though in giving of his being without restriction the Son were fully absorbed into the Father. As a creaturely image, consider the consequences of human gift-giving, in which one man's gift to another involves not only the object given but its emotional and spiritual entailments, the fellow-feeling and goodwill that naturally accompany the transfer of a good. Arguably the greater the gift the stronger the spiritual implication, so that when man gives all that he has and is for another man, one can say that he gives his heart to his neighbor. Joyous and grateful thoughts and feelings redound to the recipient through the gift and are present in it. The object not only symbolizes these things but carries them as intangible realities, a fact that magnifies the cruelty in deception. By receiving the gift, the recipient mirrors the generosity of the giver in thanks. Now the Son gives his being to the Father, not withholding the plenitude of his nature, and how can this not imply his heart in a way much more potent and mysterious than men discern in their own sharing of good things?

The life-outpouring of the Son makes no sense except as a gift meant for the Father. The Father makes the gift coherent because it is destined for him, because without him it becomes superfluous if not dubious in its origins and purpose. As a destined giving within the Trinitarian illumination the life-outpouring flows from the Son to the Father in faith and thanksgiving, passing from one to the other through the Spirit and toward the finality of perichoretic communion. Remove the life-outpouring from this particular Trinitarian life and it changes its goal as well as its form. Imagine that the life-outpouring has no intended goal in the Father, that it is not designed to come into his grasp. In this case it does not go anywhere, so to speak, but just is. One could conjecture the Son keeping it for himself as a witness to his life-producing power. This seems worthy enough, but if the Son produced this outpouring for his own glory he would also reject the leading of the Spirit and its testimony that the Father reciprocates. The Son would not trust the Father who begot him and would turn away from the Father to himself. In short, the Son would dwell in pride and the joyous pressure that produces the life-outpouring would suffer suspicion, ingratitude, and selfishness. How could it then be joyous? Would it retain the pressure toward life abundant and newly generating? Would the Son's abiding dwell contentedly within its limit or would the Son seek aggrandizement as a rejection of and a revolt against his origin? Certainly the latter, certainly the Son would deny the source of his life and thus his own being as a replication of that source. In this case the life-outpouring would make little sense. It must either exist as gift or exist as a pained contradiction, if it exists at all.

This mystery of the life-outpouring, this bestowal that men can describe only obliquely and without fully understanding yet in the highest terms, the Son delivers to the Father. From the harmony of the Son's life-outpouring wells up the pressure, the joyful force that the Father feels as the inclination to life. Though the Father feels this pressure its weight remains ever gentle, ever tender. Never does this pressure become the infinite as fallen men experience it, never is it harsh, impersonal, draconian, tyrannical, savage, and cruel. It leans upon the heart of the Father like the disciple who reclined upon the Lord, like one at rest in the presence of his master. The Son's life-outpouring meets with the Father's freedom such that the freedom at first retains the upper hand and rules in the affair, as though the servant had met his superior. The joy of the life-outpouring implies within it the request for more, the desire for new life, but it submits to the fact that it cannot eventuate in new life if it abstracts away from freedom. Only the divine will brings about the mystery. The affair thus involves a mutual respect and sharing of place between the Son's life-outpouring and the Father. In its exuberance, the joy that exerts pressure on the Father comes to him seeking approval, the entry into his heart.

When the Son passes the pressure for life to the Father for blessing and furtherance, he holds back his hand like a servant awaiting the response of his master. In this manner the Son, as the giver of the gift, rests in the Father. The Son's part comes to an end, his portion of the advance of life from joy to joy complete temporarily halts. He annuls his work as all turns on the Father's liberty, hinging on the latter's will to facilitate the divine life. Just as the abiding within the Father turns over the pressure of life to his freedom, passing through the death-moment as a means toward begetting, a passage revealed obliquely in the image of the burning bush, so the Son gives the form of the life-gift in the hope that it will pass through the freedom of the Father toward a reciprocal giving of life. Now the Son dies to his work, to his effort and contribution in the illumination, now his contribution is the stillness of rest.

Here the testimony of the Holy Spirit confirms the righteousness of the Son. The Spirit approaches the Father, as it were, with the request that he receive the life-gift of the Only-Begotten, accepting the overflow of the Son's being. Cautiously and with reverence we might imagine the Spirit encouraging the Father this way: "I beseech you to take up the life-gift of the Son and allow it to penetrate into your depths, becoming one with it." Rather than the possibility of rejection (if this is at all possible), the Spirit calls the Father to turn to the Son. The call includes the recognition that the Son has forwarded the illumination of life by humbling himself before the Father in his gift. This is the Son's righteousness as expressed in the Holy Spirit, who is the Spirit of mutual humility and thus of union. Turn to me, says the Son to the Father in the Spirit, as I have turned to you. I have humbled myself before and beneath you, says the Only-Begotten to the source through that same Spirit, in faith that that you will be humbled to me.

We learn in the Gospels that the Christ came to glorify the Father. There we see Jesus on his mission to reveal the Father to the world, testifying to the truth. There we see him performing miracles, healing the souls and bodies of those who appeal to him. There we see him teaching the commandments that lead to theosis and warning his followers against the pride of the world. There we see him confronting the powers that do not recognize his divinity and who wish to publicly refute it, who devise plots to kill him and label him a criminal, who subject him to pain, ignominy, and death. The Christ performs the works noted above and especially endures his sacrifice as a lowering that lifts up the Father and gives him glory. The Son's food is not physical but it is "to do the will of him who sent me and to complete his work." He teaches that he does nothing on his own, but "speaks these things as the Father has instructed him." Jesus adds, "The Father who sent me has given me a commandment about what to say and what to speak. And I know that his commandment is eternal life." He offers his life in submission to the Father and as a witness to the profundity that life continues through and beyond death. For his service in the matter the Father glorifies him in turn, as Jesus says, "If I glorify myself, my glory is nothing. It is my Father who glorifies me." After Judas leaves to betray him, setting in motion the lowering that is Christ's "lifting up" inasmuch as it implies and looks forward to his resurrection, Jesus declares: "Now the Son of Man has been glorified, and God has been glorified in him. If God has been glorified in him, God will also glorify him in himself and will glorify him at once." If the Christ has humbly glorified the Father, the Father will return glory upon the Son "in himself and at once."

This return of glory to the Son from the Father replicates the glory given to the Son because the Father loved him before the foundation of the world. When the Son comes to earth, he bows to the Father out of the promise of a glory not unlike the glory he receives in the eternity of the Trinity. Out of his confidence in this promise he says to his followers that "Whoever serves me must follow me," dying as Christ dies, "and where I am, there will my servant be also. Whoever serves me, the Father will honor." Whoever gives glory to the Son, being humbled before him as Lord and Master, is humbled before God also as Lord and Master, and those who bear fruit and become Christ's disciples glorify the Father as well as the Son. As the Father honors the Son for submitting to the divine testimony, he honors the Son's disciples for imitating that testimony in the Spirit. Behind both of these testimonies as a model and a precursor stands the immutable testimony, the unending revelation of the truth in love, the honoring of the Son by the Father in the Trinitarian illumination.

The Father bestows this honor in the acceptance of the Son's life-outpouring and in his subsequent reciprocation. The Father receives the gentle pressure for life, the experience of remarkable joy emanating from the Son's gift, and his heart is moved by both this joy and his gratitude for the Son. Taking up the gift in his freedom, the

Father wills the infinite in the divine Yes. He wills that his freedom should serve as a passage point for the Son's life-outpouring, that as the infinite it should act as the permeable barrier, the limit destined to submit into being. In the Yes of his heart the Father's freedom is annulled. His distance or objectivity with respect to the gift perishes and the Son enters in, mysteriously becoming one with the Father. This marks a great step toward the teleological union of the Father and the Son in the Spirit, whose end the mind of man cannot glimpse, for the Father accepts the gift of the Son not as an external offering but as being unified with his own, which he gathers into his person. The same freedom that limits the Father's abiding and through which he begets life now is cancelled in order to draw the Son into his being, into his very life. Otherwise the gathering of God does not come to completion, otherwise a dubious objectivity remains between the Father and the Son. The latter therefore gives his life and the Father receives it as his own, as offered through the Spirit. Now the result of freedom's self-annulment in the Father grows more glorious, for in freedom's annulment the fruition of life involves the union of the gift and the recipient as well as a new and corresponding life-outpouring that reflects the union. The Father returns the life-gift of the Son back to him augmented and bettered, compounded in joy.

In this manner the Father wills life, but in the will-to-life he affirms a subordinate and mediating absorption of death. Not that the Father wills actually to die, but that in blessing the Son's life-outpouring the Father accepts that, although the Son has given him the gift, he accepts it not by keeping it for himself but by allowing it to pass through him. When the being of the Son's life-outpouring traverses the infinitude of the Father, the latter does not withhold its movement or arrogate it as private. Nowhere does the Father say "You have glorified me" without saying "I shall glorify you," nowhere does he say "You have humbled yourself before me" without saying "I shall be humbled to you" or "I shall honor you." What the Son has given he receives from the Father, and more, for the Father gives as one who spreads generously, as one without worry or ill feeling, as one bubbling over with magnanimity and resolve. The Father reciprocates in thanksgiving for the Son's gift and his joy in receiving it.

This reciprocation reverses the relationship in which the Son looks to the Father as a servant to his master, granting the Father the upper hand. In possession of the request, the Father acquiesces by submitting to the joyous pressure of the life-gift. The Father recognizes its destiny in a greater outpouring, recognizing as well that only the divine life can absorb death toward new life. The Father thus gives in to the Son for the purpose of expanded life. For the Son's gift possesses the power of life in fact but moreso in the appeal, being oriented to its cessation in the Father; the latter, not puffed up with pride, responds toward life by annulling his freedom and bowing into the gift, allowing it to permeate and perdure through him. On the other side of this perdurance, this traversing of death, the life-gift bursts forth augmented and multiplied, the divine miracle of joy increasing without end. The gift emerges like a new dawn, now the possession of the Father just as the Father dies to himself through the gift, which is the very life of the Father conjoined with the Son's and augmented through freedom. The Father gives this gift in full to the Son, bestowing his being upon the Only-Begotten and holding back nothing for himself, dying to himself so that life should blossom in the Spirit. This is the Father's thanksgiving for and his work of union with the Only-Begotten, the humility of the Father to the Son who humbled himself before him.

When does the Christ not say that he who gives will receive back more than what he has given? "The measure you give will be the measure you get, and still more will be given to you. For to those who have"—that is, those who have the love of God that gives—"more will be given; and from those who have nothing"—who lack the same love of God—"even what they have," the grace and life that God has shed on them as he sheds it on all, "will be taken away." Or as Jesus teaches his disciples after meeting the rich man, "Truly I tell you, there is no one who has left house or brothers or sisters or mother or father or children or fields, for my sake and for the gospel, who will not receive a hundredfold now in this age—houses, brothers and sisters, mothers and children, and fields, with persecutions—and in the age to come, eternal life." Or hear the parable of the talents, in which the master rewards the servant who took five talents and made five more, commending also the slave who made two talents beyond the two given him. Yet the slave who received one talent, who hid it rather than making more from what he had received, earns condemnation from his master. The slave misunderstands his master, claiming that he "reaps where he did not sow and gathers where he did not scatter seed," as if God takes what is not his by force! Neither does the slave act on the inclination toward life intrinsic to his Lord. For this reason he meets God as one who turns away: because the slave rejected the augmentation of God's gifts toward life, God rejects him. But the augmentation, the bettering of life as it moves from God through the hands of his servants, draws its meaning from the augmentation of life through freedom within the Trinity and especially from the life-gift of the Father as it multiplies the life-gift of the Son. From the Father the Son reaps thirty, sixty, and one-hundredfold, from the Father the Son receives ten talents in place of five. The life-gift of the Son comes back to him greatly expanded and strengthened by the beneficence of the source and origin.

Like the burst of energy upon the union of atoms, so the Father's return of his very life to the Son confirms their bond. In this bond the Father lowers himself to the Son who is lowered beneath him. This mutual humility, the giving of the Son preceding the giving of the Father, sets the pattern for the divine repetition within the Spirit. For the Son accepts the Father's life-gift in a way that mirrors the Father's acceptance of the Son's, and as that gift moves through the Son's affirmation it grows again, bolstered through its union with the Son and the passage through his heart. This new and enlarged gift goes back again to the Father in the Spirit so that the Father can welcome it again in the Spirit. Although it surpasses all of man's words and explanations and renders his ideas a nullity, although he cannot begin to comprehend the fullness of the divine communion, man can say that the Trinitarian illumination reveals the endless sharing of life in reciprocal joy, the uninterrupted mutual outpouring of an impervious and advancing life, a life drawn out infinitely as it is actually infinite, a burgeoning of being whose wonder cannot be excelled.

This breathing communion is joy complete, a fulfillment that teaches the Holy Spirit as the Spirit of communion through mutual humility. Wherever there is life, unity, peace, love, and thus truth, there is the Spirit of truth. He is present in the life-giving structure of the Father, in the interaction between the Father's abiding and his heart. In the abiding's lowering before freedom and in freedom's lowering into the abiding, a movement that accomplishes union and begets life, there is the Spirit.[1] Inasmuch as the life of both the Father and the Son, as well as the life-giving power of each, implies this mutual humility within the divine persons, at least to that extent the Holy Spirit indwells both Father and Son. How the Spirit proceeds from the Father man cannot say, as the Bible gives no indication regarding this occurrence, but Scripture and Tradition instruct us that the Spirit is God, that his unifying work pervades the Trinity as it pervades the church. The Holy Spirit thus abides within the Father and the Son as a full participant in the Trinitarian life.

The Spirit abides no less as an external person who guides the illumination to its destiny in joy complete. As he who testifies to the Father's faithfulness before the Son and leads the latter's life-gift toward the Father, as he who petitions the Father's acceptance, as it were, and confirms the Father's reciprocal gift for the Son, as one who works not only within the Father and the Son but between them, the Spirit exists as one both internal to the other persons and external to them. The mutual love between the Father and the Son does not "give birth" to the Spirit as a result but presumes his activity as having proceeded from the Father alone. That mutual love reveals the Spirit in his externality, as a third person whose activity is no less necessary than the Father's and the Son's and whose engagement in and experience of the illumination of life coincides with that of the other persons. Consider creaturely procreation as an image of the Trinity: the female lowers herself beneath the male while he lowers himself to her, and out of this mutual humility comes the third, the child, who was implicit in the male's seed and the female's egg. The procreative pattern of mutual humility reveals the child not only as implicit to its participants but as externalized in the third, the new creation. The human image is not perfect (as no image is), for in the Trinity the fullness of the Spirit is implicit and actually present in the Father and the Son while the mutual humility of the two does not create the third. Yet in both the Trinity and its creaturely image the implicit becomes explicit, externalized in its distinction.

---

1. I hope that in saying this I am not far from Bishop Nikolai Velimirovich, who writes that "The All-Holy Spirit hovered over the chastity of the first hypostasis, and the Ultimate Man, the Wisdom of God, was begotten" (*Prayers by the Lake*, X). Although he says it more beautifully, we both affirm that the Spirit is present in the begetting of the Son.

In the mutual humility of the Father and the Son in the Holy Spirit men glimpse the divine love, a love grounded in the righteousness of God. In the latter each person in the Godhead trusts in the faithfulness of the others while himself remaining faithful, so that among the persons faith grounds and works through love unto the perfection of both. As mutual humility love presupposes mutual righteousness, which co-operates with mutual faith. The divine love, as dependent on the divine righteousness, is thus "through faith for faith." It matures first through the faith of the Father as he begets the Son. For the Father knows that the illumination must achieve its fullness, knowing as well that it must achieve this fullness through the free participation of the Only-begotten in the Spirit. The Father has faith that the Son will give his life-outpouring, performing his part in the mutual humility of the divine love, and in this faith the Father begets the Son. This "through faith" of confident begetting occurs "for faith," that is, so that the Son should act according to a like faith in the Father. Just as the Father begets through faith in the Son's will to give his life in humility, the Son acts on his faith that the Father will reward the gift of life-outpouring in the Spirit, sharing the divine life in an act replicating the Son's. The righteousness of God constituted in the mutual faith of the Father and the Son through the Spirit thus comes to fruition within and between the three as one, so that these three persons are one God. On the basis of the divine righteousness man understands that God is love.

The divine love likewise comes to completion as each person rests in the others. Inasmuch as the Father has faith that the Son will give freely and so facilitate the illumination, he also rests in the Son as one who fulfills his part in joy and peace through the Spirit. Inasmuch as the Son has faith that the Father will return the life-gift, rewarding the Son's giving and bringing mutual love into joy complete, the Son rests in the Father as He who brings all things to fulfillment in the Spirit. And the third, inasmuch as he has faith that the Father and the Son will freely give unto love, also rests in both. The practice of faith among the persons means that each enters into the rest of the others, not coercing or compelling them to action but trusting in them in tranquility, being still so that each can work his part in thanksgiving and gentleness.

But hear this: the Trinitarian persons rest in their neighbors as they have given to them and through them. The Father rests in the Son and the Holy Spirit as he has given his life to the Son through the Spirit. The Son rests in the Father and the Spirit as he has given the life-outpouring to the Father in the same Spirit. And the Spirit rests in each as it forwards their mutual giving. This work of giving, this life-gift that men might call sacrifice, is implied in and in a way precedes the rest that each takes in the others while it brings to completion the faith that each has in the others. Each person has faith that the others will give life and each rests in the surety that they will do so, but this resting does not occur apart from the act of offering and is unthinkable without it. How could the Father expect the Son to give life if he had had not first given life to the Son? Or how could the Son hope that the Father would reward a life-gift that he had not given? Shall faith not work through love? In a case involving men, picture

Abraham commanded by God to sacrifice Isaac, thus giving up God's promise and the human life-gift of offspring. Now imagine that Abraham says to himself, "I have faith in God and I believe that he will not take Isaac away. I believe in God's promise." Convincing himself in this manner, Abraham does not rise early in the morning, he does not go to Moriah, he does not build the altar or raise the knife to kill his son. He gives no offering and makes no effort because all along he has had faith and the work, he thinks, is irrelevant. Foolish Abraham! Would the angel call him to cease who had failed to begin to act? Would the angel say "Now I know that you fear God, since you have not withheld your son, your only son, from me"? Abraham has done no such thing! In this scenario he does not hear the angel nor does he hear God's promise that "Because you have done this, and have not withheld your son, your only son, I will indeed bless you." Understand, brothers, that a man must offer his life if he should receive it back bettered by God, and he must do this in body and soul, carrying out his faith in action as he hopes in God's rest. Understand also that this faith and rest in God has its model in the divine love, the Trinitarian mutual humility and shared life-giving. Apart from the work of giving man does not act in faith, he forfeits the divine rest, and he exiles himself from the divine love.

The righteousness and love of the Trinity provide the model for God's covenant with men. In calling Abraham and his descendants as the people of Israel God acts in faith. The Lord set his love on the Israelites alone and chose them out of all the peoples in faith and hope that these would turn to him. He chose them through the faith that the best among them would honor the covenant and serve only him, obeying the commandments and forsaking other gods, although he knew that frailty and weakness would often undermine the people at large. He selected them so that they might have faith in him, calling them out through his faith for their faith. The covenant formulary expresses the structure of this double faith: I will be your God and you will be my people. Like the Son who humbles himself beneath the Father, in "I will be your God" the Israelites humble themselves beneath their Lord. Like the Father who humbles himself to the Son, in "You will be my people" God humbles himself to the Israelites, dwelling among them alone from the nations. This union comes about through the two infinities, the freedom of each to be humbled with respect to the other. The historical double infinities along the way to the creation of Israel—the near sacrifice of Isaac and the famine in the days of Joseph, the Exodus and the Passover before entering Canaan—remind us that through the two infinities God accomplishes communion, exercising these infinities toward mutual humility. Such is the case within the Trinity, so also is it the case between God and his creatures.

In a manner similar to the Trinity and God's covenant with Israel, the church also discovers its righteousness "through faith for faith." The "through faith" belongs to Christ, who dies and rises through faith first that the Father will reward his humility and secondly that God will redeem mankind through his work. Through Christ's faith God works "for faith," for the belief of men in the righteousness of God as faithful and for their own humility within the divine love. This "for faith" lives in the life-gifts of men given to God through gifts to others and principally to their brothers, through their generosity in the name of Christ. Through the faith of these saints in their giving spreads a broader "for faith," as the imitation of Christ multiplies through those who share his faith and act upon it. Those who make up the church through this ongoing mutual sacrifice dwell together as the body of Christ, his bride. Christ says to them, in effect, "I will be your head and you will be my body," just as the marriage of man and woman serve as an image of Christ and the church. In saying "I will be your head," Christ calls the church to freely humble itself beneath him, recognizing him as its only Lord. By saying "You will be my body," Christ promises to join himself to the people and abide within and among them. This communion also matures to fulfillment through two infinities, the collective mysteries of baptism and eucharist. There Christians say as one that they rest in Christ's sacrifice while they pledge their life-gifts to one another and the surrounding community in Christ's name. Through these two freedoms Christ draws men into his heart, that they should lay down their lives for him and for their neighbors in the hope of the great undeserved rest, eternal life.

Brothers, God is love, and those who abide in love abide in God, and God abides in them. Abide in God! Every minute of every hour lower yourselves before him in prayer, remembering his righteousness and the promise of the grace of salvation for those who seek him. As St. Paul instructs, we must pray without ceasing. I say again, abide in God! When you see your brother in need, when those who have lost spouses, children, and other loved ones are near, when you encounter the sick, the infirm, the abandoned, the widows, the orphans, and the stranger, give to them the life-gift of your body as well as your heart. Share of your possessions and so fill their lack. Through your faith that the righteous God does not neglect gifts given humbly in his name, act for the faith of those who might doubt the Lord's mercy. I say again, abide in God! When men turn upon you for the name of Christ, when they despise you and persecute you and speak all kinds of evil against you, when they threaten your possessions and your person, humbly endure their anger, absorbing it into the undying love of Christ. Pray for those who hate you and bless those who curse you, ministering to the hardships of all. Through your faith in the rest of the soul in this world and the hereafter, a faith manifest in the willingness to relinquish earthly powers and comforts, witness to Christ for the faith of your adversaries. Humble yourself before God in these ways and he will honor you. Lower yourself beneath him and he will lower himself to you. In this way "as he is, so are we in the world," as his body bound to imitate the love given to us by our head. For "we" are not a collection of individuals but a single body, interwoven and mutually dependent, fulfilled in reciprocal love and so bold on the day of judgment.

Men today talk as though this judgment were an insult, as though God could not and would not judge because he lacks a reason for judging. But God judges inasmuch as he reciprocates, returning not only good for good but permitting harm to come to the wicked. Men of each kind reap what they sow, the humble to honors bestowed by God and the iniquitous to punishments that fit their crimes. As Isaiah proclaims of the righteous and the wicked, "Say to the righteous that it shall be well with him . . . and to the wicked that it shall be ill with him, for the reward of his hands shall be given him." And as Jeremiah prophecies, "Therefore all who devour you shall be devoured, and all your foes, everyone one of them, shall go into captivity; those who plunder you shall be plundered, and all who prey on you I will make a prey." Those who do evil bring it upon themselves, as God states through Ezekiel and Obadiah, "I will deal with you as you have done." Or as 2 Esdras teaches from the Lord, "Because you have forsaken me, I will also forsake you. When you beg mercy of me, I will show you no mercy. When you call to me, I will not listen to you; for you have defiled your hands with blood, and your feet are swift to commit murder. It is not as though you had forsaken me; you have forsaken yourselves, says the Lord." This revelation of the divine nature belongs no less to the New Testament. When Christ exhorts his followers to do as they would have done to them, he implicitly warns them that those who perform evil will see it visited upon them. He implies, as the psalmist long before, that he who pronounces a curse will receive its ill. He that has shown no mercy, says James, will receive judgment without mercy, while not only does God destroy the man who destroys his temple, but he also destroys those who destroy the earth. Does God have no right to mete out to men as they have stored up for themselves, gathering those who turn to him and leaving his enemies in the outer darkness? Look to the whore of Babylon, "how much she glorified herself and lived deliciously," and how she gained for herself an equal measure of sorrow and torment. "Reward her even as she rewarded you," and in an inversion of the expanding life-outpouring between Father and Son, "render her double according to her works: in her cup, fill double."

Beware those who teach that the unrepentant shall suffer no harm because God is love! At the judgment all will meet God as a consuming fire, a flame that will burn within the righteous as the peaceful and loving presence of God just as it visits the wicked as a scourge, confirming them in their sin. It is the same love of God experienced on one hand as a validation of those who have struggled on the path of healing and, on the other, as sinners' inestimable pain at the realization of what they have lost, how paradise has closed to them because they have closed themselves to it. Those who receive recompense for their sins thus meet the divine fire as holiness and justice, and through these as love. They have chosen to meet the reciprocating love of God, the fire that burns in the believer's heart, in a form inverted by their withdrawal from him.

The ontology of No begins with man's dissatisfaction with his being. Rather than eyeing the good that God has given him, accepting the form that defines him and the life toward which God has oriented him, rather than taking up his freedom as a remarkable mystery subordinated within that orientation toward life, man decides that God has given him a raw deal. He decides that he cannot and should not rest content with God's gift, that his form limits and so degrades him, and that his freedom should not confirm and facilitate life within God's commands but should explore life as man imagines it beyond them. The blessing with which God has honored man, the beauty of the divine image and the wonder of existence, reside so powerfully in men that they cannot come to this decision without being deceived. This was the case at the beginning when the serpent tempted Eve and Adam through her. The adversary persuaded them to think that God is a liar if not the author of falsehood, and by implication that their natures suffer that falsehood as his creation. Then he pointed them to the fruit, by which he suggested that they could be like God. In directing them to the fruit and to the supposedly higher way of life and wisdom implied in the eating, the tempter drew them to despise if not hate their life under God's design. "You have been made too low by the creator," he whispers, "so raise yourselves up to new and better heights." Seeing that the fruit was pleasant to the eye and useful for making one wise, and not imagining any negative consequences to result from partaking in it, each took a bite. In this the first coupled spurned God as they spurned themselves as his creatures. They said No to the creator because they refused their own creaturely form, though it bears his image.

After the Fall men arguably have a reason to despise their life and pursue a better one. In sin and death they endure suffering, loss, various types of pain, a host of furies and agonies continually besetting their minds and bodies and jubilant that they must die. Men can therefore say that they should improve their lot, that they must strive to somehow make things better, and how could God argue with them? As long as their desire to make things better merges with their desire to return to him, humbling them before the limits he has prescribed and turning their hearts to him in prayer, so long as "making things better" contributes to the larger task of union with Christ and the love of God and neighbor, God does not contend against but desires their improvement. But the evil one infiltrates the minds of men so skillfully that they do not perceive his direction of their energies away from sin as a blight upon nature to that nature itself. Especially in this later docetic age men try to improve their lives by eradicating the good of nature, to say nothing of contradicting the possibility of communion with the Savior. So Luther desired desperately to be saved, to have peace, rest, and Christ's grace in the heart, but by following the course of the infinite he unexpectedly annulled the limits intrinsic to the attainment of his desire. He attempted to "make things better" but in a way that severed his nature and drove him away from Christ, alienating him from his Lord. Men have repeated this misled attempt in various ways since Luther's era, and in these cases the man or men who set about the infinite have hoped to make things better while galloping away from God. In this manner men worsen rather than ameliorate their condition, for they seek betterment not within the divine communion but as a protest against it.

Through deception, then, and not because of any deficiency in what God has made, man despises the nature given to him. This nature becomes an offense to him, and so man decides that he must abandon his mortal existence for the beyond. Perhaps he asserts that he is lower than God but higher than men, or perhaps he believes he is a little god, an infinite potentiality destined for boundlessness. While every age has seen men whose dissatisfaction at their humanity motivated them, in the docetic age this proclivity has ballooned under the pressure of the infinite law until men dream the whole purpose of their lives as the aggrandizement of human possibilities, the destruction of boundaries, and the elevation of earth-dwellers to heaven. These values disclose man's pride just as they conceal his self-hatred, his disdain for the smallness of his life. It is this smallness, an insufferable finitude intensified by man's imprisonment in the docetic assembly-line, that turns docetic men against the creator who made them. Offended at his nature, docetic man likewise takes offense at the God who created it, rejecting the one who fashioned him not for eternal augmentation but for the mystery of communion. Man cannot feel anxiety, anger, malcontent, and hatred toward his form without propelling all of these onto God. This anxiety and anger, this jealousy for one's imagined improvement and his envy of God and neighbor drive the creature to action that repudiates both his limits and his creator.

Man's actions inevitably affect the creator of all things for good or ill. Just as the man who finds contentment and joy in the limit of nature, humbling himself to that limit as a medium for his humility before God, meets his Lord therein as one overjoyed to receive his creaturely overtures, so the man who spurns the limit of nature and regards his definition as a tyrant presses against God as an adversary. And God suffers! The divine heart yearns as a father for his sons, it is pained at the negligence of men who seek food and clothing, trifling pleasure and power, over the everlasting embrace. In the prophecy of Ezekiel, in many places so horrifying and terrible, and in which one could imagine a heartless God carrying out the punishments, the Lord says to those destined for scattering among the nations: "Those of you who escape shall remember me among the nations where they are captive, how I was crushed by their wanton heart that turned away from me, and their wanton eyes that turned to idols. Then they will be loathsome in their own sight for all the evils they have committed." Despite their smallness men can crush the God of heaven, for he loves them tenderly, and as a parent scorned by his child our God endures pain from those who abandon and insult him.

The man who abolishes his limit by expanding beyond it thus dominates and oppresses. He means to enlarge his own sphere and believes that by doing so he procures greater rest. In truth he forces out all that gives him rest, God and his neighbor, as a reflection of his unhappiness with his nature. He dominates God by pressing the thought of the Lord out of his heart, concentrating on violence while casting the life-giver into outer darkness. He dominates God also by raising his actions against the creator, proclaiming that man can improve upon what God has designed. "You have created," says docetic man, "but I can excel what you have done. I can make this world a better place, one without peril, worry, or useless impediments." In this spirit docetic man sets about the domination in which he, as one dedicated to the infinite law, refashions his world into a place without rest, a place defined by systems of domination. In order to improve the earth (that is, to make it a home for his infinite nature) docetic man must visit the infinite upon it, dominating and exploiting it, while in order to improve his society he sets the conditions of domination, even of war. Men never say to themselves that they mean to eradicate rest from the world and indulge their indifference toward it, but this they do. Nor do they say that they will dominate their neighbors, while in the language of raising the lot of all men, this they do.

Man cannot dominate God without dominating his neighbors, just as he cannot rest in God without resting in his neighbors. As he rebels against God by rebelling against his limits, he hates his neighbor both by rejecting his individual limit and, in a more cunning fashion, inviting his neighbor to envision and pursue a world in which none recognize their limit. When docetic man says to his neighbor "Let us be liberated, let us have no limits!," he does not perceive that he also says "Let us relinquish rest in one another! Let us become minions of the infinite task!" Taking up this task and abolishing rest, and in the pride of their supposed service to God, humanity, or progress, they submit to the ethos of mutual hatred. Let us look again at the history of schism in western Christendom. Men used to announce their justification by faith alone and their freedom from works and the law, implying that the form of their lives has no bearing for redemption. By casting off the law, they proclaimed that it could not limit them. From this starting point those who believed that they were saved (and thus expelled the freedom of God) rose up against the Roman Church and one another, church versus church and sect versus sect, multiplying over centuries until the church's ways of worship are as many as its towns and every man does what is right in his own eyes. In his liberation from the law of God that is the way of God, docetic man was liberated from God himself. Does it surprise anyone that docetic men thereby liberated themselves from one another, destroying Christ's body in the process? In saying "I will not be limited by the law" in one breath and "I am assured of salvation" in the next, differences of doctrinal opinion led to the combat in which each claims his own righteousness and the error of others. From these grounds each sought to dominate the others, wielding claims to truth as so many weapons of spiritual warfare against their foes, who also claimed the name of Christ.

Domination raises men against one another by way of criteria that exalt some over others within the same congregation or throw entire congregations and churches into battle. As long as those driven by the pride of certitude insist that they cannot be wrong, that they have undeniable proof of their righteousness and salvation, and as they consequently persecute rivals with the aim of destroying dissent, seeking an absolute uniformity with their own views, then the docetic spirit of domination guides their movements. This spirit does not culminate in domination, however, but exploits it as a means to another ontological end. Whether foreseen and desired by the dominators or not, their action tends to the greater goal of indifference toward the dominated.

When God says that the Jews crushed him by turning away from him, he describes both the attitude from which their actions sprouted and the actions themselves. As a presupposition for the false sacrifices, for the idolatry and abominations in the temple, for trampling the poor and needy and selling them for sandals, the hearts of Israelites had turned from the God who loved them, called them out, and sought a covenant with them. The turning away of the heart comes to life through the practical domination of God and man, grieving the love of God and abandoning the neighbor in one swoop. This domination seeks the practical fulfillment of its presupposition, aiming to materialize the indifference of the heart in concrete action, as if saying to God that one has disavowed him with the heart and the hands. Yet it cannot attain its end without the consent of God, who, after patience and opportunities for rapprochement, shows again his nature as a reciprocator. Here he does not return life for life, gift for gift, and love for love. He rather says to the people who have rejected him that he likewise rejects them. He called the Hebrews into being so that reciprocal life should bind the two parties, so that the people would humble themselves before him as God while he humbled himself to them as his people. The people's domination of God negates the first half of the covenant formulary, so distancing the people from God that they sum up their indifference by renouncing their recognition of him. "You are not our God," they say by their actions, implying their liberation from his law, their rebellion against his authority, and their indifference to his presence. In this manner the rebels press against him, cornering God, as it were, into the necessity of turning their evil back upon them. They desired formlessness, they desired freedom, and in so doing they had to crush the capacity for God to shower them with blessing. When they have accomplished this, achieving such dedication to their disobedience that their excelling of their limit all but eradicates the liberty of the Lord to will them good, he gives them over to the consequences implicit in their course. He says in response, taking the form of the people's rejection to heart, "I am not your God." He adds to this the dreadful corollary, the consequence of his recognition of man's indifference, "you are not my people."

Woe to those who reject the lifegiver, for they reject life! Woe to those who pledge themselves in liberation from the lifegiver, for they will be released from life! When God asserts that these men are not his people, when he affirms that their indifference has provoked his own, that he will turn away from them as they have turned from him, he sets in motion the completion of his promise. Man will endure the lifegiver's absence, his lack of concern for the creature that despises him. And if man must come to the indifference of God, must he not endure domination as a means to it? God wishes terror upon no man, he does not actively seek to despoil his beloved. He must only withdraw, he must only reciprocate, but when he does the cruelty of men is visited upon them. Those who sought to dominate God and men endure domination, those who crushed the heart of God and their fellows are crushed, those who took have their treasures taken, the destroyers are destroyed. When the lifegiver announces that he will cut ties with a people, from where shall they receive their life? They have nothing that does not come from him. When the lifegiver declares that he shall leave, how does the people find joy? Not in marriage, for it is forgotten; not in children, for the womb is cursed; not in the labor of the field, for the ground is barren; not in the society of men, for it is cut to pieces, distrustful, and warlike; not in the body troubled with disease and pain; and not in the mind, which succumbs to despair and horror, to visions of loss that gouge out the heart. Let no man misunderstand the anguish of the lifegiver's abandonment or the domination by which it comes: all war, all famine, all pestilence, all alienation and isolation, all the deprivation of humanity entailed in the mutual death of soul and body, point to the removal of the lifegiver's mercy and his forsaking of those who have forsaken him.

Modern men consider such punishment unnecessary if not barbaric, as though God had responded with a nuclear bomb to sins committed with a knife. Such men do not comprehend the ontological course of Docetism, they walk in blindness to the foundations of their ethos. Docetic man assumes formlessness, a freedom of infinite possibility, as the assumption of his nature and the goal of his actions. Formlessness, the something-nothing and the is-that-is-not, is matter that has not yet come to be, and its suspension in becoming consists in the annulment of a form posited and ready to assert itself. Formlessness "is" inasmuch it begins to take shape as something distinct, but immediately "is not" as the promised form disintegrates, a disintegration that negates the positing not simply by contradicting it but by a total opposition. When men under the aspect of the infinite affirm their character as destroyers, they posit a form as such. But to consummate their infinitude as destroyers—that is, to annul the apparent form unto formlessness—they must be more than "not destroyers," a simple suspension of the positing, but they must themselves suffer destruction. Or when men live by taking, hoarding power and wealth at the expense of nature and other men, the presupposition of infinitude and its eventual realization requires that they suffer the total annulment, existing as those whose goods are taken. They must suffer despoliation as they themselves have despoiled. Only in this manner do they fulfill their chosen ontology; only in this manner do they achieve the materialization of their indifference to God, by suffering his indifference toward them. Not all docetic men bear the extremity of this total opposition on earth, but woe to those to whom it comes.

Such men become spectacles to themselves and their neighbors, dwelling in the throes of death like men forced to wait in the guillotine. Their confusion at their predicament exacerbates it because they did not consider themselves enemies of life but its protectors. The ancient Israelites did not think of themselves as sinners, they did not recognize their actions as transgressions. Had those in the Northern Kingdom not multiplied altars? Were they not observant of the festivals and eager for the day of the Lord? Surely they considered themselves blessed and holy, perhaps some of them saw themselves as truly religious. Though they laid down on garments taken in pledge, surely they had arguments justifying this action. Few men knowingly walk the path to hell, few knowingly invite damnation. For this reason the curses announced by the prophets must have shocked the guilty. They did not say with their mouths that God was not their God, they did not reject him directly with their tongues. Nor did they likely set out to oppress the poor against God's command, although they lived recklessly. One should at least give them the benefit of being dupes in their malice.

For that very reason they are more to be pitied when the destruction arrived. God had announced the punishments, the agonies justly deserved, but the men did not perceive their guilt. In the midst of their anguish they might have asked whether they were their brothers' keepers, trembling at the thought that they deserved what had come upon them or that their actions had invited it. They did not see their rejection of God's rest through their desire for the infinite and how they oppressed God and men; nor did they see that to become the infinite implies the descent into formlessness, in which man becomes a thing and its opposite; thus they did not see that the consummation of their denial of rest to others entailed the denial of their own rest. To all this they remained blind, enslaved to the powerful delusion that they could forget God without incurring blame. Such is the strength and craft of the evil one, that man can walk a road whose end is death, a road that terminates in indifference toward and hatred of his own life, without comprehending his destiny.

Man's indifference in the docetic age has rarely embroiled him in conditions comparable to the Babylonian siege or the Assyrian destruction. Nonetheless indifference rules in his heart with respect to God, his fellow men, and nature, serving as his basic disposition. He does not fathom that God formed him to rest in his neighbors and that the structures of docetic existence work to annihilate that rest. He claims that he loves God and his fellows, but his love lives like an elderly and dying woman among mountebanks and suicide-assisters. On this point little separates the devout churchgoer from the atheist. Both agree that the arguments for the Wars of Religion, for example, are folly and that their spilling of blood has no justification. Both thereby condemn the domination that drove the confessional era to extremes. Both then accept the indifference resulting from that era as good, right, and true, as an expression of necessity if not the hand of God. So each side views the separation of church and state, which codified the mutual domination of religiously-inspired realms during the Wars into a law of political indifference to religion. The devout churchgoer adds that schisms in the church are regrettable, that Christians should agree and get along, that those who worship Christ should love one another as brothers. Domination, says the docetic churchgoer, has no place in the body of Christ, and he repeats his objection to the Wars of Religion while claiming that he loves his brother. Then this churchgoer accepts the current landscape of western Christendom, with its thousands of denominations, sects, and individual churches, this disintegration of the body of Christ, with indifference. In this way the domination and bloodshed, the pained denial of communion in earlier ages, finds an heir in the carelessness of the contemporary docetic heart.

1 John: On Docetism and Resurrection

When a man drinks coffee made with beans from the earth's far reaches, when those beans were gathered by men and women who work long hours through heat and whose managers pay the minimum if not less, when this occurs so that the man can enjoy his coffee at little cost and with ease, does he not condone and share the guilt for the workers' lack of wages? Does he not justify their treatment in consenting to its benefits? Does he not partake, in some small way, in the aggregate of dehumanization for some and exaltation for others? And when a man eats an egg produced by chickens held in confinement, deprived of open air, of space, and of ground to sit on, so that the birds die early for the sake of a lower price for their produce, which the man and his family eat without conscience, does the man not approve of the conditions that fill his stomach at little cost? Does he not justify and share in them as a contributor to the aggregate that demands that the lower creatures suffer as brutes while the higher ones consume their gifts? Or when a woman deplores all forms of brutality, abuse, and oppression of the poor and voiceless, and then, having life within her, a heartbeat, hands, fingernails, eyelids, and the divine image, she decides that this life is not worthy of life, perhaps that it is a burden and a curse, and so destroys her unborn child, does she not oppress and brutalize the voiceless? She might justify her action with such intricate arguments that she convinces herself that it comes at no cost, that her liberation requires no sacrifice. She might claim that she despises domination and dominates no one, whereas she has built her life upon domination and, in accordance with the stunning deformity possible at present, can smile in indifference to the life she has torn apart.

Likewise, you who harbor no sadness at the fragmentation of the body of Christ, who see no spiritual or moral disaster in the absence of the Spirit of communion, and who would consider it an injustice if an authority compelled you to attend a worship not of your choosing, look at your hands. If you believe that your freedom outweighs the scattering of Christ's body so that you would not and have not traded your liberation for obedience to the divine will to unity, and if you enjoy this freedom as a right and entitlement without conscience for Christ, know that you do so as one who condones processes and events that have made your indifference possible. How then can you love your brother as you claim? Just as the man who condemns the conditions of the bean pickers while he drinks the coffee is a hypocrite, and so for the man who condemns the industrial farmer while he eats the eggs, and so for the woman who condemns domination while she kills her unborn child, the same hypocrisy redounds to those who condemn the Wars of Religion and the anguish of schism without washing their hands of the church's disorder, which they have learned to cherish as a guarantor of freedom. The context of their supposed love for the brothers in Christ assumes that they have relinquished such love, preferring the liberty of indifference.

Docetic man answers by arguing that in these conditions, when he can choose his form of worship and find a style that meets his preferences, he better loves his neighbor. He says, "How can I love God whom I do not see when I cannot love the neighbor whom I see? In freedom I best love the neighbor, a freedom that levels all men and wipes out the barriers that divide us. In this same freedom, then, I best love God." Dear man, do you not see that you have set love of neighbor against love of God and have justified the former at the expense of the latter? God gathers all things in Jesus Christ for the church, his body, and the Christ teaches that "he who does not gather with me scatters." Against this you say, "Let the body of Christ be scattered through schism because this better joins men in the name of Christ," or again, "Let me disobey the Lord in order to better obey him." Or in a twist on the words decried by Paul, "Let us sin more so that grace may abound." But in the schism that supposedly leads to love one finds only sin and no grace.

Docetic men believe that they come together truly when they commune without regard for objective categories by which others might define them. By rejecting definition according to rank, title, or authority, by abdicating the structures of higher and lower, docetic men hope to make themselves only "human" and thereby personal. They seek to commune apart from limits and without the public bonds made concrete in rank. They come together apart from law, apart from substantive moral obligations beyond the demand that they create, sustain, and enliven the conditions necessary for such communing. In this manner they press the advance of the infinite. They must be intimate with one another, celebrating the casting off of form and excluding it in the name of shared emotion. In the ideal, the man liberated for the unhindered expression of emotion meets others as similarly liberated and their joint expression of emotion, their discovery of mutual sympathy, yields something real and true, the authentic contact of man with man in the name of Jesus Christ. In this ideal men come to know one another without prejudice, injustice, or condemnation, in complete equality, and as models of the love of God among men. This ideal underlies much that contemporary docetic churches seek, lifting up the communion of the liberated as the end of Christian striving.

The antithesis of unregulated emotional expression and its peculiar bonding against all limit, rank, and objectification has meant, in the current docetic age, the defeat of the latter by the former. This defeat has included the church as a limiting institution no less than other institutions, insofar as the church, when it understands the title "Christian," understands an office incomprehensible apart from publicly limiting bonds. Those bonds say of a man, "member in the body of Christ" or "one submitted to Christ as Lord and gatherer," subordinating the believer within the cosmic plan of God's mystery. When men threw off the implication of Christ's Lordship that the church belongs to him, that it does not obey the whim of men or lie subject to their discretion, and when they raised emotional expression above the unity of the church—a process revealed over centuries, from at least the Reformation to the present—they thereby made the unity of the church a limit and a hindrance to the extent that it does not celebrate whatever emotional effluvia men identify as "grace." The unity of the church had to suffer this way inasmuch as emotion, in the abstract sense, has no limit but comes and goes like the wind. To grant priority to emotion, which has no intrinsic limit, promises that its priority will evolve into dictatorship. Such evolution implies a tyrannical grace battling against the form of the church given through the Holy Spirit, which affirms freedom within boundaries. For the church to survive the docetic onslaught, it therefore had to transform in nature from a limited and limiting institution to an unlimited and liberating one. As such its survival exists in name only, concealing the church's defeat before Docetism's death-drive.

When the church becomes unlimited as fragmented into uncountable options, with denominations, sects, and movements dispersed along the horizon, so that it mirrors a man liberated to express his emotions as he chooses among infinite possibilities, how does this unlimited church provide rest to an unlimited man, whose lack of limit discloses his lack of rest? When the body of Christ forgoes the internal limit of unity necessary to train men in rest, it cannot give him either law or grace, nor the solace of knowing God. It rather blesses his restlessness in the name of Christ, as though God designed him to be restless! On the other hand, when this unlimited church subtly denies the efficacy of the sacrifice (as has occurred in docetic churches), how does man find rest in them? Though they claim the name of Jesus Christ and admit his sacrifice with their mouths, they know little of the rest of God in their hearts. Men cannot experience that rest when the church robs them of its means and then assures them that they are saved. And if the docetic body cannot offer men rest, how do they rest in one another or in God?

Now objections rise up from every corner of docetic Christendom, with each claiming that his church rests in God and facilitates rest among neighbors. These churches have a case to make. Their parishioners pray and care for one another, while their congregations organize relief efforts, charitable ministries, and programs designed to further the knowledge of God. Pastors deliver learned and fiery orations that seek to right social ills and convict their hearers, and church leaders work to inculcate the faith in the youth. In all these efforts the church teaches its members to love their neighbors, calling them to admirable forms of sacrifice and engagement in the lives of sufferers. Can a church perform such works of charity without its members resting in one another and in God? That these churches can point to practices that exemplify the love of others argues also that they love God whom they do not see, resting confidently in him.

Yet evil never totally eradicates good. Only in hypothetical and idealized scenarios does the darkness completely annul the light, while even the holiest churches contain some mixture of righteous and sinful actions. One should not ask, then, about the presence of righteous actions because one can assume that they will be present and that Satan, if he could not misrepresent through them, would be a poor deceiver. One should rather ask about the ontological foundation underlying the actions, for the ontological foundation tips the whole toward the good in spite of lingering evil actions or toward evil despite visible good deeds. Does the particular good occur in the larger context of disintegration and death, or do wicked deeds blemish an order tending toward beatification? If that order and context is the church, in which men come to know God and their brothers in love, what is its trajectory in the West? Has the church progressed toward life or death? Biblically speaking, has it scattered or gathered? The answer is obvious to those who observe history, who take seriously the withering of Christ's body and who gasp at the flimsiness of Christian faith in the current age. The church has all but died, with faith following and reproducing that death in only slightly mutated forms. Do not be deceived by the residue of good deeds that the churches continue to muster. They witness to the earlier life of a creature that has perished, standing out precisely because of the rarity of their occurrence. Again, do not be deceived, for the action does not speak for itself, but men must locate it within the larger vector toward form and unity or formlessness and fragmentation. Notwithstanding the presence of such actions, men can hardly rest in Christ and God where they are subjected to the negative infinite. Nor do well-meaning actions in such circumstances fully exemplify the mutual rest intended by God for men.

The church should replicate the forms of rest that the Son enjoys in the Father within the Trinitarian life, taking these as its model. The Son has his origin in the Father and receives the structure of the divine being from him, so that the former neither creates himself in an original, self-willed, and mysteriously ungrounded moment, nor does he decide what shape his God-given essence will take. The Son then rests in the Father by giving to him in the expectation of reciprocal life-giving. The church's foundation in these forms of rest progressively devolves as Docetism tightens its grip, enervating the believer's opportunities for solace in God and others if not eradicating them.

With his lips alone does docetic man acknowledge God's plan to form the body of Christ as the mystery of the cosmos. In his heart the meaning of religion originates from his life as a man, whether he refers this meaning to his emotions or intuition, his need to live a moral life, his inescapable sociability, or his self-assertion through choice. In the latter case, men have increasingly viewed Christ's body as a voluntary association and their participation in it as a function of their wills. These docetists approach the churches as a canvas for individual religious prerogatives, an inert and lifeless background awaiting the preferences that give it shape and color. Men rarely look back to a religious beginning not their own, to circumstances that drew them with greater force than their assent to these forces, but find religious meaning in the individual response and its efficacy for self-definition. Everywhere the individual reigns, creating himself almost from air. The docetic repudiation of the church, in which secular men seek meaning apart from religious structures, exerbates this tendency and so better conforms to the docetic ideal. Here men generate meaning according to guides they select through personalized criteria, so that the weight of the question of meaning, of faith and belief, falls squarely on the individual isolated in pursuit of answers. No man of intellectual depth and integrity could find such a situation restful, although he could become accustomed to the chaos implied in it. But the man inured to the lack of rest, to his personal creation of meaning, or responsible for his own spiritual genesis, cannot but doubt this endeavor on the ontological plane. This is because the pronouncement, "I am self-sufficient, independent, the author of my religious life, and a constructor of meaning" presumes that man does not depend on outside sources in forming his world, and that this formation therefore belongs to an infinitized freedom. He refuses a locus for his rest, submitting to the fiction of his infinitude in his mind against the apprehension of his finitude in fact. This apprehension disturbs him to the degree that he avoids the deceptions that distract him from it, troubling his conscience.

Docetic believers who have chosen their church, who devote their lives to it and cannot live without it, who want sincerely to give their lives to God, do not rest in their worship because from it they receive no spiritual form, no destiny of faith and practice within the body of Christ. Other than weekly attendance at a liturgy meant to liberate rather than heal and activity in groups that do little in the way of regeneration and grace, the docetic church prescribes virtually nothing to instill humility into its devotees. Docetic worship does much to comfort and care if by these terms we mean an outlawing of moral reform and an instinctive justification of one's way of living. The liberated have no use for habits, for discipline, for the practice of form or the conversion of sense into soul. It hardly occurs to many docetists that they should pray without ceasing, that they should fast and give alms, that they should cultivate a spiritual rhythm meant to reflect the Trinitarian life-giving. Should they have concerns for the acquisition of form in Christ (and this comes to the heart of the matter) the docetic church has no coherent guidance or direction for them. Should one fast? If so, how much? On what days and from what foods? For what reasons? Should one give alms? If so, to what extent? And how, in general, should one address mammon? As docetists give varied advice on these and other matters, they fail to enclose the conversation within the boundaries of an authoritative tradition. In this way they fail to guide those who wish to follow. The believer makes up his spiritual practice as he goes along, without tutors or saints to strengthen and confirm his steps. Lacking an effective tradition, he has little acknowledgment of the Holy Spirit leading his predecessors and himself. Only the Roman Church, which long ago gave up the role of docetic vanguard, retains the perspective of tradition. Sadly, its authorities resemble monarchs whose title gives them no power for rule, who receive a glory that lacks substance. The history, teachings, and disciplines of this grand Church bow to the individual barely less than in more advanced docetic circles.

Neither does the docetic church allow for the third form of rest, in which the believer seeks the reciprocation of God. Inasmuch as the docetic church misunderstands if not outlaws sacrifice, so that its believers make no petition to God through the gift, to that extent the church destroys the possibility of the believer seeking rest in God through the offering. Docetists are quick to call the sacrifice a manipulation of God, as if the believer were coercing God into giving. The chance of such abuse always remains, but focusing on it obscures the intended meaning of the sacrifice, which humbly calls the Lord to answer out of his kindness. Believers must call God to reciprocate if they should abide in the divine love, but Docetism has convinced men that this is a lie. Docetists have gloried at one point or another that they give nothing to God, that he requires no work of them, that they exalt him by refusing the necessity of their own action. In this manner they alienate themselves from mutual love with the God they presume to laud. Today men think as though God's duty requires him to accept them as they are, not wanting to change them or direct their conduct away from death and toward life. "Blessed are the merciful, for they shall receive mercy." Who is merciful if not us docetists, although we have no habit of mercy? And if we cannot point to acts of mercy, why cannot God accept us as objects of mercy in any case? If he is love, does he not owe this to us? Such sad, wicked, and deceived creatures are we, who believe that God should bestow the fullness of his love upon us when we will not lift a finger to call for that love. Though unmerciful before God, we cry foul should he withhold mercy from us.

The staggering degree to which reciprocation has vacated the life of docetic man eludes him. There is not a greater mystery to him than a life in which he acts reciprocally with others for the good of all, in which he considers others not as objects of domination but as practical sources of rest, and himself as created in order to give such rest. His indifference to life means, in his social practice, the absence of reciprocation with those close to him. The neighbor with whom man does not reciprocate, to whom he does not humbly offer the service of love, he regards from the disposition of mutual distillation. From this disposition he does not care for his neighbor, and the one for whom he extends no care is by definition a person of indifference to him. The offer of reciprocation to the neighbor is often small and internal: it consists in the prayer of the heart for the good of every person that one encounters, an interest in their struggles, and the will to meet those struggles as God allows. The Christian lives on the offense in prayer and service, whereas the docetist lives on the defense, waiting for the needs of others to come to him. The docetist does not understand that his good works, because they do not spring from a heart trained in active humility, deceive him regarding his practical disposition. Moreover, the more powerfully that docetic man asserts that he is self-sufficient and that he relies on no one, and the more his daily practice bears out his claims while he assumes the same regarding others, the more he excludes reciprocation from his dealings with men and grows comfortable in mutual indifference. Those near him become not neighbors with whom he should share meaningful obligations of rest, but others whom he does not know and for whom he takes no concern.

If a man does not rest in God with respect to his spiritual origins or the form of his spiritual life, and if he also does not rest in reciprocation with God, he cannot presume to live humbly before his Lord. He cuts off the humility that recognizes that his being drawn to God implies subservience to the unified body of Christ, he jettisons the humility that learns from the tradition alive in that body, and he forgets the humility of the offering in which he comes before God lowered by the Lord's love as lifegiver. In the latter, the believer who forgoes reciprocation simultaneously forgoes the humility bound up with it. He does not lower soul and body before God as a supplicant nor a penitent, nor does he offer his pride as a sacrifice. What is the attitude of the believer who does not give humbly to God if not pride against him? With the Lord there is no middle ground or neutrality. One either is for him or against him, one either gathers or scatters, one is either humble or proud. Ontologically, if man does not submit to God as the author of nature by living within his limit as God's creature, that man proclaims himself the author of limit and makes himself limitless. Despite this, man is not God, he does not embody the mystery of limitlessness and limit, he is not the merciful infinite. In his dismissal of humility man thus turns to pride, and rather than lowering himself before God he rises against the creator, unwittingly seeking the reciprocation that is punishment.

The man who rises against God cannot love his neighbor. When men deny rest in God as the author and perfecter of faith, they deny that he first loved them; if they deny that he first loved them, how do they love others after that first love? Docetism presents this love in contemporary circles as acceptance, as tolerance, as a lack of judgment, or as works performed to dignify and aid others. So often this love masks pride resolved to validate pride, the infinite seeking to assert its boundlessness, a fragile and unseemly congratulation of wickedness, the distancing of man from man paraded as intimacy. Satan and his angels can construct entire worlds upon lies, being sure to reserve space within these for churches assured that they walk in the truth. The veil of the good, the respectable, and the praiseworthy, if not the humble and noble, easily covers man's rebellion against God and neighbor.

A no less powerful covering has encompassed the most basic natural institution by which men abide in love, the marriage of husband and wife. Under the veneer of marriage Docetism has developed a seeming, something that presents itself as marriage but whose reality contradicts the presentation. This form of union, while it purports to bind persons together in love, hides their conflict with each other and with God, whose image it progressively abdicates as it matures.

Within the bond of husband and wife God planted procreation, and within procreation both the dual infinite of orgasm and labor cry and the mutual humility in which the woman lowers herself before the man, who lowers himself to her. Subtly Docetism unwinds the image of the Triune life in marriage as it loosens the procreative bond, until men no longer view procreation as a critical element of the union. Docetic marriage prioritizes the fulfillment of the individual over other considerations, until the bond becomes a vehicle for self-actualization. At present, docetic marriage presents itself in this manner without qualifications, although in previous centuries men encountered it in romanticism, sentimentalism, and more generally in the concept of marriage as grounded in emotion. For centuries docetic marriage carried on its plodding war against limit by virtue of feeling, transforming the legitimacy of the bond until men lodged its vitality essentially if not solely in romantic or erotic attachment. This development preceded Docetism's current stage, in which marriage has thrown off the bonds and restraints implicit in well-established social orders, bursting its boundaries unto regular divorce, cohabitation, children out of wedlock, and unions in which procreation is forsaken if not impossible.[2]

Considered in the ideal, the redefinition of marriage according to docetic principles cannot stand the imposition of limit. By grounding the union in emotional self-actualization Docetism builds upon a slippery and ever-changing foundation, but more importantly it affirms the infinite as the essence of the bond. Affirmations of law do not surround this infinitude but arise out of it, so that something so effervescent and fading as desire, or something so haphazard and variable as the individual's notion of his fulfillment, must ultimately sustain his commitment. Forgetting the unpredictability of this arrangement due to the initial harmonization of wills and desires, the couple marries, fixing the promise of a future happiness upon their incipient bliss. Their bond of matrimony might assume the language of reciprocity, as each might promise to serve and fulfill the other while being served and fulfilled. The deception occurs in the pledge of mutual service that implies mutual limit and humility, whereas the docetic ontology demands that each partner absorb this calculated humility into self-assertion and pride.

Man might say with his lips, "I humble myself before you and to you," but with his heart and his ethos he proclaims that he is boundless, a man of infinite possibility unthinkable apart from his freedom. As essentially infinite in his way of being he cannot logically commit himself to humility as an end, but can only act humbly insofar as he insists upon a return for his energy, as if one owed him a debt. When one marries for the purpose of self-realization, one's day-to-day business falls under the question of fulfillment. Such criteria lead to daily scuffles over responsibilities, preferences, and plans. Married life becomes a sullen sacrifice, and as it crawls away from the initial euphoria the days become dutiful but colorless, a task without joy. The spouse seems cold, intransigent, and cruel, while one sees himself as the consummate giver against the spouse as the taker. On such days, when they multiply into weeks and months if not years, married life negates its foundation and abdicates its legitimacy. The individual no longer enjoys fulfillment, but the routine and regular abrasiveness of life convince the docetic soul that this is no longer its joy, that the marriage has failed the self-actualization of its members and must be aborted—and this assumes that the marriage has experienced no tragedy or unusual hardship. In short, when one establishes marriage in the freedom of emotional attachment and personal actualization, the tasks, responsibilities, and daily conflicts of married life easily morph into an unbearable burden, a privatized infinite law whose logical end is divorce. In this manner the presumption of ontological freedom realizes itself through law as a mediation, consummating itself on the other side in disunion.

2. The latter does not include heterosexual couples who suffer from infertility.

Only in an era in which social safeguards against divorce have vanished could this picture become normal. The shrug with which contemporary men hear of "irreconcilable differences" as the cause of disunion witnesses that it has become so, while the prevalence of divorce frightens and saddens those who ponder it. Churchgoing men might still say that God has given marriage as a bond of genuine love, and God can indeed act through docetic marriage to achieve his purposes, but docetic structures contradict the divine image imprinted on marriage by the creator. In its most advanced stages, it assumes the infinitude of the participants and seeks to validate it to the exclusion of mutual rest.

The perfected state of docetic marriage permits rest neither at its origin nor in the life of the bond. First, the weight of finding a match lands squarely on the individual. He strikes out among strangers in order to find that singular gem, an attractive mate whose character and loyalty he does not question and whose past does not stain her present. His reason guides him in this pursuit, although he relies just as strongly on his emotions. The church, his parents, and the social order have the say that he allows them, which usually amounts to little. All sides agree that he must bear the burden while his isolation exacerbates the pressure of longing. The question of love, which wafts in contingency, can consume his adult life if he lets it. After years the arbitrariness and duration of his search provoke despair that he will ever find his happiness, and he might feel the temptation either to marry at the first spark or to give up the dream, rationalizing it as obsolete and impossible, a quaint fairy-tale of the unenlightened. Man might euphemistically describe this experience as a period of adventure, experiment, and freedom, but he cannot describe it as restful. Peace comes only with the end of the journey, with the settlement of romantic vertigo in the arms of the soul mate. Or so it would seem. Within the arrangement that the partners have constructed, they must define their stance before one another. Docetism does not grant men to take up usual tasks and women to take others because this would acknowledge limits upon the desires and self-determination of each. Instead, the couple endlessly negotiates the terms of the union, a diplomacy that slides into guerilla combat. Absent the imposition of social expectations and institutional mores, the daily attitude of the partners boils down to "I want" and their plans extend barely farther than satisfying these wants. These conditions beg the partners to probe the boundaries of their union in mundane chores if not in relationships with outside parties. Like the courtship that preceded it, this setting does not give rest to the couple but exhausts them.

With difficulty docetic thinking hides the dearth of rest in the above examples, but in the sexual act it lodges its strongest deception that the participants love one another, that their performance realizes mutual appreciation and service. On this point the contrast between Christian marriage and its docetic counterpart can elude the onlooker who considers sex as sex, who does not perceive that the same act can imply divergent ontological principles. Whereas in Christian marriage husband and wife come together physically to create life, accomplishing this in a co-operation that implies rest, in docetic marriage two persons come together in a celebration of death instantiated in the sexual exaltation of each.

Under docetic conditions, in which the partners eschew the possibility of children as the foundation for their activity, they extract and isolate a sexual infinitude from the larger process of life-giving. Just as the contemporary docetic theologian extracts the Exodus event from the larger story that reaches from the patriarchs to Canaan, exalting the infinite pressure and its end in the Israelite liberation, and as he asserts this as the model for Christian-docetic existence and the progress of Christian-docetic society, so docetic sexuality isolates and extracts sexual pleasure from its context within the arc of new life, a narration that begins with the promise of procreation intrinsic to the body, travelling through sex, pregnancy, and labor unto the newborn child. Thus the participants enact the sexual infinite as a festival of two. Together they repudiate both nature and the mutuality through which nature would join them, preferring to use one another as instruments for mutual estrangement.

How artfully does Satan appear as an angel of light, disguising hatred as love! With what genius does he dress discord and enmity in the garb of truth, brotherhood, even matrimony! The Seeming deploys such powerful deceptions that man does not begin to fathom how a similar act hides two very different realities and opposed meanings. In procreation the life of man and woman find mutual solace on the way to greater life, whereas in the docetic imitation those under the spell of the infinite merge that they should devour one another, rising up against one another in "marriage" in a way not unlike the warring sects constitutive of "Christendom." In neither the spiritual nor the natural case do men love their brothers, but the parties involved act out their infinitude in combat. They counter the admonition to be as Christ was in the world and to submit to his peace. Refusing to humble themselves beneath one another, each elevates his soul in pride and forsakes the neighbor, calling down God's anger.

Men will not escape the Judgment, but must answer for their lives. Have they turned to God through faith in Jesus Christ or have they turned away from him? Although each must at some point make this decision as an individual, fundamentally men make it as a collective. "Because as he is, so are we in this world": the plural does not refer to isolated individuals held together after their individuality. It refers to a single body whose members realize that they cannot know God apart from the mediation of this knowledge through others, and who understand that being like Christ implies that they cannot be men without humbling themselves. They love because Christ loved them and as Christ loved them, sacrificing themselves along the narrow way in the hope that God will draw near to them as they have drawn near to him. This love casts out fear because men who give of themselves have experienced a foretaste of God's drawing near, having known God to lower himself to those who lower themselves beneath him. To these God binds himself in joy, to these God says that though they still sin and are at times faithless, "he remains faithful, for he cannot deny himself." Therefore they look to the Judgment boldly and with a certain anticipation, for they have faith that God will turn to them for eternity. Not so the wicked who have refused to turn to God or humble themselves before him and their peers. Scorning rest and obedience, they have rebelled against the creator, the nature he fashioned, and those close to them. In blindness they claim to love their neighbors while hating them, just as they deny the God whom they might claim to worship. Such men have not sought God with their hearts, and as such he has not come down to them as those who struggle to lower themselves. When they say that God is not, that he is irrelevant, that he does not judge, or some other nonsense, they reveal that they have not pursued him. Having loved neither the neighbor they see nor the God whom they do not see, at the Judgment both God and their neighbors will turn away from them. The fear of that day, as well as the earthly days that approximate it, liquefies the heart.

Book II

Preface

DURING THE CARNIVAL OF Leveling that year, the Christians went out of the city to a nearby hillside. There the priests taught the heads of the families, together with their wives and children, about steadfastness and struggle, and about the joy of the Way. The Christians sought to walk in the truth and in love, and they were weary of the Carnival, which was dissolute, profane, and occasionally violent.

One evening, a while after the time of prayers, plumes of smoke began rising from the city. Starting from one part and spreading to others, the flames engulfed the whole and brought it to the ground. The Christians, having laid down to rest, did not see what had happened until the morning. They did not know if attackers had come suddenly from without or if chaos had arisen from within, but they saw that the city had descended into ruin.

"The place that we have known is dissolved before our eyes. It is no longer there for us," said one of the priests. The men agreed, and one of them spoke up. "We do not know what dangers wait for us if we return there," he said. "If there are barbarians, they will attack us, and if it is the men of this land, we cannot say whether they will think of us as friends or enemies. We should depart." When all had consented to this, the Christians prayed that God would lead them to a place of rest. The following day they set out.

As they walked, they met a wild-eyed and ragged man. His beard was frayed and his clothes torn, and he sobbed mightily. He sat on his knees, beating his breast and wiping away his tears. A priest approached him. "Do I know you?" he asked the man. "I think that I recognize you from the city."

"My city, my home!" the man burst out. "I miss her, I miss the way things were! I ate well, I would dance and sing at night, I had such enjoyments and entertainments in the day. The beautiful men and women I would meet, and our celebrations! I would give my life to have them back only for a moment. There is nothing left to me . . . but there was such oppression there, such injustice, such selfishness and power-grabbing, such lying and deceit. This is why the city burned: it was imperfect, and its imperfections far exceeded its benefits! It should have burned, it should have burned, because its people were flawed. Why did it have to burn? Because it had to burn. The Carnival revealed our sins, I suppose, and the city had to burn. I miss you, my home, but it is for the best that you are gone."

The Christians looked at the man with a mixture of bewilderment and tenderness. A woman came to him with a cup of water, and he began to drink. After a small sip, he cast the cup aside. "This does not help me!" he exclaimed. "I need wine, or something sweet, not this tasteless filth!" And he brushed her away furiously with both arms.

"God's peace be with you," said the priest as he made the sign of the cross toward the man. The other scowled at him. The priest then signaled to the Christians that they should be going, and the people began to depart. The man suddenly stood up and implored them to take him with them. "You must take me! You must, you must!" he cried. "Have you no mercy? How can followers of Christ have no mercy? Accept me and take me with you!"

"On one condition you can join us," replied the priest. "You must give up your attachment to the Leveling. You must recognize that its goals and mores seem honorable, but this is only a seeming. The Leveling has denied God, made neighbors into enemies, and brought the land to disrepair. You must therefore forsake it. If you have a longing for it in your heart, you must cut it off."

The man was appalled. "The city has come to ruin, yes, but the Carnival is not to blame," he said. "Its goals remain noble and true and worthy. If the citizens became oppressors, their faults mean only that we should redouble our efforts and try once more. They were not worthy of the ideals set before them, but where they failed others will succeed. I will find those who will rebuild the city, and when we have laid its foundations and erected its tower, you will see a place more virtuous and compassionate, more magnanimous and egalitarian than you and your God could devise. Then you will meet me again. On that day you will be humbled!" Having said this, the man stalked angrily away. The Christians looked at each other with concern. "Let's keep going, and remember him in our prayers," said one of the men. "We should find the place that God has for us before worrying that adversaries might seek us."

The next day, as the Christians journeyed, they came upon another group of families somewhat like themselves. "We escaped the city as it burned," said their leader, "and we mean to find a new home under the name of Jesus Christ." When the priests and the men replied that they also sought a new home under the Christ, the other group was overjoyed. But some among the Christians were hesitant. "Before we are sure of our brotherhood with you, we must ask if you adhere to the Leveling. Were you a contributor to the Carnival?"

"At the recent Carnival, no, many of us were not participants," they answered. "It was an excess beyond what we could stomach. Nonetheless, we claim without reservation the basic principles of the Leveling. It is our history and our way, and inseparable from all that we understand as good and right. Christ himself has blessed it, has he not?"

These words troubled the Christians, and a priest immediately spoke up. "We cannot recognize you or partner with you. You claim to hold to Jesus Christ and also to the Leveling, which led men to licentiousness and destruction. You worship an idol at the same time as Jesus Christ, even an idol disguised as the Christ. You seem to be Christians, but you are only a seeming. Our Lord does not share with the god of the Levellers, even if he calls himself the Christ."

The other group took offense at this. "Isn't it the case," said one of them, "that all who use Christ's name are Christians? One must only have the Christ's name on his tongue, and his faith is true!"

"As surely as the Israelites believed the golden calf to be the God of Abraham," responded one of the Christians, "it is not the case. One must have more than the name of Christ on the lips. One must worship in the way that he has commanded." And turning to the priests, the heads of the families insisted that they leave.

A short while later, as the Christians walked along the way, one of them came alongside a priest. "Father, the city is no more, and while we do not know exactly how it came to its end, we know that pride comes before destruction and that the city is destroyed. There is some pride hidden within the Levelling that men have not seen, a revolt against God that they have not perceived. My concern is this: we lived in the city and have known no other earthly home. Are we not also, in some sense, Levellers? Does the sickness not live also within us, although God spared us and although we seek a new home? Those others who called themselves Christians do not recognize the Levelling as a sickness that they carry within them. They will take it wherever they go, and it will eventually infect and sabotage their efforts. As for us, we call the Levelling a disease and pride, but how do we guard ourselves against it? How do we purify ourselves of it? It seems to me that the Levelling pulses in our veins, whether we wish it to or not."

"Do not despair," the priest replied. "The problem you have pointed out is real, but the power of God overcomes all challenges for the faithful. As we move forward, it is for us to refashion our minds. We must again see the cosmos, and our life together, according to the order in which God made them and not according to the principles of the Levelling. That way of seeing the world will likely not take root for us, but God willing, it will be the air that our children and grandchildren breathe. We who have lived in the city have walked in darkness, but God will give us light to see, to the extent that he deems right."

1 John 2:12-14

> I write to you, little children, because your sins are forgiven you for his name's sake. I write to you, fathers, because you have known him who is from the beginning. I write to you, young men, because you have overcome the wicked one. I write to you, little children, because you have known the Father. I have written to you, fathers, because you have known him who is from the beginning. I have written to you, young men, because you are strong, and the word of God abides in you, and you have overcome the wicked one.

I WRITE TO YOU, little children, because your sins are forgiven you for his name's sake. We Christians are ever tempted to construct our own righteousness, thinking of our own way as holy and, from our perch, looking down on those who have not done as we have. Many of us, who seek a way of life outside of the docetic milieu, will have done things that are hard. One might have left a job that he loved, that gave him meaning and occasionally filled him with exhilaration. Another might have left behind worldly accomplishments and importance, and the honors that come with position and authority. A third will have turned away from a spacious and well-furnished home, from an enviable automobile, and from any of the other prizes that the world offers to its winners. Many of us will have left a life that captured us outwardly, that beguiled us with delights of mind and body so that we wondered if we would ever leave. Some will have sacrificed family and friends, distancing themselves from father and mother, aunt and uncle, niece and nephew, even from son and daughter. Some will have broken with bitterness and longing from those dear to them, who do not see the urgency of our moment or accept that salvation requires decision. Many of us will have stepped away from the docetic world and faced the questions directed to us in the faith—what shall we eat? what shall we drink? what shall we wear?—responding to these not with firm answers in every case, but with faith that God provides for his children, that he honors the humble and will not let them go unclothed. Our struggle for humility consists in the turn from Docetism, a turn not principally understood as trading one set of material circumstances for another, not in the rejection of docetic ease and protections, docetic comforts and delights. Nor should we understand the struggle first as the escape from the threat of hardship and persecution as nations turn against the faith while their solvency crumbles. At its core, our struggle for humility concentrates on the inner life before God, pausing from externals to stand before the Lord who sees all and, admitting our sins, seeking forgiveness from him. From this we strive to lower ourselves before nature and the neighbor, placing the latter's interests above our own and loving him. But many will inevitably be tempted either to turn back to Docetism or to raise themselves above those still inured to its ways. We have all been inured, we have fought against our attachments, and the fight goes on. Without the grace of God we would fail miserably. St. Anthony reminds us to remain firm in our commitment, not to put our hand to the plough and look back, for those of us who cannot stand fast against temptation are not fit for the kingdom of God.

The sufferings that many Christians will endure are a natural part of the Christian life, and by God's grace we must resist pride on their account. It is better to set out upon the path of repentance, to have made certain steps along the way under the guidance of Scripture and the Fathers. All this "betterment" is demolished, however, when one savors it in the heart as proof of righteousness and moral superiority. It would be a tragedy for the Christian to go the way of the Pharisee in the parable, thanking God that he is not like other men, like thieves, rogues, and adulterers. We should beware that "being ignorant of the righteousness that comes from God, and seeking to establish" our own, we do not submit to God's righteousness. The evil one means either to transform the way of humility into the way of pride, so that men regard the path that humbles before God as the foundation for self-exaltation, raising themselves above others as the saved, the righteous, and the good as opposed to the deceived, foolish, and wicked, or he cloaks the way of pride as that of humility, so that men who believe that they follow the way of righteousness progress deeper and deeper into sin. The latter characterizes Docetism, which has led men into perdition while convincing them that they serve the purposes of God and the enrichment of their neighbors. Let us pray that the former does not characterize those who turn from Docetism, so that those who have come to the Orthodox faith, and who hope to imitate the Christ through the example and aid of the saints and the Fathers, do not suffer the corruption of the path of humility unto pride. We are ever at the mercy of God, toward whose love we strive to turn.

For some men, the hardest of all things is to rest in God. Our sins do not fall away because we have covered them, nor is it for us to blot them out with a multitude of good deeds. No man can cover his sins, no man can eradicate his pride, no man can confirm his salvation by his effort. If one could work without ceasing, if he could obey without end and with increasing intensity and precision, this obedience would not cover his sins but increase them. Do we not see that the path of salvation, understood as a path of limitless work, squeezes out the activity of God? Our sins, while not forgiven without the effort of repentance and conversion, are not forgiven due to that effort, as if the grace of Christ did not play the pivotal role. Docetic man, to include those of the Orthodox faith who have labored under Docetism, whether by life in the docetic world or by previous adherence to its heresies, has as his principle task to learn that he must not forgive his own sins, that he cannot work them off or by good deeds procure forgiveness. In order to come to health he must trust the divine Physician, resting in the medicine prescribed and submitting to a treatment he did not himself devise, one that will often be painful to him. And when the Physician commands him to rest, he must rest.

Docetic man does not understand rest just as he does not understand the structure of the world in which God has placed him, having constructed a different order in place of the original one. In the beginning, when God created the heavens and the earth, he spent six days fashioning the world according to his good pleasure. On the seventh day he rested, and because of his rest he called that day holy. The cosmos moves by the relationship between work and rest, a complementarity arranged for the furtherance of life and reflective of the Trinity, where the persons rest in one another. Docetism has all but destroyed this shared life and mutual rest among men while it has sundered the mutual relation of the lower and higher natures in the cosmos. It has done this in the name of freedom (or liberation), which it has enshrined as holy in place of rest. From its foundations in religious developments in the West, and culminating theologically in the doctrine of justification by faith alone, the docetic transformation of rest into freedom has finally come to surround its man, so that he breathes, eats, travels, and works according to its dictums, rendering him an oppressor all the while.

In the Christian faith man comes to salvation in the alternation of work and rest. He works by obeying the commandments, struggling against his passions, wicked thoughts, and various temptations in the attempt to love God virtuously. He rests in the sacrifice, where he trusts in Christ's death and resurrection to forgive his sins and provide him power for sanctification, the grace unto salvation that he desperately needs and cannot provide for himself. Ideally, man progresses simultaneously in these two, growing closer to God as he thinks, speaks, and acts in holiness while he experiences the blessing of God in the eucharist and in prayer, receiving peace and respite in divine grace. The saints, the Christian's guides and exemplars, his helpers, teachers, and intercessors along the path of Christ, show him what it means to grow in holiness and to fortify the inner life in God's mercy, so that he does not go astray.

Docetism undermines man's growth in obedience and sacrifice, in work and rest, by intensifying the first at the expense of the second. In it, the evil one causes the law to so expand that the work of man progressively squeezes out his rest as well as the giver of rest. At the climax, when rest is finally and definitively wiped out, when it seems as if man will suffer an ineradicable and ruthless burden, a remarkable thing occurs: man shifts the burden onto another, liberating himself from the infinite pressure at the same time that he requires the infinite law of the object or person that he wills to grind down underneath it. Man enjoys a kind of unlimited rest—for the infinite is rest without starting or stopping, without pause, interruption, or delay—while he imposes an infinite law, so that the victim suffers the burden without start or stop, without interruption or delay. The docetic world operates to a greater or lesser extent according to this logic. Its technology, its work, the means of its life amount to the theological denial of rest in the name of liberation and the assertion of man, whom God created for rest in him, as a denier of rest to his neighbors and his world.

In the medieval West, the canon law grew to immense proportions as popes battled emperors and as the concept of law as systematic took hold. The growth of this law transformed the Catholic hierarchy into an increasingly legal institution. In this manner the work of religious man, and the law of his labor, surreptitiously grew beyond its bounds. As this law grew, the sacramental cult of Catholicism became enervated, withering in tandem with the law's growth. The law and work increased without apparent limit and the opportunity for rest in the sacrament suffered, the one expanding at the expense of the other, the law of God in Christ turned to counter the grace of Christ. This trajectory reached its apogee in Luther, whose doctrine of faith alone confirmed the total emptiness of the sacrificial cult. By Luther's day, Christ no longer gave rest in the sacrament at the same time that God had become the tyrant, the holy bringer of the infinite law and its horrors. Luther's doctrine of justification reverses this scenario by revolting against God, casting off the law and putting all on Christ's grace. Now grace is rediscovered, but it is no longer grace cooperating with a law necessary for salvation, or grace in the sacrament, but grace as liberation from law and sacrament. Luther announces that man is free from the infinite law at a subtle and tremendous cost, as he makes man the enemy of Christ and his oppressor.

The justified man oppresses Christ by imposing upon him the whole burden of salvation, casting the infinite law upon him at the decisive moment. God designed man for a communion with him modeled to some degree after the reciprocal life-giving of the Trinity. In Luther's doctrine of justification, man rejects reciprocation as integral to his communion with God while Christ alone bears the responsibility, taking on the whole work. Is it any wonder that man, who had previously been subject to the perversion of the infinite law in Catholicism, now forces that infinitude upon Christ as his salvation, returning the entire weight of docetic tyranny upon the savior? God also designed man in his image so that man should rest in God as his God and that God should rest in man as his creature. As the covenant of the Old Testament states, "I will be your God and you will be my people." But Luther dictates that, while the believer finds infinite rest as liberation from the law, Christ finds no rest as he alone takes on the law as his task. For Christ, now the Christ-Idol, does not absorb the infinite as death and conquer it with his immortal life, forgiving sins and bestowing grace for sanctification. He rather suffers the infinite law as its slave, and for the sake of man's newfound freedom. Salvation supposedly turns on Christ's sacrifice on the cross, the concluding work of Christ as the abolishment of sin, and the work of man supposedly counts for nothing. But the "sacrifice of Christ" means, ontologically, that he has taken on the infinite law that man suffered not to conquer it but as its logical consummation, so that, as the Christ-Idol, he suffers it eternally. This form of salvation comes to characterize docetic man both in spiritual and mundane affairs, and validates his ethos as the liberated oppressor. He says that he shall be saved, his salvation now implying his grasp of the infinite as liberation, but he cannot arrive at this grasping, this liberated way of life, without identifying, manufacturing, or otherwise constructing someone or something that suffers his infinitude. If man wills both to worship his idol and to be a god—an ersatz god built upon ruthlessness—he must have his slaves. This applies immediately to Christ his savior, whom man jettisons in favor of the Christ-Idol and who cries out that man's wanton heart has crushed him, that the callousness of liberation has forced him into company with the downtrodden.

The transformation of Christ into Christ-Idol appears directly in the enervation of the sacrament, which ceases as the locus of power, the revelation of mysterious and benevolent forces that nourish man toward salvation, and shrinks into an empty signifier and a sociological bore. For man, in casting off rest in the mystery, decrying it and the priesthood as magic and superstition and denying the unseen powers that flow from it, facilitates the inversion of his relation to God and the cosmos. Beyond abandoning his natural inclination to rest in his Lord, man repudiates the entire spiritual realm with all its wonders, its possibilities, and the manifestations of the higher nature known as miracles. When he unwittingly seizes the infinite as his salvation, man also unwittingly affirms that the lower nature, the physical realm that he perceives with his eyes and other senses, likewise must grasp the infinite, assuming infinitude into itself. Just as the revolt of man against God in Eden presaged the revolt of the ground against man, so that it produces thorns and thistles for him, so the denial of the spiritual realm goads the lower nature, as it were, to rise up against its superior at man's own hand, as he seeks his liberatory salvation in the world that he has made. Starting with the eucharist, docetic man casts out the intermittent and often unpremeditated moments of rest in which the higher nature affirms itself, embarking in embryo toward the technological fantasy in which the lower nature ascends to replace the higher.

The lower nature should rest in the higher as man rests in God, at the same time that the higher powers bestow their blessings within the physical world. There is one nature in two aspects, higher and lower, and the two should exist in harmony. The higher nature gives meaning and purpose to the lower, but not as man grasps them cognitively, not as the conclusion of a syllogism or a point of doctrine, but as the confidence bred by experience of divine things, by the activity of God, the angels, and the saints in answers to prayer, in protection during the hardships and travails of life, in stories of holy men and their struggle to commune with God, as well as in miracles. This experience confirms man in the unspoken recognition that the lower nature points beyond itself in its beauty and goodness, that it is not all that man has to experience nor that it is fit to be the infinite. The lower realm possesses a profound degree of meaning and is good as God's creation, and the certainty of meaning and purpose within this world presumes that man has located it properly, placing it below the higher nature. The activity of that nature, most importantly the regular incursion of divine power in the eucharist, provides for the rest of the lower nature in the higher. In those moments the lower nature breathes more easily as its confidence in the higher world is reaffirmed.

When Docetism reconceives the lower nature as a realm of universal and exceptionless laws, shutting out the freedom of the higher nature to act in the lower if not the existence of the spiritual realm itself, it does not thereby oppress the spiritual order. Docetic man does attempt to prohibit the spiritual powers from accomplishing their God-given purposes, he does slander the glorious ones and consider the stories of saints quaint tales or malicious myths, but it is difficult to call this wiping out of spiritual forces oppression or subjection to an infinite burden. Man does not load down the angels and the saints with the work of salvation or some other unlimited task. He would deprive them of the good work that God has given them but he does not remove them from God's presence, certainly not enslaving them. The enslavement rather occurs ironically, as docetic man's adoption of the infinite law sows it into his world, placing it on his own shoulders *there*. Docetic man theorizes that he has placed the whole burden of salvation on the Christ, and it seems this way according to the doctrine of faith alone, but the Christ does not accept this burden. If the Trinity abides in reciprocal love, how could he? Not the Christ but the Christ-Idol assumes the infinite as his task. Whereas the former offers rest, a return to a limited law, and reciprocal love, the latter stands at the end of the infinite law to announce man as free from Christ and his neighbors. But in the latter case man's imposition of the infinite law upon the Christ-Idol does not really free man from the burden. As the worshipper of the Christ-Idol, man must assume the burden himself as the prelude to casting it upon his god, a dynamic that repeats itself with such regularity that man always remains under the infinite law. His moments of release from the infinite, when he feels that the burden now belongs to Christ and that he is liberated, give birth to new iterations of the tyranny, new and more intensified forms of oppression that he must himself undergo. Rather than the Christ who draws man to him through a merciful law, granting him forgiveness and rest from the burden so that he can return to the way of righteousness refreshed, docetic man worships the demon-god who whips him with the law until he finds release through revolt, the retribution that casts the burden upon the Christ-Idol—who then bears a reinvigorated and doubly terrifying law back upon his man. In this way the Christ-Idol drives man to achieve his salvation, his exoneration from limits, as he progresses along the way of limitlessness. His salvation has made him a slave to the world he must create in its name, a world in which there is no higher nature, no law of God and therefore neither sin nor forgiveness of sins, few friends and neighbors, and from which man has all but expelled the great enemy, death.

1 John: On Docetism and Resurrection

The imposition of the infinite upon man appears likewise in his thirst for meaning and purpose, these two that elude him especially when he steps back from the civilizational task of eradicating rest. His notion of "progress" entails the denial of God and the higher nature and the project of establishing the lower as infinite, wiping out the solace provided by immaterial powers in tandem with the expansion and intensification of his political and social freedom as well as his technological capacities. Buried within his activity and hopeful for glory, he presses on toward spiritual death, toward the scattering that is the world without respite, a world that openly mocks the powers of the higher nature. With each successful turn of the revolutionary screw, he finds that what he thought would build and tighten has loosened and torn down, until he stands on the disorganized pieces of what was his shelter. Yet the deception is so strong, and the sickness so entrenched, that he cannot allow the possibility of action and influence to powers that are not real to him. At this point even the most devout docetic religionist, if he has breathed the docetic air fully and singularly, cries out with the biblical father who hoped for his child: "Lord, I believe. Help my unbelief!" Apart from God's grace, I am afraid that docetic man cannot rediscover the higher nature, so decisively has his spirit snuffed it out. The docetic world, a wasteland without purpose, without mission or mystery, weighs him down with its inescapability. It is the infinite within, the terror of the soul deprived of God.

Those who have received forgiveness of sins and who labor toward righteousness enjoy consolation against this terror and the deceptions that stoke it. By faith if not by experience they understand that the higher nature, the invisible and eternal realm of powers beyond docetic calculation, permeates the visible and lower nature, and this often as an expression of joy and salvation. Forgiveness of sins implies the interweaving of the visible and the invisible, the lower and the higher, both as an objective statement about the cosmos and as the tacit order that man bears within him. The man striving in light of forgiveness in Christ acknowledges the invisible powers without and within, just as Scripture teaches the activity of those powers in space and time.

By the Spirit of God, the prophet Ezekiel saw the abominations occurring in the temple: all kinds of creeping things and loathsome animals on the walls, the idols and the burning incense, the women weeping for Tammuz and the men putting the branch to the nose, all desecrations occurring in the visible world. After this he had a vision of the invisible acting within the visible realm. He saw six men carrying weapons for slaughter and a seventh with a writing tablet, the last dressed in linen. They entered the temple and stood beside the altar, and there God commanded the man in linen to mark those who were troubled at the abominations in Israel. God instructed the others to follow him and kill all who did not receive the mark. Men and women, the old and the young, fell because of the sins of Israel and the punishment carried out by the men with weapons. Were these seen by the Israelites? Likely not at all. As angels, God might have allowed a few men to see their activity, but not many. They correspond in the visible world to the Babylonian army that bore God's wrath in flesh and blood. God carries out his will on two levels, the higher and the lower, and the higher realm expresses the deepest truth about physical events. Not the arrogance and ambition of Babylon, not the thirst for glory of king or captain, but God's punishment of sin and the sanctity of the temple count in the interpretation of the destruction of Jerusalem. He who strives after holiness through the forgiveness of sins recalls the spiritual meaning, remembering God's wisdom and his ordering of the cosmos.

The New Testament affirms the intertwining of higher and lower natures no less than the Old, emphasizing the double meaning of Christ's sacrifice on the cross. Hebrews refers to Christ as a priest "according to the order of Melchizedek," citing the prophecy in Psalms to highlight the activity of Christ in the heavenly sanctuary as the heavenly high priest. The Christ died on the cross physically, in the visible world and before the eyes of men. The onlookers saw his side pierced and that his legs did not require breaking, they saw him lowered from the cross and his body taken away. They did not see Christ the high priest in heaven, the one without earthly father or mother, having neither beginning of days nor end of life, remaining a priest forever. They did not see the heavenly sanctuary, the greater and perfect tent not made with hands of men and not of this creation, the eternal house of worship of which the earthly replica is a sketch and a shadow. They did not see him enter the Holy Place there and offer his own blood rather than the blood of goats and bulls, appearing once and for all at the end of the age to remove sin by the sacrifice of himself. They did not see him sitting as heavenly high priest at the right hand of the throne of the Majesty in the heavens, an eternal minister in the sanctuary by his blood. These things take place in a manner beyond man's grasp and in concert with the death on the cross. We envision the man on the cross perishing as if we were spectators, and with the eyes of faith we believe in its heavenly counterpart, for the man's visible death on the cross directs us to what occurs invisibly, the temporal turning our eyes to the eternal. Let us not separate these two, both of which are critical, lest we lose the forgiveness of sins! For the reconciliation of the cosmos with God, from the inner hearts of men to the entire visible order, happens essentially in that heavenly temple, where Christ performs the heavenly ritual. There man discovers purity of conscience, there he finds forgiveness from his iniquities. Christians should not dismiss the priority of the higher realm, lest we invert the higher and the lower and again relinquish the forgiveness of sins, as if Christ were no better than a goat or bull. Our atonement, though not without a vital and corresponding visible act, draws us toward the love of the eternal just as Christ acts in eternity.

The priority of the higher over the lower realm has a partner in the superiority of Christ's work over man's in the joint accomplishment of salvation. The Christ performs the heavenly sacrifice on man's behalf, completing the work necessary for salvation that no other could accomplish. At the same time he calls upon us, having taken on the crucial and significant burden himself, to bear our part and work out our salvation with fear and trembling. He has conquered, he has redeemed the creation

1 John: On Docetism and Resurrection

and vanquished death, and as the master he directs his slaves to participate in his work according to his commandments. We once followed the ruler of the power of the air, the spirit that is now at work among the disobedient, the invisible and wicked force that directs men by falsehood toward passion and perdition. Now we have the Holy Spirit written on our hearts by grace, we have received the heavenly gift, and so we struggle as the lesser workers whose contribution pales before the savior's. We have forgiveness of sins in his name, not in ours, and under that name we live the life to which he has destined us. We persevere in suffering, we abstain from the desires of the flesh that war against the soul, we discipline ourselves for the sake of our prayers, we forgive the trespasses of others as the Lord has forgiven us, and above all we maintain constant love for one another. The Christ, acting in the invisible and eternal realm, has purified our consciences so that we no longer hand ourselves over to dead works, freeing us to come to know him.

I write to you, fathers, because you have known Him who is from the beginning. In the church there are little children, we who should remember that our sins are forgiven on account of Christ's name, because of his work, and who, in our day, have wandered long under Docetism. Apart from these there are fathers, men of holiness and courage, of commitment and zeal, gentleness and patience, who remind we who have progressed little if at all what it means to know the One from the beginning. When John wrote to the fathers, he may or may not have immediately envisioned the history of witnesses, teachers, and wonder-workers from whom contemporary Christians take their cues under Christ and the Holy Spirit. The spirit of his writing nonetheless remains the same, as the church in our day needs and, by God's grace, possesses leaders in the faith. We rejoice that we have fathers, men and women whose testimony is pure, who looked after orphans and widows and kept themselves unstained from the world. We rejoice that Christ has not abandoned us to the deception that, hand-in-hand with the Bible, the individual can decide upon the doctrine and practice of Christianity. We rejoice that our signposts point us to the goal of holiness that Christ intends for us. Our saints, our illumined fathers, prescribe the path that, despite the diversity of the Spirit's gifts, applies to each and every Christian as a member of Christ's body. For all sin in thought, word, and deed, and Christ commands all to struggle against that sin. The fathers commend that struggle to us as markers along the way, abiding in God as so many smaller lights directing us to God the Son, the great light that shines in our hearts by the Spirit.

The fathers know him who is from the beginning, the Word made incarnate as Christ. What is the beginning? There are two beginnings, one in Genesis and the other in John's Gospel, and man should consider the two together with regard to knowing Christ. "In the beginning was the Word, and the Word was with God, and the Word was God. He was in the beginning with God." The first beginning steps outside of man's time into the life of the Word with the Father in the Spirit, confirming this beginning's relevance to man. When the Christian comes to know him who was from the beginning, he experiences Christ as one active in the spiritual realm, an experience gained at a certain distance from man's material concerns. This way of knowing Christ, the primary and fundamental one, depends upon man's rest and inactivity, his stillness before God. "All things came into being through him, and without him not one thing came into being. What has come into being in him was life, and the life was the light of men." The second beginning occurs in God's forming all things, as he commands the matter created *ex nihilo* to become the world that men know, a cosmos of wonder that bears the divine image. Here man comes to know Christ within the material world, as he in whom all things hold together. This holding together applies practically to man's love of his neighbor, to whom Christ binds him as a brother in the church and as a fellow image-bearer in the broader world, as well as man's love of the natural order, in which he perceives the divine power and nature. To these two beginnings we can add a third, one no less important for the life of the church. This beginning refers to the teaching of Christ and the life he lived, the proclamation of resurrection that he embodied and handed on to his disciples so that he remains as the light of men after his ascension.

    The Christian desires union with Christ and participation in the energies of God, loving him in spirit and in truth. He cannot do this without rightly ordering the form of his striving, acknowledging the higher as higher and the lower as secondary. Although the first two beginnings noted above exist not apart from one another, although man cannot love God inwardly without loving him outwardly and vice versa, although one cannot isolate either way of love and focus singularly upon it, man should orient his pursuit of Christ first within the spiritual realm and secondly in the created order. Man should see Christ in all things and come to know him everywhere, but he cannot rightly perceive Christ in all things if he does not first see him in the Trinity, he cannot love all things in Christ if he does not first seek Christ as the immortal principle of life, as one whose immortal life communes with man's spirit. The principle life with Christ occurs inwardly, in the spirit or the mind in the heart, and following this, outwardly. St. Paul writes concerning the Jewish preoccupation with external obedience that "A person is not a Jew who is one outwardly, nor is true circumcision something external and physical. Rather, a person is a Jew who is one inwardly, and real circumcision is a matter of the heart—it is spiritual and not literal." Likewise, true obedience and communion with God is inward, of the mind and the heart, the outer moral life being subordinate to this. The Christian should know Christ in both the spiritual and physical realms, then, but let him first know Christ as the Son, the Word in the beginning with God, seeking him in rest and distance from worldly activity. Subordinate to this man should seek God in the works of the created order, as the light of its life. As the Christ teaches, we must clean the interior of the dish first, and the exterior second.

    Docetic man knows nothing of the inner life, at times excoriating it. Inasmuch as his science divides and dichotomizes, and inasmuch as he has little notion of higher and lower, of primary and secondary, he will decry the forwarding of the inner life over the outer and active ethic as the latter's rejection. He must admit, if he is honest, that his rejection of the inner life in favor of the outer mirrors his scorn for the spiritual realm, with a total dismissal of both. Only the smallest fraction of docetic men have thought for the dynamics of the inner life, whether maintaining a robust guard over the thoughts and tremors of feeling by which the evil one draws one into sin, or training oneself in the concentration by which man turns to God in humility. Sadly, such humility is hardly possible for the docetist, grounded as he is in the infinite, the ontology of pride. He has so eradicated the inner life that even among the devout, who pay lip service to prayer and the heart, there prevails a unilateral preoccupation with ethics, with morals, with the social order and its sins, with habits and institutions, with behaviors and forms of communication that scientists can quantify and compare from one man or group to another. According to his spirit, docetic man must act in the world. Prayer, hope, love, and faith mean for him not stillness and waiting but promptings to decision, to seizing upon the proper course of action post haste. Anything less than this activity, which likes to pray for a thing before expending every effort oneself to gain it, strikes the docetist as counterproductive if not foolish. He cannot understand how a man can claim that God will act without taking up action on God's behalf. Must man not, as God's instrument, be the one through whom God's will should be done? How shall God act, if not through this man? How shall men learn to love one another if docetic man, empowered and authorized by his god, does not refashion the world according to docetic love? How shall his society become more just if he does not work ceaselessly for Docetism's justice? How can suffering be defeated in God's name without self-appointed cadres on a mission to repeal the effects of suffering until they cancel it as a cause? And how can man claim to work in the name of God, to have faith and love his neighbor, if he does not immerse himself straightaway in this external and urgent task?

By this task, through which man believes that he moves closer to God, he in fact springs away from him and runs headlong into the infinite. In his restless pursuit of "a better world" man forgets that the higher world exists beyond this one, that the lower nature testifies to the higher and that loving the lower world as though it were higher amounts to hatred of both worlds. Restless man, who knows his pride in the place of Christ and suffers in ignorance of the Holy One, whose mind has become the playground of evil, scattered in iniquity, worry, and ambition! Cleanse your hands and purify your heart, forsake your ways, and be still, so that men of God might speak of his presence and of our proper orientation to what is higher and spiritual:

> "During the divine services, during the celebration of all the sacraments and prayers, you should be as trusting as a child with his parents. Remember what great Fathers of the Church, what inspired luminaries, enlightened by the Holy Spirit, are guiding you! Be simple, trusting, undoubting as a child in what concerns God. Lay all your cares upon the Lord, and be entirely free from sorrow.
> *"Do not worry about how or what you should speak. For it will be given to you*

in that hour what you should speak; for it is not you who speak, but the Spirit of your Father, which speaks in you" (Matt 10:19–20). The Lord has long ago freed us from this care, this sorrow, having taught our God-fearing Fathers through His Spirit what to say and how to pray to the Lord at divine services, at the celebration of the sacraments, and during various other occasions and events in human life, when one prays to call down divine blessing from above. It should be easy for us to pray. But the enemy troubles us! But what does it matter, if our heart is firmly established in the Lord? The only misfortune is if we do not rest in God, if there is no firm faith in us, if we have bound ourselves to worldly attachments, if our intellect is proud and presumptuous. Then, even in the holiest, purest service to God—the celebration and communion of the Holy Mysteries—the enemy will greatly hinder us." (St. John of Kronstadt)

To rest in God belongs to the liturgy and the sacraments. It comes as worshippers put aside their worldly cares, casting out the thoughts by which the evil one tempts us and drags us down, seeking to imprison us in anger, jealousy, lust, and sorrow. If the Christian should rest in God, he must fix the mind upon spiritual rather than worldly things and pray with the whole heart. So says St. John, and so says the tradition with him. Christians come together and worship, pausing from their activity as they cry out for God's mercy, at ease in the confidence that God hears the one who worships him and obeys his will.

The Christian should approach the sacraments with contrition and thanksgiving, if not with awe and wonder. This "holiest, purest service to God" constitutes the pre-eminent and regular miracle of God's work in the lower nature, the point where God offers his presence, mediated through physical matter, to the man whose soul has turned to accept it. "Marvel, Christian, still more at the wisdom, omnipotence and mercy of the Creator! He changes and transforms the bread and wine into His Most-pure Body and Blood, and He takes up His abode in them Himself, by His Most-pure and Life-creating Spirit, so that His Body and Blood together are Spirit and Life. And why does He do this? In order to cleanse you, a sinner, from your sins, to sanctify you and to unite you, thus sanctified, to Himself, and thus united to deify you and make you blessed and immortal" (St. John). At the eucharist man sees the cup and the priest, the bread and the wine, but he must understand that more is present than this. Just as one man's encounter with another does not mean that a body meets a body only, as if there were no unseen thoughts and powers within each person, so when the Christian comes to the eucharist he comes to unseen powers, to the Life-giving Spirit carried with the elements for the sake of the sinner. Christ has made simple, physical matter into Spirit and Life, a mystery that man cannot comprehend. "In order to commune of the life-giving Holy Mysteries with undoubting faith and to vanquish all the snares and attacks of enemy," St. John writes, "imagine that that which you receive from the Cup is 'He Who is,' He Who alone exists. If this is the disposition of your thoughts and heart, then by receiving the Holy Mysteries you will obtain peace, joy, and new life, and you will recognize in your heart that the Lord truly dwells within you, and you dwell in the Lord. This is from experience." The presence of God in the eucharist is the spiritual reality of God given to man in grace and love. So the saints tell us as they testify to the experience of their hearts.

Come to the mystery with the eyes of faith, the eyes that Docetism blinds by its thoughts and assumptions, and seek God in the higher nature. The unexplainable perdures, the miraculous thrives, where men approach God in confidence that he draws near to those who draw near to him, humbly submitting themselves to his rule. "O, Almighty Power, able to accomplish everything in a single moment, do not leave us on account of our sins, and above all on account of our incredulity and despair, to be tormented by our own infirmities" and by our lack of faith, "lest we be destroyed like earthen vessels. Grant that we may believe with all our hearts in Your Almighty Power, and that we may never doubt in the fulfillment of our every proper request," especially that your grace will descend to us in your mysteries, sanctifying us in truth and love (St. John). In this we rest: God has acted in Jesus Christ once-for-all and finally, and he acts again and again in the mystery for the nourishment of Christ's body. If and when the miracle occurs, be humbled but do not be shocked, for the higher power acts naturally within the lower.

In the prayer of faith the believer concentrates on every word, not only thinking but feeling, until the Holy Spirit comes to him. "Prayer gives us this grace [of the Holy Spirit] most of all, for it is always at hand, as an instrument for acquiring the grace of the Holy Spirit," says St. Seraphim. Prayer, as the saint writes, means stillness. Man's activity must stop so that God can fill him. The saint adds:

> "Many explain that this stillness refers only to worldly matters; in other words, that during prayerful converse with God you must 'be still' with regard to worldly affairs. But I will tell you in the name of God that not only is it necessary to be dead to them at prayer, but when by the omnipotent power of faith and prayer our Lord God the Holy Spirit condescends to visit us, and comes to us in the plenitude of His unutterable goodness, we must be dead to prayer too."

> "The soul speaks and converses during prayer, but at the descent of the Holy Spirit we must remain in complete silence, in order to hear clearly and intelligibly all the words of eternal life which he will then deign to communicate. Complete soberness of soul and spirit, and chaste purity of body is required at the same time. The same demands were made at Mount Horeb, when the Israelites were told not even to touch their wives for three days before the appearance of God on Mount Sinai. For our God is a fire which consumes everything unclean, and no one who is defiled in body or spirit can enter into communion with Him."

When a man prays, according to St. Seraphim, he becomes totally quiet, even without thought, so that he shall not impede the Spirit's communication. Man must maintain this stillness as his work of self-negation, his work of rest. The power present to him in this moment—which might come after years of prayer and contrition—is not his, and it fills him in his silence of mind and heart, a silence prepared by purity. If man should come into contact with God the Trinity, if he should know God as eternal through the experience of the Spirit, he does so not in restless labor but in rest from all labor, as if to say: You are my God, and no other; you are my thought, and no other; you are my feeling, and no other. You fill me, and I take solace in you. I hand myself over to you, and you commune with me.

This communion with God does not occur apart from knowledge of Him in the world of action, through purification of soul and body and love of neighbor. The two realms intertwine, as love of neighbor and moral purity prepare the way for the inner experience of rest, benefiting also from that experience. As St. Seraphim teaches, "However prayer, fasting, vigil, and all the other Christian practices may be, they do not constitute the aim of our Christian life. Although it is true that they serve as the indispensable means of reaching this end, the true aim of our Christian life consists in the acquisition of the Holy Spirit of God. As for fasts, and vigils, and prayer, and almsgiving, and every good deed done for Christ's sake, [these] are the only means of acquiring the Holy Spirit of God." Christians should not despise the means, though they are only means, but should regard them as intrinsic to the acquisition of the Holy Spirit, as fundamental to the rest in God that we seek. "Make the most of your time getting heavenly blessing through earthly goods," the saint adds, as "Earthly goods are the good works done for Christ's sake that confer the grace of the All-Holy Spirit on us." Christians can therefore look to obedience with anticipation and firmness, recalling the joy bestowed when it is performed in faith and in the expectation of God's presence. Once man has set his heart on that nearness of God, or perhaps has tasted it, he begins to see distraction, disobedience, and all kinds of temptations as the enemies they are. In them he must daily choose: shall I accept this bodily and earthly pleasure that tempts me, and which will draw me away from God? Or shall I deny this temptation for the good of my soul, keeping God nearer to me and purifying my heart, so that my spirit should better commune with him as he wills? Just as man denies worldly pleasures for the next life, he denies transient and fading pleasantries for what is spiritual, for the inner closeness of the divine. In addition to this, he understands his time and resources as given so that he can give rest to others, living to carry out this means to God's Spirit.

Thus the second "beginning" in Eden, where the rest of man in woman and woman in man provides a template for human relations. I have explained elsewhere how man does not rest in God without resting in his neighbor, how the "not good" of Eden means that God had not yet fully established man's rest. God placed Adam in the Garden "to till it and keep it," and God created Eve to aid him in this so that the two create life together. God explicitly commands that the couple should be fruitful and multiply, filling the earth and subduing it, and that they should have dominion over the birds, the fish, and every living thing on the earth. He lastly directs them not to eat of the tree of good and evil, the first explicit break upon man's free will. He does not explicitly command Eve to help Adam nor Adam to aid Eve, but God writes this commandment into their nature as well as the others. In every case the commandment reinforces what God had created by nature by appealing to man's will, guiding man's natural inclination toward life and away from death. As made in the image of the creator, man naturally yearns for the multiplication of life and its fruitfulness. As rational and made for communion with him, man assumes a place above the other forms of life on earth and rightly rules over them. As God's creature, his nature inclines also to worship his creator, not falling into idolatry. As a natural imitator of the Trinity both in his relation with God and others, he tends toward giving and receiving love as the basis of his interactions, bearing the burdens of others as they bear his own. The first commandment sets man to his natural task of producing life, the second deputizes him to oversee the lower creatures in their own orientation toward life, the third confirms that he performs the first two in trust and obedience before his creator, and the fourth demands that he share the burden equitably with his neighbor, so that each rests in the other as they rest in God.

I write to you, little children, because you have known the Father. You little children "have known and are coming to know," in the perfect tense, the Father. This means that the little children have repented in Jesus Christ. "Come to me, you who labor and are heavy laden," he says, "and I will give you rest. For my yoke is easy and my burden is light." We come to know the Father through the Son, if he has chosen to reveal the Father to us. This we receive as we progress along the way prescribed by Christ, the way of prayer, almsgiving, and fasting, of worship and obedience, of eucharist and love of neighbor. This way requires purity of mind and heart, wherein man does not succumb to distraction or give in to passions but holds his peace as he restrains them. It is a life of generosity, of mercy to the unfortunate and sharing of bread with the hungry, of visiting the sick and the poor. When in his mind distractions tempt him and he casts them out, declaring that he rests in God; when in his heart desires, troubles, and emotions disturb him and he negates these quietly, affirming his peace in God; and when the insistence to act pulls at his will, directing him in errant paths and urging him to break the commandments, but he resists and maintains a godly habit, reigning in his words and his hands; when he is obedient in thought, word, and deed, striving to love God within and without, then we might say, timidly, that a man knows the Father, although such a man would not say this, much less would he state it over and against others.

You who know the Father know that he gives rest rather than freedom. He commands not liberation but mutual care, not equality but mutual humility. He regards as holy not the breaking of boundaries, the transgression of law, and the satiety of desire but the humility of the obedient and their will to suffer with and for their brethren. If we should know the Father, we recognize that he alone determines what is good, calling us to know it. The prerogative that determines good for ourselves we relinquish, and in this abdication we respect God's commandment that we love one another. One must repent of liberation if he wishes to give his neighbor rest. How can he know God while his liberation distances him from God? How can he give meaningful and true rest while he cherishes freedom from his neighbor? Docetic man cannot say "I am free" and "I love my neighbor" at the same time, for in docetic freedom he expels and oppresses his neighbors, assuming this as the good that he chooses for himself. God has announced that rest is holy, and the man who denies that holiness for freedom's sake also denies God, embarking upon a different way. In proclaiming his freedom—in docetic terms, his enslavement to the Christ-Idol—he admits that God is not his god, and that he does not know the Father.

I write to you, young men, because you have overcome the wicked one. . .I have written to you, young men, because you are strong, and the word of God abides in you, and you have overcome the wicked one. If any of us have broken from Docetism in a meaningful way, we should give thanks to God. If any of us have rejected in belief and practice, to the best of our ability, the notion that the ground of existence is freedom and have accepted that it is rest, we should give thanks. If God has indeed plucked us out from the powerful delusion of which St. Paul writes, and that permeates the world, removing us from the muddy and burdensome landscape of docetic thoughts and habits, guiding us away from the Christ-Idol or any of the other idolatries within its realm, let us give thanks. If God has distanced us from the scattering whose lifeblood is freedom and competition, the alienation of man from man and their mutual antagonism, we should give thanks. If God has given us a mind to seek what is spiritual first, to love him inwardly through eucharist and prayer, to rightly order our lives so that the we clean the interior of the cup before the exterior, struggling to open our hearts to the Holy Spirit, then let us humbly give thanks. If there is in this a kind of conquering, we should be grateful to God that his grace, and his grace only, has brought us this far. We are not "competent of ourselves to claim anything as coming from us; our competence is from God." We should not take pride in conquering, for to conquer means not merely escape from the deceptions by which the evil one ensnares us, but to willingly suffer in this world. In the docetic era no less than others, men who prioritize the inner and spiritual will suffer. It is for them to humbly accept this suffering as the Christian's destiny while hoping for salvation in the world to come.

Salvation after the example of Christ implies that man lowers himself before God, who then honors him. The life of the Christian in this world requires that humility, a suffering that he bears while understanding its necessity as a preliminary, as intrinsic to the blessing that follows. Thus the Christian patiently endures, thus he counts himself blessed when God forces upon him all kinds of trials and troubles, from chronic sickness and poverty to war, famine, and shame. The lives of the saints, in many cases, amount to a long testimony of suffering, sometimes willingly as a spiritual struggle and other times as a result of external circumstances allowed by God. Consider St. Seraphim, who lived such a pure and holy life, and who in his holiness was beaten by robbers nearly to death, so that he was injured for the rest of his life. Consider St. Galaction, who read the Holy Scriptures in his cell until the Roman soldiers found him, taking him away to torture and death. Consider his betrothed Episteme, who went with him out of love. The humiliation and faith of these I cannot but revere. They said to God "Thy will be done," and accepted their sufferings as God's will, rejecting pride and opening themselves to the joy of the next world. Docetism would have men conquer by the illusion of suffering eliminated, of pain and disease banished from the earth, while Christianity conquers in the wisdom that comprehends suffering, rightly practiced, as the prelude to joy.

Many are the sufferings of the righteous, and the Lord delivers them from them all. "How great and evil are the afflictions you showed me, and you returned, and made me live; and you raised me up again from the depths of the earth. You multiplied your greatness, and you returned and comforted me; you brought me up again from the depths of the earth," says the Psalmist. As St. Paul writes, "For I consider that the sufferings of this present time are not worthy to be compared with the glory which shall be revealed in us . . . Who shall separate us from the love of Christ? Shall tribulation, or distress, or persecution, or famine, or nakedness, or peril, or sword? As it is written, 'For your sake we are killed all day long; we are accounted as sheep for the slaughter.' Yet in all these things we are more than conquerors through Him who loved us." He continues in Hebrews, citing Proverbs that "'For whom the Lord loves He chastens, and scourges every son whom he receives.' If you endure chastening, God deals with you as with sons; for what son is there whom a father does not chasten? But if you are without chastening, of which all have become partakers, then you are illegitimate and not sons . . . now no chastening seems to be joyful for the present, but painful; nevertheless, afterwards it yields the peaceable fruit of righteousness to those who have been trained by it." And remember that those who conquer, in the Apocalypse of John, have suffered unto death, testifying in this way to Christ our Lord. For "our brethren . . . overcame [Satan] by the blood of the Lamb and by the word of their testimony."

If we Christians would conquer, then we must suffer all that the Lord imposes upon us as we strive for holiness. Not that this conquering depends on us, not that it is matter of a steeled will or manliness, but that it convinces us of our weaknesses and drives us to Christ. "You, Lord Jesus Christ, are everything, and I am nothing. I am powerless, I am infirm," says St. John of Kronstadt. If before our suffering we feel dread and dismay, let us recall the reward for those who persevere in meekness and be joyful. If we abide in God and remain strong in him, then by his grace, and in the midst of our sorrows, we shall overcome the evil one.

1 John 4:13–16a

> By this we know that we abide in him, and he in us, because he has given us of his Spirit. And we have seen and testify that the Father has sent the Son as Savior of the world. Whoever confesses that Jesus is the Son of God, God abides in him, and he in God. And we have known and believed the love that God has for us.

By this we know that we abide in him, and he in us, because he has given us of his Spirit. The Holy Spirit bestows communion as mystery and truth. In him, we perceive that the coherence and unity of being have their ground in mutual humility, but we cannot say why this is so beyond acknowledging that God is in this way and that this humility unto love bears all things and holds them together in Christ. And Christ has given us his Spirit so that we should abide in a world that holds together, loving one another in mutual humility after the form of God. In every case we humble ourselves before and as the lower, so that we may be humbled to by the higher. We humble ourselves before God by obedience and worship, and especially in prayer, charity, and eucharist, with faith and hope that he will condescend to us. We humble ourselves before the cosmos as God has structured it, the world of visible and invisible in which the former takes its place as lower while the latter is higher. We humble ourselves before the neighbor, hoping that he will turn to us and reciprocate our goodwill. These three, each expressive of the truth, exist in unison: as man humbles himself before God, he humbles himself before God's cosmos and the neighbor. Thus he abides in holy communion with all that is. In this man apprehends that he abides in God, and God in him, because man dwells in the Spirit that joins all things in harmony.

How does man conform to the shape of the cosmos? How does he further its unity by dwelling in the Spirit? When men breathe the air according to docetic principles and see with docetic eyes, they forget the shape of the world as crafted by God though it daily confronts them. Their movements, born by docetic directives and guided by lying thoughts, alienate them from the design of the world and their design within that world. They become creatures of a new magnitude, a foreign and amorphous way that wanders until its end, drunk with possibility but sobered by despair and catastrophe. In the latter moments man's choice crystallizes before him, if he has ears to hear. Will he continue on the path of the Christ-Idol or will he worship the true God? Will he enslave himself to folly or wisdom? Will he take seriously the invisible realm, naturally known to other ages and regions but ejected from the docetic consciousness, and will he respect the interweaving of visible and invisible powers that mark his true home? Docetism has propelled all its energy against these invisible powers, castigating them as superstition and childishness, presenting technological and thus controllable unseen powers in their place, and marshalling a chorus of voices and institutions, of words, mores, and criteria, until the docetic path seems the only sensible one and the alternative a fable.

The physical world exists according to general and predictable laws. Gravity, motion, and force exist in the world such that man can measure their effects. He observes these laws and uses them for his benefit, providing for the improvement of human life within its limit, employing them for the betterment of civilization and the preservation of life according to nature. Laws of power and energy, of heat and cold, and the various repetitions of human experience surround man with a certain necessity and regularity, so that he can count upon their consistency for his advantage. These laws, however predictably he might experience them, are not universal or irresistible, nor are they exceptionless and unilateral. They remain general and usual, leaving room for a freedom not nameless and chaotic, not haphazard and meaningless, but born of rational beings who desire good or evil. These influence the course of events in the physical world as God allows, carrying out God's will directly or seeking to subvert it. Whether one speaks of angels and saints on the one hand or demons and their ilk on the other, they live not as forces or anonymous powers but as willed persons that, as they exist in the higher and invisible order, can act to suspend the laws of the visible world. This action does not contradict the supposed universality of the laws governing the physical world but confirms their limited character, giving rest to physical laws and, in the case of benevolent powers, complementing them (the rest given to physical laws by demonic powers is at best ambivalent). With angels, saints, and heavenly powers, the invisible's suspension of visible laws reveals immortal powers so that man, who raises himself up as he bows to the visible, should not construe the temporal as the eternal. In this way man views the world as composed of two kinds of powers, seeing that he can measure and make use of the visible to his advantage while submitting to the priority of the invisible as a higher law, a realm that can attempt to influence him by its own initiative and which he can supplicate for mercy. He cannot measure and calculate the powers of this realm, nor can he manipulate and control them, yet he has been shown that they abide according to principles not so unlike those of the visible world, principles of integrity as well as freedom.

It takes time and patience for man to unlearn the deceptions that Docetism instills within him, those opinions that, in its view, anyone with the least intelligence should hold and whose denial renders man a buffoon. In prayers repeated not about the inhabitants of the spiritual realm but to them as intercessors with real powers, man slowly realizes that these forces populate the world and that men can interact with them. He senses distance between this realization and the world of uncompromising and exceptionless laws, the mechanical and closed world in which Docetism entraps him. As his understanding of the world as systematic and everywhere determined fades, and as he permits a space for the interplay of free and self-determining powers, he comes not so much to the acknowledgment that spiritual beings exist and are active as he converses with them, calling for angels and saints to hasten to his aid in tribulation and hearkening to their wonders in previous eras. The parameters of his experience shift and expand as the glorious ones whom he mocked become objects of adoration and supplication. If the spiritual world exists, partaking of God's glory and abiding eternally in his presence, how can man pray to God without humbling himself before it? How can he look to God, crying out for his salvation, without asking his ancestors in the faith to pray for him, confident that God's ear inclines to those who have sought him in obedience, purity, and longsuffering?

In the akathist to the Archangel Michael, the Christian who prays with faith both recognizes his miracles and asks for his protection from visible and invisible enemies. When he prays, the Christian sings of how Michael "withstood the arrogant daystar Satan—who was exceedingly proud and breathing out evil when he and his dark servants had been cast down into the nethermost parts of the world." Against him Michael led the heavenly hosts to victory in battle as commander of God's army. The same Michael "appeared in the Church of Khony as a divinely flowing fountain of great miracles. Not only was a large and fearful serpent dwelling there destroyed by [his] strength, but a stream of pure water was revealed there healing all bodily ailments." The Archangel also in the form of a man "stood before Joshua, son of Nun, saying 'Take off your shoes, for I am the Supreme Commander of the hosts of the Lord.'" He carried off the prophet Habakkuk at God's command, taking him "from Judah to Babylon to give food to Daniel, a prisoner in the den of lions. Amazed at the mighty effect of your strength," Habakkuk cried out, "Alleluia!" According to the tradition and the akathist hymn, Michael destroyed the 185,000 warriors of the Assyrian king Sennacherib, an event recorded in the Old Testament (4 Kgdms 19:35–36, Isa. 37:36–37). Much later, the monks of Athos saw him save "the God-fearing child who was thrown into the depths of the sea, with a stone around his neck, by money-grubbing men," so that the monastery that took in the boy was named after Michael. The Archangel acted against the spiritual powers of darkness, he performed miracles of various kinds to protect the faithful, he aided the prophets in their service to the Lord, and he carried out the divine command by laying low enemies who had blasphemed God's name.

The one praying sings of these wondrous deeds not merely as a celebration of the past but as an appeal for Michael to act in the present. The Archangel lives, and while he is "entirely in the heights" of the heavens, standing before God's heavenly throne, he is also "not far from men and women below on earth." The Christian prays for Michael "to set us free from all distress that we may cry to you with faith and love," asking also that he will "entreat for us a clear understanding and a release from passions." Christians exult that they have in Michael "a mighty defender and helper in battle against the adversary" who delivers them from "all the storms of temptation and trouble. Be our mighty helper in every affliction and our preserver and defender in the hour of death," Christians say, "so that we may cry aloud to our Lord and our Lady: Alleluia." Michael, who ever fights "against the enemies of mankind's salvation," and who is "a secure wall for all who believe and a sturdy pillar in the struggle with visible and invisible enemies," receives the following closing prayer: "We come to you, O leader of the archangels and angels, in our need for defense against unbelief and for enlightenment over doubt. Grant us shelter beneath your strong and glorious wings, that we may discern and overcome all temptations and attacks. Help us to live in fidelity to our Mother the Church and our Father in Heaven. Amen."

By the Holy Spirit men pray to God and Jesus Christ, and by the Spirit also men call upon the heavenly powers to act on their behalf. By the Spirit man perceives the visible and invisible realms in their unity, and by the Spirit he humbles himself as body and soul before the immaterial and benevolent powers, so that bodiless and angelic beings should respond in their humility to him. In this mutual humility, this fundamental work of the Spirit, lies the mystery of union and of faith, for man cannot explain why humility draws all things together beyond saying that God has ordained life to conform to his image. In this humility man rests in the Spirit, inasmuch has he relieves himself of burdens that God has not meant for him to bear. It is easy to say that docetic man has discarded faith in heaven and its hosts in order to raise earth to heaven (what frightful foolishness!), but it is considerably more difficult to affirm with one's soul and spirit that heaven is, and that its legions will act for the faithful to do what they cannot do for themselves. What mortal did God intend to withstand the arrogant daystar Satan? What mortal carries prophets through the air or destroys armies nearly 200,000 strong? What mortal saves those about to die by drowning or redirects the flow of waters? What mortal, by his power alone, can do such things? Man rests in knowing that the highest angels act in his aid, having received his supplications. In the Spirit man has faith in that action as God grants him the ability to believe.

The docetist smirks at the above as myth and falsehood, as delusion and stupidity. If one believes in angels as active and influencing the visible world, he reasons, one must also believe in demons who are active but malevolent. And let us not stop there: what of fauns and unicorns, of orcs and wizards, of sprites and fairies? Where do our imaginary creatures and spiritual powers end, once we allow them to begin? So he scoffs and returns to the infinite, flushed with pride and the comfort that he and his authorities know all, that he and his companions tower above history as giants over babes. I do not deny the existence and activity of demons, who mean to drag men into all kinds of sin in thought, word, and deed, who trouble the hearts of those who long for God by enticing them into dalliance, distraction, and dismay. Whereas Docetism raises itself up by doing away with all "superstition," referring to the invisible realm destroyed by negation, the Christian absorbs the reality of supernatural powers while keeping an eye open for unfounded beliefs. The allowance of these powers does not entail that the Christian accepts any and every wondrous story or that he surrenders all criteria for reasonable judgment, or that he must believe every tale that tickles his ears. Did the leaders of the early Church, validating the canonical Gospels with their miraculous claims, not reject the Gospels of Mary, Thomas, Peter, and James? Did they receive every miraculous story about the Christ as true? They did not. They lived in the world prior to and without Docetism, a world of active spiritual powers and the ready acknowledgement of miracles, but this did not render them naïve.

Docetism's proponents would have men believe that they differ from their adversaries principally by advancements in knowledge. "We know," say the docetists, pointing confidently to their scientists, their philosophers, their technological achievements and their cultural prowess. They claim to live in the light, to be the vanguard of civilization and to bear its progress, they promise the betterment of the world and its liberation from darkness. Those who believe in the supernatural suffer from this darkness. They are unconverted, recalcitrant, backward, and above all ignorant. Whether they choose not to know or do not possess the requisite intelligence, they slumber in the past, their eyes shut. They believe in what men cannot prove and so they misunderstand the world utterly. This contrast between those who know and those who do not, between the sophisticated and the ignorant, misleads those who consider it. The true contrast concerns the heart: the docetist dwells in his pride, the limitlessness of his methods of liberation, manipulation, and control, while the Christian who confirms his belief in the supernatural humbles himself before what he cannot know by Docetism's measurements and means. It secondly consists in the form of law by which man lives: the docetist lives by the infinite, a choice he makes more or less consciously, willing knowledge and mores as the infinite directs him, while the Christian accepts a law of limit, tailoring his knowledge of the world to the limits of this law. But what the Christian learns as he struggles against sin—the knowledge of God as the infinite and the indwelling of that infinitude as peace and joy—the docetist does not and cannot know. His sorrowed pride, and the darkness of his infinitude, will not allow it.

The division of the higher nature from its visible counterpart, of the unseen and spiritual powers from the seen, has happened through Docetism's leading thinkers and teachers. Predictably, John Calvin denied miracles in his day, announcing that their age has concluded: "But those powers and manifest workings, which were dispensed by the laying on of hands, have ceased; and they have rightly lasted only for a time . . . when the Lord ceased from these [unheard of and extraordinary miracles], he did not utterly forsake his church, but declared that . . . the dignity of his word had been excellently enough disclosed." With this assertion Calvin lodged a bold stroke for Docetism against the Holy Spirit, for he relegates miracles to the limited purpose of witnessing to the Gospel rather than, in addition to this purpose, allowing that their occurrence expresses the pattern by which God unifies the cosmos. Calvin rejects the ongoing mutual humility between the natural and the spiritual, the visible and the invisible, to which miracles testify. In Calvin's wake, the Protestant docetist broadens the denial of the higher nature so that he does not appeal to the saints, he does not call upon the angels to aid and guide him, he does not expect the higher nature to suspend the lower's laws and give it rest. To this extent he eliminates the practice of humility before the higher powers so that they might be humbled to the visible. What shame Calvin brings upon himself by planting this seed, as well as shame upon the Theotokos, the Archangel Michael, and the host of the saints! Yet all this follows from Calvin's thought, for he who destines both human nature and the law to Christ's "grace," unwittingly understanding the latter as the culmination of the infinite, sets his believer upon that infinite as his practical ethos. Thus Calvin introduces the infinite as the ethic definitive for man's relationship with the visible world, and with the infinite established what room remains for rest? Under the influence of the infinite, man has no rest in the sacrament as the locus of God's grace and of miraculous power, pursuing his salvation by "ceaseless activity" not in contemplation or mystical prayer but in ethical diligence and work. In these conditions, how can Calvin expect the eternal to give rest by suspending the laws of the lower realm? He has made the lower realm the arena of restless activity! Beyond this, in remaking man's nature and his path as the infinite, Calvin adopts a view of the world that mirrors that infinitude, prohibiting the eternal from breaking in upon the finite just as he implies man's outward activity as the vehicle of his infinity. In this manner Calvin unknowingly authored a gigantic step in Docetism's division of the world. In light of this I offer a hypothesis, which further study could establish as a general rule: since the Christ-Idol, where one finds the infinite or universal applied to the visible world and man in it, one finds the invisible powers, if not the realm of the eternal *per se*, expelled.[1]

---

1. While I do not have the space to investigate this hypothesis, I can suggest some lines of inquiry that would illumine the topic. One could engage Hobbes's casting God out of the state of nature and his criticism of certain forms of religion, which occur hand-in-hand with his description of "natural" man as boundlessly rapacious and driven by appetite; or one could explore Locke's removal of God from a meaningful relation to political theory at the same time that he opens the door for men to accumulate money without limit, since it does not spoil; or one could point to Marx's disdain for religion while advocating the universality of man as both "species being" and as unconditioned by the division of labor. One could also ponder Nietzsche's hatred of Christianity in conjunction with his espousal of the *Übermensch* and the revaluation of all values, by which men live without moral limitations imposed by God while determining morality for themselves. These are some of the more stimulating tracks that one could follow.

One could also study the combination in the thought of Immanuel Kant of, on the one hand, the division of the world between the phenomenal and the noumenal and the outright rejection of spiritual powers (in *Religion Within the Bounds of Reason Alone*) and, on the other, the affirmation of man as "universal" in the moral sense of adherence to the categorical imperative. Likewise, Hegel's *Phenomenology of Spirit* relocates Absolute truth and knowledge in the present world, leaving off the spiritual one. It is an open question how and to what extent this defines man according to a certain creaturely infinitude. Investigations of these and other thinkers could lead in different directions, with different implications for the meaning of the infinite as applied to man. Yet the rejection of the work

1 JOHN 4:13–16A

And we have seen and testify that the Father has sent the Son as savior of the world. We have seen that the Father has sent his Son as the savior in that the Christ, by dying and rising from the dead, arose as the first fruits of the resurrection and the perfect unity between the invisible power of God and man, a creature visible and invisible. We have seen that as savior he redeems the world by putting back together what sin had torn apart, sealing the cosmos where evil had severed it. In the present age we continue the struggle against forces bent upon ripping the world into pieces, mangling what God made whole and rending it into parts. Thank God that he has given us the long train of saints who have testified and still testify to Jesus Christ as the savior! Thank God that we can look to their examples in this life, their miracles, and the deaths they suffered as sure guides for our testimony to the Lord! Christ ensures us that the one lowered in this life will be raised up in the next, and that this visible and spiritual world, enslaved to the evil one, will be reborn in the age to come. The saints witness to the same things in Christ's name, and in them we see both the promise regarding glory in the next world and a present image of that glory. In their persons and in their faith they bind the two worlds together, submitting to humiliation and pain here for the sake of the beatitude to follow. In this manner they bring that beatitude into the present world just as they raise the current age toward the eternal.

Consider St. Phanourius, of whose background we know virtually nothing. We learn from the tradition that, when the Muslims conquered the island of Rhodes around the end of the fifteenth century, they wished to rebuild the fortress there. They discovered the ruins of a church during their work, including several icons on its floor. The majority of these had sustained damage, but the icon of St. Phanourius looked like new. The Christians there called the local bishop to view the icon, which bore the saint's name.

The icon portrayed twelve scenes from the saint's life: his questioning under an official, soldiers beating him with stones, his whipping by soldiers while he laid outstretched on the ground, iron hooks raking his sides, his being locked in a jail, a second time of questioning before a local official, his being burned with candles, the rack, his confrontation with wild animals, and his suffering under a large stone. Another scene shows him standing in front of idols while holding burning coals, with a demon grieving over the saint's victory over him. In the final scene the saint stands in a fire while praying, his arms raised toward heaven. How did you suffer such agony, St. Phanourius? Which of the tortures anguished you most? Or was it the time in prison, when you had already suffered much and had to suffer again, that plagued you above all? At what point did the demons bring their fullest onslaught, and at what point did they nearly convince you to fall? These are the wrong questions! We should rather ask how the grace of God sustained you through these trials. How did the Lord give you firm and unrelenting hope in the age to come? How did he steel your nerves so that you spat in the face of physical pain? Or did he give you joy already, a foretaste

---

of spiritual powers, or of the spiritual world on the whole, would likely remain constant.

of divine light, so that you withstood cheerfully? Did angels stand at your side and encourage you? Did they come to you in prison and minister to you? Did the prayers of the saints surround you with comfort? Were you who mourned also given solace? Did the Holy Spirit not descend on you, dwelling in your heart as you prayed in the midst of the fire? At what point, great martyr and witness of Christ, did the Lord relieve you of your mortal tent and take you to himself? We venerate you, great St. Phanourius, who reminds us of the transience of this world. We thank you for lifting our gaze beyond the trials of the flesh and to the eternal.

What also of the Protomartyr and Equal of the Apostles St. Thekla? We cannot meditate upon courageous saints without mentioning the young woman, full of learning and beautiful, who spurned her betrothed in order to give herself to Christ. Her parents had dedicated her to a young man for marriage, but after hearing the teaching of St. Paul she decided to give her life singularly to God. She ran away from her parents to the prison where St. Paul was incarcerated, staying there until her parents found her and compelled her to come home. When she insisted that she would not marry her fiancé, her mother wanted the authorities to put her to death. The sentence was burning, from which the Lord rescued the saint by his presence and a divine light, so that the flames did not harm or even touch her. Later, when St. Thekla helped St. Paul and his comrades preach the gospel in Antioch, again the rulers sentenced her to death for following Christ. This time they tried to beset her with hungry animals, but they would not injure her. Instead, they laid down on the ground before her and licked her feet. When subjected to further torments she continued to survive, as when torturers tied her to two oxen and ran after her with hot irons only to see the cords broken and the oxen running away. Many years after these trials, at the age of 90, pagan sorcerers sent their devotees to defile the saint because she treated the sick at no charge. As they came after her, St. Thekla cried out to God for help. A rock opened up to hide her and in this way she gave up her life to the Lord.[2]

Like St. Phanourius, St. Thekla stands before posterity as a witness and a guide. She shows us the unity of the physical and the spiritual, the temporal and the eternal. She came before torturers at various instances ready to die for Christ, humbling herself in the present for the sake of honors in eternity, and the Lord chose to save her by miracles that manifest the presence of the divine and immortal in our world. She witnesses to the interweaving of the lower and the higher natures in two ways, showing both how the lower nature attests to and humbles itself before the higher (in her willingness to be martyred) and how the higher humbles itself to the lower by appearing within it (in miracles). This dynamic occurs in many of the saints, and St. Thekla embodies it with particular respect to miracles that allowed her to persevere

---

2 Poulos, *Orthodox Saints*, 145–146. For a different account of St. Thekla's youth, see the *Reference Book for Clergy Servers* by Nastol'naya Kniga Svyaschennosluzhitelya. Unless otherwise noted, the *Reference Book* is the primary source for the remaining accounts of the saints, in addition to other sources recognized by the Orthodox Church in America.

through attempts to kill her. She witnesses uniquely to the power of immortality over death and to the unconquerable life that grounds our world. Such stories contradict the apprehension of docetic man, who considers them as fables just as he lacks knowledge of the inner reality to which the saints testify. For in severing the eternal from the temporal in order to eliminate the former, he has annulled both the eternal within himself and the sensibility that the inner room for the eternal implies.

St. Procopius of Palestinian Caesarea knew of the eternal and had the sensibility for divine things, acquiring this by a direct encounter with the Lord. His father having died while he was young, his mother provided the pagan youth with a thorough secular education. As a child from an eminent Roman family, he entered government service under Diocletian when he came of age. The emperor sent him to Alexandria to persecute the Christians there, but Procopius—at this point known by his pagan name, Neanius—received a vision of Christ much like St. Paul's. He heard a voice that inquired why Neanius meant to persecute him and that identified itself as Jesus Christ the crucified and Son of God. Neanius then saw a cross appear in the sky and at once became a follower of Jesus. This transformation brought him trouble, as his mother reported to the authorities that her son no longer worshipped the ancestral gods. When he appeared before the procurator, he was given the law of Diocletian against Christians, which he tore into pieces. As punishment for his crime, the authorities sent him to Caesarea in Palestine, leaving him in prison. The Lord appeared to him a second time during his stay, this time baptizing Neanius and giving him the Christian name Procopius.

The Romans led Procopius before the court multiple times, subjecting him to tortures between his questionings and demanding that he abandon his faith, but he steadfastly refused to abdicate Christ. Several of those who witnessed his courage came to claim Christ and lost their lives, including his pagan mother Theodosia. Having seen her son endure such sufferings, she repented of her unbelief and joined those executed for the faith. The Great-Martyr Procopius finally died by beheading. He is the first martyr known at Caesarea during the Great Persecution.

Prior to that era, the martyr St. Tryphon suffered under Decius (249–251 AD). God granted wondrous gifts to the saint from a young age, including the power to exorcise demons and heal the sick. It is reported that his prayers saved the city of Lampsacus from a swarm of locusts that were consuming local crops, leaving the fields barren. He also received notoriety by casting an evil spirit from the daughter of the emperor Gordian, who ruled a few years before Decius. When the latter ascended to the throne, he mandated a persecution of Christians that led to the arrest and questioning of Tryphon for preaching the name of Christ and baptizing converts. When he confessed Christ before the judge, St. Tryphon received the penalty of severe tortures. They burned him with fire, tore at his body with iron hooks, struck him with clubs, and paraded him through the city with iron nails driven through his feet. He died by beheading. St. Tryphon is said to have prayed prior to his execution, thanking God for the strength to sustain his tortures and asking the Lord to heed those who seek help in his name.

In the century before St. Tryphon, the martyrs Florus and Laurus gained heavenly glory by their service to God in the face of paganism. These brothers lived at first in Byzantium, later moving to Illyrium. They shared a profession as stone masons, with the prefect of the realm hiring them to work on a temple to pagan gods. They took up the task while distributing their wages to the poor, keeping a strict fast and praying always. At one point, the local pagan priest's son was hit in the eye by a chip of stone at the work site. This hurt him very badly, and Florus and Laurus assured his father that the eye would be healed. When they had roused the son from unconsciousness, the brothers told him to believe in Jesus as Lord and God, with the result that the young man confessed faith in him. The brothers then supplicated God on his behalf and the eye was restored. In light of this miracle the pagan priest also converted to Christianity. When they finished work on the temple, Florus and Laurus gathered fellow Christians before moving through it, smashing the idols. After erecting a cross in the eastern portion of the structure, they spent the night in prayer under a light from heaven. When the leader of the region heard of it, he sentenced 300 Christians to death by fire, including the former priest and his son. Florus and Laurus appeared before the prefect before being thrown into a well and smothered with dirt.

At the end of the third century lived the martyr Andrew Stratelates, a Roman military commander under Maximian (284–305 AD). When Persian forces invaded Syria, the governor Antiochus gave leadership of the army to Andrew, who selected the soldiers to follow him and set out to meet the enemy. Although unbaptized and a leader of pagan military men, Andrew believed in Jesus Christ. Prior to taking his soldiers into battle, he convinced them to put their faith in Jesus Christ rather than pagan gods that were really demons. He explained to them that Jesus gives help to all who have faith in him, and the soldiers, taking after Andrew's words, called on Christ for help as they went into battle. God gave them victory over the Persians despite smaller numbers, but the event turned awry for Andrew when envious men revealed him as a Christian to Antiochus, saying that he had led his subordinates to follow Jesus. When Antiochus called for Andrew to stand before him, the latter declared himself a Christian. They then tortured him, laying him on a bed of hot copper. When Andrew prayed to the Lord, however, the bed lost its heat. Seeing this, the Romans decided to kill Andrew's soldiers, crucifying them on trees, while they left Andrew in prison until the emperor should decide the fate of the renowned soldier.

The emperor released Andrew and those still with him but commanded that they be executed on false charges. When Andrew later resided in Cilicia, Antiochus wrote to the ruler there to arrest and kill him on the claim that he had forsaken his military duty. Seleucus, the Cilician governor, approached the saint in the mountains. St. Andrew encouraged those with him not to fear death, knowing that their martyrdom was at hand. Soon the cohort and Andrew were laid low by beheading. In that place a spring of water appeared that was known to possess healing powers, curing a clergyman who had long ailed under an evil spirit.

These saints and countless others have perished as a testimony to Christ, imitating his unification of the invisible and the visible by their faith. The Lord died and after three days rose again, witnessing to the redemption of the world as the power of the immortal permeating and restoring what must die. The saints have died and await the final resurrection of which Christ's was the first fruits. They have followed his example in suffering and humiliation so that, when he returns in power to purify and repair all nature, liberating it from its subjection to futility and its bondage to decay, they will obtain the freedom of the glory of the children of God. The new birth for which nature longs, groaning in labor pains, and for which the saints also groan as those enduring hardship, affliction, and persecution, means the re-unification of what sin had fractured, the visible beaming with the power of the eternal, the harmony of the higher and lower orders as each dwells rightly within the other. To this redemption the saint says "Yes" in his suffering and death, suspending the fallen and mortal body in order to receive an immortal and perfect one. "What is sown is perishable, what is raised is imperishable. It is sown in dishonor, it is raised in glory. It is sown in weakness, it is raised in power. It is sown a physical body, it is raised a spiritual body . . . just as we have borne the image of the man of dust, we will also bear the image of the man of heaven."

In practice, Docetism knows no resurrection of the dead. It might have martyrs with their sacrifices, but these do not belong to the crucified and resurrected Christ. They belong to the Christ-Idol, the ontological way of folly and the infinite law dressed up as the way, the truth, and the life. We know this because docetic Christians, particularly in Protestantism, affirm the Christ whereas they deny the saints and claim a church without saints. Protestant Docetism (a more mature form than Catholicism due to the full appearance of the Christ-Idol) in many cases allows that the Christ performed miracles, that he is fully God and fully man, that he rose from the dead, and that in him the mortal and immortal exist in union. But in these cases—to say nothing of the later stages of Protestantism, which deny miracles entirely and wipe away much if not all of the truth about Christ—docetists restrict the fusion of lower and higher to Christ alone, or perhaps to Christ and the apostolic age. I have noted how John Calvin believed the age of miracles to have ended with the apostolic era, so that docetists should have no expectation that the visible realm, rightly humbled before God, could receive the power of the invisible. While docetists might claim to have seen that "the Father sent the son as savior of the world," they therefore cannot testify to this in the sense that they cannot walk in the path of the savior. In this manner the docetist becomes one who claims Christ with his lips but whose ways wander from God.

In Calvin's estimate, men cannot judge who are elect and who reprobate, and often "no distinction can be made between the godly and the ungodly." God alone knows, by his "secret election and call" those who belong to him and those who do not.

"We must leave to God alone the knowledge of his church," Calvin declares, "whose foundation is his secret election." Men cannot judge because in the visible church "are mingled many hypocrites who have nothing of Christ but the name and outward appearance . . . just as we must believe, therefore, that the former church, invisible to us"—Calvin's true church, in which the verification of salvation lies beyond man's purview—"is visible to God alone, so we are commanded to revere and keep communion with the latter [visible, outward church] which is called 'church' in respect to men." In this way Calvin distinguishes the visible from the invisible without providing substantive means for discerning the saints. Laying the emphasis on the mystery of God's secret election, he cuts off the visible world from the recognizable life of holy men and women. Rather than saints who imitate Christ in part by the benign power of the invisible flowing through the visible, joining the two realms under his headship, Calvin condemns his followers to an unbridgeable gulf between the two realms. Docetists in Calvin's wake have left this severance largely unquestioned, having dismissed the intercessory power of those reposed in the Lord.

Calvin admits that God has given men "a certain charitable judgment whereby we recognize as members of the church those who, by confession of faith, by example of life, and by partaking of the sacraments, profess the same God and Christ with us." He appears to leave a sliver of light for recognizing the elect, but this is to no avail inasmuch as the Reformed churches deny and have historically failed to produce visible saints in whom the fissure of the world is repaired. By this statement Calvin might call one of the Fathers or anyone else he chooses a saint, but it matters more that he has undercut the possibility of real sainthood among his adherents. On the other hand, other docetic sects do claim to perform miracles, notably healings and exorcisms, as God has supposedly allowed and as evidence of their progress toward salvation. Of these the words of the savior ring true: "On that day many will say to me, 'Lord, Lord, did we not prophesy in your name, and cast out demons in your name, and do many deeds of power in your name?' Then I will declare to them, 'I never knew you; go away from me, you evildoers.'" The Lord sees that these, despite their powers, do not do the will of the father in heaven. They fail the surest test of sainthood: they do not gather all things under Christ but contribute to the scattering. They have strayed from the path of peace and humility, and in their pride they have chosen how they shall worship rather than submitting to the way given by God. These docetists dot the Protestant landscape in various churches and denominations, witnessing to deceptive spirits among the deceived.

Whoever confesses that Jesus is the Son of God, God abides him, and he in God. We confess Jesus Christ as "the image of the invisible God, the firstborn of all creation; for in him all things in heaven and on earth were created, things visible and invisible, whether thrones or dominions or rulers or powers—all things have been created through him and for him. He himself is before all things, and in him all things hold together. He is the head of the body, the Church; he is the beginning, the firstborn

1 JOHN 4:13–16A

from the dead, so that he might come to have first place in everything. For in him the fullness of God was pleased to dwell, and through him God was pleased to reconcile to himself all things, whether on earth or in heaven, by making peace through the blood of his cross." As he in whom all things hold together, we confess the Christ who reconciles the visible and invisible powers, binding them in mutual harmony. We confess the Christ who simultaneously holds the visible world together, for all things come together in their intended union as they submit to him as head and Lord. A rending beyond human imagination has beset the world since the Fall, and Docetism stands at its apex. The most profound severance of all things from each other, invisible from visible and visible from itself, the docetic age culminates in apostasy and scattering. For in turning aside from the image of the invisible God, he who holds together all things, the world crumbles into pieces. We confess that, despite Docetism's presentation of its ways and knowledge as natural if not superior to nature, its dominance signals that the lie has triumphed. The possibility of reconciliation men now consider a myth, and its natural manifestations as legends.

Through Christ God reconciles the faithful first to himself, and then to the visible and invisible orders. The stories of the saints bear witness to man's reconciliation with the natural world, in particular his relationship with the animals. Consider St. Gerasimos of Jordan, who abandoned a life of leisure and wealth to pursue monastic labor. He left his home to live in a cloister in the desert, where he attracted others to toil spiritually with him. One day, as he was near the Jordan river, he heard the roar of a lion. Interrupting his prayers to investigate, he turned and saw the creature in pain and licking its paw. Still in the peace acquired from his meditation, the saint approached the lion and saw a sizable sliver buried in its flesh, which he removed without threat from the animal. After this, St. Gerasimos began to return to the monastery but found that the lion followed him like a pet. From this point forward the two of them lived in friendship, the lion remaining with him as he took up his monastic work and staying at his side through his days. This took some getting used to for the other monks, who eventually came to see the king of the wild as a pet for the group and not a danger. Students, pilgrims, and other monks witnessed the lion at the side of St. Gerasimos, so that his relationship with the animal was not rumor or gossip but verified fact, a witness to the reconciling power of God between man and his natural environment. For who, if not those stilled before God in prayer and purified from passions, can approach untamed and dangerous beasts with equanimity?[3]

The story of the nun Matrona Pescheyev, speaking of St. Seraphim of Sarov, echoes the account regarding St. Gerasimos:

> "As I approached the hermitage I suddenly saw that Fr. Seraphim was sitting on a tree trunk near his cell, and beside him stood a huge bear. I was paralyzed

---

3. Poulos, 39–40.

with fear, and shouting with all my might: "Father, this is my death!" I fell down.

On hearing my voice, Fr. Seraphim hit the bear and waved his hand at him. And the bear, as though he were a rational being, went at once in the direction pointed out to him by the Elder, into a thicket. Seeing all this I was shaking with fear, and even when Fr. Seraphim came up to me with the words: "Don't be scared, don't be afraid," I continued to shout as before: "This is my death!" The Elder said in reply: "No, mother, this is not death; death is far from you; this is joy."

... We had hardly had time to sit down when that same bear came out of the thicket and lay down at St. Seraphim's feet. Finding myself close to such a terrible beast I was at first trembling with terror, but afterwards seeing that Fr. Seraphim treated him as a gentle lamb without any fear and even fed him with his own hands with bread which he had brought from his bag, little by little my confidence revived. Then the face of the Elder seemed to me especially wonderful; it was as joyful and radiant as an angel's. At last, when I had grown quite calm and most of the bread had been eaten, the Elder gave me the remaining bit and bade me feed the bear myself ... then I took the bread he gave me, and the feeding gave me such pleasure that I wished I could feed him longer, for the beast was gentle even with me a sinner. Seeing me quiet, Fr. Seraphim said to me: "Do you remember, mother, how a lion served St. Gerasimus on the Jordan? As for poor Seraphim, a bear serves him. You see, even the beasts obey us!"

Abbess Alexandra, accompanied by a sister Anna, tells a comparable story of St. Seraphim:

> Without stopping at the monastery we went straight to the distant hermitage, and on approaching it we saw Father sitting on a log. Suddenly an enormous bear walked out of the wood on its hind legs. Our hands became clammy; our eyes grew dim.
>
> The Father said, "Misha, why do you frighten my orphans? Better go back and bring us some kind of consolation, as I have nothing to offer them." The bear turned round and went off into the forest.
>
> About two hours had passed in sweet converse with Fr. Seraphim in his cell when that same bear suddenly appeared again, scrambled clumsily into the cell and roared. The Elder went up to it and said: "Well, well, Misha, show me what you have brought us." The bear rose on its hind legs and gave Fr. Seraphim something wrapped in leaves and somehow tangled together. The contents of the parcel proved to be a fresh honeycomb of pure honey. The Elder took the honey and silently pointed at the door. The beast seemed to make a bow and the Elder, taking a bit of bread out of his bag, gave it to him. Then the bear went off into the forest.

Docetic men cannot bring themselves to believe such stories of reconciliation between men and animals. How could they? On the one hand, they have never seen such events and their faithlessness outlaws the humility needed to behold them. On the other hand, the docetic world justifies all kinds of torture and degradation of animals, whom docetic man exploits as fodder for his experiments and trials, and whom he has forgotten as part of God's creation and the reconciliation of all things. Docetic man laughs at these accounts, revealing his ignorance of the world that he believes he has mastered. His "mastery" applies the infinite to the natural world, fashioning slaves and horrors that he commands without conscience, coercing them into service under his progressive division from nature. This mastery amounts to a new form of self-enslavement inasmuch as it bars man from rest in the place God has assigned, simultaneously suffocating God's place in his heart.

Man first is reconciled with God, not the natural and visible world nor the invisible world intertwined with it. God dwells in man, and those who confess God discover that he abides in them. To confess means not only to have the name of Christ on one's lips as Lord, although it includes this. It means submitting the heart and the body, the mind, soul, and strength to God, so that one lives toward and as a participant in the reconciliation of all things. Upon these, whose lives consist in the purity of prayer and love, the humility of obedience and meekness, and who mourn over their sins, God deigns to bestow his Spirit. God has shown us sinners a glimpse of this bestowal through his vessel, St. Seraphim, who offers us a vision of the experience of God in his conversation with Mr. Motovilov (recorded in the latter's diary):

> Fr. Seraphim replied: "I have already told you, your Godliness . . . I have related in detail how people come to be in the Spirit of God and how we can recognize his presence in us. So what do you want, my son?"
>
> "I want to understand it well," I said.
>
> Then Fr. Seraphim took me very firmly by the shoulders and said: "We are both in the Spirit of God now, my son. Why don't you look at me?"
>
> I replied: "I cannot look, Father, because your eyes are flashing like lightning. Your face has become brighter than the sun, and my eyes ache with pain."
>
> Fr. Seraphim said: "Don't be alarmed, your Godliness! Now you yourself have become as bright as I am. You are now in the fullness of the Spirit of God yourself; otherwise you would not be able to see me as I am."
>
> Then, bending his head towards me, he whispered softly in my ear: "Thank the Lord God for His unutterable mercy to us! You saw that I did not even cross myself; and only in my heart I prayed mentally to the Lord God and said within myself: 'Lord, grant him to see clearly with his bodily eyes that descent of Thy Spirit which Thou grantest to Thy servants when Thou art pleased to appear in the light of Thy magnificent glory.' And you see, my son, the Lord instantly fulfilled the humble prayer of poor Seraphim. How then shall we not thank Him for this unspeakable gift to us both? Even to the greatest hermits,

my son, the Lord God does not always show His mercy in this way. This grace of God, like a loving mother, has been pleased to comfort your contrite heart at the intercession of the Mother of God herself. But why, my son, do you not look me in the eyes? Just look, and don't be afraid! The Lord is with us!"

After these words I glanced at his face and there came over me an even greater reverent awe. Imagine in the centre of the sun, in the dazzling light of its midday rays, the face of a man talking to you. You see the movement of his lips and the changing expression of his eyes, you hear his voice, you feel someone holding your shoulders; yet you do not see his hands, you do not even see yourself or his figure, but only a blinding light spreading far around for several yards and illumining with its glaring sheen both the snow-blanket which covered the forest glade and the snowflakes which besprinkled me and the great Elder. You can imagine the state I was in!

"How do you feel now?" Fr. Seraphim asked me.

"Extraordinarily well," I said.

"But in what way? How exactly do you feel well?"

I answered: "I feel such calmness and peace in my soul that no words can express it."

"This, your Godliness," said Fr. Seraphim, "is the peace of which the Lord said to His disciples: My peace I give unto you; not as the world gives, give I unto you. (John 14:21) If you were of the world, the world would love its own; but because I have chosen you out of the world, therefore the world hates you. (John 15:19) But be of good cheer; I have overcome the world. (John 16:33) And to those people whom this world hates but who are chosen by the Lord, the Lord gives that peace which you now feel within you, the peace which, in the words of the Apostle, passes all understanding. (Phil. 4:7) The Apostle describes it in this way, because it is impossible to express in words the spiritual well-being which it produces in those into whose hearts the Lord God has infused it. Christ the Saviour calls it a peace which comes from His own generosity and is not of this world, for no temporary earthly prosperity can give it to the human heart; it is granted from on high by the Lord God Himself, and that is why it is called the peace of God. What else do you feel?" Fr. Seraphim asked me.

"An extraordinary sweetness," I replied.

And he continued: "This is that sweetness of which it is said in Holy Scripture: 'They will be inebriated with the fatness of Thy house; and Thou shalt make them drink of the torrent of Thy delight.' (Ps. 35:8) And now this sweetness is flooding our hearts and coursing through our veins with unutterable delight. From this sweetness our hearts melt as it were, and both of us are filled with such happiness as tongue cannot tell. What else do you feel?"

"An extraordinary joy in all my heart."

And Fr. Seraphim continued: 'When the Spirit of God comes down to man and overshadows him with the fullness of his inspiration, then the human soul overflows with unspeakable joy, for the Spirit of God fills with joy whatever He touches. This is that joy of which the Lord speaks in His Gospel: 'A woman when she is in travail has sorrow, because her hour is come; but when she is delivered of the child, she remembers no more the anguish, for joy that a man is born into the world. In the world you will be sorrowful; but when I see you again, your heart shall rejoice, and your joy no one will take from you.' (John 16:21-22) Yet however comforting may be this joy which you now feel in your heart, it is nothing compared to that of which the Lord Himself by the mouth of His Apostle spoke: that joy which eye has not seen, nor ear heard, nor has it entered into the heart of man what God has prepared for them that love Him. (1 Cor. 2:9) Foretastes of that joy are given to us now, and if they fill our souls with such sweetness, well-being and happiness, what shall we say of that joy which has been prepared in heaven for those who weep here on earth? And you, my son, have wept enough in your life on earth; yet see with what joy the Lord consoles you even in this life!

"Now it is up to us, my son, to ad labours to labours in order to go from strength to strength, (Ps. 83:7) and to come to the measure of the stature of the fullness of Christ, (Eph. 4:13) so that the words of the Lord may be fulfilled in us: But they that wait upon the Lord shall renew their strength; they shall grow wings like eagles; and they shall run and not be weary; (Is. 40:31) they will go from strength to strength, and the God of gods will appear to them in the Sion (Ps. 83:8) of realization and heavenly visions. Only then will our present joy (which now visits us little and briefly) appear in all its fullness, and no one will take it from us, for we shall be filled to overflowing with inexplicable heavenly delights. What else do you feel, your Godliness?"

I answered: "An extraordinary warmth."

"How can you feel warmth, my son? Look, we are sitting in the forest. It is winter out-of-doors, and snow is underfoot. There is more than an inch of snow on us, and the snowflakes are still falling. What warmth can there be?"

I answered: "Such as there is in a bath-house when the water is poured on the stone and the steam rises in clouds."

"And the smell?" he asked me, "Is it the same as in the bath-house?"

"No," I replied. "There is nothing on earth like this fragrance. When in my dear mother's lifetime I was fond of dancing and used to go to balls and parties, my mother would sprinkle me with the scent which she bought at the best shops in Kazan. But those scents did not exhale such a fragrance."

And Fr. Seraphim, smiling pleasantly, said: "I know it myself just as well as you do, my son, but I am asking you on purpose to see whether you feel it in the same way. It is absolutely true, your Godliness! The sweetest earthly fragrance cannot be compared with the fragrance which we now feel, for we are now enveloped in the fragrance of the Holy Spirit of God. What on earth can be like it?"

"Mark, your Godliness, you have told me that around us it is warm as in a bath-house; but look, neither on you nor on me does the snow melt, nor does it underfoot; therefore, this warmth is not in the air but in us. It is that very warmth about which the Holy Spirit in the words of prayer makes us cry to the Lord: 'Warm me with the warmth of Thy Holy Spirit!' By it hermits of both sexes were kept warm and did not fear the winter frost, being clad, as in fur coats, in the grace-given clothing woven by the Holy Spirit. And so it must be in actual fact, for the grace of God must dwell within us, in our heart, because the Lord said: 'The Kingdom of God is within you.' (Luke 17:21)

"By the 'Kingdom of God' the Lord meant the grace of the Holy Spirit. This Kingdom of God is now within us, and the grace of the Holy Spirit shines upon us and warms us from without as well. It fills the surrounding air with many fragrant odours, sweetens our senses with heavenly delight and floods our hearts with unutterable joy. Our present state is that of which the Apostle says: The Kingdom of God is not food and drink but righteousness and peace and joy in the Holy Spirit. (Rom. 14:17) Our faith consists not in the plausible words of earthly wisdom, but in the demonstration of the Spirit and power. (1 Cor. 2:4) That is just the state that we are in now. Of this state the Lord said: There are some of those standing here who shall not taste death till they see the Kingdom of God come in power. (Mark 9:1)

"See my son, what unspeakable joy the Lord God has now granted us! This is what it means to be in the fullness of the Holy Spirit, about which St. Macarius of Egypt writes: 'I myself was in the fullness of the Holy Spirit.' With this fullness of His Holy Spirit the Lord has now filled us poor creatures to overflowing. So there is no need now, your Godliness, to ask how people come to be in the grace of the Holy Spirit. Will you remember this manifestation of God's ineffable mercy which has visited us?"

The account of Fr. Seraphim with Motovilov stands on its own as a witness to the reconciliation of God with man. What can any one of us add to it? We learn from it the abiding of God in man by his Holy Spirit, an abiding given to those who rightly confess. Let us strive for this, just as we strive also to love our neighbors.

And we have known and believed the love that God has for us. Reading of the saints forces one to confront mysteries, and no less than that one sees their holiness and sacrifice for others. As individuals and as a group, the saints carry within them the binding of all things in Christ. That they abide in the Holy Spirit, and that the visible and the invisible intertwine in them goes hand in hand with their binding people in harmony through mercy for the needy and love of neighbor. The saints bear the neighbor's burden and give him rest according to the graces bestowed on them. One testifies to the Kingdom of Heaven in the next world; another witnesses to the spiritual powers by faith, and in miracles meant to aid the weak and convert the pagan, freeing those ensnared by lies; a third loves by embracing poverty, giving all to the poor and using this world's goods as a means to life with God; a fourth reveals spiritual bliss, the truth of man's existence too often smothered by distractions and idle pleasures.

Have you heard of the terrible sorrow of St. Sophia, Mother of Orphans, and of her profound love? Raised in a devout home, the saint was given in marriage and conceived six children. During this time her worldly responsibilities occupied her, but she obeyed the commandments and struggled to live virtuously. Then the sickness came and destroyed her family totally. She lost her husband and all six of her children, but in the profound anguish of her losses she did not succumb to despair. The heaviness of her heart, and the grief incurred by many deaths, raised her devotion to new heights. Over twenty years following her catastrophe, St. Sophia adopted 100 children and raised them in the fear of the Lord. She liquidated her belongings and gave the money to the impoverished and other widows, while adhering to a diet of bread and water. She is known to have had the Psalms on her heart and lips at all times. Due to this way of life, the Lord showed favor on her by means of a miracle, for she was one in whom the Holy Spirit ruled, who made the bond of love where the curse had torn children from families. The Lord ensured that the container of wine that she reserved for the poor always remained full, no matter how much she had removed. As St. Sophia set her heart on alleviating the plight of the suffering, the Lord blessed her desire with his own hand. This miracle continued until she told someone of it and gave glory to God, at which point it ceased. St. Sophia grieved at this, increasing her struggle against the flesh as a result.

The Unmercenary Physicians also loved, bearing their crosses for the infirm and the mendicant, not charging for services rendered through faith. Saints Cyril and John, Mocius and Anikita, Hermolaus and Diomedes, Samson and Thalaleus we mention with honor before highlighting the healer Panteleimon, the all-Merciful, in whom men see combined a great love of others, the testimony of miracles, and martyrdom as his end.

After his Christian mother died, Panteleimon's pagan father sent him to school as a prelude to his study of medicine. The saint's skill as a doctor later became known to the emperor, who wanted to enlist him as the royal physician when his training was complete. During this time Panteleimon met St. Hermolaus, a Christian hiding in the city, and received teachings about Christ from him. Panteleimon came to baptism in the following way: finding a child on the street who had died from a snakebite, Panteleimon resolved that he should pray to Jesus to restore him. If the prayer were answered, he would receive baptism and follow Christ. The child returned to life after the prayer while the snake died, and Saint Panteleimon became a Christian. From this point he dedicated his energies to the sick and the poor, not taking a fee for his services and acknowledging Christ in his medical practice. He also visited Christians in prison and healed their wounds, so that news about him permeated the city and the patients of other doctors flocked to him.

When Panteleimon's activities reached the ear of the emperor, he called the holy doctor forward to sacrifice to idols. Saint Panteleimon refused and, confessing Christ, asked for a terminally ill person to be brought before them. After the manner of Elijah, the emperor's doctors could call upon their gods before St. Panteleimon called upon Christ, with all seeing which deity would answer by healing the man. When a paralyzed man was brought in, the pagan doctors failed to heal him. St. Panteleimon then restored the man by praying to Jesus, with the consequence that the emperor ordered the death of the former paralytic and sentenced St. Panteleimon to torture.

The Romans inflicted severe tortures upon the saint, all to no avail. They suspended him from a tree, they scraped him with iron hooks, they stretched him on the rack, they burned him with fire, they threw him into boiling tar, and they tossed him into the ocean with a stone tied around his neck. St. Panteleimon endured these trials unharmed, later surviving a contest with wild beasts in which the animals approached him and licked his feet. He finally died by beheading, but only after he heard a heavenly voice call him to his place in God's kingdom. The soldiers heard the voice and did not want to carry out the order of execution, but St. Panteleimon bid them do so lest they not be with him in the future life. In this way St. Panteleimon brought men together with God as he loved his neighbors, witnessing to the unity of the visible and the invisible through miracles and martyrdom.

The unity of man with his neighbors, a unity grounded in God who loves us and works through us, we see best in works of mercy. Concern for the poor and indigent, and for those suffering various trials, sicknesses, and forms of want, marks the Christian who is dedicated to the true Church, so that the life humbled before God and in love of neighbor is the same. Such was the case with St. Juliana of Lazarevo, whose way of life brings the devout to sorrow over their own unworthiness, so powerfully did she embody the sacrifice of the self for the unfortunate.[4] From her youth she did not waste time in childish pastimes, giving herself over to sewing clothes for orphans, the sick, and widows. She labored for them tirelessly, often to her own physical detriment. Although later married, the concerns of worldly life did not distract her from the health of the soul. She rose early to pray long to God, doing the same before going to sleep, so that her habit influenced her husband to take part in her supplications. Her husband served in the army, an occupation that removed him from the home for long stretches, and during this time St. Juliana would spend entire nights at prayer or making handiworks for the benefit of the poor. She sold what she sewed or spun in order to distribute the proceeds to the poor, a habit that she kept concealed from her in-laws. Despite her position in the upper ranks of her society, she cared for widows and orphans as their mother, feeding them, making clothing for them, and giving them drink as for her children.

---

4 Lambertsen, *The Lives of the Saints in the Russian Language, As Set Forth in the Menology of Saint Dmitri of Rostov,* Supplemental Vol. II (January-April): *The Lives of the Russian Saints.*

1 JOHN 4:13–16A

When famine struck her village in 1570, Juliana took food from her mother-in-law apparently for herself, but in reality for distribution to the starving. Her interest in food pleased her mother-in-law, who had been distressed over the saint's habit of self-denial, but Juliana kept her almsgiving secret from her. In this manner she put others above herself during times of distress. She similarly stayed near the sick during times of contagion, washing them and treating them as she could, praying to God to restore their health. In her home, St. Juliana was known not to rely on her servants, wanting no one to wait on her hand and foot, no one to dress her or take her shoes, in short, no one to treat her as the member of the noble class to which she belonged. She rather prayed that quarrels among the servants would abate while she refused to condemn them, but took care for their nourishment and clothing. She gave birth to ten sons and three daughters, of whom several died in childhood. After misfortunes led to the deaths of certain of her adult children, she besought her husband to go to a monastery. He denied her request, citing the words of the priest who had spoken at their wedding and the advice of other Church fathers: "Black garments will not save us if we do not live monastically, and white garments will not destroy us if we do what is pleasing unto God. If anyone departs to a monastery, not desiring to care for children, he seeks not the love of God, bur rather peace. And the children, orphaned, will weep and curse their parents . . . if it is commanded to feed the orphans of others, it follows that one ought not starve one's own children." With this message among others, St. Juliana's husband convinced her not to seek the monastic life and to strive for holiness in the familial place that God had provided.

When St. Juliana's husband passed, and after she had buried and commemorated him as was proper, she turned more fully to the service of God and the poor. Her children mourned the loss of their father, and she built them up by encouraging them to love one another and give alms. While the saint loved prayer and fasting, above all she gave to the poor. At times she gave so much as to have none left for herself, and in winter her children gave her money to buy warm attire which she promptly gave to the destitute. For ten years after her husband's death, St. Juliana gave virtually all she owned to the poor. She kept for her house the barest necessities and no more, planning such that her supply of food not pass from one year to the next. Any excess she gave to the disadvantaged and to orphans. When another famine struck, she sold all that remained in her home, including livestock and vessels, in order to buy grain for the impoverished with the income. With these funds she fed both the poor and her own household until she could no longer keep her servants, giving them freedom if they chose it. During this time, as over the course of her life as a wife, mother, and lady, she did not grumble or complain about her hardships. She died in January of 1604, signing the cross three times over herself before emitting her last words: "Glory to God for all things! Into thy hands, O Lord, do I commit my spirit!"

When her son George died roughly a decade later, a place was prepared for him in the crypt owned by the family. Those in the crypt saw that the coffin of the saint remained intact, although they did not know whose body was in it. After the funeral service, some women of the village who had attended decided to open the coffin to see the body, and were shocked to find the coffin full of fragrant myrrh. The women told the remaining children of Juliana about this, and they rushed to the crypt to verify the report. Seeing that the ladies had told no lie, they took a small amount of myrrh as evidence to the local cathedral. News of this spread throughout the region, so that many people came to the saint's coffin for anointing with the myrrh. Many received healing of their sicknesses in this way. When the myrrh was almost spent, on several occasions visitors used the sand from beneath St. Juliana's coffin as a supplication for healing. Jeremiah Chervev went to her coffin with his two sick children, both of whom had suffered over two years from a severe illness of the hands and feet. Completing a service of supplication and a panikhida at the saint's coffin, the parents rubbed the sand upon their children. Within a week the sickness had left them completely, with their hands and feet fully restored. On another occasion, a peasant from another village who suffered from an abscess on his leg came to the crypt for healing. Having heard of the miracles occurring at her grave, the sick man convinced his friends to carry him there. After the service of supplication he rubbed dirt from the grave on his ulcer and soon returned to health. These are only a few examples of the healings that occurred at St. Juliana's gravesite. Others are not hard to find.

From first to last, the saints have "known and believed the love that God has for us." The Holy Spirit abiding within them has shown them the love of God, and by their faith they have embraced the divine commandments and the promises. From this foundation they are able to love without limit, to give freely and abundantly, and to sacrifice themselves. In them men see the unity of man with God and of the invisible with the visible. Man also sees what amounts to the test of the prior two, that the saint loves his neighbor, binding himself to others through humility and service. The proof of sainthood and righteousness does not lie in miracles or in exalted states and experiences, the latter especially not coming without profound and habitual humility and recognition of sin, and both of which God gives to his children sparingly and as he sees fit. Nor does the proof of veracity lie in one's claim to love God with one's lips, nor in the fervor of devotion for one's cause. Miracles have and will occur as performed by the demons to deceive men, and many have said and will say "Lord, Lord," but the Christ will not recognize them. The test lies in the way of one's life, whether he follows the commandments by worshipping God rightly and loving his neighbors, giving rest to the weary. If a man performs works of power, then, we should not immediately give him our trust, and if he opens to us contact with spiritual beings and powers, remember that Satan can appear as an angel of light. Ask instead if he gathers or scatters, if he honors God or himself, if he gives men rest in God or liberates them from God and each other, and pray diligently that you not be deceived. The schismatic does not rightly worship God as he seeks to scatter the church; the docetist does not love his neighbor as he preaches freedom rather than rest and mutual love. And the antichrist, who will come with signs and wonders and works of power, will gather all unto himself in pride rather than humility—and in deception!—before all is destroyed, both him and the world with him. We should remember the saints, therefore, and seek Christ through them as our guides, that we may know and believe the love of God for men, and that the Holy Spirit may dwell within us.

1 John 2:15–17

> Do not love the world or the things in the world. If anyone loves the world, the love of the Father is not in him. For all that is in the world—the lust of the flesh, the lust of the eyes, and the pride of life—is not of the Father but is of the world. And the world is passing away, and the lust of it; but he who does the will of God abides forever.

Do not love the world or the things in the world. If anyone loves the world, the love of the Father is not in him. Having eliminated the interior realm and its treasure, there remains nothing to docetic man except the world, which he loves because "the world" is not the creation of God but the perversion of that creation according to man's striving to be God. In his immediate experience, the world consists of the objects and forces, people, and events that make up man's encounter with what is outside of him. It includes the phenomena enumerated in the account of creation in Genesis, the realms that God created by separation and gathering and the population of those realms with the entities and life-forms that call them home. It also includes the spiritual powers that impinge upon him, influencing him for good or ill. All of these things, inasmuch as God has created them, giving to each a nature and a place of rest, are good. Man does not sin in loving them so long as he does so properly, not raising these things above their rank in God's order. "Do not love the world or the things in the world" does not exhort us to disdain God's creation but to keep it in its place, admiring it in subordination to God who fashioned its beauty and gave it to us as our home.

Man loves the world wrongly not because he has raised it immediately to the status of God, lowering himself before it as though it were the creator rather than a creature. He does this mediately, to be sure, and as an outgrowth of the primal error in which he raises himself to the status of God, making himself the infinite. When he asserts himself as God, rising up to the boundlessness of the divine, he transforms the meaning of the world that God has given him. Whereas God created him to rest in his place and submit before his limit as a nature, coming to know the Maker by obeying the purposes inscribed in his being, man's grasping of himself as God recasts the world as the arena for realizing this new self-understanding. Rather than the realm that limits man and thus points him toward God, in whom alone man should experience the infinite, the world becomes the realm in which man exercises his powers of choice and self-assertion, his bent toward possibility, exploration, and control. Man seizes the world as the means for his experience not of God as the infinite but of himself in his striving to be the infinite, usurping the position of God. He raises up the world as an object of worship because he first raises himself to this level. This attitude toward his own nature and secondly toward the world has defined man under sin since the writing of 1 John if not since the Fall. Under Docetism its tendencies have multiplied abundantly, for Docetism has legitimized man as the infinite to a degree unimagined before it, taking man's love of the world to heights he had not known or dreamed.

"To love the world and the things in the world" means to love oneself in the place of God, and so is idolatry. Rather than savoring God in his heart and mind, securing a place for God there and guarding it dutifully, man enthrones himself as a monarch in his inner realm. This means not that he exercises newfound rulership and control over his inner life but that he hands over that rulership to his passions, to the thoughts and feelings that wash over him from day to day and moment to moment. When God rules over the mind in the heart, man turns inwardly to him in concentration and stillness, resting in the inner encounter with the divine. When man presumes to govern himself in God's place, the impressions of the outer realm pour into him unobstructed, turning him in one direction or another until they guide him along their chosen course. The demons and his own thoughts deceive him, the words of others persuade and beguile him, and the drumbeat of his social order inevitably coerces him into falling in line. He becomes a product not of the indwelling of the Holy Spirit and his communion with the eternal but of his slavery before the evanescent and trivial, the petty and irritable. His idolatry manifests itself as the worship of many and varied idols, as subservience to pleasure, power, and comfort in their diverse appearances.

So is the heart of man, and particularly docetic man, lost to himself and to God. What does God desire more earnestly than the heart? God wants communion with man and obedience from his beloved creature, but this communion and obedience do not pertain first to the body. They refer to the heart and mind, the inner world of man, as their primary locus and as the preliminary to outward obedience. As God says to Moses when discussing the essence of his covenant with Israel, "So now, O Israel, what does the Lord your God require of you, but to fear the Lord your God, to walk in all his ways, to love him, to serve the Lord your God with all your heart and with all your soul, and to keep the commandments of the Lord your God . . . the Lord chose your fathers to love them: and he chose their seed after them, you above all the nations, as it is this day. Therefore circumcise the foreskin of your heart, and do not be stiff-necked any longer." God calls upon us to love him with our hearts and to seek him with our souls, circumcising our hearts. This means that men resist the urge to worship themselves, pursuing instead the presence of God in the inner man. We circumcise our hearts not as lifeless men or automatons, not as bondsmen to a merciless and cruel master, but as those who seek rest in the God who has set his heart on us. "You shall put these words of mine in your heart and soul, and you shall bind them as a sign on your hand, and fix them as an emblem on your forehead." Putting the words of God in the heart and soul takes time, it necessitates the circumcision in which man steps back from the world in order to give his attention to God. "Do not be stubborn" encourages men to turn inwardly to God, casting out the array of thoughts that present themselves to men for their pleasure and pride, their sense of honor and self-worth, subtly affirming them as their own gods. Christians struggle to direct ourselves away from these thoughts and their attendant feelings, for these are of the world.

After defeating the prophets of Baal and on the run for his life, Elijah met God at Horeb. "Now there was a great wind, so strong that it was splitting mountains and breaking rocks in pieces before the Lord, but the Lord was not in the wind; and after the wind an earthquake, but the Lord was not in the earthquake; and after the earthquake a fire, but the Lord was not in the fire; and after the fire a sound of sheer silence. When Elijah heard it, he wrapped his face in his mantle" and went out to converse with the Lord, who spoke to him as he stood at the mouth of the cave. Not in power, not in the forces that cause the world to quiver and crack, nor in the fire that consumes all, but in stillness God approaches man. Where do you encounter him, you of the West? Where shall we meet him, we who have borne and still bear heavy burdens under the docetic way? He is not in our high towers, our offices and penthouses, nor does he shine in our glittering lights. He does not traverse the country on our highways or wear the white coat in our labs, he does not attend the concerts and games at our stadiums, march in our parades, or attend our protests. He does not participate in our galas or visit our clubs, he does not learn in our classrooms or add to our civic associations, he does not advance with our equality or celebrate with us our cultural achievements. Nor will we find God through our screens. We will not encounter him as we lose our hours there, engaging the infinite in a most seductive and inescapable way, drying up what was left of our nature. Although God fills all things and is everywhere present, he reveals himself to man in the stillness of the heart, in the inner room not unlike the sheer silence heard by Elijah.

The Christ withdrew regularly to pray, turning to his inner closet to meet the Father there. Truly, the love of the Father was "in him," in his heart and his mind, when "in the morning, having risen a long while before daylight, he went out and departed to a solitary place; and there He prayed" (Mk 1:35). The Father dwelled in him when, after saying farewell to his disciples, "he departed to the mountain to pray" (Mk 6:46) and at another time when "he himself often withdrew into the wilderness and prayed" (Lk 5:16). Concentrating on the teachings of Jesus to his disciples and the crowds, focusing on the Lord's passion and resurrection, or meditating on his parables, men can forget the amount of time Jesus spent in the wilderness in prayer, turning away from the inhabited world and toward the inner room where he communed with the

Father. His 40 days in the wilderness prior to the temptation was not a unique or singular event inasmuch as he regularly withdrew to the wilderness to be with God. At that time he did so as a preparation for facing the evil one, but the habit of praying in the desert stayed with him after the temptation as it had certainly been with him before. If the forerunner of Christ, John the Baptist, spent his life in the wilderness as one turned to God and was sent to prepare the way of the Lord, surely the Christ walked along that way, meeting God in the heart while set apart in deserted areas. Thus the transfiguration witnesses to the presence of the Father alive in the Son, a presence revealed once to the disciples but which was with the Lord often (if not always!) in his reclusion. The prayer of the Lord in Gethsemane carried on a habit of inner encounter that was with him throughout his ministry, here intensified by the nearness of the cross.

In his conversation with the Pharisees, the Christ criticized their focus on outward things. Quoting Isaiah, he laments of them that "This people honors me with their lips, but their hearts are far from me." He teaches regarding ritual defilement that "There is nothing that enters a man from outside which can defile him; but the things which come out of him, those are the things that defile a man . . . For from within, out of the heart of men, proceed evil thoughts, adulteries, fornication, murders, thefts, covetousness, wickedness, deceit, lewdness, an evil eye, blasphemy, pride, foolishness. All these evil things come from within and defile a man." He who spent such time in his heart, circumcising the flesh and keeping the world at a distance in order to dwell there, teaches that man must fix his attention not on the things that go into the body but those that emerge from the heart. He must watch out for the things that defile, taking care to cleanse himself of them, washing the hands of his heart from attitudes and thoughts that condemn him while nourishing those that give life. When asked of the greatest commandment, Jesus replies that man must "Love the Lord your God with all your heart, and with all your soul, and with all your mind, and with all your strength." At least the first three, if not the fourth also, apply fundamentally to the inner life of man, and when the Lord went into the desert to pray he did so to love the Father wholeheartedly with these. The Christ commands us to do as he did so that God will be "in us" as he occupies our hearts, as we remain vigilant in casting out the machinations of the evil one just as we dedicate our inner energy to loving God with heart, soul, mind, and strength.

But docetic man has no knowledge of the heart, and those struggling to escape docetic ways, myself among them, have made virtually no progress in the inner life. Not that docetic man does not have thoughts and emotions and that these do not remain hidden from his neighbors. To this insignificant extent docetic man has a heart and a mind and can distinguish the inner from the outer. That he can write and speak at length about the heart as this inner form of experience hardly qualifies his predicament. *The heart does not exist for docetic man, for he has no means of gathering himself before God, locating himself in his inner chamber to meet God there.* If docetic man went into the wilderness in imitation of Christ and determined to pray, this outward exercise would add nothing to him. He is no less lost for asking what Jesus did and would do because he has not imagined the habit of inner prayer that brought the Lord into communion with the Father. Docetism has stripped this tradition from him entirely, so that those who disavow Docetism and start along this path writhe like newborn babes. What St. Dimitri of Rostov wrote applies to us: "There are many among you who have no knowledge of the inner work required of the man who would hold God in remembrance. Nor do such people even understand what remembrance of God means, or know anything about spiritual prayer . . . as for secret communion with God in the heart, they know nothing of this, nor of the profit that comes from it, nor do they ever taste of its spiritual sweetness." Docetic man and his heirs do not comprehend the unilaterally outward quality of their lives because they wallow in ignorance of the inner life. The first hints of this life, when experienced, subject the docetist to profound shame as he begins to perceive the godlessness in which he has lived. There has been in him nothing except the love of the world.

If man would have the love of God in him rather than the love of the world, he must dedicate himself to the former love by discipline and patience. He must understand that closing the heart to the world and opening it to God, both developments that take time and effort, amount to a request for God to descend as he wills, entering the heart of his own accord. Let the Christian gather himself in prayer, let him "stand with the attention in the heart, and . . . hold the whole body in a vigilant tension of the muscles, and not . . . allow attention to be influenced and diverted by exterior impressions of the senses." Let him descend from the head into the heart, for while "you are still in your head, thoughts will not easily be subdued but will always be whirling about." The head "is a crowded rag market: it is not possible to pray to God there." The head should be empty when one prays because the thoughts have descended into the heart, which is the reception room of the Lord. "Find a place in your heart, and speak there with the Lord . . . Everyone who meets the Lord, meets Him there; He has fixed no other place for meeting souls." And again, "You preserve inner attention and solitude in the heart. May the Lord help you always to remain thus. This is the most important thing in our spiritual life" (St. Theophan the Recluse). The world permeates the inner life of docetic man because he has lost the heart, losing the foundation of communion with God and the possibility of his indwelling. If, in our attempt to escape the vice-grip of Docetism, we would love God with our heart, soul, mind, and strength, we Christians must first set the world aside inwardly, casting out all worldly cares, and from there approach God in the stillness of humility. Without this practice we will fall before the love of the world.

For all that is in the world—the desire of the flesh, the lust of the eyes, and the pride of life—is not of the Father but is of the world. The Fathers note that the desire of the flesh, the lust of the eyes, and the pride of life correspond to sins of pleasure, greed, and glory (Archbishop Averky). If these are not of the Father, then our pursuit of them, our giving of our heart, mind, soul, and strength to them, is idolatry. By loving these things above God we deny our rest in him and locate it in ourselves, inasmuch as we deem for ourselves what is good and choose what gods we shall worship. Due to our desire for these things we also murder our fellow men, unjustly taking from their lives in order to add to our own. The desire of the flesh, the lust of the eyes, and the pride of life appear in the middle ground between our putting ourselves in the place of God and the murder of our neighbor, linking our denial of rest received from God with our denial of rest given to our neighbor. For idolatry and murder intertwine in several ways, with the desires through which man asserts himself as God often connecting them.

At the opposite pole from idolatry and murder, those most unholy and abominable acts, is the rest that God proclaims as holy. God created men to rest in him and in one another, such that he joins the two rests into one. In the Garden the Lord commanded Adam and Eve not to eat of the tree of Good and Evil, implying at once that they should rest in him as possessor of that knowledge and worship him in their obedience, recognizing him in both ways as God. He simultaneously makes them for the shared purpose of creating life, a task that entails mutual rest inasmuch as they partake in it together. As man rests in God, so he rests in and gives rest to his neighbor, and as he spurns rest in God he denies rest to his neighbor. But there is more at work here: to give rest is to give life while to deny rest is to deny life. We know this because God meant to give Adam a helpmate, bringing to him all the animals so that he should name them. "But for Adam there was not found a helper comparable to him." The ox, the donkey, and the mule did not provide the adequate rest needed for Adam in his work, so that God put a trance on the man and, during his sleep, removed the rib through which he created Eve. In her Adam has a mate who helps him in tilling and keeping the ground, and whose giving of rest extends beyond tasks in the field. Adam receives one with whom he can become one flesh, joining with her physically for procreation. This intimates the profound connection between rest and life, for the proper rest-giver for Adam is also a life-giver for him, and one through whom he contributes to life. As one gives rest, one gives life, and this giving moves along a continuum. One gives rest by bearing another's burdens, aiding in the tasks allotted to him, just as one gives rest in distributing alms and visiting the sick. Performing these tasks gives life to the worker and the sufferer. One gives another, physically profounder rest by giving life itself, in the creation of life according to God's design in pregnancy and childbearing. Rest is holy as life itself is holy; rest is intrinsic to life and is life, inasmuch as it preserves and refreshes that which acts, and by its action lives. Up to the cry of the newborn if not spiritually beyond this, the gift of rest implies the gift of life. And I have said nothing of the spiritual life and its rest.

If to give rest means to give life, with these two progressing along a physical continuum unto childbirth as absolute, what can we say of the denial of rest? Is it not the denial of life, moving along a continuum in the negative direction unto death as absolute? This death contemporary man rightly calls murder, for the denial of bodily life is indeed murder. Yet the biblical writers and the Fathers understood murder to include both the absolute and the continuum that culminates in it, grasping the overlap between the denial of rest and the denial of life. In the Christian tradition, therefore, murder means death and what leads to death, including anguish, despair, physical pain, and want. To "take" or seize another's due, to cast him aside with harshness, and to deprive of life in the broad sense—as men do because of greed, for pleasure, or for glory—is to murder. To oppress or inflict unjust hardship is to shed innocent blood.

St. James asks, "Where do wars and fights come from among you? Do they not come from your desires for pleasure that war in your members? You lust and do not have. You murder and covet and cannot obtain. You fight and war." When he says that the Christians commit murder, he does not mean that the congregants go to the extreme of physical death, killing each other's bodies. Those who act in this way would not last long in any society, much less the church. He points out that Christians deprive one another of rest, harming their neighbors in soul and body. "To murder" in this sense does not differ markedly from fighting and warring, as each causes distress and anguish for the neighbor. Or consider the following from the same letter, where James criticizes the rich: "You have heaped up treasure in the last days. Indeed the wages of the laborers who mowed your fields, which you kept back by fraud, cry out; and the cries of the reapers have reached the ears of the Lord of Sabaoth. You have lived on the earth in pleasure and luxury; you have fattened your hearts as in a day of slaughter. You have condemned, you have murdered the just; he does not resist you." The murder of the just refers to withholding the wages of workers, a taking of life not directly to physical death but inflicting a hardship that tends toward death. The murderer oppresses by denying bread and pay, taking the life of others and giving nothing in return, exploiting his excess for indulgence. Sirach says this plainly: "The bread of the needy is the life of the poor; whoever deprives them of it is a man of bloodshed. Whoever takes away his neighbor's livelihood murders him, and whoever deprives a hired worker of his wages sheds his blood," and St. John adds that "Whoever hates his brother is a murderer, and you know that no murderer has eternal life abiding in him," pointing not to outward action but inward malice. Murder means the death of the body, but it can just as easily refer to the deprivation of rest and the wickedness of the heart. To give rest is to give life, while to refuse rest means the refusal of life, and thus murder.

The prophet Ezekiel makes this point loudly. The leaders in Israel, he states, "conspired together in you, each with his relatives, to shed blood." Expounding on this, he exclaims that "within you they speak evil of father and mother, and behave unjustly toward the resident alien. Within you they oppress the orphan, and with you, the widow." In Jerusalem "they accept gifts so as to shed blood. Within you they receive interest and unjust gains, and by oppression you bring your evil to the full. But you forgot me," says the Lord. "Therefore, if I strike my hands against the evils you bring to the full—against the things you are doing—and against the bloodshed occurring in your midst, will your heart endure, will your hands remain strong in the days I deal with you?" The city's officials "are like wolves seizing their prey, so as to shed blood and exploit others for greed . . . they oppress the people of the land in wrongdoing, commit robbery, oppress the poor and needy, and do not treat the resident alien with upright judgment." For Ezekiel, "to shed blood" refers less to death than to oppression and extortion, to theft and the destruction of another for dishonest gain. It means the ruin of the neighbor's life so that one can prosper, driving another to anxiety, despair, and want for the sake of one's abundance.

Under the sixth commandment, the preparation of confession for Orthodox Christians asks if the believer has "caused the injury or death of any one, or wished that I were dead? Have I done anything to shorten my own life or that of someone else by injuring health, or through evil and intemperate living? Have I given way to anger, or harmed others with words or actions? Have I defamed others who needed help, or failed to stand up for those unjustly treated? Have I been cruel to anyone? Have I been cruel to animals or destroyed any life unnecessarily? Have I failed to forgive anyone or harbored evil thoughts against them?" The interrogation of the sin of murder does not end with whether one has taken another's breath but begins there, inasmuch as one more easily avoids this extreme than the measures that build up to it. What man has never caused harm or injury? What man has never been cruel? What man has never taken from another or desired his hurt? In all these actions man murders by exerting himself against his neighbor, but the warning against harmful action applies also to inaction. Hear the lesson St. Basil draws from the experience of hunger and those who do not mollify it for others. Death by starvation, he writes, "prolongs the pain and draws out the agony, so that sickness is ensconced and lurks within the body, while death is ever present yet ever delayed. The body becomes dehydrated, its temperature drops, its bulk dwindles, its strength wastes away. Skin clings to bone like a spider's web . . . The body takes on a mottled hue, with yellow and black patches mingling in a manner terrible to see . . . The belly is empty, shrunken to nothing, possessing neither girth nor the natural tone of the bowels, so that the bones of the spine are visible from the front." Given this portrait of horror and forsakenness, St. Basil asks "How many torments does the one who neglects such a body deserve? What extreme of cruelty does such a person not surpass? Does not someone like this deserve to be numbered among the savage beasts, being accounted accursed and murderous? For whoever has the ability to remedy the suffering of others, but chooses rather to withhold aid out of selfish motives, may properly be judged the equivalent of a murderer" ("In Famine and Time of Drought"). Here the example is extreme but the principle, elsewhere discussed by St. Basil, holds true. "You are thus guilty of injustice toward as many as you might have aided, and did not" ("I Will Tear Down My Barns"). To murder can mean physical death; it can mean cruel and vicious thoughts that want another's pain; it can work through oppression, vengeance, and forced deprivation of diverse kinds; and it can occur in the lack of compassion for those whose suffering cries out to us, whose plight we daily ignore. God gave men to one another that they should neither actively harm their neighbors nor be indifferent to their afflictions, but that they should give each other rest. This is the natural law intrinsic to man, and to transgress it is murder.

At times the Scripture connects idolatry (want of rest in God) to murder (denial of rest to the neighbor, often unto death), as with the murder of Abel by his brother Cain. "Now in the process of time Cain brought a sacrifice to the Lord from the fruits of the ground. Abel also brought a sacrifice from the firstborn of his flock and of their fat." The Lord accepted the sacrifice of Abel but not of Cain, for Abel offered the firstborn, and thus the immediate proceeds of his bounty if not the highest and best, while Cain only offered "from the fruits of the ground," deciding among his produce and keeping the first fruits for himself. In this lies a subtle form of idolatry in which one worships the right God in the wrong way. One says to God, "I will worship you" and does so outwardly, simultaneously raising oneself above God in that worship. This falsifies worship because it does not recognize God as God. He remains subordinate to man in a covert manner, with the implication that man pretends to rest in him while not doing so. The man who claims that God is God while exalting himself above the deity in worship says "I rest in God" while expressing that he rests in himself, squeezing God out of his place as Lord and rest-giver. His lips pronounce the name of God but his heart remains far from him.

Cain's false sacrifice and Abel's acceptance provokes the former to worry and jealousy, emotions premised upon the pride of his position as firstborn. Cain has fallen below Abel in the worship of God; shall he now also fall below Abel in the society of men? Cain raised himself up above God in his sacrifice; shall Abel now raise himself above Cain in rebellion? With such thoughts Cain's mind darkens and his heart grows desolate, and he considers the denial of rest to his brother even unto death. "So the Lord said to Cain, 'Why are you extremely sorrowful? And why has your countenance fallen? Did you not sin, even though you brought it rightly, but did not divide it rightly? Be still: his recourse shall be to you; and you shall rule over him.'" God points out Cain's sin, noting that it was good for him to bring a sacrifice but that he must do so in the right way. God also acknowledges Cain's discontent and seeks to reassure him that his brother will not overtake his position. If Cain gives his sacrifice rightly in the future God will accept it, while Abel in his humility will not overtake Cain's position as firstborn. But having lost his rest in God in both his idolatry and his inability to be consoled, sin crouches at Cain's door and compels him to master it. Cain does not do this, turning against his brother when they had gone into the field. There "Cain rose up against Abel his brother and killed him," committing the Scripture's first murder.

God gives Cain an opportunity to confess his crime by asking the whereabouts of his brother. "I do not know," Cain replies, "Am I my brother's keeper?" The implied "yes" to this question cuts to the heart of God's creation of men to love one another by bearing each other's burdens. There is no middle ground, Christian, as God has called you to give rest to your neighbor. As St. Chrysostom writes about witnessing to Christ before men, "Nothing is more frigid than a Christian, who cares not for the salvation of others." He adds shortly thereafter that,

> "Every one can profit his neighbor, if he will fulfill his part. See ye not the unfruitful trees, how strong they are, how fair, how large also, and smooth, and of great height? But if we had a garden; we should much rather have pomegranates, or fruitful olive trees: for the others are for delight to the eye, not for profit, which in them is but small. Such are those men who only consider their own interest: nay, not such even since these persons are fit only for burning: whereas those trees are useful both for building and for the safety of those within. Such too were those Virgins, chaste indeed, and decent, and modest, but profitable to none (Matt. 25:1) wherefore they are burned . . . for observe that none of those are charged with particular sins of their own, with fornication, for instance, or with perjury; in short, with no sin but the having been of no use to another. Such was he who buried his talent, showing indeed a blameless life, but not being useful to another. How can such an one be a Christian? . . . For it is easier for the sun not to give heat, nor to shine, than for the Christian not to send forth light: it is easier for the light to be darkness, than for this to be so." (*Homilies on the Acts of the Apostles*, XX).

Or as St. Ambrose teaches about God's making men to aid one another,

> "What the pagan philosophers take to be the first duty of justice is not acceptable to us. They maintain, in fact, that the first duty of justice is to hurt no one, unless provoked to do so by the wrongs received. This opinion is contradicted by the authority of the Gospel. For the Scripture wills that we should imitate the spirit of the Son of Man, who came to give grace, not to harm . . . That man was made for the sake of man we find stated also in the books of Moses, when the Lord says: 'It is not good that man should be alone, let us make him an helpmeet for him.' Thus the woman was given to the man to help him. She should bear him children, that one man might always be a help to another . . . Thus, in accordance with the will of God and the union of nature, we ought to be of mutual help one to the other, and to vie with each other in doing duties, to lay all our advantages as it were before all, and (to use the words of Scripture) to bring help one to the other from a feeling of devotion or of duty. . ." (*On the Duties of the Clergy*, I, XXVIII)

Christian justice acts positively for the good of others, not leaving them to their burdens while providing the assistance needed for the neighbor to rest. As God gives men to one another for their mutual benefit, they should help one another to the best of their abilities. I add that the command to do good to others belongs not only to Christians but to all men inasmuch as God has implanted it in man's nature. He wills that their love for one another be grounded in their love for him, their giving of rest to one another being grounded in their resting in him. Having cut off his rest in God through idolatry, Cain contradicts his natural inclination to give rest to his brother Abel and becomes a murderer. Thus the pride of life consumes him who indulges it.

The kings of the Old Testament regularly succumb to the connection between idolatry and murder. Having put himself in the place of God, David murders to hide his adultery, shedding blood to conceal the lust of his flesh; Ahab murders in order to grasp Naboth's vineyard, killing his neighbor to satisfy the lust of his eyes; and Solomon, the wisest of men, murders his people through oppression, subjecting them to heavy loads while he basked in the pride of life. The three were each idolaters in his own way, just as each took from his neighbor so that he should gain, murdering the helpless to secure his own advantage.

At the time when kings go out to battle, David sent out his army while he remained in Jerusalem. One evening, as he walked along the roof of his palace, David saw a beautiful woman bathing. We do not know how long he gazed at her or what thoughts he allowed to seize his mind, what wickedness he permitted to reign in his heart. He asked about the woman and found her to be the wife of one of his soldiers. Knowing the husband to be at war, "David sent messengers and took her. And she came to him, and he lay with her." Already David is an idolater and a murderer, already he worships another than the God of the patriarchs and already he destroys the life of his neighbor. When David submits to the lust of the flesh, his mind turns away from God and to himself and his desires. With his thoughts he tacitly declares, like Adam and Eve, that he shall know good and evil, defining these for himself. Not that David explicitly rejects God or renounces him with his lips, but David's heart goes wildly astray, following a foreign deity. His disobedience, as arguably in the breaking of any commandment, implies the idolatry of man's making himself God's equal, an equality that immediately usurps God's position by flaunting his decree. "You are my God," David might say to himself on the roof, "but I am my god as well, and I say that the deed is right!" So he acts, following the god who destroys him and makes him a murderer.

And Uriah! He sleeps in the field unaware that his home is destroyed, that a demon has invaded his house and poisoned his marriage. With his adultery David already murders, for if Uriah had known the deed his agony would be no less than the slaying of the heart, whereas if David had succeeded in hiding his behavior, with Bathsheba not becoming pregnant but carrying on for years with the act buried in her breast, surely it would eviscerate her life with her husband while making her soul a tomb—and this assumes that David does not call her again, making a habit of his sin. But David has impregnated her and she informs him of it. Imagine that, when David calls Uriah to Jerusalem, the latter goes to his house and lays with Bathsheba, so that David's sin goes underground. Now Bathsheba raises the child knowing that it is David's, she knows that David manipulated events to cover his sin, and she knows Uriah to be duped (although he has suspicions). Does this knowledge not murder her?

Her life consists of lies to her husband, to her child, and to her neighbors. She shows everyone her family but in her mind the truth dogs her, the reality that nothing is as it seems burrows beneath her skin like a maggot. When David sent for her and took her, he took much more than her body.

David sees that he cannot convince Uriah to go to his house, so he plots to kill him on the battlefield. He instructs his general, Joab, to put Uriah where the fighting is fiercest and abandon him there. Joab carries this out, becoming an accomplice in David's murder. In this way David progresses from the murder of his neighbor's heart to the murder of his body, depriving Uriah of life as he deprives Bathsheba of her husband. In all this he has first squeezed out God, who cries out to him through the prophet Nathan, "I am the one who anointed you king over Israel, and I am the one who delivered you from the hand of Saul. I have given you your master's house and your master's wives into your arms, and have given you the house of Israel and Judah. And if that had been too little, I also would have given you much more!" Why did you despise the Lord, O David, and refuse to rest in him? Why did you put yourself on his throne to hold sway in your heart? You have taken and murdered, denying your neighbor's life and his resting place, stealing his breath after staining his marriage bed! As you eject God as your Lord, so you eject your neighbor as your friend, and as you murder your neighbor so you crush God, who has set his heart on you.

Like David, who murdered to conceal the lust of the flesh, Ahab with his wife Jezebel murders to satisfy the desire of the eyes. Ahab sees the vineyard of his subject Naboth near his house and desires to own it, offering money or a better vineyard in return for it. Naboth refuses, declaring that "The Lord forbid that I should give the inheritance of my fathers to you." This response exasperates Ahab, who lies on his bed and will not eat. This is the way of those who set their heart on earthly goods, aligning their happiness with their belongings, whether luxuries, lands, houses, or money! The queen sees his behavior and reproaches him not because he acts like a child nor because his heart has turned away from God, but because he has not planned to use his power to take what Naboth denies him. "Do you not now exercise authority over Israel?" she asks, implying that he should seize as he wills, as though he has a right to all things as king. "Arise, eat some food, and be yourself. I will give you the vineyard of Naboth." With this, Jezebel initiates her plot to murder the latter, planting false accusations meant to bring about his death. She has two scoundrels sit opposite Naboth at an assembly, men who have agreed to charge him with cursing God and the king. When they denounce him publicly, those present take Naboth out and stone him. The cunning of the wicked bears fruit in murder, the lust of the eyes and the pride of power impose injustice on the innocent, Naboth dies the victim of a hidden scheme.

When Jezebel hears of Naboth's death, she relays the fact to Ahab with an instruction. "Arise," she says, "and take possession of the vineyard of Naboth the Jezreelite, which he did not give you for money; for Naboth is not alive, but dead." Ahab follows this direction with guile, for upon hearing of Naboth's death he tears his clothes and puts on sackcloth as if to mourn for the deceased. He gives the appearance of sadness, portraying that he had no hand in Naboth's demise. "After that, he arose and went down to take possession of the vineyard of Naboth."

Ahab and Jezebel indulged in idolatry no less than murder, if not moreso. "It was not enough for [Ahab] to walk in the sins of Jeroboam the son of Nebat," who established golden calves for worship in Israel, but having taken the Sidonian Jezebel as his wife, Ahab "went and served Baal and worshipped him." He set up altars for Baal among his idols, also planting a sacred grove to the god. Under Ahab, the prophet Elijah lamented that he alone remained of the Lord's seers, whereas four hundred and fifty prophets of Baal inhabited the land. Under Ahab, Elijah challenged those prophets to the duel in which the true God sent fire from the sky upon his sacrifice to devour it, shaming the prophets of Baal before their death under Elijah's authority. Despite this loss, Ahab continued to limp along with two opinions, serving the God of Israel and the idol Baal, pushing out the Lord before whom his followers have no other god by making him equal with a false god. He presses out God because he will not recognize him as God, foreshadowing his pressing out of his neighbor Naboth because he refuses to see him as his neighbor. He sees both God and the neighbor as little more than vehicles to the fulfillment of his desire, and when they cease to serve as this vehicle, or do not serve as effectively as he would like, he murders his neighbor and chooses other gods.

Ahab and David together do not compare to Solomon, that most ambivalent of Israelite kings. On the one hand the wisest of men, blessed by God with a mind to govern in truth and righteousness, the builder of the temple and the overseer of Israel's golden age, no ruler rivals Solomon's opulence and international reputation. No one comes close to his glory, replete with building projects, enormous wealth, and the majesty of his administration. Of Solomon we can certainly say, "may the king live long and benefit his realm"! And yet, and yet—a shadow follows Solomon, a foul spirit taints him, drawing him down among sinners. The wise man who knew that wisdom holds all things together was not without fault, possessing errors so profound that they tore his kingdom in two. It was his folly to commit both of the sins lambasted by the prophets, worshipping other gods and oppressing his neighbor. It was Solomon of whom Samuel warned when he said that the king shall take, Solomon the mighty and unsurpassed, the noble and esteemed, who defiled Israel and murdered his people.

It displeases Samuel when the people ask for a king. Samuel then prays to God regarding the request, who tells him to give the people what they want. However, God adds a severe warning:

> "This will be the custom of the king who shall reign over you. He will take your sons and put them in his chariots, and among his horsemen, and running before his chariots; and for himself, he will appoint them as captains over his thousands, and captains over his hundreds; and to harvest his crop and gather his vintage; and to make his weapons of war and instruments for his chariots.

He will take your daughters to be perfumers, cooks, and bakers. And he will take the best of your fields, your vineyards, and your olive groves and give them to his servants. He will take a tenth of your grain and your vintage and give it to his eunuchs and servants. And he will take your male servants, your female servants, and your finest cattle, and your donkeys, and take a tenth of them for his work. He will take a tenth of your sheep. And you will be his servants. Then in that day you will cry out before your king whom you chose for yourselves, and the Lord will not hear you in those days, because you chose a king for yourselves."

Over and over again God warns that the king will "take," a synonym in the Old Testament for oppression and intimating murder. Possessed of an authority that could support the rest of men in their neighbors, the king will abuse that authority to steal rest from his subjects, leaving them anxious and without a place before their superiors. The king will take your sons and your daughters, your crops and your vineyards, your servants and livestock, until finally he comes for you, forcing you to be his servant and his slave. When you call out to God in your oppression, suffering the burden of your murderous ruler, God will not hear you. For Israel has rejected its rest in God.

More than any other king whom the Scripture describes with detail, Solomon fulfills the warning of Samuel concerning royal rapacity. While Solomon "increased beyond the understanding of all the ancient men, even beyond the learned men of Egypt; and he was made wise beyond every man," he also had an enormous amount of food required for one day, "thirty measures of the finest wheat flour, sixty measures of beaten ground meal, ten chosen calves, twenty pastured oxen, a hundred sheep, and besides this, deer and gazelles, and choice fatted hens, because there was a governor all along the opposite shore of the river." Who prepared this food, if not the daughters of Israel that he had taken to be cooks and bakers? And where did the sheep come from if he did not take them from the people? And while Solomon crafted three thousand proverbs and gained an encyclopedic knowledge about the world, so that people from all around came to hear his wisdom, he also "had four thousand female horses for chariots and twelve thousand horsemen, whom he stationed in the chariot cities and with the king in Jerusalem," making the sons of Israel "his men of war, his servants, and those in charge of his chariots and servants." Solomon took the sons of his subjects and put them in front of his chariots to run before them, appointing them as captains over his thousands and over his hundreds, realizing the warning of Samuel that the king will gather all unto himself at the price of his subordinates.

In other ways Solomon made the people his servants if not his slaves, coercing them to hard labor. In order to build the temple "the king raised up a labor force out of all Israel," a collection of thirty thousand men. These he sent to Lebanon in shifts, ten thousand at a time to stay for one month. Solomon also had "seventy thousand who carried burdens," bearing the weight of the temple materials on their backs, and "eighty thousand who quarried stone in the mountain" in addition to thirty-six hundred supervisors who oversaw "the people who labored in the work." But the Scriptures also testify that in all of his building projects, from the temple of the Lord, Solomon's palace, and the wall of Jerusalem to the fortifications of various cities, he made the conquered peoples perform the work and "did not deliver any of the sons of Israel" to it. Given that the witness to Solomon's policies is mixed, it tips toward Solomon's oppression of the people. After his death, they came to his son Rehoboam with the message that "Your father made our yoke a heavy burden; but if you now lighten the harsh servitude and the burdensome yoke under which your father placed us, then we will serve you." No greater evidence that Solomon oppressed his people could be sought, short of rebellion against him. Whether Solomon oppressed them with harsh servitude and a heavy yoke only at the end of his reign or throughout it, we cannot say. We can say that he made their burden hard, depriving them of rest and subjecting them to murder so that they cry out to his son for mercy. "Lighten our burden" is their plea, their request for rest so that they might live and not die, not persisting under the death-like hardship that Solomon imposed upon them.

They ask for rest and therefore for life, but Rehoboam responds with greater murder, intensifying their burden. His father was harsh, and he would exceed Solomon's harshness with cruelty. "I will add to your yoke. Whereas my father chastised you with whips, I will discipline you with scorpions." At this announcement the people rebel, stoning the head of the Israelite labor and installing Jeroboam, who had led the labor force of the house of Joseph, as king.

This turn of events brings to bear the prophecy against Solomon because of his idolatry, a sin that appears at both the beginning and the end of his kingship. Prior to requesting wisdom from God in his dream, Solomon allowed the people to burn incense at the high places and did this himself, going to Gibeon to offer "a thousand burnt offerings on the altar." The Scriptures say that Solomon did this because the Lord did not yet have a temple, the house of worship that Solomon built. Perhaps when he had finished the construction, and after receiving his wisdom, Solomon abandoned the worship of idols and turned singularly to God. Perhaps he humbled himself in purity and piety, lowering his heart before the Lord and not straying from him. At the end of his rule, however, Solomon fell before his foreign wives and worshipped their gods. In his old age his heart did not remain loyal to the Lord, and his wives influenced him to build "a high place for Chemosh, the idol of Moab, and for their king, the idol of the children of Ammon, and for Ashtaroth, the abomination of the Sidonians." Solomon clung to the gods of his wives, sacrificing to them and burning incense, and for this sin the Lord promised to sever the kingdom from his hand and give it to another, retaining only the tribe of Judah and Jerusalem for the line of David.

As David gave in to pleasure and Ahab to greed, Solomon succumbed to the pride of life, the glory of magnificence and reputation. In securing this glory for himself he fulfills the warning of Samuel that the king will take, placing a burdensome yoke and harsh servitude on the people. The possibility of such oppression appears in

Solomon's early habit of idolatry, as he who regularly denies rest in God opens the way for oppressing his neighbors. In his great projects Solomon gathered glory to himself at the expense of the Israelites, pressing them down in order to raise himself up, shedding their blood so that he should gain in splendor. In the end this shutting out of the neighbor dovetails with his overt rejection of God, as Solomon neglects the Lord for the deities that his foreign wives bring to him. In Solomon idolatry and murder coincide, the lack of rest in God aligning with the denial of rest to the neighbor.

The kings' love of pleasure, greed, and glory caused enormous pain to others, up to and including murder as physical death. Their outward brutality implies an inner companion, a form of harm that docetic man, ensnared by things visible and external, strains to recognize as oppression because he cannot conceive of anything better. In his turn from God to the world, forgetting the former in order to seize upon the latter, man willingly submits himself to the oppression that inwardly trades the higher for the lower. He relinquishes true peace and joy, the children of devout fixation upon heavenly things and the way of piety, for a weak and exasperated inner life, a heaviness of heart and mind that drags him to the pit. In place of rest in God, which he acquires by the Lord's grace and not apart from solitude and concentration in prayer, he suffers a torrent of arrows shot by his enemy. Now worry and fear assail him, here lust and ambition, there sorrow at his failures, preoccupations with ills from the past and anxiety about the future, fierce anger at injustices real and perceived, a host of demons eager to betray and perturb him. Man imagines himself as king, he dreams of illicit and lascivious activity, he plots vengeance, he bows before greed and visions of luxury. He becomes a creature of this world in his heart and mind, wiping from his consciousness the communion for which God created him, cutting himself off from the spiritual bliss for which he should yearn. This is his primal oppression, the inner darkness that exchanges the glory of the immortal God for what is temporal and doomed to die.

The Christ-Idol redirects man to this suffering, deceiving him toward inversion by means of visible pleasures. For the Christ-Idol is the great inversion, holding within himself the key to Docetism's inverted world. Over the centuries prior to the Christ-Idol's arrival, salvation consisted of two elements: works, which are primarily outward and visible, and the inner faith of the soul. This faith maintained the primary position as it affirmed man's rest in God, in the eternal, in his neighbor, and in the natural world. Man's works oriented him to this rest, whether fasting and prayer, almsgiving, right worship, obedience to superiors, control of the passions, or any of the ways that men love their neighbors by putting the latter's interest above their own. The outward among these works confirmed the priority of the inward, depending on faith as well as the believer's will for their legitimacy. For centuries the Christ-Idol germinated in secret beneath this way of salvation as its antithesis, being birthed in the Reformation to mutilate its mother. The Christ-Idol unveils himself when works attain their limitlessness, when the law grows to such boundlessness that it undermines and squeezes out the soul's respite in prayer, sacrifice, and faith. The progressive intensification of the law and the elimination of rest periods, which suffer starvation as the distance between them grows, ruins the cycle of work and rest by finally wiping out the second element. At the decisive moment, Luther's heresy of justification "by faith alone"—a gross and hellish, damnable falsehood—salvation changes its meaning from rest in the context of God's limited and merciful law to liberation from Docetism's infinite law. Given the eradication of rest that is salvation, however, rest no longer holds its place above works as their support and orientation. It steps aside entirely and in its place one finds works and only works. There is a kind of faith, of course, but this faith believes that the law consummates itself in freedom, the liberation that drives the fool to further restlessness. It facilitates the infinite law rather than interrupting and limiting it, and thus allows no escape other than the eradication of law.

That works usurp priority over faith (as rest) is the primary inversion, the seed of others that transform the world after the Christ-Idol's whims. The eradication of rest first means that man does not seek the sources of that rest, so that God, the eternal and the soul, the neighbor and the natural world, fade as man travels along his new path of salvation. This loss grounds the new transition, the enthronement of works as the deformers of his world. For rest, as fundamentally inward, prioritized the invisible and eternal world over the visible, and as the way of justification by faith (as rest) it guides man into the invisible while properly loving the visible. Contrary to this, works belong principally to the visible and physical world. Their way of salvation emphasizes this world no longer as the lower before the higher but as the higher itself. As he pushes away the priority of the invisible, man sets his eyes increasingly on the visible as the arena of justification by works and the ultimate realm of meaning. But the nature of his works must also change according to the idol that he serves. If the Christ-Idol imposes salvation as the infinitizing of the law and the destruction of rest, the works that bring about this salvation must infinitize the law while severing man from sources of rest, prohibiting the avenues toward refreshment commanded by the Christ. Gone are fasting, prayer, and meditation, gone is almsgiving, gone are control of the passions and sacrifices, as well as works of love and self-denial once understood as the way of life. Though it takes hundreds of years, the Christ-Idol ensures that these fall into disuse if not scorn. The only outward form of Christianity left to docetic religion, it sometimes seems, is the command to spread the name of Jesus, a name now concealing the Christ-Idol. In place of the earlier works one finds a bevy of new ones, works in society meant to transform it, works "in the world" for the sake of the new docetic order. Man must build the world of the Christ-Idol in which he does not know any source of rest; in which all men are the infinite, or at least strive to be; in which he celebrates the slavery that confuses freedom and efficiency; in which men mock God; in which they smirk at the eternal as a myth contrived by meaning-making Neanderthals; in which nature is an alien and empty shell; and in which the neighbor lacks a face. Man calls this order progress and liberation, calling it equality while constructing it as the exaltation of the lower over the higher. It is the salvation of the Christ-Idol, the visible and physical work erected over the tomb of faith as rest.

In this world man adopts the pattern of docetic salvation as his way among his fellows. According to that pattern, congealed particularly in the early Protestant form of Docetism, man suffers the infinite law from God until he returns it, casting the infinite upon the Christ-Idol as savior. In the wake of this salvation he approaches his neighbor more or less as he approaches the Father of the Christ-Idol. Just as he knows the Father as a tyrant rather than a rest-giver, man encounters his neighbor not as a source of rest but as an enemy and a competitor. He does not bear the unspoken recognition that the neighbor implies a just law and a requirement of joint labor for life, nor does he see comfort and companionship in those close to him. Man implicitly understands his neighbor as a carrier of the infinite who would impose terrors upon him and hold him down, humiliating him if the chance arises. In response the docetist affirms his freedom from the neighbor, standing aloof from his fellows in pride and fear. Not that men consciously think of their comrades as enemies, and not that they consciously believe that those near them are criminals in waiting, scoundrels searching for an advantage to exploit. Far from it. On the surface man attempts to be friendly and sociable, cooperative and innocent, and might consider his associates to be the same. But he thinks this from the distance of liberation in which no force, internal or external, coerces him into a relationship with his neighbor. Man chooses to what extent he will commit himself to his neighbors and by what criteria he will do so. He chooses what sacrifices he will make, what trials he will endure, what gifts he will give, and no one shall compel him to act against his will. Traditions, social mores, institutional expectations, family, culture, and nationality, blood and sex have little hold on him, serving as gaunt and feeble guides. Introduce his neighbor as a law to him, by contrast, and bring the two together under the auspices of obligation, tie them together with cords of mutual debt that neither has chosen, restrict the freedom of each in order to strengthen their shared life, give them a single task that involves sweat and exertion, and at the farthest extent, put one of them under the authority of the other in a manner of which neither has consciously approved, but which the commonwealth has handed down to them: then you will see each run from the other as though his neighbor were a hungry lion or a rabid dog. For each believes, in his core, that the other is essentially selfish and cruel, and will place his own interest far above his neighbor's. Each man no longer sees a companion but an enemy from whom he must run with full speed. At this point the neighbor ceases to be a docetic friend, having become a law to him. In the unspoken consciousness of the docetic world, however, all laws are infinite, all know neither beginning nor end. The neighbor bearing such a law threatens oppression, his smile conceals machinations. Man comes quickly to this law's culmination by fleeing from his neighbor, abandoning his former companion.

When man runs from his neighbor—that is, when he accepts the distance of liberation as the starting point for his social life—he turns the infinite law back upon the latter inasmuch as he denies his place as a source of the neighbor's rest. Man says to the neighbor "I will not be a just law to you, neither will I give you solace." The two then agree to live at this distance, being convinced for the present that mutual liberation is the better bargain. Yet each is disposed toward oppression just as he sees this disposition in the neighbor. Each bears the infinite law within him, carrying the misery of Docetism's DNA in his heartbeat and his thoughts. Beneath his conversation and his dreams, his logic and his intuition lies the docetic mantra that he cannot rest until he has proven himself above his neighbors, until he has in some way exalted himself over them, even dominated them. Just as Docetism's salvation once consisted in forcing the infinite law upon his god, so docetic man's ethos compels him to force his superiority, his pride and his infinitude, upon his neighbor. The spirit of the Christ-Idol overwhelms him inwardly with such success that he cannot fathom the stillness that rests in God, while it raises him up on every front to defend and justify himself. His competition against his neighbor merges with the heart of his oppression, that he has raised himself up against God by liberating himself from his creator. Docetism realized this inner liberation in "justification by faith alone" as the annulment of both good works and the sacrifice of rest, so that man cannot but exalt himself against God, compulsively ascending in pride. The Christ-Idol simultaneously swings the whip and jolts man into action, to the salvation that demands that men dominate and oppress as they progress along the infinite law. This domination does not often appear in its starkness, as anonymous neighbors strive in small ways to outdo and defeat one another. Through the desire for pleasure, the lust for possessions and wealth, and the search for glory the Christ-Idol impels man against his peers, driving him to overshadow and humiliate them.

Could docetic man, all along an idolater, really be a murderer? He only compares his house or his car to his neighbor's, he only thinks himself slightly more attractive, intelligent, or accomplished, he only believes that his children are a bit smarter or more athletic. To his knowledge, he has not pulled the trigger to kill another man, nor has he broken into another's house to purloin his goods. His no murderer, no thief, no criminal deserving of time behind bars. His sins are peccadilloes, and men do not suffer eternal torment for peccadilloes.

But these trifling competitions, as well as his business, his entertainments, and his social contacts, make up the life of man. He goes about his day doing as he pleases, noticing the achievements and admirable qualities of his neighbors in order to find in himself what surpasses them. What he misses, what fails to cross his mind and what curses him, is his forgetfulness of the principle commandments that God issues to him. He shall the love the Lord his God with all his heart, soul, mind, and strength, and he shall love his neighbor as himself. To these commands gives no thought while the cares of the world consume his mental habits and his perceptions. The second commandment he misunderstands, believing that he loves the neighbor to the extent that he recognizes the latter's freedom for self-determination, or in other words, the latter's liberation. The docetic love-commandment dictates that men remain at the distance of "the individual," of mutual liberation, acknowledging above all that they cannot make demands of one another nor that they have concrete obligations toward one another. This hate-commandment denies the recognition of oneself as a source of rest and the neighbor as a rest-giver. Yet the commandment of Christ regarding the neighbor does not say "You shall respect the neighbor's liberation" but "You shall love your neighbor," meaning that the Christian shall bear the neighbor's burden and give him rest. Whose burden does docetic man bear? For whom does he go out of his way, acting in obedience and out of love? Not friends, not community or neighborhood, and rarely for family. The priest passed by and also the Levite, and also docetic man! When he sees the poor and beaten, the suffering and oppressed, he hurries to the other side of the road, his mind occupied with the concerns of the world and his competitions, forcing this burden onto "social structures" or the state while he personally scurries away. He murders not as one who beats the traveler and steals his goods, but insofar as he participates in the final act of the criminal, leaving the sufferers for dead.

Docetism has hidden man's life as a murderer beneath the designation "the individual." To be the individual, one defined by liberation from others and the rejection of the rest one could give them, is to murder. To live among men who embrace that rejection, who fail to give rest and leave their neighbors wanting, alienated, and fearful, is to be murdered. Docetic man says to himself that he is no murderer, whereas in the same breath he takes pride in being the individual, in admitting no authority that rules over him and no god to whom he must bow, no neighbor to whom he owes his life or for whom he must make sacrifices. He shouts that he is innocent and that he has not shed blood, at the same time whispering that he will pass by those doomed to pain and want. He observes his neighbors with the remark that they are basically good people like he is, simultaneously confessing that they are his competitors, that few if any come to his aid in his distress and that they have no obligation to do so. He considers them good in their alienation from him and himself as good in his alienation from them. In this way he accepts the conditions of mutual indifference, or biblically speaking, mutual murder, in which Docetism has lodged him.

God made all things for their proper places, while docetic man eschews the creator's design as fully as he can; that he and his neighbors coexist in mutual indifference presents but one form of the exile that docetic man accepts as his lot. God placed the sun in the sky by day and the moon and the stars at night, he placed the fish in the sea and the birds in the air, he placed Adam and Eve in the Garden and Israel in the Promised Land. The psalmist desired "a place for the Lord, a tabernacle for the God of Jacob," proclaiming to God, "Arise, O Lord, into Your rest, you and the ark of your holiness; Your priests shall clothe themselves in righteousness, your saints shall greatly rejoice." So he calls out for God to enter his place, the temple where his name shall dwell and where the people praise him. "For the Lord has chosen Zion; He chose her for his dwelling: 'This is my place of rest unto ages of ages; here I shall dwell, for I have chosen her... There I shall cause to spring up a horn for David; there I prepared a lamp for my anointed.'" And he says of Israel's wandering in the desert, "They shall not enter my rest," referring to Canaan as the place God had set aside for them. God rests in his place, which was once the temple and Jerusalem and is now the hearts of those who seek him. Man also rests physically in the natural world and his neighbor and spiritually in his inner communion with the Lord. Man forsakes these places in his exile, abandoning the heart as the place of God's residence as well as the neighbor and the natural world as the locales of his natural rest. In the latter cases man liberates himself from his existence as a natural being, knowing neither the rhythms and habits of the physical environment nor his way with others as neighbors rather than strangers. Men lose their places before their God, within their world, and with one another. They have chosen this fate in their darkened minds, electing to murder and suffer murder, to withhold mercy as they endure mercilessness.

For the sake of pleasure men assert themselves as the infinite, trading the momentary respite of nature for the infinitized rest of liberation from nature. Under natural circumstances of travel, for instance, men must walk or ride an animal. Both require periodic breaks especially over long distances so that living beings can rest. The man who must walk two hundred miles will occasionally sit, lest his feet and his energy give way. The distance of the trip and the time to cover it ask much of him, so that he must get off his feet for refreshment. Imagine, then, that this man is always at rest, always seated and at ease, and in this position can travel with such velocity that time and space almost cease to constrain him. Imagine that his body needs no exertion, no displacement of force or duration of energy, that it does not break a sweat while arriving at his destination with unprecedented immediacy. Is this not an adequate description of the automobile? Man travels in the position of rest, and with such breathtaking speed that distances taking days or weeks in natural conditions take hours, while he needs no physical labor to cross mountains or rivers. The American interstate is Docetism's ideal mode of vehicular travel (not to speak of airplanes), as the man in infinite rest moves in liberation from the bounds of nature, without intersection or stop sign and thus without pause or interruption. He is utterly free, entirely efficient, and wholly apart from his body. Natural existence no longer makes sense for men using such machines, which drug him into forgetting its struggles and necessities. He comes to scoff at these, for what fool would choose them over the pleasures of modern travel? Man has made progress and can smile upon his inventions. Surely the ease of rapid and uninhibited travel is innocent, harming no neighbor nor any god. Surely this liberation is good and right! Yet this technology does what docetic technologies inevitably do, alienating man from his rest. Through such machines he abdicates lived knowledge of his body and the earth as his place. How could he know these if he no longer moves according to their laws? How could he remember human existence when he has dismissed it for Docetism's infinitude?

Or think of the seasons that condition man's experience on the earth. In the summer he bears the discomfort of heat, which makes him sweat constantly. In the winter he endures the cold, the ice, and the snow, which imperil him if he lacks proper clothing or a source of warmth. Each of these remind him always of his bodily existence inasmuch as he feels bodily unease, and at their extremes each threatens his bodily way of life through sickness or death. In the winter nature provides fire for his respite, or perhaps the midday warmth will be enough to gird him. In the summer he looks forward to the breeze, to the shade, or the cool of the morning. Between the intensity of summer and winter he finds rest in the spring and the fall, which each provide a month or two of weather so comfortable that he needs neither heat nor cold to improve his condition. His life in nature thus subjects him to irritation if not complaint, with moments of solace dispersed into his servitude. If only men could pluck out the moments of relief and make them permanent, eliminating the long winter chill. If only man could cool himself at will in the summer, avoiding the stifling air in favor of unimpeded rejuvenation. This docetic man has done, infinitizing the moments of rest once sprinkled into his natural existence so that they define his ersatz environment. In this synthetic and technologically-mediated world the burden of the summer does not force him to sweat, seek shade, or wait for the breeze. The same world does not force him to seek wood for his fire in winter while it seals him from cold, frost, and snow. Nature's seasons hardly exist, remaining on the other side of the window as stunted reminders of the past. They possess as much power to compel or shape man's experience as modern royalty, whose presence is vestigial and meaningless to the government of their nations. Man lives on earth—where else shall he live?—yet he is utterly liberated from the nature characteristic of life on earth. He does not know the seasons, tolerating the winter only in fugacious walks between his vehicle and whatever building he means to enter. In summer he exposes himself to heat according to his will and no further, for what fool would willingly choose natural existence, sweating for no apparent reason? Is it not smarter and safer to stay indoors as much as possible, relaxing in the conditioned cool? This liberation from nature, man's infinite rest from nature's whoop and wharf, perverts the rest intrinsic to that nature just as it transforms God's kindness into man's denial of his world.

One could discover more examples of Docetism's infinitizing drive for pleasure against the natural world, a drive that also infects his relationship with his neighbor. Consider the recently-matured docetic sexual order, where men and women run rampant upon one another for rest, seizing one another for sexual pleasure. Some desire to love and be loved. Some desire to be loved but not to love, taking the desire and adoration of others while giving none of their own. Others, in greater darkness, forsake love as a fantasy, reducing sexual intimacy to haphazard and ephemeral unions. Man and woman join together physically, completing their sexual ritual and perhaps lying next to each other. At this point no commitment or expectation ties them to one another beyond the finished act, whose meaning was dubious from the outset. Or in deeper gloom the man discards the need for a partner, the infinitized individual now sitting before his screen, watching non-lovers playing at pleasure in acts that appall. From this objectivity he draws out his pleasure, partaking inhumanly, distressingly, so mauled and depressed is his soul. He grasps the rest inherent in pleasure for himself alone, an individual distilled from true physicality, from bond and reciprocation, from joy and life. In this the infinite tantalizes him with any woman that he could imagine and total liberation from responsibility toward her. At any time and on any day, as long as he has a screen and an object he can seek this pleasure. According to these examples and in addition to others, docetic man pursues his pleasure as the liberation in which he alienates himself from the woman and suppresses the possibility of rest. The latter depends especially upon the depth of mutual commitment. For the pleasure of sexual union overlaps mysteriously with the rest it bestows to the soul, an overlap confirmed by the union's embedding within the law of husband and wife. Their co-struggling and co-rejoicing, their mutual service, shared patience, and willingness to sacrifice for one another increase both the pleasure and the restfulness of their physical consummation. Remove the latter from the context of obligation and hope, of shared tasks, responsibilities, and pastimes, and from the orientation toward new life, and the rest-giving potential of their union crumbles. There remains for man a pleasure that gives no rest and that, as it multiplies without boundary, transforms into a burden. This pleasure deprives him of meaning because he has plucked it out of the way of life in which it makes sense, infinitizing it at the expense of himself and his partner.

For the sake of pleasure man increases his rest until it becomes the norm and context for his life, a totality that is his liberation from nature. This unlimited rest convicts him as a taker and a murderer, for on the one hand he cannot produce his liberated world without harming the natural one, and on the other he cannot indulge his liberated pleasure without damaging his neighbor. These forms of murder often intersect, as the same car that poisons the air allows him to live at great distances from friends and family, conditioning him to pass quickly by the poor. Behold the docetic everyman, this contemporary priest or Levite who is careless of God and unwilling to slow down, urged by his engines to ignore the afflicted. Likewise, the air conditioning that depletes the atmosphere encourages men to live indoors such that one can roam neighborhoods without seeing another soul. These docetic technologies that infinitize rest and liberate man from nature liberate him as well from the neighbor that God gave as part of that nature. And in his limitless striving for sexual pleasure man murders, turning against both the other sex and the divine image. He hates the woman insofar as he exploits her as an instrument for his pleasure, purchasing her beauty before casting it aside as rubbish. He hates her because he refuses to know or console her, to protect and provide for her, much less to cherish and love her, wanting only what she gives while he gives nothing. Thus he takes and murders for himself, but in this habit he digs a pit into which he himself falls. As pornographic murder in particular becomes his way of life, training him into its mores, he stabs his soul with so many thrusts of the knife. He undermines his capacity for durable relationships and moral commitment as his pleasure-habit reshapes his practical understanding of the relation between man and woman. Once he solidifies her status as object he can see her as nothing other than this, and in this manner he imprisons his soul within the search for vain and transient pleasures. He also murders his body, not understanding his disdain for the physical nature that rules him. God gave man a body with an intrinsic drive toward biological life, but Docetism's sexual libertine drowns this will to life in liberation, thereby submerging his bodily nature toward death. For what he allows to carry on under such sin he consigns to servitude under death, and what he allows to devolve unto death he cannot but hate. That the libertine announces this life as freedom and social advance adds to the tragedy, as in it he has mortally condemned his image as God's creature.

Today men have begun to take the next step, trading intercourse with woman for an inhumanity beyond description, deriving sexual pleasure from machines. Those who engage in such acts undoubtedly do so under the impression that they are harming no one, not perceiving a specific or visible victim who suffers due to their actions. While they do not see a victim, they become murderers, growing accustomed to taking pleasure without giving rest or support. They construct the embodied infinite, the machine, to be a slave for their passions, making themselves masters and commanders over their slaves. By this habit man himself becomes a machine and a slave, the victim of his iniquity. His desires control him to such an extent that he wholly casts out the neighbor, here the woman in all her humanity. His capacity for love perishes as he ceases to remember the requirements of romantic attachment and fidelity, and as he confuses the reality of the woman and the robot. This development brings the disposition of the infinite to an apparent conclusion, as the man who views others as instruments for domination and pleasure-seeking creates an object made for this purpose, jettisoning the free will of woman for the servility of the machine. He rests infinitely as he attains his pleasure without limit, but he experiences this conquest as the burden of alienation from rest in his neighbor. He murders not because he has a particular victim whom he can identify, but as he becomes incapable of providing the love intrinsic to his nature as a man. Lacking a specific victim, all women have become his victims, while the man himself, the bearer of such sadness and despair, endures the weight of the taking.

Men have desecrated the divine image for the sake of greed in addition to pleasure, seizing the natural world and their neighbors with force sufficient to pillage without consequence. Man takes what God provides for his bodily necessity and, tossing out his neighbor and his environment, he again infinitizes the gift of rest unto liberation and murder.

1 John: On Docetism and Resurrection

The creator gives man the plants of the ground and the herbs of the field for food, placing him originally in the Garden to till the soil and keep it. For the great majority of their history men have obeyed this divine directive, working in the dirt with their hands, learning the growth of the plant until the fruit matures. Men maintained a relationship with the earth as an object of local care and a partner in the work of life, and as the home that offers its bounty for them. They lived according to the seasons, knowing when to plant and when to harvest, and what fruits and vegetables to expect in their time. Bread and grain they might eat year-round, tomatoes and okra in the summer and early fall, and squash, potatoes, and other storable produce in winter. In this way men lived within the limit of nature, receiving according to its rhythm while battling its threats, notably drought, insects, and larger species that sought the crop. This way of life included its kinds of rest: the contentment of work with the land, the joy of the crop's growth and the arrival of rain, the feast of the harvest and, above all, the regularity of food. Men planted, tended the earth, and were grateful for its fare, resting in the reward that nature bestows to men abiding within its constraints.

Docetism has obliterated this order so thoroughly that little children today could expect the earth to sprout with the cans that contain their food. They know nothing of the natural world because Docetism's bearers have deprived them of it, offering instead this new and better world. In this utopia men do not sweat in the sun, they do not develop calloused hands or clean the dirt from their fingernails, they do not scatter the seed or pick the ripened fruit. They do not plant the tree or tend its branches, as this requires the wrong kind of work, work in and with nature, work in and with the body. Docetism forbids man's participation in natural work—it is under the curse!—while promising the rest of food on the table infinitized, enjoyed by docetic men without boundary. Men have always planted their crops in rows, so let us envision the rows extending over acre after acre unto the horizon. Imagine magical sprays and chemical compounds that compel the land to deliver its yield, so that the earth realizes an unlimited potential for production. Let us dream of machines that plant and harvest vast plots of earth in a single day. Imagine that the plant grows from seed to maturity without feeling a human hand, imagine men who cannot remember the last time they felt an okra or zucchini plant, imagine eyes that have never seen trees for pears, peaches, or other indigenous fruits. Imagine at the same time that this man, who lacks any meaningful relationship with the earth that feeds him, has staggering quantities of food available to him at negligible cost. Envision him eating tomatoes and other fruits in the dead of winter, ignorant of the natural limits of climate and season. Imagine sprawling and complicated transportation systems that bring his food from the other side of the world, where Docetism's invisible slaves ensure his satisfaction. Imagine that he brushes away news of drought and famine like a gnat, moving on to his meal. Imagine that he knows no way of life other than this and that he considers it right and good, that he believes all of this is necessary and natural. He draws infinite rest from the earth and is liberated from it, exulting in his liberation.

This is at once man's greed and his murder, but late docetic man, unlike Ahab, has swapped the murder of the neighbor for his vineyard with that of the vineyard itself. Man grabs ravenously, expecting that the soil should sate his hunger year-round, handing over whatever food he desires, when he desires it. He is hungry, let him eat—but let him understand the stupendous greed with which he devours, let him comprehend the cost that he imposes upon his voiceless victim. Underneath the uncountable rows of crops, maximized to guarantee the highest yearly production and to feed men who demand their produce neatly packaged, the earth pleads for rest. It bears the burden of his appetite, with man regarding it not as the womb of life or a co-worker in his sustenance but as a machine that must obey his demands. Docetic man treats the earth as his helpless slave, the beast to whom he can do no wrong. When we look at the fields that cover our countryside, we see the infinite law, boundless and uninterrupted, without mercy or rest. The earth moans, it grimaces and cries out under the weight that we force it to carry. "Six years you shall sow your field, and six years you shall prune your vineyard and gather its fruit; but in the seventh year there shall be a Sabbath rest for the land, a Sabbath to the Lord. You shall neither sow your field nor prune your vineyard. What grows by itself in your field you shall not reap, nor gather the grapes of the vines you dedicated, for it is a year of rest for the land." The spirit and practice of this injunction elude docetic man *in toto*, for his salvation coerces the land to endure the infinite burden. He cannot fathom that it might need rest, that he should moderate the load that he presses upon it out of respect for the commandment and the land's place in God's order. The holiness of rest pertains to all of creation as God's, and God wills that the creation be holy as he is holy. "While the earth remains, seedtime and harvest, cold and heat, summer and spring shall not cease by day or by night." Docetic man scoffs at this, having rid himself of seedtime and harvest, the earthy practice of summer and the necessities of winter. He exerts no energy, not lifting a finger to nurture his food toward his table while overriding the laws of nature to fill his stomach. He hands over his husbandry to the small number of men left to operate the machines, who farm by the rules of industry, and to the minority of farmers who attempt to grow apart from docetic methods. In docetic lands these bear the last memory of man with the earth, living in greater or lesser service to the infinitude in which Docetism imprisons us.

"I shall have infinite rest and be liberated," docetic man proclaims, "while you will have no rest, O earth, and will bear your burden!" To love is to bear the burden of others, to hate is to leave others alone to their burdens or otherwise increase them. Here is docetic man, well fed, strong, and exuberant, the murderer of the earth.

"By right the earth is mine," he thinks, remembering that God gave him the ground to rule over. In the same way docetic man declares that his work—an infinitizing docetic labor divorced from nature, swallowed within Docetism's social construct—belongs to himself and no other. From their youth many docetists believe that their labor belongs exclusively to themselves, that no other has a claim to their exertion or the wages it earns. John Locke has told them so, and men have adopted his word as their custom for centuries. The challenges to this way of thinking that have arisen within Docetism have borne little power against its contribution to the larger docetic stream, despite their rightly castigating it as greed. The greedy man believes that he must have more and his neighbor less, as though social life consists in ceaseless one-upmanship through the acquisition of goods. More subtly, the greedy man says that all that he has is his, whether it comes to little or much, and that the neighbor has no right in seeking his aid. The latter case, which the docetic mind considers self-evident, reveals the unspoken and intransigent denial of man's nature as an image of the rest-giving God. In it man flagrantly rejects knowledge of his nature as the complementarity of work and rest, of care for his own provision joined with his share in his neighbor's burden. Man discards this in favor of the presumption that he lives and works unto himself, that he is all law as selfishness and is thus the infinite, squeezing out the neighbor as one due support just as he undermines his capacity for rest in his neighbor. Not far from this attitude toward money one discovers another of Docetism's unwritten ideals, that the good man neither owes anyone a debt of gratitude nor knows anyone who owes him. Docetism's man neither lends nor borrows. He acts this way not out of the prudence and wisdom of the ancients, which looked upon proper reciprocation as the meat of men's lives together, but from the docetic drive to liberate himself from those close to him.

The man who declares that he owes his neighbor nothing, that no command of God or characteristic of nature impels him to lighten his neighbor's burden, hates and murders his neighbor. Docetic man does this for the sake of greed, and does more: for worldly finery he increases that burden, reducing others to the place of machines rather than men. Our economic kingmakers, leaders of empires who hold the lives of men in their hands, serve the docetic god first and recognize their neighbors secondarily if at all. That god demands profit according to efficiency, accepting as its sacrifices the humanity of those who work. These fall prey to long hours and harsh conditions as in the industrial factories and the shanty towns that stocked them. For the time being, these conditions exist at an international remove from the consumers who purchase their products, the owners exploiting free trade to find the cheapest labor beyond the ocean. Where labor laws exist, such as in the United States, the conditions have changed but the infinite spirit lingers. The world's richest men develop new ways to divest life from their subordinates, regulating their employees' every move while requiring severe standards of productivity, imposing harsh physical demands and dismissing medical complaints, provoking workers to protest that they are not robots. In the place of industrial factories stand distribution centers, with a new threat dawning. The aim of the owner and manager today, whose wealth fabulously exceeds his fellow man's, does not involve his workers living in hovels, eeking out a living while their children man assembly lines. He envisions a world in which he has done away with workers altogether, replacing them with the ideal efficiency of the machine. There is no mystery why ancient science never invented these monstrosities. It existed within cultures of rest; why would it invent a mechanism whose ontological meaning is the eradication of rest? The robot or the machine, the unique bearer of docetic culture, carries the docetic anti-soul and enlivens the vampires who benefit from that culture by wealth. If these men cannot transform others into machines for profit, they will do away with them for the sake of profit by machines. The shanty towns will return, the avenues will drip blood and the poor will cry out, and the rich, still claiming their wealth as their own, will feign innocence and say, "not I."

Docetic philosophers in their darkness deplore that men see each other as "things," preaching that they must know one another as persons. They forget that man is both law and freedom, work and rest, both thing and person. They do not perceive that knowledge of the person comes through knowledge of man as the thing, that rank or position precedes one's name. As a thing man has a place and a role, and a name in the context of that place and role. Destroy his thinghood, properly conceived, and he loses the place and the role and his name, while he might retain it, lacks grounding and thus meaning. Thingless names and nameless things, all of us. Let me keep my thinghood, let me be the thing that God created me to be: a man who bears the divine image, meant for communion with my creator as his creature, a man at home among men and on earth. Just do not pervert my nature into a machine, do not ruthlessly oppress me under Docetism's efficiency. Allow me my rest, which God has shown me is holy, and do not murder me for the sake of gain. And I, as Christ is my Lord, will bear your burdens with you.

One could be forgiven for thinking that man now rests in himself, without need of God or heaven, for he approaches the glory of the gods. The great civilizations of the past cover their mouths in shame before docetic man, whose life appears to them as a dream. The Romans did not know precision and power as the docetist does, the Greeks did not know philosophy, theater, or music like the docetist, the learned men of old marvel at the knowledge that docetic man takes for granted, that he treads over as minutiae. Not one of them could foresee the heights docetic man has attained, not one concocted the world of the infinite in which man rests without limit. Or perhaps they did envision the path to this world and, perceiving it as folly, declined to embark upon it. Perhaps the rest intrinsic to nature sufficed for them. Perhaps they knew not to go further.

Blessed is the man who knows what he should, who rests in knowledge rightly acquired. He studies the natural world to discern its laws, its regularities and habits, and from this develops a general expectation regarding nature. The same man observes human behavior and notes the general rules of long experience, so that he can pass on this knowledge and its rest to his children. In these types of knowledge man remembers his smallness, not adorning himself in presumptions like "the universal" or the intoxication of "species-being," contenting himself with the measure of knowledge appropriate to him. He knows some and cannot know all, but the part that he does not know troubles him less than his knowledge comforts him. He recalls the lesson of Ecclesiastes that making many books wearies the flesh, and that, while it is good to have wisdom, one must not seek God's wisdom as though one is God. Men must remember their lot, taking joy in the work that God has given and restraining their curiosity, knowing what God designed them to know.

What would become of man if he ceased to rest in the right measure of knowledge, destroying the boundaries for knowing about his world and his neighbor, I cannot say. If he decided that he should know everything about the natural world, vastly exceeding the knowledge of Solomon, his drive to infinitude may well push out what rest in knowing he possessed. He would never gain enough knowledge, while the natural world would step back as an alien object before his all-knowing subject. He would abuse nature from this distance, for the infinite is necessarily a drive to dominate. If man also decided that he should know all that one can about his neighbor or his society as a whole, what perverse mechanisms he would unleash I cannot predict. He might regard his neighbors more as machines than men, seeing them as programs who react in determined ways given the appropriate stimuli. He might devise schemes in which others, given the right nudge, will do as he pleases while believing themselves to be free and autonomous. He might perfect the delivery of advertisement and propaganda, of medium and message, of inundation and persuasion, so that the man-machine he intends to influence will inevitably succumb. Like the natural world, the neighbor whom he knows so well through his science and data shrinks into an object before his omniscient subject. Like nature, the neighbor endures manipulation under the infinite as the drive to dominate.

The glory of docetic knowledge leaves no stone unturned, transforming rest in the little man ought to know into liberation from both the object of knowledge and rest in knowing it. As man knows all about nature, he stops knowing nature; as man knows everything about his neighbor, he no longer has neighbors. He can, if he wishes, list a grand number of facts about natural operations and species, about photosynthesis and architectural movements. Only do not ask him to sow or reap, to build or plant. These activities he forgot long ago in favor of the uncountable facts that his docetic masters insist he learn. If he wishes, docetic man can enumerate principles of psychology, decision-making, and human development, give statistics about what people think on a variety of topics, describe the values and religions of ancient cultures, and expound on theories of group behavior. Just do not ask him about the neighbors on his street, most of whom he barely knows, or the family far away that he seldom sees, or the co-workers that tend to stay at a distance. He can tell you all about "humans" in the abstract, with charts, graphs, and indices that detail patterns of individual thought and social life, whereas he knows few men and fewer does he know well. Docetic man knows all, but this all-knowing which should mean an enormity of rest portends his liberation from rest. He knows his object infinitely, yet what he cannot know, what his knowledge prohibits him from knowing, is rest in that object.

Man yearns especially to rest in his neighbor, and for this reason he has always gathered into communities. Through these he seeks to better his life, hoping that by shared mores he could develop a deeper fellowship, by shared tasks he could establish a relative comfort, through shared recreation he could take part in simple pleasures, and through mutual compassion he could aid others in their afflictions as they prop him up to endure his own. So long as he is neither beast nor god, he requires this support and its comradeship in order to live a meaningful and prosperous life. That life consists centrally in the greatest benefit of life together, the habit of friendship. Not merely a joining of sentiments or emotional concurrence, friendship encompasses the forms of reciprocation constitutive of communal existence. One man exchanges goods with his neighbor, another gives respect and honor in return for patronage, a third gives his labor in return for material sustenance, and in their cooperation men nourish the spirit that binds them as a people, solidifying common expectations, common obediences, and common forms of rest. The habit of giving and receiving teaches them to rely on each other while the necessity of truthful speech in these circumstances trains them in mutual confidence. Men learn to appreciate one another through the history of reciprocal dealings, treasuring the growth of affect and the enjoyment of pastimes, a pride in their common heritage and commitment to the land, a kinship that they know together as home.

At the same time men have historically dwelled in societies of rank and distinction, allowing that nobles belong to their particular class while commoners abide below, with little if any substantive crossing of social barriers. Their distinctions provide the context for their friendship, which occurs in its ideal state among equals but does not exclude the reciprocal relations of higher and lower. Friendship can even exist between master and slave so long as each acknowledges the other as a man, awarding the other with the place of human dignity and the rest intrinsic to God's image. From their distances men remain relatively available to each other, normally without immediate and unimpeded access to others. The idea of rank or place prohibits unimpeded access across horizontal lines as well as vertical ones. The noble who has his place among the lesser class has it just as well among his peers, who, if they are truly noble, will be the first to respect his place. The commoner and the slave who receive their due place from their superiors will receive the same from their fellows, who shame the nobles if they better adhere to the respect due to all as bearers of the divine. In a society of rank, properly administered and permeated with the spirit of common humanity, no man has unlimited expectations of any other. The respect demanded by God toward the neighbor regardless of his rank, as well as toward one's livestock and the earth, a dignity defined as rest rather than freedom, prohibits this.

The late docetic city infinitizes the pre-docetic communities. Where men gathered in hundreds, thousands, and tens of thousands, the docetic metastasizing of population introduced cities of millions and tens of millions. It might seem on the surface that the uncountable gathering of persons ensures the rest that men have sought in their smaller city-states and towns. With such a multitude man must find somewhere to fit in, some group of like-minded persons ready to set out toward friendship and desirous of shared meaning. Thinking this, man fails to reckon with his milieu and the men who populate it, not realizing that limited and rest-bestowing men inhabit limited communities while the infinite city houses infinite men. The city that knows no boundaries upon its numbers, siphoning men from the countryside in order to swell its bowels, draws them to their individual manifestations of the infinite, seducing them into attitudes and habits that refuse the neighbor his rest. The individual city-dweller absorbs its glory, the height of its buildings, the glitter of its electricity and the power of its highways and bridges, not to mention the grandeur of its stadiums, the elegance of its museums, and the gaiety of its festivals. By virtue of his residence in the city this glory becomes his glory, causing him to wonder at both the achievements of men and himself as a man. In addition, the vastness of the population and the endless queue of strangers encourages him to shift the burden of rest onto others. They will care for the poor and the destitute, they will take up the cause of the depressed, the hungry, and the forgotten, while this man will not suffer the interruption. If he did help, what good would it do? Small efforts vanish before the city's deprivation.

In reciprocation neighbors encounter one another as mutual sources of law and rest, with man affirming that the neighbor is a law to him so that he can rest in the neighbor. In his infinitude the city-dweller wipes out both of these elements, celebrating the dismissal of his neighbor as a law. This adds to man's glory, as he considers the millions who surround him with the defiant assertion that none of them shall rule him, none shall determine or coerce him or be his master. None shall influence him unless he grants them influence and no one shall manipulate him. He shall remain in control over himself. In his mind he is liberated, and in a sense he thinks rightly. His neighbor makes no demand upon him, not telling him overtly what he can and cannot do. No rank limits him, no ossified social order or hierarchy of being binds him to a caste, no traditions or customs tell him whose company he must seek, where he will worship, or whom he shall marry. This pride, in which he exults as king over his shadow, starves the forms of reciprocation available to docetic man until he retains little more than shared tastes or political opinions, details of personality that shift with the wind, and the fruitless reciprocation of goods and services for money. His bonds to others slacken and grow stale, while the pride that fills his heart when he surveys the skyline fails to conceal the loneliness that dogs him. He knows the city as outward fascination and inward remorse, the latter the price that he laments but willingly pays for his glory.

Despite the absence of overt requirements or laws from his neighbor, in the last few decades docetic technology has accelerated the infinitude of its worshippers so that they now live under the conditions of limitless interpersonal demand. What is the meaning of docetic man's devices, the house gods that gleam in his eyes and enchant his soul, if not that man has infinitized his capacity for communication and thus alienated himself further from his neighbor? By owning the device man makes himself always available, renouncing the barriers of time and space that distanced him from those close by and far away. Expecting that they also own the device, he assumes that they remain always and immediately accessible to him, should he contact them. No man could practice the conversation made theoretically possible by the cell phone, answering every call without hindrance and engaging every interlocutor earnestly. No one is everywhere and at all times available to others. The ridiculousness of this idea reveals the tension within the infinitude that docetic man accepts in his technology. "I am always and everywhere available," he implies in his machine, while the last thing he wants is to be subject to such an availability. It would oppress him beyond all reason, and fortunately he has a ready escape in the text message. By this innovation the infinitely available man affirms his distance and the denial of access. He can answer the neighbor without hearing the latter's voice or, if annoyed, having to hang up on him. He does not need to bear the phone ringing, ignoring texts (and calls) at will. Due to its ease and the distance it affords, the text message has replaced the phone call as the purpose of the cell phone. In it the infinite man preserves his liberation while adding to his glory, proving that he is both important enough to need the device and independent enough not to allow others to disturb him.

It is impossible for man to love his neighbor through a text message. What burden of his neighbor's can he bear through this liberation? What is left of their reciprocation? How can one man know another's affliction when his habit excludes the neighbor's voice? How can he embrace the sufferer's heart or mollify his anguish? We murderers, hypnotized by docetic glory, who prefer the majesty of our machines over compassion toward those we mean to love! Out of our distances we bite and devour our neighbors, while violence blankets our world. And Docetism's labors take us, at long last, to a horror not yet known.

And the world is passing away, and the lust of it; but he who does the will of God abides forever. "Vanity of vanities," says docetic man, "vanity of vanities, all is vanity!" What advantage does a man have in all his labor in which he toils under the sun? Men are born of fathers whose names they do not know, they give birth to children whose progeny they will not meet. The sun rises and sets, returning to the place where it rises. The wind whirls in a circular motion and returns to where it began. The sea is not filled although all the rivers flow into it, and the waters return to the river's womb. All words are wearisome, and a man will not be able to say them. Neither is the eye satisfied with seeing, nor the ear satisfied with hearing. "I have created all things," says the docetist. "I have laid tracks across thousands of miles and built locomotives to run on them, I have given men tea and coffee as they race through the countryside. I have given them ease and vistas and wonders of travel. I have put them above the clouds so that they could caress the stars. I have launched them beyond the earth as if they could ride with Aphrodite on her chariot. I have healed their bones, corrected their deformities, enhanced their sight and their hearing, inoculated them against deadly sicknesses, and cured their diseases. I have taught them the names of the galaxies, the heat of the sun and the cold of distant planets, and revealed to them the structure of the atom. I have worked and constructed a new world. All is vanity! There is no remembrance of former things, and there shall be no remembrance of later things by those who come after."

"I was king over all men and all history, over all civilizations with their knowledge and achievements. I gave my heart to seek out and to prepare myself in wisdom concerning all the things done under heaven. I gave my heart to know discernment and knowledge, to learn the deep operations of the universe, its fundamental principles. I formulated laws of nature, of gravity, pressure, and thermodynamics. I harnessed unseen powers for energy and destruction. I developed biology, categorizing all the forms of life and dissecting their bodies, their organs and major systems, how they breathe, digest food, and ward off illness. I learned of single-celled organisms, of the multitudinous variety of life as well as the cells within complex animals. I commanded cadres of scientists dedicated to the study of particular species, even worms. I hypothesized the evolution of species from the least complex to the most advanced, marking the adaptation of species to their environment as the means of evolution. I tackled chemistry, examining the substances constitutive of life on earth, experimenting with their compounds and testing their volatility, devising the periodic table and expressing the relationships between the elements. I invented fiber optics, discovered microwaves, and mastered the sorcery that delivers information through the air. I have copied the human voice and recorded man's activity in one location in order to project it instantaneously to another thousands of miles away. I have made available every song or ballad of the ages so that men can access music without exertion. Vanity of vanities," says the docetist, "all is vanity. What advantage does a man have in all his labor in which he toils under the sun? For he who increases knowledge increases suffering."

Docetic man said in his heart, "Come now, I will test you with merriment and see if there is good." I filled my ears and my eyes with mockery, with scorn and laughter at those I considered fools. I sat in the seat of scoffers, inclining my heart to endless comedy, to the absurd and the stupid, the slapstick and the dark, the bevy of humor brought daily to my doorstep. I trusted the jester above the public servant, I accepted the bribery that pleases with silliness. I spent the night hours watching fruitlessly, joke after joke, and found that humor too is vanity. And I said concerning laughter, "This is madness." I also gave myself to social life, to dinners and parties, to dance clubs and sporting events and concerts, to movies and television, to infotainment and documentaries. I found strong drink among drinkers and good taste among sophisticates, I pretended to education and high-mindedness while indulging my desires. I learned the cuisines of foreign cultures, I developed an appreciation for the arts and literature, for plays and sculpture. I built vacation homes in the mountains or at the beach, I laid for hours watching the waves and visited destinations exotic and picturesque. I took pictures to record my travels, reminding me of these blessings and announcing them to my visitors. Whatever my eyes desired I did not keep from them, and I did not withhold from my heart any merriment. For my heart was made glad in all my labor, and this was my portion from all my labor. Then I looked on all the work my hands had done, and on the labor in which I had toiled, and indeed all is vanity and is the choice of one's spirit. There was no profit under the sun."

Then docetic man returned and saw a strange thing. What has been done is what will be done, and there is nothing new under the sun—and the strange thing was the foolishness of docetic man. If you see the oppression of the poor and violation of judgment and righteousness in the land, do not marvel at the matter; for there is a high official to watch over a high official, and higher ones over them. The greater the distance between the powers and their subordinates, the more likely that the higher will forget their natural bond with the lower and the divine commandment incumbent upon them. The highest must struggle to maintain the humility that binds them to the lower, and they do this by remembering God who both establishes their position and enjoins them to be merciful, to bear the neighbor's burden and love him. Docetic man saw all this and said to himself, "I will improve upon God! I will do away with oppression, even the possibility of oppression! There will be neither king nor commoner, neither higher nor lower. All will be equal, and so all will be free for the choice of the spirit." In seeking to level the array of men with regard to wealth, rank, and noble birth, he allowed that all could become the highest. At the same time he destroyed the bonds between men, including the glue of *noblesse oblige*. He undermined the duty imposed upon the materially blessed to exercise mercy. Docetic man had considered God an oppressor, lumping him in with the slaveowner and the bishop, the king and the capitalist, but in the wake of his war against them he saw greater oppression under the sun. He heard the weeping of Docetism's oppressed: from the Southern slave to the industrial worker, from the homeless and destitute to the child laborer, from the Orthodox enemy of communism to the hapless Jew! They have no earthly comforter. On the side of the oppressors was power and prestige besotted, laid low by guilt. Today they sense the blood on their hands as their own standards condemn them. On one side of the Atlantic men cannot justify their nation. Once it was manifest destiny that they conquer the plains and the mountains, now it is theft and injustice that they have done so. On the other side of the sea the shadow of the World Wars persists, such that men who have forgotten the right of self-defense cower at its necessity. Their elites, whose mercy amounts to a kind of suicide, are not far from the Americans who consider their own borders an offense against humanity. Thus the nations of the powerful mourn their ancestors as well as themselves, with no one to comfort them. They await the approaching death of their nations and erasure of their peoples, whose inability to draw boundaries proves the loss of the will to live. In the West, docetic man borrows without limit both in his nations and his households; he is ever the slave of machines that beguile him with comforts while stripping him of his nature; he cannot maintain his family bonds, trading what is firm and protective, and meant for strength and self-control, for what is malleable and porous; he does not know how to discipline his children and succumbs to weakness before them; and he absorbs sexual perversity as though it were mouthwash. But grind the fool with mortar and pestle, and the folly will not come out. So docetic man continues his leveling, his revolution and charade. He raises his standard of equity, eradicates the past as a reminder of his ancestors' sins, and proclaims that he will not repeat their offenses. He strives to change the world, to redress inequalities and eradicate oppression, forgetting where this path has led and denying where it will lead. Blessed are those who are not yet born, who have not seen the folly of docetic freedom. Vanity of vanities, all is vanity.

Remember your creator in the present moment! Docetic man feels that difficult days come soon, he perceives that they have already begun to arrive. As the Athonite Fathers have warned, they come: the years that docetic man lacks the will to face, when the sun, moon, and stars are darkened and the keepers of the house tremble, when he acquiesces to the infinite as bloodshed and desolation. On that day the men of strength will be led astray and the women who grind the grain will become idle because they are few. The doors will be shut in the marketplace and one will rise up at the sound of a sparrow. Men will look from the height and see terrors in the way, with the mourners going about the markets. The pitcher will be shattered at the sink and the screen will go dark. The automobile will lack fuel and the pundit will have no words. The dust of Docetism's civilization and its man return to the earth. "And it shall be that the people shall be as the priest, the servant as the lord, the maiden as the mistress, the buyer as the seller, the lender as the borrower, and the debtor as the creditor." They shall at last be equal, and equally forlorn.

How deep are the riches of the wisdom and knowledge of God! How unsearchable are his judgments and his ways past finding out! I said, "I will be wise," but it was far from me, and as for what is far off and exceedingly deep, who will find it out? Where can wisdom be found? What is the place of understanding? Mortal man has not known its way, nor is it found among men. The deep said, "It is not in me"; and the sea said, "It is not with me." God has established its way, and he alone knows its place. From the heavens he said to man, "The fear of God is wisdom, and to abstain from evils is understanding." He made everything beautiful in its time, and He put eternity in their hearts in such a way that man may not find out the work God made from beginning to end. For those who wish to distance themselves from Docetism's milieu and its ways, there is therefore nothing better than to rejoice and do good. Following the tradition of the Fathers, every man should love God and his neighbor, he should eat and drink and experience the good in his labor. Though he finds himself working the land and without docetic comforts, though he accepts work he once considered menial, the Christian should be thankful for the work that God has given. This is God's gift to him and the portion allotted to him.

Although all have taken part in Docetism's iniquity inasmuch as it has enveloped and directed us, we are by no means without the possibility of repentance. Those seeking God will perdure through Docetism's collapse because they have reckoned the enormity of its sins and humbled themselves, purifying their hearts from idolatry and oppression. When considering their sins, they remember Ahab. After Elijah accosted him for his murder of Naboth and the seizure of his vineyard, the king bowed before God. He fasted, tore his clothes, and wore sackcloth due to his behavior. How many tears he shed in mourning his transgression we do not know. On account of his repentance God looked upon him with kindness, delaying the recompense set in motion by his deeds until after his death. Those who perdure will bear this in mind, learning sorrow for their sins and acquiring the change of mind needed to live righteously. Or they will remember David, who fasted in sackcloth and refused food after hearing that his child by Bathsheba had become sick. But when he received news of the child's death, David washed and anointed himself, put on fresh clothes, and worshipped. He recalled that God is just in all things, and that those who suffer do so under a God whose faithfulness and love stand above all.

Those who take joy in their labor and repent of their sins have great hope! They have trained themselves in the conviction that God's providence guides all things, that he uses struggles to draw the repentant toward him, and that for his saints the hardships of this world fashion a crown in the next. They might stand to one side as thousands fall at their right hand, seeing that it does not come near them. They might find themselves in the midst of a fiery ordeal, recalling St. Peter's admonition not to be surprised at this. They might fear Docetism's end and want to escape it, but fear drives neither their spirit nor their actions. It is not fear that should drive Christians away from docetic mores and brutalities, but the promise of life. They desire good things in the age to come and the inner presence of God in this one, and they perceive the docetic barrier between them and their goals. The sense of the eternal, the love of the transcendent, the sublime, and the quiet and restful, the love of humility in the face of insults and sacrifice for the neighbor, harmonize within them like a heavenly choir. They see beyond the death of Docetism to what perdures through death, the immortal that awaits new birth within its mortal home, the return of man to God and his humanity. These seek the right order in which the spiritual exceeds the physical, in which the internal excels the external and the kingdom of God surpasses the kingdom of men who will to be gods. They take the Christ at his word when he says that God's kingdom is within us, waiting for man to delve into his heart. Though they suffer in the body, enduring the pains characteristic of human life and persecution from their adversaries, they also know God within. Their glory is to dwell always in his presence and do his will, lowered as his servants, abiding in the hope that sustains all things.

1 John 4:7–12

Beloved, let us love one another, for love is of God; and everyone who loves is born of God and knows God. He who does not love does not know God, for God is love. In this the love of God was manifested toward us, that God has sent His only begotten Son into the world, that we might live through Him. In this is love, not that we loved God, but that He loved us and sent His Son to be the propitiation for our sins. Beloved, if God so loved us, we also ought to love one another. No one has seen God at any time. If we love one another, God abides in us, and His love has been perfected in us.

Beloved, let us love one another, for love is of God; and everyone who loves is born of God and knows God. He who does not love does not know God, for God is love. In our day men mistake love for hatred and hatred for love, confusing the most virtuous and the basest of our habits and dispositions. Ask docetic man what love is and he will respond with the equality in which all are free, an equality alive in the presumption that allows men to do what is right in their own eyes, expressing themselves without judgment or reprimand, going about their lives without a concrete sense of obligation beyond the universal proscription against judgment or criticism. "Love thy neighbor" means "do not judge thy neighbor, whatever he may do or say," and this finally means not to restrict him or place any break upon his behavior. As his equal, how can one judge him? Therefore give the neighbor the widest possible latitude to form his habits, which in practice means for him to decide which desires shall rule over him and succumb to them straightaway. This false love presupposes that men conceive of the neighbor in isolation, as an individual immune to giving and receiving rest and therefore as his own master. Whereas the way of God in Jesus Christ excludes other ways such that no one comes to the Father except through Christ, the docetic way opens man to infinite ways because he is himself presumed as infinite and an equal among other infinites. Love as toleration and the apparent absence of judgment make sense only if man is the infinite, if he believes it his right to grant himself all possibilities that he desires and that circumstances permit him to attain.

This false love among men is hatred; it is pride, not humility; the alienation of men, not their unification; an unnatural perversion of nature, not its fulfillment in God; the denial of rest, not its granting; the abdication of mutual service, not its enthronement; the abandonment of the soul, not spiritual joy; the road to damnation, not beatitude; and the surety that men will rise against men as competitors, domination upon domination. Docetic man believes that the reign of higher over lower is the source of all oppression, not realizing that oppression arises from the perversion of this necessary form, a form necessary as it is intrinsic to love. Rather than pursuing the humility that curtails the possibility of form's perversion, he chooses as his solution the unraveling of hierarchy. Along this path he destroys the possibility of hierarchy's perversion but also the form itself, and thus the possibility of love, for the reign of higher over lower provides the essential means for men to live in mutual humility. Without it, they become docetic conquerors, unleashed and unhindered. Docetic man therefore knows reciprocation but in the form of competition, of repeated violence, because he assumes a love in which infinites collide in their freedom. "We have competition, we have war, and our pride is to widen the field so that those once protected from our combat can join in. Now that we have made them equals, let them partake in the fray!" So says docetic man. "I have loved you by liberating you from bond and limit. Now make war with me!" The liberated man celebrates his liberation by turning men and nations away from the mutual giving unto life that is love, directing them to mutual taking, to the bitter and fissiparous exchange which reveals friends as fiends.

"God is love" does not mean "God tolerates," as if the Holy One of Israel could stand what is unholy, as if he does not reserve holy things for those who have trained themselves in holiness. "God is love" does not mean "God does not judge," as if the word of Christ did not judge men, as if the light did not expose the darkness, and as if men do not reap what they sow. The Lord will sit on the throne with the sheep on his right and the goats on his left, and he will judge. "God is love" does not mean "God liberates," as though, like the Christ-Idol and his docetic father, God set men on the path of the infinite until they arrive at schism as salvation. Nor does God's love imply the equality in which boundaries fall away or are shattered so that a greater mass of men can clamor for infinitude.

As the contrary to the Christ-Idol, in whom men discover all pride, folly, perdition, limitlessness, perversion, taking, and deception, stands the truth that God is love. He embodies humility, wisdom, right order, nature, self-giving, and fidelity. He is all these things not apart from a notion of limit in his being but through it. In the same way he is all these things, even love, not without hierarchy in the divine being but through it. Love is not apart from the order of higher and lower and the mutual giving between them. Hierarchy does not stand opposed to love as hatred. It stands within love, so that men must say "God is hierarchical" just as they say "God is love," and so that they cannot say "God is love" without implying that God is hierarchical.

This accords with the writings of the Fathers, who affirm the Monarchy of the Father with respect to his origination of the other persons and by this criterion alone. St. Gregory Nazianzen admits "that in respect of being the Cause the Father is greater than the Son" and no less greater than the Spirit,[1] and St. John of Damascus adds that in thinking of the Godhead Christians contemplate a "difference we conceive of according to cause and effect and the perfection of the Person, that is to say, His manner of existing," for "the Father alone is cause."[2] He adds that "the Father and the Son and the Holy Ghost are one in all things except the being unbegotten, the being begotten, and the procession," so that they are of the same substance or essence. Therefore "when we hear that the Father is the principle of the Son and greater than He, let us understand this as being by reason of his being the cause" of the Son, in addition to "the Holy Ghost . . . who proceeds from the Father and abides in the Son," and "who proceeds from the Father and is communicated through the Son and is participated in by all creation."[3] This hierarchy with respect to origin or manner of existing is intrinsic to the Monarchy of the Godhead, belonging to the three Persons, a Monarchy made, as St. Gregory teaches, "of an equality of Nature and a Union of mind, and an identity of motion, and a convergence of its elements to unity—a thing which is impossible to the created nature—so that though numerically distinct there is no severance of Essence. Therefore Unity having from all eternity arrived by motion at Duality, found its rest in Trinity."[4] The divine rest intertwines with the divine love, the Persons resting in one another as they love one another. This mutual life-giving of the Father and the Son in the Spirit I have attempted to elucidate in earlier essays. The hierarchy of origin facilitates this Trinitarian unity, its assertion of higher and lower being intrinsic to the mutual giving characteristic of the Trinitarian life, the life of God as love. The Father begets the Son and the Spirit proceeds; the Son humbles himself before the Father in the Spirit; the Father humbles himself to the Son in the Spirit also. In this, the manner of life-gift between the Persons and the essence of the three remain the same.

Have I not gone too far in my earlier work when speaking of the begetting of the Son? The same St. John affirms that the Father begets "without time or change or passion and in a manner beyond all understanding, as only the God of all knows," adding that "as to the manner of the begetting and the procession, this is beyond understanding."[5] God has revealed through the Scriptures and the ancient Fathers, says St. John, "what it was expedient for us to know . . . with these things let us be content and in them let us abide and let us not step over the ancient bounds or pass beyond the divine tradition."[6]

1. *Theological Orations*, 3.xv.
2. *The Orthodox Faith*, I.8, 12.
3. *The Orthodox Faith*, I.8.
4. *Orations*, 3.ii.
5. *The Orthodox Faith*, I.8.
6. *The Orthodox Faith*, I.1.

1 John 4:7–12

I hope to make it clear that in speaking of the divine hierarchy, of the begetting of the Son and the life of love within the Trinity, I have not overstepped the bounds of Scriptural wisdom or transgressed the teachings of the Fathers. I have offered my thoughts out of a desire to counter a heresy that the Fathers did not face. These thoughts do not stray from the assertion of God as Father, Son, and Holy Spirit, their identity of Nature, and their common and singular life as love, the convergence to unity mentioned by St. Gregory. If the Church judges that I have contradicted the Fathers or threatened the possibility of salvation, I will quickly retract such statements. Let the critic remember, beyond this, that "we are unable to think or speak of the divine, lofty, and immaterial operations of the Godhead unless we have recourse to images, types, and symbols that correspond to our own nature."[7] I have employed types and symbols due to the necessity of human thought, at no point intending to demean our God or the teachings of our holy faith, and I have not meant to peer into mysteries that men should not ponder. I have attempted nothing more than to set right what is wrong (as I understand it), to open the door to the experience of God that Docetism means to close.

I have written that Docetism births an infinite law out of a formless freedom, destining that law to return to its origins as it wipes out the limit that is rest. The docetic dynamic posits freedom (as formlessness or liberation), then the law as an infinitized middle term, and freedom again as the consummation of the law. This dynamic destroys what is holy as it obliterates freedom-as-rest, inverting the right order in which rest plays the middle part between assertions of work or law. Rather than fundamentally breaking or smashing the cross, the evil one destroys it by inversion, turning it upside down. One can see this in the worship of the Satanists, who confront one another with an inverted cross. The deceiver secretly reverses the way of life to become the way of death, wearing the mask of heaven in order to lead men to hell. To turn this wickedness right side up, one must understand rest as the middle term between assertions of work, which are ontologically assertions of form, law, or being. Life works, it perseveres and creates, yet it cannot exist in its activity apart from rest, such that the total loss of rest is death. Rest preserves and protects life, nourishing it like the rain that spurs the plant to greater growth in sunlight.

In locating rest as a middle term within the divine life, I have introduced a fundamental concept not mentioned as such by the Fathers. By this, however, I have not transgressed the biblical commandment to rest nor its holiness as expressed in the creation. "Come to me, you who labor and are heavy laden, and I will give you rest," says the Christ, whose first criticism of the Pharisees points out how they lay heavy burdens upon others without lifting a finger to help them, depriving them of rest. In an era defined by the docetic abolition of rest in the neighbor and the nearly complete eradication of rest in God through prayer and eucharist, men need to discern how "God is love" relates to his giving of rest, and they should consider how rest functions

---

7. *The Orthodox Faith*, I.11.

within the Trinitarian love. Can rest make sense without a prior affirmation of work? And does life itself make sense without some labor or activity meant to provide for and further it? Men rest when we have exerted ourselves or borne a burden, wearying our souls and bodies until they require refreshment. In a similar way, to say that God rests implies that he has worked, that the "identity of motion" noted by St. Gregory, the work of love that is the Trinitarian life, is a logical prerequisite to Persons' rest in one another. This motion, through which they enact the supreme truth that God is love, binds rest within it and turns in various ways on this rest. The beginning is motion or work, and between motion and motion, life and life, form and form, comes rest, the death-moment of the burning bush that refreshes in a mysterious and inexplicable way the work of life.

St. John writes that "as to the manner of the begetting and the procession, this is beyond understanding." I agree fully, and I have said not a word especially about the procession. But some will ask how I can agree with St. John when I have argued that the begetting happens at the behest of the joy of the divine being and through the freedom of the Father, while that freedom consists not only in the rest of being but an assertion of the divine will.

Joy is not passion, according to St. Gregory. Concerning the begetting he writes, "How can this generation be passionless? In that it is incorporeal. For if corporeal generation involves passion, incorporeal generation excludes it."[8] When we consider the joy of the divine being, we do not speak of a human passion or inclination, but of a fruit of the Spirit whose nature is divine and beyond our understanding. We use human types and symbols while the reality exceeds our comprehension. But I say that this joy impinges upon the divine freedom, exerting a joyful pressure upon the will implied in that freedom. Having begun with the being of God that is activity, law, and form, we must move to its rest in freedom. Men must do this especially when considering the begetting, for if there were no relation between the divine being-in-act and the divine freedom at this point, one could arguably say that the will acts spontaneously and on its own. Could we then say that the begetting belonged to the divine nature? Would it not much moreso be the child of the divine will alone, as if that will were distinct and separate, somehow distilled from the divine essence? St. Gregory dismisses just this possibility in his *Orations* (3.vi), where he contends that the will cannot stand between the Father and the begetting of the Son as a third thing, as if the Son were a child of divine will as isolated from the divine nature. Thus the Father's activity of being must press upon the will or freedom, and I can find no better expression for this than joy. For the being of God radiates a joy beyond our comprehension and that affirms and furthers life. But how can I say that the will is involved in the begetting? Hear again St. Gregory speaking of the begetting and the procession: "For we shall not venture to speak of an 'overflow of goodness,' as one of the Greek philosophers dared to say, as if it were a bowl overflowing ... Let us not ever look on this generation as involuntary,

---

8. *Orations*, 3.iv.

like some natural overflow, hard to be retained, and by no means befitting our conception of the deity."[9] With St. Gregory we say that the will is active in such a way that it is not distilled from influence or distinct from the divine nature, so that no "partition is set up" between the Unbegotten and the Son "in the shape of Will."[10] The joy of the Father encounters the divine freedom and must pass through it, with the two working together toward begetting.

It is now repeated that the begetting lies beyond understanding and that I have tried to describe how it occurs. I respond that I have described nothing of the sort. What is the freedom of God and how does begetting happen through the will? I have no idea. We say that God created through his word, "Let there be," and in saying this we claim no knowledge of how the words produced the creation or what secret powers they contain. How does God create *ex nihilo* by his word? What mind of man could grasp this? In a similar way I say that the joy of the divine being places its pressure upon the will, but I venture no explanation of how this concludes in begetting. St. Gregory speculates that with the Father "perhaps the will to beget is generation and there is no intermediate action," but he does not say this with any firmness. Nor would I. He continues about the begetting that men must toss out their "notions of flow and divisions and sections, and your conceptions of immaterial as if it were material birth . . . How was he begotten? I repeat the question in indignation. The Begetting of God must be honored by silence . . . the manner of his generation we will not admit that even Angels can conceive . . . it was in a manner known to the Father who begat, and to the Son who was begotten. Anything more than this is hidden by a cloud" and escapes our thoughts.[11]

The Father begets the Son and from him the Spirit proceeds. "The Father is wellspring and cause of Son and Holy Ghost—He is Father of the only Son and Emitter of the Holy Ghost," says St. John of Damascus, who emphasizes that "the Father alone is Cause."[12] As he is the Cause and Unbegotten, in this respect he is the higher. This hierarchy is subordinate to the equality of nature among the Persons and in no way detracts from their unity. It contributes to that unity in the shared life of love. When I say that the Son is "humbled before" the Father in the Spirit, and that the Father is "humbled to" the Son also in the Spirit, this does not entail any difference between the three in essence or nature. The three remain equal as God, while the distinction of "humbled before" and "humbled to" derives from the Father's role as Cause, and that only. That the Son is "humbled before" the Father does not make him ontologically inferior, nor does it so designate his life-gift. Similarly, the "humbled to" of the Father to the Son does not raise the Father up as though he were more divine than the Son or the Spirit, nor does it elevate his life-gift above the Son's. In every case the Persons

9. *Orations*, 3.i.
10. *Orations*, 3.vi.
11. *Orations*, 3.vii.
12. *The Orthodox Faith*, I.12 (196).

give a life that is fully and equally divine, without imperfection or subordination in comparison to the other Persons. And yet the hierarchy of origin is intrinsic to this mutual giving that is love. From the Father comes the Son and the Spirit, so that he is in this sense higher; from his position of relative subordination the Son looks to the Father with profound joy and thanksgiving, turning his own life-gift to the Cause and Unbegotten, a lower that gives willingly to the higher. At no point does the Son say "I am equal to the Father" as if in ingratitude or presumption, but he turns to the Father humbly, handing over his life in the Spirit. Likewise the Father, receiving the gift of the Son in the Spirit, does not withdraw into himself in his superiority of origin, but returns the life-gift to the Son, completing the mutual giving in the Spirit that is the divine love. We cannot understand "God is love" without acknowledging the hierarchy intrinsic to that love. We cannot say "the Son loves the Father in the Spirit" without saying "the Son is subordinate by begetting." We cannot say that "the Father reciprocates the Son's love in the Spirit" without saying that he does so as Cause and Unbegotten, and therefore as higher. The three Persons are equal, each lacking nothing that the others possess beyond their divergent manners of existing as Unbegotten, Begotten, and Proceeding. Yet these divergent manners and the hierarchy they imply are inseparable from the convergence of the divine Persons to unity expressed in the truth that God is love.

It has not been the witness of the Son or his followers to cling to their equality. Instead, they embrace subordination and act out of it as a starting point. The Son, "being in the form of God, did not consider it robbery to be equal with God, but made himself of no reputation, taking the form of a bondservant, and coming in the likeness of men." How puzzling is it to docetic man that the Son relinquishes his equality with the Father, placing it in the background for the sake of mortal, finite, and fallen creatures, and that he does not prioritize his equality before the holy and pure, loving and gracious Father who begot him! The Christ humbles himself as God's wisdom, lowering himself as a prelude to honor as stated in Philippians, and he teaches that the first among Christians shall be the servant who lowers himself before others. When the Son humbles himself before the Father in the Trinity, we have every reason to believe that, despite his equality with the Father with respect to nature or essence, he casts off that equality in favor of the subordination due to origin. He humbles himself as an inferior rather than an equal, setting aside the ineffability and grandeur of his divinity in order to come before the Father as one lower, forgetting his own goodness, as it were, and remembering the superiority of the Father as the Begetter from which he has come. In this spirit St. Paisios remarks that the Christian, "if he's working properly spiritually . . . will rarely ever remember the good he has done, but will never forget the smallest good done to him. He can never ignore the smallest benefaction of others" ("Spiritual Counsels, Volume II: Spiritual Awakening"). How much more, then, that the Son in giving his gift of love to the Father, and in approaching the Father in general, should forget the goodness of his equality with the Father and act out of his subordination as the Begotten before the Begetter, remembering the goodness of the Father rather than his own.

In discussing the begetting of the Son and the reciprocal life-giving of the Trinity, I tried to preserve a robust space for the mystery of God, showing untainted respect for the divine incomprehensibility. I explained as much as I did for the purpose of re-presenting the Christian God to worshippers of the Christ-Idol, so that they can perceive the gulf between the god that dissolves and drives to restlessness and our God, who gives rest to all who cry out to him in faith and commands us to love others by bearing their burdens. In my arguments for my understanding of the Trinity I utilized the Scripture and the evidence of nature wherever I thought this appropriate, and at no time have I meant to render the incomprehensible as if it were so. St. Paul instructs us that we can know of the divine nature through what God has created, so that we can distinguish between what God reveals to us about himself from that of which we cannot speak. I emphasize this aspect of man's understanding of God, and of his experience of his creator, most emphatically: there is much of which men cannot speak, that far exceeds our feeble minds, a wisdom that makes us silent and a mystery that guides us to genuflect. Whether men speak of the Father, the Son, and the Holy Spirit as Persons, or of their relations of origin, or of their mutual life-giving, or of the great joy of union in the Spirit and the triumphant knowledge that God is love, they everywhere encounter the mystery of the God who condescends to their rational faculties while meeting them most directly in the heart, a place not without reason while reaching beyond reason.

In this the love of God was manifested toward us, that God sent His only begotten Son into the world, that we might live through Him. In this is love, not that we loved God but that He loved us and sent His Son to be the propitiation for our sins. God the Father sent the Son as a propitiation on our behalf, offering the Word, as the Word offers himself, for our redemption from sin, our victory over death, and the restoration of all things. Through this propitiation and our faithful imitation of it, our bearing of our crosses as the sacrifice of disciples who follow their master, we participate in the reconciliation of man with God and with his fellows. What sin had torn apart reverses course from its severance, returning toward the unity in which God created it. In propitiation men love God and others, they put the interests and needs of others above their own, they exercise the fundamental practice of placing themselves in the neighbor's position so that they can have compassion on him. Those who act in this way from faith die to themselves in Christ, a death that rises again as a new creation. "Therefore, if anyone is in Christ," writes St. Paul, "he is a new creation; old things have passed away; behold, all things have become new."

The work of Christ as propitiation conforms to the pattern of the Trinitarian life, the mutual life-giving of love. On the one hand, Christ's whole work is propitiation, it is all a sacrifice on our behalf from the incarnation in Bethlehem to the crucifixion and the resurrection. Just as we say that the whole life of the Trinity is love,

1 John: On Docetism and Resurrection

proclaiming with St. John that "God is love" and so glorifying him, we also say that the whole work of Christ is an offering for us, from the miracles and the parables to the commandments to the cross. On the other hand, the Trinitarian love consists in the passage from lower to higher and back, with the life-gift offered by the Son to the Father in the Spirit, which the Father reciprocates. Likewise, the propitiatory work of the Son passes from the affirmation of the lower to the suspension of the lower in the higher, which then gives back to the lower. "The lower" refers to all that builds up and gives life to men in this world, including man's body, his social life, and the soul as it is concerned with physical necessities. "The higher" refers to the orientation of man in soul and spirit to the next world, an orientation bound up with the lower world and which gives rest to it. The next world for the blessed is eternal and without sin, a world for the redeemed. The propitiation of Christ in the strict sense, his sacrifice on the cross, directs us to this eternal life, the spirit's participation in God. It leads us from the lower to the higher, and in the resurrection back to the lower. In that new life, the Christ gives power for his followers to become sons of God in this world, to become new creations defined by their love. In his life beyond the grave the Christ is the first fruits of the redeemed cosmos and the bestower of the Holy Spirit, who gives a foretaste of the next world in the present one.

As the propitiation of Christ reminds us of the triune God's life of love, and as, in the cross and resurrection, it progresses from lower to higher and back to lower, so his propitiation occurs within the context of hierarchy and not apart from it. Remove Christ's propitiation from its hierarchical setting and it loses its cogency, contradicting the savior's own understanding of the work that he came to do. He loves us profoundly, with the heart of God that longs for communion with his people, a love that presumes the hierarchical form as a stepping stone to unity. Thus Jesus Christ is the Son and lower before the Father as higher, and he is also the higher over his disciples as the lower. Jesus says that his food is to do the will of the One who sent him, he says that he brings a word from the Father. He said, "I do not seek my own will but the will of him who sent me," and throughout his ministry he recognizes his work as under the Father's direction. As St. Paul informs us, "It pleased the Father that in Him all the fullness should dwell, and by Him to reconcile all things to Himself, by Him, whether things on earth or things in heaven, having made peace through the blood of his cross." The Father gave to the Son his mission of salvation, and the Son fulfills it unto reconciliation. For this the Father glorifies the Son, so that he who lowered himself before the Father sees the latter humbled to him for glorification. The same Christ stands as Lord over his followers, his body the church, over which he reigns as king. He is also the church's savior, and it is subject to him as the wife to the husband. In it, the Christ receives the sacrifice of his followers as one higher. As they humble themselves before him, he humbles himself to them in the Holy Spirit, the indwelling of God according to man's nature. As the Christian's propitiation imitates his master's, the glorification of the Son by the Father extends to his disciples in inward renewal and, in the saints, the inner and outer life of the heavenly man. As the lower, Christians receive life back from the higher, just as life is given back to the Son in the Trinity.

As a predecessor to the higher, the lower in the work of Christ applies in multiple ways. First is the incarnation itself, the Christ's taking on of a body and life in this world, humbling himself to the vicissitudes of man's experience. In this way he affirms the law of man's form, the shape of his existence in the present age and his creaturely finitude. It is a wonderful miracle and a great mystery that God became one of us, and a great love that he did so. This love affirms man's nature in its goodness as created by God, a goodness that remains despite the blight of sin. Christ takes up the nature of man in every aspect save its sinfulness, he accomplishes the lower step in his work by assuming the nature he means to redeem. He becomes the law of man so that in it he can fulfill the law of God. Second, the Christ supports that same law of man through miracles of healing. He cures those with fevers, he heals the blind, he frees the lepers from their ailments, he casts out demons, he raises the dead. In all of these he affirms the lower law of life in this world, he proclaims the goodness of what God has made by his mercy. Bodily health is good because the body is good, and men should seek that health. Sight is good, hearing is good, the ability to walk is good, the ability to speak is good, soundness of mind is good, the peace of the spirit in God is good, to say nothing of the works of creation possible to man as he labors, and as he bears and raises children. All this is good, and the great Physician acknowledges and seeks its goodness. By his miracles he affirms the lower form of the body and the present world despite its fallenness. The third assertion of the lower leading to the higher involves the way of salvation as it initially passes through the law. Christ begins with this lower as he issues his commands, directing men to wisdom and piety in the Sermon on the Mount, warning them against excess and selfishness on the plain, and instructing them to love one another at the Passover. He gives the commandment that is eternal life, guiding men on the path toward by God by leading them to this humility. His criticisms of the Pharisees and the lawyers do not once denounce the law, leaving it intact. Everywhere he supports the law and offers it as a means to salvation, for he came not to abolish but to fulfill.

These three converge upon the higher to which they lead and to which they are handed over, a higher that suspends the lower as it exists beyond the latter's boundary. That higher is the cross, which breaks at death from the incarnation, the miracles of healing, and the commands of the law. In the incarnation God had joined himself with man, affirming the lower nature of his creature, the body as well as the soul. So much did God care for his creation that the Son emptied himself and took on the form of a slave, and now he suffers unto death. In this final and ultimate lowliness, the Lord gives up his bodily life, but this apparent contradiction of that life transcends it in order to renew it toward eternity. His perishing severs the divine and human natures so that the death of the latter can be gathered into the indestructible life of the former. At his death, his followers shuddered in bewilderment because they did not understand this, they did not readily absorb the wisdom that the harrowing lowliness of death conceals within it the highest form of life.

One might argue that this death contradicts life. As the mockers stated at the cross, "You who would destroy the Temple and build it in three days, save yourself, and come down from the cross!" And the priests echoed them saying, "He saved others, Himself he cannot save." He healed others, he opened the eyes of the blind, the lame walked and the dumb spoke, so how does he not descend from the cross? Did the Christ not come that men should have life, and have it abundantly? He did, and while the miracles attest to this life, they do not reveal its apex. In its higher form that life is spiritual, the healing of the soul for eternity. Thus the Christ healed diseases and also forgave sins, noting the priority of the latter as he did so. Beyond these he accomplished the great miracle, a resurrection that presumes death and thus temporarily suspends the possibility of miracles. He who affirmed the health of the sick and released men from bodily affliction now gives up the body, handing over the work of healing to the grave. This lowliness bears within it the higher that is the Christ's fundamental work. He does not die for death's sake, nor is his the wrongful death of a zealot. His death means the fleeting rejection of a lower granting of life in order to secure a higher one, the denial of lower miracles in order to accomplish the supreme miracle. His miracles healed faithful individuals, while the crucifixion points toward the comprehensive healing of all things, the unsurpassable miracle in which the Christ gathers all things in unity, restoring to life that which was doomed to die.

The Christ also suspends the law in his sacrifice at the cross. The law upholds life in this world while pointing to the next, but the sacrifice points most directly to the next world and, inasmuch as man himself is the sacrifice, cuts off his relationship with the law. The Christ obeyed as long as he lived, but dead men do not continue in earthly obedience. In his death, the Christ does not give concrete commands as when standing on the Mount or the plain. Although he commanded that his disciples take up their crosses and follow him, and although he does hang on the cross implicitly as a command that the faithful join him there, this should not obscure the essential nature of the cross as propitiation or offering. The accent of the cross lies not on the "do this" of the command to believers but the "I have done for you" of the sacrifice, of Christ's offering on behalf of undeserving sinners. There the lower of obedience passes into the higher of sacrifice, and the faith present in obedience passes into the higher form that is rest in God, that trusts that Christ's work on the cross has secured salvation from the grave and sin while giving power to believers to become children of God. Obedience is necessary for salvation as a lower element, whereas sacrifice and the faith of rest are higher, the essence of redemption as accomplished by God for men. The Christ's saving issuance of the law leads upward to the saving propitiation, an upward path of salvation that humbles the believer as he progresses upon it.

Out of the tomb, a formless void in eyes of the physical and visible world, emerges the gift of life given back by the higher. The Christ restores the incarnation as God and man come together again, the first instance of the reconciliation of all things is witnessed, and salvation comes forth from the abyss with eternal power, the promise of immortality. Jesus said, "My kingdom is not of this world," and he said, "for this cause I have come into the world, that I should bear witness to the truth." In that kingdom, and in the light of its truth, there is no sickness or death. Neither is there sin, for men abide in union with the creator. The resurrection gives back to the present, lower world by spreading abroad the power of that higher one, planting God's presence in men's hearts. If men wish to experience salvation, they should hearken to the way of the savior. As he lowered himself before God, let them lower themselves before him, and as he engaged the law as the lower preliminary to the sacrifice, let them struggle with obedience and battle the passions as the lower preliminary to the eucharist. Let them humbly hope that God, as a loving and merciful Lord, will give back to his creatures according to his wisdom.

Men live through Christ as they walk in obedience and struggle, in perseverance of affliction and temptations, toward rest in worship. There they receive the grace of Christ in the mystery, then returning to the struggle refreshed, buoyed by the divine presence and the love of God shed in the heart. They might be tempted to bring their obediences as so many small sacrifices, laying them before God at the table. But humble men do not think of this, not counting their good deeds as if God owed them recompense, indeed not recognizing their good deeds at all. They immediately perceive that their obediences amount to nothing, that man brings his sins and failings, his voluntary and involuntary trespasses, his transgressions of thought, word, and deed for which he cannot atone. He knows that his most valiant efforts will not come near attaining salvation and he cries out to God for mercy. Understanding this, believers come humbly, asking that God will accept the offering of bread and wine and send down the Holy Spirit upon them in return. In the higher, in the eucharistic sacrifice, men cease their activity and rest in God. They have faith in the sacrifice of Christ, handing their salvation over to him. In response to the faith, hope, and love of those who rest in him, the Lord gives the grace to become his children.

The evil one tries with all his might to invert the order of higher and lower, of rest over work, of faith in the sacrifice over obedience. He does this by trying to make rest into another form of law, distorting its character so that the "thou shalt" overshadows and squeezes out the rest implicit in sacrifice. When the Pharisees would not allow Jesus to heal on the Sabbath, they succumbed to this inversion of rest and law. They knew that rest is holy and that God commands the Jews to do no work on the holy day. Yet they said in their hearts that Jews must follow the commandment even if it denied rest to their neighbors, leaving them to their burdens. Thus they placed the commandment to rest *qua* law against the commandment to love the neighbor, giving him rest, and raised the former injunction above the neighbor in need. This perverts the law's relation to rest, as though man's first obligation consisted in following the law rather than loving his neighbor, making sacrifices for the neighbor's rest. The end of the law, however, is always man's sacrifice for others, loving God with all his heart, soul, mind, and strength, and his neighbor as himself. The commandment exists in orientation toward the giving of rest, and of man making himself a sacrifice as did his Lord. God does not give rest as subordinate to the commandment, as if following the commandment to rest justified increasing the burdens of others. After picking the heads of grain on the Sabbath, Jesus expresses this principle by saying that "the Sabbath was made for man, not man for the Sabbath." Man stands over the Sabbath inasmuch as God gave it for his rest, so that man can rest on that day. "Man was not made for the Sabbath": the Sabbath does not stand over man as a law, task, or burden, as if his principle task consists in obedience to the commandment *qua* commandment.

In the docetic age, the evil one has secretly transformed this Pharisaic misunderstanding, again using rest as the veil for new burdens. Under "justification by faith alone," the proclamation that salvation is entirely rest and divorced from man's effort, he has hidden the limitless law. He has taken faith, rest in God, and the sacrifice, and concealed within them the infinite, such that man must reorient the world toward that infinitude. Docetic man's "Sabbath rest" bears down on him with the whole weight of a new salvation, the construction of a world without sin and death to the greatest extent possible. He must translate the true, inner equality of men before God, wherein each can be a home of the Holy Spirit in the heart, into the ersatz external equality of all before society and state. He must imbue this lower and fallen world with heaven, a burden too great to bear and at which he has already failed. He must save himself, he must work until all is accomplished while his goals will never come to fruition and in their place he discovers ruin. The way of salvation does not change, and docetic man long ago abandoned that way. Nor do the tricks of the evil one change, as he drives the docetic world this way and that, perverting the way of rest into the infinite law.

Beloved, if God so loved us, we also ought to love one another. No one has seen God at any time. If we love one another, God abides in us, and His love has been perfected in us. The Trinitarian love has a hierarchical form inasmuch as the Persons, distinguished by their relations of origin, love one another through the recognition of the Father as higher and the Son and Spirit as lower. The salvation effected through Christ also recognizes the Father as higher and the members of Christ's body, the church, as lower. In addition, salvation as lived by the believer involves a lower element in obedience and a higher, fundamentally saving element in sacrifice, the rest of faith. In all of these the lower humbles itself before the higher, which then humbles itself to the lower, returning the gift originally directed from lower to higher. The Son gives to the Father, who gives back to the Son; the church gives to the Christ and Christians give to one another, receiving for their sacrifices the mystical presence of the Holy Spirit and inner consolation; the law stills itself, the work of obedience pauses, and the forgiveness of sins in the sacrifice gives rest to the believer and reinvigorates him for obedience. The God that Christians serve and the way of salvation he has given through his Son imply a hierarchically-grounded love.

God created man in his image, to live in a communion that imitates the divine. Just as the Persons of the Trinity, though equal, cast off that equality in the threefold work of love, God made men to do the same, casting off their equality as men in order to humble themselves, lower before higher and higher to lower. In this way men, like the divine Persons, love one another hierarchically despite being equal in nature. As God so loved us, fellow Christians, let us love one another. As God the Son gave himself as a propitiation, let us offer ourselves as propitiations, as servants to our master and for the love of God and our neighbors. The Christ has shown us that this propitiatory love occurs through hierarchy, through the mutual humility and reciprocal giving of higher and lower, that this love is thus the higher achieved through hierarchy as the lower. "No one has ever seen God. If we love one another, God abides in us, and his love has been perfected in us." We approximate the vision of God as we give reciprocally, lower to higher to lower. This is perhaps as close as we shall come to seeing God socially, and in this God abides in us and his love is perfected in us. Without humility before the naturally hierarchical shape of our existence—of our nature as soul and body, of the cosmos in which God has placed us, and of our salvation from sin—we will neither see God nor love one another.

The Christ nowhere denies the importance of hierarchy, nor does he undermine it in his teachings. He has disciples, he supports the priesthood, he assumes the context of masters and servants, and he affirms the legitimacy of the state as from God. He tells the Christian not to be proud of his work, at the end of his labors remembering that "when you have done all those things which you were commanded, say, 'We are unprofitable servants. We have done what was our duty to do.'" Jesus also teaches that "a disciple is not above his teacher, nor a servant above his master. It is enough for a disciple that he be like his teacher, and a servant be like his master." He adds elsewhere that the Gentile authorities exercise lordship over their subjects, implying that they glory in their superiority. "But not so among you," he instructs the disciples. "On the contrary, he who is greatest among you, let him be as the younger, and he who governs as he who serves. For who is greater, he who sits at the table, or he who serves? Is it not he who sits at the table? Yet I am among you as the One who serves." Jesus makes the last point not to eradicate or undermine the hierarchical form of love, but to emphasize its true character. The higher who have no love gather up what the lower gives and hoard it to themselves, keeping more than their share of power, honor, and wealth. But it is not so among us, Christians. If we find ourselves to be the higher, we must not see this higher position as something to hold on to, but humble ourselves to the lower and make ourselves his servant. We are not to lord over others, though we might have power, and we are not to deprive the needy of their bread, the worker of his wages, or the child of loving-kindness. The lower have given, humbling themselves before us in such cases, so we should hurry to humble ourselves to them, forgetting our position and remembering the good that others have done for us. The Christ excelled his disciples in holiness but humbled himself to them, as to us, in service.

We should do likewise, if we are rich, lest we lose our consolation. Let us do the same, if we are full, lest we go hungry. And we should do the same, if we govern and hold authority, lest we reap the harvest of oppression. If we return the gift of the lower with mercy as higher, making ourselves the one who serves rather than the one sitting, we shall receive mercy. This is difficult and against the inclinations of many, who hold to pride of place and say, not without reason, that it is their role to preserve right and order. But they should especially humiliate themselves inwardly before others and seek contrition in thought, word, and deed, so that their judgments proceed from a heart of love and not from self-will.

In the same manner Jesus says to Pilate, and by extension to all political authority, "You could have no power at all . . . unless it had been given you from above." The political authority comes from God, an authority meant to govern men, at the very least, by restraining the wickedness of the sinful. As St. Paul admonishes, "Let every soul be subject to the governing authorities. For there is no authority except from God, and the authorities that exist are appointed by God." For this reason one should not resist the authorities, nor should one do evil works so as not to incur their wrath. "For he is God's minister to you for good . . . for he is God's minister, an avenger to execute wrath on him who practices evil." St. Paul continues that we pay taxes for this reason, that governors attend to a duty established by God. His concluding words are of great interest: "Render therefore to all their due: taxes to whom taxes are due, customs to whom customs, fear to whom fear, honor to whom honor." In this passage St. Paul implies the form of reciprocation appropriate to government in the wake of the fall, when men bite and kill one another. Through the punishment of violence, the government secures the peace necessary for love to flourish, in this negative way supporting that love. The subjects give to the authorities the taxes, customs, fear, and honor due to them as the higher put in place by God, and the authorities give the gift back by administering justice and keeping the peace. The public form of existence involves the lower and the higher who are equal *qua* men, but who, in their assigned roles, take on positions of inferior and superior for the sake of mutual life-giving, a recognition born of reciprocal dependence and a bond of affection secured through the humility of justice. In that justice none exploits or offends his neighbor, be he superior or subordinate, recognizing the neighbor's due according to both his station and his humanity.

A similar reciprocal bond marks Christian marriage. "Wives, submit to your husbands, as to the Lord. For the husband is the head of the wife, as also Christ is the head of the Church; and He is the Savior of the body." As the church is the lower before Christ, "so let the wives be subject to their own husbands in everything." At the same time, "Husbands, love your wives, just as Christ also loved the Church and gave himself for her, that he might sanctify and cleanse her," and that he should present her as "holy and without blemish . . . he who loves his wife loves himself." St. Paul enjoins that the lower shall give obedience and respect while the higher shall give sacrificial love. The woman shall admit her lower place while the man bears the greater burden spiritually. By his position he carries the spiritual well-being and guidance of his wife (as well as his children), and he shall spare no effort in sanctifying her, not letting a day pass in which he has not led her toward the holiness that God desires for her. The lower gives to the higher, being humbled before him, and the higher is then humbled to the lower not as the one who sits but as he who serves, imitating the Christ who led his disciples as one who served.

It is shameful to need to speak of parents and children in their roles as superiors and subordinates, to need to declare that, insofar as parents abdicate their places as higher over the children as lower, they also abdicate their love for their sons and daughters. "Children, obey your fathers," St. Paul writes. "And you, fathers, do not provoke your children to wrath, but bring them up in the training and admonition of the Lord." The child gives the parent obedience and honor, obeying the father's command and respecting the love of the mother, humbling himself before his biological forebearers. They humble themselves to the child in return by bestowing spiritual and material benefits, first and foremost the direction of the mind and heart toward God. In the best cases, the parents orient the child toward spiritual treasures over material means. By their habits they teach the virtue of humility, placing the good of others before their own; they instill a regular practice of prayer and the inner pursuit of God; they gird the child to face afflictions patiently and to receive blessings with gratitude; they encourage him to seek good and avoid evil, to hate sin and all transgression and to love good and all virtue, to walk in the light of Christ through the guidance of his All-Holy Mother and the saints. After this the parents care for material goods, food, clothing, and shelter, and an education toward responsibility and charity. The child as lower hands his life over to the parents as higher, and in that handing over receives his life back bettered, enhanced by the wisdom of years and the love of faithful guardians.

In the church, in the social order, and in the family the Scripture prefers hierarchy. It teaches that the higher and the lower exist and that they love one another in mutual humility. "But," you say, "this concerns the world after the Fall. What about the world before the Fall? What of man's nature unstained by sin?" I respond that it makes no difference, that hierarchy existed prior to sin, and that God reinforced the natural hierarchy in various ways after the Fall as a correction for the chaos introduced by sin.

God put all things in their places at the creation, fixing the fish, the birds, and the land animals in their proper homes, as well as the sun, moon, and stars in the sky and Adam and Eve in Eden. In addition to this assignment of location, God instituted a vertical order, bestowing upon man "dominion over the fish of the sea, over the birds of heaven, over the cattle, and over all the earth, and over every creeping thing that moves on the earth." After the superiority of man over the animals, God gave to both the plants of the ground, so that "every seed-bearing herb that sows seed on the face of all the earth, and every tree whose fruit yields seed" belongs to man for food, while God has given "every green plant as food" to the animals. Man stands at the highest above the animals, just as men and animals together reside above the plants. Above all of these is God, who rules over the physical and spiritual realities that he has created as Lord alone. Man therefore exists within a hierarchy, receiving the place that God has assigned to him vis-à-vis other creatures and dwelling in the particular place, Eden, that God gave him to inhabit.

The man and the woman are equal, seeming to stand apart from the natural hierarchy of the creation. In making mankind, including the woman as well as her husband, God says that they are made "in Our image, according to Our likeness . . . in the image of God He made him; male and female He made them." The man and the woman bear God's image equally; in essence and nature *qua* humanity, nothing raises the one above the other. This is fundamental and not to be overlooked. It is also not the whole story, as we see in Genesis 2. There God decides to make a helper for Adam, taking one of his ribs from him while he slept and forming the woman from it. God then brought her to him as he had done the other animals that Adam had named, and he named her. "This is now bone of my bones and flesh of my flesh. She shall be called Woman, for she was taken out of Man . . . and the two shall become one flesh." That Adam names the woman proves his superiority over her, a superiority subordinate to their more fundamental equality. God establishes this subordinate hierarchy for the sake of love, as a structure necessary to the two becoming one and as a creaturely imitation of the subordinate hierarchy within the Trinity. As the Son is humbled before the Father in the Spirit, and as the Father is humbled to the Son, so the woman is humbled before the man who humbles himself to her. Through the mutual humility born of hierarchy they become one flesh, the woman respecting and obeying the husband who loves her as Christ does his body. Or does the mystery of Christ and the church, which St. Paul relates to the mystery of marriage, exemplify a fallen manner of human love? Does it not rather express the perfected form of the marital union? As the mystery of Christ and the church presumes hierarchy, and as that hierarchy finds a parallel in marriage, so the marital hierarchy belongs to God's original design rather than being a consequence of the Fall.

Likewise with children prior to the Fall, if there had been such. When we speculate on this, imagining a sinless child born to Adam, the child would certainly possess virtues unseen in us sinners. Among these virtues would be obedience to parents, as God commands at Sinai and as St. Paul echoes in Ephesians. If the well-behaved but sinful child follows the orders of father and mother, the child perfect in virtue would be perfect in obedience. The freedom of the child from sin does not free him from authority or the humility needed to be obedient to it. Rather, in this way the child learns what it means to love as the lower, to be humbled before parents who are humbled to the child. The parent still provides guidance and wisdom as well as physical sustenance, on the other hand, so that the reciprocal love of parents and children does not differ in form whether before or after the Fall. From youth the child would absorb the movement of divine love through the hierarchy of mutual humility and self-giving, the secondary affirmation of lower and higher beneath a fundamental equality of nature. For the child bears the image of God no less than the parent, and is no less human than father or mother.

If only man had rested in his place, if only he had been thankful for the gifts that God had bestowed upon him! In sinning Adam and Eve raised themselves up illegitimately, abdicating their places. When Adam decided that he should be like God, he distanced himself from his creaturely abode on earth as well as his particular place, Eden. He sought immortality wrongly, not through obedience to the creator but by usurping the creator's place. Eve also raised herself up unrighteously toward God and thereby against the divine order, including her subordination to Adam. God had created all things to rest in their places, both in the realms that He gave them as their homes and in their places in the natural hierarchy. The introduction of sin greatly disturbed that rest and threw all things into disorder. Man no longer knew his proper humility before God, the woman lost her place before God and the man, the communion of man with the animals was broken, and the ground rose up in revolt. Faced with this rupture and the prospect of further descent toward destruction, what was the loving Father to do? Those who raise themselves up in pride must fall, facing the perdition that their hands have wrought. But it was the work of God to use the punishments to draw man back to his place, re-affirming his connection to rest and his place wherever this was possible. He greatly increased the woman's pain, as "in pain [she] shall bring forth children." This pain reminds her that she sought life wrongly, outside of God's design. It ties her to her human nature as it ties her to her body, reminding her that she produces life through that nature and not apart from it. God also reprimands her with respect to Adam: "Your recourse will be to your husband, and he shall rule over you." In this way God reinforces and reconstitutes the subordinate hierarchy of man over woman, threatened as it is by the Fall's unleashing of wickedness. The woman loses a certain freedom before her husband and bears a certain need for him, but this is not so that the man should rule harshly or that the woman should grovel as a slave, as if the fundamental equality between them had been lost. God issues the consequence so that the hierarchy should retain the strength necessary to facilitate the reciprocal love that He desires for husband and wife. In this chastisement God directs the woman back to her place of rest in his order, so that she should learn to love him and others in it.

It is no different for man as he endures his passions and engages the soil. When Adam eats the fruit, he rejects his nature as a creature as his soul exceeds its knowledge, breaking mysteriously from his body. Adam means to rise in spirit as though he were God, but in doing so he cuts the tie to his bodily life. As a result, the body fills with passions and temptations—a punishment not mentioned directly in Genesis but apropos here—that distract the soul from communion with God and that compel him to humble himself toward his flesh if he would conquer them. Both the man and the woman after the Fall encounter the body as the locus of bidirectional struggle: they must look downward to the body in order to fight the passions, acknowledging in this that they cannot win the conflict apart from God's grace. This admission forces them to turn upward to God with the humility they forgot at the Fall. "God have mercy on me, a sinner, and release me from my passions," the man prays, at once suffering the punishment for his sins and remembering God as his place of rest, his Lord and Master. God thereby binds man to his body as he binds him to Himself as the source of joy and salvation. God secondly reminds man of the land as his creaturely place, the physical location for his bodily life. To the man God says, "cursed is the ground in your labors. In toil you shall eat from it all the days of your life." The ground revolts against the man, it produces thorns and thistles for him, but God gives him this struggle not only for punishment. It reminds him of his place and bids him to find rest there despite the struggle. As the woman must recall her rest before the man, he must recall his rest on the land. Like her, he sought to raise himself up, forgetting his bodily existence with its limitations. Like her, he must return to that place humbly so that God will bless him, again giving him a share in the production of life. Even death, the consequence for man raising himself beyond his boundaries, the horror that many wish to escape, reminds him of his place as a creature. It proves that he will never be like God by disobedience and that humility before the creator is proper to him.

Some would say that hierarchy among men results from the Fall, but the introduction of sin only reinforces the need for man to recognize his place. The hierarchy already existed between men and women and would have existed between parents and children. Arguably, it also would have existed in Eden as a commonwealth, had there been enough men to populate it. This conclusion arises, as with the others, from the form of love within the Trinity and man's bearing of the divine image. If the Father, Son, and Holy Spirit love in a hierarchy of mutual humility in which lower and higher draw toward one another in reciprocal giving, should men who bear the divine image not love in the same way? And do they not love God as they love their neighbor, bearing the latter's burdens? The form of government in a world without sin would establish higher over lower for the sake of mutual rest and self-giving, serving as a vehicle for man's imitation of God. The words of St. Ambrose well describe this "most perfect state of things" among men, although he does not tie the form of government he describes to Eden or the condition of sinlessness:

> "In the beginning men exercised their political power given to them by nature, following the example of bees, so that work and dignity were common. Individuals learnt to share their duties and divide their authority and rewards, so that no one was excluded either from honors or from work. This was the most perfect state of things inasmuch as no one could become arrogant by possessing power permanently or crushed by a prolonged submission. Promotion is made without envy, according to the order of the offices and the measure of time. Offices that are given by rotation are more tolerable; no one would dare to lay too heavy a burden on another who would succeed him in his office and

from whom he could receive in turn much harm. No burden would seem too heavy to anyone if he knows that eventually he will obtain honor."[13]

In this scheme no men are permanently higher while others remain permanently lower. The rotation of offices ensures the just distribution of burdens as well as the proper apportionment of dignity, or as St. Ambrose puts it, "equality in work and humility in power," so that all men learn the necessity of giving to their neighbors, whether they do so from the higher position or the lower. In all cases, the purpose of the office is to train men in the virtues of humility, obedience, and submission before God and the common good. The political order serves as a stepping stone to propitiation as it teaches its adherents the initial lesson of limit, a first step in self-giving oriented toward the height of sacrifice. This is the profoundest reason for government for men formed in God's image, a reason tied inevitably to the hierarchical structure of the order so formed. In the reciprocal giving of higher and lower, the political world reminds men of the divine love and orients them toward participation in it. "No one has ever seen God at any time. If we love one another, God abides in us, and His love has been perfected in us."

Like the hierarchy of man over wife, the hierarchy of government is reinforced after the Fall. In this case the rulers receive the power of punishment, which they wield against the wicked and against lawbreakers. For those who might disturb the common peace or unjustly harm their neighbors, the government given to draw men toward love assumes the additional duty of inspiring the fear of evil deeds, bearing the sword to ensure peace and an order in which goodwill can prosper. This new power turns men back to the humility with which they should regard one another. God gives it, as he gives certain of the punishments after the Fall, to reign in the forces of disruption released there, guiding men toward their natural places. If government leads men positively toward mutual humility prior to the Fall, after the introduction of sin it also dissuades them negatively from mutual aggression.

If hierarchy belongs to God's love, and if God has instilled it in human relationships for their good, what of St. Paul's assertion that "you are all sons of God through faith in Christ Jesus. For as many of you as were baptized into Christ have put on Christ. There is neither Jew nor Greek, there is neither slave nor free, there is neither male nor female; for you are all one in Christ Jesus"?

St. Paul writes this in response to the temptation of the Jews to raise themselves up vis-à-vis Gentiles due to their possession of the law. He argues that the law precedes faith and is superseded by it, as "before faith came, we were kept under guard by the law, kept for the faith which would afterward be revealed. Therefore the law was our tutor to bring us to Christ, that we might be justified by faith." He is battling the notion that the Jews could use the law, the way of humility unto Christ, as a means for raising themselves up above others. "For not even those who are circumcised keep the law,

---

13. *Hexameron*, V, 15, 52 (Text: CSEL 32.1.178), quoted in Phan, 166.

but they desire to have you circumcised that they may boast in your flesh. But God forbid that I should boast except in the cross of our Lord Jesus Christ, by whom the world has been crucified to me, and I to the world." On the contrary, St. Paul argues that men should be crucified to one another, bearing one another's burdens. As he states in 2 Corinthians, "For the love of Christ compels us, because we judge thus: that if One died for all, then all died; and He died for all, that those who live should live no longer for themselves, but for Him who died for them and rose again." He continues that "from now on, we regard no one according to the flesh . . . if anyone is in Christ, he is a new creation; old things have passed away; behold all things have become new."

There is no longer slave or free, Jew or Greek, male or female because all have died in Christ. They are no longer judged according to the flesh, and their differences are nullified inasmuch as they live no longer for themselves but for Him. They do not affirm themselves over against one another, as if to say "I am man" or "I am woman" or "I am a Jew" or "I am Greek," as if in competition or self-justification, but they crucify themselves for one another. How could they, then, rise against the hierarchical order that binds them? That order is temporarily suspended not because all are above hierarchy or have rejected it out of pride, as a limit upon them. It is obsolete because all live in humility, so that the order of higher over lower disappears before the order of mutual humility, of all from their various positions taking the place of the lower to bear the burdens of the neighbor viewed as higher. Following the love in the Trinity, in this manner human love transcends hierarchy while preserving it as a lower and necessary structure. Men return to that structure reinvigorated by love of their fellows, whom they view as sources of consolation and rest.

These moments of love occur mystically in the present world. The Jew is outwardly a Jew, the Greek is outwardly a Greek, man is man, woman is woman. They do not leave their bodies, they do not cease to be as they are. Nor is the hierarchical order in which they live obliterated or refuted. Yet they become mystically unified with God in the heart and the spirit, they become one spirit or one soul, and the priority of the physical existence, of the apprehension of the physical in which men live as their default experience, recedes before the priority of God and the eternal. The man humbled before God in all things, and who has sacrificed himself, experiences God in all things and loves his neighbors equally, without concern for their outward circumstances or characteristics. When all love each other in this equality, a mystical union is achieved that does away with hierarchy temporarily without denying its necessity for the physical order, even the order in which this love is achieved.

Prayer is a primary form of equality, and perhaps its purest form, just as the inner is the properly egalitarian realm. In another of the attempts to infuse the lower order with the characteristics of the higher, illegitimately translating the infinitude of the soul to the visible world, docetists have sought to transfer the equality meant for the inner experience of God to the social order. God cares not whether one comes as man or woman, Jew or Greek, slave or free, rich or poor, intelligent or dumb. He cares only for the humility that casts aside all worldly cares in order to stand in his presence and, concentrated there, seeks forgiveness for one's sins while praying for the neighbor. God comes to all equally as they come to him, he enters the hearts of all equally as they open their hearts to him, he heals all equally as they receive his grace and obey his prescriptions, he gives his joy to all equally as they love him. Though he might give one gift here and another there, he bestows without discrimination his love and the compassion of his guiding hand. This equality, which extends into eternity, supersedes all that docetic man dreams about justice and a better world.

If the social order should bind men together rather than driving them apart, there must be higher and lower among them. All people—men, women, and children—should rest in their places and give humbly of themselves. Anything more specific than this regarding society I do not venture to say. Whether one, few, or many should rule, and what should be the form of government, and how men should determine the particulars of their relations, they should learn from the Scriptures, the Fathers, the church canons, and their God-given reason. Only may they avoid the temptations to pleasure, greed, and glory by which the evil one and his demons would deceive them, and with which Docetism misleads them. May they rather love one another, that the Holy Spirit may dwell within them.

Epilogue

IF THE FOREGOING HAS sufficiently warned the reader of the presence of Docetism and its designs upon the world; if he fears the wrath of God against the spirit of dissolution and those deceived by it; and if he desires a way of being submitted to the law of his nature and seeking the divine love, a way of reconciliation with both his God and his neighbor; then I commend to him certain steps to guide him along this path. It is unwise to embark upon these too quickly. For most men their inculcation will require time and patience. Let those who spring up with haste beware lest their roots do not go deep. Equally, let those who flourish along the way regard their slower brethren with compassion, making room for their weakness.

Let the man who would reject Docetism withdraw from the churches corrupted by it and adopt a new worship. The docetic spirit has infiltrated if not defined the churches of the West, Protestant and Catholic. It has exploited their language in the service of the Christ-Idol and perverted their understanding of God, driving parishes into decay. It has abused the churches as its unwitting theological advocates. The doctrines of the Orthodox East alone have not been a theological party to the docetic spirit, having maintained the traditions of the Fathers from antiquity. In them will man find the resurrection, under their rule he will rediscover God and the soul. To the best of his ability man should turn to the East and find his home in the arms of Holy Church.

As a member of Christ's body the convert should learn to pray, bearing within himself the thoughts given as a means to God, practicing them until they have shaped his mental world and punctured his heart. When prayer has trained him toward humility, when he approaches others after praying for their well-being in a spirit of gentleness, when he has learned to fast and to regard others as higher and himself as lower, then he is best prepared to embark on the remaining steps.

The man who wishes to escape Docetism should leave the modern city, cutting off dreams of "a better world" or "social improvement" in his heart. The city proclaims love, brotherhood, and progress, but its reality is loneliness, anonymity, and divorce, along with the temptation of the flesh. In the city man forgets his nature and its law, living as though he were universal. Inasmuch as he is able, the lover of God must trade this socially constructed and virtual world for one that is natural and substantive, not because the natural world is freedom from the infinite law and thereby from all law, but because it frees man from the infinite by subjecting him to a law that is merciful.

Having relocated toward the natural world, man should submit to its rhythms and apprehend its ways. As far as it lies within his power, he should disavow his total reliance on modern conveniences and comforts, his dependence on universalized means of life, and the habits that distract and disintegrate his nature. He will again know the land, the sunrise and the sunset, the heat and the cold, as tutors in the weight of his humanity and as expressions of the grace of God. In these circumstances he can strive for a life of rest in God and his neighbor, a life of mutual support, encouragement, and love. Patience is needed especially here because docetic ways are powerful and men are addicted and intransigent. The natural world moves to its own tempo and man must approach it humbly, as a student.

A warning: do not leave the city or attempt conformity to the natural world in the name of Christ without converting to the Eastern Church. Shall the Christian work to gather and reaffirm his bodily life while leaving the body of Christ scattered and lifeless? The unity of man as a nature presupposes the unity of the body of Christ inasmuch as men understand their constitution as God's creatures. A second warning: there may be some who misunderstand, criticize, or persecute those who take this path. There will be those who regard it as foolishness and stupidity. Pray for these and show them kindness, just as Christ prayed for those who sent him to the cross. A warning and exhortation: at all times, and with all your heart, abase yourself in your own eyes and put yourself beneath others, not raising yourself up. Do not castigate others in your pride, do not curse them, do not dare to call yourself saved and they damned, do not think of them as anything less than objects of the love of God, in whom you rest. Such haughtiness leads to destruction.

Grace and peace be to those whose faith leads them on this path, whom the fear of God moves as willing servants, and who thirst for the life everlasting. May the love that perseveres through all hardship envelop them, that they might be born not of human decision or a husband's will, but from God, and receive the power to become children of God.

Appendix to the Academics

ALTHOUGH SPIRITUAL TORPOR HAS long dogged him, man has yet to see that his most cherished values and their projects are the means of his despair. It is a sorrowful task to reveal this state of affairs to him, to point out how his way of being antagonizes his nature. The deception and its annulment of man's being I call Docetism because in these I see a variation of the ancient and once-conquered heresy. The meaning of modern society, specifically its fractured and ever-shifting religious landscape, its love of freedom and equality, and its scientific profundity, exemplifies the docetic spirit and its contradiction of the mercy of God. It will disturb readers to hear that the social and political kingdom that they have sought is a realm of deprivation, and that the universal and boundaryless community that they celebrate is a slave to indefinition. The modern edifice has been built upon sand docetically disguised as rock, and my task in this volume has been to sound out Docetism's inner cacophony while suggesting a foundation for resurrection, elucidating an understanding of the Christian God removed from docetic distortions. I offer my words not as a theological exercise but as a warning and a promise: there is a religious meaning within history that bodes ill for contemporary men, but life still persists through death.

The docetic scientist of history is like a man watching a motion picture that he presumes as reality. His dissatisfaction with what he sees prompts him to walk back to the projector and stop the show. Taking the film in hand, he announces his discovery: "Ah! The film is composed of a multitude of isolated and distinct frames. The task of knowing is to recognize the frames according to their differences and focus on what makes each distinctive. As for the continuity between the frames and the coherence of the story they tell, this is an illusion produced by the projector, without basis in the thing itself." In this way the historian reduces history to a series of disconnected statements without overarching significance. With every frame that he studies, concentrating on its details, the less moral and spiritual worth that he can extract from it and the more useless it becomes for understanding his nature. At the same time the historian misses the mark in taking the motion picture as reality. Just as the film flattens the depth of man's existence, compressing three dimensions into two, so the scientist's perspective allows for space and time in the physical world but denies the potency of spiritual forces. His science permits an emaciated reflection of these powers if it acknowledges them at all, turning from them to what it can quantify according to its assumptions. The docetic historian then finds what his method provides him, proclaiming that there is no spirit at work in history nor an intrinsic connection between one age and the next. The exactitude of his method progresses until he finds little substance in his work other than the nullification of its subject.

These scientists of history, as well as the remainder of our docetic intelletuals, will find much in this work that is not to their liking. Their science divides the world at theoretical junctures that I see as unified and they will decry this unification as methodological naivety. The intellectuals will object in particular to my identification of the form of the spiritual law, which is interior, religious, and pertaining to the soul, with the dynamic at the heart of the modern social and political order. To argue that there is a form of spiritual law at work in medieval confession and that this form reaches its conclusion in Luther and Calvin is one thing. To say that the same form of law drives the political order from the Enlightenment through Marx into the present is another. The second claim will strike the academics as an absurdity because it overlooks the complex social process that they suppose to be the stuff of historical development. They will scoff at the replacement of this complexity with a singular and unifying principle drawn from the spiritual order.

With regard to the connection between the spiritual and the political orders the skeptics should attend to the words of Harold Berman, one of their most respected legal theorists:

> "Thus the Roman Catholic belief in the infusion of divine and natural law into legal institutions was carried on by Lutheranism, but only into secular legal institutions and not into ecclesiastical . . . For Protestantism, in both its Lutheran and Calvinist forms, God remained a God of justice, and the body of ecclesiastical and secular law of 'medieval' Europe (as it came to be called in the sixteenth century), was to a large extent carried over into the law of the 'modern' state." (*Law and Revolution I*, 197)

Berman finds the origin of the Western legal tradition in the canon law of the medieval Catholic Church, which influenced marriage, inheritance, property, and contracts. More importantly, canon law was the first attempt in the West at a systematic law, a law both comprehensive and exact. This method amounted to the "infusion of divine and natural law into legal institutions," or the introduction of the law into the Roman Church so that the latter matured as a distinctly legal apparatus in addition to its liturgical and theological functions. Berman asserts both the content and the form of this medieval Catholic law as the forerunner of the modern political-legal order, with the shift from religious institutions to secular ones occurring at the Reformation.

If Berman's argument is correct, then certain comparisons between the medieval Catholic Church and modern political institutions follow. One can also make comparisons between the way of life of those under Catholic canon law and those under modern political systems. I have isolated confession as a habit within the medieval Catholic system because in confession the whole weight of the law lands upon the individual seeking salvation. The Christian under Catholic law in the late medieval world made less of a distinction between political and religious law inasmuch as these were fused in the Catholic canonical collections. He knew only one religious law, a law with overt political ramifications inasmuch as the popes had used it to assert their political authority while they also referred to it as a guide for Christians toward everlasting life. This single politico-religious law, a law concentrated in the confessing conscience, had grown to such an extent that Luther complains of it extending "to infinity" and provoking the anxiety to be resolved in his doctrine of justification by faith alone.

To the extent that the internal legal development of the modern state reproduces that of the medieval Catholic Church, with both expanding over time toward an infinite set of laws, the life of the modern citizen reproduces the experience of the medieval Christian in confession. The genius of Luther's doctrine of justification is to appropriate the law's expansion to infinity, including the terror that it arouses in the conscience, and make it intrinsic to salvation. This is the crux of his dialectic of justification, in which the believer who would find grace, rest, and peace must traverse the antithetical moment in which the law convinces him that he is damned. When Protestantism, exemplified by both Luther and Calvin, "carried over" the law of the medieval church into the modern state, it carried over the expansion to infinity that is the meaning of the development of canon law. Now the modern state becomes the institution whose law must grow to infinity and the citizen becomes the man who must bear its infinite burden. Modern men find themselves coerced into a political confession that took centuries to mature into the totalitarian state. They likewise find themselves, in the aftermath of the Second World War, in a state of grace in which the totalitarian experience of damnation is annulled—at least until the dialectic repeats itself in a new horror.

Most academics will dismiss this analysis of the connection between the religious and political ethos of the West as simplistic. Could it be the case that a single dynamic supports and has produced the multiplicity and complexity of the modern order? To many, this claim will appear naive if not stupid. But who is the naive one?

There was a man who studied chemistry, examining the variety of complex reactions that can occur between elements. He conducted a multitude of experiments that tested chemicals under different pressures and temperatures, with different volumes and in varied combinations. "What a vast multitude of possibilities!" thought the man as he considered his tests. "What multiplicity! What complexity! What variation!" The more he studied the chemical interactions, the more convinced he became of the intricacy of the work, and the more he became preoccupied with the details of particular interactions.

After a while another man approached and saw the first at his work. "What are you doing?" asked the second. "I am studying all the remarkable array of possible chemical interactions under varied conditions, seeing how control factors can influence the results of their combinations and seeking a pointed description of their qualities," replied the first. The second man was puzzled. "Don't you think that you should look into the few principles of breaking and bonding? There may be a wide variety of possible interactions that might differ under various conditions, but the basic principles of pressure and release, of energy gained and lost, will mark each interaction. To study only the particularity of different interactions misses the essential forces at work."[1]

The first man was stupefied. "How can you emphasize anything other than the differences between reactions?" he exclaimed. "Each is a species unto itself and is radically unique in its details. Complex interactions require a frame of mind oriented to accept complexity." He smirked at the man who suggested a focus on simple principles and returned to his work.

The interactions represent the history through which the modern West has unfolded, a history filled with various social transformations. The first man is the contemporary scientist or academic, whom the differences within modernity so powerfully impress that he forgets the signs of unity within the data. The second man is one who believes that such unity exists, though not on the surface. To his suggestion that there are a few fixed principles that explain the social order, or possibly a single principle at its base, the academic responds with incredulity. The second man does not deny the multiplicity within culture and history, however. He affirms that such multiplicity goes hand in hand with certain simple and fundamental principles, which the first man denies. These principles are not immediately visible, indeed they are deeply hidden, but this does not disprove their presence.

If one asks the contemporary scientist whether there are differences between the various eras of history and social order, he would say yes. The Roman Empire differs from the modern world, the culture of the far East differs from that of the West, and aboriginal culture diverges from the technological world. Granting these differences, the scientist submerges them within his assumption of cultural and historical complexity. In all cases, history is a concatenation of complex and multiple interactions between political, social, economic, religious, and other factors that do not allow singular processes or vectors of development. The emergence of cultures that are coherently recognized as different is more or less accidental, a product of unpredictable forces that happen to have resulted in particular structures. The magnified study of complex historical interactions leads to a knowledge so qualified that the method of the science annuls the meaning of the subject.

Who, then, is the naive one? Is it the man who recognizes the limits of his knowledge and the intrinsic order of the world that he experiences, and so concludes that order must be the rule of the whole? He cannot always see how the natural order works but he recognizes a harmonious repetition in its processes and moves from the effects to an ordered cause. He further assumes that he, as subject to nature, must have a similar order as the foundation of his being and his society. If he is the naive one it is because he trusts what he perceives but does not fully comprehend, limiting his pride before the powers regnant within the world. Or is the naive one the scientist who hopes to achieve knowledge through a method that renders the knowledge he acquires superfluous? Is it not naivety to seek truth through a method that drowns its discoveries in qualifications and scholarly dross? It is not naive to jaunt happily, or perhaps labor slavishly, along a road that persistently leads nowhere? Who is the fool, he who trusts in the simple design of nature or he who manipulates its beauty into frustration in the search for infinite knowledge, all the while believing that he has discovered the means to truth? The academic smirks at the suggestion of his foolishness and, flushed with confidence, he returns to his monograph on the use of footnotes in William of Ockham.

The docetic mind oscillates between two alternatives, the universal and the particular, the absolute and the relative, that which applies always and everywhere and that which applies only here and now, with the latter so singular in its relevance as to be all but irrelevant. The scientist asserts the absolute as universal and the annulment of the absolute in particularity, but truth and knowledge belong to neither arm of this dichotomy. Man's knowledge is less than the systematic and comprehensive breadth of the universal, an assumption that the academic uses to appear humble ("I do not know everything. Many more books could be written on my subject!"), but which, because it presumes the infinite as the standard of his knowledge, is sheer pride. Man's knowledge also exceeds the insignificance of the particular, as if his knowing could not extend beyond the minutiae of specific eras and locales. Between these extremes lies a general knowledge that applies in a limited but significant way. I speak, for instance, of docetic freedom not as a "concept" but as an ontology in which law explodes its limits, with this notion underlying both man's spiritual development in the medieval world and his existence in the modern order. This ontological pattern gives freedom a certain definition and grounding, but the definition remains limited enough to permit the vagaries and applications that different thinkers have used in describing freedom as political or religious. Man understands according to his limitations, a stipulation that allows for liberty and difference in his definitions. The proper path of knowledge focuses on what is given and firm about the general with an accompanying and no less important eye on the liberty intrinsic to the finite, a liberty attendant to both the object and man's knowledge of it. To put it succinctly: men know through parables, which give unmistakable guidance regarding what is while preserving room for interpretation. Docetic unknowing, on the contrary, dismisses the finite, the given, and the image in favor of the universality of the concept, which recedes as a prelude to his focus on differences, on the particular and exact. In our day, docetists study these differences with such penetration that they reject that the object has meaningful definition.

Their scientists then have the audacity to name their intellectual histories, which seek to undermine their subjects as arbitrary and ultimately forgettable, as genealogies.

Theologians, philosophers, biblical scientists, and social theorists, in addition to others within the humanities and the physical and biological sciences, will complain that I have not satisfied the docetic rigor of their disciplines. Some will criticize my habit of not stating my purposes directly and from the start, though I write in this way out of the conviction that knowledge, especially the lived knowledge of God, does not come immediately but arrives through time and effort. Others will judge that I have not defined my subject and its terms with sufficient clarity, to which I respond, with Aristotle, that I have tried to gain only as much clarity as the subject affords. I refuse to succumb to the docetic ruse that knowledge requires a spotless and comprehensive clarity. The path to such clarity leads inevitably to obfuscation, as the current philosophical milieu illustrates. Others will object that I have not paid sufficient deference to the sea of marginalia politely referred to as the literature, and that I have not honored debates that are at best peripheral. Such margins exemplify the lumbering toward meaninglessness that has infected academic work and the humanities in particular. Leading docetic intellectuals will take further offense that I speak of man and nature rather than "a person" and "the self," though by my terminology I intend to speak of man as a creature determined by the givenness of nature rather than a creature whose bodily nature is annulled. Many will be outraged by my theory of law, calling me authoritarian and a dictator because I would preserve man by imposing limits upon him, though, by my argument, the docetic champions of freedom and equality, the supposed liberators of men from tyranny, do so as secret partisans of the most horrifying forms of domination. The same intellectuals will unilaterally reject my recognition of spiritual forces driving history in conjunction with the wills of men. Their science aims to obliterate the possibility of belief in such forces, which they consider mythical. I expect that few if any of them will give credence to my perspective on this point as well as the others I have noted. In short, my adversaries will charge that I do not follow the rules and values of their science, that I assert a knowledge that they consider the crudest falsehood and a laughable ignorance. These charges will come from professors who believe that knowledge, insofar as it is not annulled by the infinite standard, is determined by power, and that power is propaganda and falsehood, so that all that poses as truth conceals the lie. "To the corrupt and unbelieving," says the Scripture, "nothing is pure."

To the sincere churchgoer, lay and academic: through this writing I ask God for mercy regarding my participation in docetic processes. I also ask that he would spare me and my loved ones from his wrath. I pray the same clemency for my readers, believers evangelical and liberal, priests, preachers, lay leaders, and their children, men and women who yearn for God and seek his embrace. My relatives dead and alive, my dear and respected friends, those who have aided and nourished me and to whom I owe the highest gratitude, have labored under the docetic lie and have unknowingly taken sides with its spirit. My commiseration is with them, as well as my hope that they will break loose from Docetism's hold. When I use severe or inflammatory language to castigate Docetism's influence, including criticism of its manifestation through Christian churches and sacrosanct historical figures, I think not of those who are dear to me nor of those who seek God humbly, but of the incalculable violence that Docetism has caused, and which, I fear, it has yet to cause. I pray that the reader will not take offense at my words, but that he will see in my thoughts a heart that wishes to receive pardon and be known by his Lord.

Select Consulted Works

Adam, James Luther. *An Examined Faith: Social Context and Religious Commitment*. Boston, MA: Beacon, 1991.

"Akathist Hymn to Saint Michael the Archangel." http://www.akathistreconstructed.wordpress.com/michael-archangel.

Archbishop Averky (Taushev). *The Struggle for Virtue: Asceticism in a Modern Secular Society*. Jordanville, NY: Holy Trinity, 2014.

Archimandrite Lazarus (Moore). *An Extraordinary Peace: St. Seraphim, Flame of Sarov*. Port Townsend, WA: Anaphora, 2009.

Bellah, Robert. "Flaws in the Protestant Code." In *The Robert Bellah Reader*. Edited by Steven M. Tipton, 333–349. Durham: Duke University Press, 2006.

———. "Is There a Common American Culture?" In *The Robert Bellah Reader*. Edited by Steven M. Tipton, 319–332. Durham: Duke University Press, 2006.

Berman, Harold. *Law and Revolution: The Formation of the Western Legal Tradition*. Volume 1. Cambridge: Harvard University Press, 1983.

Calvin, John. *Institutes of the Christian Religion*. Edited by John T. McNeill. Library of Christian Classics, Vol. 20. Philadelphia: Westminster, 1960.

Chadwick, Henry. *The Early Church: The Story of Emergent Christianity from the Apostolic Age to the Dividing of the Ways Between the Greek East and the Latin West*. Penguin History of the Church, Vol. 1. New York: Penguin, 1993.

Dupré, Louis. *Passage To Modernity: An Essay in the Hermeneutics of Nature and Culture*. New Haven, CT: Yale University Press, 1993.

Elder Paisios of Mount Athos. *Spiritual Counsels, Volume II: Spiritual Awakening*. Souroti, Thessaloniki, Greece: Holy Monastery "John the Theologian," 2008.

Emerson, Ralph Waldo. "The Divinity School Address." In *Theology in America: The Major Protestant Voices from Puritanism to Neo-Orthodoxy*, edited by Sydney Ahlstrom, 296–316. The American Heritage Series. Indianapolis: Hackett, 2003.

Gonzalez, Justo. *The Story of Christianity, Volume 1: The Early Church to the Dawn of the Reformation*. Revised version. New York: HarperCollins, 2010.

Gregory, Brad. *The Unintended Reformation: How a Religious Revolution Secularized Society*. Cambridge, MA: Belknap, 2012.

Hatch, Nathan. *The Democratization of American Christianity*. New Haven, CT: Yale University Press, 1989.

Hobbes, Thomas. *Leviathan*. New York, NY: Penguin, 1982.

Hooker, Thomas. "The Activity of Faith: Or, Abraham's Imitators." In *Theology in America: The Major Protestant Voices from Puritanism to Neo-Orthodoxy*, edited by Sydney Ahlstrom, 114–148. The American Heritage Series. Indianapolis: Hackett, 2003.

Jestice, Phyllis G. *Wayward Monks and the Religious Revolution of the Eleventh Century*. New York: Brill, 1997.

King, Martin Luther. "Letter from Birmingham Jail," in *Why We Can't Wait*. New York: Signet, 2000.

———. "I Have a Dream," in *I Have a Dream: Writings and Speeches that Changed the World*. San Franciso: Harper SanFrancisco, 1992.

Lambertsen, Isaac E., translator. *The Lives of the Saints in the Russian Language, As Set Forth in the Menology of Saint Dmitri of Rostov, Supplemental Volume II (JanuaryApril): The Lives of the Russian Saints*. Moscow: Synodal, 1916, 1991.

Locke, John. *Second Treatise of Government*. Edited by Thomas P. Peardon. New York: Pearson, 1952.

Lossky, Vladimir. *The Mystical Theology of the Eastern Church*. Crestwood, New York: St. Vladimir's Seminary Press, 1976.

Luther, Martin. *Commentary on Galatians* and "Freedom of a Christian." *Luther's Works*. Edited by Jaroslav Pelikan and Walter A. Hansen. 55 vols. Saint Louis: Concordia, 1955–86.

McBrien, Richard P. *Lives of the Popes: The Pontiffs from St. Peter to John Paul II*. San Francisco: Harper SanFrancisco, 1997.

Metropolitan MAXIMOS, et al., eds. *The Orthodox Study Bible*. Nashville, TN: Thomas Nelson, 2008.

Morris, Colin. *The Discovery of the Individual, 1050–1200*. London: SPCK, 1972.

Mullins, Edwin. *The Popes of Avignon: A Century in Exile*. New York: Bluebridge, 2008.

Marx, Karl. *Contribution to the Critique of Hegel's Philosophy of Right: Introduction*. In *The Marx Engels Reader*. Second edition. Edited by Robert C. Tucker. New York: W.W. Norton, 1978.

McCue, James F. "*Simul iustus et peccator* in Augustine, Aquinas, and Luther: Toward Putting the Debate in Context." *Journal of the American Academy of Religion* 48, no. 1 (Mar 1980) 81–96.

Nevin, John Williamson. "The Mystical Presence." In *Theology in America: The Major Protestant Voices from Puritanism to Neo-Orthodoxy*, edited by Sydney Ahlstrom, 374–426. The American Heritage Series. Indianapolis: Hackett, 2003.

Niebuhr, H. Richard. *Radical Monotheism and Western Culture*. Library of Theological Ethics. Louisville: Westminster/John Knox, 1970.

O'Malley, John W., S.J. *A History of the Popes: From Peter to the Present*. New York: Sheed and Ward, 2010.

Phan, Peter C. *Social Thought*. Messages of the Fathers of the Church, 20. Wilmington, DE: Michael Glazier, 1984.

Poulos, George. *Orthodox Saints: Volume Two*. Brookline, MA: Holy Cross Orthodox Press, 1978.

A Prayer Book for Orthodox Christians. Englewood, NJ: Antiochian Orthodox Christian Archdiocese of North America, 1956, 2004.

Rauschenbusch, Walter. *Christianity and the Social Crisis*. Library of Theological Ethics. MacMillan, 1907 and Louisville: Westminster/John Knox, 1991.

Reference Book for Clergy Servers. Tomes 2–3. . Edited by Nastol'naya Kniga Svyaschennosluzhitelya and translated by Stephen Janos. Moscow: Moscow Patriachate, 1978 1979.

Robinson, Ian S. *Authority and Resistance in the Investiture Contest: The Polemical Literature of the Late Eleventh Century.* New York: Holmes and Meier, 1978.

Runciman, Steven. *The Eastern Schism: A Study of the Papacy and the Eastern Churches During the XIth and XIIth Centuries.* Oxford: Clarendon, 1955.

Saint Ambrose. *Select Works and Letters.* Edited by Philip Schaff. Nicene and Post-Nicene Fathers, Vol. 10. Peabody, Mass.: Hendrickson, 1994.

Saint Basil the Great. *On Social Justice.* Edited by C. Paul Schroeder. Popular Patristics Series 38. Crestwood, NY: St. Vladimir's, 2009.

Saint Cyril of Alexandria. *On the Unity of Christ.* Crestwood, NY: St. Vladimir's Seminary Press, 1995.

Saint Gregory the Theologian. *Theological Orations.* Philip Schaff and Henry Wace, editors. Nicene and Post-Nicene Fathers, Vol. 7. Peabody, Mass.: Hendrickson Publishers, 1994.

Saint. John Chrysostom. *Homilies on the Acts of the Apostles and the Epistle to the Romans.* Edited by Philip Schaff. Nicene and Post-Nicene Fathers, Vol. 11. Peabody, Mass.: Hendrickson, 1994.

Saint John of Damascus. *The Orthodox Faith.* Frederic H. Chase, editor. The Fathers of the Church, Volume 37: St. John of Damascus. Ex Fontibus Company, 2015.

Saint John of Kronstadt. *My Life in Christ, Part I.* Jordanville, NY: Holy Trinity Publications, 2015.

Saint Seraphim of Sarov. *On Acquisition of the Holy Spirit.* Lexington, KY: CreateSpace Independent Publishing Platform, 2014.

Spener, Philip Jacob. *Pia Desideria.* Translated by Theodore G. Tappert. Minneapolis: Fortress, 1964.

Taylor, Charles. *A Secular Age.* Cambridge, MA: Harvard University Press, 2007.

Tennent, Gilbert. "The Danger of an Unconverted Ministry." In *Sermons of the Log College: Sermons and Essays by the Tennents and their Contemporaries,* compiled by Archibald Alexander, 49–58. Ligonier, PA: Soli Deo Gloria, 1993.

———. "The Grace of God." In *Sermons of the Log College: Sermons and Essays by the Tennents and their Contemporaries,* compiled by Archibald Alexander, 375–404. Ligonier, PA: Soli Deo Gloria, 1993.

Tierney, Brian. *The Crisis of Church and State* 1050–1300. Toronto: University of Toronto Press and Medieval Academy of America, 1988.

Tuchman, Barbara. *A Distant Mirror: The Calamitous 14th Century.* New York, NY: Ballantine, 1978.

Vatican Council II: The Basic Sixteen Documents. Edited by Austin Flannery, O.P. Northport, NY: Costello, 1996.

Verhey, Allen. *Remembering Jesus: Christian Community, Scripture, and the Moral Life.* Grand Rapids, MI: Eerdmans, 2002.

Ware, Timothy, editor, Igumen Chariton of Valamo, compiler, and Kadloubovksy, E. and Palmer, E.M., translators. *The Art of Prayer: An Orthodox Anthology.* New York: Farrar, Straus, and Giroux, 1966.

Weber, Max. "Religious Rejections of the World and Their Directions." In *From Max Weber: Essays in Sociology.* Edited and translated by H.H. Gerth and C. Wright Mills. New York: Oxford University Press, 1946.

———. *The Protestant Ethic and the Spirit of Capitalism.* Translated by Talcott Parsons. New York: Routledge, 2004.

Whitman, Walt. *Democratic Vistas.* New York: Liberal Arts, 1949.

From the works of Saint Augustine:

De civitate Dei	City of God
De nuptiis et concupiscentia	On Marriage and Concupiscence
De spiritu et littera	On the Spirit and the Letter
Confessiones	Confessions
De gratia et libero arbitrio	On Grace and Free Will
De immortalitate animae	On the Immortality of the Soul
De natura et gratia	On Nature and Grace

www.ingramcontent.com/pod-product-compliance
Lightning Source LLC
Chambersburg PA
CBHW080723300426
44114CB00019B/2475